Identities in Transition

Supplements

to

Vetus Testamentum

Editor in Chief

VOLUME 142

Identities in Transition

The Pursuit of Isa. 52:13–53:12

By

Kristin Joachimsen

BRILL

LEIDEN • BOSTON
2011

BS
H10
V452
vol.142

This book is printed on acid-free paper.

Library of Congress Cataloging-in-Publication Data

Joachimsen, Kristin.
    Identities in transition : the pursuit of Isa. 52:13–53:12 / by Kristin Joachimsen.
        p. cm. — (Supplements to Vetus Testamentum ; v. 142)
    Based on the author's doctoral thesis, University of Oslo, 2006.
    Includes bibliographical references and index.
    ISBN 978-90-04-20106-4 (hardback : alk. paper) 1. Bible. O.T. Isaiah LII, 13-LIII, 12—Commentaries. I. Title.

    BS1520.J63 2011
    224'.106—dc22

                                                                    2010053813

ISSN 0083-5889
ISBN 978 90 04 20106 4

MIX
Paper from
responsible sources
FSC® C004472
FSC
www.fsc.org

PRINTED BY DRUKKERIJ WILCO B.V. - AMERSFOORT, THE NETHERLANDS

CONTENTS

PART TWO

ISA. 52:13–53:12: IDENTITIES IN TRANSITION

PREFACE

This monograph is a slightly revised version of my thesis defended for the degree of Doctor theologiae at the Faculty of Theology at the University of Oslo in May 2006. There are many people I would like to thank for contributing to this study: my supervisor Prof. Hans M. Barstad (Oslo/Edinburgh) for his advice during the writing of the thesis. Professors Martin Ravndal Hauge and Helge Kvanvig (Oslo) for their conscientious readings and constructive criticism. Professors Frederik Lindström (Lund), David J. A. Clines (Sheffield) and Reinhard G. Kratz (Göttingen), Dr. Else Kragelund Holt (Aarhus) and Dr. Rannfrid Thelle (Oslo/US), who have read and commented on parts of my work. A special thank you to the examination committee, Professors Marvin Sweeney (Clarendon), Kåre Berge (Bergen) and Dr. Marta Høyland Lavik (Stavanger), who offered valuable criticism. Prof. Terje Stordalen (Oslo) administered the examination committee and has also been responsible for the Nordic-German network "Old Testament Studies: Epistemologies and Methods" (OTSEM), at which I have presented parts of the thesis during the writing process.

In 1996/97 I was a D. Phil. student at the Faculty of Theology, University of Oxford and was supervised by Prof. John Day. His professional skill, excellent library and kindness were invaluable. In 1996/1997 I was awarded the Yates senior scholarship at St Hugh's College, Oxford. The college was most helpful in arranging my stay that year, and also my one-semester stays in 2000 and 2002. The thesis has been funded by a four-year doctoral scholarship from the Norwegian Research Council and the Faculty of Theology, University of Oslo. This includes also travel grants for the stays in Oxford in 2000 and 2002. Norwegian Research Council has also funded the proof-reading. Vemund Blomkvist and Tom Jude have assisted in linguistic matters, while Peter Glen has performed the final proof-reading. The abbreviations are taken from D. J. A. Clines, *The Sheffield Manual for Authors and Editors in Biblical Studies* (Sheffield: Sheffield Academic Press, 1997). Any faults are, of course, entirely my own. Finally, I am grateful to Brill for accepting publication of this book in their *Vetus Testamentum* series.

Many thanks also to the staff at the library of the Faculty of Theology, University of Oslo, the University Library in Tromsø, the Bodleian Library and the library of the Faculty of Theology at the University of Oxford, and the Oriental Institute, Oxford, where I have had many a good time. This study of Isa. 53 is dedicated to the suffering servant, Vanunu Mordechai. May he win the freedom he so deserves very soon.

Kristin Joachimsen, Berlin October 1, 2010

PART ONE

IN PURSUIT OF ISA. 52:13–53:12

CHAPTER ONE

INTRODUCTION

1.1. HISTORIES OF ISA. 52:13–53:12

In Isa. 52:13–53:12, there is talk of servant, exaltation, disfigurement, vision, questioning, contempt, desolation, illness, striking, sin, punishment, healing, delusion, oppression, silence, death, burial, descendants, wealth and vindication, moving readers to understandings of relationships of YHWH, "I", "he", "you", "we", "many", "numerous", "transgressors", "people", "many peoples", "kings" and "servant". In first- and third- person speech, "I", "we" and anonymous voices talk about and question broken and restored relationships between YHWH, "he", "we", "you" and "they". From early on, this text has occupied a special position in both Jewish and Christian traditions and the fifteen verses are much read and celebrated in liturgy, preaching, visual art, music, education, commentaries and so forth. Readings of Isa. 52:13–53:12 are laden with echoes, polemics, apologetics, speculation and controversies. The text has also been ignored for being too offensive. In each reading, special attention has been paid to the quest to determine the identity and fate of the servant who is mentioned, with a focus, variously, upon his suffering, humiliation, exaltation and vindication.

In Jewish traditions, witness is borne to Isa. 52:13–53:12 by virtue of a comprehensive history of interpretation: in the Qumran texts, Pseudepigrapha, the Greek LXX, the Aramaic Targumim, the Syriac Peshitta and in mediaeval and modern rabbinical literature. The servant interpreted as the Messiah is a dominant reading, focusing on his exaltation rather than his humiliation.[1] However, in both the Middle

---

[1] For a survey of interpretations of Isa. 52:13–53:12 in Jewish traditions from LXX to the nineteenth century, see S. R. Driver and A. Neubauer, *The Fifty-Third Chapter of Isaiah according to the Jewish Interpreters I–II* (LBS; New York: Ktav, 1969). In R. Loewe, "Prolegomenon", the perspectives are extended to the 1960s. For overviews of the Jewish material, see C. R. North, *The Suffering Servant in Deutero-Isaiah: An Historical and Critical Study* (London: Oxford University Press, 1948) 6–22,

Ages and in modern times, other Jewish exegetes have tended to view the servant as the Jewish people suffering in exile.

In Christian traditions, the history of interpretation of the text is similarly comprehensive as may be seen from its role in the Pseude-pigrapha, the Apocrypha, the LXX, the New Testament and the Latin Vulgate, in patristic and mediaeval literature, and in biblical scholar-ship in its growth from pre-modern times.[2] Here again, the identity

---

H. Hegermann, *Jesaja 53 in Hexapla, Targum und Peschitta* (BFCT, 2. Reihe, 56. Band; Gütersloh: C. Bertelsmann, 1954), E. Ruprecht, *Die Auslegungsgeschichte zu den sogenannten Gottesknechtliedern im Buch Deuterojesaja unter metodischen Gesichts-punkten bis zu Bernard Duhm* (Unpubl. Diss., Heidelberg, 1972) 1–73, and H. Haag, *Der Gottesknecht bei Deuterojesaja* (Erträge der Forschung, 233; Darmstadt: Wissen-schaftliche Buchgesellschaft, 1985) 1–3; 34–66, covering the time from early Juda-ism until the 1980s. See more surveys of early Jewish interpretations in E. R. Ekblad, *Isaiah's Servant Poems according to the Septuagint: An Exegetical and Theological Study* (Contributions to Biblical Exegesis and Theology, 23; Leuven: Peeters, 1999), I. Knohl, *The Messiah Before Jesus: The Suffering Servant of the Dead Sea Scrolls* (California: University of California Press, 2000), B. Janowski and P. Stuhlmacher (eds), *Der lei-dende Gottesknecht: Jesaja 53 und seine Wirkungsgeschichte mit einer Bibliographie zu Jes 53* (Forschungen zum Alten Testament, 14; Tübingen: J. C. B. Mohr {Paul Siebeck}, 1996, ET B. Janowski and P. Stulmacher [eds], *The Suffering Servant: Isaiah 53 in Jewish and Christian Sources* [Grand Rapids: Eerdmans, 2004]) and C. C. Broyles and C. A. Evans (eds), *Writing and Reading the Scroll of Isaiah: Studies of an Interpretive Tradition. Volume 2* (VTSup 70, 2; Leiden: E. J. Brill, 1997). On mediaeval Jewish interpretations, see A. Funkelstein, "Basic Types of Christian Anti-Jewish Polemics in the Later Middle Ages", *Viator* 2 (1971) 373–383, and J. E. Rembaum, "The Develop-ment of a Jewish Exegetical Tradition Regarding Isaiah 53", *HTR* 75 (1982) 289–311, which sees the paucity of references to Isa. 53 in talmudic and midrashic literature "as a form of Jewish self-censorship in the face of the Christian emphasis on the Christo-logical meaning of such passages and as an attempt to control messianic movements and speculation among Jews" (p. 291, n. 5). F. Landy, "The Construction of the Subject and the Symbolic Order: A Reading of the Last Three Suffering Servant Songs" in P. R. Davies and D. J. A. Clines (eds), *Among the Prophets: Language, Image and Structure in the Prophetic Writing* (JSOTSup, 144; Sheffield: JSOT Press, 1993) 62, describes the "Jewish response...[to Isa. 53 as] tacit demonization; Isaiah 53 is not recited in the synagogue among the readings from the prophets; there are no Midrashim about Isaiah 53".

[2] For surveys of interpretations of Isa. 52:13–53:12 in Christian traditions, see North, *The Suffering Servant in Deutero-Isaiah*, pp. 23–116, M. D. Hooker, *Jesus and the Ser-vant: The Influence of the Servant Concept of Deutero-Isaiah in the New Testament* (London: SPCK Press, 1959), Ruprecht, *Die Auslegungsgeschichte zu den sogenannten Gottesknechtliedern*, H. W. Wolff, *Jesaja 53 im Urchristentum* (Giessen: Brunnen Verlag, 1984) 55–151, A. Y. Collins, "The Suffering Servant: Isaiah Chapter 53 as a Christian Text" in R. Brooks and J. J. Collins (eds), *Hebrew Bible or Old Testament? Studying the Bible in Judaism and Christianity* (Christianity and Judaism in Antiquity, 5; Notre Dame: University of Notre Dame Press, 1990) 201–206, J. F. A. Sawyer, *The Fifth Gospel: Isaiah in the History of Christianity* (Cambridge: Cambridge University Press, 1996) 83–99, Janowski and Stuhlmacher, *Der leidende Gottesknecht*, M. Barker, *The Risen Lord: The Jesus of History as the Christ of Faith* (Current Issues in Theology;

and fate of the servant have been of key interest. In Acts 8:34, the puzzled eunuch asks Philip about Isa. 53:7–8: "About whom may I ask you, does the prophet say this, about himself or about someone else?" A Christological interest has dominated these readings, in which the text has been interpreted as the passion story of Jesus Christ, including his death, atonement and resurrection. R. Loewe (1969) has described Isa. 52:13–53:12 as:

> the Christian *locus classicus* for the meaning of the passion of Jesus as allegedly foretold in the Old Testament, scholarly treatment of these fifteen verses is exposed. More perhaps than that of any other text, to an extraneous magnetism.[3]

In their presentation of the text's ancient history of interpretation, scholars' biases are brought to the fore. One illustration of this might be B. Janowski and P. Stuhlmacher's introduction to a volume called *Der leidende Gottesknecht: Jesaja 53 und seine Wirkungsgeschichte* (1996):

> With its idea of the vicarious suffering of the Servant of God, Isaiah 52:13–53:12, the focus of this volume, is one of those leading Old Testament theological texts that have had, and will continue to have, an extraordinary influence or "effective history" (German *Wirkungsgeschichte*) in Judaism and Christianity. In order to sketch the basis of this effective history, especially for the postbiblical and early Christian periods, we must have access to the foundational Old Testament text with its tradition and transmission history. Yet the problems begin precisely here.[4]

Edinburgh: T. & T. Clark, 1996), W. H. Bellinger Jr. and W. R. Farmer (eds), *Jesus and the Suffering Servant: Isaiah and Christian Origins* (Harrisburg: Trinity Press, 1998) and B. S. Childs, *Isaiah: A Commentary* (OTL; Louisville, KY: Westminster/ John Knox Press, 2001) 420–423.

[3] Loewe, "Prolegomenon", p. 8, cf. H. Gunkel, "Knecht Jahwes", *RGG* III (1912) 1542: "Nur mit tiefster Andacht aber, ganz leise, läßt sich von diesen Dingen reden; es sind die letzten Geheimnisse der Religion", S. Mowinckel, "Der Knecht Jahwäs", *NTT* 3 (1921) 68: "In die Leiden des gerechten Gottesknechtes wird sowohl Wissenschaft als Religion sich immer mit tiefer Andacht und Ehrfurcht versenken können- und müssen", and W. Brueggemann, *Isaiah 40–66* (Westminster Bible Companion; Louisville, KY: Westminster/John Knox, 1998) 149: "[W]e are very close here to what seems to be quintessential holy ground."

[4] B. Janowski and P. Stuhlmacher, "Vorwort" in Janowski and Stuhlmacher, *Der leidende Gottesknecht*, p. III. The quotation is taken from ET B. Janowski and P. Stuhlmacher, "Preface" in Janowski and Stulmacher, *The Suffering Servant*, p. vii.

Janowski introduces his reading of Isa. 52:13–53:12 as follows: "Few religious texts of antiquity have been so influential yet puzzling as the biblical stories of the 'suffering righteous'."[5] In these quotations, scholars' conceptualisations such as "vicarious suffering" (*stellvertretendes Leiden*), "servant of God" (*Gottesknecht*) and the "suffering righteous" (*leidende Gerechte*), as well as labelling the passage a "foundational text" (*Basistext*) and "leading text" (*Leittext*), are formulated to explain the centrality of the text and its role in scholarly presentations of religious traditions.[6]

Its history is also related to biblical scholarship, within which it is especially connected to Bernhard Duhm's thesis, first proposed in 1892, about the "Servant Songs". In this thesis, Duhm claimed that Isa. 42:1–4, 49:1–6, 50:4–9 and 52:13–53:12 comprised an independent group of texts which were later additions to Isa. *40–55. These four texts were only loosely related to Isa. *40–55 and depicted the fate of the servant differently from elsewhere in these sixteen chapters.[7] Most scholars have accepted Duhm's main thesis and have offered only slight correctives to it. The pursuit of the Duhmian *Gottesknecht* is still alive and is a naturalised concern when dealing with certain texts from Isa. 40–55. Duhm's thesis has, so to speak, even become part of our common cultural heritage. For instance, this may be illustrated by the heading of Isa. 52:13–53:12 in *The New Jerusalem Bible* (1985) which labels the text "Fourth Song of the Servant".

Due to the comprehensive history of interpretation of the text, studying Isa. 52:13–53:12 is intriguing in many ways. The text has been multifariously interpreted within biblical studies and theology in Judaism and Christianity: "collective", "individual", "messianic", "Christological" and "canonical" interpretations are offered to guide, correct and edify faith, worship and practice in life with God. In an ongoing wrestling with the text for meaning, readers and reading communities have contemplated experiences or visions of humiliation, suffering,

---

[5] B. Janowski, "Er trug unsere Sünden: Jes. 53 und die Dramatik der Stellvertretung" in Janowski and Stuhlmacher, *Der leidende Gottesknecht*, p. 27. The quotation is taken from ET B. Janowski, "He Bore Our Sins: Isaiah 53 and the Drama of Taking Another's Place" in Janowski and Stulmacher, *The Suffering Servant*, p. 49.

[6] These and other concepts and technical terms such as *Ebed Jahwe* (EJ), *Ebed-Jahwe-Lieder* (EJL), *Gottesknecht* (GK) and *Gottesknechtslieder* (GKL) will be treated in more detail in Chapter. 2.

[7] B. Duhm, *Das Buch Jesaia übersetzt und erklärt* (HKAT; Göttingen: Vandenhoeck & Ruprect, 1902, 2. ed.) xiii–xviii. More on this in 2.1.2. and 2.1.3.

sin, atonement, forgiveness, vindication and resurrection.[8] Readings of Isa. 52:13–53:12 are shaping and being shaped by readers' ideas of their own identities and that of the text, in which the text serves both as a source of and a witness to experiences and visions.

In biblical scholarship in general, and as regards the Book of Isaiah in particular, increasing interest has been devoted to the history of the interpretation of the biblical texts. B. Janowski and P. Stuhlmacher (eds), *Der leidende Gottesknecht: Jesaja 53 und seine Wirkungsgeschichte* (1996), has a pronounced interest in the effective history (*Wirkungsgeschichte*), tradition and transmission history of Isa. 52:13–53:12, and limits the studies historically to the Hebrew Bible, New Testament, Targumim and patristic and rabbinic literature.[9] W. H. Bellinger Jr. and W. R. Farmer (eds), *Jesus and the Suffering Servant: Isaiah and Christian Origins* (1998) is concerned with the question of the influence of Isa. 52:13–53:12 on Jesus, while C. C. Broyles and C. A. Evans (eds), *Writing and Reading the Scroll of Isaiah: Studies of an Interpretive Tradition* (1997) focuses on the Book of Isaiah from its formation up to its interpretative tradition in late Antiquity. J. F. A. Sawyer's *The Fifth Gospel: Isaiah in the History of Christianity* (1996) studies the use (and misuse) of the Book of Isaiah in the history of Christianity and wishes to shift the focus away from the standard commentaries and official academic history of exegesis towards popular uses of Isaiah and the interaction between Isaiah and the Church and society at large.[10] B. S. Childs' *The Struggle to Understand Isaiah as Christian Scripture* (2004) focuses on the exegetical tradition of the Church:

> I have chosen to trace through the centuries the different ways in which great Christian theologians have struggled to understand the book of Isaiah as the Church's sacred scripture, that is, as a vehicle for communicating the Christian gospel.[11]

Childs' aim is not to write a history of interpretation, but a study in which "the hermeneutical issues will be understood as primary".[12] He further asks whether a "family resemblance" may be emerging from

---

[8] North, *The Suffering Servant in Deutero-Isaiah*, p. 1, claims that S. R. Driver intended to write a commentary on Isaiah, but gave up the project because the question of the suffering servant's identity "overwhelmed him".

[9] Janowski and Stulmacher, *The Suffering Servant*, p. III.

[10] Sawyer, *The Fifth Gospel*, p. 14.

[11] B. S. Childs, *The Struggle to Understand Isaiah as Christian Scripture* (Grand Rapids: Eerdmans, 2004) xi.

[12] Childs, *The Struggle to Understand Isaiah as Christian Scripture*, p. xi.

his analysis of many generations of the Christian biblical study of Isaiah. The intention of C. M. McGinnis and P. K. Tull (eds), *"As Those who are Taught": The Interpretation of Isaiah from the LXX to the SBL* (2006) is "to introduce the discussion of Isaiah by a variety of commentators over the course of twenty centuries".[13] The focus is the interpretative history, including the early, premodern history of the interpretation of the book. J. Blenkinsopp's study, *Opening the Sealed Book: Interpretations of the Book of Isaiah in Late Antiquity* (2006), pursues the impact that the interpretation of biblical books can have on social realities, and elaborates:

> The specific instantiation of this general thesis will be the interpretation of the book of Isaiah as an essential and irreplaceable factor in the legitimizing, grounding, and shaping of dissident movements in late Second Temple Judaism, with special reference to the Qumran sects and the early Christian movement. The interpretation of the text is generally understood to be a scholarly and scribal activity; it is that, but it is also a social phenomenon and, typically, a group activity.[14]

In this study, Blenkinsopp offers a separate chapter entitled "The Many Faces of the Servant of the Lord" in which he relates the identification of the servant to the Teacher of Righteousness in Qumran and to Jesus of Nazareth.[15] In the treatment of Isa. 52:13–53:12 in one of the most recent commentaries on Isaiah 40–55, J. Goldingay and D. Payne's *A Critical and Exegetical Commentary on Isaiah 40–55* (2006) presents "the afterlife of the passage" in which the authors briefly refer to later texts from the Hebrew Bible, 1 Enoch, the LXX, the Peshitta, Targum, the New Testament, and from the patristic/rabbinic period, the medieval period as well as the post-Holocaust period.[16] Yet another illustration of the interest in the interpretation history of biblical texts is the recent blossoming of dictionaries of biblical interpretation.[17]

---

[13] C. M. McGinnis and P. K. Tull, "Remembering the Former Things: The History of Interpretation and Critical Scholarship" in C. M. McGinnis and P. K. Tull (eds), *"As Those who are Taught": The Interpretation of Isaiah from the LXX to the SBL* (SBLSS, 27; Atlanta: SBL, 2006) 13.

[14] J. Blenkinsopp, *Opening the Sealed Book: Interpretations of the Book of Isaiah in Late Antiquity* (Grand Rapids: Eerdmans, 2006) xv.

[15] Blenkinsopp, *Opening the Sealed Book*, pp. 251–293.

[16] J. Goldingay and D. Payne, *A Critical and Exegetical Commentary on Isaiah 40–55. Volume II* (ICC; London: T. & T. Clark, 2006) 284–288.

[17] For an overview, see McGinnis, and Tull, "Remembering the Former Things", p. 6, n. 27.

The histories of interpretations mentioned above demonstrate various theoretical reflections of this kind of historiography, in that they are more or less pragmatic overviews of empirical material and briefly mention the related discussions of "effective history". While most of the studies mentioned above would refer to themselves as "histories of interpretation", further qualified by the respective focuses they have chosen, the volume edited by Janowski and Stuhlmacher explicitly designates itself an "effective history",[18] but with no additional theoretical treatment of the concept.[19] In the studies referred to above, different terminology appears mirroring various interests: effect, tradition, transmission, reception, interpretation, influence, use and misuse, afterlife, all illustrating a complex interaction between the text and readings.[20]

---

[18] Janowski and Stuhlmacher, *Der leidende Gottesknecht*. In his review in *CBQ* 68 (2006) 168, M. A. Sweeney describes it as "a volume of essays concerned primarily with the interpretation of Isaiah 53 in the Bible and patristic Christian sources, with a number of forays into selected Jewish sources to provide background for the early Christian debate".

[19] Neither the editors of nor the contributors to this volume explain what they mean by the concept of *Wirkungsgeschichte*. The German concept of *Wirkungsgeschichte* ("effective history") is related to the history of the impact a text has on our readings. The concept is often related to the German philosopher Hans-Georg Gadamer (1900–2002), who uses it in an explanation for the way in which a reader becomes influenced by previous readings, i.e. it leads to a tradition which opens up for us some perspectives and horizons of understanding while hiding others. Gadamer thereby shows our limitations as regards understanding. H. Räisänen, "The Effective 'History' of the Bible: A Challenge to Biblical Scholarship?" *SJT* 45 (1992) 303–324, claims that some theologians, for instance Peter Stuhlmacher, regard "the effective history of the Bible [as] practically identical with the formation of the great confessional traditions in the churches", i.e. "[e]ffective history here harmoniously assimilates into the normative ecclesial-dogmatic tradition". Räisänen argues that this represents a confusion which is also partly in line with Gadamer's ambiguous use of the term (pp. 306–307). Räisänen himself emphasises how effective history is a competitive process, in which the confessions have been influenced by factors quite independent of the Bible, such as Greek philosophy, the sacking of Jerusalem, the politics of Constantine (p. 308), as well as different competitive biblical impulses (p. 317). He comments that "little distinction is made between effective history of the Bible and the history of its theological interpretation" (p. 310). *Wirkungsgeschichte* is often distinguished from *Rezeptionsgeschichte*, the latter focusing more on the creative role of the reader. See more on *Rezeptionsgeschichte* in 1.1. n. 20.

[20] Theories of reception, *Rezeptionsgeschichte* ("reception history") in the German version, are related to literary historians such as Wolfgang Iser and Hans Robert Jauss, and focus on how reception of text is both a reproductive and a creative activity. M. P. Thompson, "Reception Theory and the Interpretation of Historical Meaning", *History and Theory* 32 (1993) 255, explains how in *Rezeptionsgeschichte*,

1.2. Identities of Isa. 52:13–53:12

In "Part I: The Pursuit of Isa. 52:13–53:12", I will present Duhm's studies of the Book of Isaiah, with particular attention to Isa. 40–55 and the
"Servant Songs". Each scholarly work written about Isa. 52:13–53:12
since Duhm refers either covertly or overtly in some way to his thesis.
Although Duhm's studies have been important for all later research,
many scholars seem to ignore the principles of his theses, for example
his positivistic, neo-romantic and psychological view of the prophets,
prophecy and prophetic literature, and, hand in hand with this, his
historical-biographical interpretation of a *Gottesknecht*. My presentation of Duhm's works is followed by one Duhm reception: the Isaiah studies of Odil Hannes Steck. Representing a traditional German
historical-critical approach (though a somewhat extreme one) with a
special interest in redaction criticism, Steck has been rather influential in much recent Isaianic research, both as regards the book as a
whole and the "Servant Songs" in particular. A degree of conformity
and reproduction seems to appear within Steck's and his contemporaries' Isaiah research, where they refer to certain precursors and colleagues. Scholars seem to ignore the principles of Steck and his reading
community – as they ignore Duhm's studies – as far as the text and
historiography are concerned in referring to and evaluating these contributions to Isaianic research.

My own assessment of Steck's contribution to recent Isaiah research
will lead to my dwelling upon the way in which contexts and interests
are brought to bear on readings of Isa. 52:13–53:12. A review of its
history of research might offer some clues as to the context and conventions of "The Fourth Servant Song Research". Although reading
always refers to other literary works, both identifiable and anonymous,
in an extraordinary way Duhmian readings of Isa. 52:13–53:12 seem to
involve re-covering the meaning of the text through some kind of homage to Duhm's "Servant Song" thesis: a confirmation, reproduction or
corrective, or an expression of ambivalence or uncertainty towards the
text as an established "Servant Song". A study such as J. N. Oswalt's
The Book of Isaiah: Chapters 40–66 (1998) might exemplify this:

changing receptions are accounted for in terms of the changing horizons of
expectation [*Erwartungshoizont*], horizons of expectations which are now generally taken to be conditioned not solely by accumulated literary experience, but by
readers' social, economic, and political experiences as well.

However one may evaluate Duhm's conclusions, one cannot fault his observations: there is an atmospheric change at these four places in the text…It is difficult to define that change, yet most readers will acknowledge it. The language becomes more exalted and sweeping; the Servant is either left unidentified or identified in the broadest terms; the descriptions tend to be graphic and detailed; and there is a unique emphasis on what the Servant will accomplish for the world. It is even more difficult to ascertain what these data mean. In all four instances the person being addressed or described is identified as the Lord's Servant (42:1;49:3;50: 10;52:13)…My position is that in these passages Isaiah is speaking of an individual, almost certainly the Messiah, who will be the ideal Israel. Through his obedient service to God, Israel will be enabled to perform the service of blessing the nations that had been prophesied in Gen. 12:3 and elsewhere.[21]

To recent attempts to bid farewell to the "Servant Songs" as a separate group of texts, J. Blenkinsopp's *Isaiah 40–55* (2002), responds: "[B]y now it is clear that they play a critical role in chs. 40–55 and in the Book of Isaiah as a whole and that they present the reader with a unique set of problems. They are not going to go away."[22] He identifies the servant in the first song as Cyrus and in the last three as the prophet, and regards 52:13–53:12 as added to the first three songs "soon after the prophet's death".[23] Due to the scholarly consensus since Duhm, readers have become participants in a narrow discursive space restricting signifying practices. This narrowing of the text is, however, not the result of complete conformity: as will be shown, within this discursive space different interpretations of the identities of the actors and events in Isa. 52:13–53:12 are offered.

After the readings of Duhm and Steck are presented, the potential as well as the challenge in reading such a controversial text are highlighted. Readings of Isa. 52:13–53:12 are often performed by scholars who regard themselves as "mere scholars", "traditional critics" or "theologians", claiming that they are just researchers or commonsense observers. As is becoming more and more apparent, there are no non-theoretical positions but only degrees of awareness.[24] Although

---

[21] J. N. Oswalt, *The Book of Isaiah: Chapters 40–66* (NICOT; Grand Rapids: Eerdmans, 1998) 107–108.

[22] J. Blenkinsopp, *Isaiah 40–55: A New Translation with Introduction and Commentary* (AB, 19A; New York: Doubleday, 2002) 76.

[23] Blenkinsopp, *Isaiah 40–55*, p. 76.

[24] See, for instance, how in the *Historical Commentary to the Old Testament* series, the historical perspective of J. L. Koole, *Isaiah III. Volume 1/Isaiah 40–48* (Historical

more space may seem to be devoted to reading the text in question than to explicating contemporary theories, readings of Isa. 52:13–53:12 are, like all readings, theoretically contemporary.[25] In recent biblical scholarship, greater attention than before has been paid to the different forces at work in the text and reading, and a variety of possible focuses has come to the fore, e.g. biographical, historical, sociological, psychological, theological, literary and political. The significance of gender and ethnicity is also brought to the fore. Arguments have been developed based on the way in which certain details support a certain hypothesis, and the basic function of readings might be described as a reaffirmation of a system of, for example, historical or theological constructions. When paying attention to forces at work in texts and in reading, it is often asked how meaning is produced. When confronted

---

Commentary on the Old Testament; Leuven: Peeters, 1997) is made clear, and is specified as "historical interpretation" in Judaism and Christianity. In C. Houtman, W. S. Prinsloo, W. G. E. Watson and A. Wolters, "Editorial preface (I)" to this series, this is contrasted with:

> the ahistorical approach of much of contemporary reader-oriented exegesis, in which it is mainly the interaction between the modern reader and the final text that matters…The editors are committed to the view that the Old Testament was and is a vehicle of the knowledge of God – a knowledge that was originally imparted at specific times and places within the bounds of human history…Generally speaking, everything that brings the concrete historical world of the text closer to the modern reader – whether that be specific data regarding climate, geology, geography, minerals, flora and fauna, or whatever – should be treated extensively in the scholarly exposition (pp. xi; xiii).

Blenkinsopp, *Isaiah 40–55*, p. 126, explains his reading as follows: "In keeping with the character and aims of the Anchor Bible series, the commentary that follows is in the historical-critical manner, while remaining open to other readings." O. H. Steck, "Israel und Zion: Zum Probleme konzeptioneller Einheit und literarischer Schichtung in Deuterojesaja" in O. H. Steck, *Gottesknecht und Zion: Gesammelte Aufsätze zu Deuterojesaja* (Forschungen zum Alten Testament, 4; Tübingen: J. C. B. Mohr {Paul Siebeck}, 1992) 174, contrasts his own redaction-critical reading with what he designates *dramatische Endtextlesung*, see 2.2.5. J. D. W. Watts, *Isaiah 1–33* (WBC, 24; Waco, Texas: World Books: 1985) describes his commentary (including J. D. W. Watts, *Isaiah 34–66* [WBC, 25; Waco, Texas: World Books: 1987]) as distinct from historical exegesis. He reads the Book of Isaiah as "a Vision that dramatically portrays God's view of history, rather than a source book from which the historian is to piece together his view of what happened" (p. xxiv). However, in his second volume, Watts makes many attempts to locate particular passages at certain stages during the reigns of various Persian kings.

[25] This is discussed as an aspect of texts in general in P. de Man, *The Resistance to Theory* (Theory and History of Literature, 33; Minneapolis: University of Minnesota Press, 1993) 3–20. Recent attention given to theory in general might be related to an interdisciplinary discourse and a criticism of common sense as a historical construction rather than a given. In this study, discussions of theory will be particularly related to "the linguistic turn", with key terms such as text, narrative and intertextuality.

with texts, readers pursue signs. In one sense, all readings involve interpretation by way of selecting and describing signs. But signs are never simply given: they are produced by the reader through her or his reading. Accordingly, in the reading of Isa. 52:13–53:12, the reader handles details in the text and relates them to her or his answers. As interpretation is a social practice involving different protocols, different accentuations appear. In Part I of this study, this will be discussed under the headings "historising", "traditionalising", "theologising" and "textualising" (2.3.8.).

1.3. IDENTITIES IN TRANSITION

Readers of Isa. 52:13–53:12 have pursued identity in different ways. Two frequently posed questions are "who is the servant?" and "what is his fate?" Other questions pertain to textual corruptions and peculiarities, the identification of a textual unit defined as 52:13–53:12, its genre designation "Servant Song" and the question of when the text was added to Isa. *40–55.

"Identity" is a term used in many contexts, for instance in discourses more or less loosely derived from philosophy, psychoanalysis, politics, sociology, social anthropology and semiotics. In such contexts, identity is related to construction, classification, focalisation and the prioritization of one or more elements in relation to others, in which inclusion and exclusion are decisive. Identity is a matter of similarity and difference. It has been framed in terms of polarisation, for example "us" vs "them", "man" vs "woman", and on very different levels, e.g. ethnic, religious, national, political, social, sexual, psychoanalytical, textual, narrative and intertextual. In recent discussions, identity is regarded not as a state or some fixed and stable essence, but as a process, emerging relationally and constituted by discourse. In this regard, it may be asked whether identity is given or constructed, represented or produced.[26]

---

[26] S. Hall, "Introduction, Who Needs 'Identity'?" in P. de Gay, J. Evans and P. Redman (eds), *Identity: A Reader* (London: SAGE Publications, 2002) 15–30, A. Jaworski and N. Coupland, "Editors' Introduction to Part Five" in A. Jaworski and N. Coupland (eds), *The Discourse Reader* (London: Routledge, 1999) 407–414, and F. Lozada, Jr., "Identity" in A. K. M. Adam (ed), *Handbook of Postmodern Biblical Interpretation* (St. Louis, Missouri: Chalice Press, 2000) 113–119.

In "Part II: Identities in Transition", I will present a textual, a narrative and an intertextual reading of Isa. 52:13–53:12. In these three readings, the text is identified in different manners. The readings offered are not three alternatives, but supplement one another. Each reading is preceded by a brief theoretical introduction to "text", "narrative" and "intertextuality" respectively. All three readings are related to theoretical discussions concerning unstable signs and with an extended concept of text as a point of view.

The first reading, "3: Text", focuses on the linguistic relations of Isa. 52:13–53:12 and forms the basis of the two subsequent readings. The translation of the Hebrew text and textual critical issues are discussed.

The second reading, "4: Narrative", concerns the rhetorics of narrative, with special attention paid to the levels of story and narration. In the narratological reading, the trope personification and the collision of the two narrative levels of "story" ("what is told") and "narration" ("how is it told") are key. This reading shows, *inter alia*, how the two actors "he" and "we" have both become ill as punishment for their transgressions. As such, the dominant reading of Isa. 52:13–53:12 as a text about "vicarious suffering" is rejected. In this reading, attention will also be paid to the role of performativity.

The third reading, "5: Intertextuality", shows how Isa. 52:13–53:12 participate in many discourses related to humiliation and exaltation involving Israel and other peoples, sin, illness and recovery, death and descendants, and rhetorics of personification. In the intertextual part, various literary motifs in Isa. 52:13–53:12 are read in dialogue with other personification texts in the Hebrew Bible, primarily from the prophetical literature, Psalms, Lamentations and the Book of Job. In this, female personifications are also central.

CHAPTER TWO

PERSONIFYING READING

2.1. Bernhard Duhm

Bernhard Duhm (1847–1928) is a key figure in the study of
Isa. 52:13–53:12. Duhm's studies of the Old Testament have born fruit
in the study of the history of religion, prophecy and exegesis. His Isaiah research conveys both an account of the compositional history of
the Book of Isaiah as a whole and an exegesis of its sixty-six chapters.
Two theses which are later especially related to his Isaiah studies are
the thesis concerning a "Third Isaiah" and that concerning the "Servant Songs". His studies have greatly influenced all later prophetic
research in general, and Isaiah research in particular.[1]

2.1.1. *Prophecy and Prophetic Literature*

Duhm and his Protestant context presupposed a sharp opposition
between moral and cult, a high appreciation of the religious personality and a positivistic point of view. In the "Prolegomena" to his study,
*Die Theologie der Propheten als Grundlage für die innere Entwick-
lungsgeschichte der israelitischen Religion* (1875), Duhm described a
methodical ideal of allowing the subject "to speak for itself", without
rejecting the theological character of his work.[2]

---

[1] For overviews of Duhm's scholarship, see H.-J. Kraus, *Geschichte der historisch-
kritischen Erforschung des Alten Testaments* (Neukirchen-Vluyn: Neukirchener Verlag, 1982) 275–283, R. E. Clements, *A Century of Old Testament Study* (Guildford:
Lutterworth Press, 1983) 61–66, and H. G. Reventlow, "Die Prophetie im Urteil Bernhard Duhms", *ZTK* 85 (1988) 259–274.
[2] B. Duhm, *Die Theologie der Propheten als Grundlage für die innere Entwicklungsgeschichte der israelitischen Religion* (Bonn: Marcus, 1875) 2. Theologically, he did not
claim a *voraussetzungslos* attitude (an absence of presuppositions), but emphasised a
distinction between presupposition (*Voraussetzung*) and prejudice (*Vorurteil*), the last
leading to *Tendenz*. From an ideal-historical point of view, Duhm pursued a historical
continuity between the Israelite and the Christian religion. He rejected the theology
of the history of salvation as well as the concept of revelation in connection with the
theological presuppositions.

According to Duhm, in any study of the religion of Israel, beginning with the prophets was essential.[3] Duhm's view of the prophets
was connected to a theory about the way in which the Israelite religion
was originally a simple "popular religion of nature".[4] The prophets distinguished themselves from the preceding thanks to the new religious
insight they had acquired, which was later eroded with the Law.[5] At
the centre of the religion of the prophets was devotion: comprehend-
ing God as personality and standing in a moral relation to him.[6] The
religion of Israel was closely connected to the people, expressed by
the formula "Israel, the people of YHWH and YHWH, the God of
Israel".[7]

Duhm regarded the theology of the prophets as the driving force
behind the evolution of Israel's religion, and claimed there was a clear
separation between the "earlier" prophets (in the "historical books")
and the "writing" prophets.[8] He was especially interested in the personalities of the prophets and offered a detailed portrait of each. They
were described as "historiographers", "poets" and the "choirmasters of
the public religious and political life".[9] The early prophets were bound
to nature and an emotional religion (like Hosea), while prophets such
as Amos and Micah represented a more moral judgment.[10] Amos'

---

[3] Duhm, *Die Theologie der Propheten*, p. 15.

[4] Duhm, *Die Theologie der Propheten*, pp. 51; 60.

[5] Duhm has often been regarded as confirming the Graf-Kuenen-Wellhausen thesis about the post-Exilic origin of the priestly source, implying the disappearance of
the Mosaic law period as a basis for prophecy (see *Die Theologie der Propheten*, e.g.
pp. 17–19). Reventlow, "Die Prophetie im Urteil Bernhard Duhms", p. 263, nuances
Duhm's involvement in the Pentateuch discussions by claiming that the source critical thesis is not the basis of Duhm's study of the prophets, but that Graf's thesis that
the prophets precede the Law supports Duhm's own ideas. Whereas the romanticists
Herder and Eichorn had earlier emphasised the individuality of the prophets, and
the idealists and historians Ewald and Gesenius had emphasised their historical basis,
Duhm melded the two aspects into what he presented as a continuous history of evolution of the religion of Israel. Thus, his presentation of a theology of the prophets also
implied an account of the evolution of the religion of the ancient Israel.

[6] Duhm, *Die Theologie der Propheten*, p. 53.

[7] Duhm, *Die Theologie der Propheten*, p. 96.

[8] In a later study, B. Duhm, *Israels Propheten* (Lebensfrage, 26; Tübingen: J. C.
B. Mohr {Paul Siebeck} 1916) a distinction was more strongly accentuated between
the "earlier" and "later" prophets by relating the first ones to a pre-literary, oral (and
anonymous) level as a contrast to the later writing ones. Cf. 2.3.1.

[9] Duhm, *Die Theologie der Propheten*, p. 24.

[10] Duhm, *Die Theologie der Propheten*, pp. 80; 101; 103; 186. Kraus, *Geschichte der
historisch-kritischen Erforschung des Alten Testaments*, p. 281, shows how Duhm's

preaching could be described as "ethical idealism", but the idea of the moral personality still hovered "in the objective sphere of judicial acts and natural humaneness" without a personal relation between God and man and without an inner aim.[11] With Isaiah, prophecy remained bound to this level. However, Isaiah also added a moral basis and an emphasis on the word of YHWH.[12] Additionally, with Isaiah a new comprehension of YHWH's people appeared, which involved their being regarded as a community of faithful.[13] The still imperfect relationship between YHWH and his people was partly overcome by Jeremiah, whose prophecy introduced a period of subjective piety and a religion borne by spiritual personalities.[14] Jeremiah also broached universalistic ideas and ideas of a religious community standing above the individually pious. With "Second Isaiah", the idea of election was introduced. Like "First Isaiah", the majesty of God was at the centre of the message of "Second Isaiah", but through his universalism "Second Isaiah" lost the moral obligation of YHWH's people, by announcing salvation and comfort to the children of God.[15]

2.1.2. The Book of Isaiah

After *Die Theologie der Propheten*, Duhm's subsequent study of prophecy was a commentary in 1892 on the Book of Isaiah.[16] In the preface

---

focus on the prophet's "ethical idealism" is further expanded in Duhm, *Israels Propheten* (1916). In this study, Duhm also distinguished between prophets of salvation (*Heilspropheten*) and prophets of doom (*Unheilspropheten*), who had irreconcilable messages. The prophets from Amos and onwards were prophets of doom, conveying a new type of revelation. Kraus, p. 278, describes Duhm's perspective as idealistic and anthropocentric. Reventlow, "Die Prophetie im Urteil Bernhard Duhms", p. 260, ascribes Duhm's emphasis on the moral side of religion to the Kantian climate of his time, although Duhm himself is no "Kantianer".

[11] Duhm, *Die Theologie der Propheten*, pp. 103; 126.
[12] Duhm, *Die Theologie der Propheten*, pp. 83–84.
[13] Duhm, *Die Theologie der Propheten*, pp. 174–175.
[14] Duhm, *Die Theologie der Propheten*, pp. 246–247. Unlike Jeremiah, Ezekiel has not much to do with prophetic religion; the religious personality is placed in the background, while temple and sacrifice are brought to the fore ("wir befinden uns schon in der Luft des Judaismus und des Talmud", p. 260).
[15] Duhm, *Die Theologie der Propheten*, p. 291, regarded the thoughts of "Second Isaiah" as close to those of the apostle Paul.
[16] Between *Die Theologie der Propheten* (1875) and *Das Buch Jesaia* (1892), Duhm only published his inaugural lecture in Basel, "Über Ziel und Methode der theologischen Wissenschaft" in 1889. I have not been able to find this, but it is referred to in Reventlow, "Die Prophetie im Urteil Bernhard Duhms", p. 269, n. 53. Duhm's *Das*

to *Das Buch Jesaja*, he presupposed that the prophets wrote correctly and sensibly. He claimed that an analysis of metre allowed individual speech units to be recognised, and for glosses, additions and other secondary material to be discovered and removed. The exploration of the authentic text, the prophet's *ipsissima verba*, was one corrective to dogmatic readings.[17]

In *Die Theologie der Propheten* (1875), Duhm regarded Isa.* 40–66 as a unit written by the prophet himself in two phases: Isa. 40–49 before the wars of Cyrus, and Isa. 50–66 afterwards.[18] In the later *Das Buch Jesaja*, he claimed that Isa. *1–39 constituted "First Isaiah", Isa. *40–55 "Second Isaiah", and Isa. *56–66 "Third Isaiah".[19] Behind

---

Buch Jesaia was published in four different editions; the first in 1892, the second in 1902, the third in 1914 and the fourth 1922 (reprinted in 1968), with only slight alterations. Since the differences between the four editions are rather insignificant, it is of no decisive importance which one is taken as a point of view. In this study I will refer the second edition, since this is the one easiest available to me.

[17] Duhm, *Das Buch Jesaja*, p. iii. This attitude to the prophetic texts is also visible for example in his commentary *Das Buch Jeremia* (KHAT, 11; Freiburg: Mohr, 1901), in which he distinguished between secondary, inauthentic material, which included a large collection of prose sermons closely related to the Deuteronomistic writings, and authentic Jeremianic poetic parts, i.e. the main prophecies of Jer. 1–25.

[18] Duhm, *Die Theologie der Propheten*, p. 275.

[19] Duhm did not develop his theses in a vacuum. M. A. Sweeney, "On the Road to Duhm: Isaiah in Nineteenth-Century Critical Scholarship" in McGinnis and Tull, *"As Those who are Taught"*, pp. 243–261, offers an overview of some of Duhm's precursors in depicting the formation of the book of Isaiah. Sweeney dwells especially on Eichhorn, Gesenius, Hitzig, Ewald and Dillmann. It is often assumed that the literary unity of the Book of Isaiah was doubted even in the twelfth century by Ibn Ezra. Within critical biblical scholarship, it has been claimed that the thesis of "Second Isaiah" was first put forth by J. C. Döderlein, *Esaias ex recensione textus hebraei ad fidem codicum manuscriptorum et versionum antiquarum latine vertit notasque varii argumenti subiecit* (1775). According to J. M. Vincent, *Studien zur literarischen Eigenart und zur geistigen Heimat von Jesaja, Kap. 40–48* (Beiträge zur biblischen Exegese und Theologie, 5; Frankfurt am Main: Peter Lang, 1977) 17–18, Döderlein did not claim this until his third edition from 1798. Vincent claims that J. B. Koppe, *D. Robert Lowth's Jesaias übersetzt mit einer Einleitung und kritischen philologischen und erläuternden Anmerkungen* (Leipzig, 1780), was the first to suggest an exilic authorship for Isa. 40–55. R. Smend, *Deutsche Alttestamentler in drei Jahrhunderten* (Göttingen: Vandenhoeck & Ruprecht, 1989) 31, claims that the thesis about "Second Isaiah" was not provided by Döderlein in 1775, but by J. G. Eichhorn, *Einleitung in das Alte Testament 3* (1783) 84–86, whereas M. Mulzer, "Döderlein und Deuterojesaja", *BN* 66 (1993) 15–22, goes for Döderlein and his second edition in 1781. None of the writings of Döderlein, Koppe nor Eichorn has been available to me. For brief overviews of the discussions of the theses of "Second Isaiah" as a literary unit, see H. M. Barstad, *The Babylonian Captivity of the Book of Isaiah: "Exilic" Judah and the Provenance of Isaiah 40–55* (The Institute for Comparative Research in Human Culture. Serie B: Skrifter CII; Oslo: Novus Forlag, 1997) 53, n. 1, and P. T. Willey, *Remember the Former Things:*

these different "Isaiahs" there were questions of geographical, temporal and theological discontinuity. Duhm was also interested in the religious personality.[20] Of the three main parts into which he sorted the Book of Isaiah, 1–39 and 40–66 remained isolated from each other until they were joined in the time of the Common Era, whereas 40–66 might be a closed unit in the time of the Chronicles.[21] In his view of Isa. 40–66, he clearly distinguished between three different authors and offered an individual portrait of each: the earliest author is the anonymous one labelled "Second Isaiah", who wrote Isa. *40–55 around 540 BCE. According to Duhm, "Second Isaiah" lived neither in Babylon nor Palestine, but probably in Lebanon and possibly in a Phoenician place (cf. 49:12).[22] Isa. *40–55 consist of a chain of "prophetical-lyrical poetry", proclaiming that YHWH would soon lead his people back from Babylon to Jerusalem. Central in Isa. *40–55 is comfort for YHWH's favourite, Israel, forgiveness for transgressors, a splendid future, Cyrus as YHWH's tool in his plan, a fight against other peoples and an admonition for them to also turn to the true religion. "Second Isaiah" participates in the prophetic religious evolution, but is also characterised by a "naïve subjectivity and world view".[23]

The second author is the one behind the "Servant Songs" (*Die Ebed-Jahwe-Lieder, EJL*). In *Die Theologie der Propheten* (1875), Duhm regarded Isa. 40–66 as a unit and 42:1–7, 49:1–6, 50:4–9 and 52:13–53:12 as an exceptional group of texts which he labelled "Servant Songs".[24] He treated these four texts as a separate source and a later

---

The Recollection of Previous Texts in Second Isaiah (SBLDS, 161; Atlanta: Scholars Press, 1997) 12, n. 5. Cf. 2.3.3.

[20] Kraus, *Geschichte der historisch-kritischen Erforschung des Alten Testaments*, p. 280, describes Duhm's understanding of prophecy as psychological and neo-romantic, with reference, *inter alia*, to the preface in Duhm, *Das Buch Jesaia*, and more clearly in Duhm, *Israels Propheten* (1916).

[21] Duhm, *Das Buch Jesaia*, p. xiii. He divided the redactional unit of Isa. 40–66 into three parts: 40–48, 49–57 and 58–66. He also claimed that the redactor had taken 48:22 from 57:21, so that the first part (40–48) acquired a closing similar to the second and third parts (49–57 and 58–66), thereby indicating that the three parts belonged together. Other redactional additions are 42:5–7, 44:9–20, 46:6–8, many in 48, as well as 50:10–11, 52:3–6, 58:13–14, 59:5–8, 66:23–24. In the later editions of his Isaiah commentary, Duhm only slightly altered which verses he regarded as authentic and which were later additions, cf. 2.1.2. n. 16.

[22] Duhm, *Das Buch Jesaia*, pp. xiii; xviii.

[23] Duhm, *Das Buch Jesaia*, pp. xvii–xviii. In *Die Theologie der Propheten*, p. 278, Duhm characterised "Second Isaiah" as poet more than prophet.

[24] According to Ruprecht, *Die Auslegungsgeschichte zu den sogenannten Gottesknechtliedern*, p. 59, this delimitation of the texts was known from the *parashot*.

emendation by the prophet himself, who had reused a prophetical biography of Jeremiah.[25] In *Das Buch Jesaja*, Duhm regarded 42:1–4, 49:1–6, 50:4–9 and 52:13–53:12 as added to *40–55, relying on both "Second Isaiah", Jeremiah and Job, but not known to "Second Isaiah". He dated the four *EJL* to the post-exilic times, although probably before the "Third Isaiah", and he thought that they might not have been written in exile.[26] Duhm proposed literary critical arguments for this separation, and contrasted the style, language, symmetry of stichoi and strophes, temperament and theme of the author of the *EJL* with the utterances of the exilic prophet. He asserted that the four texts had been inserted at random wherever there was space on the scroll, without any connection to either the preceding or the following verses.[27] The texts might once have existed as a separate book, and some of the original pieces may not have been preserved.[28]

The third part, Isa. *56–66, due to both its form and content, was a result of an individual and independent author, although marked by a redactor of the final book as a whole.[29] Duhm called this author "Third Isaiah". He dated his activities to late post-exilic times, in the time of Ezra and Nehemiah, and his location was Jerusalem, according to Duhm. He regarded "Third Isaiah" as an important source for any movement which grew out of the theocracy of Ezra and the Samaritan congregation.[30] Thus, Isa. *56–66 were separate from Isa. *40–55 on historical, theological and literary grounds. In addition, Isa. *40–55 and *56–66 were independent of Isa. *1–39 because they had an absolutely separate tradition-history, only vaguely related to questions of original setting.[31]

Duhm's contribution is not the delimitation of these units, but his description of them as literarily independent units, ascribed to another author than for the literary surroundings (p. 134).

[25] Duhm, *Die Theologie der Propheten*, pp. 288–289.

[26] Duhm, *Das Buch Jesaia*, pp. xiii; xvii–xviii; 277. According to him, this author influenced Trito-Isaiah and Malachi.

[27] Duhm, *Das Buch Jesaia*, p. 285.

[28] Duhm, *Das Buch Jesaia*, pp. xv; xx.

[29] Duhm, *Das Buch Jesaia*, p. xiii.

[30] Duhm, *Das Buch Jesaia*, p. xix.

[31] C. R. Seitz, *Zion's Final Destiny. The Development of the Book of Isaiah: A Reassessment of Isaiah 36–39* (Minneapolis: Fortress Press, 1991) presents a comprehensive review of Duhm's theses concerning the composition of Isa. 1–66. He claims that Duhm argued from two directions: *historically* from Isa. 1–39 forward to Isa. 40–66, and *editorially* from Second and Third Isaiah back to First Isaiah. According to Seitz, this is of special interest in relation to current Isaiah research:

2.1.3. *Servant Songs*

In *Das Buch Isaiah*, Duhm proposed his thesis about the "Servant Songs", claiming that 42:1–4, 49:1–6, 50:4–9 and 52:13–53:12 were an independent group of texts not original to Isa. *40–55, but later additions. He designated the four separate texts mainly as *Gedichte*, and twice with the synonymous *Lieder*. He asserted the unity of the authorship of the songs, though he had some doubt as to 52:13–53:12 (cf. 2.1.4.), and identified the servant as the same in all four songs, i.e. as an individual.[32]

In *Die Theologie der Propheten*, Duhm had already drawn special attention to a figure he labelled *Gottesknecht* and to Isa. 42:1–7, 49:1–6, 50:4–9 and 52:13–53:12 as a special group of texts.[33] He identified the servant in these four texts as "the ideal Israel, who has the word of God", as opposed to the "empirical" Israel depicted elsewhere in Isa. 40–55.[34] Whereas YHWH is the highest and only God in the

---

No one disputes the historical distance of chapters 40–66 from what precedes… [T]he intriguing thing to note is that Duhm never assumes that the *historical* independence of Second Isaiah necessitates its *editorial* independence as well…Put in another way, just because Second Isaiah chapters presuppose the Babylonian debacle does not mean they must be independent of Isa. 1–39 on compositional grounds. Much material within Isa. 1–39 likewise presupposes the events of 587 BCE, and yet, according to Duhm's theory this material has circulated within a compositional orbit utterly independent of Isa. 40–66, yet wholly at home within the evolving First Isaiah book (pp. 2; 5, his italics).

[32] He thereby challenged the collective interpretation, which had been based upon the assumption that Isa. 40–55 (66) were a literary unit, and that the servant must be Israel throughout, because in a number of other passages, Israel is explicitly called servant (See 5.17. n. 324). Duhm, *Das Buch Jesaia*, pp. 279–280, depicted his own earlier collective interpretation of the servant as the most superficial interpretation, and explained this as follows: when it is said that the servant shall bring the religion to the peoples, this does not mean that he shall carry it himself; "he did not cry" (42:2) means that he did not try to play a political role (as the contemporaries of Isaiah attempted); the faint-hearted are the Gentiles etc. According to Duhm, the question of who the servant is is best answered when the first three *EJL* are also considered: nothing could be more absurd than for an exilic writer to say that Israel was morning by morning inspired (50:4–9); no Old Testament writer would ever claim that Israel has suffered completely innocently nor the ridiculous assumption that Israel "has not opened its mouth" (53:7) (p. 375).

[33] Ruprecht, *Die Auslegungsgeschichte zu den sogenannten Gottesknechtliedern*, pp. 130–131; 171, n. 42, comments on the use of the term *Knecht Gottes*, which appeared in scholarship about what was later called *Ebed-Jahweh-Lied* in a study by F. W. Umbrett in 1828. Moreover, the term *Ebed-Jahweh-Lied*, which has later become a *terminus technicus* for these four texts, was used only three times by Duhm, who mostly alternated between the designations *Gedicht* and *Dichtung*.

[34] Duhm, *Die Theologie der Propheten*, p. 292.

world, YHWH's servant represents the true religion, with his obedience and recognition of God. The true servant of YHWH has received the Word of God consciously and willingly so he cannot be identified as the whole of Israel. Compared to this historical, prophetical figure, the people have a rather different status. The servant people of YHWH constitute a future and ideal figure rather than something contemporaneous. YHWH's people shall be created by the insight and task of the prophet.[35] If the Lord's servant is understood as "the ideal Israel", this contact with God is passed on to the empirical Israel and also to the whole world.[36]

According to Duhm, the idea of the Lord's servant appears in both "Second Isaiah" and the "Servant Songs". In *Das Buch Jesaja*, he described the difference of this idea between "Second Isaiah" and "Servant Songs". According to "Second Isaiah", Israel is YHWH's servant; elected, protected and determined for a promising future, but at present the people are blind and deaf, imprisoned and plundered, despised by peoples and full of sin. However, the servant of the four *EJL* is superior to the people: he is innocent, YHWH's disciple, called for a mission for the sake of the people and peoples – and he attends to his vocation in silence. He is suffering like Jeremiah and Job; molested of faithless, stricken by leprosy by YHWH – not like Israel, whom foreigners became oppressed by.[37] In *Die Theologie der Propheten*, Duhm interpreted the servant of the *EJL* as "the ideal Israel, who has the word of God", and the *EJL* as written by a younger contemporary and taken over by "Second Isaiah".[38] In *Das Buch Jesaja* he changed his mind. The servant was identified as a historical person; not a prophet proper, but a disciple of the prophets, a teacher of the law, a spiritual advisor and a dying, righteous man. He suffered and was abused, first and foremost by his own people. The author of the songs is a humble spirit, more thoughtful than "Second Isaiah".[39] He talks about the guilt of the people, but also about the hope of the future of a YHWH-based world religion. The author of the songs and his protagonist are figures of light (*Lichtgestalten*) in the "first dark century" of the post-exilic

---

[35] Duhm, *Die Theologie der Propheten*, pp. 278–279.
[36] Duhm, *Die Theologie der Propheten*, p. 292.
[37] Duhm, *Das Buch Jesaia*, p. 277.
[38] Duhm, *Die Theologie der Propheten*, p. 275, claimed that a funeral speech by Jeremiah underlies Isa. 53, but that this is of no importance as "Second Isaiah" has completely rewritten it.
[39] Duhm, *Das Buch Jesaia*, p. xviii.

community. The author speaks to the unhappy, faint-hearted and despairing, whether Jews or Gentiles, proclaiming blessings, expectations and comfort.[40]

In the first *EJL*, Isa. 42:1–4, the servant and his task are made known. He is identified as a "post-prophetic figure" (*nachprophetische Gestalt*) who proclaimed nothing new, but rather taught truth revealed from long ago, and admonished and comforted the individual.[41] Duhm described him as a post-exilic figure, belonging to a period when religion was no longer the driving force in history. Nevertheless, through religion, he perceived the absolute truth and the perfect way of life.[42] The second *EJL*, Isa. 49:1–6, is conveyed in first-person speech and concerns the equipping of the servant for Israel and the world. YHWH has rescued him, and also has the deity caused the return of the Diaspora to be a part of his higher aim: to illuminate the Gentiles. In this, the poet expresses the universal tendency of the prophetic religion. The emphasis is on the formal side of religion, on religion as absolute truth.[43] In the third *EJL*, Isa. 50:4–9, the servant's bad experiences, acquired through his vocation, are depicted, but also his patience and firm conviction in YHWH's help and justification.[44]

2.1.4. *Isa. 52:13–53:12*

According to Duhm, in Isa. 52:13–53:12 the servant's coming elevation is placed over his previous inferiority.[45] The servant has been misjudged, despised, and has suffered and died for his people, and just because of this he has deserved this coming glory. 52:13–53:12 may consist of two originally separate pieces; 52:13–15; 53:11 (from after צדיק)–12 and 53:1–11 (until צדיק), with YHWH the speaker in the first part, and the prophet in the second, but the two harmonise with each other.[46] An unheard-of wonder is prophesied. Duhm claimed that

---

[40] Duhm, *Das Buch Jesaia*, pp. xviii; 279.
[41] Duhm, *Das Buch Jesaia*, p. 278.
[42] Duhm, *Das Buch Jesaia*, p. 278–279.
[43] Duhm, *Das Buch Jesaia*, pp. 331; 334.
[44] Duhm, *Das Buch Jesaia*, p. 341.
[45] Duhm, *Das Buch Jesaia*, p. 355.
[46] Duhm, *Das Buch Jesaia*, p. 355. He also moved 52:14, apart from the first four words, to after 53:2 ("Keine Gestalt hatte er noch Hoheit und kein Aussehen. So unmenschlich entstelt war sein Aussehen und seine Gestalt den Menschen nicht mehr ähnlich"). According to him, this is unnecessary, but also not disruptive, and it makes the verses correspond better. He further emended עָלֶיךָ to עָלָיו, i.e. 52:14a–15: "Wie

it is not the suffering and the death of the servant which are of significance, but how this leads to restoration and exaltation.[47]

Duhm identified the "we" from 53:1 onwards as including both the
poet and his people.[48] In 53:3, the servant's illnesses are understood literally as his suffering from leprosy. In 53:4, the illnesses are explained
as really "ours" due to sin, but imposed upon the servant instead of
on "us". "We" regard him as stricken by God, with his leprosy stigma-
tising him as a great sinner.[49] The "piercing through" and "crushing"
of 53:5 describe the effects of leprosy. Thus, the servant died of this
disease, and was not put to death by men (despite 53:8–9).[50] According to Duhm, the innocent servant did not suffer for the sin of man
in general; in that respect, he was no precursor to Jesus. However, he
suffered and died for the sins of his עַם "people " (53:8); it was not God
who put him to death.[51] What is new in this is not that an innocent
man is punished for the guilty people of his time (cf. Saul and David
in 2 Sam. 21:1ff); the significance lies in the personality of the one suffering and in his voluntary and conscious sacrifice.[52] In this regard,
"we" are not godless or impious, as the "we" do believe that YHWH
metes out punishment for sins. But the "we" do not have any deeper
sense of guilt, and even less sense of the self-denying power of bearing

---

über ihn sich viele entsetzen, so wird er erglänzen vor vielen") (pp. 355–357). For
עָלָיו...יַזֶּה in 52:15, see Appendix 2.

[47] Duhm, *Das Buch Jesaia*, pp. xviii; 357.

[48] Duhm, *Das Buch Jesaia*, p. 358. He interpreted Isa. 53:1 as a prophetic vision
(cf. Isa. 28:18), in which the prophet says something almost unbelievable; it can only
be believed by those who have already had the wonder of YHWH revealed; those
who possess the prophetic capability of seeing and hearing (pp. 356–357). Thus, he
interpreted "our" questions as pointing forwards, expressing incredibly good news
and expecting positive answers: the questions point to "our" belief, knowledge and
insight.

[49] Duhm, *Das Buch Jesaia*, p. 359.

[50] Duhm, *Das Buch Jesaia*, pp. 361–362.

[51] Duhm, *Das Buch Jesaia*, pp. 359; 362. In Duhm, *Die Theologie der Propheten*,
p. 296, he explained that the servant did not suffer for the whole world, but only for
Israel (53:4–6; 8). The harsh punishment was deserved (42:23–25). The people had also
done penance, but not in the same way as the servant. It was his suffering, death and
acknowledgement (53:11) which made the restitution of the people possible (54:1ff).

[52] Duhm, *Das Buch Jesaia*, p. 359, explained this as a sacrifice, but did not use the
term *Stellvertretung*. As regards the sheep imagery of Isa. 53:7, he commented that
while in Jer. 11:19 the gullibility of Jeremiah is emphasised, Isa. 53:7 concerns the
endurance and compliance of the servant (p. 361). Duhm did not comment on the
slaughter motif.

others' sin.[53] According to Duhm, in Isa. 52:13–53:12 the servant is, if possible, even more individually depicted than in the three previous songs, and an interpretation of him as the real or true people of Israel is absolutely impossible.[54] Both his biography as well as the depiction of his future indicate that this is an individual, not a collective. After he has been stricken by God to death and burial, he does not only live (like a collective) or continue to live (*wieder leben wird*, like a people whose power is impossible to eliminate, and like a root which always bursts), but he himself lives on for a long time and also gains children.[55]

A clear difference between the author of the "Servant Songs" and that of "Second Isaiah" appears from the following: while the former allowed the innocent servant to suffer and die for the guilty people, the second sacrificed the peoples for the far-from innocent Israel (Isa. 43:3–4).[56] In Isa. 53, the question of how the blind people could be set free from their sin and guilt is in some way answered: the servant's role is to wipe out the consequences of the sin (*Tilgung der Folgen der Sünde*) of the people.[57]

---

[53] Duhm, *Das Buch Jesaia*, pp. 359–360. He then described how the "we" thank "him" ("partly shyly, partly haughtily", *halb scheu, halb hochmütig*) and feel sympathy for him, but are mere human beings with their naïve selfishness and thoughtlessness.

[54] Duhm, *Das Buch Jesaia*, p. 355.

[55] Duhm, *Das Buch Jesaia*, p. 367.

[56] Duhm, *Das Buch Jesaia*, p. 361.

[57] Duhm, *Das Buch Jesaia*, p. 277. In *Die Theologie der Propheten*, p. 297, Duhm described vicarious suffering (*Stellvertretung*) as a dismal alienation of religion (*traurige Veräusserlichung der Religion*), in accordance with his assessment of the exterior as inferior, and (individual) moral activity as the most valuable. He interpreted the servant's suffering as vicarious (*stellvertretend*), but emphasised that the people suffer as much as him. Whereas the servant knows the cause of the suffering and that it is necessary to do penance for sin, the people are ignorant of why they are blind and dumb, and have only superficial thoughts about what it means to do penance (cf. 58:1ff.). In his interpretation of Isa. 53 in Duhm, *Das Buch Jesaia*, p. 359, he explained the servant's fate as sacrifice, but did not use the term *Stellvertretung*, cf. 2.1.4. n. 52. Interesting is Duhm's treatment of the textual problems of 53:10–11, instances which have later become decisive for the interpretations of the servant's vicarious suffering. In *Das Buch Jesaia*, p. 365, he emended תָּשִׂים to יָשֵׂם and אָשָׁם to מְשָׁם "Lust", and interpreted the expression *Lust der Seele* as a parallel to children. He translated 53:10: "Doch Jahwe gefiels, ihn zu reinigen, Neu sprossen zu lassen sein Alter; Die Lust seiner Seele wird er sehen, Samen lang von Leben." He also rendered rather freely 53:11: "([E]r rettet) von Mühsal seine Seele, lässt sie sehen das Licht, satt werden, von seinem Übel spricht er ihn gerecht. Ein Spott ist mein (?) Knecht den Vielen, doch ihre Sünden, er lud sie auf", p. 366. Reventlow, "Die Prophetie im Urteil Bernhard Duhms", p. 267, explains Duhm's judgment of *Stellvertretung* as follows: "Er ist ein typischer Vertreter des religiösen Liberalismus mit einem pelagianischen Anstrich".

2.1.5. *Summing up*

Duhm's studies bore fruit in the history of Ancient Israel's religion, prophetic research and exegesis. His studies into the Book of Isaiah explicate the long and complex process of formation behind the prophetic texts. Duhm presupposed that a foundation of historical fact can be attained by using appropriate methods and that this historical foundation can shed light upon the true nature of biblical faith. According to him, the prophets brought a new ideal into religion. They prepared the way for the gospel, not as foretellers of Christ or according to a promise-fulfilment programme, but through their preaching of moral earnestness, the rejection of cult and an individual relationship to God. In his description of a religious development, Duhm's idea of the dualism of "nature" and "moral spirit" is connected to romantic-idealistic concepts. The presuppositions of his theses are related for example to his positivistic, neo-romantic and psychological view of the prophets, prophecy and prophetic literature.

Aspects of his understanding of the Hebrew texts and their authors have been of immense influence on the biblical exegesis in terms of textual and literary criticism, for instance, his attempt to reconstruct an *Urtext* and a metrical analysis. He sought to find the relative chronology of the biblical texts as well as the sources the authors had used. As he argued, Isa. 1–39 and 40–55; 56–66 are obviously separate from each other due to historical, geographical and theological reasons, but according to him, they were primarily separate on editorial levels.[58]

Duhm's thesis about the "Servant Songs" is characterised by a historical-biographical interpretation of a *Gottesknecht* and his general emphasis on great men as driving forces in the evolution of the history of religion in Ancient Israel. Interestingly, in his pursuit of the historical biography of the servant, a concept of vicarious suffering was not of great importance. As regards the identity of the servant, he changed his mind: from initially identifying him as the ideal Israel in *Die Theologie der Propheten* (1875), to a contemporary of the prophet, suffering from leprosy, in *Das Buch Jesaja* (1892).

---

[58] Seitz, *Zion's Final Destiny*, p. 13, emphasises that in Duhm's studies, it is of importance that:

> Second Isaiah was not independent of First Isaiah because he was a prophet in Phoenicia (or Babylon); chapters *40–55 and *56–66 were independent of *1–39 because they had an absolutely separate tradition-history, only vaguely related to questions of original setting.

2.2. ODIL HANNES STECK

I have chosen the studies of the Book of Isaiah by Odil Hannes Steck (1935–2001) as an illustration of a reception of Duhm's reading of Isa. 52:13–53:12. In articles and monographs, Steck has covered a broad range of areas of biblical studies, comprising biblical theology, historiography, method and exegesis, where he has been especially concerned with prophetic and apocryphal literature.[59] He follows the Duhmian tradition, while contesting some points of Duhm's theses. Steck's studies of Isaiah represent a traditional historical-critical approach with a special interest in redaction criticism. His studies are comprehensive and details from his interpretations are often referred to in the secondary literature. Most of the studies by Steck to which I refer were published in the 1980s.[60] I have chosen to focus especially on these studies not because they are the most recent, but because they are comprehensive and influential, and might function as an illustrative example of personifying reading.

2.2.1. *The Book of Isaiah*

Steck has offered a redaction-critical approach to the Book of Isaiah. This is based on what he terms a model of development (*Werdemodell*), according to which he explains Isa. 1–66 as consisting of individual words (*Einzellogien*), collections (*Sammlungen*) and additions (*Zusätze*). He outlines an inner-Isaianic reception on a total of nine

---

[59] Steck's studies mainly pertain to prophetic literature, but he has not written extensively on the phenomenon of prophecy itself. See, however, O. H. Steck, "Prophetische Prophetenauslegung" in H. F. Geißer, H. J. Luibl, W. Mostert and H. Weder (eds), *Wahrheit der Schrift-Wahrheit der Auslegung: Eine Zürcher Vorlesungsreihe zu Gerhard Ebelings 80. Geburtstag am 6. Juli 1992* (Zürich: Theologischer Verlag Zürich, 1993) 198–244. In O. H. Steck, *The Prophetic Books and their Theological Witness* (St. Louis, Missouri: Chalice Press, 2000), he is "historically inquiring synchronic reading of the entire book" (p. 20), i.e. he is pursuing the legacy of redactional tradents and their presentation of YHWH's acts in history.

[60] O. H. Steck, "Aspekte des Gottesknechts in Deuterojesajas 'Ebed-Jahwe-Liedern", *ZAW* 96 (1984) 372–390, which is about the three first songs, and O. H. Steck, "Aspekte des Gottesknechts in Jes 52,13–53,12", *ZAW* 97 (1985) 36–58, which is about the fourth, were republished in Steck, *Gottesknecht und Zion* (1992), together with six articles about the Zion material in Isaiah, which are slightly revised versions of previously published articles, as well as one new article about the reception of the Servant Songs at various redactional levels. In yet another article, Steck presents an elaboration of the Zion image in Isa. 40–55 within a broader literary and theological context. These articles will also be referred to below.

levels.[61] He employs the terms "First Isaiah" for Isa. *1–39, "Second Isaiah" for Isa. *40–66 and "The Great Isaiah" (*Großjesaja*) for the final Isa. 1–66.[62] Steck claims that "Second Isaiah" originated independently of "First Isaiah" on literary, editorial and traditional-historical grounds, with Isa. 35 as a redactional bridge between "First" and "Second" Isaiah.[63] He (re-)constructs an independent *Grundschrift* of "Second Isaiah" consisting of 40:1–52:10, as well as the first three *EJL* and 52:13–53:12.[64] The main message of "Second Isaiah" concerns the bringing home of Jacob/Israel from Babylon.[65]

2.2.2. *Servant Songs*

Steck introduces his *EJL* research by regretting the lack of historical information in these texts, before he proceeds on to treat the first three *EJL* "in their classical and repeatedly well-founded delimitation".[66] His treatment of the first *EJL* is initiated with a reference to Elliger's view that in Isa. 42:1–4, YHWH presents the servant (*Gottesknecht*) from three different aspects, and that this probably occurs in the heavenly court. The three aspects are: how he is equipped for (42:1), how he carries out (42:2–3a), and finally his successful completion of his commission (42:3b–4).[67] After a presentation of the triadic scheme related to a

---

[61] In 2.2.5. I will focus on the five redactional levels to which Steck relates the four *EJL*.

[62] O. H. Steck, *Bereitete Heimkehr: Jesaja 35 als redaktionelle Brücke zwischen dem Ersten und dem Zweitem Jesaja* (Stuttgarter Bibel-Studien, 121; Stuttgart: Katholisches Bibelwerk, 1985) 9.

[63] Steck, *Bereitete Heimkehr*, pp. 11; 101. According to him, Isa. 35 was composed in the Ptolemaic period, long after Isa. 1–34 and 40–62 had been completed as two distinct literary units. Isa. 35 has been closely developed on the basis of Isa. 34 and 40, its "surrounding texts" (*Nachbartexten*, pp. 13–37). Isa. 35 has borrowed from both chapters in order to form a bridge spanning the two Isaiahs. Seitz, *Zion's Final Destiny*, p. 18, comments on Steck's model of development for Isa. 1–66: "[A] basic independence is still in force for the 'two Isaiahs', and in this sense the legacy of Duhm regarding editorial independence applies in a modified form."

[64] O. H. Steck, "Die Gottesknechts-Texte und ihre redaktionelle Rezeption im Zweiten Jesaja" in Steck, *Gottesknecht und Zion*, p. 150.

[65] Steck, "Israel und Zion", p. 176. In K. Joachimsen, "Steck's Five Stories of the Servant in Isaiah lii 13– liii 12, and Beyond", *VT* 57 (2007) 210–224, I provide an abridged presentation of Steck's Isaiah studies.

[66] O. H. Steck, "Aspekte des Gottesknechts in Deuterojesajas 'Ebed-Jahwe-Liedern'" in Steck, *Gottesknecht und Zion*, p. 3. Steck refers to K. Elliger, *Deuterojesaja. 1. Teilband Jesaja 40,1–45,7* (BK XI/1; Neukirchen-Vluyn: Neukirchener Verlag, 1978) 199–221.

[67] Steck, "Aspekte des Gottesknechts in Deuterojesajas 'Ebed-Jahwe-Liedern'", p. 3. Steck also refers to O. Kaiser, *Der königliche Knecht: Eine traditions-geschichtlich-*

heavenly court tradition and the way in which the three aspects appear in Isa. 42:1–4, Steck concludes that the presentation of the servant's task appears as a new interpretation of a traditional genre.[68]

Also in Isa. 49:1–4, Steck identifies a triadic scheme. Although this second *EJL* does not have the same structure as the first, he claims that this is also based on the heavenly court tradition, but the pattern is not as explicit as in the first *EJL*.[69] Central to this *EJL* is *Lehreröffnungsformel* and election (49:1), equipment (49:2), the servant's task towards the nations and his *Ebedgewißheit* (49:4). Steck describes the third *EJL*, 50:4–9, as a prophetical psalm of trust in three parts (50:4–5aα; 5aβ–6; 7–9), which concerns the enmity of the servant. This *EJL* is closer to the triadic pattern than the second *EJL*.[70]

According to Steck, the prophet "Second Isaiah" presents the way in which he has been delegated as servant (*Gottesknecht*) in each of these *EJL*.[71] After his examination of them, Steck concludes that each is oriented around the three aspects which originate in a tradition of a commission in the heavenly court. Where the texts differ from this tradition, the special form of the aspects within each song is clarified and allows Steck to determine precisely the direction and theological subject of each. This also explains the exceptional position of the texts and their status as a separate collection.[72]

---

exegetische Studie über die Ebed-Jahwe-Lieder bei Deuterojesaja (FRLANT, 70; Göttingen: Vandenhoeck & Ruprecht, 1962). The sources for the tradition of a commission in the heavenly court are 1 Kgs 22:19–22 (and Isa. 6 and extra-biblical parallels), where the assignment of a commission (*Auftragsvergabe*) is presented through the following aspects: commission (*Auftrag*; 1 Kgs 22:20a), how he performs his commission (*Art der Ausführung des Auftrags*; 1 Kgs 22:22a) and assurance of its success (*Zusicherung des Gelingens*; 1 Kgs 22:22bα), see O. H. Steck, "Bewahrheitungen des Prophetenworts. Überlieferungs-geschichtliche Skizze zu 1. Könige 22, 1–38" in H.-G. Geyer and J. M. Schmidt (eds), *"Wenn nicht jetzt, wann dann?". Aufsätze für Hans-Joachim Kraus zum 65. Geburtstag* (Neukirchen-Vluyn: Neukirchener Verlag, 1983) 87–96, and O. H. Steck, *Wahrnehmungen Gottes im Alten Testament: Gesammelte Studien* (TBü, 70; Munich: Chr. Kaiser Verlag, 1982) 153ff.

[68] Steck, "Aspekte des Gottesknechts in Deuterojesajas 'Ebed-Jahwe-Liedern'", p. 4.

[69] Steck, "Aspekte des Gottesknechts in Deuterojesajas 'Ebed-Jahwe-Liedern'", pp. 6; 12.

[70] Steck, "Aspekte des Gottesknechts in Deuterojesajas 'Ebed-Jahwe-Liedern'", pp. 14–20.

[71] Steck, "Aspekte des Gottesknechts in Deuterojesajas 'Ebed-Jahwe-Liedern'", pp. 3–21, and O. H. Steck, "Aspekte des Gottesknechts in Jesaja 52,13–53,12" in Steck, *Gottesknecht und Zion*, p. 22.

[72] Steck, "Aspekte des Gottesknechts in Deuterojesajas 'Ebed-Jahwe-Liedern'", pp. 20–21.

2.2.3. *Isa. 52:13–53:12*

In his reading of Isa. 52:13–53:12, Steck also identifies which of the
three aspects of the heavenly court tradition is visible in the text, and
how the fourth *EJL* relates to the first three *EJL*. He regards the classical delimitation of 52:13–53:12 as clear without providing any further arguments, and claims that the text does not come from "Second
Isaiah" but concerns the prophet as God's servant (*Gottesknecht*) and
all his obstacles. According to Steck, 52:13–53:12 are especially problematic because the death of the servant is described, thereby indicating that the text cannot have been written by the servant himself.
He claims that Isa. 53 might have been added to the first three *EJL*
to constitute a separate collection of texts, with a tension appearing
between the self-expressions of the servant in the first three and his
actual state in the fourth.[73]

Steck continues by asking three preliminary questions (*Vorfragen*)
about 52:13–53:12 based on his and others' observations of the first
three *EJL*. The questions concern structure, genre and the identity of
the servant and רַבִּים "many". Regarding structure, he states that unlike
the first three *EJL* (most prominent in the first and third), the fourth is
not based on the triadic basic pattern. It is divided in three, based on
whoever is speaking. The text begins and ends with YHWH oracles:
the introduction oracle in 52:13–15 (*Eingangsorakel*) and the final
oracle in 53:11aβ–12 (*Schlußorakel*). In the middle part 53:1–11aα,
the "we" speech in vv. 1–6 is based on the previous YHWH oracle.
Characteristic of the text as a whole is a temporal perspective. In the
first oracle, from 53:10aγ onwards, and in the second oracle, the future
of the servant is emphasised, while 53:2–10aαβ concern his past.[74]

Steck's second question is about genre. He discusses various possibilities: for example, the middle part as a public lament (*Volksklagelied*), an individual psalm of lament (*Klagelied des Einzelnen*) or a
psalm of thanksgiving (*Danklied*). He argues that the structure of
Isa. 52:13–53:12 cannot be related to any known *Gattung* by arguing
that if the middle part were an individual psalm of lament, it could not
be preceded by a YHWH oracle, and if it were a psalm of thanksgiving,
it could not have been followed by an oracle, and so forth. At best, the

---

[73] Steck, "Aspekte des Gottesknechts in Jesaja 52,13–53,12", p. 22.
[74] Steck, "Aspekte des Gottesknechts in Jesaja 52,13–53,12", pp. 23–24.

YHWH oracle of 52:13–15 could be a salvation oracle related to the words of confidence (*Vertrauensäußerung*) in the third *EJL*.[75]

Steck proceeds by discussing the identity of the "we" and the "many". Due to the context, the "we" in 53:1–6 is rather undisputedly identified as Israel.[76] More problematic is the identity of the "many", which appears only in the YHWH oracles: in 52:14 in confrontation with "him", in 52:15 in relation to גּוֹיִם רַבִּים "many peoples", and in 53:11–12 indirectly related to "us". By brief references to linguistic relations between the "we" part and the YHWH oracles, Steck concludes that the "many" can also be identified with Israel.[77]

After his treatment of structure, genre and identity, Steck asks which aspects of the servant event (*Ebedgeschehen*) are brought to the fore in the fourth *EJL*. The first YHWH oracle (52:13–15) concerns his coming prosperity (52:13) and the effect this will have in the world (*die Völkerwelt*), that is, for Israel (52:14) and the peoples (52:15).[78]

In the "we" part (53:1–11aα), 53:1 has a transitional function: whereas the peoples do not know about the exaltation of the servant (52:15), Israel does (53:1).[79] The rest of the "we" part is a composite of three sections: 53:2–6, 53:7–10aαβ and 53:10aγ–11aα. The first (53:2–6) is held together by "our" perspective of the servant. 53:2–3 concern the repulsive existence of the servant (*Ebedexistenz*), which isolated him from any fellowship. 53:4–6 contrast with the preceding verses: in 53:2–3; 4b, the "we" thought that the servant's state was due to YHWH's punishment because of the servant's transgression.[80] In

---

[75] Steck, "Aspekte des Gottesknechts in Jesaja 52,13–53,12", pp. 24–25. According to him, one problem related to the psalm genre is that in Isa. 53:1–6, a collective "we" depict the fate of an individual.

[76] Steck, "Aspekte des Gottesknechts in Jesaja 52,13–53,12", pp. 25–26, relates the "we" speech to a well-known cultic speech pattern in Jerusalem.

[77] Steck, "Aspekte des Gottesknechts in Jesaja 52,13–53,12", p. 26. This is explained by a connection between illness and sin in relation to "him" and "us" in Isa. 53:4–6; 10–12. Less clear is his explanation of the relation between the "many" in the first YHWH oracle and the "we" in 53:1–6.

[78] Steck, "Aspekte des Gottesknechts in Jesaja 52,13–53,12", p. 27. Regarding this first oracle, he claims that just as the Israelites reacted to the servant's shameful appearance (52:14), so shall the peoples react to his coming exaltation (52:15a). According to Steck, the exaltation of the servant in 52:13 is also the content of the perception of 52:15b.

[79] Steck, "Aspekte des Gottesknechts in Jesaja 52,13–53,12", p. 28, n. 25, explains the received announcement of 53:1 as the content of the oracle in 52:13–15, working as a transition to the middle part 53:2ff (with reference to P. Voltz), where "we" see the consequences of the announcement.

[80] Steck, "Aspekte des Gottesknechts in Jesaja 52,13–53,12", p. 28.

53:4a; 5–6, this appears not to be the case: rather, his success shows that his state was due to vicarious suffering because of "our" transgressions. He carried out YHWH's actions so that Israel might be healed (53:5b). This clarifies how the exaltation of the suffering servant through YHWH's actions for "us" is for Israel. "Our" confession leads to the second section (53:7–10aαβ),[81] where his suffering has reached an end, in death, and he offers his life for Israel – he himself being innocent (53:9b).[82] The third and last section of the "we" part (53:10aγ–11aα) concerns his future, corresponding to his prosperity in the first YHWH oracle (52:13).

The last YHWH oracle (53:11b–12) serves as a divine confirmation of the "we" part, conveying reflections from the preceding "we" speech. As a contrast to the previous assessment of the "many" of the servant (52:14), in this final oracle YHWH depicts the positive relations between the servant and the "many", where it is explained how his sufferings on behalf of Israel have brought salvation (53:11aβ; b; 12b) and how the "many" were delivered to him (53:12a). The isolation between him and the people is removed (cf. 52:14, 53:2f; 4b; 6a) and the peoples are made prey (cf. 45:13ff, 49:14ff). The active role of the servant is returned to (53:11aβ בְּדַעְתּוֹ צַדִּיק, cf. 53:7–10a), as well as the meaning of his suffering in 53:4–6.[83]

After his reading of Isa. 52:13–53:12, Steck pursues the relation between this text and the first three *EJL*. According to him, the pervasive triadic scheme proves that 52:13–53:12 are based on the previous three *EJL* and their triadic aspects of the servant event (*Ebedgeschehen*). He demonstrates this by describing a structure of the "we" part (53:1–11aα), consisting of the three aspects of the commission (i.e.

---

[81] From 53:7 onwards, the "we" perspective is absent.

[82] Steck, "Aspekte des Gottesknechts in Jesaja 52,13–53,12", pp. 28; 43–44. Steck depicts the servant's active, willing and patient acceptance of his suffering, but does not explicitly state that the servant is not sinning. However, due to his comprehension of the servant's vicarious suffering, this seems to be implied. The discussion of the "servant's death" is treated in 5.14.1. n. 251.

Steck does not comment on the sheep image of Isa. 53:7, while H.-J. Hermisson, "Das vierte Gottesknechtslied im deuterojesajanischen Kontext" in Janowski and Stuhlmacher, *Der leidende Gottesknecht*, p. 15 (ET H.-J. Hermisson, "The Fourth Servant Song in the Context of Second Isaiah" in Janowski and Stulmacher, *The Suffering Servant*, p. 37) rejects any sacrificial context in the imagery. Cf. Janowski in 2.2.4. n. 93.

[83] Steck, "Aspekte des Gottesknechts in Jesaja 52,13–53,12", pp. 30–31. According to Steck, לָרַבִּים...יַצְדִּיק in 53:11aβ corresponds to the salvation in 53:5b, 53:11b to 53:4 (סבל) and 53:5–6 (עָוֹן), 53:12b to 53:4 (נשׂא) and 53:5; 8 (פֶּשַׁע), as well as 53:12a to 53:5; 10a and 53:12a to 53:10aγ; 11aα and 53:10b (cf. 52:15).

the vicarious suffering, *stellvertretendes Leiden*, in 53:2–6): how he is equipped (53:6b), how it is carried out (53:7–10aαβ) and his success (53:10aγ–11aα). In the last YHWH oracle (53:11aβ–12), all three aspects appear, whereas in the first YHWH oracle (52:13–15), success is at stake.[84] This is followed by Steck's description of changes in aspects of the servant's fate (*Veränderungen gegenüber den Ebed-Aspekten*) when related to the first three *EJL*. The decisive differences concern the servant's relation to the peoples (*Völkerrelation*) and to Israel (*Israelrelation des Ebeds*). Whereas in the first three *EJL* the servant acted by his words, in the fourth he acts by his suffering towards Israel and by his exaltation towards the peoples.[85] Whereas in the first three *EJL* his task is executed within his lifetime, in the fourth it is divided into two phases: in his lifetime up to his death and burial, he serves Israel by his suffering, and in his exaltation his success towards the peoples is expressed.[86] In the first three *EJL*, the servant's task towards Israel is depicted (*Israelwirken*, 49:4b; 5b, 50:7–9) and is related to his success towards the peoples (42:4aβ; b; 49:3b; 6bβ). In the final oracle of the fourth *EJL*, 53:11aβ–12, both the success of the servant in relation to Israel and their special relationship (*Sonderstellung des Ebeds in der*

---

[84] Steck, "Aspekte des Gottesknechts in Jesaja 52,13–53,12", pp. 31–33. The success (*Gelingen*) of the servant in 53:10aγ–11aα corresponds to 42:4aα, 49:4b; 5b, 50:7–9. The servant's innocence in the way in which he carries out his commission (*Art der Ausführung*) in 53:7–10aαβ corresponds to 42:2–3a, 49:4a, 50:5aβ-6. His task (*Auftrag*) in 53:4a; 5; 6b corresponds to his task for Israel (*Israelauftrag*) in 49:5aβ; 6aβγ, 50:4aβ; bβ, etc.

Janowski, "Er trug unsere Sünden", p. 32, explains a connection between the four *EJL* through an assumed הן formula: as the servant from the very beginning was with YHWH (first *EJL*, הן in 42:1a), so is it also at the end of the third *EJL* (הן in 50:9aα), and by 52:13 (הִנֵּה), also the future of the servant is in the hand of YHWH. The function of Janowski's הן formula in 42:1a, 50:9aα and 52:13 might be due to his superior pursuit of the biography of the servant within the four *EJL*, where his designation "formula" for these four occurrences of הִנֵּה/הן seems to be an *ad hoc* formalisation of a more or less accidental phenomenon. Janowski does not regard biography as a literary genre, but as core expressions of the servant's "reduced life depiction" (*reduzierte Lebensbeschreibung*), where 53:2–3 and 53:10aβ; 11aα work as "previous and later history" (*Vor-und Nach-geschichte*) and 53:8–9 as his way of suffering – with "our" refusal and persecution –, ending with his unworthy burial (p. 38, incl. n. 30). Also Hermisson, "Das vierte Gottesknechtslied im deuterojesajanischen Kontext", pp. 4–6 (ET, pp. 20–22), who interprets Isa. 52:13–53:12 as a depiction of the prophetic office (*Amt*), pursues a connection between the four *EJL*.

[85] Steck, "Aspekte des Gottesknechts in Jesaja 52,13–53,12", p. 34.

[86] Steck, "Aspekte des Gottesknechts in Jesaja 52,13–53,12", p. 34. I will not go into Steck's detailed presentation of the changes between the first three *EJL* and the fourth, only note that in this regard he also uses the terminology related to the triadic scheme of the heavenly court.

Israelrelation) are strengthened.[87] This special relationship between Israel and the servant also finds its extraordinary expression in his fate of suffering and death.[88] In accordance with Steck's historical-biographical approach, the life of the servant is read with a rise from his vocation in 42:1–4 to 49:1–6, 50:4–9 to the climax of death and revival in 52:13–53:12.

2.2.4. Stellvertretung

Steck explains the servant's sufferings in Isa. 53 using the concept of *Stellvertretung* and the first three *EJL* prepare for his explanation.[89] He doubts any cultic meaning of אָשָׁם in 53:10, and by the expressions מוּסַר שְׁלוֹמֵנוּ עָלָיו "chastisement for our healing" (*Züchtigung zu unserem Heil*) and נִרְפָּא־לָנוּ "we shall be healed" (*geheilt werden*) he exemplifies that other traditions also lay behind, as the text bears features from individual psalms of lament (e.g. the themes of enemies and illness).[90] Such psalms carry a logic that the suffering one is punished by YHWH because of transgression, cf. 53:4b (possibly also 53:8aβ). However, in 53:4a; 6b it appears that the suffering servant is not being punished for his own sins, but that YHWH has stricken the innocent because of "our" sins. In this, a logic fails that claims that the innocent is rescued from his enemies by YHWH (or if not rescued, it means he was not innocent).[91] This (failed) logic is called *Vergehen-Ergehen-Zusammenhang*. YHWH acts through the innocent and righteous servant (53:7–10a; 11aβ), who suffers for the transgressions of Israel, and Israel is returned to its point of departure in Isa. 40:1–2.[92]

One scholar who has been especially interested in the concept of *Stellvertretung* is the Tübingen biblical scholar, Bernd Janowski, who works in the tracks of Steck and his forerunners and colleagues. According to Janowski, Isa. 52:13–53:12 revolves around "our" per-

---

[87] Steck, "Aspekte des Gottesknechts in Jesaja 52,13–53,12", pp. 34–35.

[88] Steck, "Aspekte des Gottesknechts in Jesaja 52,13–53,12", p. 37.

[89] Steck, "Aspekte des Gottesknechts in Jesaja 52,13–53,12", p. 38.

[90] Steck, "Aspekte des Gottesknechts in Jesaja 52,13–53,12", pp. 38–39. This is supported by Hermisson, "Das vierte Gottesknechtslied im deuterojesajanischen Kontext", pp. 15; 20 (ET pp. 36–37; 42), who claims that there is a clear connection between sin and punishment, but that YHWH does not punish the sinner.

[91] Steck, "Aspekte des Gottesknechts in Jesaja 52,13–53,12", pp. 41–42. For a criticism of such a logic, see 2.3.8.3. n. 178.

[92] Steck, "Aspekte des Gottesknechts in Jesaja 52,13–53,12", pp. 42–43. See also details of his description of the vicarious suffering in 3.10.17.2.h.

spective (53:1–6) before and after the servant's death and around the subsequent YHWH oracle concerning the servant's coming exaltation. Using a form-critical argument from the psalms of lament, he concludes that since the "we" are described in language reminiscent of the enemies of the righteous in the Psalms, the historical "we" within Israel during exile must have behaved as the servant's enemies, persecuting him and leading to his death and burial among the wicked (53:7–10).[93] As a part of God's plan, the servant surrenders his life as אָשָׁם, which is a "wiping out" provided when the guilty acknowledge their guilt and take responsibility for it. Since this is precisely what the exilic community fails to do, the servant does it for them.[94] Janowski connects this to two different temporal levels: a previous and a present one. In the previous level, the "we" were relying on an idea of a deed-consequence connection (*Tun-Ergehen-Zusammenhang*) in which actions have consequences and people get what they deserve. According to this, the servant bore his own sins (53:4b). On the present level, i.e. after the two YHWH oracles (52:13–15, 53:11b–12), the "we" realise that the logic of the deed-consequences connection fails in the servant's case. He did not bear his own sins, but the sins of the guilty. The "we" realise that he, who is the prophet according to Janowski, was not a justly punished sinner but a righteous servant.[95]

---

[93] Janowski, "Er trug unsere Sünden", pp. 40–41. He comments on v. 7 only in passing: "As we all know from other contexts, meekness and truthfulness can arouse aggression and force those who exemplify them into the role of victims (*Opferrolle*). The images of a lamb or a sheep led to be slaughtered or sheared speaks a clear language" (*sprechen eine deutliche Sprache*) (ET p. 65). It seems that Janowski is over-interpreting a victim theme. Hermisson, "Das vierte Gottesknechtslied im deuterojesajanischen Kontext", p. 15 (ET p. 37), reads 53:7 as a presentation of the way in which the servant behaved to his appointed suffering: He bowed down and did not rebel, cf. 50:5–6. Hermisson claims that the comparison (*Vergleich*) cannot be used as proof of an underlying sacrificial idea.

[94] Janowski, "Er trug unsere Sünden", p. 43. He regards אָשָׁם "wiping out guilt" (*Schuldtilgung*) as a key term in Isa. 52:13–53:12. He ascribes the origin of אָשָׁם not to a cultic context, but to:

> contexts in which…guilt-incurring encroachments and their reparation are the theme [cf. Gen. 26:10, 1 Sam. 6:3–4, 8:17]. From there the term made its way, after several intermediate stages and *after the composition of Isaiah 53*, into the priestly sacrificial tora [*Opfertora*, cf. e.g. Lev. 4–5; 7]. Its meaning is determined by the *situation of obligation arising from guilt*, in which the guilty person [*der Schuldpflichtige*] must provide material compensation to discharge this guilt" (pp. 41–43, the quotations are taken from ET pp. 68–69, his italics).

See more on this in Appendix 6.

[95] Janowski, "Er trug unsere Sünden", p. 33, n. 20, does not treat the textual-critical problems of 53:11, but relates the verse to the two מִי questions in 53:8. He relates

The servant will, however, succeed by releasing others from the fate of suffering (as the consequences of sin) to fulfil his mission of "bringing Israel back" from exile (Isa. 49:5–6). Janowski explains this as *Stellvertretung*.[96] More than most exegetes, he clarifies some of the premises of the theological pre-suppositions of his reading.[97] Using a mix of historical criticism, exegesis and dogmatics, he performs a reading in which the concept of *Stellvertretung* is the real subject matter: the core of Isa. 52:13–53:12 is the way in which Israel comes to recognise both her guilt and the cancellation of it so as to be saved.[98]

---

the questions to YHWH's justification or vindication (*Rechtfertigung*) of the servant. מַצְדִּיקִי "my vindicator" of 50:8 ("an expression predicated of God only here in the OT") becomes transformed into an active quality of the servant in 53:11aβ: "By his knowledge (of God) the righteous one, my Servant, will justify the many". The quotation is taken from ET p. 56, n. 20. The "many" are identified as empirical Israel (p. 37, ET p. 61). Janowski's reading is also guided by a pursuit of the servant's biography of the four *EJL*, cf. 2.2.3. n. 84.

[96] Janowski, "Er trug unsere Sünden", p. 27, introduces his study by describing a paradox related to the concept of "suffering righteous" (*leidende Gerechte*): "The righteous live by their faithfulness and suffer *because* they are righteous". The quotation is taken from ET p. 49, his italics. Janowski supports this with Mesopotamian and Egyptian parallels. He regards the punishment of the innocent instead of the guilty as a core of Isa. 53, and claims that this raises the problem of the transference of guilt between persons that is discussed by Kant. After God makes it clear that the one has taken the place of the many, the sufferings are substitutionary because something is done for the "we" that they could not do for themselves and representative because what the servant suffered represented their fate and not his. Moreover, "vicarious suffering" (*Stellvertretung*) concerns both Israel and the peoples (pp. 35; 41).

[97] Janowski, "Er trug unsere Sünden", pp. 28–31, comments on how the German noun *Stellvertretung* first came into being in the course of the Socinian criticism of the doctrine of satisfaction within Old Protestant orthodoxy in the eighteenth century. Luther did not use the noun, but a verbal paraphrase: "Jesus Christ, God's Son, came 'in our stead'". Supported by OT and NT terms, Janowski explains how it expresses "that one person has done or suffered something 'instead of' (*anstatt*) or 'in place of' (*an Stelle*) other persons" (The quotation is taken from ET p. 53). He further refers to E. Jüngel, "Geheimnis der Stellvertretung: Ein dogmatisches Gespräch mit Heinrich Vogel" (1983) 53. A related concept in Janowski's explanation is "suffering righteous" (*leidende Gerechte*), which is not used by Steck.

[98] In accordance with his historical-biographical pursuit of the servant's life within the four *EJL*, Janowski, "Er trug unsere Sünden" p. 35, explains how vicarious suffering is prepared for by the election in the first three *EJL*: "'Vicariousness' or 'representation' consequently has a double meaning. The prophetic Servant represents Yahweh's מִשְׁפָּט in all its consequences before the nations (first and second Songs) and before Israel (third Song), and he thereby brings 'the servant' Israel back to Yahweh, though Israel acknowledges this only after the fact (Isa. 53:4–6, cf. the closing oracle in 53:11aβ–12)" (the quotation is taken from ET p. 59). For a criticism of a concept of vicarious suffering in Isa. 53, see 2.3.8.3.

2.2.5. *Redactional Reception of the Servant Songs*

Using a redaction-critical approach, Steck explains the role of the four *EJL* within Isa. 40–66. This he terms "redactional reception" (*redaktionelle Rezeption*).[99] Important in the message of the four *EJL* is the servant's task towards Israel and the peoples (*Israelaufgabe und Völkeraufgabe des Gottesknechtes*) within a divine worldwide order of salvation (*umfassende göttliche Weltordnung des Heils*).[100] Steck outlines an inner-Isaianic reception of the four *EJL* on five levels dating from the time of Second Isaiah to the Ptolemaic period (from 539 to 270 BCE), explaining the changing identity and role of the servant on each of the five levels of each of the four *EJL*.[101]

The first level concerns three separate collections: the *Grundschrift* *40–55 and the first three *EJL* (which are gathered together), which belong to the prophet Isaiah, as well as 52:13–53:12 as a separate text. Steck dates this level to just after the Persian King Cyrus' conquest of Babylon in 539 BCE.[102] On this level, the servant texts within the *Grundschrift* (apart from the four *EJL*) concern YHWH's people as *Gottesknechte* ("servants of God"), whereas in the four *EJL* the prophet

---

[99] O. H. Steck, "Beobachtungen zu den Zion-Texten in Jesaja 51–54: Ein redaktionsgeschichtlicher Versuch" in Steck, *Gottesknecht und Zion*, p. 125, traces in detail at least nine levels of redactional composition in Isa. 47–55 (62), ranging from the sixth to the early third century. Below, I will present the five levels which involve the four *EJL*.

[100] Steck, "Die Gottesknechts-Texte und ihre redaktionelle Rezeption im Zweiten Jesaja", p. 150.

[101] Steck, "Die Gottesknechts-Texte und ihre redaktionelle Rezeption im Zweiten Jesaja", pp. 149–172, refers to R. G. Kratz, *Kyros im Deuterojesaja-Buch. Redaktionsgeschichtliche Untersuchungen zu Entstehung und Theologie von Jes 40–55* (Forschungen zum Alten Testament, 1; Tübingen: J. C. B. Mohr {Paul Siebeck}, 1991), who outlines five redactional levels in Isa. 40–55 (*Grundschrift, Zion-Fortschreibungen* [49–54]), *Kyros-Ergängzungsschicht, Götzenschicht* and *Ebed-Israel-Schicht* [40–48], dated from 539 to the first or middle part of the fifth century (see table at p. 217). While Kratz concentrates on 40–48, Steck focuses on the redaction of 40–66, especially *Gottesknecht*, Israel and Zion.

In his pursuit of a *Grundschrift*, H.-J. Hermisson, "Einheit und Komplexität Deuterojesajas: Probleme der Redaktionsgeschichte von Jes. 40–55" in H.-J. Hermisson, *Studien zu Prophetie und Weisheit: Gesammelte Aufsätze* (Forschungen zum Alten Testament, 23; Tübingen: J. C. B Mohr {Paul Siebeck}, 1998) 132–157, operates with five redactional levels within Isa. 40–55: *Ältesten Sammlungen (Grundbestand, vor 539), Kombination der ältesten Sammlungen mit der Gotteskneckts-liedern, Die qarob-Schicht (Naherwartungsschicht?), Götzenbilder* and *Übrige Texte* (p. 155).

[102] Steck, "Die Gottesknechts-Texte und ihre redaktionelle Rezeption im Zweiten Jesaja", pp. 150–151, cf. Kratz, *Kyros im Deuterojesaja-Buch*, pp. 169ff; 216.

is *Knecht Jahwes* ("servant of YHWH") for Israel and the peoples.[103]
Steck refers to Hermisson's depiction of the difference between the
two servants: the servant-prophet's task is to bring YHWH's word to
the world, whereas this word is realised through the servant-people,
in whom the salvation becomes known to the world.[104] The fourth *EJL*
has an exceptional position. Here, the task of the servant in the previous three *EJL* (*Wortamt*) is carried further, as the innocent prophet
is willing to suffer to bring to an end Israel's guilty status towards
YHWH. Additionally, his exaltation as well as the salvation and return
of Israel bring insight to the peoples.

Steck regards his second level as standing in continuation with
*40–55 and dates it to the time before 520 BCE.[105] On this level, focus
is put on the return of the exiles and the reconstruction of Jerusalem.
The Persian king Cyrus is the embodiment of YHWH's rule. The first
two, and possibly all the *EJL*, are integrated into Isa. *40–55.[106] In the
first and second *EJL*, Cyrus is *Gottesknecht* for mankind and Israel,
whereas in the last two Zion is *Knecht Jahwes* for Israel, and with

---

[103] Steck, "Die Gottesknechts-Texte und ihre redaktionelle Rezeption im Zweiten
Jesaja", p. 152. On the second and third levels, Steck distinguishes between an identification of a *Gottesknecht* in the first and second *EJL* and a *Knecht Jahwes* in the third
and fourth *EJL*. He also separates between what he designates *Ebed-Israel-Schicht* for
Isa. *40–49 and *Zion-Fortschreibungen* for Isa. *49–54.

[104] H.-J. Hermisson, "Israel und der Gottesknecht bei Deuterojesaja" in Hermisson,
Studien zu Prophetie und Weisheit, p. 201, comments on the double role of the people
of Israel as blind and dumb – and as witness for the uniqueness of YHWH. Hermisson
claims that Israel is a *passive* witness by its very existence as the people of YHWH,
as object for divine action, in which YHWH shows his uniqueness. However, both
Israel and the servant have a task of proclamation, cf. Israel in 48:20 and 55:5 and the
servant as the prophet speaking from the heavenly court, cf. 42:1–4 (pp. 203–205).
Moreover, Hermisson, "Einheit und Komplexität Deuterojesajas", p. 148, claims that
both Jacob and Zion represent Israel as a whole, but from different perspectives. Jacob
the patriarch represents the elected Israel from the perspectives of departure and way
(*Aufbruchs-und Wegperspektive*); he is the wanderer and servant of the Lord (*Knecht
Jahwes*). As the elected mother city of all Israelites, Zion represents Israel from the
perspective of arrival (*Ankunftperspektive*). Kratz, *Kyros im Deuterojesaja-Buch*, pp.
148–157, claims that in Isa. 40–48, the exiles are called Jacob and Israel, but that they
return in 49–54 (i.e. *Zion-Fortschreibung*, see 2.2.5. n. 101) as the children of Zion,
the wife and bride of God. While the first concept is concerned with the twelve tribes
and the renewal of the divine acts of resettling and repopulating the land, the last is
concerned with the restoration and repopulation of Jerusalem.

[105] Steck, "Die Gottesknechts-Texte und ihre redaktionelle Rezeption im Zweiten
Jesaja", p. 151, refers to Kratz, *Kyros im Deuterojesaja-Buch*, pp. 175–206; 216–217,
who designates this *Kyros-Ergänzungs-Schicht*, dating it to about 535–520 BCE.

[106] Steck, "Die Gottesknechts-Texte und ihre redaktionelle Rezeption im Zweiten
Jesaja", p. 151.

Israel for the peoples.[107] Whereas on the first level (dated to 539 BCE), Cyrus appeared as a provisional tool in YHWH's plan of salvation, on this level the Persian world dominion as a lasting political mediator of YHWH's world dominion is expressed by the *Gottesknecht* Cyrus as *Reichsgründer*. The fourth *EJL* concerns Zion's vicarious suffering because of her sinful children (50:1), as a presupposition regarding the salvation of YHWH's people which is mediated by Cyrus.[108]

On the third level, Steck regards Isa. 60–62 as being connected with Isa. *40–55. This level is dated to the first and middle part of the fifth century BCE, at the time of Nehemiah's activity in Jerusalem and during the decline of the Persian Empire.[109] In the first two *EJL*, the returned exiles (Gola) are *Gottesknecht* for the dispersed Israel (Diaspora), and in the last two *EJL*, Zion is *Knecht Jahwes* for God's people and the peoples. This is the first level at which the *Gottesknecht* in the (first and second) *EJL* and elsewhere in Isa. 40–55 is the same, i.e. Israel/Jacob as the Israelite Gola.[110] On this level, Isa. 40–48 are concerned with the ingathering of the people of YHWH in Zion, while in Isa. 49–54, the peoples are also taken into consideration, as Zion becomes "a light to the nations".[111] Salvation is mediated by YHWH alone, and not through an earthly power, as Cyrus was on the second level. Polemics against the idols (from the time of Darius I) and the hope of Isa. 60–62 are combined.[112] The presentation of the topics on this level indicates a Palestinian rather than a Babylonian provenance.[113]

---

[107] Steck, "Die Gottesknechts-Texte und ihre redaktionelle Rezeption im Zweiten Jesaja", p. 155.

[108] Steck, "Die Gottesknechts-Texte und ihre redaktionelle Rezeption im Zweiten Jesaja", p. 158.

[109] Steck, "Die Gottesknechts-Texte und ihre redaktionelle Rezeption im Zweiten Jesaja", p. 151, refers to Kratz, *Kyros im Deuterojesaja-Buch*, pp. 192–217, who labels this *Götzenschicht* and dates it to the late period of Darius I (522–486 BCE) within the *Ebed-Israel-Schicht* (Isa. *40–49).

[110] Steck, "Die Gottesknechts-Texte und ihre redaktionelle Rezeption im Zweiten Jesaja", pp. 161; 163, supports Kratz in claiming that, at this level, "Israel" was added to 49:3.

[111] Steck, "Die Gottesknechts-Texte und ihre redaktionelle Rezeption im Zweiten Jesaja", pp. 164–165.

[112] Steck, "Die Gottesknechts-Texte und ihre redaktionelle Rezeption im Zweiten Jesaja", p. 161. Steck does not comment on any vicarious suffering of Zion in the fourth *EJL* at this level. On his next level, he comments that the servant no longer suffers innocently, which might imply that the fourth level is the first level where vicarious suffering is not at stake. More on this below.

[113] Steck, "Die Gottesknechts-Texte und ihre redaktionelle Rezeption im Zweiten Jesaja", pp. 161–166.

On the penultimate level, "Second Isaiah" (*40–62) is connected
with "First Isaiah", and *56:9–59:21 are also included. This level is
dated to 311–302/1 BCE, and both the returned and the returning
Israel and Zion are regarded as *Gottesknecht*.[114] The unstable political
situation in Palestine leads to both religious and social tension among
the people of YHWH, and the servant no longer suffers innocently.
Thus, vicarious suffering is no longer a topic. YHWH acts through a
prophetic admonition.[115] Perspectives of hope for the empirical Israel
are announced, though still without any mission or salvation for the
peoples.

The final redaction (*Schlußredaktion*) is dated to 301–270 BCE and
is influenced by Ptolemy I's campaign in 302/1 BCE. The prayer of
Isa. 63:7–64:11 is included, as well as its answers in chapters 65–66.
The identification of YHWH's servants is altered once again: the servants are the true people of YHWH from Israel and the peoples, who
are the numerous descendants of the single *Gottesknecht* of the four
EJL.[116] Like in the fourth level, here too perspectives of hope for the
empirical Israel are prominent.

After Steck's (re-)construction of five historical levels of interpretation of the four *EJL* in the Book of Isaiah, he admits that his expressions about Zion (*Zion-Aussage*) in Isa. 49–54, which he has arranged
within the Israelite history of theology from the late Babylonian and
the early Persian time (between 539 and 520 BCE), are presented as a
mere impulse (*Anregung*). He explains this in short, thesis-like suggestions replete with uncertainties that more precise definitions and
correctives might challenge.[117] He bases his own diachronic reading
on Hermisson's and Kratz' contributions and legitimates it as obvious
(*selbstverständlich*) and unquestionable (*fraglos*). He also compares his
diachronic approach with alternative readings, which he terms syn-

---

[114] Steck, "Die Gottesknechts-Texte und ihre redaktionelle Rezeption im Zweiten
Jesaja", pp. 152 (incl. references in n. 16); 166: *Heimkehrredaktion* (Isa. *1–62), which
Kratz, *Kyros im Deuterojesaja-Buch*, p. 120, n. 461, regards as the fifth and final redac-
tion of the *Ebed-Israel-Schicht* (Isa. *40–49).

[115] Steck, "Die Gottesknechts-Texte und ihre redaktionelle Rezeption im Zweiten
Jesaja", p. 167. At this level, the servant's suffering in the fourth *EJL* is read in relation
to Isa. 56:9–57:21.

[116] Steck, "Die Gottesknechts-Texte und ihre redaktionelle Rezeption im Zweiten
Jesaja", pp. 170–172.

[117] Steck, "Israel und Zion", pp. 190–191.

chronic perspective and "dramatic final form readings" (*dramatische Endtextlesung*).[118]

2.2.6. *Summing up*

All readings involve interpretation by the selection and description of signs. Signs are never simply given, but are produced through the reading. This is true of Steck's reading of the Book of Isaiah as much as my own reading of Steck. In my treatment of some of Steck's studies of the Book of Isaiah, I merely suggest some features and tendencies. His writings are very compact: points of view are postulated rather than argued for, or they are argued for by referring to precursors or colleagues in footnotes without any additional argument. Elsewhere he is very detailed, for instance, in his distribution of verses and semi-verses in exact sources.

In Steck's redaction-critical study, various levels evolve in response to changes that have taken place in history or theology. Coherent thematic aspects also seem to be a criterion for discerning different levels. Important in his redaction-critical study of the *EJL* within the Book of Isaiah is what he designates *Israelaufgabe des Gottesknechtes* and *Völkeraufgabe des Gottesknechtes*, which also include the role of Cyrus and Zion within a divine worldwide order of salvation (*umfassende göttliche Weltordnung des Heils*).[119] Other themes are for instance related to the heavenly court tradition, conceptualisations of *Ebed*, the Babylonian exile, *Stellvertretung* and a supposed logic of transgression-state-connection (*Vergehen-Ergehen-Zusammenhang*).

Decisive for Steck's reading of Isa. 52:13–53:12 is his mapping out of a triadic pattern relating to a tradition of a heavenly court. Using this, he refers to certain past origins, traditions and mythologies, which are (re-)constructed. This "heavenly court" reading also concerns the connection of the text to the first three *EJL*.

An *Ebed* conceptualisation is also entangled in Steck's and others' exegesis, with sub-categories such as *Ebed-Aspekte, Ebed-Auftrag, Ebed-Aussage, Ebed-Dienst, Ebed-Einschätzung, Ebed-Existenz, Ebed-Gelingen, Ebed-Geschehen, Ebed-Gewißheit, Ebed-Jahwe-Lieder, Ebed-Leiden, Ebed-Perspektive, Ebed-Rezeption, Ebed-Schicksal, Ebed-Sicht,*

---

[118] Steck, "Israel und Zion", p. 174.
[119] Steck, "Die Gottesknechts-Texte und ihre redaktionelle Rezeption im Zweiten Jesaja", p. 150, and 2.2.5.

Ebed-Verhalten, Ebed-Widerfahrnisse and *Ebed-Wirken*. In the readings of Isa. 52:13–53:12 of Steck, Hermisson, Janowski and other scholars, a concept of *Stellvertretung* emerges as both a core and a *terminus technicus* of the text. A logic explained as a transgression-state-connection (*Vergehen-Ergehen-Zusammenhang*) is also taken for granted. In Steck's reading, the concept of *Stellvertretung* is identified on the first three redaction-critical levels. On the first level, *Stellvertretung* is related to the *Knecht Jahwes* identified as the prophet "Second Isaiah" suffering vicariously for Israel and with Israel for the peoples; on the second and third levels, the concept is related to Zion identified as *Knecht Jahwes* suffering vicariously for Israel, and with Israel for the peoples.[120]

By virtue of Steck's redaction-critical approach, Isa. 52:13–53:12 appear as five stories about a servant identified as the prophet "Second Isaiah", Zion, those who have returned from exile, those who remained at home in Judah, as well as the servant's descendants as the true Israel, including other peoples. Steck dates these servant stories to different times in Ancient Israel within a period from 539 to 270 BCE. Below, Steck's and others' studies of the Book of Isaiah will be related to historising (2.3.2., 2.3.3., 2.3.7. and 2.3.8.1.), traditionalising (2.3.8.2.) and theologising (2.3.8.3.).

2.3. EVALUATION AND FURTHER PROSPECTS

> Es wird für alle Zeiten das Verdienst Duhms bleiben, nicht nur Jes 56–66 Dtjes abgesprochen und einem "Tritojesaja" zugeschrieben, sondern auch die vier Perikopen vom GK als selbständiche literarische Größen, aber mit gemeinsamer Thematik, aus dem Buch Jes 40–55 herausgelöst und einem eigenen, später lebenden Verfasser zuerkannt zu haben. Er hat auch für die vier Perikopen die Bezeichnung "Ebed-Jahwe-Lieder" eingeführt, die sich seither weithin eingeburgert hat.[121]

In Haag's history of research of *EJL*, the axiomatic status of Duhm's theses is expressed. The claim of Duhm's Servant Song thesis has stood for more than a century as the prevailing manner in which Isa. 42:1–4, 49:1–6, 50:4–9 and 52:13–53:12 should be interpreted. Although his

---

[120] It seems that at the third level, vicarious suffering is not at stake in the fourth *EJL*, cf. 2.2.5. n. 112.

[121] Haag, *Der Gottesknecht bei Deuterojesaja*, p. 4.

thesis has been modified in different ways since 1892, certain questions asked about the texts have become a common denominator. For
example, classical Duhmian questions about the four Servant Songs
include: Who is the servant? Who can have a commission towards
Israel? Who is both innocent and suffers? Who can suffer vicariously
for the people? How did the servant die? When were the texts added
to the Second Isaianic corpus? Since Duhm's thesis was proposed,
Gottesknecht has become a technical term, *Ebed-Jahwe-Lied* a genre,
Stellvertretung an established theological concept and "Servant Song
Research" a special discipline within Old Testament scholarship. As
regards Isa. 52:13–53:12 in particular, the debate is complicated by
the fact that this is a most difficult text laden with textual corruptions and other problems, which have led to it often being dealt with
as an exception to the theories proposed about the first three *EJL*.
One might ask whether the consensus concerning the peculiarity of Isa. 52:13–53:12 has obstructed scholars' reading of the text.
Biblical scholars remain largely loyal to some kind of approxi-
mate version of Duhm's thesis. However, no undisputed consensus
or unified methodology has ever existed. Rather, there has been a
constant assault on the thesis and readings of Isa. 53 are complexly
heterogeneous.[122]

Duhm's studies of Isaiah were based on certain presuppositions
related for example to his positivistic, neo-romantic and psychological
view of the prophets, prophecy and prophetic literature, and his adjacent historical-biographical interpretation of a *Gottesknecht* (cf. 2.1.).
Also in the case of Steck's Isaiah research, certain debatable presuppositions regarding the text and historiography are at stake (cf. 2.2.).
In recent biblical scholarship, increased attention has been paid to the
different forces at work in the text and the reading, where a variety of
possible focuses has come to the fore, such as biographical, historical,
sociological, psychological, theological, ideological, literary and political ones (cf. 1.2. and 2.4.). This concerns both the study of prophecy

---

[122] For surveys on the history of research of the "Servant Songs", see North, *The
Suffering Servant in Deutero-Isaiah*, pp. 28–222, Ruprecht, *Die Auslegungsgeschichte
zu den sogenannten Gottesknechtliedern*, pp. 91–180, Haag, *Der Gottesknecht bei Deuterojesaja*, pp. 34–195. Especially concerning Isa. 53, see Janowski and Stuhlmacher,
Der leidende Gottesknecht, and D. P. Bailey, "The Suffering Servant: Recent Tübingen
Scholarship on Isaiah 53" in Bellinger and Farmer, *Jesus and the Suffering Servant*, pp.
251–259. Cf. some recent studies on Isa. 52:13–53:12 referred to in 2.4.

and prophetic literature in general, including the Book of Isaiah as a whole as well as the "Servant Songs".[123]

2.3.1. Prophecy and Prophetic Literature

Prophecy is a debatable field within Hebrew Bible and ANE research, with some scholars reacting against an overly uncritical following of conventional analyses, while others accept at face value statements about the prophetical literature. Duhm's studies of this literature were characterised by an idealistic-speculative view of the prophets, as well as an idea of prophecy's foundational role in the religion of Ancient Israel (cf. 2.1.1.). "Classical writing prophets" were interpreted within a romantic-historicist frame with a distinction drawn between "early"

---

[123] A frequently used metaphor for depicting changes in biblical studies in recent decades is that of "paradigm". I have also used this metaphor in a previous study, Joachimsen, "Steck's Five Stories of the Servant in Isaiah lii 13– liii 12, and Beyond", p. 216. The concepts of "paradigm" and "paradigm shift" in scientific discourses are often related to T. S. Kuhn, *The Structure of Scientific Revolutions* (Chicago: University of Chicago Press, 1970). Kuhn defines paradigms as such: "These I take to be universally recognized scientific achievements that for a time provide model problems and solutions to a community of practitioners" (p. x). According to Kuhn, "normal science" is that stage in history at which scholars accept the validity of a particular paradigm and contribute with reproduction and refinements. A scientific revolution occurs when a dominant paradigm is found inadequate, is abandoned and is substituted by a new paradigm. One example where the idea of paradigm shift is applied to describe the changes is in biblical studies on prophecy, see F. E. Deist, "The Prophets: Are We Heading for a Paradigm Switch?" in V. Fritz (ed), *Prophet und Prophetenbuch: Festschrift für Otto Kaiser zum 65. Geburtstag* (BZAW, 185; Berlin: W. de Gruyter, 1989) 1–18.
   The theoretician M. Foucault might share Kuhn's interest in the way in which models of knowledge are generated in social, historical and intellectual contexts. Also Foucault explains how authority and power work in institutions. However, while Kuhn speaks of paradigm, Foucault focuses on *episteme*, cf. M. Foucault, *The Order of Things: An Archaeology of the Human Sciences* (Routledge Classics; London: Routledge, 2002, first published in French in 1966) 168: "In any given culture and at any given moment, there is always only one *episteme* that defines the conditions of possibility of knowledge" (his italics). In the later M. Foucault, *The Archaeology of Knowledge and The Discourse on Language* (New York: Pantheon Books, 1972, first published in French in 1969), he is more nuanced, arguing that various discursive formations might undergo similar transformations at different times and that several *epistemes* might exist simultaneously and interact with each other. While Kuhn focuses on how one paradigm dominates science, Foucault shows how opposing theories can exist within a science. While Kuhn speaks about a scientific revolution, Foucault argues that the move from one episteme to another creates a discursive break or discontinuity. In the present study, Isa. 53 will be read within an endless discursive practice of both continuity and discontinuity. Attention will be drawn to different forces at work in the text and reading, in which "Duhm" also remains a part of our reading legacy.

and "latter" prophets, and between prophets of salvation and prophets of doom.[124] Such distinctions have been upheld,[125] yet have been both nuanced and criticised.[126] Adjacent to such criticism is also less interest in the personality of the prophet, which is accentuated by the view of the headings of the prophetic books as much later additions. A recent trend in research regards prophecy as it is presented in the texts not as a historical reflection or the words of a particular prophet. Prophecy is mainly available to us through texts, which can only tell us something about the phenomenon of prophecy.[127] Moreover, prophecy participates in a continual actualisation of the "original" message of the prophetic texts, where it becomes impossible to separate the "original" from later interpretations, as the interpretation itself is an integrated part of the text. From the most radical angle, the Ancient Israelite prophets are regarded as being invented in post-exilic times.[128]

---

[124] On the history of research of prophecy, see Kraus, *Geschichte der historisch-kritischen Erforschung des Alten Testaments*, Clements, *A Century of Old Testament Study*, pp. 59–91, and Deist, "The Prophets".

[125] See e.g. J. Blenkinsopp, *A History of Prophecy in Israel: From the Settlement in the Land to the Hellenistic Period* (Philadelphia: Westminster Press, 1983).

[126] See e.g. R. P. Carroll, "Prophecy and Society" in R. E. Clements (ed), *The World of Ancient Israel* (Cambridge: Cambridge University Press, 1991) 203–225, R. I. Thelle, *Ask God: Divine Consultation in the Literature of the Hebrew Bible* (Beiträge zur biblischen Exegese und Theologie, 30; Frankfurt am Main: Peter Lang, 2002).

[127] Examples of recent trends in the study of the prophetic literature are found in R. P. Gordon (ed), *"The Place is Too Small for Us": The Israelite Prophets in Recent Scholarship* (Sources for Biblical and Theological Study, 5; Winona Lake, IN: Eisenbrauns, 1995), H. M. Barstad, "No Prophets? Recent Developments in Biblical Prophetic Research and Ancient Near Eastern Prophecy" in P. R. Davies (ed), *The Prophets* (Biblical Seminar, 42; Sheffield: Sheffield Academic Press, 1996) 106–126, R. P. Gordon, "From Mari to Moses: Prophecy at Mari and in Ancient Israel" in H. A. McKay and D. J. A. Clines (eds), *Of Prophets' Visions and the Wisdom of Sages: Essays in Honour of R. Norman Whybray* (JSOTSup, 162; Sheffield: JSOT Press, 1993) 63–79, P. R. Davies, "'Pen of Iron, Point of Diamond' (Jer. 17:1): Prophecy as Writing" in E. Ben-Zvi and M. H. Floyd (eds), *Writings and Speech in Israelite and Ancient Near Eastern Prophecy* (SBLSS, 10; Atlanta: SBL, 2000) 65–81, M. Nissinen (ed), *Prophecy in its Ancient Near Eastern Context: Mesopotamian, Biblical, and Arabian Perspectives* (SBLSS, 13; Atlanta: SBL, 2000), E. Ben-Zvi, "The Prophetic Book: A Key Form of Prophetic Literature" in M. A. Sweeney and E. Ben-Zvi (eds), *The Changing Face of Form Criticism for the Twenty-First Century* (Grand Rapids: Eerdmans, 2003) 276–297, M. Nissinen, "Introduction" in M. Nissinen (ed), *Prophets and Prophecy in the Ancient Near East* (Writings from the Ancient World, 12; Atlanta: SBL, 2003) 1–11, and M. H. Floyd and R. D. Haak (eds), *Prophets, Prophecy, and Prophetic Texts in Second Temple Judaism* (Library of Hebrew Bible/Old Testament Studies, 427; New York: T. & T. Clark, 2006).

[128] R. P. Carroll, "Poets No Prophets: A Response to 'Prophets through the Looking Glass'" in Davies, *The Prophets*, pp. 43–49.

Another approach is canonical.[129] Moreover, in the study of prophecy, interdisciplinariness is also at stake, as scholars have employed analytical tools from e.g. anthropology and sociology,[130] Marxism,[131] feminism[132] and liberation theology.[133]

2.3.2. *The Book of Isaiah*

Duhm's theses concerning the Book of Isaiah are based on an assumption that a long and complex process of formation lies behind the prophetic texts. Whereas his thesis about a "Third Isaiah" for Isa. 56–66 has been much disputed, a thesis about a "Second Isaiah" for Isa. 40–66 had remained prevalent until recently. When related to later research, it is interesting to note that Duhm's separation of the Book of Isaiah into three main parts was not based primarily on the obvious historical diversity, but on editorial independence (2.1.2.). Whereas the composite character of Isa. 1–66 has been based on assumed contrasts in theology and edition, it has increasingly become a matter of dating and geography.

The threefold division of the Book of Isaiah (1–39, 40–55, 56–66) is no longer standard, as scholars have become more and more aware of a unity and disunity and of "intertextual" overlap within Isa. 1–66. Some scholars still presuppose to a greater or lesser extent a long and

---

[129] C. R. Seitz, *Prophecy and Hermeneutics. Toward a New Introduction to the Prophets: Studies in Theological Interpretation* (Grand Rapids: Baker Academic Press, 2007). This study might also be called a theological reading or a reading of the final form of the prophetic texts. Another version of reading the prophetic books as a whole is Steck, *The Prophetic Books and their Theological Witness*, commented upon in 2.2. n. 59.

[130] Deist, "The Prophets", R. C. Culley and T. W. Overholt (eds), *Anthropological Perspectives on Old Testament Prophecy* (*Semeia*, 21; Chico: Scholars Press, 1982), T. Overholt, *Channels of Prophecy: The Social Dynamics of Prophetic Activity* (Minneapolis: Fortress Press, 1989), Carroll, "Prophecy and Society".

[131] N. K. Gottwald, "Ideology and Ideologies in Israelite Prophecy" in S. B. Reid (ed), *Prophets and Paradigms: Essays in Honor of Gene M. Tucker* (JSOTSup, 229; Sheffield: Sheffield Academic Press, 1996) 136–149, as well as a Marxist approach to Isa. 40–55 in N. K. Gottwald, "Social Class and Ideology in Isaiah 40–55: An Eagletonian Reading", *Semeia* 59 (1992) 43–57, where he argues that the prophecy of Isa. 40–55 is framed against the dominant ideology of the ruling social class.

[132] A. Brenner (ed), *A Feminist Companion to the Latter Prophets* (A Feminist Companion to the Bible, 8; Sheffield: JSOT Press, 1995), A. Brenner (ed), *Prophets and Daniel* (A Feminist Companion to the Bible, Second Series, 8; Sheffield: Sheffield Academic Press, 2001).

[133] N. Lohfink, *Option for the Poor: The Basic Principle of Liberation Theology in the Light of the Bible* (Berkeley: BIBAL Press, 1987) 53–70.

complex history of formation, explained in variations of a redaction-critical approach. Steck takes into account what he designated the redactional reception as part of the process of interpretation.[134] Steck and precursors and colleagues present detailed "refinements" of supposed redactional processes which have led to a number of hypothetical "sources", editorial additions and glosses to such an extent that it is impossible to speak of a historical-critical consensus. This obvious arbitrariness has led to a widespread scepticism of the plausibility of literary and redactional criticism as a basis for constructing the history of the formation of the texts.

While some scholars maintain an Isaiah tradition which regards Isa. 1–66 as a composite work by several authors and redactors in post-exilic times, others focus on the canonical[135] or finally received text.[136] Also, the view that the eight-century prophet Isaiah ben Amoz wrote the entire Isa. 1–66 persists.[137] In this regard, it has been suggested that through the book various assumed themes are developed, e.g. "(not) seeing and hearing", "Israel's Holy One",[138] the role of

---

[134] In recent decades, a vast array of redactional-critical studies on the Book of Isaiah has emerged. Accordingly, I shall refer only to some brief overviews: see, G. T. Sheppard, "The Book of Isaiah: Competing Structures according to a Late Modern Description of Its Shape and Scope" (SBLSP, 31; Atlanta: Scholars Press, 1992) 549–582, M. A. Sweeney, "The Book of Isaiah in Recent Research", *Currents in Research* 1 (1993) 141–162, D. M. Carr, "Reading Isaiah from Beginning (Isaiah 1) to End (Isaiah 65–66): Multiple Modern Possibilities" in R. F. Melugin and M. A. Sweeney (eds), *New Visions of Isaiah* (JSOTSup, 214; Sheffield: Sheffield Academic Press, 1996) 188–218, P. K. Tull, "One Book, Many Voices: Conceiving of Isaiah's Polyfonic Message" in McGinnis and Tull, "*As Those Who are Taught*", pp. 279–314, R. F. Melugin, "The Book of Isaiah and the Construction of Meaning" in Broyles and Evans, *Writing and Reading the Scroll of Isaiah. Volume 1* (VTSup 70, 1; Leiden: E. J. Brill, 1997) 39–55.

[135] Childs, *Isaiah*. Cf. a variation in J. Goldingay, *Isaiah* (NIBCOT; Massachusetts: Hendrickson, 2001), which interprets each part of the book in the light of the whole. In a foreword, the editors of the NIBCOT series describe the perspective of the series as "believing criticism" (p. viii).

[136] L. Alonso Schökel, "Isaiah" in R. Alter and F. Kermode (eds), *The Literary Guide to the Bible* (London: Fontana Press, 1989) 165–183, Sheppard, "The Book of Isaiah", P. D. Miscall, "Isaiah: The Labyrinth of Images", *Semeia* 54 (1992) 103–121, P. D. Miscall, *Isaiah* (Readings; Sheffield: JSOT Press, 1993), P. D. Quinn-Miscall, *Reading Isaiah: Poetry and Vision* (Louisville, KY: Westminster/John Knox Press, 2001), M. A. Sweeney, "On Multiple Settings in the Book of Isaiah" (SBLSP, 32; Atlanta: Scholars Press, 1993) 267–273, K. P. Darr, *Isaiah's Vision and the Family of God* (Literary Currents in Biblical Interpretation; Louisville, KY: Westminster/John Knox Press, 1994).

[137] J. A. Motyer, *The Prophecy of Isaiah: An Introduction and Commentary* (Illinois: Intervarsity Press, 1993) 13–33.

[138] On (not) seeing and hearing, see 5.9.; on "Israel's Holy One", see 5.8.2. n. 55.

Isa. 35 and 36–39.[139] The book as a whole has been characterised both as a drama[140] and as a "sweeping vision".[141]

2.3.3. *Isa. 40–55 (66)*

A commonsensical view of Isa. 40–55, both earlier and nowadays, is that the texts were part of the activities of an unknown prophet, "Second Isaiah", and that they are connected to a crisis related to the exile of the people of Judah after the Babylonian destruction of Jerusalem in 587/586 BCE, as well as Cyrus' rescue and restoration of Judah from 539 BCE onwards. When related to this almost canonised reading of Isa. 40–55, Duhm's conviction that the prophet who wrote these sixteen chapters was definitely not located in Babylon is interesting (2.1.2.). However, both earlier and more recently, this traditional opinion regarding the history, geography and ideology of the "Babylonian exile" has been discussed.[142]

Within Second Isaianic scholarship in general, and regarding the "Servant Song Research" especially, discussions since Duhm have mainly revolved around whether Isa. 40–55 consist of more or less independent parts or whether the sixteen chapters can be read as a composite unit. In descriptions of the message of the prophet "The Second Isaiah", various issues have been emphasised, for instance, election, the ingathering and restoration of people and land, Zion tra-

---

[139] P. R. Ackroyd, "Isaiah i–xii: Presentation of a Prophet" in W. Zimmerli (ed), *International Organization for the Study of the Old Testament: Congress Volume Göttingen 1977* (VTSup, 29; Leiden: E. J. Brill, 1978) 16–48, Steck on 2.2.1. and 5.11.14. n. 203.

[140] Watts, *Isaiah 1–33* and *Isaiah 34–66*.

[141] Quinn-Miscall, *Reading Isaiah*, p. 3.

[142] P. R. Ackroyd, *Exile and Restoration: A Study of Hebrew Thought of the Sixth Century B.C.* (OTL; London: SCM Press, 1968), P. R. Davies, *In Search of "Ancient Israel"* (JSOTSup, 148; Sheffield: JSOT Press, 1992) 40–42, R. P. Carroll, "The Myth of The Empty Land", *Semeia* 59 (1992) 79–93, R. P. Carroll, "Deportation and Diasporaic Discourses in the Prophetic Literature" in J. M. Scott (ed), *Exile: Old Testament, Jewish, and Christian Conceptions* (Supplements to the Journal for the Study of Judaism, 56; Leiden: E. J. Brill, 1997) 63–85, H. M. Barstad, *The Myth of the Empty Land: A Study in the History and Archaeology of Judah During the "Exilic" Period* (Symbolae Osloenses. Fasc. Suppl., 28; Oslo: Scandinavian University Press, 1996), Barstad, *The Babylonian Captivity of the Book of Isaiah*, L. L. Grabbe (ed), *Leading Captivity Captive: "The Exile" as History and Ideology* (JSOTSup, 278= European Seminar in Historical Methodology, 2; Sheffield: Sheffield Academic Press, 1998) 22–39; 62–79, B. Becking and M. C. A. Korpel (eds), *The Crisis of Israelite Religion: Transformation of Religious Tradition in Exilic and Post-Exilic Times* (OTS, 42; Leiden: E. J. Brill, 1999).

dition, *Gerichtsrede*, universalism/particularism and a "new exodus".[143] Many scholars aim to reconstruct the exact history of the origin and development of the Second Isaianic texts by distinguishing with great precision between different layers which are ascribed, for example, to "the prophet", "the redactor" or an "Isaianic school". In such readings, not only the "Servant Songs", but also the texts about Zion, Cyrus, Babylon and the idol polemic (among others) have been viewed as later additions to Isa. *40–55.[144] Also as regards Isa. 40–55, questions are raised as to the plausibility of literary and redactional criticism as a basis for constructing the history of the formation of the texts. As a reaction to such fragmented readings, others have presented what they label holistic or synchronic readings of Isa. 40–55.[145] To illustrate the extreme points in this discussion, I might quote Kratz, who sees the "final canonical form (*kanonische Endgestalt*) of Isa. 40–55 as the interpretive problem, not the solution".[146]

2.3.4. *Servant Songs*

A growing minority of scholars have challenged the validity of separating the "Servant Songs" from the rest of Isa. 40–55.[147] For example,

---

[143] On election, see 5.8.2. n. 60, ingathering and restoration of people and land, see 5.15.5. n. 297, Zion tradition, see 5.12.6. n. 235, *Gerichtes-rede*, see 5.16., universalism/particularism, see 5.8.5., a "New Exodus", see 5.15.2. n. 288.

[144] For a survey of the traditional debate about Isa. 40–55 as a composition, see A. Schoors, *I am God your Saviour: A Form-Critical Study of the Main Genres in Is. xl–lv* (VTSup, 24; Leiden: E.J. Brill, 1973), R. F. Melugin, *The Formation of Isaiah 40–55* (BZAW, 141; Berlin: W. de Gruyter, 1976), Hermisson, "Einheit und Komplexität Deuterojesajas", pp. 132–157. On polemics against the idols, see K. Holter, *Second Isaiah's Idol-Fabrication Passages* (Beiträge zur biblischen Exegese und Theologie, 28; Frankfurt am Main: Peter Lang, 1995) and G. L. Glover, *Getting a Word in Edgewise: A New Historicist Interpretation of Deutero-Isaiah's Idol Rhetoric* (Princeton: Princeton Theological Seminary, 1999).

[145] See, for instance, F. Matheus, *Singt dem Herrn ein neues Lied: Die Hymnen Deuterojesajas* (Stuttgarter Bibel-Studien, 141; Stuttgart: Katholisches Bibelwerk, 1990), Holter, *Second Isaiah's Idol-Fabrication Passages*. On diachronic and synchronic, see 3.4.

[146] Kratz, *Kyros im Deuterojesaja-Buch*, p. 10.

[147] J. Muilenburg, "The Book of Isaiah: Chapters 40–66", *IB* 5 (Nashville: Abingdon Press, 1956) 407, T. N. D. Mettinger, *Farewell to the Servant Songs: A Critical Examination of an Exegetical Axiom* (Scripta Minora. Regiae Societatis Humaniorum Literarum Lundensis, 3; Lund: C. W. K. Gleerup, 1982–1983), P. Wilcox and D. Paton-Williams, "The Servant Songs in Deutero-Isaiah", *JSOT* 42 (1988) 79–102, Matheus, *Singt dem Herrn ein neues Lied*, pp. 118–124, Miscall, *Isaiah*, pp. 123–125, H. M. Barstad, "The Future of the 'Servant Songs': Some Reflections on the Relationship of Biblical Scholarship to its own Tradition" in S. E. Balentine and J. Barton (eds),

it has been maintained that the four texts in question are not that characteristic as to be reckoned as extraneous matter, either linguistically or in terms of content. Moreover, their "inner coherence" is not so distinct as to designate them a separate and united group of texts. This minority of scholars might still be characterised as belonging to the "Servant Song Research Guild", as they work within the frames of Duhm and his proponents, and are occupied with invalidating one or other version of the Duhmian servant song thesis. With Hägglund (2008) as a clear exception, all these works treat Isa. 52:13–53:12 only briefly. All of them are collective interpretations.

2.3.5. Isa. 52:13–53:12: Delimitation and Genre

While most scholars regard the classical delimitation of Isa. 52:13–53:12 as clear without further argument, other suggestions have been offered. Duhm has discussed whether Isa. 52:13–53:12 consisted of two originally separate parts; 52:13–15, 53:11b–12, and 53:1–11a, with YHWH as the speaker in the first part, and the prophet speaking in the second part. However, this was not of great importance to him, as the two harmonise with each other.[148] Others regard Isa. 53:1–12 as constituting a distinct literary unit.[149] As we shall see below, debates

---

Language, Theology, and The Bible: Essays in Honour of James Barr (Oxford: Clarendon Press, 1994) 261–270, Willey, *Remember the Former Things*, pp. 175–181; 219–221. F. Hägglund, *Isaiah 53 in the Light of Homecoming after Exile* (Forschungen zum Alten Testament, 2. Reihe; 31, Tübingen: J. C. B. Mohr {Paul Siebeck} 2008) 103–117, reads Isa. 53 in relation to the whole Book of Isaiah.

[148] Cf. 2.1.4. K. Elliger, *Deuterojesaja in seinem Verhältnis zu Tritojesaja* (BZWANT, 11; Stuttgart: W. Kohlhammer, 1933) 6–27, regards Isa 52:13–53:12 as "typical" Trito-Isaianic. Due to the inconsistent presentation in 52:13–15, Duhm, *Das Buch Jesaia*, p. 355, also transferred 14b to follow 53:2, and is, among others, followed by G. R. Driver, "Isaiah 52:13–53:12: 'The Servant of the Lord'" in M. Black and G. Fohrer (eds), *In Memoriam Paul Kahle* (BZAW, 103; Berlin: Alfred Töpelmann, 1968) 91–92, G. Fohrer, *Das Buch Jesaja: Kap. 40–66* (ZBK; Zürich: Zwingli Verlag, 1964) 158, C. Westermann, *Isaiah 40–66 – A Commentary* (OTL; London: SCM Press, 1969) 258–259, and Blenkinsopp, *Isaiah 40–55*, pp. 345–345 (e).

[149] H. M. Orlinsky, *The So-Called "Servant of the Lord" and "Suffering Servant" in Second Isaiah* (VTSup, 14; Leiden: E. J. Brill, 1967) 17–23 (he regards 52:13–15; 53:11b–12 as later additions) and R. N. Whybray, *Thanksgiving for a Liberated Prophet: An Interpretation of Isaiah Chapter 53* (JSOTSup, 4; Sheffield: JSOT, 1978) 143, n. 1. Whybray also assumes that 52:13–15 (apart from כִּ...אָדָם in 52:14b, which has been displaced from its original position after 53:2) have a separate origin and the identities of the servant differ in the two songs. N. H. Snaith, *Isa. 40–55: A Study of the Teaching of the Second Isaiah and Its Consequences* (VT, 14; Leiden. E. J. Brill, 1967) 194, takes 52:13–15 as "a separate piece, though it may well stand as a title or summary of chapter 53". J. Lindblom, *The Servant Songs in Deutero-Isaiah: A New Attempt to*

about the delimitation of a text might be related to a recent discussion of an extended concept of text.[150]

Genre describes the relation of a text to other texts and also to reading, with the reading distinguished by choices of focus (cf. 5.4.). For example, it has been debated whether Isa. 52:13–53:12 should be labelled "Servant Song", an "individual psalm of thanksgiving",[151] "oracle of salvation",[152] "lament",[153] "song of penance",[154] "prophetical liturgy",[155] "vision",[156] "ideal biography",[157] *Leichenlied*[158] or *Prozeßbericht*.[159] Once again one might ask whether the consensus concerning the peculiarity

---

Solve an Old Problem (Lunds Universitets Årsskrift, N. F. Avd. 1, 47: 5; Lund: C. W. K. Gleerup, 1951) 37–42, regards 52:13–53:1 as a unit and 53:2–12 as another. L. Ruppert, "'Mein Knecht, der Gerechte, macht die Vielen gerecht, und ihre Verschuldunger trägt sie (Jes 53,11)': Universales Heil durch das stellvertretende Strafleiden des Gottesknechtes?", BZ 40 (1996) 9–10, regards the YHWH speech of 52:13–15 and 53:11b–12 as redactional additions and as interpretations of the "we" speech in 53:1ff. He takes Isa. 53:1–10aα.β.b as the *Grundschrift*, in which the servant is identified as the prophet, whereas at a redactional level, the servant is regarded as a collective: the Gola community of Zion.

[150] Cf. 3.7–3.9., 5.3, 5.6, 5.7.

[151] J. Begrich, *Studien zu Deuterojesaja* (TBü, 20; München, Chr. Kaiser Verlag, 1969) 56–60; 145–151, Kaiser, *Der königliche Knecht*, p. 88 (for 53:1–6), Westermann, *Isaiah 40–66*, pp. 256–257 (for 53:1–9, 53:1–11a he also designates "report"), Whybray, *Thanksgiving for a Liberated Prophet*, pp. 110–115 (for 53), Mettinger, *Farewell to the Servant Songs*, p. 17 (for 53:1–6).

[152] Kaiser, *Der königliche Knecht*, p. 88, designates Isa. 52:13–53:12 an oracle of salvation (and 53:1–6 as an individual thanksgiving, which is also related to a lament, pp. 93–127), cf. Melugin, *The Formation of Isaiah 40–55*, p. 74, Mettinger, *Farewell to the Servant Songs*, p. 17 (for 52:13–15, 53:11–12), H. D. Preuß, *Deuterojesaja: Eine Einführung in seine Botschaft* (Neukirchen-Vluyn: Neukirchener Verlag, 1976) 99–100; 104, J. L. Koole, *Isaiah III. Volume 2/Isaiah 49–55* (Historical Commentary on the Old Testament; Leuven: Peeters, 1998) 262.

[153] Kaiser, *Der königliche Knecht*, pp. 93–127 (for 53:1–6).

[154] Elliger, *Deuterojesaja in seinem Verhältnis zu Tritojesaja*, p. 19, or "confession", cf. Westermann, *Isaiah 40–66*, p. 257.

[155] Elliger, *Deuterojesaja in seinem Verhältnis zu Tritojesaja*, pp. 19; 291–292, n. 4, Fohrer, *Das Buch Jesaja*, pp. 160–161.

[156] Duhm, *Das Buch Jesaia*, pp. 356–357, Lindblom, *The Servant Songs in Deutero-Isaiah*, p. 46 (for 53:2–12) and as "a symbolic narrative, an allegorical picture" (p. 47), J. Goldingay, *God's Prophet, God's Servant: A Study in Jeremiah and Isaiah 40–55* (Exeter: Pater Noster, 1984) 140.

[157] K. Baltzer, *Deutero-Isaiah* (Hermeneia; Minneapolis: Fortress Press, 2001) 394.

[158] H. Jahnow, *Das hebräische Leichenlied im Rahmen der Völkerdichtung* (BZAW, 36; Giessen: Alfred Töpelmann, 1923) 256–266.

[159] Preuß, *Deuterojesaja*, pp. 99–100; 104, in which the servant is rehabilitated before the heavenly court: "In der *Form* einer himmlischen Prozeßszene hat das vierte GKL doch die *Funktion* eines Heilsorakels, denn dem Knecht, der gelitten hat und gestorben ist, wird von Gott zukünftige Verherrlichung verheißen" (p. 104, his italics). Preuß also refers to Balzer.

of the text has obstructed reading, or whether "the poem as problem", to quote Clines,[160] indicates the magnitude of the problem of finding an appropriate Great Story for the text. Steck discusses different possibilities, but concludes that the structure of Isa. 52:13–53:12 cannot be related to any known *Gattung* (2.2.3.). As Steck's discussion of which genre Isa. 52:13–53:12 belong to illustrates, clearly, designations of genre might be rather restrictive for a text. Concerning Steck's struggle to try to fit Isa. 53 into a certain pattern, one might ask whether the tight pattern rather than the text itself is the problem. As Steck is unable to find a fitting genre for Isa. 53, this might be due to an idea that genre is a type of literary conceptualisation whose ideal form could be reconstructed from the present text. [161]

2.3.6. Identification of the Servant

Another obsession in Duhmian readings of the "Servant Songs" has been the pursuit of the identity of the servant. As a result of the historical-critical interest of the text, the identification of a modern biblical figure of *Gottesknecht* has become one of biblical scholarship's *cruces interpretum*. Almost all other questions asked about the text are in one way or another related to this quest. In Duhmian exegesis, no-one has adopted Duhm's identification of an unknown contemporary of the prophet Second Isaiah suffering from leprosy (cf. 2.1.4.). The abundance of suggestions concerning the identity of the servant can be categorised in two groups: individual or collective. The identifications of the servant as an individual include: the prophet Isaiah, "Second Isaiah", an anonymous contemporary of the prophet "Second Isaiah", King David, King Uzziah, King Hezekiah, King Josiah, King Jehoiachin, the Persian kings Cyrus or Darius, Zerubbabel or his

---

[160] D. J. A. Clines, *I, He, We, and They: A Literary Approach to Isaiah 53* (JSOTSup, 1; Sheffield: JSOT Press, 1983) 59.

[161] For overviews of discussions of genre related to Isa. 52:13–53:12, see Goldingay and Payne, *A Critical and Exegetical Commentary on Isaiah 40–55. Vol. II*, pp. 281–284, and J. W. Adams, *The Performative Nature and Function of Isaiah 40–55* (London: T. & T. Clark, 2006) 190–192. In his examination of my dissertation, Professor Sweeney emphasised how "more recent form critics have stressed the adaptability of genre to the rhetorical needs of the text at hand". See more recent form-critical contributions to prophetic literature by D. L. Petersen, E. Ben-Zvi and M. H. Floyd in Sweeney and Ben-Zvi, *The Changing Face of Form Criticism for the Twenty-First Century*. More on genre in 5.4.

son Meshullam, Shesbazzar, the prophets Ezekiel, Jeremiah, or Moses, Job, an unknown teacher of the Law, Eleazar (a martyr in the time of the Maccabees), the high-priest Onias, an eunuch, a vaguely defined mythical figure, Christ or a forerunner of Christ, and an eschatological or Messianic figure. The collective identifications include: the servant understood as an image of an empirical or eschatological Israel, either a part of Israel or all Israel or as Zion/Jerusalem. Others consider the servant to be the "idealised prophets" (*Idealpropheten*) or the priests. A number of combinations of individual and collective identifications have also been proposed, for instance, the servant as the people *and* the prophet, or the exiled people *and* the exiled King Jehoiachin. In recent scholarship, the servant is most often identified either individually as the prophet "Second Isaiah" or collectively as a figurative allusion to Israel.[162]

Within traditional German historical-critical readings, the servant mentioned outside the "Servant Songs" in the original version is interpreted *collectively* as Israel, while the servant in the four *EJL* is almost unanimously identified *individually* as the prophet, marked by a historical-biographical approach, where the life of the servant is read with a rise from his vocation in 42:1–4 to 49:1–6, 50:4–9 to the climax of death and revival in 52:13–53:12 (2.2.5.). In Steck's case, a collective identification of the servant in the "Servant Songs" is possible on a redactional level only. In his reading, five different identities of the servant of the four *EJL* are offered within a time span of 539 to 270 BCE. The servant is identified as the prophet Second Isaiah (Steck's first level, dated to just after Cyrus' conquest of 539 BCE, as well as on the third level, dated to the first and middle part of the fifth century Babylon), Zion (the last two *EJL* on the second level, dated to the time before 520 BCE), those who have returned from exile (the first two *EJL* on the third level, and the four *EJL* of the fourth level, dated to 311–303/2 BCE), those who remained at home in Judah (the four *EJL* on the fourth level), as well as the true Israel, which includes other peoples (the four *EJL* on the fifth level, dated to 301–270 BCE).[163]

---

[162] For an overview of this, see the surveys of the history of research of the "Servant Songs" in 2.3. n. 122.
[163] See 2.2.2., 2.2.3. and 2.2.5.

2.3.7. Redaction-Critical Approaches to the Servant Songs

Redaction-critical approaches to Isaiah 1–66 are widespread. In these, complex models of a number of redactions which took place based on a basic writing are presented, with the "Servant Songs" interpreted as an integrated part of this process of literary development. We have seen the way in which a certain "division of labour" appears between Hermisson, Kratz and Steck, as they concentrate on some parts and are dependent of each other concerning other parts of the Book of Isaiah (2.2.5.). In a recent article on German-speaking redaction criticism, Conroy's "The 'Four Servant Poems' in Second Isaiah in Light of Recent Redaction-Historical Studies", introduces his presentation with a pragmatic attitude to such studies:

> It is no secret that redaction-historical studies of this type suffer from a severe credibility crisis on the part of many English-speaking scholars. These critics often point to the substantial difference between the various histories of redaction proposed by such works (all of them extreme precise and complex), and argue that this must mean that the method, as practiced, is unsuited for the particular textual material that we have in Isaiah 40–55. In spite of these and similar criticism, however, it is worthwhile giving these important works a fair hearing, at least for the light they may throw on the understanding of the individual texts. In fact, even if one might fail to be convinced by the entire concatenation of more or less probable but interdependent arguments that generate the concluding proposal of a detailed redaction-historical stratification, it is nonetheless certain that, at the very least, there are many valuable observations of detail that can be gleaned from the pages of such redaction-historical studies and that are valid independently of the general conclusions.[164]

Conroy continues his study by presenting four recent redaction-critical works on Isaiah, by Kratz, Oorschot, Berges and Werlitz respectively.[165] Conroy presents these scholars' different proposals for the internal stratification of the Book of Isaiah, and relates them to one other. He

---

[164] C. Conroy, "The 'Four Servant Poems' in Second Isaiah in Light of Recent Redaction-Historical Studies" in C. McCarthy and J. F. Healey (eds), *Biblical and Near Eastern Essay: Essays in Honour of Kevin J. Cathcart* (JSOTSup, 375; Sheffield: Continuum, 2004) 81.

[165] Kratz, *Kyros im Deuterojesaja-Buch*, J. van Oorschot, *Von Babel zum Zion: Eine literarkritische und redaktionsgeschichtliche Untersuchung* (BZAW, 206; Berlin: W. de Gruyer, 1993), U. Berges, *Das Buch Jesaja: Komposition und Endgestalt* (Herders Biblische Studien, 16; Freiburg: Herder, 1998) and J. Werlitz, *Redaktion und Komposition: Zur Rückfrage hinter die Endgestalt von Jesaja 40–55* (BBB, 122; Berlin: Philo, 1999).

focuses especially on these scholars' various views on the redactional levels in the "Servant Songs".

Another illustrative example of a pragmatic assessment many scholars make concerning Steck's redactional critical studies of Isaiah might be seen in Tull's "One Book, Many Voices" (2006):

> While others disagree with Steck's confidence in redactional reconstruction and in assigning historical contexts to several successive redactional layers, his work has offered many helpful insights especially into Third Isaiah, a portion that had received relatively little attention but is emerging as an important key to understand the present form and theological tensions of the book.[166]

Also in her earlier study *Remember the Former Things* (1997), Tull (Willey) comments both on questionable assumptions as well as the difference between the studies of Steck and Kratz and their predecessors:

> In the US and Great Britain, their [Steck's and Kratz'] work has been received with admiration for attention to detail mixed with scepticism over their hypercritical methodology, their precise matching of posited historical settings and hypothetical redactional layers, and their confident conclusions. Despite the questionable assumptions on which their claims are founded, it is important to note that the aims of these redaction scholars differ significantly from those of their predecessors. Rather than devalue the work of biblical redactors as effacers of an originally pure prophetic word, they perceived theological and compositional coherence in the strata of rewritings they posited.[167]

The conclusion Gelston draws seems to be the opposite of others' pragmatic attitude to a redaction-critical analysis, here with regard to Steck's studies:

> Not all scholars…will be convinced that it is possible to determine with this degree of precision the exact stages in the redactional process by which ultimately the whole book of Isaiah reached its final form, and the conclusions drawn depend on the validity of the redactional analysis as a whole.[168]

---

[166] Tull, "One Book, Many Voices", p. 286.

[167] Willey, *Remember the Former Things*, p. 25.

[168] A. Gelston, "Review: O. H. Steck, *Gottesknecht und Zion: Gesammelte Aufsätze zu Deuterojesaja* (Forschungen zum Alten Testament, 4; Tübingen: J. C. B. Mohr {Paul Siebeck}, 1992)", *JSS* 40 (1995) 118. However, he does not neglect the importance of the study: "This is a stimulating and suggestive work, but one which will require close reading and careful sifting by scholars before its conclusions can be accepted. In the meantime it is a book which no commentators on Second Isaiah can afford to ignore."

I do not share the pragmatic attitude of, for instance, Conroy and Tull, as I find it hard to value details in the interpretations of these redaction-critical approaches without taking the overall assumption and methodology into consideration. The critique raised against redaction-critical approaches will be treated in more detail below under the heading "historising" (2.3.8.1.).

2.3.8. *Historising, Traditionalising, Theologising and Textualising*

The controversy within scholarship regarding what occurs in Isa. 52:13–53:12 signals the problem of constructing a larger context for the text. Since the perspectives and points of view seem incommensurable of the proponents of various interpretations and conflicting delimitations, genre recognitions, identifications etc. of Isa. 53, no easy resolution or compromise exists for specifying a single Great Story portraying what happened or happens. This involves questions of whether a "historical text" constitutes knowledge of the past as well as the motives of choosing particular concepts (e.g. *Gottesknecht, Stellvertretung, Tat-Ergehen-Zusammenhang, leidende Gerechte*) or constructing a particular narrative (related for example to a "heavenly court tradition" or the Babylonian Exile). As seen above, readings of Isa. 52:13–53:12 pose particular challenges, as the text is characterized by a long history of interpretation in Judaism, Christianity and biblical scholarship.

The majority of scholars since Duhm have supported his thesis about the "Servant Songs". Scholars who work within the bounds of this thesis reproduce the "same" questions as him, taking their point of departure in the scholarly myth that these texts are *special* and *cannot* be read as an integrated part of the rest of Isa. 40–55. But Duhm's thesis is nothing but a *thesis* whose arguments and tenability must always be subjected to criticism. In recent biblical scholarship, greater attention than earlier has been paid to the different forces at work in the text and reading, where the variety of possible focuses has come to the fore. The role and status of interpretation have been deeply challenged. One might ask whether a critical approach must justify itself by virtue of its interpretive results or by virtue of its understanding of text and reading. In the following, different forces of reading will be treated

---

Blenkinsopp, *Isaiah 40–55*, p. 44, discusses details in Steck's work without taking his overarching presuppositions into account.

under the headings "historising", "traditionalising", "theologising" and "textualising", before "new visions of Isaiah" are presented.

2.3.8.1. *Historising*

Duhm's thesis about the "Servant Songs" is based on a literary-critical approach. In this, and all other historical-critical approaches (such as textual criticism, form criticism, redaction criticism, tradition criticism), scholars explain biblical texts based on historical reconstructions of assumed earlier oral and/or written sources. In pursuing the origin of the text, the concern has been to recover the intention of the writer by identifying the sources he has used, as well as the history of the reception of the sources culminating in the present texts as redactional end-products. In this regard, it is presupposed that the author's or redactor's sources are indicated explicitly or implicitly by quotations, allusions and so forth in the text. The historical-critical concentration on sources and traditions that are presumed to underlie the biblical texts is in part based on a presupposition that historical relationships between texts are single and traceable.

Historical-critical studies are author- and work- oriented and regard texts as having one intended meaning which it is the scholars' task to find. This correct meaning and unified message is the authentic text. Moreover, in historical-critical exegesis a text is viewed as a source and vehicle for representing the past as history. In Steck's redaction-critical approach, his construction of the text is primarily shaped by his interpretation (cf. 2.2.5.). The author, redactors and historical settings are heuristic fictions created by him as hypotheses or additional stories to account for the meaning of the text. A circularity appears between a literary criticism of the text and theories concerning textual growth and a "re-interpretation" of a total of five historical levels in the four *EJL*. In Steck's description of all the different historical levels, he assumes a consistency, for example in the use of imagery, as a criterion of authorship and date.[169] His five redaction-critical interpretations of the servant's identity (based on reductive and

---

[169] R. N. Whybray, "Review: O. H. Steck, *Gottesknecht und Zion: Gesammelte Aufsätze zu Deuterojesaja* (Forschungen zum Alten Testament, 4; Tübingen: J. C. B. Mohr {Paul Siebeck}, 1992", *JTS* 45 (1994) 182. Similarly, Goldingay and Payne, *A Critical and Exegetical Commentary on Isaiah 40–55. Vol. I*, p. 7, criticises Kratz's view that "repetitions, syntactical unevenness, varying theological emphases, and varying symbolism suggest diversity in authorship".

objectifying readings) might unanimously be assumed to be constructions, but he does not regard them as particularly arbitrary as they are
legitimated by being related to certain German reading conventions.
Steck's redactional criticism of the Book of Isaiah as a whole is also
characterised by a distribution of verses and words in sources which
might be somewhat speculative in their precision, and with much
ad hoc argumentation.[170] Certain details support a certain hypothesis,
where the basic function of readings might be described as a reaffirmation of a system of historical constructions. Unfortunately, Steck does
not explain what should count as evidence or arguments, and provides
only biblical or bibliographical references. No account is provided for
the criteria which enable him and his reading community to identify different literary levels and sources in this text. The complicated
process of transforming sources into facts is abridged, without much
reflection on text production and reception. However, there are no
non-theoretical positions, but only degrees of awareness.

The criticism of Duhmian readings of Isa. 52:13–53:12 may be
related to recent debates concerning traditional historical-critical
research within biblical scholarship in general.[171] This is related to
an increased awareness of the way in which facts and knowledge are
scholarly constructions. Interpretations not only determine which facts
they comprise through selection and organisation, but the interpretations themselves also constitute facts. To historise material is to "do"
history; it might be depicted as a process of naming things in a certain

---

[170] J. L. McLaughlin, "Review: O. H. Steck, *Gottesknecht und Zion: Gesammelte Aufsätze zu Deuterojesaja* (Forschungen zum Alten Testament, 4; Tübingen: J. C. B. Mohr
{Paul Siebeck}, 1992", *JBL* 113 (1994) 714.

[171] For a criticism of traditional historical-critical readings in biblical studies, see e.g.
H. M. Barstad, "History and The Hebrew Bible" in L. L. Grabbe (ed), *Can a "History
of Israel" Be Written?* (JSOTSup, 245= European Seminar in Historical Methodology,
1; Sheffield: Sheffield Academic Press, 1997) 37–64, F. W. Dobbs-Allsopp, "Rethinking Historical Criticism", *BibInt* 7 (1999) 235–271, R. D. Miller II, "Yahweh and His
Clio: Critical Theory and the Historical Criticism of the Hebrew Bible", *CBR* 4 (2006)
149–168, and G. Aichele, P. D. Miscall and R. Walsh, "An Elephant in the Room:
Historical-Critical and Postmodern Interpretations of the Bible", *JBL* 128 (2009) 383–
404. Especially in relation to prophetic literature, see E. W. Conrad, "Prophet, Redactor and Audience: Reforming the Notion of Isaiah's Formation" and R. F. Melugin,
"Figurative Speech and the Reading of Isaiah 1 as Scripture" in Melugin and Sweeney,
New Visions of Isaiah, pp. 142–160; 282–305, R. F. Melugin, "Prophetic Books and the
Problem of Historical Reconstruction" in Reid, *Prophets and Paradigms*, pp. 63–78,
and G. M. Tucker, "The Futile Quest for the Historical Prophet" in E. E. Carpenter
(ed), *A Biblical Itinerary: In Search of Method, Form, and Content. Essays in Honor of
George W. Coats* (JSOTSup, 240; Sheffield: Sheffield Academic Press, 1997) 144–152.

way, for instance, similar to what the historian, Hayden White, has called "emplotment".[172] In historical-critical readings, the debate concerning the identification of "true" meaning turns into a discussion of who has correctly identified the author's or redactor's intentions. But an author's choices cannot be reduced to a very few causal relationships or sources. A reading of the Hebrew Bible, the Book of Isaiah or Isa. 52:13–53:12 is a function of the dynamics of social and cultural power promoting one ideology (or theology) over others in the contemporary world. As will be examined in Chapter 5, an intertextual reading regards a text as a collection of possibilities, with attention paid to the different driving forces at work in reading and interpretation.

2.3.8.2. Traditionalising

Both the "authentic" sources and traditions are the scholar's own reconstructions of the biblical texts. One example is Steck's reading of an assumed heavenly court tradition within Isa. 52:13–53:12 and within the other three *EJL* (cf. 2.2.2. and 2.2.3.). Steck identifies which of the three aspects of the heavenly court tradition are visible in Isa. 52:13–53:12, and how the fourth *EJL* relates to the first three *EJL*. Thereby, the text becomes more or less paralysed by the tradition he constructs around it.[173] Instead of reifying tradition by connecting

---

[172] Hayden White, "Historical Pluralism", *Critical Inquiry* 12 (1986) 487: "[H]istorical accounts cast in the form of a narrative may be as various as the *modes of emplotment* which literary critics have identified as constituting the different principles for structuring narratives in general" (his italics). Hayden White designates this "a work of construction rather than of discovery". This is related to what characterizes a historical inquiry: it seeks to "determine what certain events might *mean* for a given group, society, or culture's conception of its present tasks and future prospects" (his italics). He also refers to Ricoeur, who says that in historical interpretations, a given emplotment of historical events is a performative, not a constative, utterance (p. 489). On performativity, see 4.6.

[173] On an assumed heavenly council tradition in German scholarship, see 2.2.2. n. 67. Anglo-Saxon contributions to such a tradition are found in, for instance, F. M. Cross, "The Council of Yahweh in Second Isaiah", *JNES* 12 (1953) 274–277, R. N. Whybray, *The Heavenly Counsellor in Isaiah xl 13–14: A Study of the Sources of the Theology of Deutero-Isaiah* (SOTSMS, 1; Cambridge: University Press, 1971), R. N. Whybray, *Isaiah 40–66* (NCB; London: Oliphants, 1975) 33; 48; 71, C. R. Seitz, "The Divine Council: Temporal Transition and New Prophecy in the Book of Isaiah", *JBL* 109 (1990) 229–247, A. Malamat, "The Secret Council and Prophetic Involvement" in R. Liwak and S. Wagner (eds), *Prophetie und geschichtliche Wirklichkeit im alten Israel: Festschrift für Siegfried Hermann zum 65. Geburtstag* (Stuttgart: W. Kohlhammer, 1991) 231–236, and M. Nissinen, "Prophets and the Divine Council" in U. Hübner and E.-A. Knauf (eds), *Kein Land für sich allein: Studien zum Kulturkontakt in Kanaan, Israel/Palestina und Ebirnari für Manfred Weippert zum 65. Geburtstag*

historical success of cognate texts, a possible tradition might be viewed as a discursive and interpretative achievement, as will be illuminated by the intertextual approach in Chapter 5. Traditionalising might concern a process of naming things in a certain way, which is, like historising, related to a discourse in the present. Of interest, however, are not origins and dating as such, but how statements about authenticity, dating and other values inherent in the concept of tradition shape the present interpretation.[174] As regards Steck and his narrative production, one might say that he refers to the past to authorise a present interpretation.

2.3.8.3. *Theologising*
In his survey of the history of research into the "Servant Songs", Haag treats the following theological concepts he finds inherent to the four *EJL*: servant, mission, universalism, mediation (*Mittlerschaft*), vicarious suffering (*Stellvertretung*), offering to death (*Sühnetod*) and resurrection.[175] I will exemplify such theological conceptualisations with a key theme in my presentation of Steck, the German concept of *Stellvertretung* (cf. 2.2.4.). Interestingly, vicarious suffering (*Stellvertretung*) was not of great importance in Duhm's reading. To Steck, however, it is at the core of his interpretation of Isa. 52:13–53:12 in its original version, as well as the next two redactional levels. On the first level, *Stellvertretung* is related to *Knecht Jahwes*, identified as the prophet "Second Isaiah" suffering vicariously for Israel and with Israel for the peoples. On the second and third levels the concept is related to the collective Zion identified as *Knecht Jahwes* (as regards the third and fourth *EJL*), suffering vicariously for Israel, and with the people for the peoples. However, it is odd that a concept which is so strongly accentuated on his first three levels completely disappears from the last two. One might get the impression that the concept of *Stellvertretung* is rather coincidentally or arbitrarily used. Bailey claims that to a non-German like himself, "explaining *Stellvertretung*…becomes almost a

---

(Göttingen: Universitetsverlag Freiburg, 2002) 4–19. Of these, only Whybray relates this tradition to the *EJL*.

[174] R. Bauman, *A World of Others' Words: Cross-Cultural Perspectives in Intertextuality* (London: Blackwell, 2004) 27. Inspired by D. Hymes and M. Bakhtin, Bauman sees traditionalisation as a communicative strategy for producing certain forms of intertextuality, thereby authorising utterances. On Bakhtin, see 5.2.

[175] Haag, *Der Gottesknecht bei Deuterojesaja*, pp. 185–195.

matter of linguistic tautology".[176] Bailey discusses "the problems of formulation and method that may hinder international communication" of concepts of *Stellvertretung*,[177] and describes its centrality in German scholarship as follows:

> The term *Stellvertretung* does not occur in any major German translation of Isaiah 53, but it does occur almost of necessity in German-language theological exegesis concerned with the relationships of the "one" and the "many" – certainly one of the central questions of Isa. 52:13–53:12 on any reckoning. Different languages have different terms for this relationship, but German excels, both because of the theologians who make the language and because of the theologians who are made by the language, in focusing attention not only upon the role of the Servant and upon the role of the many, but upon the thing that now exists between them because of their related destinies.[178]

---

[176] D. P. Bailey, "Concepts of *Stellvertretung* in the Interpretation of Isaiah 53" in Bellinger and Farmer, *Jesus and the Suffering Servant*, p. 238. This might be exemplified by H. Spieckermann, "Konzeption und Vorgeschichte des Stellvertretungsgedankens im Alten Testament" in J. A. Emerton (ed), *International Organization for the Study of the Old Testament: Congress Volume Cambridge 1995* (VTSup, 66; Leiden: E. J. Brill, 1997) 281–295, ET: H. Spieckermann, "The Conception and Prehistory of the Idea of Vicarious Suffering in the Old Testament" in Janowski and Stulmacher, *The Suffering Servant*, pp. 1–15. Concerning the identity of the servant, Spieckermann claims: "In the realm of prophecy, the Servant is to a certain extent a 'utopian' figure who must remain nameless because no identification can do justice to the claims about vicarious suffering" (p. 293, ET p. 14). Bailey also comments on the way in which certain passages of Kant's writings have become a "canon" for atonement discourses in Germany, with a "complex and anything but uniform" response (p. 233, incl. n. 23). Hägglund, *Isaiah 53 in the Light of Homecoming after Exile*, argues that what is at stake is vicarious suffering, but not atoning suffering. Cf. 2.2.4. and 5.12.

[177] Bailey, "Concepts of *Stellvertretung* in the Interpretation of Isaiah 53", p. 227.

[178] Bailey, "Concepts of *Stellvertretung* in the Interpretation of Isaiah 53", p. 223. In this regard, see the telling subtitle of B. Janowski, *Stellvertretung: Alttestamentliche Studien zu einem theologischen Grundbegriff* (Stuttgarter Bibel-Studien, 165; Stuttgart: Katholisches Bibelwerk, 1997).

The same might concern the related deed-consequence connection (*Tun-Ergehen-Zusammenhang*). K. Koch, "Gibt es eine Vergeltungs-Dogma", *ZTK* 52 (1955) 1–42, and K. Koch, "Der Spruch 'Sein Blut bleibe auf seinem Haupt' und die israelitische Auffassung vom vergossenen Blut", *VT* 12 (1962) 396–416, argue that a twofold meaning illustrates a *Tun-Ergehen* principle in OT: the act and its consequences are regarded as one and the same thing because the act bears within itself – irrespective of any punishment which might be imposed from without – its own inevitable consequences. Further, Koch claims that divine retribution does not exist in the Hebrew Bible. What does occur is a kind of reflex between actions and consequences, where both good and bad actions are repaid in kind. YHWH has some relationship to this process, but according to Koch this is not a juridical relationship. J. Barr, *The Semantics of Biblical Language* (London: SCM Press, 1991) 109, criticises Koch's analysis for being based on an etymological understanding of root meanings of Hebrew words for e.g. sin. Also Koch's term *Vergeltungsdogma* limits the idea of retribution on the basis

Steck belongs to a school of thought which may be described as based
on (a) German common-sense reading(s), constructed on a legacy of
more than one hundred years of German-speaking theological (Protestant) scholarship. Scholars who work within the "same" conventions
include Hermisson, Kratz and Janowski, whose studies are strongly
marked by a traditional literary criticism influenced, for example, by
Duhm and Elliger.[179] For those who are not familiar with this scholarship, it might seem somewhat inaccessible, because the premises are
not articulated, and have long been taken for granted within a certain
reading community. This might be a local (German) version of what
P. R. Davies has termed "Academic Bibspeak", by which he means a
socio-religious status of biblical scholarship in which biblical concepts
are built into one's academic discourse. Davies offers sample entries
in "A Critical Dictionary of the Old Testament", with entries such as
"Old Testament", "Theology", "Israel", "Canaanites" and "Covenant".[180]
In our context, entries such as *Gottesknecht, EJL, Stellvertretung* (and
the related logic of deed-consequence-connection/*Tat-Ergehen-Zusammenhang*) and *der leidende Gerechte* might be added. Steck's reading of
the Book of Isaiah definitively shows how arbitrary a reading might be
and how closely reading is related to reading communities.

Orlinsky describes "suffering servant" and "vicarious suffering" as
"theological and scholarly fiction".[181] At least, this might be related to

---

of a pre-existing norm. It has further been discussed how his theory about actions
and consequences fits into the larger picture of the religion of ancient Israel. J. Barton,
"Natural Law and Poetic Justice in the Old Testament", *JTS* 30 (1979) 14, argues that
"texts which speak of poetic justice may probably be seen as making appeal to the
idea of natural law". Also J. S. Kaminsky, *Corporate Responsibility in the Hebrew Bible*
(JSOTSup, 196; Sheffield: Sheffield Academic Press, 1995) 24–29, criticises Koch's
analysis and relates it to the debate about a concept of corporate personality, see 4.7.
He describes Koch's theory as "insightful, but overstated" (p. 24).

[179] To the list might also be added e.g. Begrich, *Studien zu Deuterojesaja*, Westermann, *Isaiah 40–66* and E. Kutsch, *Sein Leiden und Tod – unser Heil: Eine Exegese von
Jesaja 52,13–53,12* (BS, 52; Neukirchen-Vluyn: Neukirchener Verlag, 1967).

[180] P. R. Davies, "Do Old Testament Studies Need A Dictionary?" in D. J. A. Clines,
S. E. Fowl and S. E. Porter (eds), *The Bible in Three Dimensions: Essays in Celebration
of Forty Years of Biblical Studies in the University of Sheffield* (JSOTSup, 87; Sheffield:
JSOT Press, 1990) 321–335. Cf. on discourse in 5.5.

[181] Orlinsky, *The So-Called "Servant of the Lord" and "Suffering Servant" in Second
Isaiah*, pp. 51–59, cf. H. M. Orlinsky, "The So-Called 'Suffering Servant' in Isaiah
53" in H. M. Orlinsky, *Interpreting The Prophetic Tradition: The Goldenson Lectures
1955–1966* (New York: Ktav, 1969) 227–273. Also Whybray, *Thanksgiving for a Liberated Prophet*, pp. 58–76, rejects any idea of vicarious suffering and argues that the
people of Israel have already suffered for their sins leading to the destruction of their

a discussion about whether scholars are uncritically following conventional analyses, accepting at face value statements and so promoting one ideology (or theology) over others. Landy puts it thus:

> [I]t is very hard to read Isaiah 53 except through the lens of its history of interpretation and its traumatic consequences: the vindication of the New, and the theodicy of substitutionary atonement.[182]

He continues:

> How can we innocently read Isaiah 53 as Christians and Jews, without or across the appalling memories of dialogue as persecution? How can we come to terms with the notion of vicarious suffering? Perhaps I, as a biblical critic, can avoid this history. But I would do so only in the face of my responsibility as a person and as a Jew.[183]

---

land and their captivity (cf. Isa. 40:2). The servant can only participate in their suffering, cf. Whybray's argument:

> No person has relieved them, or could relieve them, of this suffering by suffering for them. What the speaker in chapter 53 is saying is that the Servant, who deserved no punishment, has, as a result of *their* sins, which had necessitated his dangerous and fateful prophetical ministry, received the largest share of it. This is not vicarious suffering (p. 61, his italics).

Cf. J. J. Collins, "The Suffering Servant: Scapegoat or Example?", *Proceedings of the Irish Biblical Association* 4 (1980) 62, S. Croatto, "Exegesis of Second Isaiah from the Perspective of the Oppressed: Paths to Reflection" in F. F. Segovia and M. A. Tolbert (eds), *Reading From This Place 2: Social Location and Biblical Interpretation in Global Perspective* (Minneapolis: Fortress Press, 1995) 234, and Landy, "The Construction of the Subject and the Symbolic Order", p. 61. Interestingly, of the most recent commentaries on the Book of Isaiah, neither Brueggemann, *Isaiah 40–66* nor Goldingay and Payne, *A Critical and Exegetical Commentary on Isaiah 40–55. Vol. II* comment on the idea of vicarious suffering in their interpretations of Isa. 53. However, J. Goldingay, *The Message of Isaiah 40–55: A Literary-Theological Commentary* (London: T. & T. Clark, 2005) 481–488, does treat the issue.

[182] Landy, "The Construction of the Subject and the Symbolic Order", p. 62. N. K. Gottwald, *The Hebrew Bible – A Socio-Literary Introduction* (Philadelphia: Fortress Press, 1985) 21, comments on Christian and male biases in servant interpretation. Both Rembaum, "The Development of a Jewish Exegetical Tradition Regarding Isaiah 53", p. 289, and Haag, *Der Gottesknecht bei Deuterojesaja*, p. 66, comment on how Jewish interpreters both in mediaeval and modern times incorporated certain Christian concepts into their readings. J. F. A. Sawyer, "Isaiah" in J. Hayes (ed), *Dictionary of Biblical Interpretation. Vol. 1* (Nashville: Abingdon, 1999) 553, comments on the Christian presuppositions of Duhm's Servant Songs: "Much of the exegesis of these passages in the twentieth century has been, often unintentionally, the modern critical equivalent of early Christian interpretation", identifying the servant with Jesus. R. F. Melugin, "Reading the Book of Isaiah as Christian Scripture" and B. D. Sommer, "The Scroll of Isaiah as Jewish Scripture, or, Why Jews Don't Read Books" (SBLSP, 35; Atlanta: Scholars Press, 1996) 188–203; 225–242, describe particularities with their respective faith traditions that condition a modern critical reading of Isaiah.

[183] Landy, "The Construction of the Subject and the Symbolic Order", p. 62.

Certainly, no reading is an island. In Landy's case, this is related to his additional and deeper problem, that "[t]he text resists interpretation".[184] Landy's own reading is characterised by the splitting of subject and text, leading to indeterminacy and ambiguity.[185]

2.3.8.4. *Textualising*

One characteristic feature of recent literary theories is the turn from the text to the reader, which may be described as a shift from the reader's reproduction of meaning to her or his production of meaning. Texts are open to many different, even contradictory, readings. There can be no truly "literal" interpretation of any text, as all interpretations are performed by readers. Meaning is neither "in" the text, implanted there by an author, nor "behind" the text in an original socio-cultural setting. Meaning is not something added to the text (as an additional text), but rather the way in which texts are juxtaposed with one another by the reader. The reader "produces" the text as a meaningful sign. However, the readers cannot interpret the text just as they wish. Although there is no one true reading of any text, incorrect readings are possible.[186]

Traditional literary criticism pays close attention to language, justifying this attention by treating literature as a special use of language requiring readers to have what Culler has called "literary competence": "a set of conventions for reading texts [as literature]".[187] According to Culler, three basic conventions of analysis inform traditional literary competence: universal significance, metaphorical coherence and thematic unity.[188] Literary competence is a social and socialising practice, reproduced through various institutions. They are institutionalised as

---

[184] Landy, "The Construction of the Subject and the Symbolic Order", p. 62. Cf. an open-ended reading of Isa. 53 in Clines, *I, He, We, and They*.

[185] On psychoanalysis and reading, see 5.3.

[186] J. Barton, "Classifying Biblical Criticism", *JSOT* 29 (1984) 19–35.

[187] J. Culler, *Structuralist Poetics: Structuralism, Linguistics and the Study of Literature* (London: Routledge, 1975) 118. By "literary criticism", Culler is speaking here of the study of literature in general. In biblical criticism, literary criticism is used in a much narrower sense, as a method to sort out different sources behind a text. On the relation between "secular" and "biblical" literary criticism, see J. Barton, *Reading the Old Testament: Method in Biblical Study* (London: Darton, Longman and Todd, 1996) 20.

[188] Culler, *Structuralist Poetics*, p. 115. A biblical scholar who relies "heavily on Culler's ideas" of literary competence and the related emphasis on genre recognition is Barton, *Reading the Old Testament*, quoted from p. 11, n. 3. Cf. 5.4.

universal givens about essential qualities of literary works, codified, taught and so legitimised as indisputable rules. However, a reader's literary competence is subject to change. What and how people read differs from time to time and place to place.

While literary conventions are valuable tools of analysis, they are not neutral.[189] The expectations of a work's significance, coherence and unity define an agenda for reading which has political, social and theological implications in terms of what it excludes and includes.[190] The language of a text can largely cooperate with literary conventions. But language itself disrupts the coherence and unity which seemingly confirm the way in which texts have been traditionally read as "literature".[191] This might be exemplified by Steck's readings of Isa. 52:13–53:12, in which he attempts to stabilize conventions by identifying which of the three aspects of the heavenly court pattern is visible, and shows how the fourth *EJL* relates to the first three. Moreover, in his redaction-critical reading, he offers five different identities for the servant of the four *EJL* within a time span from 539 to 270 BCE.[192] Whereas Steck labels synchronic readings *dramatische Endtext-Lesung*, his own might be called *dramatische Ebene-Lesung*!

2.4. Visions of Isaiah

Traditional readings of Isa. 52:13–53:12 seem to have been preserved and legitimated more by biblical scholarship's own conventions than by any tenable methodological reflection on biblical exegesis. The Duhmian thesis about the "Servant Songs" is an illustrative example of the way in which a thesis which was created in very different times and from wholly different methodological presuppositions has survived for more than one hundred years and become an axiom for many Old Testament scholars. However, the legitimacy of the Duhmian readings

---

[189] For criticism of the idea of literary competence and its implications, see F. Lentricchia, *After the New Criticism* (Chicago: University of Chicago Press, 1980) 103–112, and T. Eagleton, *Literary Theory. An Introduction: A Study in Marxist Literary Theory* (Cambridge, MA: Basil Blackwell, 1996) 107–108.

[190] This might be related to Foucault's criticism of the reproduction of the social system through forms of selection, exclusion and domination. More on Foucault in 5.5.

[191] This will be treated in more detail in the theoretical introductions in Part II: 3. Text, 4. Narrative and 5. Intertextuality.

[192] Cf. 2.2.2., 2.2.3. and 2.2.5.

seems to lie more within the conventions of scholarly tradition than in any theoretical reflection on the production of text and reading. This has obviously created more problems than it has solved, and led to much scholarly confusion. Against this background, it is remarkable that so little attention has been paid to a discussion of the criteria for the traditional readings. The pursuit of the historical-critical identity of the servant has been driven far too far, and it is obvious that scholarship has reached a deadlock. However, instead of striving for agreement, it would be more constructive to regard any reading as situated. This might be related to the increased attention brought to the different forces at work in the text and reading, where a variety of possible focuses has come to the fore. As regards Isa. 53, many different strategies of reading can be shown, e.g. historical-critical, reception-historical,[193] theological,[194] linguistic,[195] literary,[196] rhetorical,[197] sociological,[198] popular cultural,[199] in Christian-Muslim dialogue[200] and read with Martin Buber.[201] I will briefly present a canonical, a feminist and a liberation-theological reading of the text.

---

[193] Cf. 1.1.

[194] Janowski, "Er trug unsere Sünden" and M. Rae, "Scripture and the Divine Economy", *Journal for Theological Interpretation* 1 (2007) 15–21. Rae explains a theological interpretation as a combination of a text's different contexts – historical, literary, Jewish, Christian and so on – and the place of the contexts "within the larger context of the divine economy to which Scripture itself bears witness" (p. 21).

[195] M. Rosenbaum, *Word-Order Variation in Isaiah 40–55: A Functional Perspective* (Studia Semitica Neerlandica; Assen: Van Gorcum, 1997).

[196] Clines, *I, He, We, and They.* As to the discussions of the identifications of the actors in Isa. 52:13–53:12, Clines comments:

> It is not my purpose here to attempt to decide this issue; it is rather to point to the ambiguity of the poem, and in so doing to suggest that it is of its essence that unequivocal identifications are not made and that the poem in this respect also is open-ended and allows for multiple interpretations (p. 33). See also E. W. Conrad, *Reading Isaiah* (Overtures to Biblical Theology, 27; Minneapolis: Fortress Press, 1991).

[197] R. L. Bergey, "The Rhetorical Role of Reiteration in the Suffering Servant Poem (Isa. 52:13–53:12)", *JETS* 40 (1997) 177–188.

[198] D. G. Likins-Fowler, "Sociological Functions of the Servant in Isaiah 52:13–53:12", *Proceedings-Eastern Great Lakes and Midwest Biblical Societies* 21 (2001) 47–59.

[199] L. Kreizer, "Suffering, Sacrifice and Redemption: Biblical Imagery in Star Trek" in J. E. Porter and D. L. McLaren (eds), *Star Trek and Sacred Ground: Explorations of Star Trek, Religion, and American Culture* (Albany: State University of New York, 1999) 139–163.

[200] B. J. Nicholls, "The Servant Songs of Isaiah in Dialogue with Muslims", *Evangelical Review of Theology* 20 (1996) 168–177.

[201] S. D. Breslauer, "Power, Compassion, and the Servant of the Lord in Second Isaiah", *Encounter* 48 (1987) 163–178.

In a canonical reading, Childs examines the relation of Isaiah 53 to the New Testament and also to the suffering servant in Christian theology. He claims that:

> [Isa. 53] cannot be interpreted either as simply a future prophecy or as a timeless metaphor of the suffering nation of Israel…[T]he servant of Isaiah is linked dogmatically to Jesus Christ primarily in terms of its ontology, that is, its substance, and is not simply a future promise of the Old Testament awaiting its New Testament fulfilment.[202]

Bond's feminist reading of Isa. 53 does not necessarily aim to undermine the text, but the sexist and individualistic interpretations of it that confirm gender stereotypes such as a triumphant king language, romantic, middle-class ideas about being kind and humble or a Christian servant rhetorics which suppresses women, children and other "small and weak". A feminist approach might emphasise how suffering is not a virtue to endure and abuse not something one should just forgive. Bond claims that the potential becomes very different if the servant ideology is moved from an individualistic "I" who is alone to the servant as a collective "we" standing together against oppression.[203]

In liberation theological readings, the servant of Isa. 53 is interpreted as the people suffering in imprisonment, and with a vision of the victory of the justice of God and the servant over the injustice of humans.[204] From a Nicaraguan perspective, Jorge Pixley reads in a social context of martyrdom:

---

[202] Childs, *Isaiah*, pp. 422–423. He refers to the distinction between the "economic" Trinity, i.e. "God's revelation in the continuum of Israel's history", and the "immanent" Trinity, "the ontological manifestation of the triune deity in its eternality" (p. 423). Childs questions the fundamental confusion of hermeneutical categories of both conservative and liberal scholars when discussing the historical Jesus' self-understanding as suffering servant, because the concept of an individual figure as suffering servant is a modern concept, first clearly formulated by Duhm. Some of the contributions in Bellinger Jr. and Farmer, *Jesus and the Suffering Servant*, and Janowski and Stuhlmacher, *Der leidende Gottesknecht*, are motivated by an interest in a supposed relation between the suffering servant and Jesus (cf. 1.1.)

[203] S. L. Bond, "What, Me Suffer? Women's Suspicions and the Servant Songs: Lectionary Readings for Epiphany, Year A.", *Quarterly Review* 18 (1998) 299–317. See also P. Trible, *Texts of Terror: Literary-Feminist Readings of Biblical Narratives* (London: SCM Press, 2002), who applies Isa. 53 as a co-text in her reading of texts of violence in the Hebrew Bible, see, for instance, pp. 24; 40.

[204] C. Mesters, *The Mission of the People Who Suffer: The Songs of the Servant of God* (Cape Town: Theology Exchange Programme, 1990), C. Mesters, "The Servant of Yahweh: The Patient Endurance of the Poor, Mirror of God's Justice" in T. Okure, J. Sobrino and F. Wilfred (eds), *Rethinking Martyrdom* (Concilium, 2003/1; London: SCM Press, 2003) 67–74, C. J. Dempsey, *The Prophets: A Liberation-Critical Reading*

In Nicaragua, this experience of national death and resurrection is a vivid reality related to the Sandinist revolution, which compasses past, present, and – hopefully – future.[205]

Different strategies of readings produce different pursuits and identities of the servant of Isa. 53. These examples illustrate how reading is contextual and situated. In this regard, the Duhmian reading is but one reading community.[206]

(A Liberation-Critical Reading of the Old Testament; Minneapolis: Fortress Press, 2000) 171–181.

[205] J. V. Pixley, "Isaiah 52:13–53:12: A Latin American Perspective" in P. P. Levinson and J. R. Levinson (eds), *Return to Babel: Global Perspectives on the Bible* (Louisville, KY: Westminster/John Knox Press, 1999) 95–100, quoted from p. 98. Cf. F. L. Kabasele and N. Grey, "Isaiah 52:13–53:12: An African Perspective" and C. H. S. Moon, "Isaiah 52:13–53:12: An Asian Perspective" in Levinson and Levinson, *Return to Babel*, pp. 101–106, 107–113.

[206] S. Fish, *Is There a Text in This Class? The Authority of Interpretive Communities* (Cambridge, MA: Harvard University Press, 1980).

PART TWO

ISA. 52:13–53:12: IDENTITIES IN TRANSITION

CHAPTER THREE

TEXT

3.1. LINGUISTICS

In traditional philology, language may be regarded as subservient to some idea, intention or referent which lies outside language, i.e. as existing independently of the medium in which language is formulated.[1] This approach is structured by conceptual oppositions, with primary terms such as the idea, content, intelligible, inside, essence ("the tenor") and so forth and secondary terms such as the medium, form, sensible, outside, accident ("the vehicle"). Meaning is regarded as belonging to these primary categories and language to the secondary ones. This view of language has been challenged by what has been labelled "the linguistic turn", which is associated with the Swiss linguist Ferdinand de Saussure (1857–1913). He regards language as primary and, in his view, meaning does not precede language but is an effect produced by it. Culler claims that the Saussurean legacy is revolutionary because it can be adopted only as an alternative to, not as a supplement to, traditional philology.[2]

Culler presents Saussure as contemporary with Sigmund Freud and Emile Durkheim within a new epistemological context, and describes this as a move from individual, autonomous objects to structure and system of relations. Regarding this, Culler quotes the French theoretician Michel Foucault (1926–1984):

---

[1] In a presentation of his predecessors, F. de Saussure, *Course in General Linguistics* (Glasgow: Fontana Press/Collins, 1974) 1–5 distinguishes between two stages of comparative linguistics: philosophical philology and historical philology. The philosophical philology of the eighteenth century is characterised by its etymological interest. The study of language is founded on a notion of representation: words are taken as signs which represent fundamental categories of experiences. The historical philology of the nineteenth century rejects this link between language and mind and the view of a word as a representation. It is concerned with the demonstration of the form's resemblance to and historical links with other forms. On philology, see de Man, *The Resistance to Theory*, pp. 21–26, and J. Ziolkowski (ed), *On Philology* (University Park, Pennsylvania: Pennsylvania State University Press, 1990).

[2] J. Culler, *Ferdinand de Saussure* (Ithaca, NY: Cornell University Press, 1986) 84ff.

[T]he researches of psychoanalysis, of linguistics, of anthropology have "decentered" the subject in relation to laws of its desire, the forms of its language, the rules of its actions or the play of its mythical and imaginative discourse.[3]

The subject is no longer master in its own house or language. Saussure's definition of the sign and his linguistic model have exercised an enormous influence, as may be seen, for example, in formalism, Bakhtinian dialogism, psychoanalysis, Marxism, hermeneutics, (post-) structuralism and deconstruction. At the same time, the linguistic model has undergone subsequent transformations. Whereas Saussure is primarily concerned with *la langue* at a phonological level, Barthes focuses on the reading of "text" and Derrida on *différance* as a chain of signification which can never be completely stated. In all cases, language is seen as constituting reality rather than imitating it, and in all instances the main question is how signs are interpreted or read.

3.2. SIGN

Saussure argues that language is a system of signs. The sign is a unit consisting of a form (sounds or letters), which he calls signifier (*signifiant*), and an idea, which he calls signified (*signifié*).[4] Moreover, the relation between the signifier and the signified is *arbitrary*, as there is no inevitable link between them: in English *s-e-r-v-a-n-t* (signifier) means "servant" (signified) not by natural resemblance or causal connection but by convention. *A-l-f* or *c-o-m-t* could serve equally well as signifiers if they were accepted by members of an English-speaking community. The signified "servant" has the signifier *K-n-e-c-h-t* in German, *t-j-e-n-e-r* in Norwegian and *e-b-e-d* in Hebrew.

In addition to the arbitrariness of the signifier and the arbitrary relation between the signifier and the signified, Culler emphasises how the signified is also arbitrary. Language is not a nomenclature which

---

[3] Culler, *Ferdinand de Saussure*, p. 93.

[4] Saussure, *Course in General Linguistics*, pp. 66–67. This study, first published in French as *Cours de linguistique générale* (1915), is based on students' notes of Saussure's lectures. The background of this book is treated in J. Culler's "Preface" in *Course in General Linguistics*, pp. xvi–xvii, and Culler, *Ferdinand de Saussure*, pp. 21–26.

names "existing categories"; each language articulates its own categories, and they change over time.[5]

Both the signifier and the signified belong to a system in which they become defined by their relations to the other members of that system. Since both the signifier and the signified are arbitrary, Saussure explains how a sign means by what it is *not*.[6] This might be exemplified by the sign עֶבֶד, which is a composite of the signifier *e-b-e-d* and the signified "servant" (or "slave", "Israel", "the prophet", "*Gottesknecht*", etc.). No sign is independently defined by some essential property, but is defined by its relation to other signs. Phonetically, the sign עֶבֶד differs from עֵבֶר (the name "Eber") and כָּבֵד ("heavy"). Semantically, it differs from עֶלֶם ("young man"), בֶּן־אָמָה ("son of serving-maid"), אָמָה ("maid", "serving-maid"), שִׁפְחָה ("maid", "maid-servant") and מַס (coll. "body of forced labourers"). It is the system of relations and distinctions which creates the sign and enables the articulation of meaning, not vice versa.[7]

3.3. *La langue* and *La parole*

According to Saussure, sign is the basic element of meaning, and structure of differentiation is the fundamental principle by which signs mean. He distinguishes between the system of *la langue* ("the language") and enunciations of it, *la parole* ("the speech").[8] In claiming that language works as a system of signs, he challenges the understanding of the relation between language and meaning. Language does not transcribe meaning, but constitutes reality. Since language is

---

[5] Culler, *Ferdinand de Saussure*, pp. 33–34. For a nuanced discussion of linguistic relativity, see J. J. Gumperz and S. C. Levinson, "Rethinking Linguistic Relativity", *Current Anthropology* 32 (1991) 613–623.

[6] Saussure, *Course in General Linguistics*, pp. 117; 120.

[7] Saussure, *Course in General Linguistics*, pp. 22–23, exemplifies using the game of chess that the identity of the signifier, for example, is purely relational and not necessarily material: substituting ivory for wooden chessmen would not affect the game, but a decrease or increase in the number of chessmen would transform the entire game as well as the value of each element in it. A consequence of Saussure's appreciation of the arbitrariness of and difference between the signifier and the signified is that the signified is not the same as the referent, the object of reality.

[8] When referring to the Saussurean concepts of *signifiant* and *signifié*, I use the standard English translations of signifier and signified. His concepts of *la langue* and *la parole* are less standardized in English. Accordingly, I apply the French words (their respective English translations are "the language" and "the speech").

a self-sufficient system, meaning is not determined by the subjective intentions of its speakers: it is not the speaker who gives meaning to her or his utterance, but the linguistic system as a whole which produces it. If the system "claims" that the signifier *s-e-r-v-a-n-t* means "servant", I cannot say *a-m-t* means "servant" and expect to be understood by an English-speaking community. It is due to the conventional nature of language that signs communicate ideas.

Saussure prioritises *la langue* over *la parole*. *La langue* is a socially and conventionally conditioned system which exists independently of a specific utterance.[9]

> In separating language [*la langue*] from speaking [*la parole*] we are at the same time separating: (1) what is social from what is individual; and (2) what is essential from what is accessory and more or less accidental.[10]

Saussure's prioritising of *la langue* over *la parole* prevents him from considering that, while signs are regulated by a system, they are produced in *la parole*. The relationship between *la langue* and *la parole* is not hierarchical: *la parole* is not simply the realisation of *la langue*, as *la parole* also continually revises *la langue* to allow for new conditions by which meaning is produced. After Saussure, theoreticians have highlighted more radical implications by focusing on how, in *la parole*, a sign is not always bound by a system since a signifier can transgress the system.[11]

The French linguist Émile Benveniste (1902–1976) described the pronouns "I" and "you" as signifiers without conventional signifieds.[12] Moreover, the signifier "I" always implies a speaker to whom it refers – a "you" – just as the signifier "you" always implies a listener to whom

---

[9] Saussure, *Course in General Linguistics*, pp. 9; 77.

[10] Saussure, *Course in General Linguistics*, p. 14. He also operates with a third distinction which he calls *langage* ("language in general"). *La parole* concerns the act of utterance, while *langage* concerns every conceivable *parole* which might be generated from the system of *la langue*. V. N. Volosinov (and M. M. Bakhtin), *Marxism and the Philosophy of Language* (Studies in Language, 1; New York: Seminar Press, 1973) 58ff criticise the Saussurean linguistics for what they designates as "abstract objectivism". Important for Bakhtin is what he labels "utterance", which comprises the human-centred and socially specific aspect of language which, according to him, is absent from Saussurean linguistics. On the relationship between the authorship of Bakhtin and Volosinov, see 5.2. n. 3. More on Bakhtin in 5.2.

[11] This will be further illuminated in 3.7.

[12] E. Benveniste, *Problems in General Linguistics* (Miami Linguistic Series, 8; Coral Gables: University of Miami Press, 1971) 226.

the speaker is talking. Further, "I" itself becomes a "you" when "you" addresses "me", "here" turns into "there", etc. These orientation features, called deictics, are dependent upon *la parole* and are characterised by subjectivity, and are thus unstable.

Benveniste distinguished between two sorts of subject which are involved in any discursive event: *the speaking subject* (or "referent", "narrator") and *the subject of speech* (or "referee", "actor").[13] Whereas *the speaking subject* is linked to the individual human originator, *the subject of speech* concerns the verbal entity itself. When I speak to someone, my words are linked to me as *the speaking subject*; when I write those words down and they are read by someone else, my position as a subject is no longer directly involved and "I" have become *the subject of speech*. The words (e.g. "I love you") are double-voiced (clichéd, already written and said again by the "I"), but so too is the subject position of the person speaking (e.g. the utterance "I am lying" has no stable signified). Therefore, in writing, we can only know the apersonal, constantly shifting, pronominal subjects.[14]

3.4. SYNCHRONIC AND DIACHRONIC

Saussure distinguished between a synchronic analysis of language at a static, given moment in time within the system, and a diachronic analysis concerned with changes to the system that occur over time. The synchronic level comes under *la langue* and so concerns the linguistic system as a whole, while the diachronic level belongs to *la parole* and concerns concrete utterances. Saussure claims that synchronic and diachronic "are not of equal importance... [T]he synchronic viewpoint predominates, for it is the true and only reality to the community of speakers".[15] This is due to his prioritisation of *la langue*, in which diachronic facts are irrelevant. This interest in *la langue* does not, however, imply a de-historisation, but contributes to the historising of the specific utterance by placing it into a system of historically conditioned rules, conventions and differences. It is equally a historical

---

[13] Benveniste, *Problems in General Linguistics*, p. 218.
[14] More on this in relation to subjectivity and ideology in 4.5. and in relation to intertextuality in 5.3.
[15] Saussure, *Course in General Linguistics*, p. 90.

task to describe synchronic states or systems of the past and to describe
diachronic changes.[16]

3.5. Syntagmatic and Paradigmatic

According to Saussure, the study of a language concerns relationships
of difference and arbitrariness. In a linguistic sequence, a sign's value
depends both on relations with the signs which precede and follow
it, and on the contrast between it and others which might have been
chosen instead. Saussure termed these relationships syntagmatic and
associative, later called paradigmatic.[17]

Syntagmatic relations concern the linear continuity between one sign
and others, as in a sentence, i.e. at *la parole* level. Syntactically, the sign
עֶבֶד can serve as the head of a noun phrase or as the subject or object of

---

[16] Saussure, *Course in General Linguistics*, p. 182. Culler, *Ferdinand de Saussure*, pp.
49–50, comments: "[A] diachronic statement related a single element from one state
of a linguistic system to an element from a later state of the system…[D]iachronic
identity depends on a series of synchronic identities." F. E. Deist, "On 'Synchronic'
and 'Diachronic': Wie es eigentlich gewesen", *JNSL* 21 (1995) 37–48, argues that
according to Saussure, a diachronic approach is a presupposition for a synchronic
approach. Deist claims that it is impossible to carry out a synchronic reading of the
biblical texts in a Saussurean way, because these texts are instances of *la parole*, and
because "the composite nature of ancient Near Eastern texts makes them unlikely
candidates for the successful application of a synchronic approach" (p. 46). Whenever
possible, a synchronic approach must be based on *Literarkritik* (p. 43). Deist points
out how conservative exegetes, for example, choose what they label a "synchronic
approach" as an "excuse to ignore historical questions in dealing with biblical literature and to focus on the biblical text 'as it presents itself in its present form'" (p. 37).
I would add that what they in fact practise is a holistic or canonical reading based on
their own theological preconceptions. A similar evaluation of a synchronic approach
related to the biblical texts is found in J. Barr, "The Synchronic, the Diachronic and
the Historical: A Triangular Relationship?" in J. de Moor (ed), *Synchronic or Diachronic? A Debate on Method in Old Testament Exegesis* (OTS, 34; Leiden: E. J. Brill,
1995) 4–5. Like Deist, Barr emphasises how both the synchronic and the diachronic
aspects of language belong within a historical method "and are not in opposition
to it" (p. 8). Volosinov (and Bakhtin), *Marxism and the Philosophy of Language*,
p. 60, argue against Saussure that "there is no real moment in time when a synchronic
system of language could be constructed" because language is always in a "ceaseless
flow of becoming". This is related to what they claim about "the utterance", which is
commented on in 3.3. n. 10 and 5.2. For a nuanced depiction of the role of history in
the relation between diachronic and synchronic by Saussure, see D. Attridge, "Language as History/History as Language: Saussure and the Romance of Etymology" in
D. Attridge, G. Bennington and R. Young (eds), *Post-Structuralism and the Question
of History* (Cambridge: Cambridge University Press, 1987) 183–211.

[17] Saussure, *Course in General Linguistics*, pp. 122–127.

a sentence, and it can be modified by other signs surrounding it, e.g. by an interjection and predicate, as in הִנֵּה יַשְׂכִּיל עַבְדִּי יָרוּם וְנִשָּׂא וְגָבַהּ מְאֹד "See, my servant shall prosper and be exalted, he shall be lifted and be very high!" (Isa. 52:13–53:12)

Paradigmatic relations concern oppositions between components which can replace one another, i.e. organising relations of similarity between one sign and others on the level of *la langue*. Paradigmatic relationships can be based on a similarity between two signs on the level of the signifier, the signified or both, and can be shown at phonetic, syntactic and semantic levels: the signifier עֶבֶד differs phonetically from e.g. כָּבֵד ("heavy"). Syntactically it is a noun, as opposed to a verb or a preposition. Semantically, the signifier עֶבֶד "servant" differs from אָמָה ("maid", "serving-maid") and מַס ("body of forced labourers"). Moreover, the signified of one sign can become the signifier of another signified, i.e. the signified "servant" can for example signify "humility" or "awe".

Whereas Saussure was mainly concerned with the level of phonology, the Russian formalist Roman Jakobson (1896–1982) focused on syntagmatic and paradigmatic relationships in texts. This is related to his more comprehensive depiction of language in general. According to Jakobson, all instances of language fulfil at least six functions.[18] One of these, the poetic, he describes as follows: "The poetic function projects the principle of equivalence from the axis of selection into the axis of combination."[19] This distinction between the axis of selection and the axis of combination corresponds to Saussure's distinction between associative (paradigmatic) and syntagmatic relationships. According to Jakobson, every linguistic message is the product of the act of

---

[18] The six functions he describes are: the *referential* function, which directs the message towards the referent or context (to extra-textual reality); the *emotive* function, which focuses on the addresser, expressing her or his attitude about the message; the *conative* function, which orients the message towards the addressee (e.g. by vocatives or imperatives) and conveys no information, but rather seeks to produce a response in the message's recipient; the *phatic* function, which establishes a contact between the addresser and addressee (e.g. by stereotypes); the *metalingual* function, in which language is used to explain itself; and the *poetic* function, which "focus[es] on the message for its own sake", in R. Jakobson, *Selected Writings III: Poetry of Grammar and Grammar of Poetry* (The Hague: Mouton, 1981) 25. The first three are functions of the signifieds, the last three of the signifier (pp. 21–26). All six functions may appear in the same text, but a text may be dominated of one or some of these functions, see R. Jakobson, *Language in Literature* (Cambridge, MA: Belknap Press, 1987) 66.

[19] Jakobson, *Selected Writings III*, p. 27.

selecting elements not present in the message but associated with it in the code (i.e. in *la langue*) and the combination of the elements selected into a sequence (i.e. in *la parole*).[20] A paradigmatic relationship with an element not present in the sequence is one of *similarity* or *equivalence* (the elements perform an equivalent function and can therefore replace one another). A syntagmatic relationship between elements present in the sequence is one of *contiguity*. Jakobson claims that the paradigmatic aspects dominate in poetry and the syntagmatic in narrative. Temporal continuity and causality are not required in poetry, while a narrative is characterised by the continuity of signs in a linear structure.[21]

3.6. PARALLELISM

For Jakobson, parallelism is the core of poetic language through its selection and combination of linguistic elements.[22] In accordance with Jakobson, the biblical scholar Adele Berlin claims that parallelism activates all levels of language and can be read in terms of different aspects, e.g. semantic, grammatical (morphological and syntactical) and lexical, and at different levels, e.g. word, sentence and text.[23] She describes biblical parallelism as follows:

> [T]he tension between the paradigmatic and the syntagmatic...is at the heart of parallelism, which after all, imposes similarity upon contiguity...[P]arallel lines are doubly connected; once by virtue of their role in a coherent text (with or without connective particles), and again by the linguistic equivalences which constitute parallelism.[24]

---

[20] Jakobson, *Selected Writings III*, p. 27.

[21] R. Jakobson, "Two Aspects of Language and Two Types of Aphasic Disturbances" in R. Jakobson and M. Halle, *Fundamentals of Language* (Janua Linguarum. Series Minor, 1; The Hague: Mouton, 1971) 95–96. Both syntagmatic and paradigmatic aspects are found in both poetry and prose, but the paradigmatic aspects dominate in poetry and the syntagmatic in narrative. A less nuanced contribution to a poetry-prose distinction within Biblical Hebrew literature is found in Niccacci, *The Syntax of the Verb in Classical Hebrew Prose* (JSOTSup, 86; Sheffield: JSOT Press, 1990) 193–197, and A. Niccacci, "Analysing Biblical Hebrew Poetry", *JSOT* 74 (1997) 77–93. Niccacci claims that there are completely different verbal systems for poetry and prose: the first is characterised by a non-detectable and the second by a detectable verbal system.

[22] Jakobson, *Selected Writings III*, p. 98, with reference also to G. M. Hopkins.

[23] A. Berlin, *The Dynamics of Biblical Parallelism* (Bloomington: Indiana University Press, 1985).

[24] Berlin, *The Dynamics of Biblical Parallelism*, pp. 91; 93.

This might be exemplified by Isa. 53:4a:

אָכֵן חֳלָיֵנוּ הוּא נָשָׂא וּמַכְאֹבֵינוּ סְבָלָם

Yet surely he bore our illnesses and carried our sicknesses

Isa. 53:4a is composed of two verbal clauses in which the surface structure is similar in syntax, but not in morphology. Apart from the introductory אָכֵן "yet surely", which might serve for both clauses, the syntactical components in the first clause appear in variations in the second: the first clause is followed by object (חֳלָיֵנוּ "our illnesses"), subject (הוּא "he") and predicate (נָשָׂא "he bore"); the second clause by copulative *waw*, object (וּמַכְאֹבֵינוּ "and our sicknesses") and predicate (with subject and object; סְבָלָם "he carried them"). Morphologically, variations appear: while the first clause expresses the subject doubly (in the independent personal pronoun and the predicate), the second clause expresses the object twice (in the independent object and the suff. of the predicate). Semantically, "our" illnesses are doubly expressed in variations: חֳלָיֵנוּ הוּא נָשָׂא "he bore our illnesses" וּמַכְאֹבֵינוּ סְבָלָם "and he carried our sicknesses". The copulative *waw* indicates two coordinate situations, but the second clause provides more clues. It ensures the delivery of the information given in the first clause, and simultaneously it offers an alternative interpretation. In Isa. 53:4a, two clauses correspond as regards both grammar (i.e. syntactical similarities and morphological variations) and semantics. Paradigmatically, a grammatical equivalence appears through morphologic and syntactic "substitution". Although the two grammatical structures differ, they are equivalent to one another.[25] The parallelism demonstrates both

---

[25] R. Lowth, *Lectures on the Sacred Poetry of the Hebrews. Vol. I* (The Major Works/ Robert Lowth; London: Routledge/Thoemmes Press, 1995) viii, presents a semantic definition of parallelism categorised as synonymous, antithetic and synthetic. The examples he offers are multifaceted:

> The correspondence of One Verse, or Line, with another I call Parallelism. When a proposition is delivered, and a second is subjoined to it, or drawn under it, equivalent, or contrasted with it, in Sense, or similar to it in the form of Grammatical Construction, these I call Parallel Lines; and the words or phrases answering one to another in the corresponding Lines Parallel Terms.

In the decades since Lowth, scholars have been dissatisfied with his definition because it reduces the trope of parallelism to semantic similarity only. Although some have adjusted or expanded this, only recently has scholarship broken with his categories, using different theoretical and heuristic tools, primarily based on literary, comparative and linguistic methods. J. L. Kugel, *The Idea of Biblical Poetry: Parallelism and Its History* (New Haven: Yale University Press, 1981) claims that there is no principal difference of parallelisms, only degrees of low or elevated style. Also R. Alter, *The Art of*

prosaic linearity and poetic equivalence because of its paradigmatic location in *la langue* and its syntagmatic location in *la parole*.

3.7. Structure and *Différance*

As seen in 3.3., Saussure regarded sign as the most basic element of meaning within a system of language. He further claimed that these semiological (called by later scholars semiotic) principles are valid for all aspects of culture:

> Language is a system of signs that expresses ideas, and is therefore comparable to a system of writing, the alphabet of deaf-mutes, symbolic rites, polite formulas, military signals etc. But it is the most important of all these systems. A science that studies the life of signs within society is conceivable; it would be part of social psychology and consequently of general psychology; I shall call it semiology...Linguistics is only a part of the general science of semiology, the laws discovered by semiology will be applicable to linguistics, and the later will circumscribe a well-defined area within the mass of anthropological fact.[26]

All words are signs, but not all signs are words. The arbitrary and conventional sign is especially clear in language, but wherever there is sign, there is system. Structuralism is a systematic extension of the Saussurean "phonetic revolution". By using linguistic concepts of sign and system, literary critics, psychoanalysts, sociologists, social anthropologists and so forth analyse structures at various levels of "text", comprising the arbitrary and conventional signs within systems of literature, advertising, psychoanalysis, ritual, politeness, fashion, play, cooking, botany, medicine and so on. Just as it is possible to utter a grammatical or ungrammatical sentence, so "various social rules make it possible to marry, to score a goal, to write a poem, to be impolite".[27]

Biblical Poetry (New York: Basic Books, 1985), seems to describe parallelism in much the same way as Kugel, but they disagree on its role in the description of poetry and prose: while Alter claims that parallelism is key to the recognition and interpretation of Biblical Hebrew poetry, Kugel does not regard it as peculiar to poetry at all. Based on linguistic arguments, Berlin, *The Dynamics of Biblical Parallelism*, argues for the manifold nature of the parallelism and its appearance in both prose and poetry. For an overview of recent studies on Hebrew poetry in general and parallelism in particular, see J. K. Kuntz, "Biblical Hebrew Poetry in Recent Research. Part I", *CRBS* 6 (1998) 31–64, and J. K. Kuntz, "Biblical Hebrew Poetry in Recent Research. Part 2", *CRBS* 7 (1999) 35–79.

[26] Saussure, *Course in General Linguistics*, p. 16. Cf. 5.1.
[27] Culler, *Structural Poetics*, p. 5.

In structuralistic applications of a linguistic model, *la langue* is prioritised over *la parole*, and the synchronic over the diachronic. Also, binary opposition is seen as a meaning-producing unit. Structuralism is interested not first and foremost in analyses of particular cases, nor indeed in meaning itself, but rather in how meaning is produced. Also, the sign is regarded as stable and the structure as closed and self-contained.[28]

The French philosopher Jacques Derrida (1930–2004) agrees with Saussure that "in language there are only differences",[29] but questions the concepts of sign and structure. Whereas Saussure claims that it is the difference between signs that enables them to signify, ultimately he totalises the sign. Saussure describes the signifier and the signified as inseparable as the two sides of a single sheet of paper, but presupposes the possibility of an independent signified existing prior to its signifier, explaining language as "a system of signs that expresses ideas".[30] Derrida criticises the concept of a signifier as a substitute for a signified which is transcendental and logocentric, i.e. of sounds (or writing) as a representation of meanings which are present in the unconsciousness of the speaker (or writer).[31] Derrida claims that the sign is a structure of exclusion: it is internally divided and different from itself. He makes up the word *différance* from the French *différer* which means "to defer", "postpone", "delay" and "to differ", "be different from". The two senses of *différance* explain both that any element of language relates to other elements in a text (i.e. that which precedes and follows it) and also that it is different from them.[32] *Différance* conveys paradigmatic/syntagmatic and diachronic/synchronic elements, but according to Derrida they cannot be distinguished: these elements are seen as part of a chain of relationships which cannot be reduced to an object within a structure.[33] *Différance* replaces the concept of structure,

---

[28] See, for instance, R. Barthes, "The Struggle with the Angel: Textual Analysis of Genesis 32:22–32" in R. Barthes, *Image-Music-Text* (London: Fontana Press, 1977) 125–141.

[29] Saussure, *Course in General Linguistics*, p. 117.

[30] Saussure, *Course in General Linguistics*, p. 16.

[31] J. Derrida, *Of Grammatology* (Baltimore: Johns Hopkins University Press, 1976) 79; 99, uses the term "logocentrism" to describe thoughts which are based on some external point of reference, e.g. truth.

[32] J. Derrida, *Speech and Phenomena and Other Essays on Husserl's Theory of Sign* (Evanston: Northwestern University Press, 1973) 141.

[33] A. Jefferson, "Structuralism and Post-Structuralism" in A. Jefferson and D. Robey (eds), *Modern Literary Theory: A Comparative Introduction* (London: BT Batsford, 1996) 114.

which, even though it appears to be based on relationality, seems ultimately to carry an inherent origin and stability.[34]

Différance cannot exist without logocentrism. While not accepting that language is a system of signs that expresses underlying ideas, the existence of a system of signs is still presupposed. Culler comments that "escape from logocentrism is impossible because the language we use to criticise or to formulate alternatives works according to the principles being contested",[35] i.e. the meaning of *différance*! Jefferson claims that we can never get outside logocentrism, but we can work against it from within. Logocentric oppositions at work in a text might be reversed and questioned in such a way as to "neutralise" them.[36] She comments on how the ironic presence of logocentrism is clearly visible in all secondary literature on Derrida, where "Derrida" refers to an actual person, who has certain ideas, which he expresses in particular texts which are treated as signifieds.[37]

3.8. READING AND WRITING

The exegetical craft is concerned with reading, cf. the Greek verb *exægeomai*, "to lead out of", "to draw out", "to read out of". This has been contrasted with *eisægeomai* "to add", "to read into". It has been said that exegesis and eisegesis must not be confused.[38] However, when greater attention is paid to the reader's contribution in the reading of a text, it may be seen that every exegesis also reveals eisegesis, as the reader in some way or other brings herself or himself into the text as, for example, a woman or man, a homosexual or heterosexual, black or white, Norwegian or Asian, atheist, Jew or Muslim.[39]

The French literary critic Roland Barthes (1915–1980) defines text in opposition to work. When traditionally used, the term "work" des-

---

[34] For a criticism of structuralism, see J. Derrida, "Structure, Sign and Play in the Discourse of the Human Science" in J. Derrida, *Writing and Difference* (London: Routledge, 1995) 278–293.

[35] C. Culler, *The Pursuit of Signs: Semiotics, Literature, Deconstruction* (London: Routledge, 1992) 41.

[36] Jefferson, "Structuralism and Post-Structuralism", p. 119.

[37] Jefferson, "Structuralism and Post-Structuralism", p. 119.

[38] C. R. Holladay and J. H. Hayes, *Biblical Exegesis: A Beginner's Handbook* (London: SCM Press, 1988) 17.

[39] This might also be treated in relation to Stanley Fish and reading communities, see 2.4. n. 206.

ignates writing read as a finished product that conveys an intended meaning which it is the critic's taks to find and explicate.[40] By "repeating" the intention of the author, a work places its meaning outside of the play of signifiers that is language.[41] The concept of work involves meaning, unity and the authority of a transcendent source. A work is complete, exists in space and its meaning is stable across time and culture.[42]

In contrast to the work, Barthes depicts text as "a methodological field...the work can be held in the hand, the text is held in language; it only exists in the movement of a discourse".[43] A text is an ongoing "production" rather than a finished product because "its field is that of the signifier", which offers the reader "a serial movement of disconnections, overlappings, variations".[44] Since it continually defers a final signified, the text is "restored to language; like language, it is structured but off-centred, without closure".[45] The signified is infinite, and so the text too becomes "plural" and cannot be reduced to a single, final meaning.[46] The text is a "texture, a weave of signifiers" where the signifiers go beyond a final signified.[47] A text inhabits and is inhabited by language, without any external authority (an origin or source) to authorise its meaning. The source of each text is always another text, but there is always another text before that. No text lies outside the endless play of language, and no text is complete: each shows endlessly traces of other texts without any final origin.[48] Also, "text" itself is a signifier caught up in the play of language, as Robert Young reminds us.[49]

---

[40] R. Barthes, "Theory of the Text" in R. Young (ed), *Untying the Text: A Post-Structuralist Reader* (Boston: Routledge & Kegan Paul, 1981) 43.

[41] R. Barthes, "The Death of the Author" in Barthes, *Image-Music-Text*, p. 143.

[42] Cf. Culler's literary competence in 2.3.8.4.

[43] R. Barthes, "From Work to Text" in Barthes, *Image-Music-Text*, pp. 157–159.

[44] Barthes, "From Work to Text", p. 158.

[45] Barthes, "From Work to Text", p. 159.

[46] Barthes, "Theory of the Text", p. 43.

[47] Barthes, "From Work to Text", pp. 157–159.

[48] Also Derrida criticises the limitations of traditional concepts of text. His well-known sentence *Il n'y a pas de-hors texte* (J. Derrida, *De la grammatologie* [Paris: Les Editions de minuit, 1967] 227) expresses how the text has no out-side, i.e. it is impossible to distinguish between the inside and outside of a text. More on this related to Kristeva in 5.3.

[49] R. Young's introductory comments to Barthes, "Theory of the Text", pp. 31–32.

Whereas traditional criticism is consuming and stabilising, textual analysis is producing.[50] A variation on Barthes' distinction between work and text is one between what he labels readerly and writerly texts. In the readerly text, the reader is a consumer searching for structure and stable meaning; in the writerly, she or he is a producer. The writerly text is plural, and not a product, but a production and structuration.[51] Every text is both readerly and writerly, but some texts are more readerly than others.[52]

3.9. Reading Isa. 52:13–53:12

My reading of Isa. 52:13–53:12 is based on Biblia Hebraica Stuttgartensia (BHS), which reproduces the mediaeval Leningrad Codex (L) of the Hebrew Bible (ca. 1009). The proto-masoretic Isaiah scroll from Cave 1 of Qumran 1QIsa^a "The Great Isaiah Scroll" is our most ancient witness and almost identical to the mediaeval MT, although written with a somewhat different orthography.[53] It is more or less completely preserved. Another manuscript from the same cave is 1QIsa^b "The Small Isaiah Scroll", which is dated to the Herodian period and which is even closer to MT than 1QIsa^a is.[54] Both these, and the Greek trans-

---

[50] R. Barthes, *S/Z* (Oxford: Blackwell, 1998) 4–6, and Barthes, "Theory of the Text", p. 44.

[51] Barthes, *S/Z*, pp. 3–4.

[52] Jefferson, "Structuralism and Post-Structuralism", p. 108.

[53] P. W. Flint, "The Isaiah Scrolls from the Judean Desert" in Broyles and Evans, *Writing and Reading the Scroll of Isaiah. Vol. 2*, p. 483, dates this to ca. 100 BCE while E. Tov, "The Text of Isaiah at Qumran" in Broyles and Evans, *Writing and Reading the Scroll of Isaiah. Vol. 2*, p. 494, claims 150–125 BCE.

[54] Also, Isa. 52:13–53:12 is attested in the fragmentary 4QIsa^b, 4QIsa^c, and 4QIsa^d in Cave 4, where both 4QIsa^b and 4QIsa^d are close to L, while 4QIsa^c has a somewhat different orthography. Flint, "The Isaiah Scrolls from the Judean Desert", pp. 484–485, dates 4QIsa^b to approximately the third quarter of the first century BCE, 4QIsa^c to about the middle third of the first century CE, and 4QIsa^d to the middle of the first century BCE. He describes the orthography of 4QIsa^b as "mixed", and that of 4QIsa^c, which in addition uses the Paleo-Hebrew letters for the divine name יהוה, as "quite full". The orthography of 4QIsa^d he describes as "sparing". While Tov, "The Text of Isaiah at Qumran", pp. 508; 511, claims that there existed a certain Qumran scribal practice underlying, among other texts, 1QIsa^a and 4QIsa^c, which he calls a "Qumran orthography", E. Ulrich, "Pluriformity in the Biblical Text, Text Groups, and Questions of Canon" in J. T. Barrera and L. V. Montaner, *The Madrid Qumran Congress: Proceedings on the International Congress on the Dead Sea Scrolls Madrid 18–21 March 1991* (STDJ, 11, 1; Leiden: E. J. Brill, 1992) 29–31, doubts on a general level that something like a "Qumran orthography" existed. On the Book of Isaiah in relation to Qumran and MT, see Flint and Tov, as well as E. Ulrich, "An Index

lation LXX, which is dated to approximately the middle of the second century BCE,[55] will be referred to where necessary during the following reading of Isa. 52:13–53:12. Isa. 53:11 is an example where MT has a minor reading, that is, where a significantly longer variant appears in 1QIsaᵃ, 1QIsaᵇ and 4QIsaᵈ, as well as LXX; the Qumran readings having אור and LXX has δεῖξαι αὐτῷ φῶς.[56]

After having mapped out a theoretical landscape, I will present a reading of Isa. 52:13–53:12 inspired by a linguistic model from a Saussurean legacy. In this reading, I wish to attend to the many tensions, heterogeneities and levels in the text, which does not have a comfortable sense of unity. Rather than suppressing textual details that contradict a grammar, I seek to preserve the complexity of Isa. 52:13–53:12 and not reduce it to a stable meaning. I have tried to keep a rein on the terminologisation and to encourage a dynamic relation between the text and analytical language. Although the reading has some theoretical basis, it emerges from the specific complexities of the text.[57]

My own delimitation is rather pragmatically defined. As will be clear from the summing up of the following reading of Isa. 52:13–53:12 (3.10.16.), the verses of this text run into each other. In such a pragmatic delimitation, the previous chapter 52 and the adjacent chapter 54 could also have been included, and would merely have given a

---

to the Contents of the Isaiah Manuscripts from the Judean Desert" in Broyles and Evans, *Writing and Reading the Scroll of Isaiah. Vol. 2*, pp. 477–480, D. W. Parry and E. Qimron, *The Great Isaiah Scroll (1QIsa): A New Edition* (STDJ, 32; Leiden: E. J. Brill, 1999) and P. Pulikottil, *Transmission of Biblical Texts in Qumran: The Case of the Large Isaiah Scroll (1QISa)*, (JSPSup, 34; Sheffield: Sheffield Academic Press, 2001).

[55] A. van der Kooij, "Isaiah in the Septuagint" and S. E. Porter and B. W. R. Pearson, "Isaiah through Greek Eyes: The Septuagint of Isaiah" in Broyles and Evans, *Writing and Reading the Scroll of Isaiah. Vol. 2*, pp. 513–529; 531–546. For most scholars, LXX Isaiah remains valuable primarily as a witness to its *Vorlage*, where a reading of the document in itself might be lacking. LXX Isaiah is a Hellenistic document and a free translation, with various levels of interpretation, including its context within the book as a whole, and historical, cultural and theological actualizations.

[56] D. A. Sapp, "The LXX, 1QIsa, and MT Versions of Isaiah 53 and the Christian Doctrine of Atonement" in Bellinger and Farmer, *Jesus and the Suffering Servant*, pp. 170–192.

[57] The terminology of the Biblical Hebrew grammar is not standardised. For pragmatical reasons, I use the definitions in B. K. Waltke and M. O'Connor, *An Introduction to Biblical Hebrew Syntax* (Winona Lake, IN: Eisenbrauns, 1990) of linguistic terms such as phrase, clause, sentence, as well as the classifications of nouns and verbs (fientive/stative, transitive/intransitive, verbal stems and conjugations), subject/object and agens/patient. These definitions will be referred to during the reading. One exception to Waltke and O'Connor's terminology is that I designate the verbal forms perfect and imperfect, and not suffix and prefix conjugations.

different structure of the presentation of my reading. As will become clear later in this study, with its focus on personification (chapter 4) and intertextuality (chapter 5), Isa. 53 will be brought into communication with many other texts, which will extend the text even further. In 5.15.5., for instance, Isa. 54:1–3 is read with Isa. 53, and in 6.1., it is commented how Isa. 52:13–53:12 are encircled by proclamations and exhortations to Zion/Jerusalem to prepare for a victorious return and the restoration of people and land (51:17–52:12 and 54).

3.10. Text

3.10.1. *Isa. 52:13*

הִנֵּה יַשְׂכִּיל עַבְדִּי יָרוּם וְנִשָּׂא וְגָבַהּ מְאֹד:

> See, my servant shall prosper and be exalted, he shall be lifted and be very high!

An interjection הִנֵּה "see" precedes two couplets of verbal clauses in succession. In the first couplet, there is a break between the two predicates, where the subject "he" of the compound sentence is introduced by עַבְדִּי "my servant" (noun, 1cs poss. suff.). In the suffix, a speaking "I" appears. The interjection הִנֵּה, which is rendered as a visual predicate ("see", "look", "behold") acts as a sign in an address to an implied "you". By the deictic and volitional force of הִנֵּה "see", "your" attention is drawn to the adjacent utterance.

In the string of four predicates, the first is יַשְׂכִּיל (imperf. internal hi. 3ms of שׂכל "prosper", "succeed") "he shall prosper". In this one-place hiphil, the subject and object are the same, expressing how the double-status subject causes "himself" to prosper. The verb is also fientive, describing an action, and since the object is elided it is formally intransitive as well.[58] The next predicate, יָרוּם (imperf. qal 3ms of רום "be exalted", "high"), is also fientive and intransitive: "he shall

---

[58] Waltke and O'Connor, *An Introduction to Biblical Hebrew Syntax*, § 20.2k; l, define "group aspect (*Aktionsart*) phenomena [which] involve *fientivity* and *transitivity*. [*Fientivity*] refers to the type of movement or activity inherent in the verb. A verb may be stative (describe a state) or fientive (describe an activity)... *Transitivity* refers to the contour of movement or activity inherent in the verb. An intransitive verb is one which customarily takes no object... A transitive verb is one which takes object(s)" (their italics). On scholarly discussions of יַשְׂכִּיל in Isa. 52:13, see Appendix 1.

be exalted".[59] The third predicate, נִשָּׂא (perf. ni. 3ms of נשׂא "be lifted", "exalted"), which is prefixed by a *waw*, is pass. and fientive, i.e. "he" is the patient, receiving of an action: "he shall be lifted".[60] No agent is mentioned. The fourth and last predicate, גָּבַהּ (perf. qal 3ms of גבה "be high", "exalted"), is stative, prefixed by a *waw* and modified by the adverb מְאֹד "very", which signifies degree: "he shall be very high".

In both the last two predicates, the subject עַבְדִּי "my servant" appears as patient, the one who undergoes the verbal action of being exalted, and no agent is mentioned. All the four verbs are intransitive: no action passes over from agent to goal. Both predicates in the second couplet, נִשָּׂא "he shall be lifted" and גָּבַהּ "he shall be high", are prefixed by a copulative *waw*, expressing situations coordinate with one another.[61] The first three predicates are fientive and the last is static. Whereas the predicates in the first couplet are imperfect, in the second they are perfect. This morphological contrast of perfect/imperfect appears between equivalent situations, where all four predicates signify an action or state in a time that is future to the speaker: יַשְׂכִּיל יָרוּם "he shall prosper and be exalted"; וְנִשָּׂא וְגָבַהּ מְאֹד "he shall be lifted and be very high".[62]

---

[59] Waltke and O'Connor, *An Introduction to Biblical Hebrew Syntax*, § 20.2j, connect the agent/patient relation to *Aktionsart*, which "refers to the category of morphological phenomena that describe the kind of situation a verb refers to... With an active verb the subject is an agent and actor, while with a passive verb the subject is a patient (one who undergoes or suffers the action)". In LXX יָרוּם is not rendered, supported by Fohrer, *Das Buch Jesaja: Kap. 40–66*, pp. 158; 161.

[60] Waltke and O'Connor, *An Introduction to Biblical Hebrew Syntax*, § 23.2.2a; e:
By "passive" we mean that the subject is in the *state* of being acted upon or of suffering the effects of an action by an implicit or explicit agent... Passive constructions in Hebrew may be incomplete or complete. In the *incomplete passive* the agent is not indicated (their italics).

[61] A *waw* can have many functions in a sentence, related to both syntagmatic and paradigmatic aspects. A syntagmatic *waw* organises relations of continuity between one sign and others in the sentence or text, rendered "but", "while", "whereas" etc. A paradigmatic *waw* organises relations of similarity or contrast, i.e. "and", "or". Waltke and O'Connor, *An Introduction to Biblical Hebrew Syntax*, § 32.1.1:
The suffix conjugation [*qtl*] preceded by *waw* is associated with two semantically distinct constructions, one with relative force and the other with coordinate force... We call the first construction *waw-relative* and the second *waw-copulative*. (Traditionally the former has been called either *waw-conversive* or *waw-consecutive*), (their italics).

[62] Berlin, *The Dynamics of Biblical Parallelism*, pp. 35–36; 136–137. "[T]he *qtl-yqtl* shift... occurs not for semantic reasons (it does not indicate a real temporal sequence) but for what have been considered stylistic reasons. But it is not just vaguely 'stylistic'; ...it is...a kind of parallelism" (p. 36).

The four predicates in the string are joined together with the subject עַבְדִּי (noun ms cstr. of עֶבֶד "servant", "slave", "subject", "worshipper", 1cs poss. suff.) "my servant". The predicates give the subject attributions which emphasise the coming state or situation of עַבְדִּי "my servant". עַבְדִּי "my servant" is modified by features realised by the predicates, with an accumulation of verbs of exaltation calling attention to the way in which servanthood implies a promising future. In the predicates, the implied subject עַבְדִּי "my servant" is mentioned, and not addressed. In עַבְדִּי "my servant" a close relationship between the subject "he" (3ms) and a speaking "I" (1cs) is implied. עַבְדִּי "my servant", "slave", "subject", "worshipper" is modified in the poss. suff. by the contrasting "your lord", "master", "head", "superior", "god", a hierarchical relationship appearing between an inferior, dependent, subordinate position and the superior, speaking partner by whose will and action the inferior is terminated.

Related to the rest of the sentence, the deictic הִנֵּה "see" introduces an exclamation of perception and calls attention to situations and actions both near and far. The "seeing" involves a more active capacity than that of a mere immediate "listening", as it also includes a prospective future to be perceived: הִנֵּה "see", עַבְדִּי "my servant" shall be exalted! "I", "you" and "he" are all signifiers of identity, realised by the relations in which they stand. In עַבְדִּי "my servant", "I" and "he" are related. While עַבְדִּי "my servant" is depicted at a distance in a 3ms description, "you" (2ms) is implied by the speaking "I"'s (1cs) direct address in the interjection הִנֵּה "see".

3.10.2. *Isa. 52:14*

כַּאֲשֶׁר שָׁמְמוּ עָלֶיךָ רַבִּים
כֵּן־מִשְׁחַת מֵאִישׁ מַרְאֵהוּ וְתֹאֲרוֹ מִבְּנֵי אָדָם׃

As many were appalled at you
– such a disfigurement from that of man was his appearance and his form from that of humanity

A subordinating conjunction כַּאֲשֶׁר "as" introduces both a situation and an argument which are commented upon by an adjacent subordinate conjunction, כֵּן "such". In this subordinating verbal clause, the reactions of רַבִּים "many" to a "you" are described. This is followed by two subordinate nominal clauses introduced by the conjunction כֵּן "so", where the appearance of a "he" is further depicted. A speaking "I" is indicated by the address to a "you" (2ms).

The conjunction כַּאֲשֶׁר "as" precedes the subject רַבִּים "many". The subject is connected to the predicate שָׁמְמוּ (perf. qal 3mpl of שׁמם "appalled", "astonished", "dismayed", "scorn") "appalled", which is stative, intransitive, and signifies a state in time that is past to the speaker. Then follows the prep. phrase עָלֶיךָ (prep. עַל "at", 2ms suff.) "at you", acting as an indirect object.[63] In a numerical inequality, reactions of רַבִּים "many" (mpl of רַב "much", "many") witnessing "you" (sg) are depicted. By the address to "you", a first-person "I" speech is indicated.

The subordinating כַּאֲשֶׁר "as" clause is followed by the subordinate conjunction כֵּן "such" and the predicate מִשְׁחַת "disfigurement", which both work elliptically for two adjacent nominal clauses.[64] In the nominal clauses, the subjects are expressed by the noun phrases מַרְאֵהוּ (noun ms cstr. of מַרְאֶה "appearance", "sight", "vision", 3ms suff.) "his appearance" and תֹּאֲרוֹ (noun ms cstr. of תֹּאַר "form", "shape", "outline", 3ms suff.) "his form". Both subjects, which concern "his"

---

[63] The 2ms suff of the prep. phrase עָלֶיךָ "at you" has raised difficulties because it disrupts the surrounding 3ms forms. Some exegetes have solved this by means of harmonisation, amending עָלֶיךָ to עָלָיו, cf. Duhm, *Das Buch Jesaia*, pp. 355–356, Muilenburg, "The Book of Isaiah: Chapters 40–66", pp. 616–617, Kutsch, *Sein Leiden und Tod – unser Heil*, pp. 12;16, Clines, *I, He, We and They*, p. 14, Hermisson, "Das vierte Gottesknechtlied im deuterojesajanischen Kontext", p. 6, n. 12 (ET p. 23, n. 12). This 3ms rendering is supported by Targum, Peshitta etc., cf. 52:15.

Lindblom, *The Servant Songs in Deutero-Isaiah*, p. 38, n. 53, argues for MT of 52:14 on the basis of the prophetic style elsewhere, cf. Kaiser, *Der königliche Knecht*, pp. 85–86, Whybray, *Isaiah 40–66*, p. 170, Koole, *Isaiah III. Vol. 2*, p. 373, n. 53, Oswalt, *The Book of Isaiah: Chapters 40–66*, p. 267. 1QIsaᵃ, 1QIsaᵇ, LXX and the Vulgate render 2ms. About the common shift of persons in Biblical Hebrew in general, see 3.10.2. n. 68.

[64] W. G. W. Watson, *Classical Hebrew Poetry: A Guide to its Techniques* (JSOTSup, 26; Sheffield: JSOT Press, 1984) 303–304:

Ellipsis, i.e. omission of a particle, word or group of words within a poetic unit, where its presence is expected. In other words, ellipsis is the suppression of an element demanded by the context…Ellipsis, of course, belongs to ordinary language as well as poetry – but the problem with ellipsis in poetry…is that an obscure passage or an ambiguous context can make its recognition difficult.

Kugel, *The Idea of Biblical Poetry*, pp. 46–47; 90–94, explains ellipsis – or "gapping" – such as the elimination of particles, articles, conjunctions and the suppression of a major constituent in a "double-duty" construction, as effecting a de-emphasis, where the emphasis is given to the words that are paralleled, and in which the disjunctive, difficult and strange nature of poetic language becomes emphasised. Alter, *The Art of Biblical Poetry*, pp. 23–26, criticises the traditional "ballast variant" explanation of ellipsis, and claims that it expresses intensification, development, focusing of meaning or isolation for attention. Also, ellipsis touches upon doubling and displacement of language in general, see 4.4.

corporeal appearance, are modified by the predicate מָשְׁחַת (noun ms) "disfigurement",[65] also carrying bodily connotations.[66] This is further expanded by prep. phrases linked to each of the subjects; מֵאִישׁ "from that of man" and מִבְּנֵי אָדָם "from that of humanity". The noun in the first prep. phrase, אִישׁ (noun ms "man", "each", "every", "any one", "fellow"), is singular and "particular", whereas the noun phrase in the second, בְּנֵי אָדָם (noun mpl cstr. of בֵּן "son", noun ms אָדָם "man", "mankind", "humanity") is plural and collective. As both these noun phrases are connected to the disjunctive prep. מִן "from", they act as forceful depictions of how "he" is separated or cut off from any human fellowship. By the nominal clauses, both comparison and separation

---

[65] מָשְׁחַת is a *hapax legomenon*, and the explanation of MT vocalisation is unresolved by scholars. Scholars have chosen between a derivation from משׁה "to anoint" (cf. 1QIsaᵃ מָשׁחתי) and שׁחת "to corrupt", "destroy", "ruin", and taken it to be adj. or pt, ho or ni. Apart from 1QIsaᵃ, the mss, including 1QIsaᵇ, support MT. LXX renders ἀδοξήσει ἀπὸ ἀνθρώπων "will be dishonoured by men".

E. Y. Kutscher, *The Language and Linguistic Background of the Isaiah Scroll (IQIsa)* (StDJ, 6; Leiden: E. J. Brill, 1974) 262, translates 1QIsaᵃ שׁחתי "I have anointed", relating to the Messiah identity at Qumran. A. Guillaume, "Some Readings in the Dead Sea Scroll of Isaiah", *JBL* 76 (1957) 41–42, claims that the verb in 1QIsaᵃ cannot have been שׁחת "anoint", which is "inconceivable without Christian ideas", but rather a homonym. He regards מָשְׁחַת as a derivation of משׁה, which he correlates with an Arab. cognate for "to spoil". He is supported by J. Barr, *Comparative Philology and the Text of the Old Testament* (London: SCM Press, 1983) 284–285.

J. Komlosh, "The Countenance of the Servant of the Lord, Was it Marred?", *JQR* 65 (1974/75) 217–220, argues that 52:14 cannot give a negative description of the servant when both 52:13 and v. 15 depict his exaltation. He refers to מָשְׁחָא "measure" (as in Aram.) for a more coherent presentation of the servant. He emends מָשְׁחַת to מָשְׁחָתוֹ (cf. 1QIsa). With an additional change in the verse division, he translates 52:14b: "his stature more than any man, and his visage and his form unlike the sons of men". This presentation of the servant becomes strengthened as Komlosh reads שָׁמְמוּ as signifying not astonishment, but the sense of surprise, cf. 1 Kgs 9:8.

C. C. Torrey, *The Second Isaiah: A New Interpretation* (Edinburgh: T. & T. Clark, 1928) 416, takes the original reading to be נִשְׁחַת, whereas A. Rubinstein, "Isaiah LII 14 מָשְׁחַת and the DSIa Variant", *Bib* 35 (1954) 475, reads pt cstr. ho., supported by Driver. Driver, "Isaiah 52:13–53:12", p. 92, argues that the reading of 1QIsaᵃ is only a *hireq compagnis* (cf. Isa. 49:7 and GKC § 90l), which does not differ from MT. He explains the MT form as derived from שׁחת "spoiled", "transformed", "marred", "ruined", "damaged", "destroyed", "desolated", thus "disfigurment". Oswalt, *The Book of Isaiah: Chapters 40–66*, p. 373, n. 54: "The proposal (Cf. BHS) to correct the MT reading from an adjective in place of a participle is unneccessary. This use of a substantive or an adjective in place of a participle is a characteristic of this poem (cf. 53:3: 'a cessation of men'; 'a hiding of face')."

[66] Waltke and O'Connor, *An Introduction to Biblical Hebrew Syntax*, § 4.5b;c: "In a *verbal clause* the predicate is a verb...In a *verbless* (or nominal) *clause* there is no verbal marker of predication. Hebrew...may predicate an adjective, or noun directly, without a *copula* (i.e. some form of היה...)", their italics.

are expressed: "he" was so disfigured as to appear hardly human. Not only did "he" have a shameful appearance, but due to this "he" was also separated from human fellowship. The second subordinate clause is introduced by a copulative *waw* expressing situations coordinate to each other. After the conjunction and the predicate, a chiastic structure appears: the first nominal clause continues with the prep. phrase מֵאִישׁ "from man" and the subject מַרְאֵהוּ "his appearance", while the second has the subject תֹּאֲרוֹ "his form" and then the prep. phrase בְּנֵי אָדָם "from that of humanity". Both this criss-cross placing of repeated syntactical elements and the numerical shift provide difference within similarity: the inverted syntax and the morphological contrast of number appear between the equivalent expression of one situation.[67]

The subordinating conjunction כַּאֲשֶׁר "as" introduces both an event and an argument. The reactions of רַבִּים "many" as appalled at "you" in the past (52:14a) are modified when a cause is given by the subordinate conjunction כֵּן "such" (52:14b): due to מִשְׁחַת "disfigurement", מַרְאֵהוּ "his appearance" and תֹּאֲרוֹ "his form" separate "him" מֵאִישׁ "from that of man" and מִבְּנֵי אָדָם "from that of humanity". With temporal and explanatory force, the conjunction כֵּן "such" introduces further information about the event. In the relation between the subordinating and the subordinate clauses, a shift in participants and a change from action to state appear: the argument beginning with the appalled reactions of רַבִּים "many" to "you" is developed by a portrait of "his" disgusting appearance. Also, an enunciative distancing and impersonalisation appear between "you" (52:14a) and מַרְאֵהוּ "his appearance" and תֹּאֲרוֹ "his form" (52:14b), whereas the reactions of רַבִּים "many" to "you" are comparable to the relation of אִישׁ "man" and בְּנֵי אָדָם "humanity" to "him". Moreover, in the temporal and causal relation between שָׁמְמוּ עָלֶיךָ רַבִּים "many were appalled at you" and "his" מִשְׁחַת "disfigurement", an identification appears between "him" and "you", but an identification which is conveyed through different accentuations: "you" are the one at whom "we" are appalled,

---

[67] Blenkinsopp, *Isaiah 40–55*, p. 346e, regards 52:14 to be defective, where, among others, v. 14b seems to be out of place. He claims that:

> it is unlikely that successive verses would begin with [כֵּן]; the word breaks into the contrast between the former humiliation and the future glorification of the servant [כַּאֲשֶׁר...כֵּן]; and 14b fits better after 53:2, especially in view of the pair [מַרְאֵהוּ וְתֹאֲרוֹ] repeated in reverse order

(p. 346e). This transposition is also made by, among others, Duhm (2.1.4. n. 46), Driver, "Isaiah 52:13–53:12", p. 91, Westermann, *Isaiah 40–66*, pp. 253; 258–259, Whybray, *Isaiah 40–66*, p. 169.

while "he" is disfigured.[68] Working as orientation features within the situation of the utterance, the suffixes of "his" and "your" play with each other and their context in a way that prevents an assumed coherent enunciation of the text in terms of the relation between "you" and "he".

"I", "you", "he" and "many" are signifiers of identity. In the crisscrossing of implicit or explicit first-, second- and third-person suffixes, signs of different language situations are given. By the address in the second-person "you" (cf. the prep. phrase עָלֶיךָ "at you"), an "I" and a "you" are related. The deictic pronouns "I" and "you" differ from "he", רַבִּים "many", אִישׁ "man" and בְּנֵי אָדָם "humanity".

To the list of agents, "I", "you" and "he" in 52:13 are added רַבִּים "many", אִישׁ "man" and בְּנֵי אָדָם "humanity" in 52:14. The addressee "you" is signified by הִנֵּה "see" in 52:13, and by being regarded as appalling by רַבִּים "many" in 52:14. עַבְדִּי "my servant" shall prosper in 52:13, whereas מַרְאֵהוּ "his appearance" and תֹּאֲרוֹ "his form" were a disfigurement מֵאִישׁ "from that of man" and מִבְּנֵי אָדָם "from that of humanity" in 52:14. While 52:13 concerns the future, 52:14 is about the past.

3.10.3. *Isa. 52:15*

כֵּן יַזֶּה גּוֹיִם רַבִּים עָלָיו יִקְפְּצוּ מְלָכִים פִּיהֶם
כִּי אֲשֶׁר לֹא־סֻפַּר לָהֶם רָאוּ וַאֲשֶׁר לֹא־שָׁמְעוּ הִתְבּוֹנָנוּ׃

– so he יַזֶּה (will startle?) many peoples before him, kings shall shut their mouth;
for what has not been told them, they shall see, and what they did not hear, they shall understand.

The introductory subordinate conjunction כֵּן "so" relates to the subordinating כַּאֲשֶׁר "as" in 52:14. It is followed by two clauses, in the first of which a relation between "him" and גּוֹיִם רַבִּים "many peoples" is described. In the second clause, the reactions of מְלָכִים "kings" are depicted. Then yet another subordinate conjunction כִּי "for" follows,

---

[68] The sudden transition from 2ms "you" to 3ms "he", which breaks with the norms of standard language in Isa. 52:14, elsewhere in Isa. 40–55 and in the Hebrew Bible in general, is commented on in e.g. GKC §144p, Kugel, *The Idea of Biblical Poetry*, p. 22, Berlin, *The Dynamics of Biblical Parallelism*, p. 40, and M. C. A. Korpel and J. C. Moor, *The Structure of Classical Hebrew Poetry: Isa. 40–55* (OTS, 41; Leiden: E. J. Brill, 1998) 545. Both Kugel and Berlin emphasise the widespread use of shifts in person as a morphological parallelism in Biblical Hebrew poetry.

which is related to the כֵּן "so" clause(s) by offering two further comments upon it (them), where "they" are related to sense perceptions
in negative utterances about the past and positive utterances about
the future.

The subordinate conjunction כֵּן "so" precedes the predicate יַזֶּה עַל,
which may be imperf. hi. 3ms of either נזה I "sprinkle" or נזה II "startle". In both alternatives, "he" is the subject and agent acting towards
the patient גּוֹיִם רַבִּים (noun mpl of גּוֹי "people", "nation" and noun
mpl of רַב "much", "many") "many peoples". However, the transmission of יַזֶּה in 52:13 has been regarded as both cryptic and corrupt,
and I support those who emphasise its uncertain meaning.[69] The prep.
phrase עָלָיו (prep. עַל; "before", 3ms suff.) might be reflexive "before
himself" or might introduce a new participant "before him". A numerical inequality appears in the relation between the subject "he" (sg) and
the object גּוֹיִם רַבִּים "many peoples" (pl). Related to the subordinate כֵּן
"so" in 52:15, יַזֶּה...עָלָיו ("he will startle... before him"?) offers a future
response which is the opposite of that of the explanatory כֵּן "such" in
52:14 (see more below).

The next clause is not connected to the preceding clause by *waw* or
other signs of relation. The predicate יִקְפְּצוּ (imperf. qal 3mpl of קפץ
"shut", "draw together") "shut" is fientive and transitive and is followed by the subject מְלָכִים (noun mpl of מֶלֶךְ "king") "kings" and the
object פִּיהֶם (noun ms cstr. of פֶּה "mouth", 3mpl suff.) "their mouth".
Related to the subordinate conjunction כֵּן "so", the clause יִקְפְּצוּ מְלָכִים
פִּיהֶם "kings shall shut their mouth" is presented as a future response
contrasting with the explanatory conjunction כֵּן "such" of 52:14. Both
the conjunction כֵּן "so" and the prep. phrase עָלָיו "at him" might work
elliptically in the two subordinate clauses of 52:15a. In the first clause,
"he" is the subject and agent and גּוֹיִם רַבִּים "many peoples" is the
object and patient. In the second, מְלָכִים "kings" are the subject and
agent, without any patient mentioned. The two clauses are syntactically similar and morphologically contrasting. The relation between
"him" and גּוֹיִם רַבִּים "many peoples" in the first clause is not brought
to the fore in the second. While "he" acts towards גּוֹיִם רַבִּים "many
peoples", מְלָכִים "kings" react by being silent. There might be both a
temporal and a causal relation between the two כֵּן "so" clauses: "he
('will startle'?) many peoples before him" might lead to "kings shutting

---

[69] On scholarly discussions of יַזֶּה...עָלָיו in Isa. 52:15, see Appendix 2.

their mouth", in terms of both a cause and progression. Alternatively, the two clauses might act as simultaneous responses to the "same" event (of 52:14), expressing the kings' astonishment at "his" disfigurement (or at the servant's exaltation in 52:13, see more below), but due to the uncertainties of יָזֶה this is hard to tell.

After the two subordinate כֵּן "so" clauses, yet another subordinate conjunction כִּי "for" appears, followed by a negative statement which is contrasted with a positive one. The predicate סֻפַּר (perf. pu. 3ms of ספר "be told", "recounted", "related") is pass., preceded by the negation לֹא "not", and no agent is mentioned: "what has not been told". The object and patient of the action appears in the prep. phrase לָהֶם (prep. and object marker לְ, 3mpl suff.) "them". In a contrasting positive utterance, רָאוּ (perf. qal 3mpl of ראה "see", "look", "perceive", "observe", "consider"), a plural agent "they" is implied: "they shall see". Both verbs are perfect conjugations, but have different stems[70] and agencies: the first is pu. with a 3mpl patient, and the second is qal with a 3mpl agent. "Their" agency is related to what "they" have not been told, yet react to: by emphatic force, the conjunction כִּי "for" modifies "their" preceding situation to concern מְלָכִים "kings" (and גוֹיִם רַבִּים "many peoples"?), i.e. the subject(s) of the subordinate כֵּן "so" clause(s) (see more below).

Preceded by a *waw*, yet another negative statement is contrasted with a positive one. The predicate שָׁמְעוּ (perf. qal 3mpl of שמע "hear", "listen", "pay attention") is preceded by the negation לֹא "not": "what they did not hear" and followed by the contrasting positive הִתְבּוֹנָנוּ (perf. hitpal. 3mpl of בין "understand", "perceive", "become aware of") "they shall understand". Both verbs are perfect, but have different stems (qal and hitpal.), both denoting "they" as subject and agent. In the clause as a whole a past and a future situation are related, with the negative utterance temporally preceding the positive one.

In the four perfect verbs of these כִּי "for" clauses, utterances about "their" future reactions to past events appear, with negative utterances temporally preceding positive ones. Three of the four verbal actions have a 3mpl agent (רָאוּ "they shall see", שָׁמְעוּ [לֹא] "they did [not]

---

[70] Waltke and O'Connor, *An Introduction to Biblical Hebrew Syntax*, p. 693, defines stem as "a major inflectional category of the verb marking *Aktionsart*, e.g. *himlīk* is a *Hiphil* stem form..." Conjugation is defined as "a major inflectional category of verbs, the principal Hebrew conjugations being the *qatal* (or perfective or suffix) conjugation and the *yiqtol* (or non-perfective or prefix) conjugation", p. 690, their italics.

hear" and הִתְבּוֹנָנוּ "they shall understand"), while the last (לֹא] סֻפַּר[
"was [not] told") has a 3mpl patient expressed by the adjacent prep.
phrase לָהֶם "to them". Both verbs in the positive statements, as well
as the negated verb of the second clause (רָאוּ "they shall see", הִתְבּוֹנָנוּ
"they shall understand" and לֹא שָׁמְעוּ "they did not hear"), are bound
up with the subject "they" (3mpl). Moreover, all three of these are
verbs of perception.

In the first כִּי "for" clause, the object is expressed through the prep.
phrase לָהֶם "to them", whereas in the second it is expressed through
a 3mpl suff. of the verb הִתְבּוֹנָנוּ "they shall understand". Moreover,
the negated predicate of the first clause is sg (לֹא סֻפַּר "what has not
been told"), while the negated predicate in the second is pl (לֹא שָׁמְעוּ
"what they did not hear"). Apart from these differences, the surface
structure of the two כִּי "for" clauses is identical in both syntax and
morphology. However, the second clause both provides more information and informs about other signs in the text: the negative and
passive utterance לֹא־סֻפַּר לָהֶם "what has not been told to them" in
the first clause is contrasted with the active לֹא שָׁמְעוּ "what they did
not hear" in the second, while the positive statement רָאוּ "they shall
see" in the first is related to הִתְבּוֹנָנוּ "they shall understand" in the
second. The second clause ensures the delivery of information in
the first, but also offers an alternative view of the "same" situation.
In both instance, an object for the seeing or understanding is mentioned. When related to the agencies of (עָלָיו) יִקְפְּצוּ מְלָכִים פִּיהֶם
"(before him) kings shall shut their mouth", the two כִּי "for" clauses
might explain "their" silence. The כֵּן "so" and the כִּי "for" clauses in
52:15 are contemporary with each other, as the comparison of the
future in the כֵּן "so" clause is further explained and expanded by verbal
clauses of perceiving. The subordinate כִּי אֲשֶׁר לֹא "for what was not"
introduces two explanations of the future situation(s), and is contemporary with כֵּן "so" in 52:15.[71] Thus, the elliptical כִּי "for" might introduce object clauses when related to the preceding כֵּן "so" by offering
further comments upon it (them): "(so) he יַזֶּה ('will startle'?) many
peoples before him…; for what has not been told them, they shall
see", etc.

---

[71] Above, the relation between the two כֵּן "so" clauses of 52:15 is described as
ambiguous in temporality and causality. Due to the obscurities as regards יַזֶּה עָלָיו
in 52:15, it is difficult to say much about the relation between that clause and the
subordinate כִּי clauses.

52:14 and v. 15 together form a complex sentence. In 52:14, רַבִּים "many" were appalled when confronted with "you" due to "his" dis-figurement. The subordinate כֵּן "such" in 52:14 has a causative and temporal force when related to כַּאֲשֶׁר "as", providing a past-tense situation with a similarly past-tense explanation. When related to the argument beginning with the subordinating כַּאֲשֶׁר "as" in 52:14, the subordinate כֵּן "so" in v. 15 has no causal force, as no explanation is given for the change from past to future. However, the subordinate כֵּן "so" in v. 15 has both a temporal and a comparative force when related to כַּאֲשֶׁר "as", contrasting a past situation with a future one. It works as a response in a comparison, with the argument pointing to the future: "as many were appalled at you" due to "his disfigurement" (52:14) – so he יַזֶּה ('will startle'?) גּוֹיִם רַבִּים "many peoples" before him, מְלָכִים "kings" shall shut their mouth (52:15). When related to the subordinate כֵּן "so" of 52:15, the silence of the kings appears as a future response in contrast to the explanatory כֵּן "such" of 52:14, i.e. as a response pointing to a reversal of past events. What "they" were not told and did not hear, they shall see and understand. Thus, the argument comes together by way of a change from past to future, whereas the situations begin to differ due to a change in both actors and actions.

In 52:13–15, contrasts appear between the past humiliation of "you"/"him" and "his" vindication, and between the past and future of "many peoples"/"kings": while 52:13 concerns the future prosper-ity of עַבְדִּי "my servant" and "your" witnessing of it, in 52:15 גּוֹיִם רַבִּים "many peoples" and מְלָכִים "kings" are related to the seeing, with new actors and situations involved. עַבְדִּי "my servant" shall be exalted (52:13) and "he יַזֶּה ('will startle'?) many peoples before him" (52:15). In-between v. 13 and v. 15, the humiliation of the "you"/"him" of the past appears (52:14). The roles change – "you"/"he" shall be vindi-cated and were humiliated (52:13–14) and the "many" were appalled and shall see (52:14–15) – in both instances related to appearance. In 52:14, a linguistic pressure point appears disrupting the poten-tial coherence of the text. This occurs because of confusion between "him" and "you" as regards both similarity and difference: both "you" and "he" are related to the dismay of the "many", but a discrepancy appears in the argument: "his" disfigurement is the cause and "you" are the one at whom "many" are appalled. This invites us to attempt to interpret the relation, but it also places pressure on the text which impedes attempts to find a single, decisive meaning. When the relation is worked out through interaction and difference, some aspects become suppressed, while others are brought into focus and expanded. A grammatical analysis falls short if consistency is expected.

3.10.4. *Isa. 53:1*

מִי הֶאֱמִין לִשְׁמֻעָתֵנוּ וּזְרוֹעַ יְהוָה עַל־מִי נִגְלָתָה׃

> Who believes what we hear? And the arm of YHWH – to whom is it revealed?

An interrogative pronoun מִי "who" introduces a question. A 1cpl suff. of the prep. phrase characterises the question as "we" speech. A second question is related to the first by a *waw*. Due to the two interrogative pronouns מִי "who", both questions concern identity.

In the first question, the pronoun and subject מִי "who" is a sign of uncertainty referring to persons, but does not vary in gender or number. The identity of this "who" is elicited by its interaction with the predicate הֶאֱמִין לְ (perf. hi. 3ms of אמן "believe", "give credence to", "trust to"). In this causative internal hi., the subject and object are the same, i.e. the interrogative pronoun מִי "who" "causes itself to believe". Since the object is not grammatically expressed, the verb is formally intransitive: no action is depicted as passing over from agent to goal. The verb of believing concerns "us", and it might be rendered either in the past or in the present tense.[72] The identification of the person in the pronoun מִי "who" is also related to the prep. phrase לִשְׁמֻעָתֵנוּ (prep. and object marker לְ "to", noun fs or pt. pass. fs of שמע, i.e. שְׁמֻעָה "message", "tidings", "report", 1cpl poss. suff.) "what we hear". In the suff., a plural speaking "we" is made known. The object

---

[72] Duhm (cf. 2.1.4. n. 48) interprets "our" questions as pointing forwards (prolepsis), expressing "incredible good news" and expecting positive answers, i.e. pointing to "our" belief, knowledge and insight, cf. Steck in 2.2.3. n. 79. Kutsch, *Sein Leiden und Tod – unser Heil*, pp. 18–19, translates 53:1 "Wer glaubt der Kunde, die uns ward", and explains the announcement as that which one perceives, not one to hand over. Hermisson, "Das vierte Gottesknechtslied im deuterojesajanischen Kontext", p. 6, ET p. 24: "Who could have believed (*or*: who can believe) what we have just heard? Upon what sort of figure has the arm of the Lord now been revealed?", (his italics).

Most often, the questions are taken to regard the past (analepsis), in expectation of a negative answer, i.e. expressing "our" disbelief, blindness and ignorance, see most recently in Koole, *Isaiah III. Vol. 2*, pp. 275–278, Blenkinsopp, *Isaiah 40–55*, pp. 345; 349, Oswalt, *The Book of Isaiah: Chapters 40–66*, pp. 374; 381–382, Goldingay and Payne, *A Critical and Exegetical Commentary on Isaiah 40–55. Vol. II*, pp. 296–298.

marker לְ makes the predicate a two-place verb, with an external object in addition to the internal one.

The second question is related to the first by a *waw*. It continues with the noun phrase זְרוֹעַ יְהוָה (noun fs cstr. of זְרוֹעַ "arm", "strenght") "arm of YHWH", which is an attributive or rather anthropomorphic metonymy for YHWH and the subject of the interrogative clause. This is followed by the prep. phrase עַל־מִי (prep. עַל "to", "upon", expressing direction, interrogative pronoun מִי "who") "to whom". The clause closes with the predicate נִגְלָתָה (perf. ni. 3fs of גלה "revealed", "be uncovered", "disclosed") "revealed",[73] implying a confrontation between the subject זְרוֹעַ יְהוָה "arm of YHWH" and מִי "who" and might be rendered in either the past or the present tense. In ni., the subject זְרוֹעַ יְהוָה "the arm of YHWH" is the patient, as "we" ask to whom זְרוֹעַ יְהוָה "the arm of YHWH" is (not) revealed.

The interrogative pronoun מִי "who" is a signifier of identity. Whereas the pronoun in the first question works as the subject and agent of the verb of believing, in the second it acts as an indirect object in the prep. phrase עַל־מִי "to whom". Apart from the different syntactical placement of the interrogative pronoun, a chiastic relationship appears between the questions. Whereas the first question opens with the pronoun מִי "who" as its subject, the second begins with the subject זְרוֹעַ יְהוָה "the arm of YHWH". The first question continues with the predicate (הֶאֱמִין לְ "believed") and prep. phrase (לִשְׁמֻעָתֵנוּ "what we hear"), while in the second a prep. phrase (עַל־מִי "to whom") follows and then the predicate (נִגְלָתָה "is revealed"). In both cases, the interrogative pronoun is related to a confrontation between participant and situation. "We" are the agent of the first question "who believes what we hear?", and no patient is mentioned. In the second question, זְרוֹעַ יְהוָה "the arm of YHWH", the patient is "being revealed upon", and no agent is mentioned. In both questions the predicates are in the perfect; the first in active (הֶאֱמִין hi.) and the second in pass. (נִגְלָתָה ni.). Thus, the two situations are similar in temporality and different in agency. With interrogative force the questions signify the reception of לִשְׁמֻעָתֵנוּ "the message to us", which is further illuminated by the revelation of זְרוֹעַ יְהוָה "the arm of YHWH". As regards the *waw*,

---

[73] Ni. of גלה and the prep. עַל is an uncommon construction. Ni. pass. of גלה with the prep. לְ occurs in Isa. 23:1 and Dan. 10:1, and ni. reflexive of גלה with אֶל in 1 Sam. 14:8; 11 ("uncover oneself"), Gen. 35:7, 1 Sam. 2:27, 3:21 ("reveal oneself" [God]), Isa. 22:14. Cf. עָלֶיךָ "at you" in Isa. 52:14 and עָלָיו "before him" in 52:15.

relations of similarity might be expressed by a coordinate, a copulative *waw*. Alternatively, an aspect of progression might be seen, as זְרוֹעַ יְהוָה "the arm of YHWH" in the second question might offer a hint as to לִשְׁמֻעָתֵנוּ "what we hear" in the first one, i.e. the *waw* may be conjunctive.

In two questions in the "we" speech in 53:1, the "I" speech of 52:13–15 is interrupted by new participants and a new situation. Simultaneously, the questions in 53:1 echo 52:15 by taking up its final words: as in 52:15, something which has never been heard of before is now brought to the fore. But whereas "I" speaks about לֹא־סֻפַּר לָהֶם "what has not been told to them" and לֹא־שָׁמְעוּ "what they did not hear" in 52:15, לִשְׁמֻעָתֵנוּ "what we hear" in 53:1 leads "us" to assume that something might have been both told and heard. While in 52:15 it is stated that רָאוּ "they shall see" and הִתְבּוֹנָנוּ "they shall understand", in 53:1 "we" ask whether זְרוֹעַ יְהוָה "the arm of YHWH" is revealed.[74]

3.10.5. *Isa. 53:2*

וַיַּעַל כַּיּוֹנֵק לְפָנָיו וְכַשֹּׁרֶשׁ מֵאֶרֶץ צִיָּה לֹא־תֹאַר לוֹ וְלֹא
הָדָר וְנִרְאֵהוּ וְלֹא־מַרְאֶה וְנֶחְמְדֵהוּ:

> He grew up like a shoot before him and like a root out of dry ground;
> there was no form to him and no splendour that we should look at him,
> and no appearance that we should be attracted to him.

An imperf. cons., וַיַּעַל "he grew up", is followed by two particles of comparison which introduce plant similes. The similes are supplied with portraits of "him" by two nominal clauses, both with adjacent consecutive verbal clauses working as complements to the depictions of "him". In the verbal clauses, "we" appear as the judging subject and "he" as the object being judged.

In the predicate וַיַּעַל (imperf. cons. qal 3ms of עלה "grow up", "go up", "spring up", "shoot forth") "he grew up", a situation in the past to the speaker is evoked.[75] The predicate works elliptically as it serves

---

[74] Koole, *Isaiah III. Vol. 2*, p. 259: "The chiasmus of 52:15b with chap. 53 is remarkable: לֹא־שָׁמְעוּ is matched by לִשְׁמֻעָתֵנוּ, הִתְבּוֹנָנוּ probably by הֶאֱמִין (43:10, cf. 28:9, 19), in the same way רָאוּ corresponds to נִגְלָתָה (40:5, 47:3)."

[75] Clines, *I, He, We, and They*, p. 48, claims that "it [is] impossible to establish any systematic correspondence between Hebrew 'tenses' used in the poem [i.e. Isa. 52:13–53:12] and the poem's own temporal structure". He comments further on the

both the two adjacent clauses. Each of these continues with a comparison of the subject, as "he" is כַּיּוֹנֵק (particle of comparison כְּ "like", definite article, noun ms יוֹנֵק which elsewhere means "young child", but here "shoot", "suckling", "young plant", "sapling") "like a shoot" and וְכַשֹּׁרֶשׁ (waw, particle of comparison כְּ "like", definite article, noun ms שֹׁרֶשׁ "root", "stock") "and like a root". Although the predicate concerns the past, it also brings associations of a promising future with potential growth and with progeny, prosperity and hope. In the relation between the verb for "growing up" and the similes יוֹנֵק "shoot" and שֹׁרֶשׁ "root", both human and vegetable spheres are signified and attention is drawn to appearance and visibility.

Each of the comparative noun phrases is followed by a prep. phrase which might also work elliptically. In the first, לְפָנָיו (prep. לְפָנֶה "before", "in front of", 3ms suff.) "before him", "he" might either be related to "another" or be reflexive, i.e. refer to "himself".[76] The prep.

---

imperf. cons. וַיַּעַל in 53:2 and וַיִּתֵּן in 53:9 (he incorrectly writes 53:8). Clines claims that the narrative verb forms indicate "a narrative sequence that begins with the servant's growing up and ends with the preparation of his tomb" (p. 48), and adds: "Of course, we cannot infer that the poet regards the history as having already occurred" (n. 33). Koole, *Isaiah III. Vol. 2*, p. 280:

> As regards the grammatical connection between v. 2 and v. 1, some scholars assume that the cons. imperf. וַיַּעַל more or less makes this v. formally an apodosis of v. 1, for which North refers to GKC §111f. It is true that v. 2 starts a discussion about "what we have heard" and "Yahweh's arm". But a description of events may begin with a cons. imperf., Joüon § 118c, and this seems to be the case here as well.

See more on this in the narrative reading of Isa. 52:13–53:12 in 4.8.3.1. n. 91.

[76] The reading of לְפָנָיו has been widely discussed. All the versions support MT. Koole, *Isaiah III. Vol. 2*, pp. 279–280, claims that the suffix might be read in at least three ways:

i) it may refer to "who" in v. 1, cf. e.g. L. G. Rignell, "Isa. LII 13–LIII 12", *VT* 3 (1953) 90.

ii) it may be reflexive, cf. G. R. Driver, "Linguistic and Textual Problems: Isaiah I–XXXIX", *JTS* 38 (1937) 48, who refers to 1 Sam. 5:3–4, and suggests that וַיַּעַל....לְפָנָיו "and he grew up...before him(self)" means "and he grew straight up" or "shot right up", supported with additional nuances by R. P. Gordon, "Isa. LII 2", *VT* 20 (1970) 491–492 and L. C. Allen, "Isaiah LIII 2 Again", *VT* 21 (1971) 490. Later (in 1968), Driver, "Isaiah 52:13–53:12", pp. 92; 102 withdrew his earlier proposal.

iii) it may relate to God, cf. M. Treves, "Isaiah 53", *VT* 24 (1974) 102 (regarding the high priest Onias III as the servant), Blenkinsopp, *Isaiah 40–55*, p. 347, Whybray, *Isaiah 40–66*, pp. 173–174, Oswalt, *The Book of Isaiah: Chapters 40–66*, p. 374, n. 60, Koole, p. 280.

Others suggest various emendations: Lindblom, *The Servant Songs in Deutero-Isaiah*, p. 43, renders לְפָנַי "before me" within a prophetic revelation, explaining the waw as having arisen through dittography, i.e. a doubling of the first letter of the next

phrase is related both to the main clause, i.e. וַיַּעַל....לְפָנָיו "he grew up...before him" and the simile, כַּיּוֹנֵק לְפָנָיו "like a shoot before him". Simultaneously, this "personal confrontation" is contrasted with the vegetable sphere by the last modifier, i.e. the prep. phrase מֵאֶרֶץ צִיָּה (prep. מִן "from", "out of", noun phrase אֶרֶץ צִיָּה "dry ground") "out of dry ground". This simile works in direct contrast to the potential of prosperity of the predicate, as the dry ground obstructs growth. Signs of drought and desert bring associations of a feeble and perishable plant prematurely stripped of its vitality and visibility. Thus, the two elliptical prep. phrases, לְפָנָה "before him" and מֵאֶרֶץ צִיָּה "out of dry ground", both interact and work in different directions. Within the similes, they work to compare "his" fate. The similes cross boundaries by bringing together incompatible fields: the comparison וַיַּעַל כַּיּוֹנֵק "he grew up like a shoot" encourages a future of hope, וַיַּעַל...לְפָנָיו "he grew up...before him" might concern a "personal" relation, and וַיַּעַל...מֵאֶרֶץ צִיָּה "he grew up...out of dry ground" rather obstructs hope. Through contrasts and similarities, different and distinct fields come into play. The similes, signifying appearance and visibility, touch on both human and vegetable spheres, and bring associations both of hope for the future of יוֹנֵק "a shoot" and שֹׁרֶשׁ "a root" that might grow, and lack of hope for a future doomed to wither because of the inadequacy of the parched soil to sustain such growth.

The comparisons are further modified by a portrait of "him" painted by two nominal clauses. The first, which is introduced by the negation וְלֹא,[77] is composite of two noun phrases, the second of which is introduced by a copulative *waw*. Both noun phrases refer to bodily appearance: תֹּאַר (noun ms "form", "shape", "outline") and הָדָר (noun ms "splendour", "honour", "majesty", "dignity", "glory"). The elliptical prep. phrase לוֹ (prep. לְ "to", 3ms suff. of belonging) "to him" is placed between the nominal clauses, thus modifying "his" state, and no activity is mentioned: "there was no form to him and no splendour".

---

word וְכַשֹּׁרֶשׁ. Some support an emendation to לְפָנֵינוּ "before us", see e.g. Kaiser, *Der königliche Knecht*, p. 86, Kutsch, *Sein Leiden und Tod – unser Heil*, pp. 12; 20, Clines, *I, He, We and They*, pp. 15–16. G. Schwartz, "...wie ein Reis vor ihm", *ZAW* 83 (1971) 256–257, suggests מִפִּנָּה "from a battlement".

[77] The negation is expressed by nominal clauses in compound with the particle of negation לֹא, and not the usual אֵין, see Waltke and O'Connor, *An Introduction to Biblical Hebrew Syntax*, § 39.3.3b.

After these depictions of "him", a judgment follows by way of the elliptical verb וְנִרְאֵהוּ (*waw*, imperf. qal 1cpl of ראה "look", "see", "gaze", "give attention to", "take heed", "attract", 3ms object suff.) "that we should look at him". This consecutive verbal clause is preceded by a copulative *waw* and works as a complement to the preceding clause.[78] A speaking and judging "we" (1cpl) is the subject and agent and "he" (3ms) is the object and patient. The complementary verb expresses a negative wish: due to "his" lack of form and splendour, the "we" speaking did not have any pleasure in "him". The judgment belongs to the past situation above: וַיַּעַל "he grew up".

Yet another noun phrase follows, also preceded by a negation. The noun phrase וְלֹא־מַרְאֶה (*waw*, negation לֹא, noun ms מַרְאֶה "no appearance", "sight", "vision") concerns "his" bodily appearance and is modified by the verbal clause וְנֶחְמְדֵהוּ (*waw*, imperf. qal 1cpl of חמד "attract", "desire", "take pleasure in", 3ms suff.) "that we should be attracted to him". This verbal clause is again preceded by a copulative *waw* and works as a complement to the depiction of "him", a speaking and judging "we" appearing as subject and agent with a 3ms "he" as object and patient. "Our" judgment of him regards his "bodily" appearance, for which "he" is neither respected nor deemed attractive.

While the similes call attention to a similarity of seeming opposites, i.e. a crossing of semantic fields of both human and vegetable spheres, they do not identify what, specifically, equates them. That the similes do not lead to a determinate meaning establishes a gap between the signifiers and a final signified. This invites us to interpret the similes, but it also places pressure on them, since they are only more signifiers. The similes יוֹנֵק "shoot" and שֹׁרֶשׁ "root" are supplied in "our" depiction and judgment of "him", and through interaction and conflict some aspects of the similes become suppressed, while others are brought to the fore. These are further modified by contrasting similes of growth and drought, hope and lack of hope in the comparisons of "him", יוֹנֵק "shoot" and שֹׁרֶשׁ "root". The connection between "our" portrait of "him" and the similes is strengthened as the verb עלה "grow up" is never used for human beings, but often for plants.[79] From the interaction of the similes and their explanations, we can see that the

---

[78] Cf. GKC §166a, P. Joüon and T. Muraoka, *A Grammar of Biblical Hebrew* (Subsidia Biblica, 14/II; Rome: Editrice Pontificio Istituto Biblico, 1996) § 116c.

[79] Koole, *Isaiah III. Vol. 2*, p. 279.

insignificant little plants have hardly any future. Following on from the similes, "he" is judged not for his growth (or lack of it) but for "his" appearance. "His" disfigurement makes "him" neither seen by nor attractive to "us".

The complementing verbs נִרְאֵהוּ "that we should look at him" and נֶחְמְדֵהוּ "that we should be attracted to him", which are bound up with the subject "we", are both verbs of perception with both fientive and stative characteristics simultaneously. Even though they are bound up with an object (3ms object suff.), the verbs are not notionally transitive, for no action passes over from agent to goal. But since they are still connected with an object, they might be called "quasi-fientive".[80] "Our" judgment belongs to the same past situation as depicted above: by an imperfect consecutive (וַיַּעַל) and two imperfects (נִרְאֵהוּ and נֶחְמְדֵהוּ), "our judgment" of "him" belongs to "his" growing up in the past.

Both "he" and "we" are signifiers of identity, contrasting as regards both number and roles. "Our" depiction of "him" in 53:2 echoes "my" portrait of "him" in 52:14. In 53:2, "he" is depicted as growing up like יוֹנֵק "a shoot" and שֹׁרֶשׁ "a root" and not attracting "us" to "him" because of "his" appearance and in 52:14 "he" is portrayed as so disfigured as to appear hardly human. מַרְאֵהוּ וְתֹאֲרוֹ "his appearance and his form" in 52:14 are chiastically related to "his" lack of תֹּאַר "form" and מַרְאֶה "appearance" in 53:2.[81] In both instances, a contrast with "he" (sg) appears: "many" (pl) in 52:14 and "us" in 53:2. In 52:14, רַבִּים "many" are the subjects and actors being שָׁמְמוּ "appalled", and their reactions are caused by the confrontation with "you" due to "his" מִשְׁחַת "disfigurement". In 53:2, "we" neither look at nor are attracted to "him" due to "his" (lack of) תֹּאַר "form", הָדָר "splendour" and מַרְאֵהוּ "appearance". The "I" speech and the "we" speech interpenetrate. However, whereas in the "I" speech, "your"/"his" shame is related to the dismay of the רַבִּים "many" (52:14), in the "we" speech "he" is described in a contrasting relation to "us" (53:2). In a crossing

---

[80] For this definition of "quasi-fientive", see Waltke and O'Connor, *An Introduction to Biblical Hebrew Syntax*, § 22.2.3b.

[81] On the word pair תֹּאַר "form" and מַרְאֶה "appearance" in Isa. 52:14 and 53:2, see M. L. Barré, "Textual and Rhetorical-Critical Observations on the Last Servant Song (Isa. 52:13–53:12)", *CBQ* 62 (2000) 3. Barré criticises other scholars for overreadings and misreadings of Isa. 52:13–53:12 (pp. 11–12). Many of the choices Barré himself makes are also not very sound, while others are illuminating. The most interesting observations of his reading will be referred to below.

of semantic frames, "his" fate is presented from different perspectives with various sorts of involvement, from both "my" (and רַבִּים "many") and "our" angles of vision.

After the "I" speech in 52:13–15, in 53:1 a speaking "we" emerges on the scene, and "he" is left out. The "we" speech continues in 53:2, here echoing the earlier "I" speech about "him" by working within the same semantic frameworks concerning appearance. Moreover, when "we" in 53:2 vividly recall "our" judgment of "his" past, this might be related to the revelation "we" (do not) perceive in 53:1 (זְרוֹעַ יְהוָה עַל־מִי נִגְלָתָה "and the arm of YHWH – to whom is it revealed?"). In 53:2, the relation to YHWH is pushed into the background. An "I"/"you" relation is marked by the detached prep. עָלֶיךָ "at you" in 52:14, in 52:15 either "him" or YHWH is present through עָלָיו "at him", and in 53:2, לְפָנָיו "before him" might refer to YHWH.

3.10.6. Isa. 53:3

נִבְזֶה וַחֲדַל אִישִׁים אִישׁ מַכְאֹבוֹת וִידוּעַ חֹלִי
וּכְמַסְתֵּר פָּנִים מִמֶּנּוּ נִבְזֶה וְלֹא חֲשַׁבְנֻהוּ׃

> He was despised and abandoned by men; a man with sicknesses and known with illness,
> and like one from whom men hide their faces; he was despised and we did not consider him.

Without a *waw* or other signs of connectedness, in 53:3 "his" fate is depicted by six nominal clauses related to isolation, to illness and to "his" surroundings. The last of these clauses is a repetition of the first, before the verse ends with its only verbal clause, conveying "our" judgment of "him".

In the first nominal clause, נִבְזֶה (pt. ni. 3ms of בזה "despise", "regard with contempt") "he was despised", "he" is the patient being despised and no agent is mentioned.

Then follows the nominal clause וַחֲדַל אִישִׁים (*waw*, adjective of חדל "cease", "withdraw", noun mpl of אִישׁ "man", "everyone", "fellow")[82]

---

[82] Pl אִישִׁים is a rare, but not unique form, see Ps. 14:14, Prov. 8:4. The common pl of אִישׁ is אֲנָשִׁים. Duhm, *Das Buch Jesaia*, p. 358, finds the sequence אִישִׁים אִישׁ ugly (*hässlich*) and accordingly emends the pl to אֲנָשִׁים. M. J. Dahood, "Phoenician Elements in Isaiah 52:13–53:12" in H. Goedicke (ed), *Near Eastern Studies in Honor of William Foxwell Albright* (Baltimore: Johns Hopkins, 1971) 66, explains אִישִׁים as a Phoenician element. L. Boadt, "Intentional Alliteration in Second Isaiah", *CBQ* 45 (1983) 362–363, suggests that אִישׁ אִישִׁים might be employed for its assonance.

"and abandoned by men", depicting not action, but the state of the desolation of "him". The copulative *waw* connects two coordinate situations, נִבְזֶה "he was despised" and חֲדַל אִישִׁים "abandoned by men", these are corresponding expressions for the environments' reactions to the solitary and socially excluded one; the one cut off from any company with his fellows.

The third nominal clause, אִישׁ מַכְאֹבוֹת (noun ms cstr. of אִישׁ "man", "each one", "fellow", noun fpl abs. of מַכְאֹב "sickness", "pain", "trouble", "distress")[83] "a man with sicknesses", depicts "him" as a sick man. אִישׁ (sg) contrasts with אִישִׁים (pl) in the preceding clause.

The fourth nominal clause, וִידוּעַ חֹלִי (pt. pass. qal of יָדַע "know", noun ms חֹלִי "illness", "wound", "disease")[84] "known with illness", is preceded by a copulative *waw* indicating a situation coordinate with the preceding one: "he" is familiar with illness. Both these nominal clauses concern state rather than action, i.e. "his" bodily weakness and "his" suffering from illness.

The fifth nominal clause begins with a conjunctive *waw* and is followed by a particle, כְּ "like", which introduces a comparison or correspondence and heads מַסְתֵּר (noun ms) "hiding". The plural of the

---

[83] 1QIsaᵇ renders mpl in 53:3. This might be due to מַכְאֹבֵינוּ (mpl) "our sicknesses" in 53:4. Apart from Isa. 53:3, in the Hebrew Bible מַכְאֹב occurs in ms or pl, see 5.11.1. n. 115. See also 3.10.7. n. 89.

[84] Driver, "Linguistic and Textual Problems", p. 48, and "Isaiah 52:13–53:12", p. 93, gives חדל in Isa. 53:3 an *active* sense, i.e. the servant forsakes the company of men. He asks whether an Arab. root translated "refrain from" is cognate with the Hebrew root (p. 93). He translates the expression in 53:3 as "despised and aloof of men". He is supported by D. W. Thomas, "Some Observations on the Hebrew Root [חדל]" (VTSup, 6; Leiden: E. J. Brill, 1957) 8–16, and Clines, *I, He, We and They*, p. 16. Cf. Clines' reading of the following וּכְמַסְתֵּר פָּנִים מִמֶּנּוּ, which is treated in Appendix 3.
With references to 1 Sam. 2:5, Job 14:6 and Prov. 19:27, 23:4, P. J. Calderone, "HDL-II in Poetic Texts", *CBQ* 23 (1961) 451–460, suggests a חדל II "to be fat", "full", or by extension "to be prosperous" on the basis of an Arab. cognate. P. J. Calderone, "Supplementary Note on HDL-II", *CBQ* 24 (1962) 412–419, also notes a few instances of חדלה "abstained from", "neglected", "deserted", which has been generally accepted for practically all forms of חדל. Concerning חָדֵל in Isa 53:3, he states: "[A]n adjective of the stative verb 'to be fat', can semantically be predicated in an intellectual sense as 'stupid', and religiously as 'senseless', 'gross', perhaps even 'sinful'." He translates נִבְזֶה וַחֲדַל אִישִׁים "he was despised, as the most senseless of men", and explains the parallelism in v. 3a as:

> between the mental sorrow in the first colon and physical pain in the second; and just as the contempt is accompanied by the reason, so is the suffering explained, by the servant's experience of infirmity. If [חדל] indeed means "stupid", it points up a sharp contrast with the corresponding word in the next colon, [ידע] "knowing" (p. 419).

object, פָּנִים "faces", implies a plural reading of the impersonal noun phrase כְּמַסְתֵּר, i.e. "like hiding one's faces". This is followed by the prep. phrase מִמֶּנּוּ (disjunctive prep. מִן "from", "away from", 3ms suff.) "from him", which forcefully depicts how "he" is cut off from any human fellowship. אִישִׁים "men" in the second clause might function as the subject of this impersonal expression.[85]

The sixth and last nominal clause נִבְזֶה (pt. ni. of בזה) "despised" is a repetition of the first clause. Finally, the whole verse concludes with the verbal clause וְלֹא חֲשַׁבְנֻהוּ (waw, negation לֹא "not", perf. qal 1cpl of חשב "consider", "think", "esteem", "account", "value", "regard", 3ms object suff.) "and we did not consider him". "We" are the subject and agent and "he" is the object and patient. The predicate is a verb of perception and exhibits both fientive and stative characteristics. It is bound up with an object, but no action passes over from agent to goal. "Our" judgment of "him" is temporally and causatively related to the preceding depictions of "his fate", as illness and isolation made "us" not recognise "him" in any way. The contrast between "us" and "him" is made as "he" is deprived of dignity and fellowship with "us".

In 53:3, "his" fate is elusively and tersely depicted, with disdain, illness, shame, desolation and dissociation running together. Characteristic of the nominal clauses is that "his" state rather than action is depicted. "He" is presented as אִישׁ "a man" and contrasted with those who despise "him", called אִישִׁים "men" and "we" through suff. The social and physical devaluation is underlined by "our" final judgment of "him": וְלֹא חֲשַׁבְנֻהוּ "and we did not consider him".

"Our" depiction and judgment of "him" in 53:3 echo the disapproval of "him" by רַבִּים "many" in 52:14, and "our" disregard of "him" in 53:2. In 52:14 רַבִּים "many" are appalled עָלֶיךָ "at you" due to "his" disfigurement. In 53:2, "he" is portrayed as a man without beauty or respect, and in 53:3 "he" is despised, assailed by sickness and disregarded by "us". As in 52:14 and 53:2, in 53:3 the prominent relation is the contrasting relationship between the solitary "he" (sg) and "they"/"we" (pl). In all events, "his" illnesses and disgusting appearance isolated "him" from all affairs; "he" was entirely insignificant.

---

[85] On the phrase כְּמַסְתֵּר פָּנִים מִמֶּנּוּ in 53:3, see Appendix 3.

3.10.7. *Isa. 53:4*

אָכֵן חֳלָיֵנוּ הוּא נָשָׂא וּמַכְאֹבֵינוּ סְבָלָם
וַאֲנַחְנוּ חֲשַׁבְנֻהוּ נָגוּעַ מֻכֵּה אֱלֹהִים וּמְעֻנֶּה:

Yet surely he bore our illnesses and carried our sicknesses,
whereas we accounted him stricken, smitten by God and humiliated.

The demonstrative adverb, אָכֵן "yet surely", reverses the preceding verse.[86] This is followed by two verbal clauses in which a relation between the subject "he" and the speaking object "we" concerns illness and the past. The second clause echoes the first, but with some variations in syntax and morphology. A copulative *waw* then connects to a verbal clause with three pt. phrases as its objects. In the predicate, the subject "we" appears to be judging the preceding 53:3: while in 53:4a "we" are talking about a present judgment of a past, in 53:4b "we" present "our" previous judgment of a past. In 53:4a the subject, the voiceless הוּא "he", is accented, and in 53:4b the speaking "we" are the subject thrown into relief by the pronoun אֲנַחְנוּ "we".

After the contrasting and confirming אָכֵן "yet surely", the first clause continues with the object חֳלָיֵנוּ (noun mpl of חֹלִי "illness", "wound", "disease", 1cpl poss. suff.) "our illnesses". Then the subject is expressed by an independent pronoun הוּא "he" and the predicate נָשָׂא (perf. qal 3ms of נשׂא "bear", "carry") "he bore", which may exhibit both fientive and stative characteristics, i.e. related to both action and state. The predicate is modified by the object, as the construction נָשָׂא חֹלִי "bear illness" expresses that "he was ill". Thus, even though the predicate is bound up with an object, no action passes over from agent to goal. "He" did not perform an action, but suffered illnesses as a state.

---

[86] T. Muraoka, *Emphatic Words and Structures in the Hebrew Bible* (Jerusalem: Magnes Press, 1985) 132–133: "The particle [אָכֵן] indicates a turning-point in [the] thought of the speaker and expresses the reality in opposition to his previous doubt or false presupposition." Waltke and O'Connor, *Introduction to Biblical Hebrew Syntax*, § 39.3.5d, classify אָכֵן as a restrictive adverb which reverses or restricts what immediately precedes it. Moreover, "אָכֵן has a general emphatic sense…, indicating 'a sudden recognition in contrast to what was theretofore assumed'". They interpret Isa. 53:3-4 as follows: "We did not esteem him, *but* [we were wrong because] he carried our weakness", their italics. S. A. Geller, "Cleft Sentences with Pleonastic Pronoun: A Syntactic Construction of Biblical Hebrew and Some of its Literary Uses", *JANES* 20 (1991) 30, claims that "[t]he contrast is between the former opinion of the speakers that the Suffering Servant's maladies were his own burden, just cause for shunning him, and their current recognition that his suffering were vicarious atonement for *their* sins" (his italics).

But since the predicate נָשָׂא "bear" is still connected with an object, it might be called "quasi-fientive".[87] By 1cpl suff. of the object חֳלָיֵנוּ "our illnesses", a similar state of "us" is depicted: "we" were also ill. Thus, חֳלָיֵנוּ הוּא נָשָׂא "he bore our illnesses" expresses how both the subject "he" and the object "we" are ill. In the relation between הוּא "he" and חֳלָיֵנוּ "our illnesses", an enunciative distancing and "impersonalisation" appear. Simultaneously, an identification appears between "him" and "us", but an identification which is conveyed through different accentuations.[88]

The second clause begins with the object מַכְאֹבֵינוּ (noun mpl of מַכְאֹב "sickness", "pain", "trouble", "distress", 1cpl suff.) "our sicknesses",[89] preceded by a *waw*. Then follows the predicate סְבָלָם (perf. qal of סבל "carry", "bear", 3mpl suff.) "he carried them". The predicate is bound up with the subject "he" and may exhibit both fientive and stative characteristics. Modified by the object, the predicate is related to suffering, as the phrase וּמַכְאֹבֵינוּ סְבָלָם "and he carried our sicknesses" expresses that "he" suffered illnesses. Thus, even though the predicate סבל "carry" is bound up with an object, no action passes over from agent to goal. But since the verb is still connected with an object, it might be called "quasi-fientive" (cf. חֳלָיֵנוּ הוּא נָשָׂא "he bore our ill-

---

[87] For this explanation of "quasi-fientive", see 3.10.5. n. 80. The expression חֳלָיֵנוּ הוּא נָשָׂא "he bore our illnesses" in Isa. 53:4 has most often been read as fientive, i.e. expressing an action passing over from agent to goal: "he" bore instead of or on behalf of "us" (cf. the parallel phrase וּמַכְאֹבֵינוּ סְבָלָם "and he carried our sicknesses"). A common translation is also "he takes away", see e.g. Oswalt, *The Book of Isaiah: Chapters 40–66*, p. 386: "The Servant is not suffering *with* his people (however unjustly), but *for* them", his italics. Koole, *Isaiah III. Vol. 2*, p. 290, discusses whether נָשָׂא can be rendered as "to take away" as well as "to carry": "The word has in fact this meaning in 40:24; 41:16, and in v. 5b, which correspond to this line, this aspect clearly emerges and is then elaborated in vv. 11f, when the Servant not only 'bears' and 'carries' the consequences of sin and guilt but also this guilt itself." Koole claims that as in Num 14:33 and Lam. 5:7, Isa. 53:4 "seems to be talking about the misery of the Servant, who could represent the younger, more devout generation of the exiles." Ultimately, however, Koole rejects this comparison because the servant suffers voluntarily and without sin (vv. 7; 9). On the expression נָשָׂא חֳלִי "bear illness", see 5.11.1. n. 117. On the parallel נָשָׂא חֵטְא "bear sin" in Isa. 53:12, cf. 3.10.15. n. 154.

[88] Rosenbaum, *Word-Order Variation in Isaiah 40–55*, pp. 25; 94–96, seeks to eliminate the use of the "specious term 'emphasis'" as an explanation for variations in word-order. By a pragmatic-functional approach, he explains these constituents in terms of their variety of functions rather than forcing them to all answer to the same name. Concerning Isa. 53:4, he comments: "The combination of the word-order (OV) and [הוּא] focuses attention on the *our-ness* and points to the true cause of the Servant's suffering" (p. 83, his italics).

[89] On מַכְאֹב, see 3.10.6. n. 83 and 5.11.1. n. 115.

nesses" above). וּמַכְאֹבֵינוּ סְבָלָם "and he carried our sicknesses" is an expression of being ill, with both the subject and object related to sicknesses by the predicate סְבָלָם "he carried them", i.e. "he suffered sickness" and the suff. of the object, מַכְאֹבֵינוּ "our sicknesses", i.e. "we" are sick. Again, both "his" and "our" illnesses are expressed. The preceding copulative *waw* indicates two situations coordinate with each other. The opening אָכֵן "yet surely" might serve both clauses. While the first clause continues directly with the object, the second clause is introduced by a *waw* and then continues with the object. In both clauses, the object precedes the predicate syntactically. In the first clause, the subject also precedes the predicate in the independent pronoun הוּא "he". In the second clause, the object is doubly expressed: both in the noun phrase preceding the predicate (מַכְאֹבֵינוּ "our sicknesses") and in the suff. of the predicate (סְבָלָם "he carried them"). Thus, while the first clause expresses the subject doubly, the second clause expresses the object twice.[90] The second clause confirms the first, but in so doing it encourages a second interpretation, with the two clauses signifying slightly different or similar views of the "same" situation: "he bore our illnesses and carried our sicknesses".

Introduced by אָכֵן "yet surely" in 53:4a, "our" preceding portrait of "him" is reversed or restricted by a contrast ("yet", "but") and simultaneously explained ("surely", "truly", "indeed"). In 53:3, "he" is described as וִידוּעַ חֹלִי "known with illness" and in 53:4a חֳלָיֵנוּ הוּא נָשָׂא "he bore our illnesses". In v. 3 חֹלִי "illness" occurs in ms, and in v. 4a in mpl (with suff.; חֳלָיֵנוּ "our illnesses"). Moreover, in v. 3 "he" is depicted as אִישׁ מַכְאֹבוֹת "a man with sicknesses" and in v. 4a מַכְאֹבֵינוּ סְבָלָם "he carried our sicknesses". In v. 3 מַכְאֹב "sicknesses" occur in fpl, and in v. 4a in mpl. The nouns חֹלִי "illness" and מַכְאֹב "sickness" are chiastically repeated in vv. 3–4a, i.e. אִישׁ מַכְאֹבוֹת וִידוּעַ חֹלִי "a man with sicknesses and known with illness" (v. 3), and חֳלָיֵנוּ הוּא נָשָׂא וּמַכְאֹבֵינוּ סְבָלָם "he bore our illnesses and carried our sicknesses" (v. 4a).[91] In addition to these morphological contrasts of both gender and number, a change of perspective occurs between v. 3 and v. 4a. In 53:(2–)3, "we" distance "ourselves" from "him" by judging "him"

---

[90] In the first clause the subject is expressed by the independent personal pronoun and the predicate, whereas in the second clause the object is expressed by the independent object and the suff. of the predicate.

[91] On the word pair חֳלָיֵנוּ "our illnesses" and מַכְאֹבֵינוּ "our sicknesses", see Barré, "Textual and Rhetorical-Critical Observations on the Last Servant Song", p. 4.

to be contemptible. After "our" depiction of the illnesses which "he" carried, a final and concluding judgment is offered: וְלֹא חֲשַׁבְנֻהוּ "and we did not consider him". Whereas "his" illnesses are depicted by "us" in v. 3, in v. 4 "our" own participation is included in the diagnosis of "his" fate by the addition of 1cpl suff. of חֳלָיֵנוּ "our illnesses" and מַכְאֹבֵינוּ "our sicknesses". Thus, "our" diagnosis becomes interwoven with "his", expressing how "his" aforementioned illnesses also belong to "us". The predicates of v. 4a might be described as present perf., i.e. the speaking "we" are talking about a present depiction and explanation of a past.[92] Just as "he" was ill in the past (cf. v. 3), so too were "we". Simultaneously, a contrast between "him" and "us" is upheld through an enunciative distancing and "impersonalisation" in the relation between the subject "he" (who suffered illnesses) and object "we" (i.e. חֳלָיֵנוּ "our illnesses" and מַכְאֹבֵינוּ "our sicknesses"). In a crossing of syntactic frameworks illness becomes a metaphor for a relation between "him" and "us".

After "our" depiction and explanation of the relationship between "his" and "our" fate, "our" judgment of "him" follows with interruptive force in 53:4b. An introductory copulative *waw* connects to a verbal clause with three pt. phrases as its objects. In addition to the *waw*, "our" acknowledgement is expressed through a contrast in pronouns between v. 4a and v. 4b: the voiceless subject "he" is accented by the pronoun הוּא "he" in v. 4a, against which the speaking subject "we" is thrown into relief by the pronoun אֲנַחְנוּ "we" in v. 4b. The situation shifts from description and explanation to judgment through a contrast which is developed between "him" and "us" by the verbs of v. 4b. In the predicate of this clause, חֲשַׁבְנֻהוּ (perf. qal 1cpl of חשׁב "account", "think", "esteem", "value", "regard", "consider", 3ms suff.) "we accounted him", "we" are the subject and "he" the object.[93] The predicate is followed by yet another object conveyed as a subordinate clause composed of three pt. phrases with "him" as the implied subject:

---

[92] Waltke and O'Connor, *An Introduction to Biblical Hebrew Syntax*, § 30.5.2b: "The *present perf.* signifies a resulting perf. state in present time relative to the speaker" (their italics), that is, "he bore our illnesses".

[93] As a verb of perception, חֲשַׁבְנֻהוּ "we accounted him" exhibits both fientive and stative characteristics. Even though it is bound with an object, "he", no action passes over from the agent to the goal, i.e. it is "quasi-fientive", cf. 3.10.5. n. 80. The predicate governs a double accusative in which the second expresses the judgment which the speaking "we" give of the first, "him", cf. GKC §117h.ii.

In the first pt. phrase, נָגוּעַ (pt. pass. qal ms of נגע "stricken", "plagued", "touched"), "he" is the patient of the verbal action, and no agent is mentioned: "he (was) stricken".

In the second pt. phrase, מֻכֵּה אֱלֹהִים (pt. ho. ms of נכה "smitten", "stricken", noun אֱלֹהִים "God"), "God" is the implied agent of an external pass. causative, and "he" is the patient: "he (was) smitten by God".

The third and final pt. phrase וּמְעֻנֶּה (waw, pt. pu. ms of ענה "humiliate", "degrade", "humble") is pass. and stative, in which "he" is the receiver and no agent is mentioned: "he (was) humiliated". This third phrase of "our" explanation of "his" illnesses is the only one which is connected by a copulative waw.

All three phrases are composed of pt. pass. (qal, ho., pu. respectively). Although אֱלֹהִים "God" is grammatically connected with the second phrase only, he might be related to all three expressions in terms of implied agency. With reference to a past state of affairs, the participles describe circumstances accompanying the principle event, i.e. "our" account of "him". In this threefold juxtaposition, the severity of "his" sufferings is made clear by piling one phrase upon another. By "our" judgment of "him", the ill man's sufferings are both explained and made comprehensible for "us": "his" illnesses are a punishment from YHWH. "Our" explanation of "his" situation in 53:4b is different from the one given in 53:4a. V. 4a might be described as present perf., i.e. the speaking "we" are talking about a *present* judgment of a *past*. In this present perf., the diagnosis is presented in terms of an identification between "his" and "our" illnesses: אָכֵן חֳלָיֵנוּ הוּא נָשָׂא... "Yet surely he bore our illnesses..." etc. In v. 4b, וַאֲנַחְנוּ חֲשַׁבְנֻהוּ "whereas we accounted him" might signify a past perf., i.e. the speaking "we" are talking about their *past* judgment of a *past*.[94] Here "we" explain "our" (previous) consideration of "him": that it was Elohim that struck, smote and humiliated "him". Not only do "we" regard "him" as one laden and bowed down because of the burden of sicknesses, but the illnesses "he" carried are also God's punishment in the past. The copulative waw has a bearing on both the terseness of the

---

[94] Waltke and O'Connor, *An Introduction to Biblical Hebrew Syntax*, § 30.5.2b: "The *past perf.* (*pluperf.*) signifies a resulting state in time that is past relative to the speaker", that is, "he had been stricken" (their italics).

text and its connectedness, and is rendered as adversative ("whereas", "while").

In addition to the contrast between the subject הוא "he" of 53:4a and the subject אֲנַחְנוּ "we" of 53:4b, "we" appear in the objects of v. 4a (חֳלָיֵנוּ "our illnesses" and מַכְאֹבֵינוּ "our sicknesses") and "he" in the objects of v. 4b (the pt. phrases). The focused word order, in which the contrast between הוא "he" and אֲנַחְנוּ "we" might express a change of perspective, reveals a dissymmetry between the identification of "him" and "us" in v. 4a and a renewed polarisation of the relation between "him" and "us" in v. 4b. In the relation between "him" and "us" in v. 4a, an enunciative distancing and "impersonalisation" appear within an identification, with the speaking "we" reflecting upon the relation between "his" and "our" illnesses in the past. Whereas in v. 4a both "he" and "we" were ill, in "our" past judgment of "him" in v. 4b the focus is placed on the punishment of "him" only. Whereas in v. 4a both "his" and "our" illnesses are described, in v. 4b only "his" fate is explained: "he" was stricken by God. A dissonance appears, but in a crossing of syntactic frameworks the contrast between "him" and "us" might not be brought so sharply into focus: in v. 4a, an identification between "him" and "us" is expressed in a present perf., with both subject and object ill, whereas in the past perf. of v. 4b a contrast appears, with the subject "we" judging "him" as object, and "we" explain "his" sufferings as YHWH's striking of him.

In both 52:14–15 and 53:2–3, a contrast between "him" (sg) and "many"/"we" (pl) is prominent. Both in the "I" speech in 52:14 and in the "we" speech in 53:2–3, the disdain expressed towards "you"/"him" is due to "his" disfigurement. His solitary fate in 53:2–3 was to be isolated and ill, ashamed and disgraced. Whereas in 53:3 "we" appear as an agent judging "him", drawing a contrast in the relationship between "him" and "us", in 53:4a this contrast vanishes, as their common fate – illness – is revealed. "He" is the subject in both instances, whereas "we" are related to the objects חֳלָיֵנוּ "our illnesses" and מַכְאֹבֵינוּ "our sicknesses". A particular connection is expressed between the afflictions of "him" in 53:2–3 and "our" experience of these same illnesses in 53:4a. After "he" was judged at a distance in 53:3 and then seen as deeply involved in "our" fate too in 53:4a, in 53:4b "we" again distance "ourselves" from "him", as "his" illnesses are explained as punishment from YHWH.

3.10.8. *Isa. 53:5*

וְהוּא מְחֹלָל מִפְּשָׁעֵנוּ מְדֻכָּא מֵעֲוֹנֹתֵינוּ
מוּסַר שְׁלוֹמֵנוּ עָלָיו וּבַחֲבֻרָתוֹ נִרְפָּא־לָנוּ:

But he was wounded because of our transgressions and injured because
of our iniquities;
chastisement was upon him for our healing and by his wound is recovery for us.

53:5 is connected to 53:4 by a *waw* indicating contrast. This *waw* is
followed by two nominal clauses depicting "his" illnesses and "our"
explanation of them. In the explanation, a causal relation is drawn
between "his" wounds and "our" transgressions. After dwelling upon
the past illnesses and sins, a restitution is pronounced: by one nominal and one verbal clause the illnesses are depicted as chastisement of
"him" for "our" rehabilitation. As suff. of the prep. phrases, "we" are
still the speaking voice.

The subject of 53:5a, וְהוּא (*waw*, independent personal pronoun 3ms) "he", is connected with the predicate מְחֹלָל (pt. pu. ms
of חלל "wound", "pierce") "he (was) wounded".[95] The pt. expresses
a state of affairs or circumstances rather than action. The cause or
means of the wounding of "him" is connected with the prep. phrase
מִפְּשָׁעֵנוּ (prep. מִן "because of", "for", noun mpl of פֶּשַׁע "transgression", "sin", "crime", "rebellion", "guilt", 1cpl suff.) "because of our
transgressions".[96] The prep. מִן "because of" signifies a causal relation
between the wounding of "him" and "us": "his" wounding is explained
as "because of our transgressions".[97] In the relation between הוּא מְחֹלָל

---

[95] מְחֹלָל is most often taken to be חלל II "pierce", cf. Isa. 51:9, supported by, among
others, the parallel מְדֻכָּא in v. 5b. For a brief presentation of different alternatives, see
Koole, *Isaiah III. Vol. 2*, p. 293. Cf. further discussion in 53:10, cf. 3.10.13. n. 132.

[96] Dahood, "Phoenician Elements in Isaiah 52:13–53:12", p. 68, explains MT pl.
פְּשָׁעֵנוּ as a *scriptio defectiva*, where 1QIsaᵃ and 1QIsaᵇ supply the *mater lectionis* י,
reading pl פְּשָׁעֵינוּ, cf. the following עֲוֹנֹתֵינוּ.

[97] Waltke and O'Connor, *An Introduction to Biblical Hebrew Syntax*, § 11.2.11,
show that the prep. מִן might have separative, causal and privative functions. Most
scholars take מִן in 53:5 to have a causal function (cf. Pss. 38:19, 107:17 and Lam. 4:14,
where it occurs in connection with sin), but with different accentuations.

It is frequently assumed that מִן here denotes a kind of exchange or vicariousness,
see for instance, Hermisson, "Das vierte Gottesknechtlied im deuterojesajanischen
Kontext", p. 7 (ET p. 25) and Janowski, "Er Trug unsere Sünden", p. 39 (ET p. 64),
who interpret the innocent servant as brought down and his opponents are freed of
their guilt: "he was wounded for/because of our transgressions", as opposed to the
psalms of lament in which the innocent sufferer is saved and his enemies must be
brought down on account of their guilt.

"he (was) wounded" and פְּשָׁעֵנוּ "our transgressions", the punishment is explained in terms of an identification between "him" and "us", with various accentuations, with sin, guilt and punishment becoming inseparable. This is framed by an enunciative distancing, where "he" is wounded and "we" have committed sin.[98]

Then follows yet another predicate, מְדֻכָּא (pt. pu. ms of דכא "injure", "crush")[99] "he (was) injured", also expressing a state of affairs or circumstances. The cause or means of the injury of "him" is further connected with the prep. phrase מֵעֲוֹנֹתֵינוּ (prep. מִן "because of", "for", noun mpl of עָוֹן "iniquity", "sin", "guilt", 1cpl suff.) "because of our iniquities". In the prep. מִן "because of", a causal relationship between the injury of "him" and "us" appears: "his" injury is explained as "because of our iniquities". Again, an identification through pun-

---

Orlinsky, *The So-Called "Servant of the Lord" and "Suffering Servant" in Second Isaiah*, pp. 57–58, argues that if a sense of vicariousness were intended it would be expressed not by מִן but by בְּ, which he has further designated "the *beth* of exchange". Whybray, *Thanksgiving for a Liberated Prophet*, pp. 61–62, claims that מִן in 53:5 (twice); 8 is used in the sense of "in consequence of", "as the result of". By this, the servant "did not suffer in the place of others to allow them to escape from the consequences of their sin". Cf. 2.3.8.3. and 3.10.17.2.

Oswalt, *The Book of Isaiah: Chapters 40–66*, p. 388, claims that a vicarious suffering is implied not by 53:5a, but by v. 5b. He argues that taken alone, v. 5a could express "only sharing in result". But in the context of v. 5b, "[w]hat the servant does in bearing the undeserved results of his people's sin brings about positive results for the people. He is not merely participating in their suffering, he is bearing it away for them so that they may not labor under its effects anymore…"

The prep. מִן has also been given a separative function. L. Watermann, "The Martyred Servant Motif of Is. 53", *JBL* 56 (1937) 28, claims that the suffering of the servant comes "from", that is, by "our" sinful treatment of him. Against this, Koole, *Isaiah III. Vol. 2*, p. 294, argues that if "we" are the logical subject, the instrumental prep. בְּ would have been used instead of מִן. Cf. 3.10.8. n. 104 about *beth pretii* and *beth instrumenti*.

[98] Cf. "you"/"he" in 52:14 and "we"/"he" in 53:4.

[99] Muilenburg, "The Book of Isaiah: Chapters 40–66", pp. 622; 627, translates "bruised" for both 53:5 and v. 10, while Driver, "Isaiah 52:13–53:12", p. 103, does so only for v. 5. Dahood, "Phoenician Elements in Isaiah 52:13–53:12", p. 71, reads "crushed" in both 53:5 and v. 10, cf. R. J. Clifford, *Fair Spoken and Persuading: An Interpretation of Second Isaiah* (Theological Inquieries; New York: Paulist Press, 1984) 174, Hermisson, "Das vierte Gottesknechtlied im deuterojesajanischen Kontext", pp. 7–8 (ET pp. 26–27), Bergey, "The Rhetorical Role of Reiteration in the Suffering Servant Poem", pp. 183; 185, Oswalt, *The Book of Isaiah: Chapters 40–66*, pp. 384; 398, Koole, *Isaiah III. Vol. 2*, pp. 292; 317; 319, Blenkinsopp, *Isaiah 40–55*, pp. 345–346; 348z ("in spite of numerous efforts to construe or emend v 10, it remains obscure and the original sense almost certainly irretrievable; any translation will be tentative"), Barré, "Textual and Rhetorical-Critical Observations on the Last Servant Song", p. 26. LXX renders μεμαλάκισται as "to crush" in v. 5, but not in v. 10. Cf. on v. 10 in 3.10.13. n. 131.

ishment which has different accentuations appears: "he" is injured, whereas the iniquities belong to "us".

The introductory *waw* has a bearing on both the terseness and the connectedness of the text, but its relationship to the adjacent and preceding clauses is left unspecified. In the two verbless clauses of 53:5a, the participles and the prep. phrases are in parallel and express a relationship between "our" sins and "his" illnesses. The participles work as circumstantial clauses and denote an action simultaneous to that of the main clause (in 53:4b).[100] The copulative *waw* might be disjunctive, emphasising a contrast to v. 4b, in which "our" earlier reflection on "his" fate is offered by a past perf.: "we" regarded "him" as laden and bowed down with the burden of "his" sicknesses due to God's smiting, wrath and will. In this diagnosis, "his" fate is distinguished from "ours". The introductory *waw* in 53:5 opposes this notion that "his" fate contrasts with "ours", as "he was wounded because of our transgressions…" (v. 5a). Similarity and difference appear through the various accentuations of the diagnoses: "he" is ill, "we" are ill, "we" (and "he"?) have sinned, and "he" (and "we"?) is/are punished (more about this below).

In addition to the contrast between "him" and "us" in 53:4a and v. 4b, a continuation might be seen in the relationship between "him" and "us" in v. 5a and v. 4a. In v. 4a the diagnosis is made in present perf., an identification between "his" and "our" illnesses is presented, and no explanation is given for why this is so. "We" reflect upon the relation between "his" and "our" illnesses in the past: "Yet surely he bore our illnesses…". In v. 4a, both "he" and "we" are depicted as having been ill, and in v. 5a this illness is explained as due to sin. In v. 5a, when "his" wounds are explained as due to "our" sins, an identification emerges between "him" and "us", but with different accentuations: …וְהוּא מְחֹלָל מִפְּשָׁעֵנוּ "but he was wounded because of our

---

[100] GKC §141e, describes a *waw* preceding noun clauses, i.e. circumstantial clauses, as indicating contemporaneity with the principal clause, but in some instances as also indicating a contradictory fact. Whereas the main clause in 53:4 has הוּא with perf.: חֳלָיֵנוּ הוּא נָשָׂא "he bore our illnesses", the circumstantial clause of 53:5 has הוּא with pt.: וְהוּא מְחֹלָל "but he was wounded". Clines, *I, He, We and They*, p. 12, explains: "And yet – they were our sufferings that weighed on him; our pains were the burden he bore. While we – we accounted him smitten by God, struck down by God, humiliated by God!" He comments: "The force of vv. 4–5 lies entirely in the contrast between what 'we' *believed* was the source of his suffering (God) and what was in fact its source ('our sins'); I have repeated the phrase 'by God' with each of the participles in order to emphasise that contrast" (p. 17, his italics).

transgressions..." The punishment is depicted as corporal and relational and the 1cpl suff. expresses "our" responsibility.

Without any *waw* or other signs of connectedness, 53:5b offers two explanations for the punishment of "him". These are conveyed through one nominal and one verbal clause. In the first nominal clause, the subject מוּסַר (noun ms "chastisement", "discipline", "correction", "punishment") is related to the prep. phrase עָלָיו (prep. עַל "upon", "over", 3ms suff.), expressing how "he" was burdened: "chastisement was upon him". Then follows the object שְׁלוֹמֵנוּ (noun ms cstr. of שָׁלוֹם "healing", "completeness", "soundness", "welfare", "peace", "safety", 1cpl suff.), expressing "our" relief: "our healing". The noun phrases שְׁלוֹמֵנוּ "our healing" and מוּסַר עָלָיו "chastisement (was) upon him" modify each other as regards both temporality and causality.[101] In the phrase מוּסַר עָלָיו "chastisement was upon him", the focus is placed on "his" past humiliation, whereas the phrase שְׁלוֹמֵנוּ "our healing" concerns "our" future restitution. A causal relationship appears between the two phrases, expressing how punishment of "him" brought healing to "us". In the relation between שְׁלוֹמֵנוּ "our healing" and מוּסַר עָלָיו "chastisement upon him", שְׁלוֹמֵנוּ "our healing" might concern both restitution of illness and reconciliation as opposed to sin.

The second clause of v. 5b, which is introduced by a copulative *waw*, is a verbal clause composed of the prep. phrase וּבַחֲבֻרָתוֹ (*waw*, prep. בְּ "by", definite article, noun fs cstr. of חֲבֻרָה "wound", "stripe", "blow", "stroke", 3ms suff.) "by his wound",[102] and the verbal phrase נִרְפָּא (perf. ni. 3ms of רפא "recover", "heal", "relieve"), which is an impersonal, incomplete pass., with no agent indicated: "it is recovered". This

---

[101] Dahood, "Phoenician Elements in Isaiah 52:13–53:12", p. 68, reads the *hapax legomenon* expression מוּסַר שְׁלוֹמֵנוּ as a "legal metaphor": "The penalty we should have paid was upon him". GKC §128q, describes the expression מוּסַר שְׁלוֹמֵנוּ "the chastisement designed for our peace", as a use of the genitive that includes "statements of the purpose for which something is intended" (cf. Isa. 51:17). Waltke and O'Connor, *An Introduction to Biblical Hebrew Syntax*, § 9.5.2, explain it as a genitive of effect, where "the relationship of C [designating the construct, head or first term of the chain] and G [designating the genitive, absolute or second term] is a directly causal one, that is, roughly, C causes G: מוּסַר שְׁלוֹמֵנוּ the punishment *that brought us peace* " (their italics).

[102] Dahood, "Phoenician Elements in Isaiah 52:13–53:12", p. 68, comments on how sg חֲבֻרָתוֹ "his stripe" is often taken to have a collective meaning. However, he also refers to 1QIsaᵃ חברתים as a blend of noun sg and 3ms suffix- יו of noun pl. Thus, he regards MT חֲבֻרָתוֹ as due to *scriptio defectiva* and suggests a repointing to חֲבֻרֹתָיו "his stripes".

predicate, which is the only finite verb in the verse, involves a 3ms without an explicit agent, while the adjacent prep. phrase לָנוּ "to us" governs the subject and receiver of the pass. נִרְפָּא: "by his wounds is recovery for us".[103] The prep. phrase and the verbal phrase modify each other as regards both temporality and causality. In the prep. בְּ "by", a causal relationship emerges between "his" wounds and "our" healing: punishment of sin by chastisement of illness is followed by healing.[104] The focus in the expression בַּחֲבֻרָתוֹ "by his wound" is placed on "him" and "his" past, whereas נִרְפָּא־לָנוּ "it is recovery for us" concerns "us" in the present or future. In the two expressions explaining the treatment of "him", the first, מוּסַר שְׁלוֹמֵנוּ עָלָיו "chastisement was upon him for our healing" is ambiguous as to whether it concerns illness or sin, whereas the second, בַּחֲבֻרָתוֹ נִרְפָּא־לָנוּ "by his wound is recovery for us" expresses "his" diagnosis in terms of illness. Likewise, the adjacent depiction of the recovery, the first, שְׁלוֹמֵנוּ "our healing",

---

[103] Boadt, "Intentional Alliteration in Second Isaiah", p. 359, comments on the unusual use of prepositions in Isa. 53:5b-6a. According to him, נִרְפָּא־לָנוּ, that is, ni. רפא in impersonal use with לָנוּ working as dative is unattested elsewhere in Biblical Hebrew (he would have expected נִרְפָּאנוּ). Boadt explains the present form as due to an alliterative pattern in relation to כֻּלָּנוּ of v. 6. Waltke and O'Connor, *An Introduction to Biblical Hebrew Syntax*, § 11.2.10g: "The preposition *l* is used to make the *topic* of a verb of saying (…), a use not far removed from the *lamed* of specification" (their italics). Morphologically, נִרְפָּא־לָנוּ could also be imperf qal 1cpl "we heal ourselves", but not here.

[104] C. R. North, *The Second Isaiah: Introduction, Translation and Commentary to Chapter XL–LV* (Oxford: Clarendon, 1964) 240 (with reference to GKC § 119") and W. Zimmerli, "Zur Vorgeschichte von Jes. LIII" in W. Zimmerli (ed), *International Organization for the Study of the Old Testament: Congress Volume Rome 1986* (VTSup, 17; Leiden: E. J. Brill, 1969) 238–239, regard the prep. בְּ in v. 5 as *beth pretii* and seem to read this as equivalent to the three occurrences of מִן in vv. 5; 8. Waltke and O'Connor, *An Introduction to Biblical Hebrew Syntax*, § 11.2.5.d., explain *beth pretii* as a preposition that "can govern the material with which…the price is paid", cf. 1 Kgs 10:29. In Isa. 40:2, a punishment accepted for sin is described by *beth pretii*: לָקְחָה מִיַּד יְהוָה כִּפְלַיִם בְּכָל־חַטֹּאתֶיהָ "she has received from Yahweh's hand double *for* all her sins", their italics (cf. 5.12.5.).

Waltke and O'Connor (§ 11.2.10g) regard the prep. בְּ in 53:5b as instrumental with no agent specified, expressing a causal relationship similar to the prep. מִן "for" in v. 5a. Whybray, *Thanksgiving for a Liberated Prophet*, p. 149, n. 138:

> If בְּ here means "in exchange for", the whole phrase must be translated by "we were healed in exchange for his wounding", not "he was wounded in exchange for our healing", which would be the form analogous to that of the other phrases. There is no reason to suppose that this is *beth pretii*, which used in a metaphorical sense (which would be the case here) is much less frequent than *beth instrumenti* (his italics).

is more general than the next, נִרְפָּא־לָנוּ "recovery for us", which is closely related to illness.

Just as in 53:5a "he" was מְחֹלָל "wounded" for "our" transgressions and מְדֻכָּא "injured" for "our" iniquities, in v. 5b מוּסַר "chastisement" and חֲבֻרָה "wound" are related, and the punishment of "him" leads to "our" healing. Also, in the depiction of "our" recovery, "our" past illnesses are alluded to. In v. 5b, when "we" state that "we" are healed because of "his" wounds, a(n) (antithetical) causal relationship between the punishment of "him" and "our" healing is offered. In relation to the preceding verses, different focuses appear: the illness is connected with "him" and the sin and recovery with "us". In the relation between "his" sufferings and "our" healing in v. 5, a turning point is expressed. The recovery gained (for "us") by ("his") wound implies removal of punishment and suffering. Both phrases concern state rather than action, and no agent/patient relationship appears. "His" and "our" common fate is deepened. The healing gained (for "us") by the punishment (of "him") is to both "our" and "his" benefit: both "we" and "he" shall be healed. The depiction of "our" healing implies that "we" too have been hurt. Like "him", "we" shall suffer no more. In the explanation of "his" illness and "our" recovery, the relation between "him" and "us" is distorted. A possible centre of the text becomes more unreachable, and the relation between illness and recovery appears somewhere in-between: as "he" is ill and punished, "he" has also sinned and shall be healed. No agent is mentioned as regards either the wounding of "him" or the restitution of "us".

Following a depiction of "his" wound because of "our" sins in 53:4, in v. 5a a restoration appears. What began with "our" contemplation of "his" experience in v. 2 continues with a consideration of these same experiences as "our" own from v. 4 onwards. In v. 4a, the ill one's condition is diagnosed and explained: "he" carried "our" illnesses. In v. 4b this is explained as due to YHWH. However, in v. 5 a sudden transition from one state to another emerges: the illnesses are here explained as due to "our" sins and transgressions! By way of the introduction of sin, a new crisis appears – and a reconciliation: YHWH's punishment, which was partly introduced in v. 4, is further developed here. It provokes a new crisis which leads to restitution. Healing gained for "all" by wounds also implies the removal of punishment and suffering. "His" and "our" fates are deeply involved with each other, as everyone has been changed.

3.10.9. *Isa. 53:6*

כֻּלָּנוּ כַּצֹּאן תָּעִינוּ אִישׁ לְדַרְכּוֹ פָּנִינוּ
וַיהוָה הִפְגִּיעַ בּוֹ אֵת עֲוֹן כֻּלָּנוּ׃

All of us like sheep went astray; everyone turned his own way
and thus YHWH struck him by the iniquity of all of us.

53:6 opens and closes with the noun כֻּלָּנוּ "all of us", indicating "we" speech. The first כֻּלָּנוּ "all of us" works as the subject and is followed by a כְּ "like" particle of comparison and a simile of sheep going astray. Then a verbal clause explains the simile as illustrative of "our" delusion. Finally, a conjunctive verbal clause explains how YHWH struck "him" because of "our" iniquities.

The collective speaking subject כֻּלָּנוּ "all of us" in the main clause describe themselves with a simile where the particle of comparison כְּ "like" heads הַצֹּאן (definite article, noun fcoll. צֹאן "sheep", "small cattle", "flock") "sheep".[105] This subject of the subordinate comparative כְּ clause is followed by the predicate תָּעִינוּ (perf. qal 1mpl of תעה "go astray", "err") "we went astray". Both כֻּלָּנוּ "all of us" and צֹאן "sheep" are related to the predicate as subjects and agent as the ones going astray in delusion.

The simile is modified by an explanation, with אִישׁ (noun ms אִישׁ "man", "everyone", "fellow") as subject, לְדַרְכּוֹ (prep. לְ, noun ms cstr. of דֶּרֶךְ "way", "road", "manner", 3ms suff.) "his own way" as object and פָּנִינוּ (perf. qal 1cpl of פנה "turn") as predicate: "everyone turned his own way". The predicate is finite and transitive with אִישׁ "everyone" as its agent. While the simile calls attention to a similarity between seeming opposites from the human and animal spheres, it does not identify what makes them comparable, though both might be connected with delusion. That the simile does not have one single meaning establishes a gap between the signifiers and a final signified. The collective כֻּלָּנוּ "all of us" is split up by the singular אִישׁ "everyone", in which the unity of the flock is lost: everybody was breaking away and going their own way.

Then follows a clause which is introduced by a copulative *waw* marking a continuity by being temporally posterior to the preceding clause. In this final and concluding statement by "us", a confession

---

[105] The generic definite article in the כְּ comparison is left untranslated.

of "our" own transgressions is made: YHWH struck "him" due to עָוֹן
כֻּלָּנוּ "the iniquity of all of us". The predicate הִפְגִּיעַ בּוֹ (perf. external
hi. 3ms of פגע "strike", "cause to light upon", "encounter", "crush",
prep. בְּ, 3ms suff.) is fientive, with YHWH as the subject and agent
and "he" as the object and patient: "[YHWH] struck him by...",[106] i.e.
YHWH caused "him" to suffer. Related to the preceding clauses, this
works as an explanation of the consequences of "our" delusion (53:6a).
The explanation is developed by the additional phrase אֵת עֲוֺן כֻּלָּנוּ
(object marker אֵת, noun ms עָוֺן "iniquity", "sin", "guilt", noun כֻּלָּנוּ
"all of us") "the iniquity of all of us", where YHWH's punishment of
"him" is related to "our" sins.[107] In this reflection on "our" own guilt,
an awareness of having been chastised by God and prompted by "our"
own delusion is expressed.

YHWH's striking of "him" due to עֲוֺן כֻּלָּנוּ "the iniquity of all of us"
in 53:6 is a conflation of the two parts of v. 4, where "his" and "our"
illnesses are identical, and where "we accounted him stricken, smitten
by God and humiliated". "Our" assumptions in v. 4 that "his" illness
was due to YHWH's striking of "him" is additionally confirmed in v. 6.
But whereas the focus was on illness in v. 4, in v. 6 sin is emphasised.
A sheep motif is prominently used as an illustration of the delusion of
the people. This is a deepening and expansion of פְּשָׁעֵנוּ "our iniquities" and עֲוֺנֺתֵינוּ "our transgressions" in v. 5. Whereas YHWH was not
mentioned as the one striking in v. 5, he is in v. 6. V. 6 acts as a further
expression of the explanation of YHWH's punishment of "him" for
"our" sins. After the turning point to recovery in v. 5, v. 6 is again in
the past, presenting the very background which leads to a forthcoming
reversal of the situation: "our" delusion and YHWH's punishment of
"him". A chiastic relationship appears where "we"/"he" in v. 4 is the
"core", of which the details that follow are parts. On the basis of gram-

---

[106] For more about the verbal phrase הִפְגִּיעַ בּוֹ "he struck him" in 53:6, cf. פגע in
53:12 in 3.10.15. n. 155.

[107] Whybray, *Thanksgiving for a Liberated Prophet*, pp. 60–61, describes the expression הִפְגִּיעַ אֵת עֲוֺן as unique, and without any connection to sacrificial rites (due
to a word play with v. 12, more on this in 3.10.15. n. 155). Koole, *Isaiah III. Vol. 2*,
p. 298, argues that although this is correct,

> the verb *is* used for the avenger of blood who "comes towards" the guilty man
> and "strikes" him to pay of the debt, Num. 35:19... [and also that] the symbolism
> of the lamb (in v. 7) has been prepared for by the image of the flock (in v. 6a)
> and our line, too, probably operates on this level

his italics. Whybray again claims that what is concerned here is shared suffering, not
vicarious, cf. 3.10.17.2.f.

matical criteria, it is impossible to decide the outcome of the struggle between what is said about "him" and about and by "us".[108]

3.10.10. *Isa 53:7*

נִגַּשׂ וְהוּא נַעֲנֶה וְלֹא יִפְתַּח־פִּיו
כַּשֶּׂה לַטֶּבַח יוּבָל וּכְרָחֵל לִפְנֵי גֹזְזֶיהָ נֶאֱלָמָה וְלֹא יִפְתַּח פִּיו:

He was oppressed and he was humble(d), but he did not open his mouth,
like a sheep led to slaughtering, and like a ewe before those who shear her is dumb,
and he did not open his mouth.

With no *waw* or other signs of connectedness to the preceding verse, 53:7 opens with a verbal clause expressing how "he" was oppressed, followed by a nominal clause about how "he" was humble(d), and a verbal clause expressing how "he" reacted with silence. Then follows two כְּ "like" particles of comparison likening the preceding situations to similes of שֶׂה "sheep" and רָחֵל "ewe". Adjacent to these is a repetition of his silent reaction.

The verse opens with the pass., intransitive predicate נִגַּשׂ (perf. ni. 3ms of נגשׂ "oppress", "treat harshly") "he was oppressed", where the subject "he" is patient, the one suffering the effects of an action by an agent who is not mentioned, but assumed. A nominal clause then follows, which is related to the preceding by a *waw*. The subject is indicated by the independent 3ms personal pronoun הוּא "he", followed by the participle נַעֲנֶה (ni. ms of ענה "be humble", "afflict", "become bowed"), expressing a circumstance accompanying the preceding situation. Pt. ni. of the circumstantial clause might be rendered as either pass. or reflexive. If read as pass., "he" is the patient, i.e. burdened by humiliation brought upon him by an unnamed agent.[109] The *waw* then presents two situations as coordinate with each other: נִגַּשׂ וְהוּא נַעֲנֶה "he was oppressed and he was humbled". If read as reflexive, "he" is the agent, i.e. the double-status subject "he" humbles "himself", which

---

[108] In the narrative analysis in 4.8., the relation between "him" and "us" will be further developed in the trope of personification, in which a confusion appears between the personifier "he" and the personified "we".

[109] In 53:4, מְעֻנֶּה pt. pu. ms is rendered pass. as "humiliated".

means that the subject and the object are the same.[110] The *waw* might
then present the circumstantial clause as bringing out a situation of
the subject which is temporally and logically posterior or consequent
to the first one, i.e. the oppression of "him" was met with "humbleness": נִגַּשׂ וְהוּא נַעֲנֶה "he was oppressed and (so) he humbled himself", i.e. "he" made no resistance.

The third clause is verbal and connected to the preceding clause by
a *waw*. The predicate יִפְתַּח (imperf. qal 3ms of פתח "open") is transitive and modified by the preceding negation לֹא "not" and the adjacent
object פִּיו (noun ms cstr. of פֶּה "mouth", 3ms suff.) "he did not open
his mouth". The subordinate *waw* clause might be related to the first
clause(s) by way of a contrast working as a comment of opposition,
i.e. "although he was oppressed, he did not open his mouth", (lack
of) action being expressed with "him" as (pseudo-) agent. The verbal
clause might also be read as a consequence, working as an explanation,
i.e. "because he was oppressed, he did not open his mouth". Linked
with the preceding clauses, this imperf. also has a past meaning: "He
was oppressed, and he was humble(d)" וְלֹא יִפְתַּח פִּיו "but he did not
open his mouth".

The description of "him" as humbled and eventually humble is followed by two clauses which are both introduced by כְּ "like", working
as a subordinate conjunction and a particle of comparison. Each of
these particles heads a noun phrase, כַּשֶּׂה "like a sheep" and כְּרָחֵל "like
a ewe", which is followed by a prep. phrase, לַטֶּבַח "to slaughtering"
and לִפְנֵי גֹזְזֶיהָ "before those who shear her", and finally a predicate,
יוּבָל "led" and נֶאֱלָמָה "is dumb" respectively. The second simile is connected to the first by a copulative *waw*.

In the first simile, "he", in that "he" has been described as humbled
and humble is compared to שֶׂה (noun ms שֶׂה "sheep", "the one of a
flock") "a sheep".[111] In the predicate יוּבָל (imperf. ho. 3ms intransitive
of יבל "be led", "conducted"), the subject שֶׂה "sheep" is acted upon by
an unnamed agent. The action is modified by the prep. phrase לַטֶּבַח
(prep. לְ, definite article, noun ms טֶבַח "slaughtering", "slaughter")

---

[110] Waltke and O'Connor, *An Introduction to Biblical Hebrew Syntax*, § 37.6,
claim that when a pt. is used as a predicate of a verbless clause, the subject is usually
expressed by an independent pronoun. Also, the pt. circumstantial clause represents
a situation as continuing without interruption or progression but does not focus on
the inception of the situation (31.2c).

[111] This simile also includes a generic article.

"a sheep led to slaughtering". In the second simile, "his" situation is compared to that of רָחֵל (noun fs, no generic article) "a ewe". By the predicate נֶאֱלָמָה (perf. ni. fs intransitive, stative, pausa of אלם "be dumb"), the subject רָחֵל "ewe" is depicted as "dumb". "Her" state is modified by the prep. phrase לִפְנֵי גֹזְזֶיהָ (prep. לִפְנֵי "before", "in front of", "in the presence of", pt. pl of גזז "shear", 3fs suff.) "before those who shear her". In relation to the main clause, the כְּ clauses work as complex and relative clauses of simple co-ordination.[112] Whereas in the main clause "he" is נִגַּשׂ "oppressed" (patient), נַעֲנֶה "humble" (agent), וְלֹא יִפְתַּח־פִּיו "but/and did not open his mouth" (pseudo-agent), in the first simile שֶׂה "a sheep" is patient, and no agent is mentioned. Just as in the first simile, the passivity of שֶׂה "a sheep" when לַטֶּבַח יוּבָל "led to slaughtering" is focused on, in the second simile רָחֵל "a ewe" is לִפְנֵי גֹזְזֶיהָ נֶאֱלָמָה "dumb in front of those who shear her". The comparison with a sheep is framed in the imperfect (יוּבָל ho. "he is led") and that with a ewe in the perfect (נֶאֱלָמָה ni. "she is dumb"). The morphological contrast of these conjugations appears between equivalent situations, i.e. the passivity of שֶׂה "a sheep" and that of רָחֵל "a ewe".[113]

The comparisons of "his" situation in two similes are followed by a repetition of the last verbal clause from the first line, again connected by a waw.[114] Again (lack of) verbal action is expressed: "His" humble reaction, silence, is commented upon once more. The verb (לֹא) יִפְתַּח פִּיו is imperf. and related to a situation in the past. In the first line, the waw clause וְלֹא יִפְתַּח פִּיו "but he did not open his mouth" is temporally posterior and consequent to the preceding clause(s). The waw is subordinate to the depiction of "him" as being humbled, where "he" reacted by being humble, and so the waw is rendered "but". This last waw clause may, however, refer to a situation coordinate with the preceding ones by expanding on how "he", like שֶׂה "a sheep" and רָחֵל

---

[112] Clines, *I, He, We and They*, p. 17, takes נִגַּשׂ and נַעֲנֶה הוּא as pt., and יוּבָל and נֶאֱלָמָה as the principal verbs of the sentence. With reference to Dahood, "Phoenician Elements in Isaiah 52:13–53:12", p. 68, he also reads נֶאֱלָמָה as an archaic 3ms (cf. מָלְאָה צְבָאָהּ in Isa. 40:2, see 5.12.5.).

[113] For a possible sacrifice terminology in Isa. 53:7;10, see 5.13.1. n. 237 and Appendix 6.

[114] Duhm, *Das Buch Jesaia*, p. 361, suggests deleting וְלֹא יִפְתַּח־פִּיו in the second line: "Das zweite 'und öffnete seinen Mund nicht' ist zu streichen, weil übel nachhinkend, die Strophe überfüllend und hinter [נֶאֱלָמָה] völlig überflüssig." This is supported by e.g. S. Mowinckel, *He That Cometh* (Oxford: Basil Blackwell, 1959) 197, Kaiser, *Der königliche Knecht*, p. 86, Kutsch, *Sein Leiden und Tod – unser Heil*, p. 26. The repetition is represented in all the versions and fits the repetitive character of the text.

"a ewe", was humble(d), and so the *waw* is rendered "and": וְלֹא יִפְתַּח
פִּיו "and he did not open his mouth". All this is about the absence of
opposition and protest to other's treatment.

Between "him", שֶׂה "a sheep" and רָחֵל "a ewe", the roles of humbled
and humble become confused. The oppression of "him", "his" humbleness and "his" silence are compared to שֶׂה "a sheep" led to slaughtering and רָחֵל "a ewe" which is dumb before shearing. The comparisons
do not identify what makes "him", "a sheep" and "a ewe" comparable:
being humble, being humbled or being silent. In the comparisons no
statements about actions or afflictions are made, but the passivity of
שֶׂה "a sheep" led to slaughtering and the silence of רָחֵל "a ewe" before
those who shear "her" are depicted, i.e. the state of ones that have
fallen into the hands of others. 53:7 is concerned with passivity and
the past, and the verbs describing this are in both the perf. (נִגַּשׂ ni.
"he was oppressed"), pt. (נַעֲנֶה ni. "he was humble[d]") and the imperf.
(לֹא יִפְתַּח qal "he did not open"). When the humbled one is described
in the two similes, "his" humbleness and silence are stressed. Thus, the
slaughtering and shearing in the similes become part of a more comprehensive depiction of silence as/and humbleness. Whereas in the
preceding situation "he" was humbled (patient) and silent (pseudo-
agent), the simile might refer to שֶׂה "a sheep" as being either humbled
or humble, thus working elliptically for both aspects of the preceding
situations in which "he" is described: "he was oppressed", "humble"
and "he did not open his mouth". Also, the comparative clause וּכְרָחֵל
לִפְנֵי גֹזְזֶיהָ נֶאֱלָמָה "and like a ewe which is dumb before those who
shear her" might link up with both the following line and the preceding וְלֹא יִפְתַּח פִּיו "but/and he did not open his mouth".

The comparison of "him" to שֶׂה "a sheep" and רָחֵל "a ewe" evokes
the simile of 53:6, where "we" liken ourselves to צֹאן "sheep". "We"
participate as the speaking voice from 53:1 up to and including v. 6.
Whereas the similes of שֶׂה "a sheep" and רָחֵל "a ewe" in v. 7 focus on
being humble, humbled and silent, in v. 6 "we" liken "ourselves" to
צֹאן תָּעִינוּ "sheep that went astray", a comparison which is modified by
an explanation: אִישׁ לְדַרְכּוֹ פָּנִינוּ "everyone turned his own way". Also,
by a concluding statement in v. 6, a confession of "our" own transgressions is made. In this reflection on "our" own guilt, an awareness of
having been punished by God because of "our" own delusion is apparent. "He" is identified with "us" and "his" sufferings are a consequence
of "our" delusion.

וְהוּא נַעֲנֶה "and he was humble(d)" in 53:7 echoes מְעֻנֶּה "humili-ated" (pt. pu.) in v. 4, where it is connected to a more comprehen-sive presentation of how אֲנַחְנוּ חֲשַׁבְנֻהוּ נָגוּעַ מֻכֵּה אֱלֹהִים וּמְעֻנֶּה "we accounted him stricken, smitten by God and humiliated". Whereas the sinful "we" describe themselves as צֹאן "sheep" going astray in v. 6, in v. 7 "he" is compared to שֶׂה "a sheep" being led to slaughtering and רָחֵל "a ewe" being shorn in silence. V. 7 concerns the silence of the humiliated one, where "he", although oppressed and humbled, did not open "his" mouth. No reason is offered as to why "he" was humble and humbled. Neither "his" relation to "us" nor "his" relation to YHWH is explicitly mentioned, and the speaking voice is not clearly identified.

3.10.11. *Isa. 53:8*

מֵעֹצֶר וּמִמִּשְׁפָּט לֻקָּח וְאֶת־דּוֹרוֹ מִי יְשׂוֹחֵחַ
כִּי נִגְזַר מֵאֶרֶץ חַיִּים מִפֶּשַׁע עַמִּי נֶגַע לָמוֹ׃

> By restraint (?) and by execution (?) he was taken – but who of his time considered
> that he was cut off from the land of the living and because of the trans-gression of my people was his stroke?

After a depiction of how "he was taken", a question follows with the interrogative pronoun מִי "who" as subject, expanded by the prep. phrase וְאֶת־דּוֹרוֹ "and of his time". The question concerns "who of his time considered" and is filled in by a subordinate clause in which a situation is related to the preceding clause: כִּי נִגְזַר מֵאֶרֶץ חַיִּים "that he was cut off from the land of the living". Finally, a nominal clause depicts a causal relation between פֶּשַׁע עַמִּי "the transgression of my people" and נֶגַע לָמוֹ "his stroke", where the causality is expressed by the preposition מִן and the speaker is also revealed as "I" (in 1cs poss. suff. of עַמִּי "my people").

In both prep. phrases, the prep. מִן "by" heads a noun. The rare עֹצֶר (noun ms עֹצֶר "restraint", "oppression") "restraint" (?) is paralleled by the more common מִשְׁפָּט (noun ms מִשְׁפָּט "execution", "judgment", "sentence", "case", "procedure") "execution" (?).[115] The prep. מִן has

---

[115] The expression מֵעֹצֶר וּמִמִּשְׁפָּט is disputed. While some scholars interpret it in a concrete sense, others see a more general sense of unjust sentence. The noun עֹצֶר occurs elsewhere in Prov. 30:16 and Ps. 107:39 only. The vb עצר "imprison", "shut up" is more common, cf. 2 Kgs 17:4, Jer. 33:1, 39:15. As will be shown in various readings presented in Appendix 5, also מִשְׁפָּט might here be connected to a "legal", "profane" claim.

been taken to be causal ("as a result of", "by"), separative ("from") or privative ("without").[116] The predicate לֻקַּח (perf. qal pass. 3ms of לקח "take") "he was taken"[117] serves both prep. phrases. The verbal clause depicts a situation in the past, where "he" is the subject and patient, and no agent is mentioned. Modified by the prep. and the predicate, the nouns עֹצֶר "restraint" (?) and מִשְׁפָּט "execution" (?) might concern how "he" is treated badly by others.

By virtue of the deictic interrogative pronoun and subject מִי "who", the next clause is conveyed as a question. The clause opens with the prep. phrase וְאֶת־דּוֹרוֹ (waw, prep. אֶת "from", "of", "with"; expressing proximity, noun ms cstr. of דּוֹר "time", "generation", "age", "contemporaries", "fate", 3ms poss. suff.) "his time", which in the suff. marks out "his" further belonging.[118] The whole expression מִי וְאֶת־דּוֹרוֹ "but who of his time" elicits a closer identification of a new participant who enters the scene and is the subject and agent of the predicate יְשׂוֹחֵחַ (imperf. polel 3ms of שׂיח "consider", "pay attention")

---

[116] The different renderings of the prepositions depend on the interpretations of the nouns of the prep. phrases, cf. Appendix 5.

[117] R. J. Williams, "The Passive Qal Theme in Hebrew" in J. W. Wevers and D. B. Redford (eds), *Essays on the Ancient Semitic World* (Toronto Semitic Texts and Studies; Toronto: University of Toronto Press, 1970) 43–50, explains לֻקַּח as a pass. qal of לקח together with 51 other Hebrew roots which may preserve this form in MT (Isa. 53:8 is not mentioned in his list). He also notes the existence of pass. qal in Ugaritic and Phoenician. However, as in these other West Semitic languages, ni. came to be used to express the pass. Among his examples, he points out how all the verbs which have perf. forms exhibit a vocalisation identical with pu. Koole, *Isaiah III. Vol. 2*, p. 304, on the other hand, describes the form as pu., translating it as "he was taken".

[118] דּוֹר has been translated as "dwelling", e.g. Duhm, *Das Buch Jesaia*, p. 362 (related to Akk. cognate for "circular wall" and Arab. cognate for "building"). P. R. Ackroyd, "The Meaning of Hebrew דּוֹר Considered", *JSS* 13 (1968) 6–7, suggests "community", "royal house", "dynasty", based on F. J. Neuberg's study, and related to Ugar. cognate for "gathering", that is, "that grouping to which he belongs", cf. Isa. 38:12, as well as G. Gerlemann, *Studien zur alttestamentlichen Theologie* (Franz Delitzsch-Vorlesungen 1978, Neue Folge; Heidelberg: Lambert Schneider, 1980) 41. H. S. Nyberg, "Smärtornas man: En studie till Jes. 52,13–53,12", *SEÅ* 7 (1942) 53, assumes an original verbal abstract "waste", cf. Arab. cognates and Ps. 24:6.

Most scholars take דּוֹר "period of time"/"generation" as their point of view (cf. Isa. 41:4, 51:8–9) or "plight", "fate", cf. Driver, "Linguistic and Textual Problems", p. 403, and "Isaiah 52:13–53:12", pp. 94–95, with reference to Akk. cognate for "lasting state" and Arab. cognate for "role (in life)", "turn", "time", "change (of fortune)", translating 53: 8ab, "...and who gave a thought to his plight". This is supported by, e.g. North, *The Second Isaiah*, p. 65, Blenkinsopp, *Isaiah 40–55*, pp. 345; 348, Hermisson, "Das vierte Gottesknechtlied im deuterojesajanischen Kontext", p. 7 (ET p. 26). Dahood, "Phoenician Elements in Isaiah 52:13–53:12", p. 69, refers to the parallel between דּוֹרִי and חַיָּי in Isa. 38:12, rendering "and who gave his life a thought?", while Westermann, *Isaiah 40–66*, pp. 254; 265, renders "and who gave a thought to his stock?"

"who…considered". This verb of perception exhibits both fientive and stative characteristics. It is bound up with an object (i.e. the adjacent subordinate כִּי clause), but is not notionally transitive, since, as will be seen below, no action passes over from agent to goal, and so might be called "quasi-fientive".[119] The predicate, which is imperf., refers to the past and might express either the ignorance of "his" time ("who understood?") or indifference ("who cared?") towards "him".[120] The prep. phrase וְאֶת־דּוֹרוֹ "of his time" is preceded by a copulative *waw* which relates to the preceding situation by way of contrast. Thus it is rendered "but". The subject "he" of the previous clause is related to the prep. phrase אֶת־דּוֹרוֹ "his time" by the suff. of the noun. The object of the interrogative clause is a subordinate clause introduced by the conjunction כִּי "that", followed by the predicate נִגְזַר (perf. ni. 3ms of גזר "cut of", "separate", "exclude from"), which is pass., where "he" is patient, and no agent is mentioned: "he was cut off". The dissociation of "him" is further emphasised by the prep. phrase מֵאֶרֶץ חַיִּים "from the land of the living". The disjunctive prep. מִן "from" forcefully depicts "him" as cut off from any human fellowship; dissociated, solitary, even dead.[121] Whereas in the first part of the question

---

[119] On "quasi-fientive", see 3.10.5. n. 80.

[120] אֶת־דּוֹרוֹ has been regarded as both a prep. phrase (working as subject) and the object of the clause. I take it to be a prep. phrase, cf. e.g. Elliger, *Deuterojesaja in seinem Verhältnis zu Tritojesaja*, p. 11: "was seine Zeitgenossen anbelagt", Kutsch, *Sein Leiden und Tod – unser Heil*, pp. 13; 27: "doch wer von seinen Zeitgenossen denkt darüber nacht?"
Rendered as an object: Rignell, "Isa. LII 13–LIII 12", p. 88, translates "who takes his generation into consideration", while Clines, *I, He, We and They*, p. 18, reads "and against his generation who protested?" Due to the expected negative answer to the rhetorical question, Clines' reading would imply that no one raised a protest to his fate. Blenkinsopp, *Isaiah 40–55*, pp. 345; 348, translates "who gave a thought to his fate", Oswalt, *The Book of Isaiah: Chapters 40–66*, p. 390, has "and his generation, who has considered it?" and Koole, *Isaiah III. Vol. 2*, pp. 303; 307: "who considered his generation".

[121] J. A. Soggin, "Tod und Auferstehung des leidenden Gottesknechtes – Jes. 53:8–10", *ZAW* 87 (1975) 346–355, argues that נגזר מן is a general expression for a hopeless situation, like those in the individual psalms of lament, cf. Pss. 31:23, 88:6, related to being abandoned by God. The phrase also appears in "we" speech in Ezek. 37:11 and Lam. 3:54. Soggin distinguishes נגזר מן from נכרת מן, in which he relates the last to concrete, physical death. However, נגזר מן in Isa. 53:8 might function as an equally general description of a hopeless situation as e.g. נכרת מן in Isa. 48:9 (hi.), and in v. 19 כרת (ni.) occurs with שמד "destroy", cf. 5.15.3.
Driver, "Isaiah 52:13–53:12", p. 104, translates אֶרֶץ חַיִּים as "the world of living men" referring to "solitary confinement away from the society of men". Gerlemann, *Studien zur alttestamentlichen Theologie*, pp. 41–42, reads אֶרֶץ חַיִּים as the opposite of a place without life, e.g. a desert. L. Barré, "[אֶרֶץ חַיִּים] – 'The Land of the Living'?",

(מִי) וְאֶת־דּוֹרוֹ "(who) of his time" is the subject, in this subordinate כִּי "that" clause, "he" is the subject. After the obscure statement מֵעֹצֶר וּמִמִּשְׁפָּט לֻקָּח "by restraint (?) and by execution (?) he was taken", another description of "his" fate is given: כִּי נִגְזַר מֵאֶרֶץ חַיִּים "that he was cut off from the land of the living". It is unclear whether this expression is juxtaposed with the previous one as a further explanation, an expansion of "his" fate or is an alternative: "by restraint (?) and by execution (?) he was taken" and "cut off from the land of the living" might illuminate each other as simultaneous and similar events or stand in a causal relation: "by restraint (?) and by execution (?) he was taken", therefore he was "cut off from the land of the living", i.e. "he" was sentenced to death. In any case, the question מִי וְאֶת־דּוֹרוֹ יְשׂוֹחֵחַ "but who of his time considered" regards the relation of דּוֹרוֹ "his time" to "his" fate – as ignorant or indifferent.

Finally, yet another explanation is given by a nominal clause composed of a prep. phrase and a noun phrase working as subject. In the prep. phrase מִפֶּשַׁע עַמִּי (prep. מִן "because", noun ms cstr. of פֶּשַׁע "transgression", "sin", "crime", "rebellion", "guilt" noun ms cstr. of עַם "people", "nation", "fellow countrymen", 1cs poss. suff.)[122] "because of

---

JSOT 41 (1988) 37–59, claims that אֶרֶץ חַיִּים is often an expression for the temple, and argues that in Isa. 53:8 the servant's illness excludes him from the temple, cf. 2 Chron. 26:16–21. אֶרֶץ חַיִּים is related to humiliation in stereotypical laments in Isa. 38:11 (cf. 5.11.14.), Jer. 11:19 (with כרת, cf. 5.13.2.), Pss. 27:13, 52:7, 116:9, 142:6, Job 28:13, Ezek. 32:23; 27; 32 (cf. 5.14.5.). On a supposed כרת formula and death as a consequence of sin, see R. C. Cover, "Sin, Sinners (OT)", *ABD* 6 (1992) 39. On death, cf. 5.14.

[122] All versions apart from 1QIsa^a (which renders עמו "his people") support MT עַמִּי "my people". Blenkinsopp, *Isaiah 40–55*, pp. 345; 348w supports 1QIsa^a, while Dahood, "Phoenician Elements in Isaiah 52:13–53:12", p. 69, reads the MT suffix as 3ms. Many have claimed to emend עַמִּי "my people":
i) עַמִּי taken to be an abbreviation for עַם יהוה "people of YHWH", see G. R. Driver, "Once Again Abbreviations", *Textus* 4 (1964) 79.
ii) עַמִּי נֶגַע לָמוֹ "peoples of a striking to them", i.e. "people who deserved to be stricken", see North, *The Second Isaiah*, pp. 230–231.
iii) Whybray, *Isaiah 40–66*, p. 177: "1QIsa^a has 'his people'…Possibly the suffix -י(עמ) was intended to be the first letter of the next word, which, as has been suggested, may have been [ינגע] (imperf.). If so, the phrase would read, 'for the people's transgression he was grievously smitten'".
iv) a. מִפְּשָׁעָם "for their rebellions", see BHSapp (ed. D. W. Thomas), and מִפְּשָׁעֵימוֹ "for their rebellions", see K. Elliger, "Nochmals textkritisches zu Jes. 53" in J. Schreiner (ed), *Wort, Lied und Gottesspruch. Festschrift für Joseph Ziegler. Vol. II: Beiträge zu Psalmen und Propheten* (FzB, 1–2; Würzburg: Echter Verlag, 1972) 138.
b. מִפְּשָׁעֵנוּ "for our rebellions", see Elliger, *Deuterojesaja in seinem Verhältnis zu Tritojesaja*, p. 7, Westermann, *Isaiah 40–66*, pp. 254; 266.

the transgression of my people", the two nouns express two possessive relations: פֶּשַׁע "transgression" belongs to עַמִּי "my people" and עַמִּי "people" belongs to the speaking "I". The noun עַמִּי has connotations of ("your") "lord", "head", "god" (the antithesis of "people"), which is modified by the poss. suff., implying a hierarchical relationship where a subordinate position is terminated by the claim of a superior. This relationship is between the superior speaking partner "I" and עַמִּי "my people".

The prep. phrase מִפֶּשַׁע עַמִּי "because of the transgression of my people" is related to the noun phrase נֶגַע לָמוֹ (noun ms נֶגַע "stroke", "plague", "wound", "mark", prep. לְ with 3ms suff.)[123] "his stroke" by the prep. מִן "because of", "for".[124] A causal relationship is revealed between "him" and עַמִּי "my people", as נֶגַע לָמוֹ "his stroke" is explained as due to פֶּשַׁע עַמִּי "the transgression of my people". Through this juxtaposition

---

For different interpretations of עַמִּי "my people" in 53:8, see 3.10.17.3.

[123] נֶגַע לָמוֹ "the stroke to him", i.e. due to the people's transgression he has been stricken. 1QIsaᵃ has נוגע, while LXX renders ἤχθη εἰς θάνατον, where למו might have been taken as an abbreviation for or a corruption of למות נֶגַע לָמֻּת "he was stricken to death"). LXX is supported by Driver, "Isaiah 52:13–53:12", p. 95: "[I]f נֶגַע לָמֻּת or נגע 'he was stricken to death' is read, this is equally ambiguous, as it may mean only 'he was grievously stricken'; for 'to death' is a well known Semitic idiom for 'grievously', 'severely' (Isa. 53:12.)" LXX is also supported by e.g. Duhm, *Das Buch Jesaia*, p. 362, Elliger, "Nochmals Textkritisches zu Jes. 53", p. 13, Westermann, *Isaiah 40–66*, p. 254c, Whybray, *Isaiah 40–66*, p. 177, Blenkinsopp, *Isaiah 40–55*, p. 348w. Hermisson, "Das vierte Gottesknechtlied im deuterojesajanischen Kontext", p. 8, n. 30 (ET, p. 26, n. 29) says:
> Emend MT נֶגַע לָמוֹ to the above נֶגַע לָמֻּת, cf. 1QIsaᵃ, and LXX (…). MT has מִפֶּשַׁע עַמִּי נֶגַע לָמוֹ 'On account of the transgression of *my* people – a stroke to him (לָמוֹ)'. The translation "a stroke *for them*" would be more fitting for לָמוֹ but even further removed from the context. It is striking that the traditional Masoretic Text disallows a collective interpretation of the Servant. The expression the 'transgression of *my* people (מִפֶּשַׁע עַמִּי)' differentiates the people from the Servant, who is without transgression (cf. 53:9), and this expression also finds an exact counterpart differentiating the Servant and the people, v. 5 וְהוּא מְחֹלָל מִפְּשָׁעֵנוּ, "But *he* was wounded for *our* transgressions" (…). To the advocates of the collective interpretation, which sees the Servant as Israel, I can offer a conjecture which to my knowledge has not yet been proposed: מִפֶּשַׁע עַמִּים נֶגַע לוֹ [=On account of the transgression of the peoples – a stroke to him]. It is not the best Hebrew, but it is better than Lindblom's attempt…(his italics).

This might also be related to the discussion of the "servant's death", see 5.14.1. n. 251.
לָמוֹ has also been taken as both sg "upon him", e.g. Clines, *I, He, We and They*, p. 13), Oswalt, *The Book of Isaiah: Chapters 40–66*, p. 390, Koole, *Isaiah III. Vol. 2*, pp. 303; 310–311, Blenkinsopp (pp. 345;348) and pl "upon them", see L. G. Rignell, "A Study of Isaiah Ch. 40–55" (Lunds universitets Årsskrift. N.F. Avd. 1. 52:5; Lund: Gleerup, 1956) 82, cf. his collective interpretation of the servant referred to in 3.10.17.2.a.

[124] On the prep. מִן in מִפֶּשַׁע, see 3.10.8. n. 97.

of literary codes, an identification between "him" and "my people" is presented by a dissymmetry with פֶּשַׁע "transgression" belonging to עַמִּי "my people" and נֶגַע "stroke" to "him": "he" is stricken and עַמִּי "my people" have sinned.

The prep. phrase מִפֶּשַׁע עַמִּי "because of the transgression of my people" might be connected to the preceding elliptical conjunction כִּי "that". Through this conjunction, the question is not only related to "him" and דּוֹרוֹ "his time", but also to עַמִּי "my people": "...but who of his time considered that because of the transgression of my people was his stroke?" The question as a whole works as a commentary upon the situation just depicted. In v. 8a, "he" was patient and humbled. Commenting on this and providing further information, the interrogative clause begins with a copulative *waw* followed by two subordinate clauses specifying circumstances contemporary to the preceding clauses. When מֵעֹצֶר וּמִמִּשְׁפָּט לֻקָּח "by restraint (?) and by execution (?) he was taken" and מֵאֶרֶץ חַיִּים נִגְזַר "he was cut off from the land of the living", it was מִפֶּשַׁע עַמִּי "because of the transgression of my people". The subordinate conjunction כִּי "that" has an asseverative function as "his" fate in v. 8a is strongly confirmed and elaborated by v. 8b. Despite the change of scene and actors, the interrogative clause might have causative, temporal and consequential relations to the preceding clause. The situations are depicted in the past by verbs in perf. (לֻקָּח qal pass. "he was taken" and נִגְזַר ni. "he was cut of") and imperf. (יְשׂוֹחֵחַ polel "considered"). "He" was oppressed, isolated and stricken. Only in the very last clause is an explanation for this given: נֶגַע לָמוֹ "his stroke" was due to פֶּשַׁע עַמִּי "the transgression of my people". Here again, different actors appear: YHWH as the speaking voice related to עַמִּי "my people", the interrogation of דּוֹרוֹ "his time" and "him" are all signifiers of identity. From the perspective of the speaking "I", דּוֹרוֹ "his time" is depicted as having understood neither "his" nor עַמִּי "my people"'s fate.

In the expression מֵעֹצֶר וּמִמִּשְׁפָּט לֻקָּח "by restraint (?) and by execution (?) he was taken", no agent is presented, but only assumed. The same applies to the treatment of "him" in 53:7, where נִגַּשׂ וְהוּא נַעֲנֶה "he was oppressed and he was humbled". Whereas in v. 7 no reason is given for the oppression of "him", in v. 8 נֶגַע לָמוֹ "his stroke" was due to עַמִּי פֶּשַׁע "the transgression of my people". This explanation echoes 53:4b, where "we" regarded "him" as stricken (נָגוּעַ pt. pass. qal ms., cf. noun ms נֶגַע "stroke" in v. 8), smitten by God and humiliated. After "he" was depicted as punished by God in v. 4b, in v. 5 it is stated that "he" was stricken because of "our" sins. In the question in v. 8, the ignorance of דּוֹרוֹ "his time" is revealed, where "his" and the people's fate is related through sin and stroke: נֶגַע לָמוֹ "his stroke" is due to פֶּשַׁע עַמִּי "the transgression of my people". Also in the "we" speech of 53:2–6, the relation between "his" and "our" fate was characterised by both contrast and identity. In v. 4a both "he" and "we" are described as ill, while in v. 4b YHWH's punishment is related to "him" only. An identification between "him" and "us" in terms of illness appeared and was developed from v. 4 onwards. This becomes even more remarkable in vv. 5–6, i.e. after the sin is introduced, in which "we" explain "his" humiliation as due to "our" sins. The question in v. 8 assumes an ignorance or indifference of דּוֹרוֹ "his time". From the perspective of the speaking "I", דּוֹרוֹ "his time" is depicted as having understood neither "his" nor עַמִּי "my people"'s fate. This might be related to "our" account of "him" in v. 4: אֲנַחְנוּ חֲשַׁבְנֻהוּ נָגוּעַ מֻכֵּה אֱלֹהִים וּמְעֻנֶּה "…we accounted him stricken, smitten by God and humiliated", which also expresses how "we" (mis-) understood "his" illnesses. This is followed by an explanation of the relation between sin and illness in v. 4a and v. 5, where "we" are deeply involved in both "his" illness and ("our") sin. A significant change occurs between vv. 4–6 and v. 8: whereas vv. 4–6 are uttered by "us" in relation to "him", in v. 8 it is expressed in "I" speech about "he" and עַמִּי "my people". Just as the closeness between YHWH and "him" was emphasised by the expression עַבְדִּי "my servant" in 52:13, so too there is a close relationship expressed by עַמִּי "my people" in v. 8.

3.10.12. *Isa. 53:9*

וַיִּתֵּן אֶת־רְשָׁעִים קִבְרוֹ וְאֶת־עָשִׁיר בְּמֹתָיו
עַל לֹא־חָמָס עָשָׂה וְלֹא מִרְמָה בְּפִיו:

He was given his grave with wicked ones and אֶת־עָשִׁיר (with a rich?) in his death,
  although he had not done any violence, and there was no deceit in his mouth.

An imperf. consecutive, וַיִּתֵּן "he was given", works elliptically for two prep. phrases concerning "his" death. Then follows a subordinate clause commenting on the situation by telling how "he" had done neither violence nor spoken deceitfully.

The introductory predicate וַיִּתֵּן (imperf. cons. qal 3ms of נתן "give", "put") hides an impersonal agent: "one gave" or "he was given".[125] The clause continues with the prep. phrase אֶת־רְשָׁעִים (prep. אֵת "with", noun mpl of רָשָׁע "wicked", "guilty", "criminal") "with wicked ones". The prep. phrase is modified by the noun phrase קִבְרוֹ (noun ms cstr of קֶבֶר "grave", "sepulchre", 3ms suff.) "his grave", which works as the object. By counting "him" among רְשָׁעִים "wicked ones" and mentioning קִבְרוֹ "his grave", a situation of disgrace and unworthiness is expressed.

Introduced by a *waw*, yet another prep. phrase follows: וְאֶת־עָשִׁיר בְּמֹתָיו (*waw*, prep. אֵת, noun ms עָשִׁיר "a rich" [?],[126] prep. phrase with

---

[125] 1QIsaᵃ renders 3mpl ויתנו "they gave him" and MS Kennicott pass. וַיֻּתַּן "and it (his grave) was appointed", supported by Driver, "Isaiah 52:13–53:12", p. 95, who claims that since no subject is expressed for וַיִּתֵּן, it must be the indefinite 3ms or the verb must be read as pass. וַיֻּתַּן. As he claims, "[w]hich is read makes no essential difference to the sense" (p. 95), cf. Deut. 34:6. 3mpl of 1QIsaᵃ is a more common way of expressing virtual pass. "they have assigned", but MT 3ms is acceptable, cf. GK § 144d. Blenkinsopp, *Isaiah 40–55*, p. 348x, suggests either repunctuating to qal pass. or emending to 3mpl, cf. 1QIsaᵃ. The narrative *wyqtl* form וַיִּתֵּן is commented in 3.10.5. n. 75 and 4.8.3.1. n. 91.

[126] The translation of עָשִׁיר has been widely discussed, and one common suggestion is "rich", cf. Oswalt, *The Book of Isaiah: Chapters 40–66*, p. 390 (n. 18); 397–398, and Koole, *Isaiah III. Vol. 2*, p. 314–315. This is also rendered by all the versions. However, sg עָשִׁיר "rich" has been regarded as difficult to explain as a counterpart to pl רְשָׁעִים "wicked ones".

Driver, "Isaiah 52:13–53:12", pp. 95–96, refers to Reider's suggestion of the Arab. cognate for "stumbling", "liar" and Guillaume's suggestion of the Arab. cognate for "rabble". In addition, Driver alters to pl (cf. 1QIsaᵃ), and comments on the two Arab. cognates "even though it does not offer quite so appropriate sense and requires a pl form…Either interpretation is preferable to altering the text to עושי רע "evildoers" (Böttcher); for all Vss. support the consonants of MT". According to Koole (p. 315), Guillaume later abandoned his earlier view. Unfortunately, I have not managed to find the references to Guillaume.

Many other emendations have also been suggested:

i. עֹשֵׂי רע "evil-doers", see E. J. Kissane, *The Book of Isaiah: Translated from a Critically Revised Hebrew Text with Commentary* (Dublin: Browne and Nolan, 1941–43) 182; 189, Fohrer, *Das Buch Jesaja: Kap. 40–66*, p. 160, Westermann, *Isaiah 40–66*, p. 254d, Kutsch, *Sein Leiden und Tod – unser Heil*, pp. 13; 30, Elliger, *Deuterojesaja in seinem Verhältnis zu Tritojesaja*, p. 9, Soggin, "Tod und Auferstehung des leidenden Gottesknechtes – Jes. 53:8–10", p. 349, Hermisson, "Das vierte Gottesknechtlied im deuterojesajanischen Kontext", p. 8, n. 31 (ET p. 27, n. 32), Blenkinsopp, *Isaiah 40–55*, p. 345y.

ii. שְׂעִירִים "demons", see W. F. Albright, "The High Place in Ancient Palestine", *International Organization for the Study of the Old Testament: Congress Volume Strasbourg 1956* (VTSup, 4; Leiden: E. J. Brill, 1957) 244 ff, Kaiser, *Der königliche Knecht*, pp. 86;114–115.

iii. עֹשֵׂי רִיב "quarellers", "makers of strife", see M. J. Dahood, "Isaiah 53,8–12 and Massoretic Misconstructions", *Bib* 63 (1982) 567–568.

prep. בְּ "in", noun mpl of מָוֶת "death", 3ms suff.)[127] "and with a rich (?) in his death". Again, by counting "him" among עָשִׁיר "a rich" (?) and mentioning מֹתָיו "his death", a situation of disgrace and unworthiness is expressed. In v. 9a, a numerical chiasmus appears between רְשָׁעִים "wicked ones" (pl) followed by קֶבֶר "grave" (sg), and עָשִׁיר "rich" (sg) followed by בְּמֹתָיו "in his deaths" (pl). Moreover, קֶבֶר "grave" in the first prep. phrase is "concrete", while בְּמֹתָיו "in his deaths" in the second is "abstract". Both have 3ms poss. suff. connected. The predicate וַיִּתֵּן "he was given" works elliptically for both clauses and the *waw* indicates two situations coordinate with each other.

Then follows a subordinate עַל which might work either as a concessive conjunction "although", or as a causal prep. "because".[128] It is followed by two comments of protest against the preceding situation. The first is conveyed by a verbal clause, the second by a nominal. The predicate of the verbal clause is עָשָׂה (perf. qal 3ms) "do", expressing non-action when modified by the negative לֹא־חָמָס "non-violence".[129]

---

[127] בְּמֹתָיו "in his deaths" is rendered sg in LXX, Vulg. and Pesh, while 1QIsaᵃ renders sg בומתו "height" or "tomb" with *plene* spelling, and 3ms suff. Driver, "Isaiah 52:13–53:12", pp. 95–96, emends to מֹותוֹ ('b=) בֵּית "his tomb" on the analogy of an Acc. cognate "house of death" as "grave". Albright, "The High Place in Ancient Palestine", p. 247, emends to בָּמָה "place of burial where the deceased were interred according to pagan rites…, improper burial place, where a pious man could not be interred", cf. his emendation of עָשִׁיר to שְׂעִירִים "demons". He translates the whole line: "And his funerary installations with demons". Albright is supported by, among others, Kutsch, *Sein Leiden und Tod – unser Heil*, pp. 13; 30, Whybray, *Thanksgiving for a Liberated Prophet*, p. 103, n. 145, Blenkinsopp, *Isaiah 40–55*, p. 348y. P. Vaughan, *The Meaning of "Bama" in the Old Testament: A Study of Etymological, Textual and Archaeological Evidence* (SNTSMS, 3; London: Cambridge University Press, 1974) 16, criticises Albright's argument: "A totally subjective emendation is made on the basis of an assumed practice; the emended text is then used to demonstrate the existence of the practice." Vaughan relates the 1QIsaᵃ rendering בומתו to קִבְרוֹ in the sense of shape, as a description of a "large stone chair- a man-made hill- which commonly was heaped over a dug-grave" (p. 17), translating 53:9: "They made his grave with the wicked, and his burial-mound with the rabble" (p. 18). Also W. B. Barrick, "The Funerary Character of the 'High-Places' in Ancient Palestine: A Reassessment", VT 25 (1975) 565–595, criticises Albright's arguments. Oswalt, *The Book of Isaiah: Chapters 40–66*, p. 390, n. 19, wonders if the 1QIsaᵃ reading is a misplacement of the *mater lectionis*, thus במותו.

[128] עַל is translated "although" by Kutsch, *Sein Leiden und Tod – unser Heil*, p. 12, Hermisson, "Das vierte Gottesknechtlied im deuterojesajanischen Kontext", p. 8 (ET p. 27) and Oswalt, *The Book of Isaiah: Chapters 40–66*, p. 398, "though" by Blenkinsopp, *Isaiah 40–55*, p. 345, "because" by Koole, *Isaiah III. Vol. 2*, p. 317, and "for" by Clines, *I, He, We and They*, p. 20.

[129] The negation אַיִן is more common than לֹא in nominal clauses, cf. 53:2 in 3.10.5. n. 77.

Thus, "he" appears as a pseudo-agent in a non-causal clause: the preceding situations of disgrace have occurred despite "his" not having behaved violently. The last comment is conveyed by a nominal clause, where the negation לֹא "not" precedes the noun מִרְמָה and the prep. phrase בְּפִיו (abstract noun fs מִרְמָה "deceit", "treachery", prep. בְּ, noun ms cstr. of פֶּה "mouth", 3ms poss. suff.) "and there was no deceit in his mouth". In this clause, "his" state is expressed. When related to the subordinate conjunction עַל "although", which works elliptically, this becomes a non-causal clause: "his" death and unworthy grave are explained as brought upon "him" despite "his" not having talked treacherously. The violent and treacherous behaviour of which "he" is not guilty is the behaviour of רְשָׁעִים "wicked ones",[130] with whose dispositions of wrong-doing "he" is by implication associated in the first line of the verse.

The whole verse concerns the past, with one verb in imperf. consecutive; וַיִּתֵּן (pi.) "he was given" and one in perf. עָשָׂה לֹא (qal) "he had not done", both related to passivity or non-action. The nominal clause also concerns state and not agency: וְלֹא מִרְמָה בְּפִיו "and there was no deceit in his mouth". אֶת־רְשָׁעִים קִבְרוֹ "his grave with wicked ones" and בְּמֹתָיו אֶת־עָשִׁיר "a rich (?) in his deaths" are connected to "his" lack of violent behaviour and deceit by non-causal clauses in a blurring of the semantic field. In 53:9, the speaking voice is not identified.

Just as "his" death sentence is described in 53:8 by the expression נִגְזַר מֵאֶרֶץ חַיִּים "he was cut off from the land of the living", so too is the unworthiness of "his" burial place among "wicked ones" and "a rich" (?) depicted in 53:9. In v. 8, "his" stroke is explained as due to פֶּשַׁע עַמִּי "the transgression of my people". In v. 9, nothing is said about why "he" was struck by death and given an unworthy tomb. רְשָׁעִים "wicked ones" might be compared to sinners, cf. vv. 5–6; 8, and contrasted with an absence of violence and deceit, cf. v. 7, where "he" is depicted as oppressed, humbled and silent. The two comparisons with sheep make no statements about "his" actions, but depict the silence of one who has fallen into the hands of others. As in v. 9, so too in v. 7 "his" silence and lack of violent behaviour are prominent. However, whereas in v. 7 "he" is merely afflicted, in v. 9 the punishment

---

[130] The function of עָשִׁיר "a rich" (?) in connection with this is uncertain.

seems to be unmitigated and the suffering endless, as "he" is struck by an irrevocable judgment: there is no hope after death. "He" is a man upon whom every conceivable indignity is heaped, and death and an unworthy grave become "his" last enemy. The rhetorical question of v. 9 might allude to "our" ignorance (cf. 53:1).

3.10.13. Isa. 53:10

וַיהוָה חָפֵץ דַּכְּאוֹ הֶחֱלִי אִם־תָּשִׂים אָשָׁם נַפְשׁוֹ
יִרְאֶה זֶרַע יַאֲרִיךְ יָמִים וְחֵפֶץ יְהוָה בְּיָדוֹ יִצְלָח:

But YHWH was pleased to strike him by making him ill אִם־תָּשִׂים אָשָׁם נַפְשׁוֹ;

he shall see offspring and live long, and it is YHWH's pleasure that his hand shall prosper.

A *waw* connects this verse to the preceding 53:9 and the *waw* is followed by a verbal clause describing and explaining "his" illness. YHWH is the subject of the clause, acting towards "him" by making "him" ill. There then follows a (corrupt) clause which relates the preceding explanation of illness to sin. Then two verbal clauses turn to completely opposite situations in the future in which "he" shall see offspring and live long. In a third and final verbal clause, the future is depicted with חֵפֶץ יְהוָה "YHWH's pleasure" as subject, and his wish that בְּיָדוֹ יִצְלָח "his hand shall prosper".

The introductory copulative *waw* is followed by the subject יְהוָה and then by the predicate חָפֵץ (perf. qal 3ms of חפץ "be pleased to", "take pleasure in", "delight"), which is stative and transitive and expresses will: "but YHWH was pleased to". This is further modified by the verb דַּכְּאוֹ (inf. cstr. pi. fientive of דכא "crush", "strike", 3ms suff.), working as an object[131] and the verbal apposition הֶחֱלִי (perf. hi. fientive 3ms

---

[131] Most scholars translate דַּכְּאוֹ in MT Isa. 53:10 as "to crush" or something equivalent. LXX renders καθαρίσαι "to purify", which has been taken to be a rendering of Aram. דכא, cf. 1QIsaᵃ. Driver, "Isaiah 52:13–53:12", p. 96, who translates מְדֻכָּא in 53:5 as "bruised" (p. 103), supports LXX reading in v. 10 and equates the Aram. vb דכא with דכה "be pure", "innocent", "justified". He translates v. 10a "But the Lord was pleased to give him the victory and restored him…" (p. 104). Cf. Duhm, *Das Buch Jesaia*, pp. 360; 363–364, who translates מְדֻכָּא in 53:5 as "crushed" (*zerschlagen*) and דַּכְּאוֹ in 53:10 as "pure" (*reinigen*).
Gerleman, *Studien zur alttestamentlichen Theologie*, p. 42, connects דַּכְּאוֹ in 53:10a to the elevation, expressing that the servant will be freed from his pains, and translates: "Und es gefiel Jahwe, seine Plage zu beenden; wenn er Gelassenheit erwiese…", while in 53:5 he translates מְדֻכָּא as "crushed" (*zerschlagen*). K. Elliger, "Jes. 53:10: 'alte

of חלה "make sick"), which elaborates on דִּכְּאוֹ by expressing consequences: "strike him by making him ill".[132] Thus, three things are involved: a will, an action and a consequence. YHWH is agent and "he" is patient: by his will, YHWH struck "him", causing "him" to be ill in the past.

Nearly every word of the next clause is unanimously regarded as beset by uncertainties by scholars. The (conditional?) conjunction אִם makes an abrupt transition from the preceding clause. The אִם clause might be read as a dependent temporal clause, with the subordinate clause contemporary to its main clause. The main clause concerns the past, which also places the conjunction אִם and the predicate תָּשִׂים (imperf. qal 3fs of שִׂים "put", "place", "make") in the past.[133] נַפְשׁוֹ (noun fs cstr of נֶפֶשׁ "life", "myself", "person", 3ms poss. suff.) is the subject of the clause, and אָשָׁם (noun ms "offence", "guilt", "guilt-offering", "compensation for guilt") its object. The illness brought upon "him" by YHWH in the main clause is in this dependent clause related to אָשָׁם as "guilt-offering" or "guilt". Tentative renderings could be either "when he made himself a guilt-offering" or "when he himself made guilt". However, as the transmission אִם־תָּשִׂים אָשָׁם נַפְשׁוֹ is corrupt, I support those who regard the clause as too obscure to interpret.[134]

Without any hints from a conjunction or other sign, the event and comments in the past are interrupted by a completely opposite situation in the future, expressed by three verbal clauses. In the first, יִרְאֶה

---

crux-neuer Vorschlag'", *MIO* 15 (1969) 228–233, suggests דִּכְּאוֹ "humiliated" instead of דִּכְּאוֹ. He is supported by Begrich, *Studien zu Deuterojesaja*, p. 65.

[132] הֶחֱלִי is often taken as חלה "make sick", but also חלל II "to pierce", "mortally wound", cf. 53:5. Dahood, "Phoenician Elements in Isaiah 52:13–53:12", p. 71:

> Repointing [דִּכְּאוֹ הֶחֱלִי]; the final -[וֹ] of [דכא] is taken singly written consonant to be shared by the next word…That the root [חלל], "to pierce", underlies consonantal [החלי] is inferred from v. 5b…Consonantal [החלי] may be analyzed as the hiphil infinitive construct followed by the third person suffix-[י]; hence vocalized [הֶחֱלִי]. Thus both infinitive constructs depend upon [חָפֵץ]…[cf.] Job 33:32. 1QIsaᵃ [ויחללהו], "and he pierced him", sustains our translation which, however, preserves the consonantal text.

Hermisson, "Das vierte Gottesknechtlied im deuterojesajanischen Kontext", p. 8, n. 35 (ET, p. 28, n. 35):

> Instead of the MT's hiphil perfect הֶחֱלִי (חָלָה), "he has made him sick" (RSV margin), the above translation ["But it was the Lord's plan to crush him, to make him sick {הַחֲלִי}] reads the hiphil infinitive construct…Alternatively, we may read the noun חֳלִי or delete החלי entirely as a gloss.

Elliger, "Jes. 53:10", p. 228, deletes הֶחֱלִי as inauthentic.

[133] Waltke and O'Connor, *An Introduction to Biblical Hebrew Syntax*, § 31.1.1a, n. 2.

[134] On the translation of אִם־תָּשִׂים אָשָׁם נַפְשׁוֹ, see Appendix 6.

(imperf. qal 3ms of רָאָה "he shall see") is predicate with "he" as the subject and agent, and זֶרַע (noun ms זֶרַע "seed", "offspring") is the object: "he shall see offspring", with connotations of growth, progeny and hope. In the second clause, יַאֲרִיךְ (imperf. hi. 3ms of אָרַךְ "prolong") is predicate with "he" as the subject and יָמִים (noun mpl of יוֹם "day") as object: "he shall live long", also with connotations of prosperity. Both clauses are conveyed as promises regarding "him", where "he" is agent, and concern state rather than action. A third and final promise of the future then follows by means of a verbal clause. The noun phrase חֵפֶץ יְהוָה "YHWH's pleasure", "delight", is subject and is modified by the predicate יִצְלָח (imperf. qal fientive, intransitive 3ms of צלח "prosper", "advance", "be successful") and the prep. phrase בְּיָדוֹ (prep. בְּ "by", "into", "under the authority of", noun fs יָד "hand", "strength", 3ms suff.), which may refer either to YHWH's or "his" hand: "and it is YHWH's pleasure that his hand shall prosper". While the first two verbal clauses are not connected to each other by a *waw* or other signs of relation, the third and last one is prefixed by a copulative *waw*, indicating a situation coordinate with the preceding ones.

The corrupt אִם־תָּשִׂים אָשָׁם נַפְשׁוֹ may be related to the chiastic structure of the whole verse. Whereas 53:10a concerns "his" past, v. 10b concerns "his" future. The relation between the past and the future appears in a blurring of semantic fields. "His" past humiliations are related to illness and guilt, whereas promises for the future concern offspring, a long life and prosperity. Both the past humiliations and the future prosperity are presented in terms of a relation between YHWH and "him". The situations of both the past and the future are presented as YHWH's pleasure.[135] This is chiastically formulated: in the first component, v. 10a, יְהוָה חָפֵץ "YHWH was pleased" (vb); and in the second component, v. 10b, חֵפֶץ יְהוָה "YHWH's pleasure" (noun) is described. In v. 10a, YHWH's pleasure is related to his making "him" ill; in v. 10b, it is related to "his" prosperity.

The introductory *waw* of 53:10 might both complete one episode and introduce a new one. As a copulative *waw* it introduces an explanation for "his" unworthy burial without reason (v. 9): the humiliations of

---

[135] One of the verbs describing the past is in perf. (דִּכְּאוֹ), whereas the second is in imperf. (תָּשִׂים), and the two verbs describing the future are in imperf. (יִרְאֶה and יִצְלָח).

"him" are depicted here as illness and then related to sin. In relation
to v. 9, new participants appear: in v. 9 "he" is the subject, in v. 10a it
is YHWH. In v. 10a, YHWH is the agent behind "his" illnesses. וַיהוָה
חָפֵץ דַּכְּאוֹ הֶחֱלִי "But YHWH was pleased to strike him by making him
ill" echoes "our" diagnosis of "him" in 53:3–5, where "he" is וִידוּעַ חֹלִי
"known with illness" (v. 3), חֳלָיֵנוּ הוּא נָשָׂא "he bore our illnesses" (v. 4)
and הוּא מְחֹלָל מִפְּשָׁעֵנוּ מְדֻכָּא מֵעֲוֹנֹתֵינוּ "he was wounded because
of our transgressions and injured because our iniquities" (v. 5).[136] In
v. 10, like in vv. 5–6; 8, "his" wounds are seen as consequences of sin
and as punishment from YHWH: מְדֻכָּא מֵעֲוֹנֹתֵינוּ מוּסַר שְׁלוֹמֵנוּ עָלָיו
"he was injured because of our iniquities; chastisement was upon him
for our healing…" (v. 5), וַיהוָה הִפְגִּיעַ בּוֹ אֵת עֲוֹן כֻּלָּנוּ "and YHWH
struck him by the iniquity of all of us" (v. 6) and מִפֶּשַׁע עַמִּי נֶגַע לָמוֹ
"because of the transgression of my people was his stroke" (v. 8).

A turning point appears between "his" humiliation and death in
vv. 8–9 and prosperity expressed in promises of descendants and a
long life in v. 10. The promise of prosperity echoes the exaltation of
"him" in 52:13. Neither in 52:13 nor in 53:10 is any reason for the
turning point given. In 53:5, turning points are expressed in terms of
healing and recovery, where the humiliations of "him" seem to explain
the reason for the turning point for "us".

In 53:10 YHWH, who has not been mentioned since 53:6, is again
brought onto the scene (apart from being implied in the expression
עַמִּי "my people" in v. 8). When "his" fate is depicted as YHWH's will,
"his" life acts as a witness to who YHWH is, cf. 53:1. With interrogative force, the two questions of v. 1 indicate the reception of שְׁמֻעָתֵנוּ
"the message to us" which is further illuminated by the revelation of
זְרוֹעַ יְהוָה "the arm of YHWH": "Who believes what we hear? And the
arm of YHWH – to whom is it revealed?" When 53:10 is related to
the preceding verses, a new voice appears, as neither "I" (52:13–15)
nor "we" is speaking here (53:1–6). The introductory *waw* in 53:10
might relate to v. 9, where the speaking voice is not identified, while
YHWH's words in v. 8 might occupy an isolated place in a context
which does not have YHWH as speaker.

---

[136] In 53:3; 4 the noun חֹלִי "sickness" occurs, in 53:5 the parallel verbs מְחֹלָל (pt.
pu. of חלל) and מְדֻכָּא (pt. pu. of דכא) and in 53:10 דַּכְּאוֹ (inf. cstr. pi. fientive) and
הֶחֱלִי (perf. hi. fientive 3ms).

3.10.14. *Isa. 53:11*

מֵעֲמַל נַפְשׁוֹ יִרְאֶה יִשְׂבַּע בְּדַעְתּוֹ
יַצְדִּיק צַדִּיק עַבְדִּי לָרַבִּים וַעֲוֺנֹתָם הוּא יִסְבֹּל:

After his travail he shall see and be sated by his knowledge;
The righteous one, my servant, will cause the many to be righteous and
he carried their iniquities.

A change from "his" past to "his" future is depicted: "after his travail
he shall see and be sated by his knowledge". Yet another verbal clause
then follows about "his" future, in which "he" is further identified as
עַבְדִּי צַדִּיק "the righteous one, my servant", who יַצְדִּיק לָרַבִּים "shall
cause the many to be righteous". In 1cs poss. suff. of עַבְדִּי "my servant", the speaker becomes revealed as "I". Finally, a relation between
"him" and "them" linked to past sin is expressed: "he carried their
iniquities".

The verse opens with the prep. phrase מֵעֲמַל, where the prep. מִן
might be given both a temporal force "after", and a causative force "as
a result of". The prep. is connected with עֲמַל (noun ms cstr of עָמָל
"travail", "toil", "trouble", "sorrow", "labour", "gain") and נַפְשׁוֹ (noun
fs cstr. of נֶפֶשׁ "life", "myself", "person", 3ms poss. suff.) "after his
travail". The prep. phrase is contrasted with two verbal phrases of the
future. The first clause begins with the predicate יִרְאֶה (imperf. qal
3ms of רָאה "see") "he shall see". This is a verb of perception with no
object mentioned.[137] The adjacent verbal clause is composed of a predicate יִשְׂבַּע (imperf. qal 3ms of שׂבע "be sated", "satisfied") "he shall

---

[137] 1QIsa[a] and 1QIsa[b] do not render רָאה, but רוה, and the additional אור, both
with equivalents in LXX. This is supported by the majority of biblical scholars, but
not e.g. Muilenburg, "The Book of Isaiah: Chapters 40–66", pp. 629–630, Dahood,
"Phoenician Elements in Isaiah 52:13–53:12", pp. 64; 72, and Koole, *Isaiah III. Vol.
2*, pp. 327–329, who claims: "Graphically speaking [...] an addition of אור after יראה
is just as easily explainable as its omission" (p. 329). Driver, "Isaiah 52:13–53:12",
pp. 97–98:

> In V. 11 the first clause is rhytmically defective, lacking one beat, and the verb
> has no object; the LXX supplies φῶς, whence אור has long been conjecturally
> restored..., and its restoration has now been confirmed by Scroll A, which
> has this very word. The verb, however, is not רָאה "saw" but רוה = רָאה "was
> drenched, sated" as the parallel שׂבע "was full, satisfied" shows.

Cf. Jer. 31:14 and Lam. 3:15, and uses of רָאה in a metaphorical sense, e.g. in
Job 10:15 and Ps.1:23, 91:16. Driver refers also to a Syr. cognate "drank to satiety",
"was intoxicated". Cf. Thomas, "A Consideration of Isaiah LIII", pp. 125–126. Dahood,
pp. 64; 72, supports Driver's reading of רָאה as רוה "was drenched", "sated", but not
a haplography of אור "light", and thus, his translation reads: "with the anguish of his
soul he was sated".

be sated", and the prep. phrase בְּדַעְתּוֹ (prep. בְּ, noun fs cstr. of דַּעַת "knowledge", "insight", 3ms suff.) "by his knowledge".[138] Both verbs are imperfects rendered in the future. Related to the preceding prep. phrase, both temporally "after" and causatively "as a result of" "his" earlier travail, "he" shall gain insight and knowledge in the future.

The next clause conveys an additional depiction of "his" future. The predicate יַצְדִּיק לְ (imperf. hi. 3ms causative, fientive of צדק "cause... to be righteous", "vindicate", "justify", "save"), might be either transitive, external hi. or intransitive, internal hi., followed by the apposition עַבְדִּי "my servant" and the object and prep. phrase לָרַבִּים (prep. לְ, definite article and adj. mpl of רַב "much", "many") "the many". A transitive external hi. denotes an action performed by "him" which in some way transforms הָרַבִּים "the many" or alters their status, where "he" is the subject and agent and הָרַבִּים "the many" the object and patient: "he will cause the many to be righteous". If read as intransitive, internal hi., "he" is both subject and object: "he will show himself to be righteous towards the many (for the benefit of the many)". Here, a judicial function is at work.

The subject is modified by a compound noun construction, where צַדִּיק (adjective "righteous", "just") works in apposition to עַבְדִּי (noun ms cstr. of עֶבֶד "servant", "slave", "subject", 1cs poss. suff.) "the righteous one, my servant",[139] which is modified by 1cs poss. suff., where a hierarchical relationship might appear between a subordinate superior, speaking partner, whose will and action terminate the subordinate's position. עַבְדִּי "my servant" is further modified by selectional features realised by the predicate and the prep. phase. The predicate יַצְדִּיק "he will cause to make righteous" works as an attribute of the subject, expressing how the servanthood shall imply a promising future, whereas the object לָרַבִּים "the many" explains to whom. Both "he" and "the many" shall become righteous. They thus have a common fate in terms of righteousness, but different focuses are placed on them, for while "he" is agent, the "many" are patients: "the righteous one, my servant, will cause the many to be righteous."

---

[138] דַּעַת is usually comprehended as cognate to the verb ידע "to know", but alternative readings have also been offered, cf. Appendix 4. Muilenburg, "The Book of Isaiah: Chapters 40–66", pp. 629–630, moves בְּדַעְתּוֹ to the beginning of the next clause of the verse, and translates "by his knowledge shall the righteous one, my servant, make the many to be accounted righteous". See further discussion of this in Appendix 7.

[139] For the interpretation of צַדִּיק in Isa. 53:11, see Appendix 7.

A copulative *waw* connects what precedes it and what follows, i.e. the object עֲוֺנֹתָם (noun mpl cstr. of עָוֺן "iniquity", "sin", "guilt", "punishment", 3mpl poss. suff.) "their iniquities", the subject, which is the independent pronoun הוּא "he", and the predicate יִסְבֹּל (imperf. qal 3ms of סבל "carry", "bear") "he carried", where the imperfect is rendered in the past.[140] The predicate is bound up with the object עֲוֺנֹתָם "their iniquities", but no action passes over from agent to goal. The expression "he carried their iniquities" works as a depiction of a state of being a sinner or an act of sinning. But since the predicate is still connected with an object, it might be called "quasi-fientive".[141] The sinner incurs guilt through iniquities and is made to carry the weight of the guilt. Simultaneously, a state of "them" as object is depicted by עֲוֺנֹתָם "their iniquities", which implies that "they" too have sinned. Thus, עֲוֺנֹתָם הוּא יִסְבֹּל "he carried their iniquities" expresses how both the subject "he" and the object "they" are related to "sin" by the predicate and the suff. of the object: both "he" and "they" have committed sin. "Their" iniquities and how "he" carried them in the past are contrasted with how "he" shall make the "many" righteous in the future.[142] While the preceding clauses conveyed "his" future and that of the "many", this presents both their pasts.

"His" insight and knowledge, as well as "his" righteousness and that of the "many" are described in the imperf. (יִשְׂבָּע "he shall be sated", יִרְאֶה "he shall see" and יַצְדִּיק לְ "he shall cause [the many] to be righteous", but so too is the humiliation יִסְבֹּל "he carried" [עֲוֺנֹתָם

---

[140] Dahood, "Phoenician Elements in Isaiah 52:13–53:12", p. 72, takes the imperf. as a stylistic variation of the perfect, having preterite meaning, cf. 53:7. Koole, *Isaiah III. Vol. 2*, p. 336, explains it as *futurum exactum*.

[141] On "quasi-fientive", see 3.10.5. n. 80. Apart from Isa. 53:11, the phrase סָבַל עָוֺן occurs only in Lam. 5:7 Q: אֲבֹתֵינוּ חָטְאוּ וְאֵינָם וַאֲנַחְנוּ עֲוֺנֹתֵיהֶם סָבָלְנוּ "Our fathers have sinned, they are no longer, and we carry their iniquities". The focus here is not the sin itself, but the consequences of sin, i.e. the sufferings of the community. However, the guilt of the fathers is not contrasted with "our" present undeserved sufferings, cf. אוֹי־נָא לָנוּ כִּי חָטָאנוּ "Woe to us, for we have sinned" (v. 16). Cf. Exod. 20:5, where עָוֺן "iniquity" of the fathers is visited on the children up to the third and fourth generation (and Num. 14:33). The more common expression נָשָׂא עָוֺן "bear iniquity" suggests that the consequences of the iniquity rest on those who have perpetrated it, see e.g. Whybray, *Thanksgiving for a Liberated Prophet*, pp. 31–57, and Hägglund, *Isaiah 53 in the Light of Homecoming after Exile*, pp. 82–94. Cf. 3.10.15. n. 154.

[142] On the identification of רַבִּים "many" in 53:11, see 3.10.17.1. In the narrative analysis in 4.8., the relation between "him" and "them" will be further amplified in the trope of personification, in which a confusion appears between the personifier "he" and the personified "they".

"their iniquities"]). The tenses are ambiguous as regards the turning point from past to future, as the verbs describing both the past and the future are in imperf. The servant is related to the speaking "I" in עַבְדִּי "my servant". "He" is also related to הָרַבִּים "the many" in both past and future: "he" will cause "the many" to be righteous and "he" carried their iniquities. The verse as a whole is characterised by a blurring of the semantic fields of "his" past עָמָל "travail" and the carrying of (their) iniquities, and "his" future of seeing, being sated by knowledge, being righteous and making the "many" righteous.

After the anonymous 3ms speech from 53:7 onwards (apart from the "I" speech in v. 8), in the last part of 53:11 "I" speech reappears. The expressions יִרְאֶה "he shall see" and יִשְׂבַּע בְּדַעְתּוֹ "he shall be sated by his knowledge" might echo what is said about "them" in 52:15 and "us" in 53:1, where something which has never been heard of before is brought to the fore. But whereas "I" speaks about אֲשֶׁר לֹא־סֻפַּר לָהֶם "what has not been told" and אֲשֶׁר לֹא־שָׁמְעוּ "what they did not hear" in 52:15, by לִשְׁמֻעָתֵנוּ "what we hear" in 53:1 "we" assume that something might have both told and heard. While in 52:15 it is stated that רָאוּ "they shall see" and הִתְבּוֹנָנוּ "they shall understand", in 53:1 "we" ask whether זְרוֹעַ יְהוָה "the arm of YHWH" has been revealed. In 53:11 "his" future seeing is contrasted with "his" past travail. In the YHWH discourse in 52:14, רַבִּים "many" are appalled at "him" and in 52:15 "he" is related to the future of "many peoples" and "kings" who shall see and understand.

As in YHWH's proclamation of his servant's prosperity in 52:13, in 53:11 עַבְדִּי "my servant" also appears, here with the apposition צַדִּיק "the righteous one". In 52:13 the servanthood is realised by his future exaltation, while in 53:11 it is related to his causing הָרַבִּים "the many" to be righteous. The righteousness of "him" and הָרַבִּים "the many" might be contrasted with the sin throughout Isa. 53. עֲוֺנֹתָם הוּא יִסְבֹּל "he carried their iniquities" in 53:11 might be a variation of 53:4: אָכֵן חֳלָיֵנוּ הוּא נָשָׂא וּמַכְאֹבֵינוּ סְבָלָם "Yet surely he bore our illnesses and carried our sicknesses". In the treatment of "his" carrying of "our" illnesses in v. 4, it was emphasised how "he" too was ill. Just as the ill "he" also bears "our" illnesses, "he" also carries "their" iniquities.[143] A further correspondence might be seen in the

---

[143] The syntax of 53:11 is the same as in 53:4a, while a morphological contrast appears between a perfect in 53:4 and an imperfect in 53:11.

relation between "his travail" and "his carrying of their sins", cf. 53:5: הוּא מְחֹלָל מִפְּשָׁעֵנוּ מְדֻכָּא מֵעֲוֹנֹתֵינוּ "he was wounded because of our transgressions and injured because of our iniquities". The identification between "him" and "us", which was established in 53:4a and further developed in 53:5–6, is echoed: being sick like "us", "he" is also a sinner like "us" and "them".

Similarly, the turning point to the future in 53:5 is expressed as chastisement upon "him" for "our" healing and "his" wound as recovery for "us". In 53:11, "his" future is related to how "he" shall "see and be sated by his knowledge", and how "the righteous one, my servant, will cause the many to be righteous".

3.10.15. Isa. 53:12

לָכֵן אֲחַלֶּק־לוֹ בָרַבִּים וְאֶת־עֲצוּמִים יְחַלֵּק שָׁלָל
תַּחַת אֲשֶׁר הֶעֱרָה לַמָּוֶת נַפְשׁוֹ וְאֶת־פֹּשְׁעִים נִמְנָה
וְהוּא חֵטְא־רַבִּים נָשָׂא וְלַפֹּשְׁעִים יַפְגִּיעַ׃

Truly, therefore I will allot the many to him and numerous he shall allot
   to spoiling,
because he was slain to death and reckoned with transgressors,
he bore the sin of many and was struck because of transgressors.

The adverb לָכֵן "truly", "therefore", introduces a promise: "I will allot the many to him". This is followed by a parallel: "and numerous he shall allot to spoiling". The two clauses of the promises of the speaking "I" for "his" future are followed by a conjunction phrase תַּחַת אֲשֶׁר "because" and four clauses explaining "his" past; the first related to death, the last three related to transgressors: "he" was slain to death and reckoned with transgressors, "he" bore the sin of many and was struck because of transgressors. This "I" speech concerns both the past and the future of "him" and רַבִּים "many" (with and without definite article).

The deictic adverb לָכֵן "truly", "therefore", introduces a response of a promise or declaration in relation to the preceding verse. Then follows the predicate with object אֲחַלֶּק־לוֹ (imperf. pi. transitive 1cs of חלק "allot", "give a portion", "divide", "share with", object marker לְ, 3ms suff.) "I will allot to him". The "I" is the subject and agent and "he" is the object and patient. The additional phrase בָרַבִּים "the many" (prep. בְּ, definite article and adjective, mpl of רַב "much", "many") might work as an object or a prep. phrase. If working as an object, it expresses double transitivity, i.e. הָרַבִּים "the many" shall become "his"

possession: "I will allot to him the many".[144] If הָרַבִּים "the many" is
taken to be a prep. phrase, this expresses how "he" takes part in בָּרַבִּים
"the many".[145]

A conjunctive *waw* connects the preceding clause to a following
phrase אֶת־עֲצוּמִים, which has been taken both as an object and as
prep. phrase. If אֶת is read as an object marker, עֲצוּמִים (noun mpl of
עָצוּם "numerous", "great", "mighty") "numerous" becomes the object
of the predicate יְחַלֵּק (imperf. pi. 3ms of חלק "allot", "give a portion",
"divide", "share with") "he shall allot numerous".[146] "He" is the subject
and agent of the predicate, whereas עֲצוּמִים "numerous" are those who
have opposed him (cf. בָּרַבִּים "the many" as object in the previous
clause).[147] If we read אֶת as the prep. "with" or "among", "he" will be
dividing spoils with the victor (cf. בָּרַבִּים "the many" as prep. phrase
of the previous clause).[148] This is followed by the object שָׁלָל (noun ms
"spoil", "booty", "plunder", "prey") "spoiling", where the reward of

---

[144] Thomas, "A Consideration of Isaiah LIII", p. 120, Muilenburg, "The Book of
Isaiah: Chapters 40–66", pp. 630–631, Koole, *Isaiah III. Vol. 2*, p. 337, regard בָּרַבִּים
as object. Koole argues that this is:

> dictated not by grammar but by content. The epilogue should correspond to
> the prologue with its description of the Servant's exaltedness recognized even
> by "many peoples" and their "kings", cf. 49:7. The other explanation in which
> he shares with "many"…fails to do justice to this because their share is at the
> expense of the Servant's.

Koole translates 53:12a: "Therefore I will divide to him the many".

[145] בָּרַבִּים is most often interpreted as a prep. phrase, cf. Clifford, *Fair Spoken and
Persuading*, p. 175: "Therefore I will bestow on him a portion with the many", Wes-
termann, *Isaiah 40–66*, p. 255: "Therefore I will give him a portion with the great
(*Großen*)", cf. Hermisson, "Das vierte Gottesknechtlied im deuterojesajanischen Kon-
text", p. 9 (ET p. 29), Blenkinsopp, *Isaiah 40–55*, p. 346, Oswalt, *The Book of Isaiah:
Chapters 40–66*, p. 399: "Therefore, I will apportion for him among the many".

[146] עֲצוּמִים in Isa. 53:12 has been translated in different ways:
i.   "mighty", see Clifford, *Fair Spoken and Persuading*, p. 175, Oswalt, *The Book of
     Isaiah: Chapters 40–66*, p. 399.
ii. "numerous" (*Zahlreichen*), see Hermisson, "Das vierte Gottesknechtlied im deu-
     terojesajanischen Kontext", p. 9 (ET p. 29), Koole, *Isaiah III. Vol. 2*, pp. 336; 338.
iii. *Gewaltigen*, see Kutsch, *Sein Leiden und Tod – unser Heil*, pp. 12; 37–38.
iv. "powerful", see Thomas, "A Consideration of Isaiah LIII", p. 120, Blenkinsopp,
     Isaiah 40–55, p. 346, Barré, "Textual and Rhetorical-Critical Observations on the
     Last Servant Song", p. 27.
v.   "strong"/"great", see Westermann, *Isaiah 40–66*, p. 255 (*Mächtigen*), Clines, *I, He,
     We and They*, pp. 13; 22, who renders it rather freely as: "he may take a hero's
     portion".

[147] אֶת־עֲצוּמִים taken as an object, see Thomas, "A Consideration of Isaiah LIII",
p. 120, and further references in Koole, *Isaiah III. Vol. 2*, p. 338.

[148] אֶת־עֲצוּמִים taken as prep. phrase, see Westermann, *Isaiah 40–66*, p. 255: "with
the strong", Hermisson, "Das vierte Gottesknechtlied im deuterojesajanischen Kon-

"him" is expressed as the distribution of captured booty after military victory.

Then the complex prep. phrase תַּחַת אֲשֶׁר "because", "in return for that" works as a conjunction which introduces a causal clause.[149] Thus, after the conclusion in the first part of the verse, the cause follows. The predicate הֶעֱרָה (perf. hi. 3fs of ערה "uncover", "pour out", "bare", "become naked")[150] is external hi. and the event belongs to the past. "He" is the patient and the agent is unnamed. This is modified by the prep. phrase לַמָּוֶת (prep. לְ, definite article, noun ms מָוֶת "death") "to death" and the subject נַפְשׁוֹ (noun fs נֶפֶשׁ "life", "myself, "person", 3ms poss. suff.): "he was slain to death".[151]

A second clause about the past follows, introduced by conjunctive *waw*, then the object אֶת־פֹּשְׁעִים (pt. qal mpl of פשע "transgress", "rebel") "transgressors", and finally the predicate נִמְנָה (perf. ni. 3ms of מנה "reckon", "assign", "count")[152] "and he was reckoned with

---

text", p. 9 (ET p. 29): "with numerous", Oswalt, *The Book of Isaiah: Chapters 40–66*, p. 399: "with the mighty".

[149] The complex prep. phrase תַּחַת אֲשֶׁר in Isa. 53:12 has been variously interpreted:

i.   "yet" (*dafür*), see Kutsch, *Sein Leiden und Tod – unser Heil*, p. 14, Hermisson, "Das vierte Gottesknechtlied im deuterojesajanischen Kontext", p. 9 (ET p. 29).
ii. "in exchange for this", see Koole, *Isaiah III. Vol. 2*, pp. 336; 339, i.e. "the conjunction relates...to the exchange of the Servant's humiliation for his merited elevation" (p. 339).
iii. "because", see Muilenburg, "The Book of Isaiah: Chapters 40–66", p. 630, Clifford, *Fair Spoken and Persuading*, p. 175, Oswalt, *The Book of Isaiah: Chapters 40–66*, p. 399.
iv. "since": Blenkinsopp, *Isaiah 40–55*, p. 346.

[150] The majority of exegetes translate the expression הֶעֱרָה לַמָּוֶת נַפְשׁוֹ as "he poured out his soul to death" or something similar, cf. Westermann, *Isaiah 40–66*, p. 255, Blenkinsopp, *Isaiah 40–55*, p. 346, Oswalt, *The Book of Isaiah: Chapters 40–66*, p. 399, Koole, *Isaiah III. Vol. 2*, p. 250. A variation is offered by Clifford, *Fair Spoken and Persuading*, p. 174: "because he has exposed his soul to death". Whybray, *Thanksgiving for a Liberated Prophet*, p. 105, claims that the expression הֶעֱרָה...נַפְשׁוֹ means that the servant "'exposed' himself or left himself defenceless, in other words that he consciously put himself into a position in which he was at the mercy of his enemies or persecutors". Here, the servant's willingness is emphasised.

[151] Torrey, *The Second Isaiah*, p. 423, and Thomas, "A Consideration of Isaiah LIII", p. 126, interpret לַמָּוֶת as a way to express a superlative, cf. Driver, "Isaiah 52:13–53:12", pp. 102–104, who translates 53:12 "he has exposed his life even to (the danger of) death". Whybray, *Thanksgiving for a Liberated Prophet*, claims that it is irrelevant whether לַמָּוֶת means "to death" or "to the uttermost", as the whole expression הֶעֱרָה לַמָּוֶת נַפְשׁוֹ means that the servant "risked death rather than that he died" (p. 105). On the debate about the "servant's death", cf. 5.14.1. n. 251.

[152] Koole, *Isaiah III. Vol. 2*, p. 340, interprets ni. נִמְנָה as tolerative, cf. his emphasis on the servant's willingness in his translation of הֶעֱרָה לַמָּוֶת נַפְשׁוֹ, see 3.10.15. n. 151.

transgressors". Because of the pass. stem, "he" is subject and patient, i.e. in the state of being acted upon by an implicit agent. The prep. phrase תַּחַת אֲשֶׁר "because", "in return for", that works elliptically for both clauses and motivates the forgoing statement about the exaltation of "him". Being reckoned with transgressors, "he" is regarded as among those who have committed sin. Thus, "he" dies as one of the transgressors.

The third clause is introduced by a conjunctive *waw* and an independent personal pronoun 3ms הוּא "he", followed by a composite object חֵטְא־רַבִּים (noun ms חֵטְא "sin", noun mpl of רַב "much", "many") and finally a predicate (perf. qal 3ms נשׂא "bear") "he bore the sin of many". The predicate is bound up with the composite object חֵטְא־רַבִּים "the sin of many", but no action passes over from agent to goal. The expression הוּא חֵטְא נָשָׂא "he bore sin" works as a depiction of a state of being a sinner or an act of sinning. But since the predicate is still connected with an object, it might be called "quasi-fientive".[153] The sinner incurs guilt through transgression and is made to carry the weight of the guilt. Simultaneously, a similar state of the object רַבִּים "many" is depicted through a noun phrase: חֵטְא־רַבִּים "the sin of many". Thus, in the phrase הוּא חֵטְא־רַבִּים נָשָׂא "he bore the sin of many", both the subject הוּא "he" and the object רַבִּים "many" are related to sin by the predicate and the suff. of the object: הוּא "he" has brought upon himself his own punishment, and not only "he", but also רַבִּים "many" have committed sins.[154]

Cf. similar explanations by e.g. Thomas, "A Consideration of Isaiah LIII", p. 120, Westermann, *Isaiah 40–66*, pp. 255; 268, Whybray, *Isaiah 40–66*, p. 182, Clines, *I, He, We and They*, pp. 14; 22, Oswalt, *The Book of Isaiah: Chapters 40–66*, pp. 399; 406. Furthermore, when explaining the perf., Koole opts "for the view that the divine word predicts both the humiliation and the elevation of the Servant; these forms have the value of a *futurum exactum*". He also explains the perf. of vv. 7; 10; 11b (pp. 336; 340, quotation is taken from p. 340, his italics).

[153] On "quasi-fientive", see 3.10.5. n. 80.

[154] Zimmerli, "Zur Vorgeschichte von Jes. LIII", pp. 238–39, quoted in Spieckermann, "Konzeption und Vorgeschichte des Stellvertretungsgedankens im Alten Testament", p. 281, ET, p. 2:

> The langugage [of bearing iniquity] was by no means used for the first time with reference to the Suffering Servant. It existed previously in other contexts, but now in a novel way it is applied to the Servant and his suffering. To be sure, the original formula נשׂא עון "to bear iniquity", is varied with great freedom in Isa. 53. Hence סבל in vv. 4,11 can replace נשׂא in vv. 4 and 12. Similarly, חלי, "infirmity", in v. 4, מכאב, "disease", in v. 4, and חטא, "sin", in v. 12 can each be substituted by עון, "iniquity", in v. 11. Nevertheless, unmistakably behind all

The fourth and final clause about the past begins with a conjunctive *waw* and the object לַפֹּשְׁעִים (prep. לְ, definite article, and pt. mpl of פשע "transgress", "rebel") "transgressors". This clause has been taken to be either a circumstantial clause depending on the previous line, "while he…", or a new, independent clause expressing contrast between "him" and "many", where the *waw* is given a copulative, adversative value. Then follows the predicate, יַפְגִּיעַ לְ (imperf. hi. intransitive 3ms of פגע "strike", "cause to light upon", "encounter", "crush", and prep. לְ) "he was struck".[155] Thus, the *waw* introduces a clause restating or paraphrasing the previous clause, clarifying the immediately preceding material.

The first line concerns the future of "him", הָרַבִּים "the many" and עֲצוּמִים "numerous", with "him" as both agent and patient: "I will allot the many to him and numerous he shall allot to spoiling". In this, the predicate חלק "allot" is repeated, first with "I" as subject and "he" as object, then with "he" as subject and עֲצוּמִים "numerous" as object (or prep. phrase). The two last lines concern the past of "him", פֹּשְׁעִים "transgressors" and רַבִּים "many", again with "him" as both agent and patient: "he" was slain to death and became counted among

---

these variations, there still stands a common idea which has a wide range of application in the Old Testament.
Zimmerli relates this to priestly traditions of atonement, cf. Lev. 10:17, 16:11, and the prophet Ezekiel's symbolic portrayal of Israel's punishment, cf. Ezek. 4:4–8, the latter without any atoning effect. The phrase נָשָׂא חֵטְא "bear sin" occurs in eight passages apart from Isa. 53:12, each in the context of priestly legislation (Lev. 19:17, 20:20, 22:9, 24:15, Num. 9:13; 18:22; 32, Ezek. 23:49). Barré, "Textual and Rhetorical-Critical Observations on the Last Servant Song", p. 4, explains the appearance of נשא and סבל as a "distant parallelism" within Isa. 52:13–53:12, cf. 52:13b, 53:4ab; 11d; 12e. He also comments on the repetitive variations of פֶּשַׁע, "transgression" and עָוֺן "iniquity" in 53:5ab and 53:11d; 12f (p. 5). Cf. סָבַל עָוֺן in 3.10.14. n. 141 and נָשָׂא חֳלִי "bear illness" and סָבַל מַכְאֹב "carry sickness" in 3.10.7. n. 87.

[155] פגע occurs in perf. hi. with the prep. בְּ in Isa. 53:6 and in imperf. hi. with the prep. לְ in v. 12, and is related to the humiliation which "he" has suffered because of עֲוֺן כֻּלָּנוּ "the iniquity of all of us" (v. 6)/פֹּשְׁעִים "transgressors" (v. 12). In v. 6, it is emphasised how this is due to the will of YHWH. In both v. 6 and v. 12 YHWH is the subject of the verb, and the servant its object. While the hi. in v. 6 is perf., in v. 12 it is imperf. P. P. Saydon, "The Use of Tenses in Deutero-Isaiah", *Bib* 40 (1959) 292–293, explains v. 12 as a past *qtl* followed up by a present-future *yqtl* according to the temporal relation of the two actions: "He took away the sins of many and makes intercession for the rebellious". This is supported by Whybray, *Thanksgiving for a Liberated Prophet*, p. 152, n. 189: יפגיע "is a past frequentative the intercession [of which] is separated in time from the bearing of the punishment". Koole, *Isaiah III. Vol. 2*, p. 340, explains יַפְגִּיעַ לְ as *futurum exactum*. Also in 53:7 we saw an imperf. rendered past: וְלֹא יִפְתַּח־פִּיו "and/but he did not open his mouth" (twice). On the translation of יַפְגִּיעַ לְ in 53:12, see Appendix 8.

transgressors; "he" bore the sin of many and was struck because of transgressors.[156] The grammatical constructions in the phrases for carrying sin are identical in 53:11 (עֲוֺנֹתָם הוּא יִסְבֹּל "he carried their iniquities") and in v. 12 (הוּא חֵטְא־רַבִּים נָשָׂא "he bore the sin of many"). While the servant has earlier carried "our" illnesses (53:4: חֳלָיֵנוּ הוּא נָשָׂא וּמַכְאֹבֵינוּ סְבָלָם "he bore our illnesses and carried our sicknesses"), here it is expressed how "he" carried the sins of "all of us", i.e. "he" is both sick and a sinner. A distanciation appears between the objects of "his carrying" related to "us", "them" and "many" respectively: חֳלָיֵנוּ "our illnesses" (v. 4), מַכְאֹבֵינוּ "our sicknesses" (v. 4), עֲוֺנֹתָם "their iniquities" (v. 11) and חֵטְא־רַבִּים "the sin of many" (v. 12).

3.10.16. *Summing up*

Although Isa. 52:13–53:12 is beset with textual uncertainties, an attempt will be made to offer a summary of this reading. As mentioned earlier (3.9.), my own delimitation of this text is rather pragmatically defined.[157] In the following summing up of this reading, it will be shown how the verses of this text run into one another. In the adjacent narrative (chapter 4) and intertextual (chapter 5) readings of Isa. 52:13–53:12, elements of the text will be brought into additional dialogue with each other and with many other texts, which will extend the text even further.

The text might be briefly outlined as follows: 52:13–15: YHWH speech; 53:1–6: "we" speech; 53:7–10: anonymous 3ms speech (apart from the "I" speech in v. 8); and 53:11–12: YHWH speech.

3.10.16.1. *52:13–15*
In 52:13–15, oppositions appear between the past humiliation of "you"/"him" and "his" future exaltation, and between the past and future of "many peoples"/"kings": while v. 13 concerns "your" witnessing of the future exaltation of עַבְדִּי "my servant", in v. 15 future reactions of גוֹיִם רַבִּים "many peoples", מְלָכִים "kings" and "they" are presented. עַבְדִּי "my servant" shall be exalted (v. 13) and "he יַזֶּה ('will startle'?) many peoples before him" (v. 15). In-between v. 13 and

---

[156] Koole, *Isaiah III. Vol. 2*, p. 341, claims that stylistically vv. 11–12a form a concentric structure, with v. 12b as an extra line.

[157] When it comes to the question of delimitation, Isa. 52:1–12 and Isa. 54 might certainly be taken into consideration (cf. 3.9. and 6.1.).

v. 15, the humiliation of the "you"/"him" of the past appears (v. 14).
The roles are changed: "you"/"he" shall be vindicated and were humiliated (vv. 13–14) and the "many" were appalled and shall see (vv. 14–
15) – in relation to appearance – in both instances. In v. 14, a linguistic
pressure point appears which disrupts the potential coherence of the
text. This occurs because of a confusion between "him" and "you" in
both similarity and difference: both "you" and "he" are related to the
dismay of the "many", but a discrepancy appears in the argument: "his"
disfigurement is the cause and "you" are the one at whom "many" are
appalled (v. 14). In 52:14–15, a contrasting relationship between "him"
and "many" is prominent.

3.10.16.2. 53:1–6
In 53:1, the "I" speech of 52:13–15 is interrupted by new participants
and a new situation. Simultaneously, the questions in 53:1 echo 52:15
by taking up its final words (cf. 3.10.4.). The first question signifies the
reception of לִשְׁמֻעָתֵנוּ "what we hear" and is further illuminated by
the second question concerning the revelation of זְרוֹעַ יְהוָה "the arm
of YHWH".

The "we" speech continues in vv. 2–3 in which a contrasting relationship between "him" and "we" is prominent.[158] "He" is scorned
because of "his" disfigurement. "He" is isolated and ill, ashamed and
disgraced. Whereas "we" in v. 3 appear as witnesses to "his" fate only,
in v. 4a a connection is expressed between "his" illnesses in vv. 2–3 and
"our" experience of these same illnesses. In v. 4b "we" again distance
"ourselves" from "him", as "his" illnesses are explained as punishment
from YHWH. In vv. 5–6, the identification between "him" and "us"
becomes even more remarkable, i.e. after the sin is introduced, as "we"
explain "his" humiliation as due to "our" sins. In v. 5, the relation
between "his" and "our" common fate is deepened by the introduction of healing. The healing gained (for "us") by the punishment (of
"him") is in both "our" and "his" favour: both "we" and "he" shall
be healed. In the explanation of "his" illness and "our" recovery, the
relation between "him" and "us" is distorted. A possible centre of the
text becomes more unreachable, and the relation between illness and

---

[158] In the "I" speech of 52:14–15 and the "we" speech of 53:2–3, a contrasting
relationship appears between "him" and "many"/"we". In both instances, the disdain
towards "you"/"him" is due to "his" disfigurement.

recovery appears somewhere in-between: as "he" is ill and punished, "he" has also sinned and shall be healed. YHWH's striking of "him" due to עֲוֺן כֻּלָּנוּ "the iniquity of all of us" in v. 6 is a conflation of the two halves of v. 4, where "his" and "our" illnesses are identical, and where "we accounted him stricken, smitten by God and humiliated". "Our" assumptions in v. 4b that "his" illness was due to YHWH's striking of "him" is also confirmed in v. 6. Whereas YHWH was not mentioned as the one striking in v. 5, he is in v. 6. After the turning point towards recovery in v. 5, the situation in v. 6 is again in the past, presenting the background which leads to a future reversal of the situation: "our" delusion and YHWH's punishment of "him".

3.10.16.3. *53:7–10*

In 53:7, "he" is compared to שֶׂה "a sheep" and רָחֵל "a ewe". The similes focus on being humble, humbled and silent.[159] V. 7 concerns the silence of the humiliated one: "he", although oppressed and humbled, did not open "his" mouth. Neither "his" relation to "us" nor his relation to YHWH is explicitly mentioned, and the speaking voice is not clearly identified. In v. 7, no reason is given for the oppression of "him", whereas in v. 8 it is explained that מִפֶּשַׁע עַמִּי נֶגַע לָמוֹ "because of the transgression of my people was his stroke", and that דּוֹרוֹ "his time" has understood neither "his" nor עַמִּי "my people"'s fate. In a question, a correspondence appears between "his" and the people's fate, in that they are related through sin and stroke: נֶגַע לָמוֹ "his stroke" is due to פֶּשַׁע עַמִּי "the transgression of my people".[160] V. 8 is "I" speech about "he" and עַמִּי "my people", where the nearness between YHWH and עַמִּי "my people" is expressed.

In v. 8 נִגְזַר מֵאֶרֶץ חַיִּים "he was cut off from the land of the living"; in v. 9, the unworthiness of "his" burial place among wicked ones and a rich (?) is depicted. Nothing is said about why "he" was struck by death and given an unworthy tomb. However, רְשָׁעִים "wicked ones" might be compared to sinners, cf. vv. 5–6; 8, and contrasted with a lack of violence and deceit, cf. v. 7. As in v. 9, so also in v. 7 "his" silence

---

[159] וְהוּא נַעֲנֶה "and he was humble(d)" in 53:7 echoes 53:4, while the comparison of "him" with שֶׂה "a sheep" and רָחֵל "a ewe" echoes 53:6. Cf. 3.10.10.

[160] Cf. 53:4–6. But while 53:4–6 are uttered by "us" about "him", 53:8 is "I" speech about "he" and עַמִּי "my people". As the closeness between YHWH and "him" is emphasised by the expression עַבְדִּי "my servant" in 52:13, so too is a close relationship expressed by עַמִּי "my people" in 53:8.

and non-use of force are prominent. However, in v. 7 "he" is afflicted, but not done to death as in v. 9, in which the punishment seems to be unmitigated: after death there is no hope. The copulative *waw* of v. 10 introduces an explanation for "his" unworthy burial without reason (v. 9): the humiliations of "him" are depicted as illness and then related to sin. "His" wounds are seen as consequences of sin and as punishment from YHWH.[161]

A turning point from "his" humiliation and death in vv. 8–9 to vindication is presented in promises of descendants and a long life. "He" is promised prosperity for "his" hand. No reason for the turning point is given.[162]

In v. 10, YHWH is again brought onto the scene.[163] In the depiction of "his" fate as YHWH's will as regards past and future, humiliation and prosperity, "his" life acts as a witness to who YHWH is (cf. v. 1). By way of the introductory copulative *waw*, v. 10 might be related to the preceding v. 9, in which the speaking voice is not identified, while YHWH's words in v. 8 might occupy an isolated place in a context in which YHWH is not the speaker.

3.10.16.4. *53:11–12*

In v. 11, the future of "him" and "the many" is depicted: יִרְאֶה "he shall see", יִשְׂבַּע בְּדַעְתּוֹ "he shall be sated by his knowledge"[164] and יַצְדִּיק צַדִּיק...לָרַבִּים "the righteous one...will cause the many to be righteous". The past of "him" and "them" is also alluded to: "he" has had עָמָל "travail" and עֲוֺנֹתָם הוּא יִסְבֹּל "he carried their iniquities".[165] In v. 11, עַבְדִּי "my servant" reappears (cf. 52:13), here with the apposition צַדִּיק "the righteous one". 53:12 is a summary of what has gone

---

[161] וַיהוָה חָפֵץ דַּכְּאוֹ הֶחֱלִי "YHWH was pleased to strike him by making him ill" echoes "our" diagnosis of "him" in 53:3–5. As in 53:10, so also in 53:5–6; 8, "his" wounds are seen as consequences of sin and as punishment from YHWH.

[162] Cf. "his" exaltation in 52:13, where, similarly, no reason for the turning point is given. In 53:5, turning points are expressed as healing and recovery, and the humiliations of "him" might be explained as reasons for "our" turning point.

[163] Cf. 53:6 and "my people" in 53:8. When 53:10 is related to the preceding, a new voice appears, as neither "I" (52:13–15) nor "we" is speaking here (53:1–6).

[164] The expressions יִרְאֶה "he shall see" and יִשְׂבַּע בְּדַעְתּוֹ "he shall be sated by his knowledge" might echo what is said about "them" in 52:15 and "us" in 53:1. Cf. 3.10.14.

[165] The phrase עֲוֺנֹתָם הוּא יִסְבֹּל "he carried their iniquities" in 53:11 echoes 53:4–6: as the ill and sick one also carries "our" illnesses and sicknesses, so the (sinful) one/"he" also carries their iniquities.

before, with the conclusion stated first and then the cause. The first line
concerns the future of "him", הָרַבִּים "the many" and עֲצוּמִים "numerous" – "I will allot the many to him and numerous he shall allot to
spoiling" – while the two last lines concern the past of "him", פֹּשְׁעִים
"transgressors" and רַבִּים "many": "he" was slain to death and became
counted among פֹּשְׁעִים "transgressors"; "he" bore the sin of many and
was struck because of transgressors.[166]

3.10.17. *Identities and Difference*

In Isa. 52:13–53:12, relationships between YHWH, "I", "he", "you",
"we", עַמִּי "my people", רַבִּים "many", עֲצוּמִים "numerous", פֹּשְׁעִים
"transgressors", גּוֹיִם רַבִּים "many peoples" and מְלָכִים "kings" are
at play. In first- and third-person speech, "I", "we" and anonymous
voices tell about and question broken and restored relationships
between YHWH, "he", "we", "you" and "they". In the following, I shall
briefly present scholars' identifications of רַבִּים "many", the relationship between "him" and "us", as well as of עַמִּי "my people" in Isa.
52:13–53:12. Scholars' various identifications of עַבְדִּי "my servant" will
be commented upon in relation to their identifications of the other
actors in the text. This presentation of research is far from complete,
but is meant to illustrate the complexity both in the text and in readings of it.[167]

3.10.17.1. רַבִּים *"many"*

Both רַבִּים "many" and עַבְדִּי "my servant" appear only in the YHWH
speech in our text, in 52:14–15 and 53:11–12.[168] In 52:14, a numerical
inequality appears in the reactions of רַבִּים "many" (pl) witnessing the
disfigured "you" (sg): רַבִּים "many" were appalled at "you" due to "his"
disfigurement. In 52:15, the past situation of v. 14 is contrasted with
a future one: "he יַזֶּה ('will startle'?) גּוֹיִם רַבִּים 'many peoples'[169] before
him, מְלָכִים 'kings' shall shut their mouth". Moreover, what "they"

---

[166] 53:1 might be the beginning of a report made by "us" and set within the framework of divine utterance (52:13–15, 53:11b–12).

[167] For references to surveys of the history of research of Isa. 52:13–53:12, cf. 2.3.
n. 122.

[168] YHWH speech occurs in 52:13–15, 53:11b-12 (and v. 8?).

[169] רַבִּים "many" are here connected with גּוֹיִם "peoples", which in Isa. 40–55 is a
designation for those who are not called by the name of Israel. On the foreign peoples,
cf. 5.8.5.

were not told and did not hear, they shall see and understand. In v. 14, רַבִּים "many" appear in confrontation with "him" in the past, and in v. 15 in relation to גּוֹיִם רַבִּים "many peoples" and מְלָכִים "kings" in the future.

In 52:13, the coming prosperity of עַבְדִּי "my servant" is presented, in which "his" servanthood is realised by his future exaltation.[170] When "his" fate is related to what happens in vv. 14–15, "he" is related to the speaking "I", YHWH (as עַבְדִּי "my servant"), רַבִּים "many" (who witnessed "his" disfigurement in the past) and גּוֹיִם רַבִּים "many peoples" and מְלָכִים "kings" (who react).

In 53:11, the future of צַדִּיק עַבְדִּי "the righteous one, my servant" and הָרַבִּים "the many" is depicted. Their common fate is related to righteousness, with different focuses placed on עַבְדִּי "my servant" and הָרַבִּים "the many": "he" is righteous and will cause הָרַבִּים "the many" to become righteous in the future. This future is further contrasted with "their" iniquities which "he" carried in the past.[171] Also v. 12 has a turning point – here from future to past: "Truly, therefore I will allot the many to him", paralleled with "עֲצוּמִים 'numerous' he shall allot to spoiling", where "he" is the beneficiary who shall possess booty. This is contrasted with the past, where "he" was reckoned with פֹּשְׁעִים "transgressors", "he" bore the sin of רַבִּים "many" (here without a definite article) and "he" was struck because of פֹּשְׁעִים "transgressors". In v. 11, the future of "him" and הָרַבִּים "the many" is related to the past of "them", in v. 12, the future of "him", הָרַבִּים "the many" and עֲצוּמִים "numerous" is contrasted with the past of רַבִּים "many" and פֹּשְׁעִים "transgressors" in relation to "him".

What is the connection between רַבִּים "many", גּוֹיִם רַבִּים "many peoples" and מְלָכִים "kings" in 52:14–15 and רַבִּים "many" and עֲצוּמִים "numerous" in 53:11–12? Due to different interpretations of the identity of עַבְדִּי "my servant", various identifications of רַבִּים "many" will also appear through the text. Also, scholars do not necessarily interpret רַבִּים "many" as the same in every verse referred to in our text. Torrey draws attention to homonymous repetitions in Second Isaiah. He includes the wordplay in Isa. 52:14–15 concerning רַבִּים among these "puns", as he claims that רַבִּים in 52:14 is "many", and

---

[170] For a servant referred to elsewhere in Isa. 40–55, see 5.17. n. 324.

[171] In 53:11, עַבְדִּי "my servant"'s earlier travail leads to coming insight and knowledge. Moreover, "his" servanthood is related to רַבִּים "many" in both future and past: "he will cause the many to be righteous and carried their iniquities", see 3.10.14.

"mighty" in v. 15.[172] Payne argues that Torrey fails to relate the phenomenon to the widespread use of repetitions in the Book of Isaiah and in much other poetry in the Hebrew Bible, and also that he does not recognise that, in several of his examples, the repetition serves to extend the prophet's thought, not to lead into a totally different direction, cf. 54:1.[173]

a) Nations, Peoples, Gentiles

Hertzberg stresses that, in Isa. 40–55, everywhere the root פשע occurs, it describes the apostasy of the people of Israel.[174] However, regarding the root חטא, the picture is more complex. For instance, he claims that the expression הוּא חֵטְא־רַבִּים נָשָׂא in 53:12 refers to the two-fold task of the servant, to Israel and to the nations.[175] Israel has sinned, but so too have the Gentiles.[176] Hertzberg interprets רַבִּים "many" as the Gentiles in every verse in which the word occurs in 52:13–53:12.[177] He identifies the servant as a messenger of God (der Sendbote des Gottes),[178] and his reading is clearly universalistic: the servant's mission of salvation regards all people, Israel as well as the Gentiles.

Mettinger, who takes the servant to be Israel, identifies רַבִּים "many" in 52:14–15 to be the nations, while 53:11–12 are not treated in detail.

---

[172] Torrey, The Second Isaiah, pp. 199–202. He defines "Second Isaiah" as consisting of Isa. 34–35, 40–66.

[173] D. F. Payne, "Characteristic Word-Play in 'Second Isaiah': A Reappraisal", JSS 12 (1967) 207–229. J. W. Olley, "'The Many': How is Isa 53,12a to be Understood?", Bib 68 (1987) 336, n. 25, comments how North and Muilenburg, who both see word play as a literary device in Second Isaiah, do not see this in 53:12.

[174] H. W. Hertzberg, "Die 'Abtrünningen' und die 'Vielen': Ein Beitrag zu Jesaja 53" in A. Kutschke (ed), Verbannung und Heimkehr. Beiträge zur Geschichte und Theologie Israels im 6. und 5. Jahrhundert v. Chr.: Festschrift für W. Rudolph (Tübingen: J. C. B. Mohr {Paul Siebeck}, 1961) 98–101.

[175] Hertzberg, "Die 'Abtrünningen' und die 'Vielen', pp. 104–107.

[176] Hertzberg, "Die 'Abtrünningen' und die 'Vielen', p. 105. In connection with this he refers to Isa. 49:7, as well as 45:20, 47, 51:7; 18–23 and 52:5 (pp. 105–106).

[177] Hertzberg, "Die 'Abtrünningen' und die 'Vielen', p. 103–106.

[178] Hertzberg, "Die 'Abtrünningen' und die 'Vielen', p. 100, n. 17:
Diese Formulierung [der Sendbote des Gottes] muß hier als Interpretation des Ebed genügen. Sie paßt in jedem Falle, ob er der Prophet, der Heilskönig oder auch, wie neuerdings bei O. Kaiser (...) die Gola ist – eine mir übrigens schon deshalb sehr unwarscheinliche Lösung, weil "Israel" bei Deuterojesaja sowohl das Volk in seiner vergangenen Geschichte wie den exilierten "Rest", also die vom Propheten wiederholt Angeredeten, bezeichnen kann. An der "Abtrünnigkeit" hat das alte Volk früherer Tage genauso Anteil wie seine Vertreter in der Gegenwart des Propheten.
In his interpretation of the servant as a messenger of God, Hertzberg opens for both an individual and a collective identification.

Due to his interpretation of the servant, רַבִּים "many" in these verses should also be taken to be the nations.[179]

Oswalt identifies the servant as "an individual, almost certainly the Messiah, who will be the ideal Israel".[180] When searching for the identity of רַבִּים "many", he refers to the common understanding of 52:14–15 as "a comparison between two shocks" of the nations, the first concerning the servant's disfigurement (v. 14), the second concerning his exaltation (v. 15, cf. v. 13).[181] According to Oswalt, the basic thrust of 52:14–15 is clear: that the nations will be shocked speechless by what they see in God's servant. But the verses might additionally be read in continuity with 53:1–3. Here, the comparison is not between reactions to past disfigurement and coming exaltation, but "between a narrower group (v. 14) who is appalled and a larger group (v. 15) who is equally appalled".[182] In any case, what is expressed is the worldwide scale of the servant's shame and humiliation.[183] This same worldwide perspective also applies to Oswalt's reading of 53:11–12.[184]

b) Israelites

Westermann interprets the two instances of רַבִּים "many" in 52:14–15 as corresponding to each other, and identifies them as the Jews of the diaspora being spoken of as "nations" and as "kings".[185] Although he does not state it explicitly, it seems that he also identifies רַבִּים "many" in 53:11–12 as the Israelites.[186] To the question of the servant's identity, Westermann replies:

---

[179] Mettinger, *Farewell to the Servant Songs*, p. 38. cf. Torrey, *The Second Isaiah*, pp. 411–412, and Melugin, *The Formation of Isaiah 40–55*, pp. 167–169.

[180] Oswalt, *The Book of Isaiah: Chapters 40–66*, p. 108.

[181] Oswalt, *The Book of Isaiah: Chapters 40–66*, p. 379.

[182] Oswalt, *The Book of Isaiah: Chapters 40–66*, p. 379. Oswalt refers to Calvin and North for somewhat similar readings.

[183] Oswalt, *The Book of Isaiah: Chapters 40–66*, p. 379.

[184] Oswalt, *The Book of Isaiah: Chapters 40–66*, pp. 403–408.

[185] Westermann, *Isaiah 40–66*, p. 259. As for v. 15, he claims:
The meaning is that his [i.e. God's] work which consists in the exaltation of the Servant is so stupendous that people hear of it with astonishment in far-distant places (nations) and exalted circles (kings). Deutero-Isaiah is thinking of the widespread publicity to be given to the work, but not of heathen spheres outside of Israel.

[186] Westermann, *Isaiah 40–66*, pp. 267–269. He claims, for instance, that the conclusion of the divine utterance of 53:11b stands in continuation with the divine utterance of 52:13ff (p. 267).

One thing in particular will need to be heeded – and here the present writer disagrees with the majority of the innumerable commentaries on the songs. On principle, their exegesis must not be controlled by the question, "Who is this servant of God?" Instead, we must do them justice by recognizing that precisely this is what they neither tell nor intend to tell us. The questions which should control exegesis, are: "What do the texts make known about what transpires, or is to transpire, between God, the servant, and those to whom his task pertains?"[187]

Ruppert identifies the servant as the Gola community of Zion (*die Gola der Ziongemeinde*) and רַבִּים "many" in 52:14, 53:11–12 as the whole of Israel (*ganz Israel, Gesamtisrael*) within a particularistic horizon, where the servant of the Lord suffers a vicarious death (*stellvertretendes Todesleiden*) and makes the whole of Israel righteous.[188]

c) Both the Nations and Israelites

Rignell and Olley interpret רַבִּים "many" as having a broad meaning, embracing both the nations and Israel in both 52:14–15 and 53:11–12.[189] Rignell identifies the servant as the generation of the captivity which had the task of enduring the vicarious suffering of the nations.[190] Hollenberg regards רַבִּים "many" as "crypto-Israelites" who have merged their identity with the nations of the dispersion but who have come to recognize their true identity in the suffering Israel of the Babylonian exile.[191] He interprets the servant to be "the righteous remnant".[192]

---

[187] Westermann, *Isaiah 40–66*, p. 93.

[188] Ruppert, "'Mein Knecht, der Gerechte, macht die Vielen gerecht, und ihre Verschuldung-er trägt sie'", pp. 12–14. He regards the YHWH speech of 52:13–15; 53:11b-12 as redactional additions and as interpretations of the "we" speech of 53:1ff. He takes Isa. 53:1–10aα.β.b to be the *Grundschrift*, in which the servant is identified as the prophet, whereas at a redactional level, the servant is identified as a collective, i.e. the Gola community of Zion.

[189] Rignell, "A Study of Isaiah Ch. 40–55", p. 79, interprets רַבִּים in 52:14 and גּוֹיִם רַבִּים in v. 15 as including both the Gentiles and the unfaithful of Israel. About 53:11, he states: "The 'many'…refer above all to the children of Israel but may also have a wider meaning and refer to the Gentiles" (p. 84). He identifies the servant as the generation of the exile (p. 79). Olley, "'The Many'", pp. 353–354.

[190] Rignell, "A Study of Isaiah Ch. 40–55", p. 79. As far as I can see, Olley does not identify the servant.

[191] D. E. Hollenberg, "Nationalism and 'The Nations' in Isaiah 40–55", *VT* 19 (1969) 35–36.

[192] Hollenberg, "Nationalism and 'The Nations' in Isaiah 40–55", pp. 27–28.

d) Sometimes the Nations and Sometimes Israelites

Many scholars claim that רַבִּים "many" in 52:14 and 53:11–12 are the Israelites and in 52:15 the nations (see, for instance, Elliger,[193] McKenzie,[194] Kutsch,[195] Whybray,[196] Hermisson,[197] Steck[198] and Koole).[199] Koole identifies the servant as a coming saviour, while the others take the servant to be the prophet.[200] Whybray identifies the servant with Israel in 52:13–15 and with the prophet in Isa. 53.[201]

e) The Servant's Disciples

Blenkinsopp, who identifies the servant of 52:13–53:12 as the prophet, claims that since רַבִּים is used with the article, "it is tempting to inter-pret the term in a quasi-technical sense with reference to the Servant's disciples as [הָרַבִּים] ('the Many')".[202]

f) Summing up

In the YHWH speech of 52:13–15 and 53:11b-12, relationships between YHWH, "I", "he", "you", "we", רַבִּים "many", עֲצוּמִים "numerous", גּוֹיִם רַבִּים "many peoples" and מְלָכִים "kings" are signs of identity, where the different plural actors of the text are identified in relation to each other

[193] Elliger, *Deuterojesaja in seinem Verhältnis zu Tritojesaja*, pp. 6–27, regards Isa 52:13–53:12 as a "typical" Trito-Isaianic passage, and identifies the servant as the prophet.

[194] J. L. McKenzie, *Second Isaiah: Introduction, Translation, and Notes* (AB, 20; Garden City, NY: Doubleday, 1968) 132–136. McKenzie regards the prophet as the servant (pp. xl–xli).

[195] Kutsch, *Sein Leiden und Tod – unser Heil*, p. 18. Kutsch argues that in 53:1, it is expressed that "we" have perceived a tiding, while in 52:15b it is announced that the peoples are astonished at an event about which they have not been told. He interprets the servant as the prophet (pp. 19ff).

[196] Whybray, *Isaiah 40–66*, pp. 170; 182–183, quotation from p. 181.

[197] Hermisson, "Israel und der Gottesknecht bei Deuterojesaja", p. 13 (ET p. 34) regards "many" in 52:14 as "the larger community from which the Servant was excluded; this means first and foremost Israel", cf. the "we" of 53:1ff. גּוֹיִם רַבִּים in 52:15 points to "an expanded, universal circle that is evident only at the end, in the Servant's future of which the YHWH oracle speaks". In 53:11, רַבִּים "many" are Israel. Later on, "[w]hen Yahweh's plan through the Servant succeeds, then the nations come to salvation by noticing what happens to an Israel that has found its way to faith through the suffering, death, and exaltation of the Servant" (p. 19, ET p. 42).

[198] Cf. 2.2.3.

[199] Koole, *Isaiah III. Vol. 2*, pp. 334–338.

[200] Koole, *Isaiah III. Vol. 2*, pp. 276ff.

[201] Whybray, *Isaiah 40–66*, p. 169.

[202] Blenkinsopp, *Isaiah 40–55*, p. 350. In this regard, he refers to Dan. 12:2–4;10, the Qumran group, Mark 14:24 and Rom. 5:15. In Isa. 52:14, however, רַבִּים appears without the article.

and to "him" and צַדִּיק עַבְדִּי "the righteous one, my servant". רַבִּים "many" are identified as the nations, seen in relation to the servant as the collective Israel (Mettinger), a messenger of God (Hertzberg opens for both an individual and a collective interpretation) or an individual, for instance, the Messiah (Oswalt). רַבִּים "many" are also identified as the Israelites in relation to the servant as the "Jews of the diaspora spoken of as nations and kings" (Westermann), or as the Gola community of Zion (Ruppert). רַבִּים "many" are further taken to embrace both Israel and the nations (Olley), with the servant as the generation of the exile through which the nations had suffered vicariously (Rignell), or as "the righteous remnant of the people" (Hollenberg). רַבִּים "many" are further interpreted as the Israelites in 52:14; 53:11–12 and the nations in 52:15, seen in relation to the servant interpreted as the prophet (Elliger, McKenzie, Kutsch, Whybray, Hermisson, Steck). Finally, רַבִּים "many" are identified as the disciples of the servant, who himself is interpreted as the prophet (Blenkinsopp). The identification of רַבִּים "many" in 52:13–53:12, esp. 53:11–12, might relate to discussions of universalism/particularism, which will be commented upon in 5.8.5.

3.10.17.2. *"He" and "We"*

In two questions in 53:1, "we" ask about לִשְׁמֻעָתֵנוּ "what we hear" and to whom זְרוֹעַ יְהוָה "the arm of YHWH" is revealed, thus assuming that something is told, heard and seen.

In v. 2, a man is depicted as growing up like יוֹנֵק "a shoot" and שֹׁרֶשׁ "a root" and not attracting "us" to "him" because of "his" lack of תֹּאַר "form", הָדָר "splendour" and מַרְאֶה "appearance". Both "he" and "we" are signifiers of identity, with a relationship of contrast as regards both number and roles. "Our" portrayal of "him" continues in v. 3, in which "his" fate is elusively and tersely depicted in terms of disdain, illness, desolation and dissociation. This social and physical devaluation is underlined by "our" final judgment of "him": לֹא חֲשַׁבְנֻהוּ "we did not consider him".

In v. 4a, the contrast between "him" and "us" is abolished as their common fate – illness – is revealed: "he" carried "our" illnesses. A special connection is drawn between the afflictions of "him" in vv. 2–3 and "our" experience of these same illnesses in v. 4a. After "he" was judged at a distance in v. 3 and then seen as deeply involved in "our" fate as well in v. 4a, in v. 4b "we" again distance "ourselves" from "him", as "his" illnesses are explained as punishment from YHWH.

After a depiction of "his" wound because of "our" sins in v. 5a, in v. 5b a rehabilitation appears. What began as "our" contemplation of "his" experience in v. 2 emerges as a consideration of these same experiences as "ours" from v. 4 on. In v. 4a, the diagnosis of and explanation for "his" illnesses are given: "he" carried "our" illnesses. In v. 4b this is explained as being due to YHWH. However, in v. 5 a sudden transition from one state to another emerges: here, the illnesses are explained as being due to "our" sins and transgressions! Reconciliation is also introduced. Healing gained for "all" by wounds implies the removal of punishment and suffering. "His" and "our" fates are deeply involved in each other, as everyone has been changed.

After the turning point to recovery in v. 5, v. 6 returns to the past, presenting the background which leads to a coming reversal of the situation: "our" delusion and YHWH's punishment of "him". YHWH's striking of "him" due to עֲוֺן כֻּלָּנוּ "the iniquity of all of us" in v. 6 is a conflation of the two parts of v. 4, where "his" and "our" illnesses are identical, and where "we accounted him stricken, smitten by God and humiliated". "Our" assumption in v. 4 that "his" illness was due to YHWH's striking "him" is confirmed in v. 6. But whereas the focus was on illness in v. 4, in v. 6 sin is emphasised. A sheep motif is prominently used as an illustration of the people's delusion, cf. v. 5. Whereas YHWH was not mentioned as the one striking in v. 5, he is in v. 6.

a) A Remnant of Israel and the Whole Israel
Rignell takes the servant to be the generation of the captivity which had the task of enduring the vicarious suffering of the speaking "we", i.e. the whole of Israel.[203] A similar interpretation is given by Hollenberg, who understands the servant as "'the righteous remnant', the prophetic nucleus of Israel" and "we" as the remaining part of Israel.[204] Unlike the rest of Israel, the servant is righteous and takes upon himself the burden of the people's sins by identifying with them (53:5–6; 9; 12).[205] Clifford also takes the servant to be the faithful part of the people, while he interprets the "we" as the whole of Israel.[206]

---

[203] Rignell, "A Study of Isaiah Ch. 40–55", pp. 79–81.
[204] Hollenberg, "Nationalism and 'The Nations' in Isaiah 40–55", pp. 27; 35, and 3.10.17.1.c.
[205] Hollenberg, "Nationalism and 'The Nations' in Isaiah 40–55", pp. 28; 35–36.
[206] Clifford, Fair Spoken and Persuading, pp. 179–180.

b) The Exilic Community and the People of Judah

According to Hägglund, the servant represents the exilic community, while the "we" group represents the people of Judah.[207]

c) Israel and the Nations

Most of those who maintain that the servant is Israel interpret the "we" in 53:1ff as the nations. This includes, for instance, Torrey,[208] Muilenburg,[209] Melugin[210] and Mettinger.[211] Neither Torrey nor Melugin explicitly discusses the concept of vicarious suffering, but they seem to assume that this is what Isa. 53 concerns. Torrey depicts the theme of the text as "Israel's atonement for the Gentiles": "the servant is to endure chastisement *in the stead* of the Gentiles" so that the foreign peoples may be saved.[212] Melugin claims that, in Isa. 53:1ff, the nations confess that the servant Israel suffers for their sins.[213] Mettinger explicitly interprets Isa. 53 in terms of a collective, vicarious suffering. According to him, "[t]he concept of the scapegoat plays a decisive role in the theological deep structure of Isa. 53", with further references to the expression נָשָׂא עָוֹן "to bear iniquity" in Lev. 10:17; 16:22.[214]

Muilenburg claims that Isa. 53 indisputably talks about sin, but that the sinner and the sufferer are not the same: "The sufferer is bearing the consequences of the sins of others than himself":[215] "he" is carrying "our" sins. Muilenburg takes Israel to be the servant and the "we" to be the nations in Isa. 53. Elsewhere he states: "Israel and Israel alone is able to bear all that is said about the servant of the Lord."[216] As regards 53:5, he explains: "The punishment was borne vicariously, and the

---

[207] Hägglund, *Isaiah 53 in the Light of Homecoming after Exile*, pp. 22–32.

[208] Torrey, *The Second Isaiah*, p. 416. Cf. Torrey's presentation of the personification of Israel in Second Isaiah, pp. 135ff.

[209] Muilenburg, "The Book of Isaiah: Chapters 40–66", p. 411.

[210] Melugin, *The Formation of Isaiah 40–55*, pp. 167–169. R. F. Melugin, "Israel and the Nations in Isa. 40–55" in H. T. C. Sun (ed), *Problems in Biblical Theology: Essays in Honor of Rolf Knierim* (Grand Rapids: Eerdmans, 1997) 249–264, esp. p. 259.

[211] Mettinger, *Farewell to the Servant Songs*, pp. 38; 44–45.

[212] Torrey, *The Second Isaiah*, pp. 409; 412, his italics. Cf. his interpretation of עַמִּי "my people" in v. 8 in 3.10.17.3.

[213] Melugin, *The Formation of Isaiah 40–55*, p. 167, his italics. Cf. his interpretation of עַמִּי "my people" in v. 8 in 3.10.17.3.

[214] Mettinger, *Farewell to the Servant Songs*, p. 41. See 3.10.14. n. 141 on the expression נָשָׂא עָוֹן "bear iniquity". Cf. more about Mettinger's interpretation in Appendix 6.

[215] Muilenburg, "The Book of Isaiah: Chapters 40–66", p. 622.

[216] Muilenburg, "The Book of Isaiah: Chapters 40–66", p. 411. He also adds that Jesus might identify himself with the servant (pp. 413–414).

vicarious suffering was efficacious in the eyes of God."[217] In addition to his closer identifications of the actors in Isa. 53, Muilenburg also opens the way for a much broader interpretation as he states finally that "all Israel [including the Christian community] – in its varying distances, held succinct and understood in its maximum form as a person – is present."[218]

Kaiser identifies the servant as both the ideal Israel and the prophet who represents the people in his prophetic role – and the "we" as the nations.[219] He explains the relation between "him" and "us" in vv. 4–6 as follows:

> V. 4–6 bringt...das Bekenntnis zu seiner wahren Stellung und schließt somit das der eigenen Sünden ein. Dennoch wäre er verfelt, etwa den ganzen Abschnitt als ein Sünden-bekenntnis anzusprechen: Sein Schwerpunkt liegt ganz offensichtlich nicht auf der Erkenntnis der eigenen Schuld, sondern auf der Unterstreichung des Sühneleidens des Knechtes.[220]

d) An Individual and Israel

Koole identifies the servant as a coming saviour and "we" as Israel,[221] where the role of the servant is described as substitution and vicarious suffering.[222]

e) The Messiah and the Whole World

Oswalt identifies the servant as "an individual, almost certainly the Messiah, who will be the ideal Israel".[223] The servant does not suffer through his own fault but as a result of "our" sin – and this will lead to "our" healing. He identifies this phenomenon, as in vv. 10–12, as "the substitutionary suffering of the servant", which he defines as follows: "He does not suffer merely as a result of the sins of the people, but in place of the people."[224] As regards the identification of the "we", Oswalt speaks of an intentional ambiguity: "It is almost certainly the prophet identifying himself with his people and speaking for the

---

[217] Muilenburg, "The Book of Isaiah: Chapters 40–66", p. 623.
[218] Muilenburg, "The Book of Isaiah: Chapters 40–66", p. 631.
[219] Kaiser, *Der königliche Knecht*, pp. 65; 93–109; 116–118; 132.
[220] Kaiser, *Der königliche Knecht*, p. 88.
[221] Koole, *Isaiah III. Vol. 2*, pp. 267; 276ff.
[222] Koole, *Isaiah III. Vol. 2*, pp. 254; 292.
[223] Oswalt, *The Book of Isaiah: Chapters 40–66*, p. 79.
[224] Oswalt, *The Book of Isaiah: Chapters 40–66*, p. 385.

whole."[225] Moreover, the servant's ministry is not limited to the people as he is also to be a light to the nations (Isa. 42:6; 49:6): "Thus, all persons who recognize that their sin has caused the Servant to suffer may include themselves in the all-inclusive 'we'."[226]

f) The Prophet and One or More Disciples
Whybray identifies the servant as the prophet and the "we" as fellow Babylonian exiles, "…possibly an intimate group of his disciples, though they speak for the whole exilic community".[227] Whybray does not agree on the duality of "him" and "us". He claims that the servant is not suffering "*in place* of the exiles in such a way that they escape the consequences of their sins".[228] The "we" say that "he" has been smitten by "*our* diseases and *our* pains".[229] According to Whybray, "he" has suffered more then "us" and "he" is innocent when compared to "us". Whybray insists that "this is shared and not vicarious suffering".[230] He further stresses that the speakers are fellow exiles of the servant, and therefore they themselves, like the prophet, are suffering divine punishment. To explain this relationship, Whybray distinguishes between a literal and a metaphorical meaning of the illness phrases. Literally, מַכְאֹבוֹת "sickness" and חֳלִי "illness" (53:3) describe the actual state of the servant; metaphorically, they express "the broken state of the nation after the destruction of Jerusalem in 587 BC".[231]

Blenkinsopp regards the speaking "we" as an individual disciple who speaks on behalf of those who "revere Yahveh and obey the voice of his Servant" (50:10).[232] He identifies the servant in the last three

---

[225] Oswalt, *The Book of Isaiah: Chapters 40–66*, p. 384, n. 4. Cf. his identification of עַמִּי "my people" in 53:8, treated in 3.10.17.3.
[226] Oswalt, *The Book of Isaiah: Chapters 40–66*, p. 384, incl. n. 4.
[227] Whybray, *Thanksgiving for a Liberated Prophet*, pp. 134–139.
[228] Whybray, *Isaiah 40–66*, pp. 171–176, quotation is taken from p. 171, and Whybray, *Thanksgiving for a Liberated Prophet*, pp. 134–139. He identifies the servant with Israel in Isa. 52:13–15 and with the prophet in 53, cf. Orlinsky, *The So-Called "Servant of the Lord" and "Suffering Servant" in Second Isaiah*, pp. 17–23.
[229] Whybray, *Thanksgiving for a Liberated Prophet*, pp. 58–59, his italics.
[230] Whybray, *Thanksgiving for a Liberated Prophet*, p. 30.
[231] Whybray, *Thanksgiving for a Liberated Prophet*, p. 59. He refers to the uses of חֳלִי "illness" in the depiction of the people's fate in Isa. 1:5–6 (cf. 5.11.2.) and Jer. 6:7, and the use of מַכְאֹבוֹת "sickness" as punishment for sin in Jer. 30:15 (cf. 5.11.7.) and Ps. 38:18 (cf. 5.11.11.), as well as in the personification of Jerusalem in Lam. 1:12; 18 (cf. 5.11.9.).
[232] Blenkinsopp, *Isaiah 40–55*, pp. 350–351.

songs as the prophet and regards 52:13–53:12 as added to the first three songs "soon after the prophet's death".[233] Blenkinsopp claims that Isa. 53 in different ways tells of the way in which the servant bore the burden of the sin of the community (53:4a; 5; 6b; 10a). He did not do this voluntarily or willingly; rather, his sickness and sufferings were caused by YHWH (v. 6b). This goes against "the dominant theory of moral causality" in which one should suffer for one's own sins, cf. "our" interpretation of "his" fate: "he" was stricken, smitten by God and afflicted (v. 4b).[234] However, yet another explanation is offered:

> Yahveh had diverted the ills that should have fallen on the community onto this one individual. The change occurs between vv. 4 and 5 and the intensity and emotional immediacy of the language derive from the impact of this insight and the experience of the conversion to discipleship.[235]

Blenkinsopp sees associations both with a vocabulary of sacrifice, with the servant serving a function analogous to a reparation or trespass offering (אָשָׁם in 53:10, cf. Lev. 5:1–26, 7:2, 14:24), and with the scapegoat ritual in Lev. 16.[236]

g) The Exiled Israel and the Prophet

Snaith identifies the servant as Israel, "the first batch of exiles, those who went into captivity with the young king Jehoiachin in 597 BC" and notes "a tendency to include also the 586 BC exiles". Ultimately, he says, all the exiles in Babylon are the "true People of God". He takes the speaking "we" to be the prophet.[237] Snaith, like most other scholars, also reads Isa. 53 as concerning vicarious suffering, and adds:

> The idea of Israel as a suffering Servant, meekly redeeming the nations, is quite foreign to the thought of a prophet, and has been largely instrumental in obscuring his real thought…[238]

---

[233] Blenkinsopp, *Isaiah 40–55*, p. 79.
[234] Blenkinsopp, *Isaiah 40–55*, pp. 350–351.
[235] Blenkinsopp, *Isaiah 40–55*, p. 351.
[236] Blenkinsopp, *Isaiah 40–55*, p. 351. Cf. more about Blenkinsopp's interpretation in Appendix 6.
[237] Snaith, *Isaiah 40–55*, pp. 169–170, quotation from p. 170.
[238] Snaith, *Isaiah 40–55*, pp. 168–169.

h) The Prophet and the People of Israel

Orlinsky interprets the servant as the prophet in 53:1ff, "we" as Israel,[239] and rejects any idea of vicarious suffering.[240] He claims that what the "we" are told in Isa. 53 is that a man "bore the griefs and carried the sorrows of the people, having been wounded for their transgressions and bruised for their iniquities".[241] This is what all spokesmen and prophets of God experienced. While the people suffered because of their transgressions, the innocent prophet suffered because of his unpopular mission. "And when the people were made whole again…, it was only because the prophet had come and suffered to bring them God's message of rebuke and repentance."[242]

McKenzie takes the servant to be the prophet, and the "we" his fellow Israelites, with the innocent Israelite rescuing his fellows from suffering by carrying their sufferings.[243]

Elliger, Kutsch, Steck, Janowski and Hermisson[244] also all identify the servant as the prophet and "we", indisputably, as Israel. All of these scholars take the concept of vicarious suffering to be central in their readings. Steck describes the relation between the servant and the "we" as follows:

> Sachlich zielt dieser Abschnitt [i.e. 53:4–6] darauf auszusagen, was diese leidvolle Ebed-existenz in Wirklichkeit war: Sie war nicht Ergehen, mit dem Gott des Ebed eigene Vergehen geahndet hätte, wie die Wir früher dachten (v. 4b.2–3), sondern sie war, wie das Wissen seines Erfolges ergibt, stellvertretendes Ergehen für die Vergehen der Wir, das der Ebed als Gottes Tat an sich trug, so daß Israel damit Heil und Heilung (v. 5b) offensteht.[245]

---

[239] Orlinsky, *The So-Called "Servant of the Lord" and "Suffering Servant" in Second Isaiah*, p. 54.

[240] Cf. 2.3.8.3. and Appendix 6.

[241] Orlinsky, *The So-Called "Servant of the Lord" and "Suffering Servant" in Second Isaiah*, p. 57.

[242] Orlinsky, *The So-Called "Servant of the Lord" and "Suffering Servant" in Second Isaiah*, p. 57.

[243] McKenzie, *Second Isaiah*, p. 134.

[244] Elliger, *Deuterojesaja in seinem Verhältnis zu Tritojesaja*, pp. 81–88, Kutsch, *Sein Leiden und Tod – unser Heil*, pp. 19; 39–40. Steck, Janowski and Hermisson are treated in more detail in 2.2.3. and 2.2.4.

[245] Steck, "Aspekte des Gottesknechts in Jes. 52,13–53,12", p. 28. This interpretation concerns what Steck regards as the original text of Isa. 52:13–53:12. Additionally, he presents four redactional revisions. In the first and second redctional revisions, he relates the concept of vicarious suffering to Zion being identified as *Knecht Jahwes* suffering vicariously for Israel, and with Israel for the peoples, see 2.2.5.

Janowski correlates the "he" and the "we" in Isa. 53:1–6 with the suffering individual in the complaint psalms: "our" behavior towards the servant reminds us of the enemies in these psalms. "We" considered this unsightly, suffering man to be stricken, struck down by God and afflicted (vv. 3a; 4b), and they distanced themselves from "him".[246] Further, Janowski connects this to an earlier and a present view, which he describes as a logic which fails in terms of the *Tun-Ergehen* model in the Psalms: "They now realize that the Servant's suffering was the consequence not of his but of their actions, the actions of others."[247]

Hermisson regards the servant songs as a presentation of the prophetic office. The suffering of the servant was no punishment for his sins. When the prophet bore "our" illnesses (v. 4a), this was because "'the Lord has laid on him', the innocent one, 'the iniquity of us all'" (v. 6b).[248] This is a variation on the connection between guilt and its consequences which "we" observed in vv. 2–3, with the difference that it is not the sinner, but the innocent one upon whom Yahweh piled suffering. The relation between "his" suffering and "our" sin is explained by the concept of *Stellvertretung*.[249]

i) The Prophet and the Nations
North, who interprets the servant as the prophet whose task includes a special mission towards the nations, holds the "we" to be the nations. He claims that the "we" of 53:1–6 are the Gentiles of 52:15 within a universal setting.[250] North does not discuss, but seems to assume, that vicarious suffering is indicated.

j) Unclear Identification of "Him" and "Us"
Lindblom holds the "we" in 53:1 to be the nations, whereas for vv. 2–6, the "we" "denotes neither the Gentiles nor the Jews, but simply the bystanders in the vision".[251] Whereas Lindblom identifies the

---

[246] Janowski, "Er Trug unsere Sünden", p. 39, ET p. 64.

[247] Janowski, "Er Trug unsere Sünden", p. 39, ET p. 64.

[248] Hermisson, "Das vierte Gottesknechtlied im deuterojesajanischen Kontext", p. 15, the quotation is taken from ET p. 36.

[249] Cf. 2.2.4., 2.3.8.3. and Appendix 6.

[250] North, *The Second Isaiah*, p. 236 and North, *The Suffering Servant in Deutero-Isaiah*, pp. 151–152, cf. Kaiser, *Der königliche Knecht*, pp. 93ff. This was also claimed by the early Mowinckel, see his "Der Knecht Jahwäs", p. 37, n. 1.

[251] Lindblom, *The Servant Songs in Deutero-Isaiah*, pp. 39; 42, quotation taken from p. 44.

servant as Israel in 52:12–53:1,[252] he states as follows when it comes
to vv. 2ff:

> [I]t becomes meaningless to ask *who* is the Servant in the Fourth Servant
> Song. Is he identical with Israel? Is he the prophet himself? Is he the
> Messiah? Is he a historical individual known or unknown? The suffering
> man is none of these. He is a fictitious person, who (from the psycho-
> logical point of view) is conjured up in the prophet's imagination, and
> (from the religious point of view) is the subject of a divine revelation.[253]

To the question of vicarious suffering, Lindblom states:

> It is true that the idea of vicarious suffering is not indicated in the parts
> of the text which surround the fourth Servant oracle. But this is of no
> import. To the compiler of the Book of Deutero-Isaiah it was quite suf-
> ficient that the whole section played variations on this leading theme,
> abasement and glorifying, in accordance with the sublime plan of
> Yahweh.[254]

Clines presents a brief overview of alternative identifications of the
servant. Without offering his own identification, he concludes: "No
further comment is needed to underscore the enigmatic nature of
literature that permits such a multiplicity of interpretation."[255] When
it comes to the identification of the "we", Clines states: "Here the
range of options is more limited, but the cryptic character of the poem
is equally evident."[256] After having presented some alternatives, he
seems to support the view that the "we" are either Israel or Second
Isaiah's disciples.[257] However, he is generally keen to say that his purpose is to:

> point to the ambiguity of the poem, and in so doing to suggest that it is
> of its essence that unequivocal identifications are not made and that the
> poem in this respect also is open-ended and allows for multiple inter-
> pretations.[258]

Then Clines offers what he calls a functional analysis of the actors
in the text. He describes the relationship between "him" and "us" as

---

[252] Lindblom, *The Servant Songs in Deutero-Isaiah*, p. 42.
[253] Lindblom, *The Servant Songs in Deutero-Isaiah*, p. 46, his italics. He designates
Isa. 53:2–12 as a prophetic revelation, see 3.10.5. n. 76.
[254] Lindblom, *The Servant Songs in Deutero-Isaiah*, p. 50.
[255] Clines, *I, He, We and They*, pp. 25–27, the quotation is taken from pp. 26–27.
[256] Clines, *I, He, We and They*, p. 29.
[257] Clines, *I, He, We and They*, pp. 30–31.
[258] Clines, *I, He, We and They*, p. 33.

a duality, which is especially clear in v. 4. He claims that a resolution comes about when "the attitude of the 'we' to 'him' *changes* from hostility or scorn to appreciation".[259] Westermann similarly reads the servant as an unclearly identified individual and the "we" as "unnamed speakers".[260] Like Westermann, Clines claims that what is of importance is not who the servant is, but what he does.[261] Neither Westermann nor Clines explicitly discusses the concept of vicarious suffering, but in their dualistic reading of the relation between "him" and "us", both seem to assume that this at least might be indicated in Isa. 53.[262]

k) Summing up

The relationship between "him" and "us" in Isa. 53:1–6 is most often explained as a contrast between "his" suffering in innocence and "our" sin. "We" are most often identified as a collective, the whole of Israel (Orlinsky, McKenzie, Elliger, Kutsch, Steck, Janowski, Hermisson, Rignell, Hollenberg, Clifford, Koole), the nations (North, Torrey, Muilenburg, Melugin, Mettinger) or the whole world (Oswalt). However, individual interpretations are also offered, such as the "we" as the prophet (Snaith) or one or more disciples of the prophet (Blenkinsopp, Whybray).

The abundance of suggestions concerning the identity of the servant can also be outlined in two groups: individual and collective. The identifications of the servant as an individual include: the prophet (Whybray, Steck, Hermisson, Janowski, Blenkinsopp, Orlinsky); a Messianic figure (Oswalt, Koole); or, an unclearly identified individual (Westermann). The collective identifications include: the servant comprehended as Israel – either a remnant of Israel (Rignell, Hollenberg, Clifford); or, the whole of Israel (Torrey, Mettinger, Muilenburg, Melugin).[263]

---

[259] Clines, *I, He, We and They*, p. 38, his italics. He also provides many other analyses related to the visual aspects, actors, speech, affect and time – none of these seems to oppose this functional analysis as regards the relation between "him" and "us".

[260] Westermann, *Isaiah 40–66*, pp. 262–264. Cf. his treatment of Isa. 42:24 in 5.12.2. n. 213. Cf. the later Mowinckel, *He That Cometh*, p. 119. Spieckermann similarly does not want to identify the servant, cf. 2.3.8.3. n. 176.

[261] Clines, *I, He, We and They*, p. 59.

[262] Westermann, *Isaiah 40–66*, pp. 263–264, Clines, *I, He, We and They*, p. 63.

[263] On the abundance of suggestions concerning the identity of the servant, see also 2.3.6.

Some tendencies may be discerned in the identifications of the relation between "him" and "us": those scholars who take the servant to
be the collective Israel might identify the "we" as the nations; those
who regard the servant to be either the faithful part of Israel or an
individual take the "we" to be the nations or Israel in general.

Other scholars characterise the text as enigmatic and its actors as
unnamed or unidentifiable and thus are somewhat unwilling to identify both the servant and "us" (Lindblom, Hertzberg, Westermann,
Clines, Spieckermann). While most scholars in this brief overview take
the concept of vicarious suffering as central to Isa. 53, a few deny that
vicarious suffering is indicated. Orlinsky, for instance, describes the
prophet's suffering as due to his mission, while Whybray opts for a
"co-suffering".[264]

3.10.17.3. עַמִּי "My People"[265]

In the midst of Isa. 53:7–10, in which the speaking voice is anonymous,
in v. 8 we find "I" speech about "he" and עַמִּי "my people", with the
nearness expressed between YHWH and עַמִּי "my people". V. 8 starts
with a depiction of how "he was taken" and is followed by a question
concerning "who of his time considered that he was cut off from the
land of the living". A causal relation is then expressed between פֶּשַׁע
עַמִּי "the transgression of my people" and נֶגַע לָמוֹ "his stroke".

עַמִּי "my people" in 53:8 is often taken to be synonymous with "us"
(see, for instance, Oswalt, who identifies the "we" with the whole world
as well as Clifford, who identifies the "we" as the whole of Israel).[266]
Mettinger suggests different groupings of Israel, where the sufferings
of the servant, for example in 53:8, symbolise the minority which was
in exile, a pious remnant, and עַמִּי "my people" the sinful majority left
in Judah.[267] Snaith solves the problem of identification as follows:

---

[264] On criticism of the concept of vicarious suffering in Isa. 53, cf. 2.3.8.3., 5.12.
and Appendix 6.

[265] Many emendations of עַמִּי "my people" in Isa. 53:8 are made, see 3.10.11. n. 122.

[266] Oswalt, *The Book of Isaiah: Chapters 40–66*, p. 396, and Clifford, *Fair Spoken
and Persuading*, pp. 178–180.

[267] Mettinger, *Farewell to the Servant Songs*, p. 43.

We take 52:13–15 to be spoken by the Gentile kings, and chapter 53, certainly as far as v. 11a to be spoken by the prophet himself, which "my people" means Israel in some sense.[268]

Also scholars who interpret the "we" as the nations take עַמִּי "my people" in 53:8 to be Israel. Torrey identifies the servant as Israel and the "we" in 53:1ff as the Gentile ruler, who in v. 8 talks of his own people.[269]

Melugin claims that in Isa. 53:1ff the nations confess that the servant Israel suffers for their sins, and that in v. 8 he also suffers for the sin of עַמִּי "my people".[270] To this "solution", he adds:

> The lack of an explicit identity for the servant and for [עַמִּי] creates difficulties for the interpretation of the text. It seems to be relatively certain that he suffers for the nations, and it is probable that he suffers for Yahweh's people Israel. The lack of clarity concerning the identity of the servant and "my people" is perplexing. In all likelihood it is related to similar ambiguities in Deutero-Isaiah.[271]

Many scholars do not specify who עַמִּי "my people" in 53:8 are, perhaps because they take it for granted that they are Israel.[272]

3.10.18. *Summing up*

In an extraordinary way, Duhmian readings of Isa. 52:13–53:12 seem to be a matter of re-covering the meaning of the text through some kind of homage to his "Servant Song" thesis. Due to the scholarly consensus since Duhm, readers have become participants in a narrow discursive space restricting signifying practices. As this brief overview shows, certain tendencies might be seen in the readings of Isa. 52:13–53:12, for instance, the identification of רַבִּים "many" might be related to discussions of universalism/particularism, while the dualistic interpretation of the relation between "him" and "us" is further related to a concept of vicarious suffering. This narrowing of the text is, however, not the result of complete conformity. The Duhmian readings of Isa. 52:13–53:12 are not as homogenous as one would have expected.

---

[268] Snaith, *Isaiah 40–55*, p. 169.
[269] Torrey, *The Second Isaiah*, pp. 409; 412; 420.
[270] Melugin, *The Formation of Isaiah 40–55*, p. 167.
[271] Melugin, *The Formation of Isaiah 40–55*, pp. 167–168.
[272] Cf. 3.10.11. n. 122.

The overview also shows that there is no easy consensus, but rather a complex heterogeneity of ideas among readings of Isa. 52:13–53:12. As we have seen, within this discursive space different interpretations of the identities of actors and events in Isa. 52:13–53:12 are offered. Enormous scholarly activity has produced a great number of divergent suggestions as to how the text should be read. Past readings of it are not more homogenous than present ones. This might illuminate both the complexity in the text and in readings of it.

CHAPTER FOUR

NARRATIVE

4.1. On Narratology

"Nothing seems more natural and universal to human beings than telling stories".[1] This and similar utterances about the omnipresence of narrative in history and culture have been called "a contemporary narratological cliché".[2] The overwhelming production of literature and theories about narratology demonstrates the challenge posed by narrative. Despite the universality of story-telling, theoreticians and readers strive to determine what constitutes a narrative, what its minimum conditions are and when it is no longer a narrative. Since narrative cannot be considered separately from language, it might be useful to pick up the thread from Saussure. According to him, sign is the most basic element of meaning. Although Saussure worked primarily at the level of phonology, he called for the application of semiotic principles in all aspects of culture (cf. 3.7.). The arbitrary and conventional sign and the differentiation in language also challenge text, narration and culture. In narratology, the Saussurean linguistic model has been extended to the semiotic fields of other social constructs such as literature, myth, history, religion, sociology, anthropology, psychology, architecture, fashion and film. Narratological theories have been constructed from a number of schools of thought, including formalism, Bakhtinian dialogism, New Criticism, (post-) structuralism, psychoanalysis, hermeneutics and deconstruction.[3]

---

[1] J. Hillis Miller, "Narrative" in F. Lentricchia and T. McLaughlin (eds), *Critical Terms for Literary Study* (Chicago: University of Chicago Press, 1995) 66.

[2] M. Currie, *Postmodern Narrative Theory* (Transitions; Hampshire: Macmillan, 1998) 1.

[3] Also in studies of the Hebrew Bible, a multiplicity of narrative approaches appears, see overviews in J. L. Ska, *'Our Fathers Have Told Us': Introduction to the Analysis of Hebrew Narratives* (Subsidia Biblica, 13; Rome: Editrice Pontificio Istituto Biblico, 1990), D. M. Gunn and D. N. Fewell, *Narrative in the Hebrew Bible* (The Oxford Bible Series; Oxford: Oxford University Press, 1993) and G. Aichele et al. (eds), *The Postmodern Bible: The Bible and Culture Collective* (New Haven: Yale University Press, 1995) 70–118.

Narratology is a theory and a systematic study of narrative in which features distinctive of or relevant to narrative are isolated, characterised and classified.[4] In the following, a compressed narratology will be presented as an introduction to a narrative reading of Isa. 52:13–53:12. The narrative reading draws attention to narrative structure and the effects this has on the shape and unfolding of the text. The narrative reading explores relations of the composite parts of Isa. 52:13–53:12, for instance, the distinction between story (including events and actors) and narration (including narrator and narratee). Particular attention is paid to the collision between the levels of story and narration, in which the trope of personification is also important. The narrative reading activates forces in the text on a level other than the linguistic one previously focused upon, and shows what a story *does*, i.e. its performative dimension.

4.2. Narrative

By narration, a narrative recounts a story; and to analyse a narrative, it must be distinguished from non-narratives. Temporality and causality have been regarded as constituents of narrative, as opposed to, for example, description, exposition and argument. Rimmon-Kenan comments on how narrative and non-narrative elements are intertwined: "[N]on-story elements may be found in a narrative text just as story elements may be found in non-narrative texts."[5] B. H. Smith goes even further in describing the difficulty in distinguishing between narrative and non-narrative such as description or assertion:

> "[T]elling someone that something happened" can, under certain circumstances, be so close to "saying that something is (or was) the case" that it is questionable if we can draw any logically rigorous distinction between them or, more generally, if any absolute distinction can be drawn between narrative discourse and any other form of verbal behaviour.[6]

---

[4] G. Prince, "On Narrative Studies and Narrative Genres", *Poetics Today* 11 (1990) 271.

[5] S. Rimmon-Kenan, *Narrative Fiction: Contemporary Poetics* (New Accents; London: Routledge, 1989) 15. Jakobson claims that paradigmatic aspects dominate in poetry and syntagmatic ones in narrative, cf. 3.5. According to him, temporal continuity and causality do not constitute prerequisites for a poem, while in a narrative, meaning is basically realised through the continuity of signs in a linear structure.

[6] B. H. Smith, "Narrative Versions, Narrative Theories" in W. J. T. Mitchell (ed), *On Narrative* (Chicago: Chicago University Press, 1981) 228.

Culler claims that a distinction between *story* and *discourse* is "an indispensable premise of narratology".[7] He defines *story* as "a sequence of actions or events, conceived as independent of their manifestation in discourse" and *discourse* as "the discursive presentation of narration of events".[8] On such dichotomies in narratology, Smith comments: "[N]o single *basically* basic story [exists,] but rather, an unlimited number of other narratives that can be *constructed in response* to it or *perceived as related* to it."[9] She claims that the textual inscription of the narrative *is* the narrative itself and so *story* and *narrative* are one and the same.[10] This might be exemplified by Isa. 53. As seen in Part I, translations and interpretations of this text appear in Jewish contexts such as the Qumran texts, the Pseudepigrapha, the LXX, the Targumim, the Peshitta,

---

[7] Culler, *The Pursuit of Signs*, pp. 170–171. This relates to a distinction made in Russian formalism between the order of events as presented in the narrative, labelled *fabula*, and the events as the text arranges and presents them, labelled *sjuzet*. In French structuralism, a distinction is made between the story's chronological events, called *histoire*, and the manner in which they appear in the temporality and spatiality of the text, called *récit*. *Fabula/sjuzet* and *historie/récit* are described in e.g. P. Brooks, *Reading for the Plot: Design and Intention in Narrative* (Cambridge, MA: Harvard University Press, 1998) 12–14.

[8] Culler, *The Pursuit of Signs*, pp. 169–170. S. Chatman, *Story and Discourse: Narrative Structure in Fiction and Film* (Ithaca, NY: Cornell University Press, 1989) 19, distinguishes between the *what* of a narrative (its content) and the *how* (the way in which that content is expressed).

[9] Smith, "Narrative Versions, Narrative Theories", p. 217, her italics.

[10] Another objection to such a dichotomy is offered by Brooks, *Reading for the Plot*, pp. 13–14:

"Plot"…seems to me to cut across the *fabula/sjuzet* distinction in that to speak of plot is to consider both story elements and their ordering. Plot could be thought of as the interpretive activity elicited by the distinction between *sjuzet* and *fabula*, the way we *use* the one against the other. To keep our terms straight without sacrificing the advantages of the semantic range of "plot", let us say that we can generally understand plot to be an aspect of *sjuzet* in that it belongs to the narrative discourse, as its active shaping force, but that it makes sense (as indeed *sjuzet* itself principally makes sense) as it is used to reflect on *fabula*, as our understanding of story. Plot is thus the dynamic shaping force of the narrative discourse. I find confirmation for such a view in Paul Ricoeur's definition of plot as "the intelligible whole that governs a succession of events in any story". Ricoeur continues: "This provisory definition immediately shows the plot's connecting function between an event or events and the story. A story is *made out of* events to the extent that plot *makes* events *into* a story. The plot, therefore, places us at the crossing point of temporality and narrativity…" (his italics).

Brooks regards Ricoeur's description of plot as a corrective to the structural narratologist's neglect of the dynamics of narrative and the reader's role in the understanding of plot. M. Gignillat, "Who is Isaiah's Servant? Narrative Identity and Theological Potentiality", *SJT* 61 (2008) 125–136, focuses on narrative identity, as explicated by Ricoeur and Frei, in his interpretation of the servant's identity in Isa. 40–55.

and mediaeval and modern rabbinical literature, and in Christian contexts such as the Pseudepigrapha, the Apocrypha, the New Testament, the Vulgate, in patristic and mediaeval literature and in biblical scholarship in its growth from pre-modern times to recent feminist and liberation-theological readings. In Steck's redaction-critical reading for instance, Isa. 52:13–53:12 appear as five stories about a servant variously identified as the prophet "Second Isaiah", as Zion, as those who have returned from the exile, as those who remained at home in Judah and as the servant's descendants, the true Israel (which includes other people). All these servant stories of Steck are dated to different times in Ancient Israel within a period from 539 to 270 BCE. To the many written versions of Isa. 53 may be added pictorial ones, in which the servant is variously known as: "Man of Sorrows", e.g. by Bellini (ca. 1470–1500) and Dürer (1471–1528); "Solitary Christ Crucified", e.g. by Titian (ca. 1565), Rubens (ca. 1615) and Rembrandt (1631); and, "The Bearer of Burdens" in the 1970s painting by the Palestinian artist Suleiman Mansour.[11] Musical versions of the servant story are also told in hymns, e.g. "O Haupt voll Blut und Wunden" by Paul Gerhard (1607–1676) and "Messiah" (1743) by Händel (1685–1759).[12] On the idea of narrative versions, Smith comments:

> Among the narratives that can be constructed in response to a given narrative are not only those we commonly refer to as "versions" of it (for example, translations, adaptions, abridgements, and paraphrases) but also those retellings that we call "plot summaries", "interpretations", and sometimes, "basic stories". None of these retellings, however, is more absolutely basic than any of the others.[13]

Smith claims that the dichotomy between *story* and *discourse* "reveals its major logical and methodological limitations" in its insistence that a story exists independently of its telling and reading.[14] In a narrative reading of Isa. 52:13–53:12, I will employ a heuristic distinction between a sequence of events labelled *story* and the presentation of the events labelled *narration*. Through this distinction, the rhetorics of

---

[11] On Isa. 53 in art history, see Sawyer, *The Fifth Gospel*, pp. 83–99, and M. O'Kane, "Picturing 'The Man of Sorrows': The Passion-filled Afterlives of a Biblical Icon", *Religion and the Arts* 9 (2005) 62–100. Kane's interest is to show how the artists are not simply illustrators of biblical scenes, but active readers, who are expanding the text through their interpretations.

[12] Sawyer, *The Fifth Gospel*, pp. 83–99.

[13] Smith, "Narrative Versions, Narrative Theories", p. 217.

[14] Smith, "Narrative Versions, Narrative Theories", p. 211.

the narrative will show how shifting and unstable discourses interact with other discourses without any stable terms. In both *story* and *narration*, as well as in the relation between them, rhetorics of temporality, agency and causality are key, and "the theory of the text and its resistance to theory" is clarified.[15] Also, the role of temporality and causality as constituents of narrative is problematised.

4.3. STORY

A story is a result of a reading. The reader distinguishes a story from the text and from the narration.[16] Through the translation and labelling of a text's narrative components, such as temporality, agency and causality, a paraphrase is articulated.[17] As well as distinguishing the story from the text, a narrative reading shows how the presentation of the story is also "manipulated" by the narration.[18]

A story might be organised according to relations between events. An event might be some sort of physical or mental activity, an occurrence or a state in time, which might be caused or experienced by one or more actors. However, it might be difficult to distinguish between state and action as an event might be composite of complementary states and moments.[19] Actors have performing functions in a story, and they are differentiated from each other by traits.[20]

---

[15] Cf. Barthes, "Theory of the Text" in 3.8.

[16] Text is currently understood in a narrow sense as "a finite, structured whole composed of language signs", cf. M. Bal, *Narratology: Introduction to the Theory of Narrative* (Toronto: University of Toronto Press, 1997) 5. Bal further comments: "The finite ensemble of signs does not mean that the text itself is finite, for its meanings, effects, functions, and background are not."

[17] Bal, *Narratology*, pp. 3; 5. According to G. Prince, *A Grammar of Stories: An Introduction* (De proprietatibus litterarum: Series Minor, 13; The Hague: Mouton, 1973) 31, a minimal story requires temporal succession, causality and inversion. Rimmon-Kenan, *Narrative Fiction*, p. 18, claims that temporal succession is a minimal requirement for a group of events to form a story. Culler, *The Pursuit of Signs*, p. 171:

> Mieke Bal defines this assumption with an expliciteness that is rare among theorists of narrative: "the story [*l'histoire*] consists of the set of events in their chronological order, their spatial location, and their relations with the actors who cause or undergo them." And more specifically, "The events have temporal relations with one another. Each one is either anterior to, simultaneous with, or posterior to every other event".

[18] Bal, *Narratology*, p. 9.

[19] Rimmon-Kenan, *Narrative Fiction*, p. 15.

[20] S. Cohan and L. M. Shires, *Telling Stories: A Theoretical Analysis of Narrative Fiction* (New Accents; London: Routledge, 1997) 72.

For an event to belong to a story, it must be part of a sequence in which at least two events are needed: one establishing a narrative situation and another altering (or at least differing from) that situation. A story might order events temporally into relations of succession or concurrence, and logically into relations of comparability or causality.[21] Strict succession can only be found in stories with a single line or one, unified character. However, a character is not unified, there may be more than one character, and events may occur simultaneously, so a story might be multilinear rather than unilinear. Thus, a story is identified with an ideal chronological order which in fact never exists.[22]

A story may be as small as a single sentence, or it may consist of many sentences in a sequence. Isa. 53:6, for instance, might be described as a minimal story where both temporality and causality are at play:

> All of us like sheep went astray; everyone turned his own way
> and thus YHWH struck him by the iniquity of all of us.

This story begins with "our" going astray, followed by an explanation of how this led to YHWH's punishment of "him" due to "our" iniquities. The events might be organised into relations of going astray/ iniquities and punishment. A story might order events temporally into relations of both succession and concurrence, and logically into relations of causality: "We" are going astray/sinning and/while "he" is punished. However, in Isa. 53, two stories occur: the story about "him" and that about "us", between which temporal and causal connections are fluid (cf. 4.8.2.3.).

4.4. NARRATION

The mediation of story happens through narration, in the way it is told by a narrator. A narration might be divided into signifying components of, for instance, temporality and ordering.

Temporality concerns the narration's presentation of events in time. When the telling of a story is viewed as a retelling, events are treated as if they have already happened before they are narrated. But narration itself also occurs in time, i.e. the time of the telling as well as that of the reading, watching or hearing. Narrational time is therefore not the

---

[21] Rimmon-Kenan, *Narrative Fiction*, pp. 18–19.
[22] Rimmon-Kenan, *Narrative Fiction*, pp. 16–17; 44.

same as story-time.[23] Certain disparities between the temporal order of the story and that of the narration are called anachronies.[24] A story-event might be narrated at a point in the text after events that occur later in the story sequence (analepsis). An example is Isa. 53:6:

> All of us like sheep went astray; everyone turned his own way
> and thus YHWH struck him by the iniquity of all of us.

The narration of Isa. 53:6a turns to a past point in the story of, say, 53:1–6 by referring to events which happened before what we have been told so far in the story, in order to offer an explanation. A story-event might also be narrated ahead of events that occur before it in the story sequence (prolepsis). An example is Isa. 52:13:

> See, he shall prosper, my servant, and be exalted, he shall be lifted and be very high!

This verse evokes in advance an event that will take place later. The event is narrated at a point before earlier events in the story of, say, Isa. 52:13–15.[25]

An ellipsis occurs when the narration omits a point in the story-time. The unnarrated event can be referred to in an anachrony, it can be inferred by a reader based on supposed causality or it can be entirely omitted and unrecoverable.[26] In Isa. 53:1–6, for example, a story delineates time through a process of placement-displacement-replacements to transform one event into another. In the story about "him" and that about "us", different times are in play. As will be shown, these stories are neither chronologically nor causally interrelated, as the relation

---

[23] See G. Genette, *Narrative Discourse: An Essay in Method* (Ithaca, NY: Cornell University Press, 1980) 33–85, for a discussion of the discrepancies between story-time and text-time. P. Ricoeur, "Narrative Time" in Mitchell, *On Narrative*, pp. 165–186, claims that we do not only have different versions of stories but different versions of time which are shaped by the stories by which we live. He describes these versions of time as: 1. external and chronological; and, 2. internal and non-chronological. Whereas the former is related to natural science, the latter is related to human existence and experience.

[24] Rimmon-Kenan, *Narrative Fiction*, pp. 46–51.

[25] Frequency points out differences between story and narratorial times, e.g. single events told more than once, or a recurring event narrated only once. Duration might be narrated through summary or scene. A summary condenses time in the narration so that it is shorter than story-time. A scene coordinates the duration of story and narrational times so that they appear equivalent, cf. Rimmon-Kenan, *Narrative Fiction*, pp. 51–58. This is problematised in 4.5.

[26] Bal, *Narratology*, pp. 103–104.

between the sin and illness of "him" and that of "us" is not obvious in these stories (cf. e.g. 4.8.2.2. and 4.8.2.3.)

Deictics mean only by pointing to an antecedent located somewhere else in a text. For example, the pronouns "I" and "you" only mean because they occupy a position in a given narrative: they cannot mean outside of that narrative.[27] In Isa 52:13–15, for example, the narrative perspective is linked to, among other things, "I" and "you" (and "him") and in 53:1–6 to "us" (and "him"). The complexity of the relations between "I", "you", "us" and "him" in Isa. 52:13–53:12 will be further expounded in 4.5 and 4.8.

Just as a narrator is not the same as the author, the narratee is not the same as the reader. The narratee is inscribed in the text, for example either directly by being addressed by the pronoun "you", or by implication, through explanations, characterisations, ellipsis, questions.[28] Narration as a function of the narratee is clearest when the addressee is designated by the second-person pronoun "you", cf. the "I" speech of Isa. 52:14a: "As many were appalled at you…", and the "we" speech of 53:1: "Who believes what we hear? And the arm of YHWH – to whom is it revealed?", in which answers from a narratee are in some ways demanded to "our" questions.

4.5. TELLING, SHOWING, WRITING

In narratology, a distinction has been made between telling and showing. The distinction revolves on the distance in the relation between the narrator and the events and actors in the narrative. Telling is concerned with *who tells* (e.g. narrated monologue, free indirect speech; summary), while showing concerns *who sees* (e.g. dialogue, direct speech in general; scene).[29] Narrators are classified as in the first- or third-person. When a narrator is also an actor in the story, the narrator is character-bound, told in the first-person. When the narrator is not an actor in the story, the narration is anonymous, told in the

---

[27] Bal, *Narratology*, pp. 30–31 (who refers to E. Benveniste), Culler, *The Pursuit of Signs*, pp. 135–154, Cohan and Shires, *Telling Stories*, pp. 90–92. Cf. 3.3.

[28] G. Prince, "Introduction to the Study of the Narratee" in J. P. Tompkins (ed), *Reader-Response Criticism: From Formalism to Post-Structuralism* (Baltimore: Johns Hopkins University Press, 1980) 9. Cf. Chatman, *Story and Discourse*, pp. 253–262.

[29] On summary and scene, cf. 4.4. n. 25.

third-person. Such a categorisation identifies two fundamentally different relations between a narrating agent and the story on the basis of inclusion or exclusion from the story. The classification is useful, but according to Cohan and Shires it also poses an analytical problem: a third-person narrator is a contradiction in terms, as a third-person cannot narrate. The pronouns "she" and "he" refer to actors being narrated, not to an agency responsible for the narration. A first-person pronoun refers to a narrator only because of circumstance; the actor being narrated happens to be a narrating agent as well.[30]

Narrative agency is also related to subjectivity. *The speaking subject* is, for instance, a character speaking or thinking, whereas *the subject of speech* is the subject of the narrative act (cf. 3.3.). Also, the role of ideology has been related to the constitution of the subject. The Algerian-French Marxist philosopher Louis Althusser (1918–1990) regards interpellation as a process controlled by the text, yet the reader is under the illusion that identification is freely entered into.[31] The reader engaged in this process sees her- or himself as an individual responsible for meaning, while she or he is in fact subjected to cultural representations of meaning. In this, the "I" becomes an ideological representation of subjectivity. Falling between two poles of agency and passivity, subjectivity is the condition of being (a) subject. The enunciation of subjectivity also occurs in the interpellation of, for example, a narratee "you". Thus, a narrative does not simply represent subjectivity *to* readers, it also signifies their subjectivity *for them*.[32]

Also in Isa. 52:13–53:12, positions shift, e.g. from personal ("I") to collective ("we") to third-person ("he"). The text is a composite of "I" speech (52:13–15, 53:11–12, in both instances YHWH speech), "we" speech (53:1–6) and "he" speech (53:7–10). In a personification in 53:1–6, for instance, two worldviews clash, i.e. "we" accounted "him" smitten by God (v. 4b, where "we" act as narrator), and chastisement was upon "him" for "our" healing (v. 5, where "we" are both narrator and actor). When "we" are telling about and judging "him" in vv. 1–6, "we" also tell about and judge "ourselves", so both testimony and

---

[30] Cohan and Shires, *Telling Stories*, pp. 89–94, Bal, *Narratology*, pp. 19–31.

[31] L. Althusser, "Ideology and Ideological State Apparatuses" in L. Althusser, *Lenin and Philosophy and Other Essays* (London: New Left Books, 1971) 160–165.

[32] Cohan and Shires, *Telling Stories*, p. 108, on narrating subject (what I call *speaking subject*), subject of narration (what I call *subject of speech*) and narrated subject.

self-testimony are at play. The narratorial "we" appears as a signifier of subjectivity, and the difference between *speaking subject* and *subject of speech* is obscured. Acting as *the speaking subject* of the telling (its narrator), "we" also function as *subject of speech* in the story (as actors). Thus, both the words and the subject positions of the person who speaks are double-voiced. Dialogism might appear between narrations, in each actor's own discourse, inside an utterance, even inside an individual word.[33] This will be further illuminated in the narrative reading of Isa. 53 below.

4.6. STRUCTURE AND *DIFFÉRANCE*

Using a linguistic model, narratologists have described a general structure of stories based on the analogy of grammatical structures.[34] In formalist and structuralist versions, narratology has become a paradigm for reducing the difference between narratives to a set of structural relationships. The texts become objectified and their tensions harmonised. Barthes sees a text not as a structure or as a copy of a structure, but as practice. He prioritizes signifier over signified and structuration over structure. When applied to narratology, this implies that the assumed distance between a narrative and its reading is abolished so that the narrative and its reading become "identical".[35]

Culler describes a "double logics" of narrative, i.e. the logics of what he labels *story* ("what is told") and the logics of *discourse* ("how is it told").[36] According to him, the logics of story assume the primacy of events, taking event as a given reported by discourse. The logics of discourse treat the events as the products of meaning, as a product of discursive forces. The two logics cannot be reconciled, as each works to the exclusion of the other. A conflict arises between a reading that pursues a grammar of narrative and deconstructive interpretations,

---

[33] Cf. on Bakhtin and heteroglossia in 5.2.

[34] See e.g. A. J. Greimas, "Elements of a Narrative Grammar", *Diacritics* 7 (1977) 23–40, T. Todorov, *The Poetics of Prose* (Oxford: Blackwell, 1977) 108–119, Genette, *Narrative Discourse*, p. 30, and Barthes, "Introduction to the Structural Analysis of Narratives" in Barthes, *Image-Music-Text*, pp. 79–124.

[35] Barthes, "Theory of the Text", p. 38, cf. his distinction between readerly and writerly texts, treated in 3.8. In a readerly text, the story dominates narration, whereas in the writerly text, narration dominates story.

[36] Culler, *The Pursuit of Signs*, pp. 169–187, cf. 4.2.

which in showing the work's opposition to its own logic suggest the impossibility of such a grammar. Since both logics are necessary in narrative, they call into question the possibility of a coherent, uncontradictory reading.

Narratives tell about a past in the present for a future, but no version is the true version. Attention to how a narrative is a version of events rather than a description of them in their true state shows how it is performative rather than constative, or inventive, not descriptive. Performativity concerns how a text is doing by saying. A central element in this is how the reader is a self-involved participant with the text.[37]

4.7. ON PERSONIFICATION

A journey through the Hebrew Bible will illustrate the manifoldness and complexity of the trope of personification. Personifications of many sorts populate the Hebrew Bible, such as vices and virtues like Wisdom, Understanding, Evil, Sin, Righteousness, Peace, Happiness and other abstractions like Death, Sheol and the word of YHWH. Also geopolitical entities such as nation, people or cities are personified as king, son, slave, young girl, sister, bride, princess and whore.

---

[37] The interest in the performative dimensions of language is especially related to the speech act theory of Austin and Searle. A fine introduction to this is given by Adams, *The Performative Nature and Function of Isaiah 40–55*, p. 1–45. Adams applies speech act theory to Isa. 40–55. He focuses especially on four servant texts, Isa. 41:21–29, 49:1–6, 50:4–11 and 52:13–53:12, and concludes:

> Through self-involvement...speakers confess and embrace the open role of Yahweh's servant...[Isa. 53] present[s] one last aspect of the confessors return – sin...In Isa. 53, the servant silently trusts in the face of unjust suffering, and his life completely revolves around others. And through self-involvement speakers confess and so become Yahweh's disciples, the children of Zion, Yahweh's servants (pp. 210–211).

Also R. F. Melugin, "Reading the Book of Isaiah as Christian Scripture", pp. 188–203, and "Isaiah in the Worshipping Community" in M. P. Graham, R. R. Marrs and S. L. McKenzie (eds), *Worship and the Hebrew Bible: Essays in Honour of John T. Willis* (JSOTSup, 284, Sheffield: Sheffield Academic Press, 1999) 244–264 treat performative dimensions of the Book of Isaiah.

In Isa. 40–55, we find personifications such as Jacob, Israel, Jeshurun,[38] friend, messenger and servant,[39] as well as "I", "you"[40] and "he".[41] The male personifications in Isa. 40–55 convey aspects of genealogy and biography as well as of the future prospects of descendants.[42] The city of Jerusalem is addressed as "I", "you"[43] and "she",[44] as well as messenger, daughter, mother, wife and widow.[45] Also, a variety of personifications appears in the presentation of peoples. The nations are personified as idol makers,[46] kings,[47] rulers[48] as well as "daughter of Babylon".[49]

Personification is mentioned in many studies of the Hebrew Bible but has not been a prominent topic of discussion. Among general works on Hebrew poetry, the trope is mainly mentioned in passing, for instance by W. G. E. Watson:

> In the case of Hebrew poetry, it [personification] was largely a matter of demythologising ancient Canaanite borrowings. Not every reference of this kind was expunged; to mention Sheol is enough proof.[50]

---

[38] Jacob and Israel appear most often together, see 40:27, 41:8; 14 (Jacob only), 42:24 (cf. 5.12.2.), 43:1; 22; 28 (cf. 5.12.3.), 44:1–2; 5; 21; 23, 45:4, 48:12; 20 (Jacob only), 49:3; 5. Jeshurun appears in 44:2.

[39] Friend and messenger in 42:19 (cf. 5.9.2. n. 90), servant in 41:8; 9, 42:1; 19, 43:10, 44:1–2; 21–22; 26, 45:4, 48:20, 49:3; 5; 6 (cf. 5.8.2.), 50:10, 52:13, 53:11. On servant, see 5.8.2. n. 58 and 5.17. n. 324.

[40] Israel is addressed as "I" in 48:16, 49:1–5, 50:4–9 and in 2ms in 40:27–28, 41:8–16, 42:20 (cf. 5.9.2.), 43:1–5; 22–28 (cf. 5.12.3.), 44:1–4 (cf. 5.15.2.); 8; 24, 48:4–10; 12; 17–19 (cf. 5.15.3.), 49:3; 6–8, 51:12–13; 15; 16, 55:5.

[41] 41:2; 25, 42:2; 20, 45:13, 46:11, 50:10, 51:10; 14, 52:13–15, 53:2–12.

[42] In 41:8, the servant Jacob/Israel is presented as a descendant of YHWH's friend Abraham, in 51:2 Abraham and Sarah are presented as father and mother.

[43] Jerusalem and "I" in 49:14; 21, and as "you" in 49:17–26 (and your children, cf. 5.15.4.), 51:12; 17; 19–23, 52:1–2, 54:1–17 (with children, cf. 5.15.5.).

[44] 40:2, 44:26; 28, 49:14–29, 50:1, 51:3 (Zion and all her ruins); 17–23 (with children), 52:1–2.

[45] מְבַשֶּׂרֶת "messenger": 40:9, daughter: 52:2, mother: 49:17–25, 50:1, 51:18; 20, 54:1–10;13, wife: 54:5–6 and widow: 54:4.

[46] 40:19–20, 41:6–7, 44:9–20, 45:16, 46:6.

[47] The texts about Cyrus contain patterns which concur with personifications, see 41:2; 25, 44:28, 45:1–3, 46:11, 48:14. On the relation between king and nations, cf. on Body Politic in 4.7.3.5.

[48] 40:23: רוֹזְנִים "princes" and שֹׁפְטִים "rulers", 41:25: סְגָנִים "rulers", 49:7: מֹשְׁלִים "rulers".

[49] Isa. 47.

[50] Watson, Classical Hebrew Poetry, p. 270.

Schökel uses the term personification:

> for those cases where an abstract quality acts like a human being, like a person in society…The personification of cities, especially capital cities, is very frequent in the female figures of young ladies (bat) or mothers (as will be seen in the marriage symbolism).[51]

Schökel (1988) regrets that the phenomenon of personification in the Bible has not yet been systematically studied, in spite of the frequency with which it occurs and its importance. Exceptions are Lowth (1787) and the more recent study by Heim (1999).[52]

Personification is frequently understood as an abstraction, for instance qualities, nations, cities or peoples, which is given a human character. It appears in cult, myth, poetry, art, philosophy and rhetorics.[53] The trope opens for many discursive possibilities: from a living creature to another living creature; from a non-living thing to another non-living thing; from a living creature to a non-living thing; from a non-living thing to a living creature.[54] In modern literary criticism, identifications of personification are closely connected to positivistic attitudes in formalisations of tropes.[55] This might be related to:

1. An anthropological personification giving an actual personality to an abstraction, for instance gods, vices, virtues.
2. A historical personification giving a fictional personality to an abstraction, i.e. "impersonating" it.[56] This concerns especially the

---

[51] L. Alonso Schökel, *A Manual of Hebrew Poetics* (Subsidia Biblica, 11; Rome: Editrice Pontificio Istituto Biblico, 1988) 123–124.

[52] Lowth, *Lectures on the Sacred Poetry of the Hebrews*, pp. 280–301, and K. Heim, "The Personification of Jerusalem and the Drama of Her Bereavement in Lamentations" in R. S. Hess and G. J. Wenham (eds), *Zion, City of Our God* (Grand Rapids: Eerdmans, 1999) 129–169. Cf. studies on personification within the Hebrew Bible which do not treat the trope's more theoretical implications in 4.7. n. 64. D. R. Hillers, *Lamentations* (AB, 7A; New York: Doubleday, 1992) 30–31; 34; 37; 39, argues that personifications are potentially misleading since they refer to a city or to citizens as a whole rather than as parts of a whole. He claims that personifications serve mainly metrical purposes, and he often omits them in translation. For a criticism of Hillers, see Heim, p. 134.

[53] J. J. Paxson, *The Poetics of Personification* (Literature, Culture, Theory, 6; Cambridge: Cambridge University Press, 1994) 12, relates the notion of *prosopopeia* to *dramatis personae* as a method of character invention, used in Greek drama and the philosophical dialogue.

[54] Paxson, *The Poetics of Personification*, pp. 20–21, with reference to Quintillian.

[55] Paxson, *The Poetics of Personification*, pp. 29–30, incl. n. 14.

[56] Paxson, *The Poetics of Personification*, pp. 7; 12ff.

personification of land and people, including the "Body Politic", the personification of land and society as the sublime "body" of the king.[57] This "non-personal" body might also take on particular features, e.g. organs, limbs, faculties, cf. Isa. 7:2: "The heart of the king and the heart of the people were shaken like forest trees in the wind."[58]

Many exegetes have been engaged in a historical identification of personifications. Some readings of geo-political personifications are connected to the concept of corporate personality. This concept has also been used to explain the individual and collective traits of the servant in the four *EJL* in Isa. 40–55, as well as the abrupt switch in some psalms from "I" to "we".[59] The concept of corporate personality has been criticised for being based on an untenable explanation of a supposed primitive mentality.[60]

The funeral dirge has been related to the mourning of the annihilation of a society and the personification of the city or state.[61] As regards female personifications of the city in the Hebrew Bible, especially in

---

[57] Paxson, *The Poetics of Personification*, p. 43.

[58] Paxson, *The Poetics of Personification*, p. 50.

[59] O. Eißfeldt, *Der Gottesknecht bei Deuterojesaja (Jes. 40–55) im Lichte der israelitischen Anschauung von Gemeinschaft und Individuum* (Beiträge zur Religionsgeschichte der Altertums, 2; Halle: Niemeyer, 1933) and "The Ebed-Jahweh in Isaiah xl–lv", *ExpTim* 44 (1933) 261–268. H. W. Robinson, *The Cross in the Old Testament* (London: SCM, 1955) based his theories regarding the Hebrew mentality on an idea of a pre-logic mentality in primitive societies, formulated by the anthropologist Lévy-Bruhl. Mettinger, *Farewell to the Servant Songs*, p. 35, seems to support this in his explanation of Isa. 49:5–6. A theory of corporate personality is also supported by W. A. M. Beuken, "Isaiah 54: The Multiple Identity of the Person Addressed" in J. Barr (ed), *Language and Meaning: Studies in Hebrew Language and Biblical Exegesis* (OTS, 19; Leiden: E. J. Brill, 1974) 29–70, and M. C. A. Korpel, "The Female Servant of the Lord in Isa. 54" in B. Becking and M. Dijkstra (eds), *On Reading Prophetic Texts: Gender-Specific and Related Studies in Memory of Fokkelin van Dijk-Hemmes* (Biblical Interpretation Series, 18; Leiden: E. J. Brill, 1996) 166.

[60] J. W. Rogerson, "The Hebrew Conception of Corporate Personality: A Re-examination" in B. Lang (ed), *Anthropological Approaches to the Old Testament* (Issues in Religion and Theology, 8; Philadelphia: Fortress Press, 1985) 43–57, has criticised Robinson for applying the idea of corporate personality in an imprecise fashion, supported by S. E. Porter, "Two Myths: Corporate Personality and Language/Mentality Determinism", *SJT* 43 (1990) 289–307. Kaminsky, *Corporate Responsibility in the Hebrew Bible*, pp. 16–29, takes much of the criticism raised against Robinson's theories into consideration, but emphasises that Robinson's "insights that corporate ways of thinking constitute part of the Israelite *Weltanschauung* are still fruitful" (p. 22).

[61] Jahnow, *Das hebräische Leichenlied im Rahmen der Völkerdichtung*, p. 164.

Lamentations, their resemblance to Mesopotamian city laments has been assessed – and disputed.[62]

Both the distinction between various kinds of personification and the distinction between personification and tropes such as allegory, metaphor, symbol and persona, are tainted by confusion. While scholars have spent much energy on discussing an adequate definition of metaphor, the trope of personification is mentioned only in passing in recent studies.[63] Other studies of personification in the Hebrew Bible do not treat its theoretical implications.[64] However, the post-structuralist de Man has proclaimed personification as "the master trope of poetic discourse".[65] Paxson regards personification as a rhetorical figure inherent in grammatical structure and considers it a trope of several principles: "[F]rom narration to characterisation, from figuration itself to Derrida's concept of *relever* as a possible concomitant of

---

[62] For brief overviews of the discussion of a supposed connection between Lamentations and the Mesopotamian city laments, see Hillers, *Lamentations*, pp. 32–39, and A. Berlin, *Lamentations: A Commentary* (OTL; Louisville, KY: Westminster/John Knox Press, 2002) 26–30.

[63] Examples of recent studies of metaphor in biblical studies, see e.g. J. Galambush, *Jerusalem in the Book of Ezekiel: The City as YHWH's Wife* (SBLDS, 130; Atlanta: Scholars Press, 1992), N. Stienstra, *YHWH is the Husband of His People: Analysis of a Biblical Metaphor with Special Reference to Translation* (Kampen: Kok Pharos, 1993), Darr, *Isaiah's Vision and the Family of God*, G. Eidevall, *Grapes in the Desert: Metaphors, Models, and Themes in Hosea 4–14* (ConBOT, 43; Stockholm: Almqvist & Wiksell, 1996) and R. Abma, *Bonds of Love: Methodic Studies of Prophetic Texts with Marriage Imagery (Isaiah 50:1–3 and 54:1–10, Hosea 1–3, Jeremiah 2–3)* (Studia Semitica Neerlandica; Assen: Van Gorcum, 1999).

[64] A. Mintz, "The Rhetoric of Lamentations and the Representation of Catastrophe", *Prooftext* 2 (1982) 1–17, U. Berges, "Personifications and Prophetic Voices of Zion in Isaiah and Beyond" in J. C. de Moor (ed), *The Elusive Prophet. The Prophet as a Historical Person, Literary Character and Anonymous Artist: Papers Read at the Eleventh Joint Meeting of The Society of the Old Testament Study and Het Oudtestamentisch Werkgezelschap in Nederland en België held at Soesterberg 2000* (OTS, 45; Leiden: E. J. Brill, 2001) 54–82, R. E. Murphy, "The Personification of Wisdom" in H. G. M. Williamson, J. Day and R. P. Gordon (eds), *Wisdom in Ancient Israel: Essays in Honour of J. A. Emerton* (Cambridge: Cambridge University Press, 1995) 222–233, M. E. Biddle, "The Figure of Lady Jerusalem: Identification, Deification and Personification of Cities in the Ancient Near East" in K. Lawson Younger Jr., W. W. Hallo and B. F. Batto (eds), *The Biblical Canon in Comparative Perspective* (Scripture in Context, IV; Lewiston, NY: Edwin Mellem Press, 1991) 173–187, M. E. Biddle, "Lady Zions Alter Egos: Isaiah 47:1–15 and 57:6–13 as Structural Counterparts" in Melugin and Sweeney, *New Visions of Isaiah*, pp. 124–139, and C. W. Miller, "Reading Voices: Personification, Dialogism, and the Reader of Lamentations 1", *BibInt* 9 (2001) 393–408.

[65] de Man, *The Resistance to Theory*, p. 48.

the process he [i.e. Derrida] calls 'metaphorisation'."[66] Personification may be read on a rhetorical, a semantic or a hermeneutic level, and cannot be reduced to "mere description" or décor.

4.7.1. *Personification Figure: Personifier and Personified*

Paxson suggests a description of personification according to Saussure's linguistic model,[67] and describes the personification figure as a compound entity consisting of

> Personifier (the material, phonic agent): servant, "he"
> Personified (conceptual, given expression through the personifier; the textual or historical referentiality of the trope): Israel, "we"

The personifier is the actual expression and narrative actant: she or he is an active human being, endowed with speech, and with a certain psychological, physiological or ideological constitution. The personified is the entity to which the expression refers and can be found among abstractions, inanimate objects, animals etc. It is figurally translated into the personifier.

4.7.2. *Personification Figure and Personification Character*

Paxson further suggests a narratological distinction between personification used in *discourse* ("how is it told"), which he labels personification figure, and in *story* ("what is told"), which he labels personification character.[68] This might, for instance, be related to the temporality of narrative. As we have seen, narrative speed divides into four tempos: ellipsis, summary, scene and pause (cf. 4.4.). Some personifications are dominated by ellipsis and scene, and so are closer to the non-narrative elements of description and illustration than to narrative ones. Paxson labels these personification figures.[69] A personification figure must at

---

[66] Paxson, *The Poetics of Personification*, pp. 5; 38. Paxson combines post-modern and traditional stances (p. 1).

[67] Paxson, *The Poetics of Personification*, pp. 40–42.

[68] Paxson, *The Poetics of Personification*, p. 35. He also refers to J. Hillis Miller, "The Two Allegories" in M. W. Bloomfield (ed), *Allegory, Myth, and Symbol* (Harvard English Studies, 9; Cambridge, MA: Harvard University Press, 1982) 355, who claims that there are two personifications: one is mostly self-contained in a phrase or a line; the other is an extension of the first into a complete narrative world (traditionally regarded as allegory). On story/narration, cf. 4.2.–4.4.

[69] Paxson, *The Poetics of Personification*, p. 35.

least be a local rhetorical ornament.[70] Paxson cites the female figure Wisdom in Wisd. 7:7; 22–24 as an example of a personification figuration "that occupies more textual space than one local site but is not necessarily narrative",[71] as the passage mainly describes abstract behavioural tendencies of the Wisdom figure.

A personification character, on the other hand, is an extension of the personification figure into a complete narrative world.[72] It occupies a role as a character, object or place of the space-time of the story, expressed by, for example, speech or gestures. The compound entity of the personification in personifier and personified becomes more explicit in the narrative personification character. Paxson illustrates this with the following expression: "Poverty walked in, and Love flew out the window."[73] He describes this as an aphoristic, localised, rhetorical figure and elaborates:

> To materialize the concepts of love and poverty as characters in a narrative world (making them walk and fly through actual doors and windows) means to *literalize* what is already a rhetorical figure. Since such literalization…is *itself* a figure, the invention of a personified character as an agent in a narrative world involves the figure of a figure.[74]

In addition, a blurring of *story* and *discourse* levels might be occuring.[75] In my narrative reading of Isa. 52:13–53:12 below, a blurring appears of what I label *story* ("what is told") and *narration* ("how is it told", what Paxson calls *discourse*). In 52:14, for instance, the distinction between the narratee "you" and the narrated "he" in 52:13 is confused. The personifier "he" and the personified "you" are blurred when a kind of identification between "him" and "you" is revealed: the narrator "I" places "you" at the same level as that about which he speaks. In doing so, the function of the narratee "you" is transferred to one of the actors, i.e. "he" (cf. 4.8.1.5.).

---

[70] Paxson, *The Poetics of Personification*, p. 35.
[71] Paxson, *The Poetics of Personification*, pp. 36–37.
[72] Hillis Miller, "Narrative", p. 75, describes three basic elements of narrative: 1. "an initial situation, a sequence leading to a change or reversal of that situation, and a revelation made possible by the reversal of that situation"; 2. "some use of personification whereby a character is created out of signs"; and, 3. "some patterning or repetition of key elements, for example, a trope or system of tropes, or a complex world".
[73] Paxson, *The Poetics of Personification*, p. 40.
[74] Paxson, *The Poetics of Personification*, p. 40, his italics.
[75] Paxson, *The Poetics of Personification*, pp. 41–42.

4.7.3. *Transformations of Personifications*

Heim speaks of four transformations in the personification of Jerusalem in Lamentations, which he describes as four levels of abstraction.[76] He cites Lam. 1:1 as an example:

> How *lonely sits the city* that was once full of people!
> How *like a widow* she has become, she that was great among the nations!

4.7.3.1. *Ideation (Reification)*
The first level of abstraction Heim labels reification, in which the personification of Jerusalem turns human beings into inanimate, abstract ideas:

Jerusalem community (reifier)
Citizens of Jerusalem (reified)

4.7.3.2. *Topification (Localization)*
At Heim's second level, the abstract concept of the Jerusalem community is transformed into an architectural site "devoid of humans: it is a city 'that was once full of people' (cf. 1:1a)".[77] Here, human beings are translated into a geographical location:

Jerusalem City (localizer)
Jerusalem community (localized)

4.7.3.3. *Personification*
At the third level of abstraction, Heim describes how the geographical location of Jerusalem City "is 'qualified' as a person by being provided with body parts, human sentiments and social relations: it sits, is lonely and a widow".[78] The widow, personified Jerusalem, represents the sum of the individuals living in the city. In this case, a nonhuman quantity is translated into a human being:

---

[76] Heim, "The Personification of Jerusalem and the Drama of Her Bereavement in Lamentations", p. 135. The first three levels are taken from Paxson, *The Poetics of Personification*, pp. 42–43.

[77] Heim, "The Personification of Jerusalem and the Drama of Her Bereavement in Lamentations", p. 137.

[78] Heim, "The Personification of Jerusalem and the Drama of Her Bereavement in Lamentations", p. 137.

<u>Widow (personifier+ human attributes)</u>
Jerusalem City (personified)

4.7.3.4. *Impersonation (Representation)*

At the fourth level of abstraction, the widow symbolizes the Jerusalem community, which again is an abstraction of the totality of individuals living in Jerusalem. Heim describes this level as the translation of a group of people into a person who speaks for them:

> <u>Widow (impersonator/representative)</u>
> Citizens of Jerusalem (impersonated/represented)

Heim explains this level as a result of the three previous abstractions, and comments how this representative function explains why the personified Jerusalem can be depicted in different and at times mutually exclusive roles:

> She is wife, prostitute, divorcée, widow, mother, daughter, and so on, thus impersonating the various individuals suffering distress.[79]

He then offers an overview of Lam. 1, highlighting the importance of personhood and relationships for the individual and communal grieving process, and explains:

> [T]he projection of personal and communal experience ("I" and "we"/"you" [pl.] onto a third person ("she") helps the individual and the community to structure their own experience of themselves.[80]

4.7.3.5. *Body Politic*

The categories might cross each others' boundaries. The Body Politic figure involves the personification of an abstract idea ("society") as a human individual, i.e. a translation of an abstraction into a geographical locus ("topification") as well as a translation of a human agent into an inanimate thing ("ideation").[81] This ideation involves a sort of dehumanisation, while topification can blur into ideation as in a Body Politic figure, where a state is personified as a king.[82]

---

[79] Heim, "The Personification of Jerusalem and the Drama of Her Bereavement in Lamentations", p. 138.

[80] Heim, "The Personification of Jerusalem and the Drama of Her Bereavement in Lamentations", p. 141. Lam. 1 is treated in more detail in 5.11.9. and Lam. 2 in 5.11.10.

[81] Paxson, *The Poetics of Personification*, p. 43.

[82] Paxson, *The Poetics of Personification*, p. 44.

Paxson comments on the way in which personification, as the "figural translation of a non-human quantity into a human being", and reification, as "the figural translation of a human agent into a non-human one", might be taken as binary oppositions.[83] However, he adds:

> [I]n true post-structuralist fashion, each of the two complementary tropes is seen to be contained in the other's structure, especially when they are reinscribed in a third and coordinate generic scheme, the Body Politic [with] the frequent personification of the land and society as the sublime "body" of the king.[84]

4.7.4. *Summing up*

Both narrative and personification have been objectified in the pursuit of their categorisation. Despite the universality of story-telling, theoreticians strive to determine what a narrative is. A narrative reading of Isa. 52:13–53:12 is motivated by rhetorics of narrative, in which an agent tells a story in language. In my narrative reading of this text, I distinguish between *story* and *narration*, and apply *narrative* as a term embracing both. By this structural distinction between *story* and *narration*, a narrative reading of the text shows counter-suggestions which overturn the hierarchy (cf. 4.2.).

Especially as regards the trope of personification in biblical studies, the interest in historical-biographical readings has dominated, or the trope has been ignored as uninteresting. As will become clear, the structural distinction between *story* and *narration* will be fruitful in identifying the trope personification. The personification contributes – whether overtly or more subtly – to the reader's perception of the subject suddenly endowed with life. It is my wish that a narrative reading of Isa. 52:13–53:12 – a text which has been so much interpreted in religious and scholarly contexts – might be opened in a new manner when the narrative forces of the text are also activated.

---

[83] Paxson, *The Poetics of Personification*, p. 50.
[84] Paxson, *The Poetics of Personification*, p. 50.

4.8. Isa. 52:13–53:12: Narrative

4.8.1. Isa. 52:13–15

52:13 הִנֵּה יַשְׂכִּיל עַבְדִּי יָרוּם וְנִשָּׂא וְגָבַהּ מְאֹד׃
¹⁴כַּאֲשֶׁר שָׁמְמוּ עָלֶיךָ רַבִּים
כֵּן־מִשְׁחַת מֵאִישׁ מַרְאֵהוּ וְתֹאֲרוֹ מִבְּנֵי אָדָם׃
¹⁵כֵּן יַזֶּה גוֹיִם רַבִּים עָלָיו יִקְפְּצוּ מְלָכִים פִּיהֶם
כִּי אֲשֶׁר לֹא־סֻפַּר לָהֶם רָאוּ וַאֲשֶׁר לֹא־שָׁמְעוּ הִתְבּוֹנָנוּ׃

52:13: See, my servant shall prosper and be exalted, he shall be lifted and be very high!

52:14: As many were appalled at you
– such a disfigurement from that of man was his appearance and his form from that of humanity

52:15: – so he יַזֶּה (will startle?) many peoples before him, kings shall shut their mouth;
for what has not been told to them, they shall see, and what they did not hear, they shall understand.

4.8.1.1. *Narration*

By the interrupting הִנֵּה "See!", a change is indicated (52:13). In הִנֵּה "See!" a telling is framed by an exclamation, as a speaking "I" tells about how עַבְדִּי "my servant" shall prosper, be exalted, be lifted and be very high. The proclamation of this event is extremely compressed, and evokes in advance something that will take place later. Then, the telling reverts to events of the past, framed by an argument, a characterisation and an explanation (52:14). The narrator "I" is telling the narratee "you" about רַבִּים "many"'s appalled reactions to "you". רַבִּים "many"'s reactions are explained as due to "his" מִשְׁחַת "disfigurement". So again the telling turns to an anticipation of future events, the scaring (?) of גוֹיִם רַבִּים "many peoples" and the silence of מְלָכִים "kings" (52:15). These events, it is explained, have never previously been told to or heard by "them", yet they shall be both seen and understood. Thus, chronological deviation frames this entire narration: it opens by picking up a story's future (v. 13) before it goes backwards to fill in a past, restoring a linear chronology (v. 14) and then finally turns forward to the future again (v. 15).

52:14–15 is framed as an argument. In v. 14, שָׁמְמוּ רַבִּים "many were appalled" at "you" due to ("his") מִשְׁחַת "disfigurement". The כֵּן "such" in v. 14b has a causative and contemporary force when related to כַּאֲשֶׁר "as", explaining a past situation with a past-state clause.

When related to כַּאֲשֶׁר "as" in v. 14, כֵּן "so" in v. 15a has not a causal, but a temporal and comparative force, contrasting a past situation (v. 14a) with a future one (v. 15) and working as a response in terms of a comparison: גּוֹיִם רַבִּים "many peoples" will become startled (?) by "him", מְלָכִים "kings" shall shut their mouth and "they" shall see and understand what "they" have neither been told nor heard. The argument takes shape through a change from past to future, while the situations differ in terms of a change in both actors and actions.

4.8.1.2. Narrator and Narratee: "I" and "You"

In this "I" speech, the telling is performed as though delivered "personally". When the narrator in 52:13 presents עַבְדִּי "my servant", this points to the position of the narrator himself as "lord". Also, through a blurring of narration, arguments and description, features are attributed to the actors by the narrator and he is able to tell about the past and/or the future of "him", "you", רַבִּים "many", גּוֹיִם רַבִּים "many peoples", מְלָכִים "kings" and "they". The "I" narrator mediates perspectives on events and actors by standing apart, but is also related to the story according to his point of view as witness and "lord".

In addition to being entangled in what he speaks of, the "I" is also involved with whomsoever it is to whom he is speaking. When the "I" addresses someone with the interjection הִנֵּה "See!", he is narrating to a "you", an immediate listener to the telling. The narratee "you" enters into the narrative by being initiated into a situation and encouraged to listen and perceive a spectacular event: the coming prosperity of עַבְדִּי "my servant". In הִנֵּה "See!" the possibility of "your" testimony of an event which is not perceptible, yet is proclaimed, appears. Thus, "you" are related to the future event of "his" exaltation as witness. The narrator "I" also introduces the narratee "you" to an event of humiliation in the past, in which "you" were regarded as appalling by רַבִּים "many" (cf. עָלֶיךָ "at you" in 52:14). The humiliation is explained as due to "his" מִשְׁחַת "disfigurement". An implicit or explicit claim of an appalling event is made, in which an enunciative defamiliarisation appears. "You" are both a narratee and an actor, whereas "he" is only an actor in the story.

4.8.1.3. Story

Through relations in which they are endowed with meaning, events and actors become identified as parts of a whole. When an end is made from a transformation of a beginning, a sequence of events involving actors and temporality is made into a story. In 52:14, the beginning of a past situation is related to the actors רַבִּים "many" who were appalled when confronted with "you". רַבִּים "many" were dismayed at "you", and this is explained through a portrait of "his" מִשְׁחַת "disfigurement". In this portrait, different claims of humiliation are made. In the mentioning of "you" and the portrait of "him", both are brought out as actors without desire, will or reactions. Through a juxtaposition of literary codes, "your" identification with "him" emerges. This occurs through a personification, in which a confusion appears between the personifier "he" and the personified "you": "you" are being regarded as appalling due to "his" disfigurement.[85] In addition, the surroundings appear as traits by the relation between רַבִּים "many" (v. 14a) and "you" and the separation of "him" מֵאִישׁ "from man" and מִבְּנֵי אָדָם "from humanity" (v. 14b). The relation is characterised by a numerical inequality: the plural רַבִּים "many" is the powerful actor, witnessing the singular, passive receiver "you"/"he".

The sequence of reflection in 52:14 allows the sentences to be organised as the first half of a story which comes to take shape when רַבִּים "many"'s humiliation of "you"/"him" is related to events leading to a change in that situation. By 52:15, the story is temporally advanced from past to future and new actors are introduced. In v. 15a, "he" יַזֶּה ('will startle'?) גּוֹיִם רַבִּים "many peoples" before "him". "His" action towards גּוֹיִם רַבִּים "many peoples" is further signified by מְלָכִים "kings", who shall be utterly subjected, responding with silence to what they witness. These coming events are amplified by being related to a reversal in the story of "them": "they" shall see/understand that something hitherto untold/unheard is going to happen, a reversal of all "their" previous seeing. A change in "their" knowledge is brought out through contrasts of negative and positive utterances. A confusion of consecutiveness and consequence appears in the identification of "them" in relation to רַבִּים "many", גּוֹיִם רַבִּים "many peoples" and מְלָכִים "kings", who are distinguished from each other by different and changing functions: רַבִּים "many" are humiliating "you"/"him" (v. 14), גּוֹיִם רַבִּים "many peoples" will be startled (?), מְלָכִים "kings" shall become silent and "they" shall see

---

[85] Cf. Heim, "The Personification of Jerusalem and the Drama of Her Bereavement in Lamentations", p. 135, on impersonation, that is, the translation of a group of people into a person who speaks for them.

and understand (v. 15). "Their" knowledge about "him" and "their" own situation becomes changed when the relations of the past in v. 14 become upset in v. 15. In the future, "their" attitude to "him" shall be both challenged and changed. The shift in relations marks out an unstable field of actor signification. Again, these relations are characterised by a numerical inequality between the plural גּוֹיִם רַבִּים "many peoples", מְלָכִים "kings" and "they" as passive receivers and witnesses *and* the singular, active, powerful "he".

A story is initiated by placing an event in a sequence to mark a beginning (52:14); what ends it is the replacement of the initial event by another to mark an ending (52:15). The story is kept going as a sequence of eventualities by displacements of both the initial and the closing events. In contrast with the disgraceful depiction of "him" in v. 14, "their" reactions in v. 15 might echo the proclamation in v. 13, where the future is foretold as a spectacular event of exaltation. The event of v. 13 concerns "him" only, and is not related to any prior, causative state of affairs. However, it might support the argument of vv. 14–15: as insignificant as "he" was in the past, so significant shall "he" be in the future. Just as no reason for עַבְדִּי "my servant"'s prosperity is given in v. 13, so in v. 14 no reason is given for why "he" was found in such miserable conditions: disfigured and dissociated from men. Through a structure of placement-displacements-replacements, a story delineates time and agency as movements in order to achieve the transformation of one event, e.g. the opening as a signifier (v. 14), into another, e.g. the closure as the opening's signified (vv. 13; 15), which is only a new signifier.

Through relations between actors and events, the identification of a story becomes revealed. As a succession of events is pursued, a chiastic pattern appears through a crisscross reversal between events and actors: exaltations and humiliations related to "him", "you", רַבִּים "many", גּוֹיִם רַבִּים "many peoples", מְלָכִים "kings" and "they". 52:14, 15 and 13 might be presented in a linear sequence where events follow after each other, but not due to each other: no explanation is given for the temporal turning point from רַבִּים "many" being appalled at "you" because of "his" מִשְׁחַת "disfigurement" (v. 14) to "his" future of exaltation (v. 13) and "his" scaring (?) of גּוֹיִם רַבִּים "many peoples" (v. 15). Whereas "he" is the only actor of the future in v. 13, in v. 15 the future of גּוֹיִם רַבִּים "many peoples", מְלָכִים "kings" and "they" is at least as prominent as "his".

In addition to performing functions for a story, actors are also differentiated according to traits distinguishing them from each other relationally. In the relation between past and future, both "his"/"your" and "their" statuses become turned around: due to "his" מִשְׁחַת "disfigurement", רַבִּים "many" became appalled at "you" (v. 14), but "he" יַזֶּה ('will startle'?) גּוֹיִם רַבִּים "many peoples" (v. 15) and be exalted (v. 13), מְלָכִים "kings" shall be silent and "they" shall see and understand. Different story-lines of "him" and "they" appear: Whereas the past events involved רַבִּים "many", "you" and "him" (v. 14), the future events are related to "him", גּוֹיִם רַבִּים "many peoples", מְלָכִים "kings" and "they" (v. 15). Characteristic of these relationships are a numerical inequality and changes of agency: the active רַבִּים "many" (pl) were appalled and witnessed the passive receiver "you"/"he" (sg), the pass. גּוֹיִם רַבִּים "many peoples" (pl) will be startled (?) by the active, powerful "him" (sg), and the passive מְלָכִים "kings" (pl) shall become silent receivers and witnesses in the future, whereas "he" (sg) shall be exalted. In all events attention is drawn to appearance. Within the clusters of seeing/not-seeing, perceiving/not-perceiving and witnessing, elements are included of transformation and reversal. The actors are also differentiated by being directly addressed ("you") or mentioned ("he", "many").

4.8.1.4. *Narrative*

In 52:13, signs of a narrative situation appear in a narrator's telling about events and actors: The "I" proclaims that "you" shall see the coming exaltation of עַבְדִּי "my servant". The story looks towards the future with a promise of things which shall become visible. In this, a double aspect appears: with the present reference to עַבְדִּי "my servant" and the future implementation of this demand, the proclamation (*narration*) and the exaltation (*story*) are so closely related that a distinction into narrative levels cannot be made. Through a transference of *narration* and *story*, an exclamation is made that is both indirect by the telling about עַבְדִּי "my servant" and direct to the narrated "you". By the verbalising of actions, events of past, present and future are triggered. The narration is happening in advance of, as well as after, the events described: the present narratee "you" is listening whereas the actor "you" shall see in the future (52:13) and became humiliated in the past (52:14).

4.8.1.5. *Narratee as Actor: "You"*

The interpellation of the narrator "I" in the narrative in turn facilitates the interpellation of the narratee "you".[86] Whereas in 52:13 "you" are implied by הִנֵּה "See!", in 52:14 the narrator "I" relates himself to the narratee by the phrase עָלֶיךָ "at you". The narratee is admonished to participate by being called upon as witness to "his" – and his own – fate.

Distinctive signs in the portrait of a fate are dissolved as the distinction between the narratee "you" and the narrated "he" in v. 13 becomes confused in v. 14. The personifier "he" and the personified "you" become blurred when a kind of identification between "him" and "you" is revealed: the narrator "I" places "you" at the same level as that about which he speaks, i.e. "you" are being regarded as appalling due to "his" disfigurement. Thus, the function of the narratee "you" is transferred to one of the actors, i.e. "he".

In addition to an identification between "you" and "he" in the event of רַבִּים "many" being appalled, the very same juxtaposition of "you" and "he" also presents a contrast between them. In the relation between *narration* and *story*, both the narratee-actor "you" and the actor "he" are created out of signs. A confusion appears between "you" and "him". The narratee-actor "you" is both humiliated and witnessing "his" humiliating מִשְׁחַת "disfigurement". The actor "you" appals רַבִּים "many", and appears also as narratee-witness when related to "him". When "your" fate is being witnessed (by רַבִּים "many") and "you" are witnessing another's fate ("his" מִשְׁחַת "disfigurement"), "you" see "yourself" and "him". Both identity and difference appear in seeing oneself as another. The dissociating humiliation of "you" raises doubt as to whether there is an uninterrupted continuity between the narratee-actor "you" and "him". Whereas "he" is involved in the event as actor, "you" are involved both by being regarded as appalling *and* by witnessing. The relation between "you" and "him" is different from that between "you" and רַבִּים "many" (actor-witnesses) and that between "him" and רַבִּים "many", as neither a clear contrast nor an unambiguous identity appears. In the confrontation between רַבִּים "many" and "you", "you" are being regarded as appalling, whereas in the explanation given for this, "his" non-belonging is depicted at a distance. This "impersonalisation" leads the narratee-actor "you" to see differently,

---

[86] On interpellation, see 4.5.

not by experiencing "yourself" as "him" in the humiliation, but by witnessing "him" from outside. By "your" seeing differently and seeing difference, the story is turned around and the actors are made different from each other. A relation is established between "you" and "him" based on closeness or distance, in connection with the narratee's role in the plot and personification: the narrative constructs the identification of the actors in constructing that of the story told. By establishing a relation between "you" and "him", the narrative becomes more than an occasion for a narrator to tell a story as it plots the duality of the narratee "you" and the actor "you"/"he". In the blurring of the *story* and *narration*, the narrative is referring to the destruction of its own illusions: "you" are divided between the source of action (witnessing) and the effect of the action (being humiliated). In terms of the syntax, the relation between subject ("you") and object ("he") points in its contradiction to a disruption of the unified subject which is the source of meaning and action.[87]

The narrative can be organised as events and actors placed in relation to each other, where each segment arranges a different relation between the narrator "I", the narratee "you" and the actors "he", "you" and "they". In the *story*, actors are related through events in a linear sequence, e.g. "he" was humiliated and shall be exalted; "many" were appalled at "you"; "he" will startle (?) many peoples; kings shall shut their mouth and "they" shall see and understand what is untold and unheard. In the *narration*, the portrait of the narratee emerges from the narrative addressed to this "you", but the significance of "you"/"him" is not unified or consistent. A pragmatic contradiction in the narrative is resolved by a temporal splitting of "you"/"him" into past/future (*story*) and present (*narration*), in which the statements about "you"/"him" and the moment of uttering them are separated.

The illusion of continuity and succession which the relation between the speaking "I" and his servant established become inverted or destabilised by the relations between "you" and "he" and between "I" and "you". This is achieved by clues that suggest that something else is going on within the story. In a narratological analysis of *story* and *narration*, the double mediation prevents the narration from being read only as an utterance of a narrator. The telling about "him" through repetition works as a way of inscribing a point of view, but it also presents others,

---

[87] Cf. Culler's double logics in 4.6.

that is, "you", רַבִּים "many", גּוֹיִם רַבִּים "many peoples", מְלָכִים "kings"
and "they", in ways which stress that repeated point of view. Given the
textual movements which result from such shifts, the narration cannot
be centred in a fixed and single point of view or personified by a narrator whose point of view is totally responsible for what is said, seen
and shown. Rather, the narrative has to be analysed in terms of how it
sets in place differing relations of agency and testimony.

4.8.2. *Isa. 53:1–6*

53:1 מִי הֶאֱמִין לִשְׁמֻעָתֵנוּ וּזְרוֹעַ יְהוָה עַל־מִי נִגְלָתָה:
²וַיַּעַל כַּיּוֹנֵק לְפָנָיו וְכַשֹּׁרֶשׁ מֵאֶרֶץ צִיָּה
לֹא־תֹאַר לוֹ וְלֹא הָדָר וְנִרְאֵהוּ וְלֹא־מַרְאֶה וְנֶחְמְדֵהוּ:
³נִבְזֶה וַחֲדַל אִישִׁים אִישׁ מַכְאֹבוֹת וִידוּעַ חֹלִי
וּכְמַסְתֵּר פָּנִים מִמֶּנּוּ נִבְזֶה וְלֹא חֲשַׁבְנֻהוּ:
⁴אָכֵן חֳלָיֵנוּ הוּא נָשָׂא וּמַכְאֹבֵינוּ סְבָלָם
וַאֲנַחְנוּ חֲשַׁבְנֻהוּ נָגוּעַ מֻכֵּה אֱלֹהִים וּמְעֻנֶּה:
⁵וְהוּא מְחֹלָל מִפְּשָׁעֵנוּ מְדֻכָּא מֵעֲוֹנֹתֵינוּ
מוּסַר שְׁלוֹמֵנוּ עָלָיו וּבַחֲבֻרָתוֹ נִרְפָּא־לָנוּ:
⁶כֻּלָּנוּ כַּצֹּאן תָּעִינוּ אִישׁ לְדַרְכּוֹ פָּנִינוּ
וַיהוָה הִפְגִּיעַ בּוֹ אֵת עֲוֹן כֻּלָּנוּ:

53:1: Who believes what we hear? And the arm of YHWH – to whom
       is it revealed?
53:2: He grew up like a shoot before him and like a root out of dry
       ground;
       there was no form to him and no splendour that we should look
       at him,
       and no appearance that we should be attracted to him.
53:3: He was despised and abandoned by men; a man with sicknesses
       and known with illness,
       and like one from whom men hide their faces; he was despised
       and we did not consider him.
53:4: Yet surely he bore our illnesses and carried our sicknesses,
       whereas we accounted him stricken, smitten by God and humili-
       ated.
53:5: But he was wounded because of our transgressions and injured
       because of our iniquities;
       chastisement was upon him for our healing and by his wound is
       recovery for us.
53:6: All of us like sheep went astray; everyone turned his own way
       and thus YHWH struck him by the iniquity of all of us.

4.8.2.1. *Narration*

In 53:1, two questions concerning the past, present and future are
posed. The questions are delivered as "we" speech, and by the inter-

rogative מִי "who", identity is asked for. The first question concerns
who believe שְׁמֻעָתֵנוּ "what we hear"; the second to whom זְרוֹעַ יְהוָה
"the arm of YHWH" is revealed. In the first question, "we" assert that
a message has been transmitted to "us", and simultaneously question
whether this is recognised. In the second question, it is asserted that
זְרוֹעַ יְהוָה "the arm of YHWH" has been revealed, and simultaneously
it is questioned whether this is acknowledged. The demands of the
questions are linked to a pursuit of testimony and self-testimony. In
both questions, "we" are both addressing "ourselves" and admonishing
"ourselves" to question "our" own experiences. The questions reveal
experiences related to oppositions of a message which is (not) believed
and a revelation which is (not) seen. The second question concerns the
relationship of "us" and YHWH, but by way of dramatising a statement about to be made, "we" speak as though uninitiated in "our"
astonishment at זְרוֹעַ יְהוָה "the arm of YHWH". A divine revelation
and a response are involved. "Our" self-questioning is also an attempt
at contact with the deity through זְרוֹעַ יְהוָה "the arm of YHWH"
being revealed or hidden. In "our" self-questioning, a narratee "you"
is bound to be artificial. But even if the questions do not seek to obtain
information from the narratee, they invite the production of answers
to the questions.

The questions are followed by "our" telling about a man's growing
up. A linear chronology is drawn and supplied with characterisation,
comments and explanation (53:2). "His" state is likened to יוֹנֵק "a
shoot" and שֹׁרֶשׁ "a root" which might have connotations of both hope
and hopelessness, promise and doom. It is further described by a portrait of "his" bodily appearance and "our" judgment of this (v. 2b).
The man is despised, ill, isolated and unacknowledged (v. 3). "We" are
talking about a *present* judgment of "his" and "our" past (v. 4a) and
"our" *past* judgment of "his" humiliations (v. 4b). While "we" had
previously regarded "his" humiliations as a punishment brought upon
"him" by God (v. 4b), "we" now claim that "he" carried "our" illnesses
(v. 4a) due to "our" sins (v. 5a). Then the telling turns to the future
by evoking in advance a later event: the chastisement and wounds of
"him" shall lead to "our" healing and restoration (v. 5b). Finally, a
flashback follows in which "we" present "our" previous interpretation
of past events (v. 6, cf. vv. 4; 5).

By means of chronological deviation, events are told before and
after they have taken place. In a blurring of description and judgment, features attributed to "him" and "us" appear. The opening
questions might introduce the unbelievable in two respects: "we" have

not believed YHWH in the past (the humiliation?) and cannot believe what is going to happen (the rehabilitation?).

4.8.2.2. *Story*

A past situation is introduced by telling of "his" growth (53:2a). "His" unattractive appearance is linked to what happens to "him": "he" is despised, forsaken and ill (v. 3a). "Our" witnessing of "his" miserable conditions makes "him" isolated and not acknowledged (v. 3b). In "our" portrait of "him", "he" is brought out as an actor, with neither will nor reactions. "He" is (de-)valued not because of "his" actions, but because of "his" state. Through relations of addition and combination, events of contempt and illnesses advance or amplify the preceding. In addition to accounting for "our" and others' non-approval of "him" as due to "his" appearance and "his" being bowed down by the burden of sickness, "we" explain "his" sufferings as due to God's smiting (v. 4b). The contrasting relationship between "him" and "us" is salient here, where "we" act as on-lookers to "his" fate.

The assumption that "he" bore "his" illnesses (v. 3) is overturned by a decisive change in perspective, where "we" make "our" own diagnosis (v. 4a). Through a juxtaposition of literary codes, "our" identification with "him" rises to the surface, expressing how "his" illnesses also belong to "us". In this identification, the subject assimilates (becomes subjected to?) an aspect of the other and is transformed according to what the other provides. In a personification, the actors are disclosed through a repetition of elements surrounding the figure(s) "he"/"we", where the personifier "he" and the personified "we" become blurred. The illusion of continuity and succession which became established by the figure "he" becomes destabilised when one set of assumptions about the relation between "him" and "us" is replaced by another, i.e. when contrast (in the past) is replaced by identity (in the present). Suddenly something is going on within the story other than what "we" have told so far. The contrasting relationship between "him" and "us" has been salient in the story, where "we" act as on-lookers to "his" fate. The story plays ironically against "our" earlier assumptions about "him" and "his" illnesses. After the testimony "we" gave about the ill man's fate, where "we" took offence at "his" illness and devastating appearance (vv. 2–3), the diagnosis is repeated with variation, where suddenly "we" are also deeply involved (v. 4a). This turn-around is in "us" seeing "him" as "us" instead of a devastating other. Suddenly we are in a double story or in crossing stories, that is, the story about "him" and that which appears to be about "us", where not only contrast, but also a common fate is created – or revealed.

After an identification between "him" and "us" related to illness is disclosed (v. 4a), the diagnosis of "him" and "us" is developed into a confession of guilt, unravelling the illnesses as punishment for "our" transgressions (v. 5a). The divine disapproval of "him" is a response to "our" iniquity (v. 6b). Vv. 5–6 work as a further reflection, interpretation and also correction of v. 4 through a dissymmetry. By "our" earlier assumption that "he" was smitten by God, the ill man's sufferings were both explained and made comprehensible to "us": God's will lay behind "his" fate (v. 4b). However, a full explanation is delayed: while it is explained that YHWH punishes "him" with illness according to his will, nothing is said about *why* the deity does this. A confusion appears when this is related to the commonality of "his" and "our" illnesses (v. 4a), when "his" illnesses appear also to be due to "our" iniquities (vv. 5–6). Thus, "our" previous mistake (v. 4b) is corrected. "Our" self-acknowledgement is that "he" is not simply punished by God: rather, the humiliations are a consequence of "our" iniquities. The illnesses are depicted as YHWH's punishment (vv. 4b; 6b) and also as self-inflicted (vv. 4a; 5a; 6).

After "his" and "our" past humiliations are depicted, "our" relation to "him" is described in terms of coming rehabilitation (v. 5b). What began as "our" contemplation of "his" experience (v. 2) continued as a consideration of these same experiences as "our" own: "he" carried "our" illnesses which were due to "our" transgressions. YHWH's punishment of sins (vv. 4b; 5a; 6) provokes a new crisis which leads to restitution. Between the prediction of "our" recovery (v. 5b) and the description of the background to this (vv. 2–5a), a dramatic tension emerges. The personifier "he" and the personified "we" are blurred, but with different accentuations: healing is gained for "us" by the chastisement of "him" (v. 5b). The relation between "him" and "us" is dissymmetrically presented: "he" is involved by virtue of מוּסַר "chastisement" and חֲבֻרָה "wound" (v. 5b, cf. vv. 2–6) and "we" by virtue of חֳלָיֵנוּ "our illnesses" and מַכְאֹבֵינוּ "our sicknesses" (v. 4a), פְּשָׁעֵנוּ "our transgressions" and מֵעֲוֹנֹתֵינוּ "our iniquities" (vv. 5a; 6), שְׁלוֹמֵנוּ "our healing" and נִרְפָּא־לָנוּ "our recovery" (v. 5b). Whereas the identification between "him" and "us" is disclosed in the common illness, the question of "his" guilt or innocence and "his" healing is in some way left open: "we" do not clearly express either that "he" has committed sin or that "he" shall be healed, only that "he" has been punished with illness.

The events in vv. 1–6 might be organised into relations of transgression, punishment, illness, contempt and recovery. Through combinations of such relations, a story orders events temporally in terms of succession or concurrence, and logically in terms of comparability or causality. "He" is despised, ill and punished, while "we" are ill and sinners and shall be healed. Moreover, "his" illnesses are "our" illnesses, whereas there is silence as far as "his" possible sins and recovery are concerned.

In 53:1–6, the effects of prior events might be reconstructed as follows: "we" (and "he"?) have transgressed (vv. 5a; 6); because of that, "he" (and "we") was/were punished with contempt (vv. 2–3) and illness (vv. 3–5; 6b), and because of that "we" (and "he") shall be healed (v. 5b). The cause-effect sequence is the product of discursive forces, but we treat it as a true order: it is not given, but constructed. The effects make us produce causes.[88] In addition to the causalities, the story is kept going as a sequence of eventualities by displacements of both the initial and the closing events. As a succession of events is pursued, a chiastic pattern appears in the reversal of events of transgression, punishment, dismay, illness and recovery. In the story, "we" offer a fluctuating explanation as "we" make YHWH "his" enemy (vv. 4b; 6b), yet blame "ourselves" for what has happened (vv. 5a; 6). Here, there is a collision between "our" explanation of "his" sufferings as due God's punishment and the explanation of the wounds as self-inflicted.

4.8.2.3. Narrative: Narrator as Actor: "We"

A narrator "we" is "written in" as the one who mediates perspectives on events and actors. "We" are telling of, judging and evaluating "him" and "our" involvement in "his" fate. "We" offer a testimony centring on "our" portrait of a humiliated one (53:2). In addition to telling of past events, the narrator "we" explains its relation to "him" (vv. 4–6). The narrator is directly related to the story, as well as standing apart with the capability of explaining what neither narratee nor actor have access to before the telling (e.g. about "our recovery" in v. 5b). In tell-

---

[88] Cf. Culler's "double logic" in 4.6.

ing also about "ourselves", "we" place "ourselves" at the same level as that about which "we" are speaking. The narrator appears as a signifier of subjectivity, and the difference between *the speaking subject* (narrator) and *the subject of speech* (actor) is obscured. Acting as *the speaking subject* of the telling (its narrator), "we" also function as *the subject of speech* in the story (as actors).[89]

That this narrating actor does mark out two different subject positions initially becomes clear in the temporality of the telling. "We" operate as the narrator in one realm of time (*narration*) and as an actor in another (*story*). A difference appears though the narrator and the actor are one and the same. The narrator is the same as the actor, but operates at a different moment from when the event happens. In "our" story about "him", the contrasting relationship between the ill, lonely and solitary one and "our" testimony to "him" at a distance is salient (vv. 2–3). However, in telling about the common fate of "him" and "us" (v. 4a), "we" appear as both narrator and actor. In a fluid relation between "him" and "us", "we", in "our" self-questioning and self-consciousness are continually self-displacing. The turning point in "our" sense of reality is expressed through echoes from v. 3 in v. 4, related to the common diagnosis. In vv. 5–6, it appears that the narrator-witness's sense of transgression may not lie simply in the knowledge that "our" own words ironically conceal another version of the figure that "we" had first mistakenly used. Seeing differently and seeing difference turn the story around and make the actors different. "We" think "we" see what "we" did not understand before. In terms of the dynamics of narrative, the plot places "us" at the cross point of temporality and narrativity, where relationships between events are endowed with meaning by being identified as parts of a whole. The shift in the telling prevents the narration from cohering around a unified and contiguous subjectivity of "us" as either narrator or actor. The story seemed to be on the verge of becoming whole and coherent. But the sign one might hope would complete it ends up deepening its complexity, functioning less as the story's centre than as a turn in its labyrinth!

In the story about "him" and that about "us", different times are at play. Establishing a chronology or causality in the crisscrossing of lines and ellipses is thus impossible. Since chronological and causal

---

[89] On the relation between *the speaking subject* and *the subject of speech*, see 4.5.

connections are not interrelated, one might ask what came first: the sin or the illness. In the *story*, priority is given to events, and present effects are seen in past events: "we" have transgressed; therefore "he" is ill. In the *narration*, events are determined by structures of signification: "He" and "we" are ill, so "he" and "we" must have transgressed. *Story* and *narration* are irreconcilable as "his"/"our" fate is either the effect of a prior event (*story*) or its cause (*narration*).[90] The "crime" exists somewhere between the past events and the present ordering of them.

The narration can be organised into segments placed in contiguous relation to each other, with each segment arranging a different relation between narrator and story. Some of the segments might assert their centrality through repetition as a way of inscribing a point of view (e.g. "he" in 53:2–3). Others might put that repeated point of view under tension (e.g. personification: "he" = "we" in 53:4a; 5–6). Given the narrative movements which result from such shifts, the narration cannot be centred either on a fixed, single point of view or around a narrator whose point of view is wholly responsible for what is said, seen and shown. Rather, the narration has to be analysed in terms of how it sets in place differing relations of agency and testimony.

53:1–6 do not only tell a story, but also offer an example of the ways in which story-telling is performative. The complexity in the narrative situation results from the instability of the distance between the narrator, the narratee and the actors. The performative dimension of the narrative consists in its power to make something happen, as opposed to its power to (appear to) give knowledge. The story dramatises how "we" see "ourselves" as "him" through repetition and confirmation of possible identifications.

4.8.3. *Isa. 53:7–10*

נִגַּשׂ וְהוּא נַעֲנֶה וְלֹא יִפְתַּח־פִּיו 53:7
כַּשֶּׂה לַטֶּבַח יוּבָל וּכְרָחֵל לִפְנֵי גֹזְזֶיהָ נֶאֱלָמָה וְלֹא יִפְתַּח פִּיו:
מֵעֹצֶר וּמִמִּשְׁפָּט לֻקָּח וְאֶת־דּוֹרוֹ מִי יְשׂוֹחֵחַ[8]
כִּי נִגְזַר מֵאֶרֶץ חַיִּים מִפֶּשַׁע עַמִּי נֶגַע לָמוֹ:
וַיִּתֵּן אֶת־רְשָׁעִים קִבְרוֹ וְאֶת־עָשִׁיר בְּמֹתָיו[9]
עַל לֹא־חָמָס עָשָׂה וְלֹא מִרְמָה בְּפִיו:
וַיהוָה חָפֵץ דַּכְּאוֹ הֶחֱלִי אִם־תָּשִׂים אָשָׁם נַפְשׁוֹ[10]
יִרְאֶה זֶרַע יַאֲרִיךְ יָמִים וְחֵפֶץ יְהוָה בְּיָדוֹ יִצְלָח:

---

[90] Cf. Culler's "double logic" in 4.6.

53:7:   He was oppressed and he was humble(d), but he did not open his mouth,
        like a sheep led to slaughtering, and like a ewe before those who shear her is dumb,
        and he did not open his mouth.
53:8:   By restraint (?) and by execution (?) he was taken – but who of his time considered
        that he was cut off from the land of the living
        and because of the transgression of my people was his wound?
53:9:   He was given his grave with wicked ones and אֶת־עָשִׁיר (with a rich?) in his death,
        although he had not done any violence, and there was no deceit in his mouth.
53:10: But YHWH was pleased to strike him by making him ill אִם־תָּשִׂים אָשָׁם נַפְשׁוֹ;
        he shall see offspring and live long, and it is YHWH's pleasure that his hand shall prosper.

4.8.3.1. *Narration*

With no *waw* or other sign of connection to the preceding, the oppression of "him" and "his" reactions to this are commented upon (53:7). An ambiguous relation between the oppression of "him" and "his" reaction appears: "he was oppressed and he was humbled", or, the oppression of "him" might be met with humbleness", i.e. "he" did not resist. In any case, although oppressed and humble(d), "he" did not open "his" mouth. This is further explained by two similes of a sheep and a ewe. These similes are also ambiguous as to whether they concern how "he" is humble or how "he" is humbled. Then we are repeatedly told that "he" did not open his mouth. The repeated clause might contrast with the previous clauses by working as a comment of opposition: *although* "he" was oppressed, "he" did not open his mouth, expressing "his" (lack of) action. It might also be read as a consequence, working as an explanation: *because* "he" was oppressed, "he" did not open his mouth.

Then we are told how he was taken "by restraint (?) and by execution (?)", which is commented upon by two questions which interrupt the flow of the narrative (v. 8). By the interrogative מִי "who", a shift in actors is introduced by the adjacent דּוֹרוֹ "his time" of the questions. In the first question, we are also told that "he was cut off from the land of the living". It is unclear whether this is set alongside the previous verse as a further explanation, is an expansion on "his" fate, or is an alternative: that "he" was taken "by restraint (?) and by execution (?)" and "cut off from the land of the living" might illuminate each other as simultaneous and similar events or stand in a causal relation: "by restraint (?) and by execution (?) he was taken", therefore "he" was "cut off from the land of the living", i.e. "he" is sentenced to death. In any case, the question regards the relation of דּוֹרוֹ "his time" to "his" fate as ignorant or indifferent. In the second question, an explanation breaks into the narrative and offers information about "him", דּוֹרוֹ "his time" and עַמִּי "my people". נֶגַע לָמוֹ "his wound" is explained as due to פֶּשַׁע עַמִּי "the transgression of my people" and an asymmetrical relation appears between the punishment of "him" and the transgression of עַמִּי "my people". The questions work as a commentary upon the situation just depicted. Despite the change of scene and actors, they might have causative, temporal and consequential relations to the preceding clause. The questions reveal the consideration of דּוֹרוֹ "his time" of "his" fate: דּוֹרוֹ "his time" has not understood why "he" has suffered. Also, "his" sufferings are explained as a question of guilt and identity: נֶגַע לָמוֹ "his wound" is due to פֶּשַׁע עַמִּי "the transgression of my people".

Then "his" disgraceful and undeserved death is depicted, and also explained as having occurred despite "his" non-violence and non-deceitful talk (v. 9).[91] "He" is related to two new actors: רְשָׁעִים "wicked ones" and עָשִׁיר "a rich (?)". The introductory *waw* in v. 10 might both complete one episode and introduce a new one. The humiliations of "him" are here depicted as illness.[92] Taken as copulative, the *waw* introduces an explanation of "his" unworthy burial without reason (v. 9). Then the telling turns to a diametrically opposite situation in the future, evoking in advance an event that will take place later: he shall see offspring, live long and prosper (v. 10b). The relation between the past and the future appears in a blurring of semantic fields: "his" past humiliations are related to illness, whereas promises for the future

---

[91] Clines, *I, He, We and They*, p. 48, comments:
[T]he narrative of the servant's history begins and ends with *wyqtl* forms (waw consecutive plus the "imperfect"): [וַיַּעַל] (53:2) and [וַיִּתֵּן] (53:8 [read 53:9]). No clearer indication of a narrative form is needed in Hebrew; the verbs bounded by these two narrative verb forms are meant therefore to be read as a narrative sequence that begins with the servant's growing up and ends with the preparation of his tomb.
My delimitation of 53:7–10 is a rather pragmatic choice, cf. the expanded concept of text in 3.9. On my delimitation of Isa. 52:13–53:12, see chapter 6.

[92] And eventually related to sin? Cf. uncertainties related to אִם־תָּשִׂים אָשָׁם נַפְשׁוֹ in 53:10 in 3.10.13. and Appendix 6.

concern offspring, a long life and prosperity (v. 10b). Both the situations of the past and those of the future are presented as YHWH's pleasure.

The evocation of the story-event in 53:7–10 is highly compressed and involves a thorough blurring of semantic fields. Depictions, comments, comparisons and questions about events of both the past (vv. 7; 8; 9; 10a) and future (v. 10b) are given without any explanation for the turning point between the two. By means of chronological deviation, events are told before and after they have taken place. In a blurring of description and judgment, features attributed to "him", דּוֹרוֹ "his time" (v. 8), עַמִּי "my people" (v. 8), רְשָׁעִים "wicked ones" (v. 9) and עָשִׁיר "rich?" (v. 9) appear.

4.8.3.2. *Narrator and Narratee*

In 53:7, the narrator is telling, comparing and judging the situation. In v. 8, a direct and "personal" discourse appears in which a speaking "I" stands apart but is related to the story as witness and also by being positioned in relation to the actors called עַמִּי "my people".

The telling of v. 7 by an anonymous voice does not refer to a narratee, but still invites him to witness the humiliation of "him". In v. 8, the questioning "I" utters signs within a dialogue between an asking "I" and a narratee "you". When "you" are narrated to by "I", the narrator interpellates the narratee as subject. The listener is not merely a listener: even though the questions do not seek to obtain information from the narratee, they do invite answers, cf. "…but who of his time considered that he was cut off from the land of the living, that because of the transgression of my people was his wound?" (v. 8).

In the presentation of עַמִּי "my people", the narrator "I" presents himself as an actor testifying to the narratee, with the latter informed about events of past humiliation and future vindication. The narrator is involved with both "you" and "my people" by explaining a relation between their fates.

4.8.3.3. *Story*

Through relations in which they are endowed with meaning, events and actors become identified as parts of a whole, where a sequence of events involving actors and temporality is made into a story. An event of the past concerns how "he" was oppressed and humiliated, and eventually humble(d) (53:7). "He" was also taken "by restraint (?)

and by execution (?)", wounded (v. 8), ill (v. 10), "cut off from the land of the living" (v. 8) and given an unworthy grave among wicked ones and a rich (?) (v. 9).

The sequences of reflection on the past in 53:7–10 allow us to organise them as the first half of a story which comes to take shape when the humiliation of "him" is related to events leading to a change in that situation. A story takes shape by moving on from the events of the earlier humiliations which formed the background for the contrasting expressions concerning "his" future. Without any explanation, "his" earlier humiliations lead to promises for the future: "he" shall see offspring, live long and prosper (v. 10).

53:7–10 might be presented in a linear sequence in which events follow one another but are not necessarily due to each other. No reason is given for why "he" is humbled, to which "he" responds with silence, nor for why "he" was taken by "restraint (?) and by execution (?)", and those treating "him" badly are anonymous (vv. 7–8). "He" was wounded due to the transgression of עַמִּי "my people" (v. 8) and stricken with illness by YHWH (v. 10). His unworthy grave among wicked ones and a rich (?) are explained as undeserved: "he" has suffered despite having neither behaved violently nor talked treacherously to those around "him" (v. 9).

No explanation is given for the temporal turning point from "him" being humiliated in different ways in the past to "his" and others' prosperity in the future. As a succession of events is pursued, a chiastic pattern appears through a crisscross reversal of events related to "him", דּוֹרוֹ "his time" (v. 8), עַמִּי "my people" (v. 8), רְשָׁעִים "wicked ones" (v. 9), עָשִׁיר "rich?" (v. 9) and "they" (v. 11).

A story is initiated by placing an event in a sequence to mark a beginning: "his" past (vv. 7; 8; 9; 10a); it is ended by the replacement of the initial event by another to mark an ending: "his" future (v. 10b). Simultaneously, the story is kept going as a sequence of eventualities by displacements of both the initial and the closing events.

A pressure point appears from the relation between "him" and others; for instance, "his" relation to דּוֹרוֹ "his time", as well as that of דּוֹרוֹ "his time" to עַמִּי "my people" in v. 8: דּוֹרוֹ "his time" did not understand that "he" was wounded because of פֶּשַׁע עַמִּי "the transgression of my people". Salient to the story has been the antagonistic relationship between "him" and those around "him": "he" was oppressed (v. 7), taken by "restraint (?)" and "execution (?)" (v. 8), stricken by YHWH (v. 10) and then dies (vv. 8; 9). The story plays on the irony

of the earlier assumptions about "him" and "his" past. After the testimony the narrator gave about "his" fate, suddenly עַמִּי "my people"
are also deeply involved in a turn-around to seeing "him" as עַמִּי "my
people" (v. 8) instead of an isolated other.[93] Through this juxtaposition
of literary codes, an identification between "him" and עַמִּי "my people"
is presented in a dissymmetry where פֶּשַׁע "transgression" belongs to
עַמִּי "my people" and נֶגַע לָמוֹ "wound" to "him": "he" is wounded
and עַמִּי "my people" have sinned. Whether this is also an explanation
for the preceding oppression and judgment of "him" is left open. In
a personification the actors are disclosed through a repetition of elements surrounding "him", in which the personifier "he" and the personified עַמִּי "my people" become blurred. The illusion of continuity
and succession which was established by the figure "he" is destabilised.
Suddenly we are in a double story or in a crossing of stories: the story
about "him" and that which appears to be about עַמִּי "my people".

4.8.4. Isa. 53:11–12

מֵעֲמַל נַפְשׁוֹ יִרְאֶה יִשְׂבַּע בְּדַעְתּוֹ[11]
יַצְדִּיק צַדִּיק עַבְדִּי לָרַבִּים וַעֲוֹנֹתָם הוּא יִסְבֹּל:
לָכֵן אֲחַלֶּק־לוֹ בָרַבִּים וְאֶת־עֲצוּמִים יְחַלֵּק שָׁלָל[12]
תַּחַת אֲשֶׁר הֶעֱרָה לַמָּוֶת נַפְשׁוֹ וְאֶת־פֹּשְׁעִים נִמְנָה
וְהוּא חֵטְא־רַבִּים נָשָׂא וְלַפֹּשְׁעִים יַפְגִּיעַ:

53:11: After his travail he shall see and be sated by his knowledge;
The righteous one, my servant, will cause the many to be righteous
and he carried their iniquities.

53:12: Truly, therefore I will allot the many to him and numerous he
shall allot to spoiling,
because he was slain to death and reckoned with transgressors,
he bore the sin of many and was struck because of transgressors.

4.8.4.1. Narration

"His" עָמַל "travail" of the past is depicted (v. 11a) before promises for
"his" future are offered: "he" shall see, know and make הָרַבִּים "the
many" righteous. "The many" are introduced as new actors. "His"
causing "the many" to be righteous in the future is further contrasted

---

[93] Simultaneously, this double voiced discourse reveals an irony in that we
know something דּוֹרוֹ "his time" does not: יְשׂוֹחֵחַ "consider" might be regarded as
equivalent to לֹא חֲשַׁבְנֻהוּ "we did not consider him" in 53:3 and אֲנַחְנוּ חֲשַׁבְנֻהוּ
"whereas we accounted him…" in 53:4, which also work as expressions for how "we"
(mis-) understand "his" humiliations.

with "his" carrying of "their" iniquities in the past (v. 11b). In the
expression עֲוֹנֹתָם הוּא יִסְבֹּל "he carried their iniquities", "he" is subject, "they" object, and both "he" and "they" have committed sin. "He"
has brought upon himself his own punishment, and not only "he", but
also "they" have sinned.

The deictic adverb לָכֵן "truly, therefore" (v. 12) responds to the preceding promises. The oscillation between "his" past and future continues, with even more actors introduced and also an "I" speech: the
speaking "I" will allot הָרַבִּים "the many" to "him" and "he" shall allot
עֲצוּמִים "numerous" to spoiling, before an explanation of "his" past is
given: "he" was slain to death, reckoned with פֹּשְׁעִים "transgressors",
"he" bore the sin of רַבִּים "many" and was struck because of פֹּשְׁעִים
"transgressors". Being reckoned with transgressors, "he" is regarded
among those who have committed sin and "he" dies as one of them.
וְהוּא חֵטְא־רַבִּים נָשָׂא "he bore the sin of many" is an expression for
being a sinner, where "he" has brought upon himself his own punishment, and not only "he", but also the "many" have sinned. Again, a
blurring of semantic fields appears, in which "his" past is related to
עָמָל "travail" and the carrying of עֲוֹנֹתָם "their iniquities", and "his"
future" to יִרְאֶה יִשְׂבַּע בְּדַעְתּוֹ "seeing and being sated by his knowledge" and יַצְדִּיק צַדִּיק לָרַבִּים "causing the many to be righteous". Also,
new actors are introduced. In addition to (הָ)רַבִּים "(the) many" (cf.
v. 11), עֲצוּמִים "numerous" and פֹּשְׁעִים "transgressors" are added.

The evocation of the story-event of 53:11–12 is highly compressed
and involves a thorough blurring of semantic fields. Depictions, comments, comparisons and questions about events of both the past
(v. 12b) and future (vv. 11; 12a) are given, without any explanation for
the turning point between the two. By means of chronological deviation, events are told before and after they have taken place. In a blurring of description and judgment, features appear attributed to "him",
"they" (v. 11), (הָ)רַבִּים "(the) many" (vv. 11–12), עֲצוּמִים "numerous"
(v. 12) and פֹּשְׁעִים "transgressors" (v. 12).

4.8.4.2. *Narrator and Narratee*

In vv. 11–12 a direct and "personal" discourse appears in which a
speaking "I" stands apart but is related to the story as witness and also
by being positioned in relation to the actor called עַבְדִּי "my servant"
(v. 11). Additionally, in v. 12, the narrator is acting towards both הָרַבִּים
"the many" and "him": "Therefore, I will allot the many to him". By

explaining the past humiliation and a promising future, the "I" demonstrates the capability of providing information and anticipating the future – to which neither narratee nor actors has access before the telling. The narrator is able to tell about the future of הָ(רַ)רַבִּים "(the) many" and עֲצוּמִים "numerous" (vv. 11–12). In the presentation of "his" and עַבְדִּי "my servant"'s past and future, the narrator "I" presents himself as an actor testifying to the narratee, with the latter informed about events of past humiliation and future vindication.

4.8.4.3. *Story*
An event of the past concerns how "he" was ill (v. 11), living in travail (v. 11) and slain to death (v. 12). The sequences of reflection on the past in vv. 11–12 allow us to organise them as the first half of a story which comes to take shape when the humiliation of "him" is related to events leading to a change in that situation. A story takes shape by moving on from the events of the previous humiliations, which formed the background for the contrasting expressions concerning "his" future. Without any explanation, "his" earlier travail leads to promises for the future: "he" shall see offspring, live long and prosper (v. 10), "he" shall see and be sated by "his" knowledge (v. 11). The blurring of semantic fields continues as regards the future of הָרַבִּים "the many" (vv. 11–12) and עֲצוּמִים "numerous" (v. 12): "The righteous one, my servant, will cause the many to be righteous" (v. 11), the "I" will allot "the many" to "him" and "he" shall allot "numerous" to spoiling (v. 12).

The story plays on the irony of the earlier assumptions about "him" and "his" past. After the testimony the narrator gave about "his" fate – "he" was living in travail (v. 11) and dead (v. 12) – suddenly someone else is also deeply involved in a turn-around to seeing "him" as "they", הָ(רַ)רַבִּים "[the] many" and פֹּשְׁעִים "transgressors" in vv. 11–12 instead of as an isolated other. Their relation becomes amplified in the trope of personification, in which a confusion appears between the personifier "he" and the personified "them": in v. 11 "he" carried עֲוֹנֹתָם "their iniquities", in v. 12 "he" was reckoned with פֹּשְׁעִים "transgressors", "he bore the sin of רַבִּים "many" and "he" was struck because of פֹּשְׁעִים "transgressors". In v. 11, promises of עַבְדִּי "my servant" are given: "The righteous one, my servant, will cause the many to be righteous", and in v. 12: "Truly, therefore I will allot the many to him and numerous he shall allot to spoiling...". No explanation is given for the temporal turning point from "him" being humiliated in different ways in the past to "his" and others' vindications in the future. Humiliations and exaltations related to "him", "they" (v. 11), (הָ)רַבִּים "(the) many" (vv. 11–12), עֲצוּמִים "numerous" and פֹּשְׁעִים "transgressors" (v. 12).

4.8.5. *Narrators in Isa. 52:13–53:12: "I", "We" and Anonymous*

In 52:13 הִנֵּה "See!" reveals a spectacular event of exaltation. The exaltation is caused by the narrator's proclamation and shall be experienced by עַבְדִּי "my servant". The proclamation is directed from an "I" to a "you", whose participation is more than that of a listener of the present, as he is also admonished to see in the future. In 53:1, a break from the foregoing occurs in a change from "I" speech to "we" speech. The narrator "we" offers a self-presentation and self-questioning about "our" own experiences of a message and a divine revelation. As a response to the announced exaltation of עַבְדִּי "my servant" that finds vivid expression in the "I" speech of 52:13–15, the "we" speech of 53:1 onwards might reflect on both an astonishing character of the past and an unanticipated future. In 52:13–15 the perspective is "external", with the "I" narrator more or less involved in the story he tells about the רַבִּים "many" and "you"/"he"/עַבְדִּי "my servant". In 53:1 the perspective is "internal" as the "we" are deeply involved in asking about "ourselves" – and "him".

The speaking "I" gave a rather unflattering portrait of the humiliated one in 52:14 which is echoed by "us" in 53:2. In 52:14, "his" shameful appearance is mentioned; 53:2 concerns "his" unattractive form. 53:1 connects the two narrations of the "I" speech in 52:13–15 and the "we" speech in 53:2. In 53:1, a speaking "we" emerge on the scene and the servant is left out. In 53:2, "our" narration continues and might also be connected to the earlier "I" story about "him". The interpenetration of the depictions, within the same semantic framework, of the disfigured one in 52:14 and 53:2, illustrates the problems with defining "units": in each narration, words extend beyond themselves to become pillars in a new structure or to develop deeper meanings.[94] From 52:14 onwards a contrasting relationship between "the servant"/"he" and "his" surroundings has been salient, where "many" (52:14) and "we" (53:2) act as on-lookers to "his" fate. Both "many" and "we" consider "him" at

---

[94] The question of delimitation of text is also discussed in relation to the expanded concept of text in 3.9. It is also touched upon in this narrative analysis, cf. 4.8.3.1. n. 91. On my delimitation of Isa. 52:13–53:12, see chapter 6.

a distance and the disdain in both instances is due to "his" disfigurement. In contrast to the "I" narrator who sees everything, the actors
see without participating in the event and the "we" narrator is also
engaged in the event as an actor.

"Our" portrayal of "him" continues: "he" is despised, ill, isolated
and unacknowledged (53:3). "We" are talking about a *present* judgment of "his" and "our" past (v. 4a) and "our" *past* judgment of "his"
humiliations (v. 4b). While "we" had previously regarded "his" humiliations as a punishment brought upon "him" by God (v. 4b), "we" now
claim that "he" carried "our" illnesses (v. 4a) due to "our" sins (v. 5a,
cf. v. 6). Then the telling turns forwards by evoking in advance an
event that will take place later: the punishment and wounds of "him"
shall lead to "our" healing (v. 5b).

Whereas "I" was speaking in 52:13–15 and "we" from 53:1 up to
and including 53:6, in 53:7 and v. 9 the speaking voice is not clearly
identified. In vv. 8; 11–12 a direct and "personal" discourse appears in
which a speaking "I" stands apart but is related to the story as witness
and also to the actors called עַמִּי "my people" (v. 8) and עַבְדִּי "my servant" (v. 11). Additionally, in v. 12, the narrator is acting towards both
(הָ)רַבִּים "(the) many" and "him": "Therefore, I will allot the many to
him". In Isa. 52:13–53:12, no first, final or dominant narrator appears.
Unstable narrators enter, leave and change, according to what Bakhtin
has called "heteroglossia" (cf. 5.2.).

4.8.6. *Variations of a Past*

4.8.6.1. *Unworthy Form*

In 52:14 and 53:2–3, "he" is depicted as having an unworthy form.
מַרְאֵהוּ וְתֹאֲרוֹ "his appearance and his form" in 52:14 are chiastically
related to "his" lack of תֹאַר "form" and מַרְאֶה "appearance" in 53:2. In
52:14 "he" is portrayed as so disfigured as to appear hardly human, and
in 53:2 "he" is depicted as growing up like יוֹנֵק "a shoot" and שֹׁרֶשׁ "a
root" and not attracting "us" to "him" because of "his" appearance. In
52:14, a contrast appears between "him" (sg) and "many" (pl), and in
53:2 between "him" and "us". In 52:14, רַבִּים "many" are being שָׁמְמוּ
"appalled", and their reactions are caused by the confrontation with
"you" due to "his" מִשְׁחַת "disfigurement". In 53:2, "we" neither look
at nor are attracted to "him" due to "his" (– lack of –) תֹאַר "form",
הָדָר "splendour" and מַרְאֶה "appearance". The "I" speech and the "we"
speech interpenetrate one other. "His" fate is presented from different

perspectives and with different sorts of involvement: from both "my"
(and רַבִּים "many") and "our" angles of vision. "Our" depiction and
judgment of "him" in 53:3 echo רַבִּים "many"'s disapproval of "him"
in 52:14 and "our" disregard of "him" in 53:2. In 53:3 "he" is despised,
assailed with sickness and disregarded by "us". Like in 52:14 and 53:2,
in 53:3 the prominent relation is also the contrasting one between the
solitary "he" (sg) and "they"/"we" (pl). In all events, "his" disgusting
appearance isolated "him" from all affairs; "he" was totally insignificant.

4.8.6.2. *Illnesses and Sins*

"We" depict "him" as וִידוּעַ חֹלִי "known with illness" (53:3) and say that
חֳלָיֵנוּ הוּא נָשָׂא מַדְכָּא מֵעֲוֹנֹתֵינוּ "he bore our illnesses" etc. (v. 4), מְדֻכָּא מֵעֲוֹנֹתֵינוּ "he
was injured because of our iniquities" etc. (v. 5), and וַיהוָה הִפְגִּיעַ בּוֹ
אֵת עֲוֹן כֻּלָּנוּ "YHWH struck him by the iniquity of all of us" (v. 6). The
beginning of the "we" speech is characterised by a contrast between
"him" and "us" (53:2), and from v. 4 onwards an identification also
appears and progresses in terms of illness and sin. Emphasis is placed
on how "he" has been stricken and punished by YHWH (vv. 4–5),
and "our" humiliations are pushed into the background. However,
after the identification between "him" and "us" is revealed in the common diagnosis (v. 4), it is further confirmed that "his" humiliation is
due to "our" transgressions (v. 5). Both "his" and "our" illnesses are
described and explained as due to sin by "our" self-acknowledgement:
the illnesses ("he") carried are due to ("our") sins. In v. 6, it is emphasised how this is due to the will of YHWH, cf. v. 4. The personification which was established in v. 4 and further developed in vv. 5–6 is
alluded to by a similar identification expressed in חֳלָיֵנוּ הוּא נָשָׂא "he
bore our illnesses" etc. (v. 4) and מְדֻכָּא מֵעֲוֹנֹתֵינוּ "he was injured for
our iniquities" and so forth (v. 5).

The explanation of the relation between "his" and "our" fate in
vv. 4–6 is echoed in an "I" speech in v. 8, but with a different emphasis.
In v. 8, נֶגַע לָמוֹ "his wound" is due to פֶּשַׁע עַמִּי "the transgression of
my people". In both the "we" speech of vv. 1–6 and in v. 8, "he" has
been humiliated by those around him and wounded because of sin.
In v. 8 the sinners are being told about, and are not "confessing" like
"us" in v. 5. Also, in the מִי question in v. 8, דּוֹרוֹ "his time" has not
understood why "he" has suffered: when "he" has been punished –
even "cut off from the land of the living" – it is מִפֶּשַׁע עַמִּי "because
of the transgression of my people". As from v. 4 onwards, in v. 8 a
change from contrast to identity appears within a confusion between

the personifier ("he" and נֶגַע לָמוֹ "his wound") and the personified (עַמִּי "my people" and its פֶּשַׁע "transgression"). "His" experiences are עַמִּי "my people"'s experiences too. פֶּשַׁע עַמִּי "the transgression of my people" is against YHWH, and the punishment of "him" is connected to their transgressions against their deity.

וַיהוָה חָפֵץ דַּכְּאוֹ הֶחֱלִי "and YHWH was pleased to strike him by making him ill" (v. 10) echoes "our" depiction of "him" in v. 3, the relation between "his" and "our" illnesses in v. 4 and the relation between "his" illness and "our" iniquities in vv. 5–6. In v. 11 עֲוֹנֹתָם הוּא יִסְבֹּל "he carried their iniquities"; אֶת־פֹּשְׁעִים נִמְנָה "he was reckoned with transgressors", הוּא חֵטְא־רַבִּים נָשָׂא "he bore the sin of many" (cf. חֳלָיֵנוּ הוּא נָשָׂא וּמַכְאֹבֵינוּ סְבָלָם "he bore our illnesses and carried our sicknesses" in v. 4) and לַפֹּשְׁעִים יַפְגִּיעַ "he was struck because of transgressors" in v. 12. In the treatment of "his" carrying of "our" illnesses in v. 4, it was emphasised how "he" was also ill. Thus, the carrying of the iniquities of הָרַבִּים "the many" might be compared to "his" bearing of "our" illnesses in v. 4: as the ill one also carries "our" illnesses, so the (sinful) one also bears their iniquities. The sinner incurs guilt through transgression and is made to carry the weight of the guilt. The guilt-laden sinner has lived under contempt, sickness and other forms of suffering. In both v. 6 and v. 12 "he" has suffered because of other's sin, "our" sin and that of the "many". The identification between the personifier and the personified is presented in two variations: being ill like "us", "he" is also a sinner like "us". In a crossing of semantic frameworks in both the "we" speech and in vv. 10–12, illness is explained as a consequence of sin. The other part of the story is told in v. 5b: "…chastisement was upon him for our healing and by his wound is recovery for us", cf. 4.8.7.2.

4.8.6.3. Death

The scale of the catastrophe which "he" has experienced is impassively depicted. "He" is depicted as having an unworthy form (52:14, 53:2; 3) and as despised and rejected by men (53:3), ill, wounded and injured (vv. 3–6), stricken, smitten by God and humiliated (vv. 4–6), oppressed and humbled (v. 7). The punishment seems unmitigated and the suffering endless, until "he" is struck by an irrevocable judgment: after death there is no hope. In v. 8 "he" is cut off from the land of the living due to "the transgression of my people", in v. 9 "he" is offered a disgraceful tomb despite having behaved neither violently nor talked treacherously to those around "him", and in v. 12 "he" was slain to death, and reckoned with transgressors, "he" bore the sin of many, and was struck because of transgressors. The other part of the story is told in v. 10b: "…he shall see offspring and live long…", cf. 4.8.7.2.

4.8.6.4. *Unjust*

In an event in the past, "he" was oppressed and humiliated, and eventually humble(d) (53:7). "He" was also taken "by restraint (?) and by execution (?)" (v. 8). No reason is given for why "he" is humbled, to which "he" responds with silence, nor for why "he" was taken "by restraint (?) and by execution (?)", and those treating "him" badly are anonymous (vv. 7–8). The motifs of injustice in vv. 7–8 are further developed in v. 9. After "his" death is described in v. 8, so too is the unworthiness of "his" burial place among wicked ones and a rich (?) (v. 9). "His" death and unworthy grave are explained as brought upon "him" despite "his" having behaved neither violently nor talked treacherously. The violent and treacherous behaviour of which "he" is not guilty is the behaviour of רְשָׁעִים "wicked ones" (cf. the silence motif of v. 7). All attention is placed on "him", as neither those treating "him" badly nor YHWH are directly mentioned. The other part of the story – the vindication – is treated in 4.8.7.1.

4.8.6.5. *Silence*

In 53:7 the oppression of "him" and "his" reactions to this are commented upon, with an ambiguous relation appearing between the oppression of "him" and "his" reaction: In any case, although oppressed and humble(d), "he" did not open "his" mouth. This is further explained by two similes of a sheep and a ewe which are also ambiguous as to whether they concern how "he" is humble or how "he" is humbled. Then we are repeatedly told that "he" did not open his mouth.

This contrasts with the silence of מְלָכִים "kings" in the future in 52:15. 52:15 is part of an argument of 52:14–15. A past situation in v. 14a is related to a future one (v. 15) and works as a response in terms of a comparison: גּוֹיִם רַבִּים "many peoples" will become startled (?) by "him", מְלָכִים "kings" shall shut their mouth and "they" shall see and understand what "they" have neither been told nor heard. The argument takes shape through a change from past to future, while the situations differ in terms of a change in both actors and actions. So while in 53:7 "he" is reacting to humiliations with silence in the past, in 52:15 kings shall react with silence to what they see and hear in the future.

4.8.7. *Variations of a Future*

4.8.7.1. *Prosperity and Vindication*

In the "I" speech of 52:13, the exaltation of עַבְדִּי "my servant" is announced by four synonymous verbs. In v. 15, "his" future vindication is deepened, as "his" relation to גּוֹיִם רַבִּים "many peoples" and מְלָכִים "kings" is taken into consideration: "…he יַזֶּה ('will startle'?) many peoples before him, kings shall shut their mouth; for what has not been told to them, they shall see"…etc. No reason for "his" promising future is offered.

In 53:1, a revelation is enquired after: "Who believes what we hear? And the arm of YHWH – to whom is it revealed?". זְרוֹעַ יְהוָה "YHWH's arm" is echoed in v. 10, וְחֵפֶץ יְהוָה בְּיָדוֹ יִצְלָח "it is YHWH's pleasure that his hand shall prosper", which here might refer to either YHWH's or "his" hand. In v. 10, both "his" past humiliations and "his" future vindication are willed by YHWH. Promises for "his" future continue within other semantic fields and with other actors involved in v. 11 (that is, הָרַבִּים "the many"), the only "cause" offered is that these promises are a contrast to "his" past: "After travail he shall see and be sated by his knowledge"; "The righteous one, my servant, will cause the many to be righteous." In v. 12, more events and actors are involved in "his" future – again with no reason given for the promises made other than "his" terrible past: "Truly, therefore I will allot the many to him and numerous he shall allot to spoiling…"[95] In a portrayal of the distribution of captured booty after military victory, the servant is presented as a victor: the one who is to receive a share of the spoils of victory and to share out those spoils with others. He will emerge victorious from his trials. Despite all the humiliations through which "he" and others have lived, "he" will "rise from death" and again live in dignity (4.8.7.2.):

4.8.7.2. *Healing and Descendants*

In the "we" speech in 53:5, a causal relationship appears between the past punishment of "him" and "our" coming healing. In the relation between שְׁלוֹמֵנוּ "our healing" and מוּסַר עָלָיו "chastisement upon him", the reconstitution might be to do with illness and the need for

---

[95] As we see, the future is not so bright for everyone. In 53:12 "he" shall allot numerous to spoiling; in 52:15 he יַזֶּה (will startle?) many peoples before him, kings shall shut their mouth, etc.

reconciliation as opposed to sin. An additional explanation, בַּחֲבֻרָתוֹ
נִרְפָּא־לָנוּ "by his wound is recovery for us" expresses "his" diagnosis
as ill, with both בַּחֲבֻרָתוֹ "his wound" and נִרְפָּא־לָנוּ "our recovery"
closely related to illness and healing. In v. 5b a turning point in the
plot appears as everyone has been changed, and a personification is
confirmed: the relation between the chastisement of "him" and "our
healing" functions as an expression of the turning point for both "him"
and "us" from humiliation to rehabilitation: after "his" – and "our" –
sufferings (vv. 2–5a; 6) everyone shall recover, "he" and "we". After a
depiction of how YHWH has stricken "him" with illnesses, suddenly
and without cause "he" is promised descendants and a long life (v.
10). Just as "his" past humiliations of illness are explained as YHWH's
pleasure, so too are the promises for the future concerning offspring, a
long life and prosperity (v. 10b). This contrasts starkly with the death
of the past (4.8.6.3.).

Moreover, in the similes in 53:2 boundaries are crossed by bringing together incompatible fields: the comparison וַיַּעַל כַּיּוֹנֵק "he
grew up like a shoot" encourages a future of hope, וַיַּעַל...לְפָנָיו "he
grew up...before him" might concern a "personal" relation, and
וַיַּעַל...מֵאֶרֶץ צִיָּה "he grew up...out of dry ground" rather obstructs
hope. Through contrasts and similarities, different and distinct fields
come into play. The similes, signifying appearance and visibility, touch
on both human and vegetable spheres, and bring associations both of
hope for the future in יוֹנֵק "shoot" and שֹׁרֶשׁ "root" that might grow,
and lack of hope for a future doomed to wither because of the inadequacy of the parched soil to sustain.

4.8.8. Summing up

The narrative constructs the identities of the characters in constructing the story told. Through this juxtaposition of literary codes, "our",
"my" and "anonymous" identifications of "I", "him", "us", עַמִּי "my
people", רַבִּים "many", גּוֹיִם רַבִּים "many peoples", מְלָכִים "kings",
עֲצוּמִים "numerous" and פֹּשְׁעִים "transgressors" emerge to the surface.
In addition, a dialogism might appear between narrations, within each
actor's own discourse, within an utterance, even within an individual
word (cf. Bakhtin in 5.2.).

Asymmetries occur between first-, second- and third-person involve-
ments. In the narrative, a relation is established between, for instance,
the narrator "I" and the narratee "you", the narrator "I" and the actor

"he", and the narratee-actor "you" and the actor "he". The actors are disclosed through a repetition of elements surrounding "him", but what one might hope would complete or ground the story ends up deepening its complexity, functioning less as the story's centre than as a turn in its labyrinth. The complexity of the narrative results from the instability of the distance existing between the narrator, the narratee and the actors. A play of incoherence appears as one way of questioning the ordered world. We are challenged to attempt to make "I", "him", "us", עַמִּי "my people", (הָ)רַבִּים "(the) many", גּוֹיִם רַבִּים "many peoples", מְלָכִים "kings", עֲצוּמִים "numerous" and פֹּשְׁעִים "transgressors" all givens of a single situation and we are doomed to fail by the dissolution of binary oppositions. We make certain assumptions about "I", "him", "us", עַמִּי "my people", (הָ)רַבִּים "(the) many", גּוֹיִם רַבִּים "many peoples", מְלָכִים "kings", עֲצוּמִים "numerous" and פֹּשְׁעִים "transgressors", but then our expectations are thwarted as we see that in the relation between narrator and actor a situation arises where the levels of *story* and *narration* produce an unavoidable collision. Between the prediction of prosperity in 52:13; 15, 53:5b; 10b; 11; 12a and the description of the very background for this in 52:14, 53:2–5a; 6–10a; 11ad; 12bc, a dramatic tension emerged which can never disappear completely: the humiliation and exaltation of sinners and the righteous in the past and future are explained as both undeserved and highly deserved.

CHAPTER FIVE

INTERTEXTUALITY

5.1. On Intertextuality

After having discussed linguistic and narratological aspects of Isa. 52:13–53:12, I shall now turn to its intertextual relations. Saussurean linguistics, with its emphasis on the difference, arbitrariness and convention of the linguistic sign, also challenges the significance of text, narration and culture. The universality of a linguistic model has been expressed by, among others, Barthes: "[C]ulture, in all its aspects, is a language".[1] This is related to an extended concept of text: a text does not exist as a closed system, but is bound up in relations of similarity and difference with other texts and with readers (cf. 3.7. and 3.8). This also has consequences for a concept of intertextuality. Intertextuality has been elaborated by various interpretative strategies. While some focus on the author and reference to stabilise the signifieds, others claim that if all signs are in some way differential, they convey a vast number of possible relations, all arbitrary and indeterminable, and no reading can be exhaustive or complete.

The concept of intertextuality is characterised by being interdisciplinary, influenced, for example, by linguistics, psychoanalysis and philosophy. "Intertextuality" is employed in structuralism, post-structuralism, deconstruction and Marxism, as well as cultural, post-colonial and gender studies.[2]

After Saussure, the linguistic sign has become a non-unitary, non-stable, relational unit, which leads into a vast network of relations of similarity and difference. Claiming that there is stable relationship between signifier and signified is the principal way in which dominant ideology maintains its power and represses marginal thoughts. If we regard the intertexts themselves as signifiers, an alternative appears.

---

[1] R. Barthes, *Mythologies* (London: Vintage, 1972). Saussure also calls for the application of semiotic principles to all aspects of culture, cf. 3.7.

[2] For an overview of intertextuality in biblical studies, see G. Aichele and G. A. Phillips, "Introduction: Exegesis, Eisegesis, Intergesis", *Semeia* 69/70 (1996) 7–18, and P. K. Tull, "Intertextuality and the Hebrew Scriptures", *CRBS* 8 (2000) 59–90.

No sign, i.e. no word, phrase, sentence, plot, trope, text, genre, etc. has a meaning of its own. As is clear already, this concerns the signifier "intertextuality" as much as anything else. Also, concepts of intertextuality are beset by a power struggle, mixed with apologetics for and polemics concerning who "owns" its definition.

5.2. Dialogicity

The concept of intertextuality is associated with the Russian literary critic Michael Bakhtin's notion of dialogism, by which he means that a writer when writing enters into dialogue with other texts and with reality. Bakhtin opposes a Saussurean tradition in which *la langue* is prioritised over *la parole*. He claims that without attention to a concrete social context, Saussurean linguistics becomes just "abstract objectivism".[3] Moreover, all utterances are in dialogue by being responses to previous utterances and addressed to specific addressees.[4] Due to this dialogicity, utterances are neither abstract nor individualised, but social, ideological and addressed to a subject by a subject.

According to Bakhtin, language reflects and transforms class, institutional, group, national and interests. He describes a struggle in language between centripetal and centrifugal forces. He explains this as unifying and disunifying forces and as oppositions between monological and dialogical utterances.[5] Monological utterances are related to the dominant ideology within society, which assumes that there is only one unified and unifying language and in which literature is dominated by the author's voice. Dialogical utterances are characterised by a heterogenity of voices not subject to the author's control.[6] Allen explains this argument as self-contradictory in that Bakhtin also

---

[3] Volosinov (and Bakhtin), *Marxism and the Philosophy of Language*, pp. 58; 65–82. Bakhtin's studies have been labelled "sociological poetics", see P. M. Morris, "Introduction" in P. M. Morris, *The Bakhtin Reader: Selected Writings of Bakhtin, Medvedev, Volosinov* (London: Arnold, 1996) 18. The authorship of Bakhtin and his relation to the possible co-authors Volosinov and Medvedev are disputed issues into which I will not go into further detail, but merely refer to the discussion in Morris, p. 18.

[4] Volosinov (and Bakhtin), *Marxism and the Philosophy of Language*, pp. 86; 93–95.

[5] M. M. Bakhtin, "Discourse in the Novel" in M. M. Bakhtin, *The Dialogic Imagination: Four Essays* (University of Texas Press Slavic Series, 1; Austin: University of Texas Press, 1981) 272.

[6] M. M. Bakhtin, *Problems of Dostoevsky's Poetics* (Theory and History of Literature, 8; Manchester: Manchester University Press, 1984).

discusses the dialogical nature of language in general.[7] Dialogicity might appear within a word, an utterance, between two speakers in a novel (actor and narrator) or at a historical or social level, and their meaning depends upon what has been said previously and on the way in which they will be received by others. Bakhtin describes this dialogicity of language as polyphony, double-voice, heteroglossia, hybridisation.[8] Due to its dialogicity, Bakhtin also stresses the otherness of language. Language is never our own and no interpretation is ever complete because every word is a response to previous words and elicits a further response. This otherness threatens any unitary, authoritarian and hierarchical concept of society, literature and life.

5.3. INTERTEXTUALITY

Kristeva combines Saussurean linguistics, Bakhtinian dialogism, Marxism and psychoanalysis. The intertextual aspects of a text concern its structuration of words and utterances that existed before and will continue after the moment of utterance (cf. Bakhtin's dialogicity). According to Kristeva, a text possesses a double meaning: a meaning in the text itself and a meaning in what she calls "the historical and social text".[9] These two texts are indistinguishable. All texts contain ideological structures and struggles inherent to society, implying that meaning is always simultaneously "inside" and "outside" the text. Whereas Bakhtin is concerned not only with the relationship between texts but also with the relationship between text and reality, Kristeva restricts intertextuality to the relationship between texts. However, she extends the concept of text so that reality also becomes a text, "the general

---

[7] G. Allen, *Intertextuality* (The New Critical Idiom; London: Routledge, 2000) 26, see also Morris, "Introduction", p. 23.

[8] Bakhtin, "Discourse in the Novel", p. 291. *Polyphony* is the simultaneous combination of voices, *double-voiced discourse* is two discourses in one character, e.g. irony and parody as a dialogue of two worldviews, *heteroglossia* concerns language's ability to contain within it many voices (one's own *and* other voices), and clashes of ideologies and past utterances, while *hybridization* is about a clash of "languages" occurring within the same utterance. For an overview, see Morris, "Introduction", pp. 1–24. Allen, *Intertextuality*, p. 17, explains how Bakhtin prioritises Saussure's *la language* over *la parole* and *la langue*: "If *parole* concerns the act of utterance, then *language* concerns every conceivable parole generatable from the system of language (*langue*)", (his italics).

[9] J. Kristeva, *Desire in Language: A Semiotic Approach to Literature and Art* (Oxford: Blackwell, 1980) 37.

text (culture)".[10] She claims that the intertextual dimensions of a text cannot be studied in terms of "sources" or "influences" or what has traditionally been called "context".[11] Opposed to the idea that texts possess a unifying meaning, she claims that words that are subjects of social conflicts and tensions in a text represent the text's *ideologeme*[12] (cf. Bakhtin's centripetal and centrifugal forces in language and the opposition of monological and dialogical utterances).

Kristeva depicts a psychoanalytic dimension of the signifying process of language by referring to the splitting of the subject between two signifying fields: the semiotic and the symbolic.[13] The semiotic involves language of drives and impulses retained from a pre-linguistic stage before the splitting of the subject during the thetic phase (i.e. the point when the subject enters the social world). The symbolic involves the social language of reason and communication, as well as the ideal of singularity and unity (cf. Bakhtin's monologicity). According to Kristeva, there is a tension between a social, symbolic discourse and an anti-rational, anti-social, semiotic language.[14] In poetic language, semiotic and symbolic fields are intertwined. In this, a polyphony of many, non-hierarchical voices is stressed; not only two, as in dialogue.

While Bakhtin regards poetry as monologic, Kristeva's poetic language is "a *signifying practice,*... a semiotic system generated by a speaking subject within a social, historical field".[15] She employs Bakhtin's emphasis on the dialogicity of language in general to attack notions of unity, which involve claims of authoritativenes, truth and society's desire to repress plurality.[16]

---

[10] Kristeva, *Desire in Language*, p. 36.

[11] Kristeva, *Desire in Language*, pp. 36–37. She coined the term intertextuality rather by chance (p. 66). To avoid the reduction of intertextuality to traditional notions of influence, source-study and context, J. Kristeva, *Revolution in Poetic Language* (New York: Columbia University Press, 1984) 59–60, replaced the term intertextuality with the term transposition.

[12] Kristeva, *Desire in Language*, p. 37, and J. Lechte, *Julia Kristeva* (London: Routledge, 1990) 103.

[13] Kristeva, *Revolution in Poetic Language*, pp. 21–24.

[14] Kristeva, *Revolution in Poetic Language*, pp. 86–89, relates this to a splitting of texts into what she labels genotext and phenotext. The semiotic genotext is the non-phenomenal aspect of language and textuality which articulates the drives and desires of a pre-linguistic subjectivity and disturbs, ruptures and undercuts the phenotext (p. 86). The symbolic phenotext uses the syntax and semantics of the text for communication, drawing on competence and performance (p. 87).

[15] L. S. Roudiez, "Introduction" in Kristeva, *Desire in Language*, p. 1, his italics.

[16] Also Barthes' "theory of the text" involves a theory of intertextuality, since the text is woven out of already existent meanings and discourses (cf. his distinction

Kristeva also applies Benveniste's concepts of *speaking subject* and *subject of speech*. Whereas the former relates to the human originator, the latter concerns the verbal entity itself. *The speaking subject* is, for instance, a speaking or thinking narrator, whereas *the subject of speech* is the subject of the narrative act ("actor").[17] Allen explains:

> The subject in writing is always double because the words that subject utters are inter-textual (clichéd, already written), and the pronominal signifiers which refer to that subject are always changing and have no stable signified ("outside" subject) to which they can be referred.[18]

Thus, whenever subjects enter language they enter into situations in which their personal identity is lost.

5.4. Genre

Genre describes the relation of a text to other texts and is thus related to intertextuality. Genre recognition applies to any categorisation of utterances: literary and non-literary, narrative and poetic, fiction and fact. Genre recognition concerns the cultural semiotics of a text, thereby making its signs intelligible within both its textual and social frameworks. Bakhtin argues that genre is not merely a literary-critical category and claims that the significance of genre is that it conceptualises reality.[19] Genre identification frames a text by relating it to a system: the relation between *la parole* and *la langue*. This involves both classifying and mastering texts, as a categorisation begins with a focalisation or prioritisation – a choice of what to read a text "as". The discussions about whether Isa. 53 should be labelled a "Servant Song", a "lament", a "thanksgiving", a "prophetic liturgy", *Leichenlied*, *Volksklagelied, Idealbiographie* or a "report" are related to the problem of finding an appropriate (form critical) Great Story for the text. After Saussure, theoreticians have brought out more radical implications of

---

between work and text in 3.8.). Texts are "quotations without inverted commas" (Barthes, "From Work to Text", p. 160.). Every quotation distorts the "primary" utterance by relocating it within another linguistic and cultural context. Meaning is always anterior and always deferred. This implies that intertextual relations can never be stabilised, exhaustively located or listed, cf. R. Barthes, *The Pleasure of the Text* (Oxford: Blackwell, 1990) 32. Cf. the Derridean *différance* (cf. 3.7.).

[17] Cf. 3.3., 4.5. and 4.8.2.3.
[18] Allen, *Intertextuality*, p 42. Cf. deictis in 3.3. and 4.4.
[19] Bakhtin, *Problems of Dostoevsky's Poetics*, p. 134.

the linguistic model by focusing on the way in which, in *la parole*, a sign is not always bound by *la langue*, for a signifier can transgress the system (3.7.).[20]

5.5. Discourse

Whereas Bakhtin focuses on heteroglossia and Kristeva on poetic language, Foucault views a text as a site of struggle between discourses. Whereas Barthes and Derrida are concerned with "boundless visions of textuality", Foucault attends to forces constraining and producing a text. In this regard, he considers more closely the social and political institutions.[21] For Foucault, discourse is more than "the general domain of all statements".[22] Discourse can be "an individualizable group of statements"[23] which are recognised as part of the same "discursive formation", e.g. the discourse of femininity, racism, medicine, religion or class. Discourse does not concern a set of coherent statements but a complex set of practices of inclusion and exclusion.[24] Foucault describes the procedures constraining and producing discourse.[25] He speaks of three groups of procedures which can control discourses:

1) social procedures related to exclusion. This includes taboos of politics and sexuality, the division between reason and madness and the distinction between true and false which legitimises what counts as knowledge in a society.[26]

---

[20] A biblical study which is especially concerned with genre recognition is Barton, *Reading the Old Testament*, p. 16, which defines literary competence "principally as *the ability to recognize genre*", (his italics). And further:
> By "genre" is meant any recognizable and distinguishable type of writing or speech – whether "literary" in the complimentary sense of that word or merely utilitarian, like a business letter – which operates within certain conventions that are in principle (not necessarily in practice) stateable.
On literary competence, see 2.3.8.4. On genre in relation to Isa. 53, cf. 2.3.5.

[21] J. Clayton and E. Rothstein, "Figures in the Corpus: Theories of Influence and Intertextuality" in J. Clayton and E. Rothstein (eds), *Influence and Intertextuality in Literary History* (Wisconsin: University of Wisconsin Press, 1991) 27.

[22] Foucault, *The Archaeology of Knowledge and The Discourse on Language*, p. 80.

[23] Foucault, *The Archaeology of Knowledge and The Discourse on Language*, p. 81.

[24] M. Foucault, "The Order of Discourse" in Young, *Untying the Text*, pp. 52–64.

[25] This might be related to Althusser and interpellation (4.5.), Bakhtin and the monological utterance (5.2.) and Kristeva and *ideologeme* (5.3.).

[26] Foucault, "The Order of Discourse", pp. 52–56.

2) internal procedures of rarefaction. This consists of discourses which
   are restricted by principles of classification, ordering and distribution. Foucault offers three examples of this:
   i. in the commentary (juridical, religious, literary), a hierarchy
      between primary and secondary text allows an endless con-
      struction of new discourses, as the primary text as a discourse
      can always be re-actualized.[27] On the other hand, the role of
      the commentary is "to say at last what was silently articulated
      'beyond', in the text".[28] This concerns the identity of the text
      (the form of repetition and the sameness), e.g. "The Book of
      Isaiah", "Isa. 40–55", "Servant Songs", "Isa. 52:13–53:12".
   ii. the author as an organising principle of texts. This grouping of
      discourses is "conceived as the unity and origin of their mean-
      ings, as the focus of their coherence",[29] e.g., to unite diverse
      texts such as "Second Isaiah", "Duhm", "Steck".[30]
   iii. as regards the organisation of disciplines (such as "biblical
      studies"), Foucault explains:

   > This is opposed to the principle of the author because a discipline is
   > defined by a domain of objects, a set of methods,...a play of rules and
   > definitions...It is also opposed to the principle of commentary. In a
   > discipline, unlike a commentary, what is supposed at the outset is not
   > a meaning which has to be rediscovered, nor an identity which has to
   > be repeated, but the requisites for the construction of new statements.
   > The distinction between primary and secondary text also concerns the
   > identity of the discipline.[31]

3) procedures to thin out of the speaking subject. This might be compared to ritual (e.g. who speaks when at the university), what counts
   as "academic" and reproduction.[32] A discourse can also refer to the
   result of a "regulated practice that accounts for a certain number of
   statements"[33] such as unwritten rules producing certain statements,
   e.g. an essay or an exegetical exercise written at university.

---

[27] Foucault, "The Order of Discourse", p. 57.
[28] Foucault, "The Order of Discourse", p. 58.
[29] Foucault, "The Order of Discourse", p. 58.
[30] Foucault, "The Order of Discourse", p. 59.
[31] Foucault, "The Order of Discourse", p. 59.
[32] Foucault, "The Order of Discourse", pp. 61–64.
[33] Foucault, *The Archaeology of Knowledge and The Discourse on Language*, p. 81.

Foucault emphasises that discourse is related to the production of knowledge. In regulating what is sayable, how it can be articulated, who can speak, where and under what conditions, a discursive practice controls what counts as knowledge, related to certain social interests. One example is statements about the Bible, used in private homes, congregations, in political, theological and other academic institutions, where, for instance, other religious and historical texts are not given the same primacy. In the case of Isa. 53, the text had a peculiar position in the history of biblical interpretation (Jewish, Christian and "critical") long before Duhm. After Duhm, versions of his "Servant Song" thesis have become a common denominator for the way in which this text should be interpreted in biblical scholarship: "Servant Song Research" has become its own "discipline" within Old Testament scholarship. This discipline may be located at institutions (e.g. departments of theology and religious studies), in practices (e.g. commentaries, sermons) and in statements using specialised vocabulary (e.g. *Gottesknecht, Ebed-Jahwe-Lied, Stellvertretung, leidende Gerechte*).

In addition to the oppressing and constraining aspects of power, Foucault stresses its productivity, its resistance to power.[34] This may be illustrated by conflicting sets of statements about Isa. 53, which appear in translations and interpretations in Jewish contexts such the Qumran texts, Pseudepigrapha, the LXX, the Targumim, the Peshitta, mediaeval and modern rabbinical literature, and in Christian contexts such the Pseudepigrapha, the Apocrypha, the New Testament, the Vulgate, in patristic and mediaeval literature, as well as in biblical scholarship since its growth from pre-modern time to recent linguistic, literary, rhetorical, anthropological, psychoanalytical, popular cultural, canonical, Marxist, feminist, liberation-theological and contextual readings. In Steck's redaction-critical reading for instance, Isa. 52:13–53:12 appears as five stories about a servant identified as the prophet "Second Isaiah", as Zion, as those who have returned from the Exile, as

---

[34] M. Foucault, *The History of Sexuality. Vol. 1: An Introduction* (New York: Vintage, 1980) 36; 100–101. S. Mills, *Discourse* (The New Critical Idiom; London: Routledge, 2004), explains the difference between discourse and ideology:

> [W]hilst within an ideological view sexism is an oppressive strategy employed by men to bolster their own power, within a discourse theory model sexism *is* the site of contestation: it is both the arena where some males are ratified in their attempts to negotiate a powerful position for themselves in relation to women, but it is also the site where women can contest or collaborate with those moves (p. 40, her italics).

those who remained in Judah and the servant's descendants, the true
Israel (which includes other people). All these servant stories of Steck's
are dated to different times in Ancient Israel within a period from 539
to 270 BCE. In addition to the many textual versions and interpretations of Isa. 52:13–53:12, pictorial and musical ones might be added
(cf. 2.4. and 4.2.). Any given discourse has a materiality and ideology
differentiating it from other discourses according to the conditions of
its formation and practice. Regarding Isa. 53, no easy consensus or
unified methodology of reading this text has ever existed. Past readings of the text are no more homogenous than present ones (cf. 2.3.8.,
2.4. and 3.10.17).

5.6. Identifying Intertextuality

Intertextuality has become a more and more diffuse and all-embracing
concept with a plethora of definitions and redefinitions. Culler warns
against the danger that the concept might lose its analytical power:

> [Intertextuality] is a difficult concept to use because of the vast and
> undefined discursive space it designates, but when one narrows it so
> as to make it more usable one either falls into source study of a tradi-
> tional and positivistic kind (which is what the concept was designed to
> transcend) or else ends by naming particular texts as the pre-texts on
> grounds of interpretative convenience.[35]

Moyise has discussed a widespread use of the term intertextuality in
biblical scholarship: it is applied to express traditional source criticism, Jewish midrash, typology, reader-response criticism, or describes
a complex texture of a work, a network of references to other texts.[36]
Moyise himself regards the term as a kind of "umbrella term" requiring subcategories. He proposes three categories be established in scholarship: intertextual echoes, dialogical intertextuality and postmodern
intertextuality.[37]

---

[35] Culler, *The Pursuit of Signs*, p. 109.
[36] S. Moyise, "Intertextuality and the Study of the Old Testament in the New Testament" in S. Moyise (ed), *The Old Testament in the New Testament: Essays in Honor of
J.L. North* (JNTSSup, 198; Sheffield: Sheffield Academic Press, 2000) 15–18.
[37] Also T. K. Beal, "Ideology and Intertextuality: Surplus of Meanings and Controlling the Means of Production" in D. N. Fewell (ed), *Reading Between Texts: Intertextuality and the Hebrew Bible* (Literary Currents in Biblical Interpretation; Louisville,

Williamson's description of the influence of Isa. 6:1 on Isa. 52:13 is
a telling example of the traditional hunt for sources:

> It is difficult not to believe...that there has...been influence from the
> same quarter [i.e. Isa. 6:1] at 52:13, where it is said of the Lord's servant
> that "he shall be exalted and lifted up, and shall be very high"...Not
> only do we find here the distinctive combination of the two roots under
> discussion from Isa. 6:1 [יָרוּם וְנִשָּׂא], but in addition there is the intro-
> duction of a third verb,... [גָּבַהּ], whose adjective also occurs in associa-
> tion with our phrase in chapter 2 (verses 12* and 15). In view of what
> we have seen of the use of these words elsewhere in Isaiah, this puts the
> exaltation of the servant, presumably following his sufferings which are
> described later, in a new and striking light.[38]

Literary works always and endlessly refer to other literary works: the
boundaries of intertextuality can never be established. A literary work
embodies endless interactions of semiotic systems and may not offer
any stable, identifiable centre or meaning. Intertextual theory explicitly attends to ideological forces at work in both text production and
text reception (e.g. forces regarding politics, religion, gender, ethnicity,
class). The shift of focus from traditional historical-critical to intertextual approaches should not be regarded as a rejection of historical
study.[39]

5.7. Intertextual Identification of Isa. 52:13–53:12

Scholars have long been aware of relations between Second Isaiah and
other biblical texts and themes. Within traditional historical-critical

---

KY: Westminster/John Knox Press, 1992) 27–39, regards intertextuality as a "covering
term" in need of subcategories.

[38] H. G. M. Williamson, *The Book Called Isaiah: Deutero-Isaiah's Role in Composition and Redaction* (Oxford: Clarendon Press, 1994) 39–40. Cf. Westermann, *Isaiah
40–66*, p. 258: "The verbs [of exaltation] are very strong ones. In the vision at the call
of Isaiah (6.1) God's throne is 'high and lifted up'; and expressions referring to Jesus'
exaltation (such as Acts 2.33) probably go back to the passage before us."

[39] R. F. Berkhofer Jr., *Beyond the Great Story: History as Text and Discourse*
(Cambridge, MA: Belknap Press of Harvard University Press, 1995) 182; 257, F. E.
Deist, "Contingency, Continuity and Integrity in Historical Understanding: An Old
Testament perspective" in V. P. Long (ed), *Israel's Past in Present Research: Essays
on Ancient Israelite Historiography* (Sources for Biblical and Theological Study, 7;
Winona Lake, IN: Eisenbrauns, 1999) 373–390, F. W. Burnett, "Historiography" in
Adam, *Handbook of Postmodern Biblical Interpretation*, pp. 106–112. Cf. 3.4. n. 16 on
the role of history in the relation between diachronic and synchronic studies.

research, the relation of Isa. 40–55 to the Pentateuch, especially its themes of Exodus, wilderness, pre-patriarchal, patriarchal and creation stories (but not Sinai), have been studied. Also its connections with the Prophets, such as First Isaiah, Jeremiah, Ezekiel, Hosea, Zephaniah and Nahum have been mapped out, as well as its common themes with Psalms and Lamentations.[40] As regards Isa. 52:13–53:12, special interest has been paid to its relation to the other *EJL* and the rest of Isa. 40–55. Recently, relations between Isa. 40–55 and its literary surroundings have been called inner-biblical exegesis, allusions, recollections and mosaics. All these approaches represent fresh thinking about such connections, the most traditional contributions being those concerning inner-biblical exegesis by Fishbane[41] and on allusions by Sommer.[42] Miscall's study of mosaics is the most radical,[43] and Willey's on recollection is somewhere in the middle.[44]

Relationality plays an important role in a formulation of intertextuality. It is not possible to delimit a priori the intertextuality of a text, but it is possible to distinguish different intertextualities. For instance, the same type of relation does not exist between Isa. 40–55 and the Book of Jeremiah as between Isa. 40–55 and Selma Lagerlof's novel

---

[40] For an overview of this, see Willey, *Remember the Former Things*, pp. 11–28.

[41] M. A. Fishbane, *Biblical Interpretation in Ancient Israel* (Oxford: Oxford University Press, 1985) describes a process which starts with a received text (traditum) whose authority is recognized. This authority requires a degree of interpretation and reapplication (traditio) to later circumstances to remain viable. The interpretation and reapplication to later circumstances revitalizes the traditum. The tradition may also undermine the traditum, which Fishbane calls a "paradox" (p. 15). He presupposes that the later text confirms the authority of the received text, and that this phenomenon of "paradox" is rare. He occasionally uses the term "intertextuality" to describe this relation between texts (e.g. p. 521)

[42] B. D. Sommer, *A Prophet Reads Scripture: Allusion in Isaiah 40–66* (Contraversions; Stanford: Stanford University Press, 1998) 1–31, adopts Fishbane's inner-biblical exegesis, mingled with allusion. This study is characterised as a pursuit of diachronic relations among a narrow range of texts in which borrowed material serves rhetorical or strategic ends. Sommer takes lexical analogies as his point of view. K. M. O'Connor, "'Speak Tenderly to Jerusalem': Second Isaiah Reception and Use of Daughter Zion", *Princeton Seminary Bulletin* 20 (1999) 281–294, supports Sommer's pursuit of lexical allusions or influence, and "adds metaphor, a literary persona, and the plot that emerges from them" (p. 282).

[43] P. D. Miscall, "Isaiah: New Heavens, New Earth, New Book" in Fewell, *Reading Between Texts*, pp. 41–56.

[44] Willey, *Remember the Former Things*, 1–104, employs Bakhtin, Fishbane and Richard Hays in her theoretical framework of intertextuality. She seeks to demonstrate a re-use of earlier biblical texts in Isa. 40–55.

Jerusalem.[45] Different relations of meaning are at play. It is the reader who establishes a relationship between a text and its intertext, where a fragment of discourse becomes accommodated or assimilated by the focused text. This does not occur by necessity.

As we have seen in readings of the Book of Isaiah, a biblical text is related to other texts, but the aims of these can be very different. The shift of focus from traditional historical-critical to intertextual approaches implies that the reading of the Hebrew Bible is something more than – or something different from – the study of a text from the perspective of the history of literature. Considering the Hebrew Bible as an intertext does not mean synthesising the messages of the books of which it is composed. It would mean establishing between them a network of similitudes, tensions, variations and transformations more beneficial to the reader than any synthesis.[46] One text defers, differs from, is differentiated from another. The critical task is not to search for an *Urtext* or original meaning which is the foundation of all others but to demonstrate differences, not commonalities.[47] Meaning in this sense seems to be the result not of pursuing originality, uniqueness, singularity and autonomy, but of an interactive process between the Hebrew language code, the text, the reader and the reading conventions to which she or he belongs.

In my intertextual reading of Isa. 52:13–53:12, I pursue neither dependence nor allusions as regards, for example, semantics or genre. My focus is the trope of personification. I shall concentrate on how nation, people and city speak and are spoken to in patterns which alternate between presentations of individuals and collectives. In Isa. 40–55, "I", "we", "you", "he", "she" and "they" are speaking and are spoken to. The people are also named as Jacob, Israel, Jeshurun and Zion, and designated as friend, messenger, servant, woman and mother. Personifications of Israel, Jerusalem, Babylon and the nations

---

[45] K. Nielsen, *Bilderna och Ordet: Om Herrens tjänare och andra bilder i Gamla Testamente* (Örebro: Libris, 1998) 14–17, relates the message of Isa. 40–55 to Selma Lagerlof, *Jerusalem I–II* (1901–1902), a novel describing a Chicago mystic sparking a religious revival in a Swedish rural community that leads people to sell their possessions and conduct a mass pilgrimage to Jerusalem.

[46] J. Delorme, "Intertextualities about Mark" in S. Draisma (ed), *Intertextuality in Biblical Writings: Essays in Honor of Bas van Iersel* (Kampen: Kok, 1989) 35–42.

[47] G. A. Phillips, "Sign/Text/Différance" in H. F. Plett (ed), *Intertextuality* (Research in Text Theory 15; Berlin: W. de Gruyter, 1991) 93.

in general populate Isa. 40–55. I will not pursue the relation of Isa. 53
to particular prior texts, a historical background or an author's intention, but the participation of the text in a discursive space. I shall concentrate on the humiliation and exaltation of fates and fortunes in the
past, present and future in Isa. 40–55 and elsewhere in the prophetic
literature, Psalms and Lamentations. Secondary literature will also
participate. *Gottesknechtlied*, for instance, is one of many intertexts,
exile another, Duhm a third, etc.

W. Müller considers that the interrelationships existing between
characters of different texts represent one of the most important
dimensions of intertextuality.[48] He argues that on an intertextual level,
the trope of personification might act as a play within a play. Simultaneously, he is surprised how little attention intertextual theory has
paid to them. He proposes that this might be due to the suspicion generally felt towards character-oriented studies, based on the idea that
"character" has been regarded by modern theoreticians as an "ideological prejudice" rather than a respectable topic for inquiry. Certainly,
purely structural identifications of personification can be difficult and
the limits of tropological formalisations are obvious. On the other
hand, it might be of some interest to study a network of relationships
that exist between figurative uses of language, without any interest in
a supposed generic order or development within the Hebrew Bible.

The following intertextual reading of Isa. 52:13–53:12 is not exhaustive. Its focus is the trope of personification. I will be treating segments
in Isa. 52:13–53:12 in relation to intertextual dialogue partners. This
concerns literary motifs such as reversals of fates and fortunes, shame,
seeing, plant imagery, illness, sin, silence, sheep led to slaughtering,
death, grave, offspring, righteousness and servant.[49]

---

[48] W. G. Müller, "Interfigurality: A Study on the Interdependence of Literary Figures" in Plett, *Intertextuality*, p. 101.

[49] Examples of verses which are treated less than others in the intertextual part of
this study include: 53:8, 53:10a, 53:11a, 53:12. In another reading, these verses might
be placed in focus, which would have given a different outcome, indeed, a very different study of Isa. 52:13–53:12. This might be clearly illustrated with those readers
who take אָשָׁם in 53:10 to be the core of the text. In such readings, the theological
concept of vicarious suffering is key and other texts are brought into dialogue. See
Appendix 6.

5.8. "As many were appalled at you...so kings shall shut their mouth..."

5.8.1. *Isa. 52:14–15*

52:14 כַּאֲשֶׁר שָׁמְמוּ עָלֶיךָ רַבִּים
כֵּן־מִשְׁחַת מֵאִישׁ מַרְאֵהוּ וְתֹאֲרוֹ מִבְּנֵי אָדָם:
15 כֵּן יַזֶּה גּוֹיִם רַבִּים עָלָיו יִקְפְּצוּ מְלָכִים פִּיהֶם
כִּי אֲשֶׁר לֹא־סֻפַּר לָהֶם רָאוּ וַאֲשֶׁר לֹא־שָׁמְעוּ הִתְבּוֹנָנוּ:

52:14:   As many were appalled at you
— such a disfigurement was his appearance from that of man and his form from that of humanity
52:15:   — so he יַזֶּה (will startle?) many peoples before him, kings shall shut their mouth;
for what was not told to them, they shall see and what they did not hear, they shall understand.

In Isa. 52:14, an "I" tells about a confrontation between רַבִּים "many" and "you", in which שָׁמְמוּ רַבִּים "many were appalled".[50] Their reactions are explained by a portrayal of "him": "his" מִשְׁחַת "disfigurement" makes "him" appear hardly human, thus separating "him" from socity.[51] An identification appears between "him" and "you", but with different accentuations: "you" are appalled at, whereas "he" is disfigured.[52] A personification emerges in this enunciative distancing in the relation of "he"/"you", with the blurring of the personifier "he" and the personified "you" (cf. 4.8.1.3.). "My" portrayal of מַרְאֵהוּ וְתֹאֲרוֹ "his appearance and his form" in 52:14 is chiastically related to "his" תֹאַר "form" and מַרְאֶה "appearance" in 53:2: As "many" were appalled at "his appearance", "we" were not attracted to "him". In both instances a contrast appears, between "him" and "many" (52:14) and between "him" and "us" (53:2). In the "I" speech of 52:14 "your"/"his" shame is related to רַבִּים "many"'s dismay, and in the "we" speech of 53:2

---

[50] For reactions of Israel's neighbours expressed by שׁמם (qal) "appalled", see Lev. 26:32, 1 Kgs 9:8, 2 Chron. 7:21, Jer. 18:16, 19:8, and for reactions towards foreigners see e.g. Jer. 49:17, 50:13, Ezek. 26:16, 27:35, 28:19, 32:9–10 and 32:15. Cf. the reactions of Job's friends in Job 17:7, 18:20 (both ni.). All these concern the response of witnesses to the devastating results of YHWH's punishment of a wicked nation, city or individual (e.g. king). For other uses of שׁמם, see 5.11.5. n. 144 and 5.11.9. n. 171.

[51] See מַרְאֶה "appearance" in a description of leprosy in Lev. 13:12; 43 and in relation to illness as listed among the curses which will strike the people if disobedient in Deut. 28:34; 67 and Lam. 4:8.

[52] On the sudden transition between 2ms and 3ms, see 3.10.2. n. 63.

"he" is related to "us". In 52:14 and 53:2 "he" is disfigured and without respect; in 53:3 "he" is also ill, despised and disregarded. Like in 52:14 and 53:2, in 53:3 a contrasting relationship also appears between the solitary figure and "them"/"us". At all events, "his" illnesses and disgusting appearance isolated "him" from society.[53]

The argument beginning in 52:14 continues in v. 15. As רַבִּים "many"'s reaction to "you" in 52:14 is described as their having been appalled, in v. 15 יַזֶּה גּוֹיִם רַבִּים עָלָיו "he ('will startle'?) many peoples before him" and (עָלָיו) יִקְפְּצוּ מְלָכִים פִּיהֶם "(before him) kings shall shut their mouth".[54] Through gesture, "they" shall show their reactions to a coming event. These reactions are further depicted through a contrast between negative utterances about the past and positive ones about the future: what "they" have neither been told nor heard, "they" shall see and perceive (52:15b). After רַבִּים "many"'s reaction to "you"/"him" in the past (52:14), the fates and fortunes of גּוֹיִם רַבִּים "many peoples" and מְלָכִים "kings" are turned around: from רַבִּים "many" being appalled to מְלָכִים "kings" shutting their mouth, but also to "their" seeing the untold and understanding the unheard. No explanation is given for the turning point from past to future.

5.8.2. Isa. 49:7

49:7 כֹּה אָמַר־יְהוָה גֹּאֵל יִשְׂרָאֵל קְדוֹשׁוֹ
לִבְזֹה־נֶפֶשׁ לִמְתָעֵב גּוֹי לְעֶבֶד מֹשְׁלִים
מְלָכִים יִרְאוּ וָקָמוּ שָׂרִים וְיִשְׁתַּחֲווּ
לְמַעַן יְהוָה אֲשֶׁר נֶאֱמָן קְדֹשׁ יִשְׂרָאֵל וַיִּבְחָרֶךָ:

> 49:7: Thus says YHWH, the redeemer of Israel's Holy one,
>   to the despised of human, to the abhorred of people, to the servant of rulers:
>   Kings shall see and rise up, princes, and they shall throw themselves down,
>   because of YHWH who is faithful, Israel's Holy one, and he has chosen you.

---

[53] For חָדֵל, see 3.10.6. n. 84 and כְּמַסְתֵּר פָּנִים מִמֶּנּוּ, see Appendix 3.

[54] The translation of יַזֶּה...עָלָיו is discussed in Appendix 2. R. E. Watts, "The Meaning of [עָלָיו יִקְפְּצוּ מְלָכִים פִּיהֶם] in Isaiah LII 15", VT 40 (1990) 335; 329, reads עָלָיו יִקְפְּצוּ מְלָכִים פִּיהֶם not first and foremost as an expression of surprise, but a metonymy "signifying the subjugation of the arrogant kings to the servant as Yahweh implements his [מִשְׁפָּט]" (p. 335). He further claims that Job 5:16 and Ps. 107:42 are metaphorical whereas Isa. 52:15 is literal. גּוֹיִם "peoples" and מְלָכִים "kings" are paralleled in Isa. 41:2, 45:1, 49:7 (cf. 5.8.2.); 22–23 (cf. 5.8.5. n. 78).

In Isa. 49:7, the expression כֹּה אָמַר־יְהוָה "Thus says YHWH" is followed by two appellatives where the quoted YHWH is presented as
"the redeemer of Israel" and "his Holy one",[55] in which a relation
between YHWH and Israel is also expressed.

Then follows a threefold depiction of the addressee. In the first
phrase, לִבְזֹה־נֶפֶשׁ "to the despised of human", a dissociation of "him"
from those around "him" is expressed by the coll. נֶפֶשׁ "human", i.e.
"everyone".[56] The phrase echoes "our" depiction of "him" in Isa. 53:3
as "despised and abandoned by men". In the second phrase of 49:7,
לִמְתָעֵב גּוֹי "to the abhorred of people", the reactions of an indefinite
coll. גּוֹי "people" echo the appalled response of רַבִּים "many" in 52:14.[57]
In 52:14 it is due to "his" מִשְׁחַת "disfigurement"; in 49:7 no reason
is given for the dissociation of "him". In the third and last phrase,
לְעֶבֶד מֹשְׁלִים "to the servant of rulers", the subject עֶבֶד "servant",
"slave" (sg) is modified by the object מֹשְׁלִים "rulers", "lords, "mas-
ters" (pl), where a hierarchical relationship might appear between a
subordinate and a superior partner.[58] An accumulation of humiliations

---

[55] The expression יִשְׂרָאֵל קְדוֹשׁוֹ "Israel's Holy one" and cognates are widespread
in Isa. 1–66. As "typically Isaianic", the expression is taken as an argument for the
unity of the Book of Isaiah (2.3.2.). H. G. M. Williamson, "Isaiah and the Holy One of
Israel" in A. Rapoport-Albert and G. Greenberg (eds), *Biblical Hebrew, Biblical Texts:
Essays in Memory of M. P. Weitzman* (JSOTSup, 333; Sheffield: Sheffield Academic
Press, 2001) 22–38, offers an overview of different positions on this. According to him,
"Isaiah himself used the title a maximum of five times…four (or possibly five) times
by those who extended his work in the late pre-exilic or early exilic period, and…the
remaining five (or four) occurrences are later" (p. 36). It is used thirteen times in Isa.
40–55. גֹּאֲלֵךְ "your redeemer" and יִשְׂרָאֵל קְדוֹשׁוֹ "Israel's Holy one" are paralleled in
41:14, 43:14, 47:4, 49:7, 54:5. See also more recently R. G. Kratz, "Israel in the Book of
Isaiah", *JSOT* 31 (2006) 103–128.

[56] See alternative readings of לִבְזֹה in Koole, *Isaiah III. Vol. 2*, pp. 31–32. I read the
construction לִבְזֹה־נֶפֶשׁ "to the despised of human", i.e. לְ (prep.), בֹּזֹה (inf. cstr. qal;
subject) and נֶפֶשׁ (ms coll.; object). For other readings of נֶפֶשׁ in Isa. 49:7, see Oswalt,
The Book of Isaiah: Chapters 40–66, p. 294. נֶפֶשׁ has a broad range of meanings: "living
being", "life", "self", "person", "desire"; here it rather generally means "everybody",
modified by גּוֹי "people" and מֹשְׁלִים "rulers". Cf. נַפְשָׁם "themselves", referring to the
Babylonians in 46:2, 47:14 and to "you" (2mpl) in 55:2–3.

[57] BHSapp Isa. 49:7 suggests pt. pu. vocalisation: לִמְתֹעַב. I read the phrase as composite of לְ (prep.), מְתָעֵב (pt. pi., subject) and גּוֹי (ms, object). גּוֹי "people" most often
occurs in pl about "nations", "other peoples", but is sg in Isa. 55:5 (with modification).

[58] In 49:7 a different use of עֶבֶד "servant" occurs from elsewhere in Isa. 40–55,
where a relation between a servant and YHWH is presented, see 5.17. n. 324. The
root עבד "serve" covers a wide range of services or obligations between unequal partners, social, political and religious: a slave serving his master, a son serving his father,
an official or people serving their king, and a king or people serving their god. In Gen.
15:13–14 YHWH tells that Abraham's offspring will be slaves for 400 years in a foreign

appears in the addressee's relation to "his" neighbours, where "he" is
בְּזֹה "despised" by, מְתָעֵב "abhorred" by and עֶבֶד "servant" to the coll./
pl. נֶפֶשׁ "human", גּוֹי "people" and מֹשְׁלִים "rulers". In 49:7, YHWH is
"the redeemer of Israel" and "his Holy one", i.e. he privileges Israel,
while the addressee is "despised of human", "abhorred of people" and
"servant of rulers".

After YHWH and his addressee are presented, a turning point in
both temporality and causality is expressed. YHWH talks about מְלָכִים
"kings" who shall see and rise up and שָׂרִים "princes" who shall bow
down. There is no object showing what they shall see, but the gestures suggest tributes of honour.[59] Following the presentation of the
addressee's past and that of "his" neighbours, a turning point to the
future appears. However, the cause of this does not concern the relationship between "him" and "they" but is explained as לְמַעַן יְהוָה "for
the sake of YHWH", expanded by two attributes: he is נֶאֱמָן "faithful"
and יִשְׂרָאֵל קְדֹשׁ "Israel's Holy one". The last attribute is a variation
of the two introductory appeals of YHWH in the verse. Both cases
regard YHWH's relationship with Israel. The appositions are followed
by YHWH's action towards the addressee: וַיִּבְחָרֶךָ "he has chosen you".[60]

---

land. Egypt was בֵּית עֲבָדִים "a slavehouse" for Israel (Exod. 13:3; 14, 20:2, Deut. 5:6,
6:12, 7:8, 8:14, 13:6; 10, Josh. 24:17, Judg. 6:8, Jer. 34:13, Mic. 6:4), the people are עֶבֶד
"a slave" (Lev. 26:13, Deut. 5:15, 6:21, 15:15, 16:12, 24:18; 22), and their activities are
עבד "to work" (Exod. 1:13–14, 5:18, 6:5, 14:5; 15ff) and עֲבֹדָה קָשָׁה "hard labour"
(Exod. 1:14, 6:6; 9).

[59] וְיִשְׁתַּחֲווּ used to be regarded as hitpal. of שׁחה, but is now most often taken as
histaph. of חוה II. Both alternatives are translated "bow (politely or respectfully)",
"prostrate oneself", "make obeisance", related to the tribute which people(s) will pay to
YHWH (or his people) in the future (Isa. 45:14 [Egypt/Kush, par. with פלל htp. "pray",
"plead with"], 49:7; 23, 60:14, 66:23) or to idols (44:15; 17, par. with פלל htp., 46:6).
For a further discussion, see G. I. Davies, "Etymology of [הִשְׁתַּחֲוָה]", VT 29 (1979)
493–495, and S. Kreuzer, "Zur Bedeutung und Etymologie von [השתחוה]/[ישתחוי]",
VT 35 (1985) 39–60. The conjunctive waw in וְיִשְׁתַּחֲווּ in Isa. 49:7 is striking. Oswalt,
The Book of Isaiah: Chapters 40–66, p. 286, n. 11: "It seems probable that we are
intended to understand the verb 'see' as continuing to function with 'princes', thus
explaining the waw conjunctive on 'prostrate' – 'princes [will see] and prostrate themselves'."

[60] In Isa. 40–55, בחר "choose" with YHWH as subject almost always appears
together with "servant", see 41:8–9 (Israel, Jacob, offspring of Abraham), 42:1, 43:10
("my witnesses"), 44:1–2 (Jacob, Israel, Jeshurun); 20 (the only place not paired with
servant), 45:4 (Jacob, Israel), 49:7, 51:2 (Abraham), 54:6 (fem. personification). בחר
"choose" is related to קרא "call" in 41:4 (the generations from the beginning); 9 (cf.
above), 42:6 (cf. "covenant for the people and light for the nations", 43:1 (created,
Jacob, formed, Israel, called by name), 45:3–4 (Cyrus called by name), 46:11 (Cyrus),
48:12 (Jacob, Israel); 15 (Cyrus) 49:1 ("from mother's womb"), 51:1 (Abraham; בחר

Whereas נֶפֶשׁ "human", גּוֹי "people" and מֹשְׁלִים "rulers" have despised,
abhorred and been served by "him", מְלָכִים "kings" and שָׂרִים "princes"
shall see, rise up and bow down because of YHWH and his elected.
The fates of "him", "you", מְלָכִים "kings" and שָׂרִים "princes" become
manifestations of who YHWH is: because of YHWH, the despised
shall be honoured and the oppressors subjected. מְלָכִים "kings" and
שָׂרִים "princes" are witnesses like רַבִּים "many" in relation to "you"
in 52:14, and like מְלָכִים "kings" who shall shut their mouth in 52:15.
In 52:15, the consequences for "them" of what is going on continue
through expressions of what "they" shall see and perceive. Like in 49:7,
no object for what "they" shall see is expressed. Also in 52:14–15, a
turning point appears in temporality, but no causality is expressed.

Whereas in 49:7b the addressee is presented as "he", in 49:7d "you"
(2ms) are mentioned. This enunciative distancing in the relation of
"he"/"you" is reminiscent of the "he"/"you" relation of 52:14–15 in
which a personification emerges (cf. 4.8.1.3.). Also in the surrounding
verses of 49:7 there are unstable changes in speaking voices and addressees. In 49:1, an "I" addresses אִיִּים "islands" and לְאֻמִּים מֵרָחוֹק "peoples
from far away", followed by a depiction of how this "I" is called and
named from the womb by YHWH,[61] the deity having equipped him
(v. 2): YHWH has made his mouth like a sharp sword and him like a
pointed arrow, and the deity hid him. Then, the speaking "I" quotes

---

in v. 2, cf. above), 54:6 (cf. above) and variations in 43:7: "everyone who is called by
my name", 40:26 (pl). J. Barr, *The Semantics of Biblical Language* and *Old and New in
Interpretation: A Study of the Two Testaments* (London: SCM Press, 1966), criticises
the concept of election as an inference from and interpretation of Israel's history with
YHWH. He also criticises the misunderstanding that a word, e.g. בחר, is a concept
with the same meaning every time it appears in the Hebrew Bible (cf. similar criticism
regarding concepts of sin in 5.12.7. n. 236). For a critique of the concept of election in
Isa. 40–55, cf. J. S. Kaminsky, "The Concept of Election and Second Isaiah: Recent Literature", *BTB* 31 (2001) 134–144. A recent contribution on election is J. S. Kaminsky,
Yet I Loved Jacob: Reclaiming the Biblical Concept of Election (Nashville: Abingdon
Press, 2007), who claims that the Hebrew Bible's doctrine of election does not consist
of a binary opposition of the elect and all the others, but a threefold division between
the elect, the anti-elect and the non-elect. Discussions of election touch upon debates
of universalism/particularism, see 5.8.5.

[61] Cf. Isa. 44:2; 21; 24, 46:3, 48:8, 49:1; 5. Cf. Jer. 1:5, Pss. 22:10–11 (cf. 5.11.12.),
71:6, 139:13, Job 31:15. Willey, *Remember the Former Things*, pp. 193–197, comments
on how similarities between the prophet Jeremiah and the servant in Isa. 40–55 have
been noted in the history of research, where Jeremiah has even been identified as the
servant. She compares the calling of Jeremiah in Jer. 1 with presentations of the servant in Isa. 40–55, which she interprets as a collective character.

YHWH's appointment of him as his servant and as Israel,[62] in whom
the deity will glorify himself (v. 3), while the "I" complains of "his"
own vain efforts in terms of his task (v. 4). "My" disappointment and
lack of honour are contrasted with trust in YHWH (v. 4).

Whereas 49:1–4 is retrospective, וְעַתָּה "and now" in v. 5 both continues and contrasts with the preceding verses. V. 5 corresponds to the
speaking "I"'s statement of trust in v. 4, as he becomes (re-)honoured
in the eyes of YHWH, and his previous futile activity (v. 4) shall succeed. V. 5 introduces a quotation by YHWH, but before this the deity
is presented as forming of the "I" as his servant "from the womb" to
his task of gathering in Jacob and Israel.[63] The quotation of YHWH
follows in v. 6, where the deity tells of how his servant shall not only
restore Israel: YHWH shall also make him a light of the nations to
bring salvation to the ends of the earth.[64]

---

[62] יִשְׂרָאֵל "Israel" in Isa. 49:3 is one of the cruces in the "Servant Song Research".
יִשְׂרָאֵל appears in all Hebrew MSS (except Kenn. 96), 1QIsaᵃ, Tg. and LXX. For many,
it is a problem that it does not fit the context (vv. 5–6), where the mission of the
servant to Israel is described. Some take it to be a gloss, e.g. Duhm, *Das Buch Jesaia*,
p. 332, Elliger, *Deuterojesaja in seinem Verhältnis zu Tritojesaja*, p. 38, Westermann,
Isaiah 40–66, p. 207, Orlinsky, *The So-Called "Servant of the Lord" and "Suffering Servant" in Second Isaiah*, pp. 83–84, Whybray, *Isaiah 40–66*, pp. 137–138, Blenkinsopp,
Isaiah 40–55, pp. 297–298, while others keep it, e.g. most recently Koole, *Isaiah III.
Vol. 2*, pp. 11–13, and Oswalt, *The Book of Isaiah: Chapters 40–66*, pp. 285; 291. Steck
regards "Israel" as added to 49:3 at the third of his five redactional levels, see 2.2.5.
n. 110. N. Lohfink, "'Israel' in Jes. 49,3" in Schreiner, *Wort, Lied und Gottesspruch*, pp.
217–229 maintains יִשְׂרָאֵל in 49:3 and regards it as secondary in v. 7.
[63] K has לֹא "not", whereas Q reads לֹו "to him", supported by BHSapp, which refers
to 1QIsaᵃ, Tg. and LXX, among others. A "classic" question raised in the "Servant Song
Research" is whether the servant Israel can have a task towards himself ("the tribes of
Jacob"), implying an objection to a collective identification of the servant. Mettinger,
Farewell to the Servant Songs, p. 35, who identifies the servant as a symbol of Israel,
"solves" this by interpreting YHWH as subject of the infinitives, supported by Willey,
Remember the Former Things, p. 182. Koole, *Isaiah III. Vol. 2*, p. 13, who identifies the
servant as the prophet, explains: "God derives honour from Israel because he derives
honour from the Servant, whose task is Israel's restoration. An Israel returned by the
Servant to God can sing God's praises and thus fulfil her vocation in the world", cf.
Hermisson, "Israel und der Gottesknecht bei Deuterojesaja", pp. 209–210, and Steck,
with regard to what they call *Israelaufgabe des Gottesknechtes*, cf. 2.2.5. Cf. 5.8.5. on
universalism/particularism.
[64] After the expression כֹּה אָמַר יְהוָה "Thus says YHWH" (v. 8), the deity addresses
"you" (2ms), whom he will answer, help and preserve when it pleases him and on his
day of salvation. YHWH will also give "you" בְּרִית עָם "a covenant of the people" to
restore the land. A discussion within "Servant Song Research" concerns the servant's
role towards the nations. This is especially related to depictions of "him" as לְאוֹר
גּוֹיִם "a light to the nations" (42:6, 49:6, cf. לְאוֹר עַמִּים "a light to the peoples" in
51:4–5) and בְּרִית עָם "a covenant for the people" (42:6, 49:8), as well as "his" task of

Through עֶבֶד מֹשְׁלִים "the servant of rulers" (v. 7), YHWH shall glorify himself by deriving honour from "him"; his servant shall gather in Jacob and Israel to be a light for the nations and bring YHWH's salvation to the earth (vv. 5–6). The crossing of 1cs, 2ms and 3ms pronouns signifies different language situations. The pronouns play with each other and their context in a way that prevents construction of a coherent enunciation of the text. A personification emerges in a confusion between Israel and the servant as to whose task it is to restore Israel. That the personification does not lead to a single meaning establishes a gap between the personifier "he" and the personified "you". The personification emerges through interaction and difference with some aspects suppressed while others are brought into focus: whereas "he" was despised, abhorred and served נֶפֶשׁ "human", גּוֹי "people" and מֹשְׁלִים "rulers", מְלָכִים "kings" and שָׂרִים "princes" shall see, rise up and bow down because of YHWH and his elected one, cf. 52:14–15, moving from "his"/"your" humiliations to "his" ("the servant"'s) vindication, as well as showing the contrasting situations of "many", "many peoples", "princes" and "kings". Through gesture, "they" shall show their reactions to a coming event. In 49:7, no causality but the glory of YHWH is expressed.

5.8.3. Mic. 7:16–17

7:16 יִרְאוּ גוֹיִם וְיֵבֹשׁוּ מִכֹּל גְּבוּרָתָם
יָשִׂימוּ יָד עַל־פֶּה אָזְנֵיהֶם תֶּחֱרַשְׁנָה:
¹⁷יְלַחֲכוּ עָפָר כַּנָּחָשׁ כְּזֹחֲלֵי אֶרֶץ
יִרְגְּזוּ מִמִּסְגְּרֹתֵיהֶם אֶל־יְהוָה אֱלֹהֵינוּ
יִפְחֲדוּ וְיִרְאוּ מִמֶּךָּ:

7:16: Peoples shall see and be ashamed of all their strength,
    they shall put the hand on the mouth, their ears shall be deaf.
7:17: They will lick the dust like the snake, like those that creep on the ground.
    They will tremble from their fastness, to YHWH, our God;
    they will be terrified and afraid of you.

In Mic. 7:16, the coming speechlessness and deafness of the peoples are expressed. In v. 17, their future situation is compared to that of snakes licking dust and living in the ground. In this humiliating state

---

"bring[ing] justice for the nations" (42:1). This is what Steck has called *Völkeraufgabe des Gottesknechtes*, cf. 2.2.5. Cf. 5.8.5. on universalism/particularism.

יִרְגְּזוּ מִמִּסְגְּרֹתֵיהֶם "they will tremble from their fastness" in fear of
YHWH. The suff. of אֱלֹהֵינוּ "our God" indicates that the words are
spoken by Israel, and "you" (2ms) in the same verse shows that the
words are addressed to YHWH. This follows a prayer raised to YHWH
to take care of his people like a shepherd (vv. 14–15).[65] The people
are depicted in the image of a flock of sheep left desolate in Carmel,
but shall be restored to graze in Basan and Gilead. Their future is
compared to YHWH's past wondrous acts for them in Egypt (v. 15).[66]
This is what the humiliations of the nations in vv. 16–17 are related
to: what Israel sees as YHWH's mighty acts of salvation for her will
become times of trembling and fear for the nations. Then follows a
hymn about YHWH's compassion and incomparability (vv. 18–20). In
v. 19 "his" (3ms) mercy is proclaimed to "us" (1cpl) before the address
is raised to the deity and "their" (3mpl) sins are mentioned.

In relation to surrounding verses, oscillations in both speakers and
times appear. In Mic. 7:1–11, a speaking "I" tells that society may
be corrupt (vv. 1–6) but this will change (vv. 7–10).[67] There shall be
no more time for the enemies to rejoice over the calamity. Although
fallen, the "I" will arise; although "I" am sitting in darkness, YHWH
will be "my" light and accomplish justice (vv. 8–9). The "I" confesses
his/her own sins and accepts that זַעַף יְהוָה אֶשָּׂא "I will carry the rage

---

[65] YHWH as shepherd, see Isa. 40:11, 42:13; 16, 49:9–10, Jer. 13:17; 20, 31:10, Ezek.
34, Pss 23:1, 44:28, 49:10, 80:2, 100:3, 107, and the people as being shepherded by
YHWH, see Isa. 63:11, Zech. 11:7; 11, Pss. 77:21, 78:52, 79:13, 80:2, 95:7, 100:3. For
variations of a sheep motif, see 5.13.

[66] D. R. Hillers, *Micah* (Hermeneia; Philadelphia: Fortress Press, 1984) 91: "The
'you' in 'when you went out of the land of Egypt' refers to God, not the people as is
more common; cf. Exod. 13:21, 33:14, and 2 Sam 5:24". A different reading is described
by E. Runions, *Changing Subjects: Gender, Nation and Future in Micah* (Playing the
Texts, 7; Sheffield: Sheffield Academic Press, 2001) 178:

> The reference to *your* going out from Egypt would seem to indicate a switch
> from addressing a ruler [v. 14] to addressing the people as a whole, though this
> does not account for the odd 3 ms *him* [v. 15]. The I would seem to be Yahweh,
> since Yahweh is usually associated with the exodus and with showing wonders
> (her italics).

Runion reads 3ms suff. of אַרְאֶנּוּ in v. 15: "I will show him", but also refers to many
other suggestions. She comments that "the historical tradition of exodus acts as proof,
it would seem, that waiting is the (historically defined) appropriate position of the
nation" when presented in a female figure, as opposed to a male. This is related to
Runion's overall focus in her reading of the Book of Micah: "female nation needing
to be rescued by male deity or ruler" or "horrifying independent woman-cities and
glorious past of male leading and rule" (pp. 196–197).

[67] For an overview of the changes in speaking voices in Mic. 7 and scholars' different identifications of them, see Runions, *Changing Subjects*, pp. 173–180.

of YHWH" (v. 9). The mocking enemies shall see not "my" shame, but their own: they will become like the mire of the street (v. 10).[68] The fate of the person is exchanged with the fate of a city, whose walls shall be rebuild and borders enlarged, and into whom people shall stream from east and west, north and south – all after the land has been laid desolate due to the actions of the inhabitants (vv. 11–13).[69] The now triumphant nations shall be utterly subjected to YHWH. In his rage, the deity has punished due to "my" sins, with expectations of a bright future to come. What the enemies have done to Israel, Israel will do to them. By the peoples' gestures, they shall react to their own despair – and Israel's hope. In Mic. 7, a characteristic shift in person appears between "I" (vv. 1; 7–10), "you" (2 ms, vv. 4–5; 11–12; 14–15) and "they" (v. 13). A personification might be seen in the exchange between the fate of a person (vv. 1; 7–10) and the fate of a city, which was desolate and shall be rebuilt (vv. 11–13).[70]

We might make sense of Isa. 52:14–15 and Mic. 7 through an interplay between them. In Isa. 52:14 רַבִּים "many"'s reactions to "you"/"him" in the past are contrasted with the fates and fortunes of גּוֹיִם רַבִּים "many peoples" and מְלָכִים "kings" (v. 15), going from רַבִּים "many" being appalled to מְלָכִים "kings" shutting their mouth, and to "their" seeing the untold and understanding the unheard. In 52:14, the appalled response of רַבִּים "many" is due to "his" מַרְאֵהוּ "disfigurement". In Mic. 7:16–17, coming times of trembling and fear for the nations are related to YHWH's mighty acts of salvation for

---

[68] Runions, *Changing Subjects*, p. 177, claims that the fs suff. in the enemies' address may indicate that a female figure has been speaking "all along".

[69] 7:11 has 2fs suff., v. 12 2ms, and v. 13 3fs and 3mpl.

[70] The Book of Micah is often taken to be composite of materials from an eighth-century prophet with redactional additions up to post-Exilic times. A more recent trend is to read the book as a coherent whole, either historically or literarily. For an overview, see M. R. Jacobs, "Bridging the Times: Trends in Micah Studies since 1985", *CBR* 4 (2006) 293–329. Hillers, *Micah*, pp. 4–8, compares the prophet's situation and his reaction to it to movements of revitalisation in Micah's Judah and the political and economical disruption caused by the fall of Samaria and the Assyrian pressure. F. I. Anderson and D. N. Freedman, *Micah: A New Translation with Introduction and Commentary* (AB, 24E; New York: Doubleday, 2000) 16–17; 21–22, focus on the present text of the Book of Micah and support the traditional threefold division of the book into chaps. 1–3 (doom), 4–5 (hope) and 6–7 (doom and hope). Runions, *Changing Subjects*, p. 23, takes MT as it stands, without "presum[ing] the text to be unitary, knowable and 'fixable' with the 'right interpretive key'". She is inspired by Althusserian ideology criticism and Bhabha's post-colonial cultural (and psycho-analytical) criticism in her reading. Runions especially focuses on issues of justice and oppression and the visions of the future in the Book of Micah.

Israel. This is in contrast to the past: a corrupt society (vv. 1–6), which might change (vv. 7–10), just as the fallen "I" will rise (vv. 8–9) and the mocking enemies shall see their own shame (v. 10). Mic. 7:16 follows words about the restoration and expansion of Zion, where the nations shall come from all the ends of the earth. The nations' reactions are explicitly to do with shame (v. 10), as their silence is a sign of humiliation. The fate of the person is exchanged with the fate of a city, which was desolate and shall be rebuilt (vv. 11–13). In Isa. 52:14–15, no explanation is offered for the change of fates, in Mic. 7:9 the "I" confesses his/her own sins and accepts that זַעַף יְהוָה אֶשָּׂא "I will carry the rage of YHWH".

5.8.4. Ps. 22:7–9; 13–14

22:7 וְאָנֹכִי תוֹלַעַת וְלֹא־אִישׁ חֶרְפַּת אָדָם וּבְזוּי עָם:
⁸ כָּל־רֹאַי יַלְעִגוּ לִי יַפְטִירוּ בְשָׂפָה יָנִיעוּ רֹאשׁ:
⁹ גֹּל אֶל־יְהוָה יְפַלְּטֵהוּ יַצִּילֵהוּ כִּי חָפֵץ בּוֹ:
¹³ סְבָבוּנִי פָּרִים רַבִּים אַבִּירֵי בָשָׁן כִּתְּרוּנִי
¹⁴ פָּצוּ עָלַי פִּיהֶם אַרְיֵה טֹרֵף וְשֹׁאֵג

22:7: But I am a worm and not a man, scorned of men and despised of people.
22:8: All who see me mock at me, they gape at me, they shake their heads.
22:9: "He trusted in YHWH, let him deliver him; let him rescue him, if he cares for him"....
22:13: Many bulls surround me; strong bulls of Basan encircle me;
22:14: they open their mouths against me, like a ravening and roaring lion.

In Ps. 22:7, a speaking "I" complains that he is treated like a worm[71] and spurned as if less than human; scorned by men and despised by people.[72] Those around him mock at him and his trust in his deity with derisory words, claiming that YHWH might have forsaken him (vv. 8–9, cf. his trust in vv. 10–11). Through gestures, they show their reactions to his miserable condition, gaping at him and shaking their heads. The enemies are further depicted as פָּרִים רַבִּים "many bulls" and אַבִּירֵי בָשָׁן "bulls of Basan", who open their mouths against him like אַרְיֵה טֹרֵף וְשֹׁאֵג "a ravening and roaring lion" (vv. 13–14). Later,

---

[71] תוֹלֵעָה: "worm", see Isa. 14:11 (cf. 5.14.4.), 41:14 (Jacob), 66:24 (related to death), Job 25:6 (man as maggot and worm).
[72] Ps. 22 is also treated in 5.11.12.

the "I" is surrounded by כְּלָבִים "dogs" and עֲדַת מְרֵעִים "a company of evils", who stare and gloat over him (vv. 17–18).[73]

Ps. 22 alternates between lament (vv. 1–3; 7–10; 13–19), prayer (vv. 12; 20–22), and praise and thanksgiving (vv. 4–6; 9–11; 23–32). In vv. 2–3, invocation and complaint are expressed by three appeals to God, אֵלִי "my God" (twice in v. 2) and אֱלֹהַי "my God" (v. 3), followed by accusations of forsakenness, and a description of "my" own toil to establish contact with "my" God (v. 3). In vv. 4–6 an affirmation of confidence is offered in an allusion to "our fathers"'s trust and YHWH's past response of delivery. The deity delivered the fathers whenever they put their trust in him and they were never put to shame (vv. 5–6) – in contrast to how the "I" is treated by his neighbours (vv. 7–9). A complaint about his present state is followed by yet another expression of trust in his God (vv. 10–11, cf. v. 2), and prayer for contact with and help from YHWH (v. 12). After the complaint about bodily conditions and his treatment by neighbours (vv. 13–19), he prays for a response from YHWH (v. 20, cf. v. 12) and deliverance from enemies (vv. 21–22). The prayer ends with an expression of trust: "You answer me!" (v. 22), where the "I" insists on a future! Then the "I" turns to thanksgiving, addressed to YHWH (v. 23) and to a collective (vv. 24–27). Due to the assurance of God's response, he will praise the deity in the congregation, and invites them to do the same (v. 24). Then a total reversal of "my" situation is expressed: YHWH did not despised or abhor the affliction of the afflicted, nor did he hide himself (v. 25). The deity listened to "my" crying (v. 25), although "my" complaint concerned how "I" was forsaken by "my" God (vv. 2–3; 12) and despised by human beings (vv. 7–9), with the "I" begging to be neither abandoned nor forsaken (vv. 2; 12), but helped (v. 20).

The despair of the speaking "I" is related to his forsaking by God, with both his fellow human beings and the animals reacting with scorn and taunting his miserable conditions: those who see him gape and shake their heads, and wild animals attack him with mouths wide-open. A contradiction appears in the relation between his experience of having been dependent upon God from birth (vv. 10–11) and his

---

[73] Berlin, *Lamentations*, p. 74, comments that "opening the mouth" is a gesture of scorn or insult, "like sticking out the tongue", and that in Ps. 22:14 "this gesture is modeled on animal behaviour". The "I" is further threatened by יַד־כֶּלֶב "the power of the dog", פִּי אַרְיֵה "the mouth of the lion" and קַרְנֵי רֵמִים "the horn of the wild oxen" (vv. 21–22).

desperate search for help. In his struggle for help, he tries different explanations, addressed to YHWH, to himself and to his enemies.[74] His problem is that he is forsaken by YHWH (vv. 2–6) and by mankind (vv. 7–9; 13–14; 17–19); his solution is to beg for God to be close (v. 12) – and also for the fellowship (v. 27).[75]

The turning point from v. 23 onwards is expressed as a vindication of the humiliated one and also collectively for Israel (vv. 23–27; 30–32) as well as as words to the nations (vv. 28–29). After the "I"'s depiction of his forsakenness as scorned and treated as less than human (vv. 1–22) and the turn to thanksgiving (vv. 23; 24–27), vv. 28–32 take both a collective and a cosmic perspective: the whole earth and all people shall turn to and worship the Lord, and the whole congregation shall join in the praise. The deity might be regarded as responsible for both the suffering and the deliverance[76] (in both death and life, and as regards descendants, cf. vv. 30–31), but no causality is expressed.

---

[74] H. Gunkel, *Die Psalmen übersetzt und erklärt* (Göttingen: Vandenhoeck & Ruprecht, 1929), the "founder" of the form-critical approach, argued for the necessity of genre recognition in the psalms. More than ninety of the 150 psalms in the Hebrew Bible have been regarded as "individual psalms of lament". On the history of research into Psalms, see J. Day, *Psalms* (OTG; Sheffield: JSOT Press, 1990), J. K. Kuntz, "Engaging the Psalms: Gains and Trends in Recent Research", *CRBS* 2 (1994) 77–106 and J. L. Mays, "Past, Present, and Prospect in Psalm Study" in J. L. Mays, D. L. Petersen and K. H. Richards (eds), *Old Testament Interpretation. Past, Present and Future: Essays in Honour of Gene M. Tucker* (Old Testament Studies; Edinburgh: T. & T. Clark, 1995) 147–156. J. Eaton, *The Psalms: A Historical and Spiritual Commentary with an Introduction and New Translation* (London: T. & T. Clark, 2005), also considers the history of reception of the psalms.

[75] A debate concerns the identification of the "I" in the individual psalms of lament, and different suggestions have been offered: "I" as an individual depicting his own experiences of humiliation (E. Balla), a personification of the nation (R. Smend) and the king, as a representative of the people (H. Birkeland). Birkeland is, among others, supported by J. H. Eaton, *Kingship and the Psalms* (Biblical Seminar, 3; Sheffield: JSOT Press, 1986), who treats the role of the king in the ritual for an autumn and New Year Festival. S. J. L. Croft, *The Identity of the Individual in the Psalms* (JSOTSup, 44; Sheffield: JSOT Press, 1987), proposes a similar theory.

Closely connected to the identification of the "I" is the question of who "his" enemies are. Here too, many suggestions are offered: the enemies as "the wicked", as the king's internal enemies or as the foreign nations – often based on "historical reconstructions", see G. T. Sheppard, "'Enemies' and the Politics of Prayer in the Book of Psalms" in D. Jobling, P. L. Day and G. T. Sheppard (eds), *The Bible and the Politics of Exegesis* (Cleveland: Pilgrim Press, 1991) 61–82, and Croft, pp. 15–48.

[76] Connections between Isa. 40–55 and the Psalms, especially related to salvation oracles of individual psalms of lament, have been widely discussed. A characteristic feature of such oracles is a turning point from lament and humiliation to thanksgiving and vindication when YHWH returns to the lamenting one. J. Begrich, "Das priesterliche Heilsorakel", *ZAW* 11 (1934) 81–92, explains Isa. 41:8–13; 14–16, 43:1–3,

In Ps. 22, the despair of the speaking "I" is related to his forsaking by God, to which both his fellow human beings and the animals have reacted with scorn and taunting. Within a stereotypical language, a dynamic appears between "my" fate and the fate the community. Both the "I", who suffered, and the larger community praise God for answered prayers. The relation between the "I" and the community is not like the personifications treated earlier, nor is it a historical biography; rather, it is a figure of identification.[77]

Unlike in Isa. 52:14–15, the neighbours' gestures in Ps. 22 are related to the "I"'s humiliation in the past: "they" mock at "me", gape and shake their heads. In 52:14 רַבִּים "many" were appalled at "you"

48:17–19, 49:7; 15–16, 51:7–8, 54:4–8 as salvation oracles, with a cultic *Sitz im Leben*. Begrich, *Studien zu Deuterojesaja*, p. 97, claims that the salvation oracles of Isa. 40–55 were not expressed in a cultic situation, but that they were poetic imitations of real priestly oracles. This regards first and foremost liturgies for individual psalms of lament. This is supported by Y. Gitay, "Deutero-Isaiah: Oral or Written?", *JBL* 99 (1980) 185–197, who emphasises the rhetorical character of the various literary forms as they are present for us as text. H. E. von Waldow, "The Message of Deutero-Isaiah", *Int* 22 (1968) 259–287, claims that in the relation between the prophetic literature and the psalms one might talk of imitation of basic structures, but stresses that both concern real cultic oracles in collective liturgies. With regard to discussions of the unity of the book or tradition of Isaiah, Eaton, "The Isaiah Tradition", pp. 58–76, for example, claims that the Isaianic texts originate with the cultic prophets of the Jerusalem temple, while E. W. Conrad, "The 'Fear not' Oracles in Second Isaiah", *VT* 34 (1984) 129–152, regards the salvation oracles in Second Isaiah as not originating in an ordinary individual lament, but in a war context. On the basis of formal and structural criteria, as well as criteria regarding content, C. Westermann, "Das Heilswort bei Deuterojesaja", *ET* 24 (1964) 355–373 and C. Westermann, *Sprache und Struktur der Prophetie Deuterojesajas* (Calwer theologische Monographien, A. 11; Stuttgart: Calwer Verlag, 1981) 117–124, distinguish between *Heilsorakel* in connection with individual laments and *Heilsankündigung* for collective laments. Von Waldow rejects Westermann's distinction between individual and collective lament, arguing that in many texts in Isa. 40–55, the prophet is speaking "individually" about Israel. For an overview of the history of research, see Schoors, *I am God your Saviour*, pp. 32–46, M. A. Sweeney, *Isaiah 1–39 with an Introduction to Prophetic Literature* (FOTL, 16; Grand Rapids: Eerdmans, 1996) 25–26 and Willey, *Remember the Former Things*, pp. 16–28.

[77] E. M. Menn, "No Ordinary Lament: Relecture and the Identity of the Distressed in Psalm 22", *HTR* 93 (2000) 301–341, focuses "on the shifting identity of the 'I' of Psalm 22 and its relation with the larger community…from its origins as a liturgical expression of an ordinary individual's suffering and restoration within the small group rites" to its role in versions where the "I" is identified as David, in Midrash Tehillim as Esther and in the New Testament as Jesus (p. 303). She points to the potential for complex relationship between the "I" of Ps. 22 in new contexts, as the fate of the individual is linked to the fate of the community (p. 341). P. C. Craigie, *Psalms 1–50* (WBC, 19; Waco, TX: World Books, 1983) 202, claims that "[t]hough the psalm is not messianic in its original sense or setting…, it may be interpreted from a NT perspective as a messianic psalm par excellence".

in the past; through gesture, "kings" shall show their reactions to a coming event in v. 15. The fates and fortunes are turned around from רַבִּים "many" being appalled to מְלָכִים "kings" shutting their mouth, but also to "their" seeing the untold and understanding the unheard (v. 15). In Ps. 22 the deity might be regarded as responsible for both the suffering and the deliverance, but as in Isa. 52:13–15, no explanation is given for the turning point from past to future.

5.8.5. *Excursus: Universalism and Particularism*

The relationship between Israel and the peoples has been greatly debated within Second Isaiah research. Words concerning foreign nations are numerous in Isa. 40–55.[78] Discussions have revolved around, among other things, the relation between universalism and particularism, and have been especially related to expressions such as מִשְׁפָּט לַגּוֹיִם "justice to the peoples" (Isa. 42:1), לְאוֹר גּוֹיִם "light to the peoples" (42:6, 49:6, 51:4) and לִבְרִית עָם "covenant for the people" (42:6, 49:8). The majority of commentators follow a traditional Christian interpretation, regarding Israel as a missionary to the nations, with the nations being given full participation in YHWH's salvation of Israel.[79] Others give a particularistic interpretation,[80] while some go

---

[78] See גּוֹיִם "peoples", which in Isa. 40–55 is a designation for those who are not called by the name of Israel, in 40:15; 17, 41:2, 42:1; 6, 43:9, 45:1; 20, 49:6; 7; 22, 52:10; 15, 54:3, 55:5. Further, pl. עַמִּים occur as a designation of the nations in 49:22, as a parallel to גּוֹיִם, as a contrast to עַם in 51:4–5. In 42:5, the meaning might be less specific: "Thus says God, YHWH, who created the heavens and stretched them out, who spread out the earth and what comes from it, who gives breath to עַם 'the people' upon it and spirit to those who walk in it...", cf. 40:7 and "daughter of Babylon". See also kings in 41:2–3; 21; 29, 43:15, 44:6, 45:1, 49:7; 22–23, 52:15, idol makers in 4.7. n. 46 and rulers in 4.7. n. 48.

[79] Cf. e.g. Hertzberg, "Die 'Abtrünningen' und die 'Vielen'", J. Blenkinsopp, "Second Isaiah-Prophet of Universalism", *JSOT* 41 (1988) 83–103, Hermisson, "Einheit und Komplexität Deuterojesajas", p. 141, O. H. Steck, "Der Gottesknecht als 'Bund' und 'Licht': Beobachtungen im Zweiten Jesaja", *ZTK* 90 (1993) 117–134, Melugin, "Israel and the Nations in Isa. 40–55".

[80] Cf. H. M. Orlinsky, "Nationalism – Universalism and Internationalism in Ancient Israel" and "'A Covenant of People, A Light of Nations' – a Problem in Biblical Theology" in H. M. Orlinsky, *Essays in Biblical Culture and Bible Translation* (New York: Ktav, 1974) 78–116; 166–186, Whybray, *Isaiah 40–66*, pp. 31–32, H. M. Barstad, *A Way in the Wilderness: The "Second Exodus" in the Message of Second Isaiah* (Journal of Semitic Studies. Monograph Series, 12; Manchester: Manchester University Press, 1989) 22, n. 53.

for a middle position.[81] This relates to a discussion regarding the construction of collective identities in terms of ethnicity, nationality, religion, gender, etc, where identities are shaped in relation to "significant others". The inadequacy of the terms universalism and particularism in relation to the Hebrew Bible has been greatly debated with regard, for instance, to suspected anachronism, critique of the terms' unifying character or the danger that one identity is framed at the expense of another.[82]

5.8.6. *Summing Up*

In Isa. 52:14–15, "many" were appalled because of his disfigurement in his past, whereas in the future "he" יַזֶּה ('will startle'?) many peoples before "him", kings shall shut their mouth and they shall see and understand what has neither been told nor heard before. "You" emerge in a personification like that in Isa. 49:7, where a confusion appears between Israel and the servant as to whose task it is to restore Israel. The personification does not have a single meaning, thereby establishing a gap between the personifier "he" and the personified "you". In 49:7 "he" was despised and abhorred, and served נֶפֶשׁ "human", גּוֹי "people" and מֹשְׁלִים "rulers", whereas מְלָכִים "kings" and שָׂרִים "princes" shall see, rise up and bow down because of YHWH and his elected one, cf. 52:(13)14–15, moving from "his"/"your" humiliations to "his" ("the servant"'s) vindication, as well as contrasting situations

---

[81] Cf. Hollenberg, "Nationalism and 'The Nations' in Isaiah 40–55", pp. 23–36, D. W. van Winkle, "The Relationship of the Nations to Yahweh and to Israel in Isaiah 40–55", *VT* 35 (1985) 446–458, G. I. Davies, "The Destiny of the Nations in the Book of Isaiah" in J. Vermeylen (ed), *The Book of Isaiah* (BETL, 81; Leuven: Leuven University Press, 1989) 93–120, A. Gelston, "Universalism in Second Isaiah", *JThS* 43 (1992) 377–398, and C. A. Franke, "Is DI 'PC': Does Israel have Most Favored Nation Status? Another Look at 'The Nations' in Deutero-Isaiah" (SBLSP, 38; Atlanta: Scholars Press, 1999) 272–291, claiming that Deutero-Isaiah is "'not concerned with consistency in detail'…especially with respect to the details of 'the nations'" (p. 298).

[82] For general critique of the topic, see M. Liverani, "Nationality and Political Identity", *ABD* 4 (1992) 1031–1037, D. L. Christensen, "Nations", *ABD* 4 (1992) 1037–1049, D. Mendels, *The Rise and Fall of Jewish Nationalism: Jewish and Christian Ethnicity in Ancient Palestine* (AB Reference Library; New York: Doubleday, 1992), M. G. Brett, "Nationalism and the Hebrew Bible" in J. W. Rogerson, M. Davies and M. D. Carroll (eds), *The Bible in Ethics: The Second Sheffield Colloquium* (JSOTSup, 207; Sheffield: Sheffield Academic Press, 1995) 136–163, M. G. Brett, "Interpreting Ethnicity: Method, Hermeneutics, Ethics" and J. D. Levenson, "The Universal Horizon of Biblical Particularism" in M. G. Brett (ed), *Ethnicity and the Bible* (Biblical Interpretation Series, 19; Leiden: E. J. Brill, 1996) 3–22; 143–169.

of "many", "many peoples", "princes" and "kings", who shall show their reactions to a coming event through gesture. In 49:7, no causality but YHWH: "because of YHWH who is faithful, Israel's Holy one, and he has chosen you."

As in Isa. 52:13–15, a contrast between past and future fates appears in Mic. 7:16–17: "Peoples shall see and be ashamed of all their strength, they shall put the hand on the mouth, their ears shall be deaf." In this the judgment of the nations/oppressors and the deliverance of the righteous are implied. YHWH's mighty acts of salvation for Israel in the future (vv. 7–11; 14–15) contrast with the past: a corrupt society (vv. 1–6), which might change (vv. 7–10), as the fallen "I" will rise (vv. 8–9) and the mocking enemies shall see their own shame (vv. 10; 16–17). The peoples shall react, through gestures, to their own despair – and Israel's hope. A personification might be seen in the exchange between the fate of a person (vv. 1; 7–10) and the fate of a city, which was desolate and shall be rebuilt (vv. 11–13). In Isa. 52:14–15, no explanation is offered for the turning point from past fates to future fates; in Mic. 7:9, the "I" admits his/her own sins and accepts carrying YHWH's rage, with expectations of a bright future to come.

In Ps. 22, the despair of the speaking "I" is related to his forsaking by God, to which both his fellow human beings and the animals have reacted with scorn and taunting. Through gestures, they show their reactions to "my" miserable conditions. Unlike the other texts presented in this chapter, the neighbours' gestures are related to the humiliation of the "I" in the past: "they" mock at "me", gape and shake their heads. Like in 52:14–15, in Ps. 22 a turning point appears in temporality, but no causality is expressed. In Ps. 22 the "I" in relation to the the community is not like the personification of Isa. 52:14–15, nor is it a historical biography; rather, it is a figure of identification.

Texts, like cultures, can be homogenised in ways that smooth over differences and authorise certain interpretations. Readers' identifications and theological positions might lead them to unify terms such as election, universalism and particularism, as well as stereotypes and narratives related to paradigmatic readings of humiliations and vindications, and turning points of past and future. Cumulative narratives and stereotypes might elevate an image to confirm or invalidate a great story. In this reading of Isa. 52:14–15, which takes gesture as its main focus, other texts are brought in as constituents of, for example, themes, tropes and displacements. Many identities and reversals of fates or fortunes are at play. The explanations for the turnaround of the actor's fates vary. In Isa. 52:14–15 no explanation is given for the turning point from past to future, in Isa. 49:7 it is explained as לְמַעַן יְהוָה "for the sake of YHWH", expanded by two attributes: the deity is נֶאֱמָן "faithful" and יִשְׂרָאֵל קְדֹשׁוֹ "Israel's Holy one". In Mic. 7:16–17, coming times of trembling and fear for the nations are related to YHWH's mighty acts of salvation for Israel. This is in contrast to the past: a corrupt society (vv. 1–6), which might change (vv. 7–10), just as the fallen "I" will rise (vv. 8–9) and the mocking enemies shall see their own shame (v. 10). In Ps. 22 the deity might be regarded as responsible for both the suffering and the deliverance, but as in Isa. 52:13–15, no explanation is given for the turning point from past to future.

5.9. "Who believes what we hear?"

5.9.1. Isa. 53:1

53:1 מִי הֶאֱמִין לִשְׁמֻעָתֵנוּ וּזְרוֹעַ יְהוָה עַל־מִי נִגְלָתָה:

53:1: Who believes what we hear? And the arm of YHWH – to whom is it revealed?

By "our" self-questioning, attention is drawn to appearance: שְׁמֻעָה "a message" and זְרוֹעַ יְהוָה "the arm of YHWH" which might be believed[83] or revealed.[84] "We" are questioning "our" own experiences. The questions reveal experiences of opposition to a transmitted message which is (not) believed and a revelation which is (not) acknowledged. In the question concerning זְרוֹעַ יְהוָה "the arm of YHWH", an attempt at contact with the deity is made. In "our" questions, surprise, insight and revelation, and inability, failure and refusal might all come into play.

The questions of 53:1 might be contrasted with the YHWH speech in Isa. 52:15. Whereas in 52:15 YHWH proclaims that "they", i.e. kings (and many peoples) have not been told, in 53:1 "we" assume that something has indeed been told. In 52:15 the deity does not state what

---

[83] Elsewhere in Isa. 40–55, "we" are speakers in 52:10 only. Apart from 1 Kgs 10:7 (par.), elsewhere שְׁמֻעָה "report", "tidings", "message" has negative connotations.

[84] גלה (ni.) "reveal", cf. the revelation of YHWH's glory for כָּל־בָּשָׂר "all flesh" in Isa. 40:5, זְרוֹעַ יְהוָה "arm (strength) of YHWH" in 40:10, 51:9 and his care for his people in 40:11. In 51:5 and 52:10, YHWH's justice and salvation are connected to his arms, which are revealed to the peoples.

"they" shall see; in 53:1 "we" ask "ourselves" whether "we" have seen the arm of YHWH revealed. In 52:15 the deity claims that "they" have not heard yet; in 53:1 "we" ask "ourselves" whether "we" can believe something which might have been heard. 52:14–15 is depicted from YHWH's point of view; in 53:1 "our" (lack of) perception is in focus. Within the clusters of (not) seeing, (not) perceiving and witnessing in 52:14–53:1, elements of transformation and reversal are included. "We" act as witnesses to "ourselves" who have (not yet) seen the testimony of YHWH; "they" have neither been told nor heard, yet "they" shall see and understand. The self-questioning points to a paradox: "we" neither hear nor see what "we" cannot be without to asking the questions. Whether the asking "we" (and "they") believe or see is left open. A personification emerges when the speaking "we" in 53:4 is related to "him", cf. the unstable relation between "you" and "him" in 52:14 (cf. 3.10.2., 4.8.1.3. and 4.8.2.2.).

The questions in 53:1 might also be related to a promise of "his" future in 53:11, stating: "After his travail he shall see". No further depiction of what "he" shall see is offered,[85] but it is framed within more promises for the future: "he shall be sated by his knowledge", "he" is identified as "the righteous one, my servant" and "he will cause the many to be righteous".[86]

5.9.2. *Isa. 42:23; 18–20*

42:23 מִי בָכֶם יַאֲזִין זֹאת יַקְשֵׁב וְיִשְׁמַע לְאָחוֹר:

> 42:23: Who among you will listen to this, who will attend and hear for the time to come?

By the elliptical interrogative מִי "who" in Isa. 42:23, three questions of hearing are introduced: who will listen, attend and hear?[87] The questions are addressed to "you" (2mpl) and might work as an appeal or admonition. The object of the questions is זֹאת "this". By the phrase לְאָחוֹר "for the time to come", the questions' significance for the future is expressed, in contrast to the past/present of the people as robbed, bounded and a prey without deliverer (v. 22). The questions in v. 23

---

[85] Cf. 3.10.14. incl. n. 137.
[86] Cf. 3.10.14. and Appendice 4 and 7.
[87] In Isa. 1–66, אזן (hi.) "listen" and קשׁב (hi.) "attend" often appear in admonitions of Israel, other peoples or heaven and earth, either together or more commonly with שׁמע "hear", e.g. Isa. 8:9, 28:23, 32:9, 51:4.

are surrounded by utterances about (a lack of) hearing and seeing. In vv. 18–20, deafness and blindness are described:

42:18 הַחֵרְשִׁים שְׁמָעוּ וְהַעִוְרִים הַבִּיטוּ לִרְאוֹת:
¹⁹ מִי עִוֵּר כִּי אִם־עַבְדִּי וְחֵרֵשׁ כְּמַלְאָכִי אֶשְׁלָח
מִי עִוֵּר כִּמְשֻׁלָּם וְעִוֵּר כְּעֶבֶד יְהוָה:
²⁰ רָאִיתָ רַבּוֹת וְלֹא תִשְׁמֹר פָּקוֹחַ אָזְנַיִם וְלֹא יִשְׁמָע:

42:18:   You that are deaf, listen, and you that are blind, look up and see!

42:19:   Who is blind but my servant, and deaf like my messenger whom I send?
Who is blind like the dedicated one (?) and blind like the servant of YHWH?

42:20:   You see many things, but do not observe (them), his ears are open, but he does not hear.

In 42:18, a paradoxical address is made as הַחֵרְשִׁים (pl) "the deaf" and הַעִוְרִים (pl) "the blind" are admonished to listen and see. No objects are mentioned.[88] This accusation and appeal concerns (in)comprehension. This is followed by four questions concerning blindness and deafness, conveyed in two couplets both introduced by the elliptical interrogative מִי "who" (v. 19). In the first couplet, עִוֵּר (sg) "blind" and חֵרֵשׁ (sg) "deaf" are related to עַבְדִּי "my servant" and מַלְאָכִי אֶשְׁלָח "my messenger whom I send",[89] and the speaking voice is identified as "I". In the next couplet of questions, עִוֵּר "blind" is repeated twice (in sg), and linked to מְשֻׁלָּם "the dedicated" (?)[90] and to עֶבֶד יְהוָה "the servant of YHWH". Whereas the first question reveals one situation by refuting another ("Who is blind but my servant?"), the other three are conveyed in comparisons, with the deaf likened to "my messenger"

---

[88] GKC §126 e.f. explains the expression בוט (imp. hi.) "look up" and ראה (inf. cstr.) "see" as inf. of purpose: "look so as to see". For transformations from being חֵרֵשׁ "deaf" to hearing and from being עִוֵּר "blind" to seeing, cf. Isa. 29:18, 35:5, 42:7, 43:8 (cf. 5.9.3.).

[89] Waltke and O'Connor, An Introduction to Biblical Hebrew Syntax, §39.3.5.d, explain the construction כִּי אִם "but" as having a restrictive force in the question, requiring a negative answer. For מַלְאָךְ "messenger", see Isa. 44:26 (pl., par. with עַבְדּוֹ "his servant"). Cf. מְבַשֵּׂר "messenger" in 52:7, the servant's mouth (49:2, 51:16), tongue (50:4) and voice (50:10), and the messengers in 48:20.

[90] מְשֻׁלָּם occurs as a proper name in 1 Chron. 3:19. In Isa. 42:19, it has been taken as משל I ("compare"), משל II ("rule", cf. LXX, which would be מושלהם "their rulers"), שלם (pt. pi./pu. "to compensate", "be in covenant with"; denominative "dedicated", cf. Arab. muslim, or hi./ho. "complete") or emended to מְשַׁלְחִי ("the one sent by me"), see Koole, Isaiah III. Vol. 1, pp. 268–269, and Oswalt, The Book of Isaiah: Chapters 40–66, p. 128 n. 59.

and the blind to "the dedicated one" and to "the servant of YHWH". עַבְדִּי "my servant" in the first question is chiastically related to עֶבֶד יְהוָה "the servant of YHWH" in the last one; the opposite part of the chiasm is מַלְאָכִי "my messenger" and מְשֻׁלָּם "the dedicated" (?). In v. 19, חֵרֵשׁ (noun, sg) "deaf" appears once and עִוֵּר (noun, sg) "blind" three times. עִוֵּר "blind" and חֵרֵשׁ "deaf" in the first line are chiastically related to v. 18 (there in pl). As in v. 18, these questions also convey paradoxes: עַבְדִּי "my servant", מְשֻׁלָּם "the dedicated" (?) and עֶבֶד יְהוָה "the servant of YHWH" are blind, and מַלְאָכִי אֶשְׁלָח "the messenger whom I send" is deaf, but their task is related to hearing and seeing. Because of their imperception they are incompetent, but are nonetheless referred to as "servant" and "dedicated".

In 42:20, "you" (2ms) are addressed in terms of seeing, followed by expressions about "his" hearing. The object of "your" seeing is רַבּוֹת "many things", followed by a negation: וְלֹא תִשְׁמֹר "but you do not observe".[91] Adjacent to this are expressions about "his" hearing and its negation: "his" ears are open, but "he" does not hear.[92] V. 20 appears to be a complaint about blindness and deafness, not in terms of a lack of senses, but in terms of imperception. V. 20 is chiastically related to v. 18. In v. 18 the deaf are admonished to listen and the blind to see; in v. 20 "you" that see do not observe, and "he" that has open ears does not hear. In an appeal to their own experiences, their failure to grasp the significance of events is expressed.

In 42:21, YHWH's will for צִדְקוֹ "his righteousness" and תּוֹרָה "instruction" is expressed. V. 22 concerns the people's past or present desperate situation involving their being plundered, despoiled and imprisoned, followed by an admonition to "you" (2mpl) in v. 23 to listen, attend and hear in the future (quoted above). The appeal is reminiscent of that raised in v. 18 in which the addressee is described as deaf and blind, but is nonetheless admonished to listen and see. In vv. 24–25, the people's present situation is explained by questions and answers within a blurring of addresser and addressee: YHWH has delivered Jacob and Israel to robbers and plunderers because "we"

---

[91] K and 1QIsaᵃ read רָאִיתָ perf. qal 2ms, while Q suggests רָאוֹת inf. abs. (see GKC §75m and Joüon and Muraoka, *A Grammar of Biblical Hebrew*, §79p) followed by תִשְׁמֹר imperf. qal 2ms. ראה "see" (or not seeing), cf. Isa. 42:18–20, 49:7 (cf. 5.8.2.), 52:15 (cf. 5.8.1.), 53:11 (cf. 5.16.1.).

[92] For expressions for the people's lack of hearing, see 40:21; 28, 42:18–24, 48:8, 52:15 (cf. 5.8.1.).

have sinned, "they" have neither walked in his ways nor observed his instructions (v. 24) and "he"/"they" has/have not understood that "his"/"their" crisis is due to "your"/"their" transgressions, which have provoked YHWH's anger and punishment (v. 25).[93] YHWH wanted to preserve and vindicate Israel (v. 21) but was prevented from doing so by their sin and failure to observe instruction (v. 24), and so he brought disaster upon them (vv. 24–25).

In Isa. 42:18–20; 23, YHWH is the speaker; in vv. 21–22; 25, the voice is anonymous, and in v. 24 it belongs to "us".[94] As in Isa. 53:1, here too a personification emerges in a fluid relation between "you", "he", "servant", "dedicated" and "messenger" within a cluster of images of (not) seeing and hearing. In a variety of paradoxical utterances in vv. 18–25, the blind and deaf "you" is admonished to listen and see (2mpl, v. 18), the servant and dedicated one are blind (v. 19), the messenger is deaf (v. 19), "you" are (not) seeing (2ms, v. 20) and "he" is (not) hearing (v. 20). "His" and "their" lack of understanding in v. 25 echoes "our" lack of seeing and "his" lack of listening in v. 20 and contrasts with the appeal to listen in vv. 18; 23. V. 19 might be explained as a conditional hope for those who are able to listen. The deafness and blindness are not a matter of sense perception, but of incomprehension and obstinacy. Similarly, the listening and seeing concern a receptiveness to the divine revelation. Within the clusters of images of (not) seeing and (not) perceiving, elements of transformation and reversal are included: "he" (vv. 19; 24; 25), "you" (2ms, v. 20, and 2mpl, addressed in vv. 18; 23), "we" (v. 24) and "they" (3mpl, vv. 23; 24) act as witnesses to themselves who have not (yet) seen the testimony of YHWH. As in Isa. 53:1, the questioning points to a paradox in "our" (not) hearing or seeing what "we" cannot be without in order to ask the question. Carroll comments upon the ambiguity of the servant's blindness due to its intertextual links:

---

[93] For Isa. 42:24–25, see 5.12.2. In Isa. 42, variations of blindness and insight appear. The servant shall open blind eyes (v. 8) and YHWH himself will lead the blind (v. 16).

[94] L. J. de Regt, "Person Shift in Prophetic Texts: Its Function and its Reading in Ancient and Modern Translations" in de Moor, *The Elusive Prophet*, p. 227, gives the person shift a structuring role in reference to the same participants (Israel and Jerusalem): "[I]n 42:18–25 the people are addressed directly in vv. 18, 20, 23, referred to in first person in v. 24c (where the prophet identifies with the people), and in third person elsewhere in the passage."

The identification of the servant of YHWH as blind may be due to the intertextual nature of the construction of the Book of Isaiah (...), but it creates the striking image of the blind, deaf servant seeking to open blind eyes and bring prisoners from their darkness. Here blindsight is *le mot juste* for describing the servant vis-à-vis the community. Blindsight and the vision thing thematically encapsulate the servant's state, task and shortcomings.[95]

5.9.3. *Isa. 43:8–13*

הוֹצִיא עַם־עִוֵּר וְעֵינַיִם יֵשׁ וְחֵרְשִׁים וְאָזְנַיִם לָמוֹ: 43:8
כָּל־הַגּוֹיִם נִקְבְּצוּ יַחְדָּו וְיֵאָסְפוּ לְאֻמִּים[9]
מִי בָהֶם יַגִּיד זֹאת וְרִאשֹׁנוֹת יַשְׁמִיעֵנוּ
יִתְּנוּ עֵדֵיהֶם וְיִצְדָּקוּ וְיִשְׁמְעוּ וְיֹאמְרוּ אֱמֶת:
אַתֶּם עֵדַי נְאֻם־יְהוָה וְעַבְדִּי אֲשֶׁר בָּחָרְתִּי[10]
לְמַעַן תֵּדְעוּ וְתַאֲמִינוּ לִי וְתָבִינוּ כִּי־אֲנִי הוּא
לְפָנַי לֹא־נוֹצַר אֵל וְאַחֲרַי לֹא יִהְיֶה:
אָנֹכִי אָנֹכִי יְהוָה וְאֵין מִבַּלְעָדַי מוֹשִׁיעַ:[11]
אָנֹכִי הִגַּדְתִּי וְהוֹשַׁעְתִּי וְהִשְׁמַעְתִּי וְאֵין בָּכֶם זָר[12]
וְאַתֶּם עֵדַי נְאֻם־יְהוָה וַאֲנִי־אֵל:
גַּם־מִיּוֹם אֲנִי הוּא וְאֵין מִיָּדִי מַצִּיל אֶפְעַל וּמִי יְשִׁיבֶנָּה:[13]

43:8: Bring forth the people who are blind, yet have eyes, who are deaf, yet have ears!

43:9: Let all the nations gather together, and let the peoples assemble. Who among them declared this, and told us the former things? Let them bring their witnesses to justify them, and let them hear and say: "It is true."

43:10: You are my witnesses, says YHWH, and my servant whom I have chosen,
so that you may know, believe and understand that I am he.
Before me no God was formed, nor shall there be any after me.

43:11: I, I am YHWH, and besides me there is no saviour.

3:12: I declared, saved and proclaimed, when there was no strange God among you;
and you are my witnesses, says YHWH.

43:13: And also henceforth I am He;
there is no one who can deliver from my hand; I work, and who can hinder it?

---

[95] R. P. Carroll, "Blindsight and the Vision Thing: Blindness and Insight in the Book of Isaiah" in Broyles and Evans, *Writing and Reading the Scroll of Isaiah. Vol. 1*, 88, his italics. P. Stern, "The 'Blind Servant' Imagery of Deutero-Isaiah and Its Implications", *Bib* 75 (1994) 224–232, sees a progression from "blind servant" to "suffering servant" in Isa. 40–55. J. Goldingay, "Isaiah 42.18–25", *JSOT* 67 (1995) 64, explains the pericope's rhetorics as confronting an audience "and preparing it for the better news of 43.1–7".

In Isa. 43:8, הָעָם "the people" are called blind and deaf: nevertheless, they have eyes and ears.[96] Then הַגּוֹיִם "the nations" and לְאֻמִּים
"peoples" are brought to court and their deities' ability to foretell is
challenged (v. 9). The nations are also admonished to bring forth their
עֵדִים "witnesses" of truth (v. 9). YHWH presents his עֵדִים "witnesses"
(pl),[97] who are further depicted as his elected עֶבֶד "servant" (sg).[98] A
sort of personification emerges within this enunciative distancing in
the relation of עֵדַי "my witnesses"/עַבְדִּי "my servant": no unified, singular subject is indicated.

The testimony of YHWH's witnesses and servant is related to their
ability to see, hear, believe and understand who YHWH is (v. 10).
In this court hearing, YHWH is the only party who offers his arguments; his witnesses are silent and presented as acknowledging their
God. The deity continues his self-presentation as the one and only
saviour in past, present and future and describes his trustworthiness
as the one who fulfils what he promises, again appealing to his witnesses (vv. 12–13). His uniqueness is also expressed by utterances such
as אָנֹכִי אָנֹכִי יְהוָה "I, I am YHWH" (v. 11) and אֲנִי הוּא "I am He"
(v. 13). Prominent in the description of Israel are paradoxical statements about the blind and deaf people as witnesses to past and present
events (vv. 10; 12).[99] In contrast to the negative judgment of the invec-
tive of Isa. 42:18–25, the attitude to the people here is more positive.
As in Isa. 53:1, rhetorics of (not) seeing, hearing or believing in language of perception are key, as well as the trope of personification and
the role of testimony concerning the past and present (vv. 10; 12).

5.9.4. *Summing Up*

In "our" self-questioning in Isa. 53:1, שְׁמֻעָה "a message" and זְרוֹעַ יְהוָה
"the arm of YHWH" might be believed or seen. In Isa. 42, within the
clusters of images of (not) seeing and (not) perceiving, elements of
transformation and reversal are included: "he" (vv. 19; 24; 25), "you"
(2ms, v. 20), "you" (2mpl, vv. 18; 23), "we" (v. 24) and "they" (vv. 23–24)
act as witnesses to themselves who have not (yet) seen the testimony

---

[96] For a transformation from not hearing to hearing, see Isa. 48:6–7 and 5.9.2.
[97] עֵד "witness", cf. 43:9 (peoples'); 10 (pl, par. "servant"); 12 (pl); 44:8 (pl, vs idols
in v. 9), 55:4 (sg). Cf. Steck's depiction of the difference between the servant Israel and
the servant-prophet in 2.2.5.
[98] On election, cf. 5.8.2. n. 60.
[99] In 43:8, the apostate Israel is presented as a blind people.

of YHWH. In 43:8–13, the dispute is about prediction and Israel and the nations are gathered as witnesses. Prominent in the description of Israel are paradoxical statements about the blind and deaf people as witnesses to events past and present (vv. 10; 12). A personification emerges within this enunciative distancing in the relation of עֵדַי "my witnesses"/עַבְדִּי "my servant": no unified, singular subject is indicated.

The use of questions is part of the dialogical style which characterises Isa. 40–55. Other features are repetition, contrasts, intensifications, short sentences or long depictions, imperatives and contradictions.[100] In the texts treated in this chapter, blindness, seeing, deafness and hearing in personifications and the turning point of the people are key. Through motifs of insight (or lack thereof), surprise, understanding, disclosure, revelation, realisation, inability, failure and refusal, whether "he", "you", "we", "they" see or hear is left open.

5.10. "HE GREW UP LIKE A SHOOT…"

5.10.1. *Isa. 53:2*

52:2 וַיַּעַל כַּיּוֹנֵק לְפָנָיו וְכַשֹּׁרֶשׁ מֵאֶרֶץ צִיָּה
לֹא־תֹאַר לוֹ וְלֹא הָדָר וְנִרְאֵהוּ וְלֹא־מַרְאֶה וְנֶחְמְדֵהוּ:

53:2:   He grew up like a shoot before him and like a root out of dry ground;
there was no form to him and no splendour that we should look at him,
and no appearance that we should desire him.

In Isa. 53:2, a man's misery is depicted in "we" speech. In a double comparison, he is likened to יוֹנֵק "a shoot" and שֹׁרֶשׁ "a root". The

---

[100] On rhetorics and Isa. 40–55, see Y. Gitay, *Prophecy and Persuasion: A Study of Isaiah 40–48* (Forum Theologiae Linguisticae, 14; Bonn: Lingustica Biblica, 1981), Clifford, *Fair Spoken and Persuading*, Ceresko, "The Rhetorical Strategy of the Fourth Servant Song", J. K. Kuntz, "The Form, Location, and Function of Rhetorical Questions in Deutero-Isaiah" in Broyles and Evans, *Writing and Reading the Scroll of Isaiah. Vol. 1*, pp. 121–141, Bergey, "The Rhetorical Role of Reiteration in the Suffering Servant Poem", Barré, "Textual and Rhetorical-Critical Observations in the Last Servant Song".

On rhetorics and the Hebrew Bible in general, see W. Wuellner, "Where Is Rhetorical Criticism Taking Us?", *CBQ* 49 (1987) 448–463, and J. D. H. Amador, "Where Could Rhetorical Criticism (Still) Take Us", *CRBS* 7 (1999) 195–222.

predicate וַיַּעַל "he grew up" depicts his past, but also bears connotations of a promising future: associations of progeny, blossoming and prosperity draw attention to potential growth and hope. The comparisons are expanded by a personal confrontation; לְפָנָיו "before him". In אֶרֶץ צִיָּה "dry ground", a vegetable sphere is indicated. Similes of drought and desert bring associations of feeble and perishable plants prematurely stripped of vitality and visibility. The comparisons are modified by a double portrayal of his bodily appearance. This is followed by a judgment: due to his lack of form and dignity, "we" did not take any delight in him; he did not have an appearance to attract "us". While the similes call attention to a similarity between the seeming opposites of human and vegetable spheres, they do not identify what makes these similar, but instead convey oppositions of life and death, hope and hopelessness. By way of the interaction between a comparison and its explanation, the insignificant little plant hardly has any future. No reason for "our" disdain for him is given other than his appearance. "Our" testimony about him underlines his isolation from his surroundings.[101] A personification emerges through the interaction of 53:2 and v. 4. In the narrative reading, the actors of v. 4 are disclosed through a repetition of elements surrounding the figure(s) of "he"/"we", where the personifier "he" and the personified "we" are blurred (cf. 4.8.2.2).

---

[101] "Our" portrayal of "him" in 53:2 echoes YHWH's presentation of "him" in 52:14 (cf. 5.8.1.), as well as a depiction of the daughter of Zion who has no splendour in Lam. 1:6. שֹׁרֶשׁ (m) "root" and יוֹנֵק (m) "shoot" are not paralleled elsewhere. יוֹנֵק "shoot" in Isa. 53:2 is the only occurrence in a vegetable context, as it elsewhere appears as "suckling" or "infant" (cf. ינק "to suck" in Isa. 60:16, 66:11–12). For יוֹנֶקֶת in a vegetable context as "sucker", "shoot", see imagery in Ezek. 17:22, Hos. 14:7, Job 8:16, 14:7, 15:30, Ps. 80:12. In Isa. 53:2, the connection between the portrayal of "him" and the similes is strengthened as וַיַּעַל (vb.) "he grew up" is never used for human beings, but often for plants, e.g. Gen. 40:10, 41:22.

Messianic interpretations of the servant are supported by North, *The Suffering Servant in Deutero-Isaiah*, pp. 207–219, H. H. Rowley, *The Servant of the Lord and Other Essays on the Old Testament* (London: Lutterworth, 1952) 49–53, Nyberg, "Smärtornas man", pp. 63–83 and I. Engnell, "Till frågan om Ebed Jahve-sångarna och den lidande Messias hos 'Deutero-jesaja'", *SEÅ* 10 (1945) 53–62. Engnell sees a Tammuz-ideological context. A. Bentzen, *King and Messiah* (Oxford: Blackwell, 1970) 48–67, argues for a liturgy used at the New Year festival when the Israelite kings suffered ritual death and resurrection. This ritual pattern, which Bentzen found in Isa. 53, Psalms and Gen. 1, makes possible a link between the suffering royal Messiah of the Old Testament and the crucified and risen Messiah of the New Testament. He identifies the servant of the *EJL* as the prophet and as a heir of David (pp. 63–64).

5.10.2. *Hos. 9:16*

9:16 הֵכָּה אֶפְרַיִם שָׁרְשָׁם יָבֵשׁ פְּרִי בְלִי־יַעֲשׂוּן
גַּם כִּי יֵלֵדוּן וְהֵמַתִּי מַחֲמַדֵּי בִטְנָם:

> 9:16: Ephraim is stricken, their root has become dry, they shall no more
> make fruit.
> And even if they have children, I will let the darlings of their
> womb die.

In "I" speech, Ephraim is depicted as stricken through the metaphor
of a plant with withered roots.[102] The root is dry, incapable of bearing fruit.[103] This metaphor of barrenness is expanded and explained as
the fruit is interpreted as children: if Ephraim begets children, מַחֲמַדֵּי
בִטְנָם "the darlings of their womb" will die.[104] The speaking deity will
bring about the death of any children born. In נכה (ho.) "smitten",
"blighted", attention is drawn to both human and vegetable spheres,
to the treatment of both Ephraim and the root of a plant. The same
is the case with the barrenness, as the dry root and unfruitfulness
express both Ephraim's and the plant's misery. In the relation between
שֹׁרֶשׁ "root", פְּרִי "fruit" and יֵלֵדוּן "they have children", attention is
drawn to the (lack of) growth and progeny of plants and human
beings. The fruitlessness of Ephraim, depicted in the image of a barren

---

[102] See נכה (ho.) "smitten", "wounded" concerning persons in e.g. Isa. 1:5 (cf.
5.11.2.), 53:4 (cf. 5.11.1.) and a tree in Jonah 4:6, as well as "be blighted" concerning
grass in Ps. 102:5. A. A. Macintosh, *Hosea* (ICC; Edinburgh: T. & T. Clark, 1997) 378,
incl. n. a, comments on Hos. 9:16:

> Since the metaphor refers back to, and reverses the sense of, that in v. 13, the
> word blighted is chosen as appropriate to a tree... The passive verb "is blighted"
> corresponds to the passive participle in v. 13 "transplanted", and hence the form
> of the first half of the verse presents the opposite sense to the (unfulfilled) prom-
> ise of v. 13... Ephraim [אֶפְרַיִם] can be characterized as fruitless [פְּרִי בְלִי־יַעֲשׂוּן];
> the pun conveys the nation's fate and served to negate the traditional blessing of
> Ephraim formulated in Gen. 41.52, and of Joseph in 49.22ff.

Cf. יָבֵשׁ "dry" about people in Isa. 40:7–8, Jer. 12:4, Ezek. 17:9–10, 19:12, Pss. 90:6,
102:12, 129:6, Job 18:16 (cf. 5.10.3.).

[103] K has the adverbial of negation בְלִי, which rhymes with פְּרִי, whereas Q has the
adverbial בַּל "not".

[104] מַחֲמַדֵּי בִטְנָם "darlings", "precious things of their womb", cf. פְּרִי־בֶטֶן "fruit of
the womb" in Gen. 30:2, Deut. 28:4; 11; 18. For שֹׁרֶשׁ "root" and פְּרִי "fruit" in the
context of giving birth, see 2 Kgs 19:30/Isa. 37:31 (Judah) and Amos 2:9 (the Amorite),
cf. Eidevall, *Grapes in the Desert*, p. 155.

tree, represents the people's fate. This arboreal metaphor for the nation closely resembles the trope of personification.[105]

The fate of Ephraim is depicted within a YHWH speech about the people's past and future (vv. 10–17). The deity is remembering his first glimpse of "your fathers", comparing it with the pleasure of finding grapes in the desert and the first ripe fruit on a fig tree (v. 10). In these paradoxical similes of grapes in the desert, a wonder is described as "found and seen"; like her fathers, she is elected by YHWH. The people are addressed as "you" (2mpl). The wonderful past of "your" fathers in the wilderness is followed by their shamefulness in Baal-peor, where they became as detestable "as that which they love" (v. 10). YHWH continues lamenting over his people, but from v. 11 onwards the people are mentioned as "them" (3mpl). As a result of their apostasy, Ephraim's כָּבוֹד "glory" is said to fly away like a flock of birds; "from birth, from pregnancy, from conception" (v. 11). Ephraim will be stripped of glory, for even if someone gives birth to children, the deity will bereave them of אָדָם "men" (v. 12). Ephraim will suffer the same fate as צוֹר (Tyre?) who was planted in well-watered ground; Ephraim shall bring his children to slayers (v. 13).[106] The addresser admonishes the deity to mete out punishment by making the womb barren and the breasts dry (v. 14).[107] Due to their evil in Gilgal, YHWH hates

---

[105] Eidevall, *Grapes in the Desert*, p. 154:
  Generally speaking, tree metaphors used about nations resemble personification metaphors, since they stress that all individuals within the people form an "organic" entity, held together by a shared identity. However, unlike the personifying metaphors, tree images allow for some differentiation within its collective identity.

[106] צוֹר (followed by pt. pass. fem שְׁתוּלָה "planted") has been read as the city of Tyre, as a "palm-shoot" (m, based on Arab. cognates) and emended to צוּר "rock" (m). For an overview, cf. Eidevall, *Grapes in the Desert*, p. 153, and Macintosh, *Hosea*, p. 371 c.

[107] Macintosh, *Hosea*, p. 380 compares this prayer of the prophet with the "laments of Jeremiah", cf. 5.11.8. n. 165. Whereas J. L. Mays (1969) and H. W. Wolff (1974) read a dialogue between divine oracle and the prophet as a prayer for mercy, D. Krause, "A Blessing Cursed: The Prophet's Prayer for Barren Womb and Dry Breasts" in Fewell, *Reading Between Texts*, pp. 191–202, reads it as ironic and judgmental, as the prophet is praying: in v. 14, a threefold repetition of "give" appears, before the content of the request: barren womb and dry breasts. Krause describes this as "an intercession for divine judgment" (p. 195), where "the found ones are cast off, [t]he fruit is dried up, the blessing is a curse", vs blessing in Gen. 49:25 (p. 199), cf. Eidevall, *Grapes in the Desert*, p. 153 n. 46. Macintosh comments further on the prayer in v. 14: "Mention here of the 'miscarrying wombs' and 'shriveled breasts' may well represent a reversal of the traditional blessing of Joseph, the father of Ephraim, as expressed in Gen. 49.25, 'the blessings of the breast and of the womb'…" (p. 374).

them and no longer loves them (v. 15). In a variation on the previous image, any possibility of growth and progeny is denied (v. 16): just as a flourishing tree can be stricken, so there will be no birth – or if any born, YHWH will cause death (vv. 11–12; 16, cf. v. 14). While in v. 14 YHWH is addressed, in vv. 15–16 the deity speaks in "I" speech, and in v. 17 the speaker explains how אֱלֹהַי "my God" will respond to the people's inability to listen to YHWH. The deity shall reject his people, and they shall go wandering among the peoples (v. 17, cf. v. 14).

In Isa. 53:2, the comparison of a man to יוֹנֵק "a shoot" and שֹׁרֶשׁ "a root" draws attention to a blending of human and vegetable spheres. In the interaction between the comparison and its explanation, it is stated: the insignificant little plant has hardly any future. "We" do not desire him because of his unattractive appearance, but no reason is offered for his fate. In Hos. 9:16, the humiliation and punishment of Ephraim are expressed in the metaphor of a dry and barren plant which has no attractiveness, splendour or future. The grapes and fig tree of the רֵאשִׁית "beginning" (v. 10) are contrasted with stricken roots and barrenness. In the depiction of the future prospects of the nation as barrenness in Hos. 9, a close connection appears between human and vegetable spheres, as it is also told how the people will be punished with childlessness (vv. 11–12; 16) because of their apostasy and wickedness (vv. 10; 15).[108]

5.10.3. *Job 18:16*

18:16 מִתַּחַת שָׁרָשָׁיו יִבָשׁוּ וּמִמַּעַל יִמַּל קְצִירוֹ׃

18:16: Beneath his roots are dry and above his boughs wither

In Job 18:16, the wicked one is depicted as suffering destruction through the image of an all-devouring fire burning the roots of a tree:

---

[108] The Book of Hosea is related to the only one of the writing prophets who is regarded as being active in the northern kingdom. The book consists of mixed material from the eight century in northern Israel and later Judean reception, and is generally divided into three parts: chapters 1–3 (Hosea, his unfaithful wife and their children; break of covenant), 4–13 (Faithful God and Unfaithful Israel; idol-seeking), 14 (Restoration). The book is characterised by poetic language and use of images. The Hebrew text is corrupt in many places. Like research on the other prophetic books, readings of the Book of Hosea are also characterised by biographical, historical, psychological, editorial and literary interests. For an overview, see C. L. Seow, "Hosea, Book of", *ABD* 3 (1992) 291–297, and Macintosh, *Hosea*, pp. li–xcvii.

from above and below, his destruction is total.[109] This is closely related to v. 15, in which the homes of the wicked are destroyed by fire, and vv. 17–20, in which the descendants of the wicked shall be wiped out.

In this second speech of Bildad (that is, 18:1–21), Bildad claims that if Job and he are to continue talking together, Job has to stop his foolish speech (v. 2). Bildad feels that he and his friends have been insulted (v. 3). In spite of Job's words, the orders of the world will not be disrupted (v. 4). In vv. 5–21 the destruction that will come over the wicked one is depicted: his light shall be extinguished (vv. 5–6), he shall be caught (vv. 7–10), he will be overpowered by terror, hunger and disease (vv. 11–14), and both he and his descendants shall be totally wiped out (vv. 13–17). Bildad sums up thus: this is the fate of the wicked one who "does not know God" (v. 21). This might imply that Job is the wicked one or that he is encouraged to change his way of living.[110]

In v. 16, the fate of the wicked one is depicted in an image of the destruction of the roots and boughs of a tree.[111] This text does not mediate any kind of personification but depicts an individual's destruction in the image of a tree which will be annihilated.[112] As in Isa. 53:2, a close connection appears between the fates of plants and humans.[113]

---

[109] Cf. similar depiction of the wicked in Bildad's first speech (that is, in 8:8–19) in 8:12.

[110] D. J. A. Clines, *Job 1–20* (WBC, 17; Dallas: Word Books, 1989) 409; 412, argues that those "who think Bildad is describing Job and those who think he portrays the opposite to Job are both wrong". He offers an alternative interpretation: Bildad aims "to encourage Job to 'seek' God with a 'pure and upright' life" so that the laws of the universe remain unshaken. Whereas vv. 2–3 are addressed to "you" (2mpl), v. 3 is addressed to Job in sg.

[111] This might be contrasted with Job 14:7, where Job claims: "There is hope for a tree, if it be cut down, that it will sprout again." In this, human and vegetable qualities are also interwoven. In vv. 7–12, the hope of a tree and the hope of humankind for a life beyond death are contrasted.

[112] The Book of Job consists of a narrative framework, i.e. a prologue in chs. 1–2 (cf. 5.11.13. n. 195) and an epilogue in 42:7–17. In between is a poetic core, consisting of a blend of hymns, laments, wisdom sayings framed in dialogue (3–31), Elihu speeches (32–37) and divine speeches (38–42:6). Suggestions for dating are offered from 6th-3rd century BCE. For an overview of different approaches to the Book of Job (both traditional historical-critical, "stable" readings and more "literary" and "unstable" ones), see C. A. Newsom, "Considering Job", *CRBS* 1 (1993) 87–118.

[113] Miscall, "Isaiah: The Labyrinth of Images", p. 103, comments on how images in biblical studies are regarded as subordinate to meaning, and gives the example of K. Nielsen, *There is Hope for a Tree: The Tree as Metaphor in Isaiah* (JSOTSup, 65; Sheffield: JSOT Press, 1989), quoting from her study: "The tree metaphors in

5.10.4. *Summing Up*

In this chapter, the humiliating fates of nations and peoples like Israel (Isa. 53:1) and Ephraim (Hos. 9:16), or of individuals like Job or the wicked ones (Job 18:16), are depicted in images of plants whose catastrophe is complete, bereft of splendour, hope and future. The fates of the servant Israel, Ephraim, Job and the wicked ones are depicted in a blurring of human and vegetable spheres.

In the interaction between the comparison and its explanations, we see that the insignificant little plant of Isa. 53:2 has hardly any future. No reason for "our" disdain of the man compared with the plant is given other than his appearance. In Hos. 9:16, the humiliation and punishment of Ephraim are expressed in the metaphor of a dry, barren plant without attractiveness, splendour or future. The pleasant grapes and figs of the desert in "the beginning" (v. 10) are contrasted with stricken roots, barrenness and childlessness (vv. 11–12; 16) because of apostasy and wickedness (vv. 10; 15). In Job 18:16, the fate of the wicked one is depicted in an image of the destruction of the roots and boughs of a tree. This text does not mediate any kind of personification, but depicts an individual's destruction in the image of a tree which is annihilated.

Considering the Hebrew Bible as an intertext does not imply synthesising the messages of the books of which it is composed. It would imply establishing between them a network of similitudes, tensions, variations and transformations. It is the reader who establishes a relationship between a focused text and its intertext, where a fragment of discourse becomes accommodated or assimilated by the focused text. In this, one might find theological positions, related for instance to Davidic, Messianic or Christological interests.[114] The trees in this chapter are not to be regarded as subordinate to meaning, or, at least, they are open to more than one interpretation. They do not (only) have the informative function of acting as theological interpretations of the political situation.

Isaiah 1–39 have the informative function of acting as theological interpretations of the political situation" (Nielsen, p. 223).

[114] Cf. 5.10.1. n. 101.

5.11. "A MAN CAUGHT BY SICKNESSES..."

5.11.1. *Isa. 53:3–6*

53:3 נִבְזֶה וַחֲדַל אִישִׁים אִישׁ מַכְאֹבוֹת וִידוּעַ חֹלִי
וּכְמַסְתֵּר פָּנִים מִמֶּנּוּ נִבְזֶה וְלֹא חֲשַׁבְנֻהוּ:
⁴אָכֵן חֳלָיֵנוּ הוּא נָשָׂא וּמַכְאֹבֵינוּ סְבָלָם
וַאֲנַחְנוּ חֲשַׁבְנֻהוּ נָגוּעַ מֻכֵּה אֱלֹהִים וּמְעֻנֶּה:
⁵וְהוּא מְחֹלָל מִפְּשָׁעֵנוּ מְדֻכָּא מֵעֲוֹנֹתֵינוּ
מוּסַר שְׁלוֹמֵנוּ עָלָיו וּבַחֲבֻרָתוֹ נִרְפָּא־לָנוּ:
⁶כֻּלָּנוּ כַּצֹּאן תָּעִינוּ אִישׁ לְדַרְכּוֹ פָּנִינוּ
וַיהוָה הִפְגִּיעַ בּוֹ אֵת עֲוֹן כֻּלָּנוּ:

53:3: He was despised and abandoned by men; a man with sicknesses and known with illness,
and like one from whom men hide their faces; he was despised and we did not regard him.

53:4: Yet surely he bore our illnesses and carried our sicknesses,
whereas we accounted him stricken, smitten by God and humiliated.

53:5: But he was wounded because of our transgressions and injured because of our iniquities;
chastisement was upon him for our healing and by his wound is recovery for us.

53:6: All of us like sheep went astray; everyone turned his own way and thus YHWH struck him by the iniquity of all of us.

In Isa. 53:3, a man's fate is depicted: he is despised, abandoned and ill.[115] His neighbours turn away and disregard him.[116] A speaking "we" also takes offence at the sick and disgusting man. A turning point is expressed through echoes of v. 3 in v. 4 as "we" realise that his illnesses are "our" illnesses too.[117] In v. 3 his illness is related to how his neighbours have despised him, and the contrast between him and "them"/"us" is emphasised, while in v. 4 an identification appears between his and "our" illnesses. "Our" self-knowledge is expressed:

---

[115] For חָדַל "abandoned", see 3.10.6. n. 84. מַכְאֹבוֹת (fpl) "sicknesses" in Isa. 53:3 is unique. Elsewhere, מַכְאֹב "illness" occurs in ms/pl, e.g. מַכְאֹבֵינוּ "our sicknesses" in Isa. 53:4 and about individuals in distress in Ps. 38:18 (cf. 5.11.11. and 5.13.3.), Lam. 1:12; 18 (cf. 5.11.9.), Jer. 30:15 (cf. 5.11.7.) and כְּאֵב "pain" in Jer. 15:18 (cf. 5.11.8.), Ps. 39:3 (cf. 5.13.4.). וִידוּעַ חֹלִי "known with illness" in Isa. 53:3, see Appendix 4. חֳלִי "illness" occurs in mpl in Isa. 53:4 and 38:9 (cf. 5.11.11.). Cf. about people, land or city in Isa. 1:5 (cf. 5.11.2.), Jer. 6:7, 10:19 (cf. 5.11.5.), Hos. 5:13 (cf. 5.11.3.).

[116] כְּמַסְתֵּר פָּנִים, see Appendix 3.

[117] See נָשָׂא חֳלִי "carry illness" as an expression for "being ill" in Jer. 10:19 (cf. 5.11.5.). Cf. carry illness/sin in 3.10.7. n. 87 and 3.10.15. n. 154.

when he carried "our" illnesses, both he and "we" were ill. In v. 3 his illness and shame were related to the reactions of those around him, and in v. 4b "we" offer "our" previous explanation for his humiliations: "we" thought him stricken and humiliated by God. "Our" present explanation then follows: his wounds are explained as punishment by YHWH because of "our" sin (v. 5).[118] In the reflection on "our" own guilt, an awareness of having been chastised with a stroke by God is prompted by "our" own delusion and self-accusation on account of "our" failure to recognise him. By acknowledging that his sufferings are due to "our" sins, "we" simultaneously confess guilt. This is framed through an enunciative distancing telling that he is wounded and that "we" have committed sin. Thus, different aspects of illness appear: he is despised and isolated because of illnesses (v. 3), his illnesses are also "our" illnesses (v. 4) and they are brought upon him by God (v. 4b) due to "our" sins (vv. 5–6).

After the humiliations of the ill, despised and abhorred one are depicted, deepened and explained in variations (vv. 3–5a), his wounds are described as chastisement for rehabilitation (v. 5b). The relation between punishment and wounds on the one hand, and healing and recovery on the other,[119] expresses a turning point for both him and "us": after his – and "our" – sufferings, "we" shall recover. What began as "our" contemplation of his fate (v. 3) continues with a consideration of these same experiences as "our" own (from v. 4 onwards). However, this is not accompanied by "our" shame and grief. As regards the past, "we" are more concerned with his fate than with "our" own inclusion in the humiliations. When the text turns to rehabilitation, it is stated that "we" shall be healed and thus suffer no more, while his inclusion in the healing is not stated, but implied.

Then, in v. 8, נֶגַע לָמוֹ "his wound" is explained as a result of פֶּשַׁע עַמִּי "the transgression of my people". It is further related to his neighbours' treatment of him and his time's consideration of it: he was taken מֵעֹצֶר "by restraint" (?) and מִמִּשְׁפָּט "by execution" (?) and נִגְזַר מֵאֶרֶץ חַיִּים "cut off from the land of the living" (cf. v. 9), while his neighbours did not consider that his fate, including his wounds and death, was due to פֶּשַׁע עַמִּי "the transgression of my people". In v. 10, his wounds

---

[118] For sin terminology in Isa. 40–55, see 5.12., esp. 5.12.7. n. 236.

[119] שָׁלוֹם "healing", "completeness", "soundness", "welfare", "peace" is related to health in Isa. 38:17, Jer. 6:14, 8:11; 15, 14:19, 33:6, Ps. 38:4. On שָׁלוֹם, cf. 5.15.3. n. 291 and 5.15.5. n. 304.

are explained as due to YHWH's will, before his splendid future is predicted: he shall be blessed with children, live long and prosper.[120] In v. 12 his suffering death is mentioned once more, and also how he was reckoned with rebels. Again, variations of the previous explanations are presented, with the common fate of עַמִּי "my people" and him explained in terms of a relation between sins (of עַמִּי "my people" and פֹּשְׁעִים "transgressors"), נֶגַע לָמוֹ "his wound" and how יֻפָּגִיעַ "he was struck" (cf. Appendix 8).

In Isa. 53, bodily conditions of pain, illness and hurt appear in variations of humiliations: he was ill, despised, isolated, even dead. Like him, "we" were also ill. This is not only a matter of illness, as the wounds are also brought upon him (and "us") by others – as punishment. He was stricken with illness by God due to "our" sins. Thus, a cause/effect relation is expressed: illness is due to sin. Also, without further explanation a turning point towards healing is expressed. In the illness, a blurring appears between human beings' diagnoses ("he", and also "we") and a diagnosis of a collective people ("we", that is, Israel). The diagnosis consists of a blurring of bodily and theological concerns. The same applies to the explanation, as illness is due to transgression.

In a personification, the actors are disclosed through a pattern of elements surrounding the figure(s) of "he"/"we", with a blurring of the personifier "he" and the personified "we". The continuity and succession which were established by the figure "he" is destabilised when one set of assumptions about the relation between "him" and "us" is replaced by another, i.e. contrast (in the past) is replaced by identity (in the present). The story plays ironically on "our" earlier assumptions about him and his illnesses. After the testimony "we" gave about him, where "we" took offence at his illness and disgusting appearance (53:3), the diagnosis is repeated with a variation: suddenly, "we" are also deeply involved (v. 4a). This about-turn is to "us" seeing him as "us" instead of as a devastated, disfigured other. The personifier "he" and the personified "we" are blurred by different accentuations: the healing is gained for "us" by the punishment of him (v. 5b). The relation between him and "us" is dissymmetrically presented. Whereas the identification of him and "us" is disclosed in the common illness, the question of his guilt, as well as his healing, is in some ways left open.

---

[120] 53:10 is treated in 5.15.1. and Appendix 6.

5.11.2. *Isa. 1:5–6*

עַל מֶה תֻכּוּ עוֹד תּוֹסִיפוּ סָרָה 1:5
כָּל־רֹאשׁ לָחֳלִי וְכָל־לֵבָב דַּוָּי:
מִכַּף־רֶגֶל וְעַד־רֹאשׁ אֵין־בּוֹ מְתֹם ⁶
פֶּצַע וְחַבּוּרָה וּמַכָּה טְרִיָּה
לֹא־זֹרוּ וְלֹא חֻבָּשׁוּ וְלֹא רֻכְּכָה בַּשָּׁמֶן:

1:5: Why will you let yourselves still be stricken? Why do you increase your apostasy?
The whole head is sick and the whole heart faint.

1:6: From the sole of the foot to the head there is no soundness; wound, sores and fresh wound not cleaned or bandaged or softened with oil.

In Isa. 1:5 two accusatory questions are raised, both addressing "you" (2mpl).[121] The first question concerns the health of the ones interrogated. This is not only a matter of illness, as the wounds are also inflicted upon "you" by others. The second question explains the first, with the responsibility for "your" own fate placed on "you" and "your" continued apostasy. The questions of wound and apostasy might express a cause/effect relation: "your" illness is due to "your" apostasy, meaning that suffering would end with "your" ending "your" apostasy. As such, the questions act as an admonition to change "your" own situation. Simultaneously, wounds and apostasy might be mutually complementary, as "you" are accused of accepting being wounded and of turning aside: "Why will you still be smitten and also continue your apostasy?" The questions of delusion, seemingly accusatory, simultaneously force inconsistencies. The illness is brought upon "you" both by others and by "yourselves". Attempting to control "your" own fate would imply denial of others, but accepting others' ways would imply abandoning "your" own will. The two questions are followed by replies, expressing the basis for the question: the whole body is broken; its head and heart, from its head to its sole (vv. 5–6).[122] The desperation of the situation is deepened by the telling of the still-bleeding, untreated, unhealed wounds. The judgment is described as having already fallen and the bleeding wounds show that a cure is urgently needed. Desperation thus lies behind the questions and an implied admonition to make a change follows them.

---

[121] For the relation between Isa. 1–39 and 40–66 and the unity of the Book of Isaiah, see 2.3.2. and 5.11.2. n. 128.

[122] For חֳלִי "sick", see 5.11.1. nn. 115; 117.

The questions about "your" acceptance of being stricken, still, and "your" continued apostasy are preceded by accusations of the people in Isa. 1:2–3. YHWH admonishes שָׁמַיִם "heaven" and אֶרֶץ "earth" to listen and bear witness to his words. This is followed by a testimony about the community in the image of a family with YHWH as a parent who has taken care of his children, while they have rebelled (v. 2). This continues with a rather unflattering comparison: unlike the ox and the ass, YHWH's people do not know who takes care of them (v. 3).[123] Then follows a הוֹי "woe" oracle (v. 4), addressing the people as sinful with a catalogue of terms for sin: גּוֹי חֹטֵא "sinning nation", עַם כֶּבֶד עָוֹן "guilt-laden people", זֶרַע מְרֵעִים "evil descendent" and בָּנִים מַשְׁחִיתִים "corrupt children".[124] Nation and people, adults and children, have gone astray and are burdened with iniquity and guilt.[125] After this fourfold address, their delusion is depicted in their relation to YHWH, קְדוֹשׁ יִשְׂרָאֵל "Israel's Holy one", who has committed himself to them, but whom they have rejected.[126]

All the images combined emphasise the people's desperate situation. They are depicted as rebellious children, a wounded body, a besieged land and a desolate woman, whereas YHWH is a caring parent. However, the suffering might end if the people change their behaviour. Unsteady shifts in pronouns occur from "they" (3mpl, v. 4) in the woe oracle to "you" (2mpl, vv. 5–8) to "we" (1cpl, v. 9). As in Isa. 53, in 1:5–6 illness is presented as brought upon "you" both by others and by "yourselves" – in both cases related to delusion. While the relation between illness and sin is conveyed in confessional "we" speech in 53:4–6 and in YHWH speech in 53:8; 12, in 1:5–6 the diagnosis is made by YHWH whose questions might act as an admonition to change "your" own situation.[127] The desperate situation of the people

---

[123] For two slightly different readings of the parallelism in Isa. 1:3, see Kugel, *The Idea of Biblical Poetry*, pp. 9; 102, and Berlin, *The Dynamics of Biblical Parallelism*, pp. 97–98. Cf. S. Niditch, "The Composition of Isaiah 1", *Bib* 61 (1980) 509–529, on metaphors.

[124] De Regt, "Person Shift in Prophetic Texts", p. 225, describes what he designates rhetorics of entrapment in the changes from 3 mpl to 2 mpl references to Israel in Isa. 1: "As long as Israel is being denounced in third person in vv. 2–4, the listener might think that these verses refer to others, but in v. 5 he suddenly learns that he is being addressed himself."

[125] On sin terminology, see 5.12.7. n. 236.

[126] For the phrase קְדוֹשׁ יִשְׂרָאֵל "Israel's Holy one", see 5.8.2. n. 55.

[127] J. Blenkinsopp, *Isaiah 1–39: A New Translation with Introduction and Commentary* (AB, 19; New York: Doubleday, 2000), relates Isa. 1:5–6 and 53:

is presented in a personification of the community as a wounded body, with a blurring of an address to "you" (2mpl) and a depiction of a sick body.[128] The rhetorical questions are addressed to a plural addressee, but the description is that of a sick and wounded individual (family metaphor in vv. 2–4).[129]

> Both passages use some of the same terms for medical conditions and proce-
> dures, but the language is really not very close. Following targumic tradition
> Rashi understood this section as a metaphoric expression of the effect of sin
> on the entire people from the leadership (the head) to the least (the sole of the
> foot).

Cf. J. N. Oswalt, *The Book of Isaiah: Chapters 1–39* (NICOT; Grand Rapids: Eerdmans, 1986) 90 incl. n. 20:

> But how can Israel bear the sufferings which have come upon her because of
> her rebellion? Must they not finally crush her and destroy her? This question
> must have become particularly real to Isaiah as he recognized more and more
> how difficult repentance was for his people. In this light, the language of Isa. 53
> suddenly stands out. What are the sickness and pains which the Servant bears?
> They are those which have been occasioned by the rebellion of his people. Ch. 53
> shows a clear conceptual unity with ch. 1, even to the use of the same metaphors.
> It is not possible to say whether this unity is conscious or unconscious. But in
> either case, any reconstruction of the supposed history of the book which does
> not do full justice to this conceptual unity is failing to do justice to the data.

On illness in the Book of Isaiah, see the redaction-critical study Z. Kustár, *"Durch seine Wunden sind wir geheilt: Eine Untersuchung zur Metaphorik von Israels Krankheit und Heilung im Jesajabuch* (BWANT, 159; Stuttgart: W. Kohlhammer Verlag, 2002).

[128] For scholars who regard Isa. 1 and 65–66 as a redactional introduction and summary of the whole book, see e.g. M. A. Sweeney, *Isaiah 1–4 and the Post-Exilic Understanding of the Isaianic Tradition* (BZAW, 171; Berlin: W. de Gruyter, 1988) 21–24, Conrad, *Reading Isaiah*, pp. 83–116, A. J. Tomasino, "Isaiah 1.1–2.4 and 63–66, and the Composition of the Isaianic Corpus", *JSOT* 57 (1993) 81–98, and D. M. Carr, "Reaching for Unity in Isaiah", *JSOT* 57 (1993) 61–80. H. G. M. Williamson, "Relocating Isaiah 1:2–9" in Broyles and Evans, *Writing and Reading the Scroll of Isaiah. Vol. 1*, pp. 263–277, opposes this by claiming that Isa. 1 is more like an exhortation to repent. Unlike Williamson, they see these chapters as later additions rather than as integrated in a uniform plan of the book as a whole. Seitz, *Zion's Final Destiny*, p. 179, claims "[t]hat sickness and moral decay infect all other levels of society is Isaiah's message in essence". In this regard, he comments on the relation between Isa. 1:5–6, 38 and 53. Cf. 2.3.2.

[129] Isa. 1–39 is generally treated as "First Isaiah", i.e. as a unit depicting historical and political events by the 8th century prophet Isaiah, as a result of redactional reworking of older material, or as a mix of various post-Exilic concerns. A more or less conventional structuring of Isa. 1–39 looks as follows: Chapters 1–12 (introductory collection of oracles from various periods [1], oracles about Judah and Jerusalem [2–12]), 13–23 (mainly oracles against foreign nations, and against the rulers in Jerusalem [22:1–25]), 24–27 (The "Isaiah Apocalypse", post-Exilic?), 28–35 (oracles mainly about the "Assyrian Crisis" [28–31], oracles about human and divine kingship [32–33], oracles of judgment of Edom and salvation for Israel [34 (post-Exilic?)-35]), 36–39 (Royal Narratives concerning YHWH's deliverance of Jerusalem and Hezekiah, cf. 5.11.14. n. 203), cf. C. R. Seitz, "Isaiah, Book of (First Isaiah)", *ABD* 3 (1992) 472–

5.11.3. *Hos. 5:13*

5:13 וַיַּרְא אֶפְרַיִם אֶת־חָלְיוֹ וִיהוּדָה אֶת־מְזֹרוֹ
וַיֵּלֶךְ אֶפְרַיִם אֶל־אַשּׁוּר וַיִּשְׁלַח אֶל־מֶלֶךְ יָרֵב
וְהוּא לֹא יוּכַל לִרְפֹּא לָכֶם וְלֹא־יִגְהֶה מִכֶּם מָזוֹר:

5:13: When Ephraim saw his sickness and Judah his wound,
then Ephraim went to Assyria, and sent to the great king.
But he is not able to heal you and he cannot cure the wound of
either of you.

Hos. 5:13 concerns Ephraim and Judah and how they make their own diagnosis: when Ephraim saw his חֳלִי "sickness" and Judah his מָזוֹר "wound",[130] they sought a remedy for the affliction. As they ask Assyria for healing, bodily and political crises become related, with the great king as a helper in both matters.[131] However, Assyria is unable to cure them.[132] Whereas in v. 13a Ephraim and Judah are depicted as "he" (3ms), in v. 13b they are addressed jointly as "you" (2mpl). They have similar fates: they are both sick and by common appeal they vainly seek help.

Hos. 5:12–15 is "I" speech by YHWH. V. 13 interweaves two opposing images of the deity. In v. 12, the deity depicts his relation to Ephraim and Judah by likening himself to עָשׁ "a moth" and רָקָב "rottenness".[133] After their incorrect diagnosis and futile attempt to be

---

488, M. A. Sweeney, "Reevaluating Isaiah 1–39 in Recent Critical Reseach", *Currents in Research* 4 (1996) 79–113 and 2.3.2.

[130] For חֳלִי "sickness", see 5.11.1. nn. 115; 117.

[131] יָרֵב "contentious", from רִיב, cf. Hos. 10:6. LXX renders Ιαριμ, identified as a personal name of an Assyrian king. F. I. Anderson and D. N. Freedman, *Hosea: A New Translation with Introduction and Commentary* (AB, 24; New York: Doubleday, 1980) 413–414, refer to Assyrian honorific titles found on the Sefire I inscription, which they relate to Hebrew מֶלֶךְ "king". This is supported by Macintosh, *Hosea*, p. 209, who refers to 2 Kgs 18:19. Hos. 5:8–6:6 is often taken as referring to the Syro-Ephraimitic war, cf. a nuanced discussion in Macintosh, pp. 193–198 and a critique of traditional reconstructions in R. Tomes, "The Reason for the Syro-Ephraimite War", *JSOT* 59 (1993) 55–71.

[132] יִגְהֶה (imperf. qal 3ms of גהה) "depart", "remove", i.e. "be cured", "healed" is a *hapax legomenon*, cf. Jer. 8:18. Cf. גֵּהָה (fs) "healing", "cure" in Nah. 3:19 (if em. כֵּהָה) and Prov. 17:22 (or em. גֵּוָה) "body".

[133] For עָשׁ "moth" related to destruction, see Isa. 50:9, 51:8, Ps. 39:12, Job 4:19, 13:28. H. W. Wolff, *Hosea: A Commentary on the Book of the Prophet Hosea* (Hermeneia; Philadelphia: Fortress Press, 1974) 108; 115 and D. Stuart, *Hosea-Jonah* (WBC, 31; Waco, TX: Word Books, 1987) 97; 105, render עָשׁ "pus", whereas Anderson and Freedman, *Hosea*, p. 412, read "larvae" because that corresponds better to the images of sores in v. 13. For an overview of alternative readings related to Arab. cognates of emaciation and disease, see Macintosh, *Hosea*, p. 207.

healed (v. 13), the deity describes his relationship to them by comparing himself to שַׁחַל "a lion" and כְּפִיר "a young lion" (v. 14). Like a
lion, YHWH will destroy, withdraw, carry away and return with his
prey to a hiding place. The deity reveals himself as the cause of the
people's sickness and as their enemy: the lion's injury will destroy
and אֵין מַצִּיל "no one will rescue them" (v. 14). The deity's power to
harm might be contrasted with the Assyrian inability to cure in v. 13.
Ephraim/Judah sought relief of their symptoms from Assyria instead
of a real cure from YHWH, who has caused their sicknesses and who
is the only one who can heal them. In v. 15, YHWH seeks to bring
his people back to him by turning away. He will withdraw from them,
and this will reveal their delusion; they will suffer from guilt[134] and so
they will seek him. Ephraim and Judah are paralleled in vv. 12–14, and
mentioned as "they" (3mpl) in v. 15.

Then, in 6:1, "we" summon "ourselves" to return to YHWH and
express trust by describing the deity as the one who both tears apart
and heals. That YHWH can tear to pieces corresponds to the lion's
destruction (5:14).[135] The deity's ability to heal contrasts with Assyria's
inability (5:13). It is made clear here that YHWH is the cause of "our"
sickness. "Our" own wrong-doing is only indirectly referred to by the
admonition to turn another way, i.e. to YHWH. The return implies
that Israel has gone astray, but no confession is directly made. When
Israel returns to YHWH, the deity's wish in 5:15 is fulfilled. When the
people suffer punishment in the form of illness, they will seek YHWH;
only when they seek him will they be healed (6:1).[136] Again, the people's illness is self-imposed by their turning away and brought upon
them by YHWH.

In Hos 5:13, different kinds of personifications are at play: Ephraim
and Judah personify land and people, while Assyria is personified

---

[134] אשם "suffer punishment", cf. 10:2, 14:1, Isa. 24:6, Zech. 11:5, Ps. 34:22–23, Prov.
30:10, and "incur guilt" in Hos. 4:15, 13:1. Cf. אָשָׁם (noun) in relation to Isa. 53:10
in Appendix 6.

[135] F. Landy, *Hosea* (Readings; Sheffield: Sheffield Academic Press, 1995) 77–78.

[136] Anderson and Freedman, *Hosea*, p. 416: "In terms of poetic arrangement being
distressed and admitting guilt are complementary, but logically the sequence is the
other way around." Whereas the summons to return to YHWH in 6:1 will lead to
healing, in 6:3 the summons to "learn to know YHWH" will lead to a restored relationship between Israel and YHWH, which will be as rewarding to the people as rain
refreshing dry land. On the illness metaphor in the Book of Hosea, see Macintosh,
Hosea, p. lxiii, and D. F. O'Kennedy, "Healing as/or Forgiveness? The Use of the Term
[רפא] in the Book of Hosea", *Old Testament Essays* 14 (2001) 458–474.

through the representation of its king (cf. Body Politic in 4.7.3.5.).
Ephraim and Judah have similar fates, where bodily and political crises
are related: they are ill and seek out the Assyrian king for help. This
king is unable to cure (v. 13) the inflictions brought upon them by
YHWH. But YHWH will withdraw from them (v. 15) and this will
reveal their delusion; they will suffer punishment in the form of illness
and will thus seek him. In Hos. 5:13, the metaphor of illness concerns
bodily and political matters. As in Isa. 53, the people's illness is both
self-imposed because of their transgression and brought upon them by
YHWH. Both "he" and "we" (Isa. 53) and Ephraim and Judah (Hos.
5:13) suffer illness due their guilt and punishment by YHWH and they
shall be healed by him.

5.11.4. *Jer. 8:21–22*

8:21 עַל־שֶׁבֶר בַּת־עַמִּי הָשְׁבָּרְתִּי קָדַרְתִּי שַׁמָּה הֶחֱזִקָתְנִי:
²² הַצֳרִי אֵין בְּגִלְעָד אִם־רֹפֵא אֵין שָׁם
כִּי מַדּוּעַ לֹא עָלְתָה אֲרֻכַת בַּת־עַמִּי:

8:21: Because of the wound of the daughter of my people I am broken;
I mourn, I am gripped with dismay.
8:22: Is there no balm in Gilead? Is there no healer there?
Why has the health of the daughter of my people not been
restored?

In Jer. 8:21, a speaking "I" is lamenting its broken heart and the wound
of בַּת־עַמִּי "the daughter of my people", i.e. a female personification.
The "I" asks three questions about healing; the first two expect no
cure is possible, while the third asks why the daughter has not been
healed (v. 22). When the misery of בַּת־עַמִּי "the daughter of my people" is depicted as שֶׁבֶר (v. 21) both the illness of the daughter and
the destruction of the city are indicated.[137] This doubleness might be
strengthened by the depiction of the people's אֲרֻכָה "health" (v. 22)
and חָלָל "slain" (v. 23). The "I" answers with his own reaction: he is
overwhelmed by tears because בַּת־עַמִּי "the daughter of my people"
was fatally wounded (v. 23).

---

[137] שֶׁבֶר "breaking", "fracture", "crushing", referring to *illness*, e.g. Lev. 21:19, Isa.
30:26, 65:14, Jer. 10:19 (cf. 5.11.5.), 14:17 (cf. 5.11.6.), 30:12;15 (cf. 5.11.7.), Lam. 2:11;
13 (cf. 5.11.10.), 3:47–48, 4:10, Ps. 60:4, Nah. 3:19 and referring to *destruction of
nation*, e.g. Isa. 15:5, 59:7, 60:18, Jer. 4:6; 20, 6:1, 48:3; 5, 50:22, 51:54.

Just as "he" interacts with "us" in Isa. 53, in Jer. 8:21–22 a dialogue appears between "I" and בַּת־עַמִּי "the daughter of my people". The personification of "he"/"we" suffers from guilt, is punished by YHWH and is promised healing. In Jer. 8:18–23, an "I" laments the city's fate. The speaker is sick and sorrowful, hearing the cry of בַּת־עַמִּי "the daughter of my people" all over the land (vv. 18–19). The "I" asks twice why YHWH is not in Zion (v. 19). In a third question, an explanation is offered: the people have been abandoned by YHWH because they have angered him by committing idolatry.[138] Then the images change: the harvest is over, but the people have nothing to reap; they are not saved and there is no healing (v. 20). Attempts are made to blame the deity for being absent, but the people's own fault is also admitted: the people have followed other deities. Both in the diagnosis and in the explanation, bodily and theological crises are blurred. The people's misery is self-imposed, as they have been abandoned by YHWH because of their idolatry (v. 19). The speaking "I" of 8:21–22 has been identified as Jeremiah as spokesman for the community: because of the suffering of the people, Jeremiah is gripped by dismay. Carroll regards Jeremiah as a mouthpiece for the city:

> It is…the city's pain which is spoken of rather than the individual speaker's pain. The people who are wounded (i.e. the community) are the wound of the city (cf. 30.12, 15; 31.15). The personification of the city…does not mean that the speaker speaks of his own feelings; he speaks of the city's response to the disaster. The fictive mode of representation does not allow for two speakers – just as in 31.15 Rachel is a personification of the community, not the matriarch Rachel mourning for the community. So in these laments there are not two figures involved, but just one – the city Jerusalem. It is an illegitimate move to argue from these poems to the personal feelings of Jeremiah or to cite them as evidence for the oneness of feeling and identity between Jeremiah and his people. The many poems and statements critical of the community

---

[138] R. P. Carroll, *Jeremiah – A Commentary* (OTL; London: SCM Press, 1986) 236, W. McKane, *A Critical and Exegetical Commentary on Jeremiah* (ICC; Edinburgh: T. & T. Clark, 1986) 194 and others regard the last sentence of the verse as a later insertion or parenthesis, since it interrupts the flow of the speech by suddenly presupposing YHWH as the speaker. It is retained by P. C. Craigie, P. H. Kelley and J. F. Drinkard Jr., *Jeremiah 1–25* (WBC, 26; Dallas: Word Books, 1991) 137 19d-d, arguing that it "is attested in the versions and completes the rhetorical form ה...אִם...מַדּוּעַ found exclusively in Jeremiah (2:14, 31; 8:4–5, 19, 22; 14:19; 22:28; 49:1)".

indicate quite clearly just how alienated that speaker felt from the community (i.e. not at one with it).[139]

The identification of him lies in his interaction with others, as one who suffers from his people's wounds. He is not a personification, but represents the people, and identifies with them.[140] Moreover, Jer. 8 is characterised by a female personification of בַּת־עַמִּי "the daughter of my people". When the misery of בַּת־עַמִּי "the daughter of my people" is depicted as שֶׁבֶר (v. 21), both the illness of the daughter and the destruction of the city are indicated: the fates of the woman and of the city go hand in hand.

---

[139] Carroll, *Jeremiah – A Commentary*, pp. 235–236, his italics. H. G. Reventlow, *Liturgie und prophetisches Ich bei Jeremia* (Gütersloh: Gerd Mohn, 1963) 195–196, explains the "I" as a lively identification of the prophet as a person with his people, but not in the sense of the prophet's private feelings. This is related to his view of the prophet as cultic mediator between nation and God, i.e. discharging a representative function as an intercessor. More on this in 5.11.8. n. 165.

[140] The relation between this figure and the people might be compared to Lam. 3:1–39; 52–66 and the identification of אֲנִי הַגֶּבֶר, a man; defeated soldier and narrator. Attempts have been made to identify this as a historical person, like Jeremiah, King Jehoiakin or Zedekiah. Alternatively, he is regarded as representing a collective, like Zion/Jerusalem/all of Israel, focusing on a figurative rather than a literal aspect. The narrator "I" relates himself to עַמִּי "my people" (v. 14) and is interrupted by a collective "we" speaking in vv. 40–47. Hillers, *Lamentations*, p. 122 interprets the man in Lam. 3 as an individual, which is:

> not a specific historical figure, but rather anyone who has suffered greatly. He is an "Everyman", a figure who represents what any man may feel when it seems that God is against him. Through this representative sufferer the poet points the way to the nation, as he shows the man who has been through trouble moving into, then out of, near despair to patient faith and penitence, thus becoming a model for the nation. This is the high point of the book, central to it in more than an external or formal way.

Berlin, *Lamentations*, pp. 84–85, sees the man as the personified voice of the exile, which she explains in two ways:

> First, the male voice is a counterpart to the female voice of the city in chapter 1…
> Second, this male persona is a Job-like figure, crying out in his suffering to a God who refuses to respond, struggling to make sense of the awful tragedy that has befallen him, trying to maintain his faith in the face of God's cruelty, and seeking to justify God's actions.

Heim, "The Personification of Jerusalem and the Drama of Her Bereavement in Lamentations", p. 154, claims that the man in Lam. 3 is "most likely…identical with the narrator of Lamentations 1–2." He further sees relations between the sufferings of the man in Lam. 3, esp. vv. 13–14, and Isa. 53, esp. vv. 3–4 (p. 155, n. 44), since the man's sufferings are seen as divine punishment for his sins. As the identification of the man in Lam. 3 might appear through interaction with the other voices in the text, he might also be compared to the narrator "we" in Isa. 53:1–6. For overviews of different identifications of the man in Lam. 3, see Hillers, pp. 120–123, and Berlin, pp. 84–85. See more in general about the Book of Lamentations in 5.11.10. n. 183.

5.11.5. *Jer. 10:19*

10:19 אוֹי לִי עַל־שִׁבְרִי נַחְלָה מַכָּתִי וַאֲנִי אָמַרְתִּי אַךְ זֶה חֳלִי וְאֶשָּׂאֶנּוּ׃

10:19:　Woe is me because of my hurt! My wound is incurable.
　　　　But I said: "Truly, this is an illness, and I must bear it."

In Jer. 10:19, an "I" expresses impassioned grief and despair: אוֹי לִי עַל־
שִׁבְרִי "Woe is me because of my hurt!" The lamenting one is heartbroken and sick with pain without the prospect of healing. The inevi-
tablility of his own fate is admitted: he must bear the illness; there is
nothing but to endure it.[141] The lament continues with a complaint
about the loss of a tent and children (v. 20). The complaint expresses
disaster and desolation, illness and the bereavement of children and
the fate of a tent-dweller whose home is scattered. Neither the identity
of the complaining one nor any reason for the suffering is given.

The "I" lament in 10:19–20 is preceded by a hint of the disaster
of the land, addressed to "you" (2fs), with the apposition "who dwell
under siege" (v. 17). A woman is told to prepare for departure from
the land as its inhabitants shall be scattered and YHWH will bring
distress upon them (v. 18).[142]

After the complaint in vv. 19–20, the shepherds are described as
stupid and as not seeking YHWH (v. 21). Due to this, they did not
succeed and their flock was scattered.[143] In a judgment of the leadership, the shepherds – and not their flock – are blamed for the disaster and dispersion. Then follows war news about the enemy from the
north, who is turning the cities of Judah into a wasteland and a haunt
of jackals (v. 22).[144] A speaking "I" acknowledges that the way of man
is not under his own control (v. 23).[145] Carroll comments how this

---

[141] For חלה (pt. ni.) "be made sick", see 5.11.7. n. 151. Vrs. have a 1cs suff. added to
חֳלִי "illness", which may be missing in MT as a result of haplography. For חֳלִי "illness",
see 5.11.1. nn. 115; 117; for נָשָׂא חֳלִי "carry illness", see 5.11.1. n. 117, cf. 3.10.7. n.
87 and 3.10.15. n. 154.

[142] Jer. 10:18 is rather obscure. I will not go into further detail, but refer to standard
secondary literature.

[143] For the people's kings or leaders depicted as good or bad shepherds, see Isa.
44:28 (Cyrus), 56:11, 63:11, Jer. 2:8, 3:15, 10:21, 17:16, 22:22, 23:1–4, 25:34–35, 49:19,
50:6; 17; 44, Ezek. 34:2; 5; 7–10; 23, 37:24, Zech. 11:16–17. See 5.12.1. n. 207 for the
people as sheep. For שכל (hi.) "prosper", "succeed" in Isa. 52:13, see Appendix 1.

[144] For שְׁמָמָה "desolation" of land, cf. Jer. 49:2; 33, 50:13, 51:26; 62, Isa. 1:7 (5.11.2.),
Joel 2:3; 20, 4:19, Mic. 7:13 (5.8.3.), Zeph. 1:13, 2:4; 9; 13, Mal. 1:3. Cf. שמם qal "to
be laid waste" about Israel's land or cities in e.g. Isa. 49:8; 19, 61:4, and ni. in Isa. 54:3
(5.15.5.), Jer. 12:11, 33:10.

[145] In v. 23, the collective אָדָם "humankind" and the particular אִישׁ "everyone"
are paralleled.

lack of control might imply irresponsibility or at least extenuating circumstances when related to an appeal raised to YHWH, in which the "I" pleads for justice when facing the disaster, and not anger (v. 24).[146] YHWH's anger would threaten the very existence of the "I". By the phrase פֶּן־תַּמְעִטֵנִי "least you make me few" (v. 24), a fear of annihilation of a collective is expressed: "I" must not be too few for survival.[147] This "I" is identified as Jacob in an address to YHWH about the peoples (v. 25). The deity is asked to direct his wrath towards the stupid and idol-seeking peoples who have devastated Jacob. Thus, Jacob's own fate turns towards his enemies: The "I" appeals to YHWH for justice for himself (v. 24) and anger towards "his" enemies.[148]

In Jer. 10, a variety of voices and actors appears in depictions of crises: in a lament over a woman in a besieged city (vv. 17–18), a person broken with illness and bereaved of his children and with his tent scattered (vv. 19–20), shepherds and their scattered flock (vv. 21–22) and Jacob's lament (vv. 23–24). Person and land are mixed, as are disaster and desolation. The responsibility for the situation seems unclear: the incurable illness might be self-imposed and inevitable (v. 19), but the leaders are also blamed (v. 21). Furthermore, YHWH is urged to show justice towards the lamenting one and wrath towards Jacob's enemies (vv. 24–25). "My" illness and the destruction of the city are interwoven beyond separation: the lamenting one is heartbroken, sick with pain without the prospect of healing, bereaved of his children and with his tent scattered (vv. 19–20). Neither the identity of the person who complains nor any reason for the suffering is given. As in Isa. 53, disaster and desolation are inseparable. Similar to Isa. 53, the illness seems both self-imposed and caused by others, but in Jer. 10 there is no prospect of healing. Also Jer. 10 touches upon a female personification (vv. 19–20, cf. בַּת־עַמִּי "the daughter of my people" in Jer. 8, see 5.11.4.).

---

[146] Carroll, *Jeremiah – A Commentary*, p. 263.

[147] Reventlow, *Liturgie und prophetisches Ich bei Jeremia*, p. 201, identifies the speaking "I" in Jer. 10 as the prophet as a representative of the people. This touches upon the question of the identity of the "I" in individual laments in e.g. 4:19–20, 8:18–9:1, 10:23–25, 14:2–10; 17, as well as the "laments of Jeremiah", see 5.11.8. n. 165.

[148] Carroll, *Jeremiah – A Commentary*, p. 264, explains vv. 23–24 as "an extract from a lament psalm" and comments on the irony in praying for anger to be poured out on the nations and justice for oneself, when the devastations of Jacob by the nations is a result of YHWH's anger, cf. Ps. 79:5. Craigie, Kelley and Drinkard, *Jeremiah 1–25*, p. 164 regard Jer. 10:25 and Ps. 79:6–7 as drawing from a common tradition, rather than the one being dependent upon the other.

5.11.6. *Jer. 14:17*

14:17 וְאָמַרְתָּ אֲלֵיהֶם אֶת־הַדָּבָר הַזֶּה
תֵּרַדְנָה עֵינַי דִּמְעָה לַיְלָה וְיוֹמָם וְאַל־תִּדְמֶינָה
כִּי שֶׁבֶר גָּדוֹל נִשְׁבְּרָה בְּתוּלַת בַּת־עַמִּי מַכָּה נַחְלָה מְאֹד:

14:17: And you shall say to them this word:
"Let my eyes weep night and day and do not stop.
For with a great wound the young girl,
the daughter of my people has been stricken with an incurable sore."

In Jer. 14:17, YHWH is quoted as instructing "you" (2ms) about what to say to "them" (3mpl). The message is conveyed as a lament in "I" speech: the "I" describes how he shed tears because of the disaster which has afflicted בְּתוּלַת בַּת־עַמִּי "the young girl, the daughter of my people".[149] She is greatly and incurably wounded, and this is brought upon her by others.

The lament follows YHWH's words to the prophet concerning a prohibition on intercession (v. 11), and the deity's refusal to hear the people's prayers and accept their offerings. Rather, the people will be consumed by the sword, famine and pestilence (v. 12). False prophets have persuaded the people to believe that there shall be no sword and famine, but שָׁלוֹם "peace" (v. 13). YHWH shall reverse this preaching so that both they and the people shall suffer what the false prophets said would never happen: by the sword and famine shall they be consumed and cast out (vv. 14–16).

"My" lament over the stricken and desolated land, people, prophets and priests (v. 18) is followed by "our" complaint (v. 19). In "we" speech, "our" distress is conveyed by three reproachful questions and complaints. The questions are raised about YHWH's attitude to the rejected Judah and abhorred Zion, whom he has stricken without the prospect of healing. After the questions concerning Judah, Zion and "us", "we" tell how "we" are vainly seeking peace and healing, but there is only "no good" and "terror". "We" are suffering without any hope of peace and prosperity (cf. vv. 14–18), and YHWH is accused of being behind the bad conditions. However, "we" also admit "our" own contribution: sins are confessed to, and the guilt of "our" fathers

---

[149] For עַמִּי "my people" in the mouth of the prophet, see Jer. 4:22, 6:26, 8:19; 21–23, 9:1, 14:17.

is acknowledged (v. 20). After this confession, "we" plead to YHWH, not only for "ourselves", but for him too. For the sake of his name, he is admonished to neither spurn "us" nor dishonour "your glorious throne" (v. 21). The deity is also reminded of the covenant, as if he, not they, should have forgotten it.

In the "I" and "we" lament, the disaster and devastation of the land and people are mixed. The "I" sheds tears because of the disaster which has afflicted "the young girl, the daughter of my people". In a female personification, the prophet describes the suffering of the people of the city as the suffering of an ill woman. She is incurably wounded, brought upon her by others (v. 17). In the metaphor of illness, a blurring of bodily, political and theological diagnoses and crises is at work. The woman becomes a personification through a set of complex transformations in the relation between "I" (the prophet), Judah, Zion and "us". The illness is both self-imposed and brought about by YHWH: Judah, Zion and "we" suffer from guilt and are punished by YHWH. False prophets (vv. 13–16), the people (v. 20) and YHWH (v. 19) are all made responsible for the catastrophe. There is no peace, no good and no healing, but rather terror, the sword, famine, pestilence and drought (vv. 13–19; 22). Both loyalty to and accusations are expressed towards YHWH (v. 21). Unlike in Isa. 53, there is no promise of healing in Jer. 14. Also Jer. 14 is characterised by a female personification of בְּתוּלַת בַּת־עַמִּי "the young girl, daughter of my people".

5.11.7. Jer. 30:12–17

30:12 כִּי כֹה אָמַר יְהוָה
אָנוּשׁ לְשִׁבְרֵךְ נַחְלָה מַכָּתֵךְ׃
¹³ אֵין־דָּן דִּינֵךְ לְמָזוֹר רְפֻאוֹת תְּעָלָה אֵין לָךְ׃
¹⁴ כָּל־מְאַהֲבַיִךְ שְׁכֵחוּךְ אוֹתָךְ לֹא יִדְרֹשׁוּ
כִּי מַכַּת אוֹיֵב הִכִּיתִיךְ מוּסַר אַכְזָרִי
עַל רֹב עֲוֹנֵךְ עָצְמוּ חַטֹּאתָיִךְ׃
¹⁵ מַה־תִּזְעַק עַל־שִׁבְרֵךְ אָנוּשׁ מַכְאֹבֵךְ
עַל רֹב עֲוֹנֵךְ עָצְמוּ חַטֹּאתַיִךְ עָשִׂיתִי אֵלֶּה לָךְ׃
¹⁶ לָכֵן כָּל־אֹכְלַיִךְ יֵאָכֵלוּ וְכָל־צָרַיִךְ כֻּלָּם בַּשְּׁבִי יֵלֵכוּ
וְהָיוּ שֹׁאסַיִךְ לִמְשִׁסָּה וְכָל־בֹּזְזַיִךְ אֶתֵּן לָבַז׃
¹⁷ כִּי אַעֲלֶה אֲרֻכָה לָךְ וּמִמַּכּוֹתַיִךְ אֶרְפָּאֵךְ נְאֻם־יְהוָה
כִּי נִדָּחָה קָרְאוּ לָךְ צִיּוֹן הִיא דֹּרֵשׁ אֵין לָהּ׃

30:12: For thus says YHWH:
        Incurable is your hurt and your wound is grievous.
30:13: There is none who pleads your cause, concerning injury; neither medicine nor healing for you.

30:14: All your lovers have forgotten you – they don't care for you.
For the blow of your enemy I have dealt you – the punishment
of a cruel one –
because your guilt is great, your sins are numerous.

30:15: Why do you cry out your hurt? Incurable is your pain!
Because your guilt is great and your sins numerous I have done
these things to you.

30:16: Therefore, all who devour you shall be devoured,
and all your foes, every one of them, shall go into captivity;
those who spoil you shall become a spoil and all who prey on you
shall become a prey.

30:17: For I will restore health to you and your wounds I will heal, says
YHWH,
because they have called you an outcast: "Zion, she for whom
no one cares!"[150]

YHWH is quoted as lamenting the incurable and grievous wound of
the addressee "you" (2fs, v. 12).[151] The woman's desperate state of illness is deepened when we are told that she has been left utterly alone
and with no prospect of healing (v. 13).[152] Her former lovers have
abandoned her and YHWH has attacked her. Her hurt, pain and desolation are caused by the deity. He compares his smiting of her to that
committed by an enemy and a cruel one, and explains the punishment
as triggered by her great and numerous sins (v. 14b).[153]

YHWH's question in v. 15 might echo v. 12.[154] The question suggests that he has heard her cry: she has lamented her state, perhaps in

---

[150] Textual criticism of Jer. 30:12–17 is commented upon below.

[151] For שֶׁבֶר "hurt", see 5.11.4. n. 137. חלה (pt. ni.) "be made sick", that is, "severely",
"incurably", occurs almost always with מַכָּה "wound", see Jer. 10:19, 14:17, 30:12, Nah.
3:19, Isa. 17:11 (corr. and without מַכָּה). For חלה (qal) "be weak", "sick" related to
sin, see Isa. 39:1, (pu.) "to be made weak" in Isa. 14:10 (cf. 5.14.4.).

[152] דָּן דִּינֵךְ "anyone to judge your cause" or "he judged your cause". W. L. Holladay, *Jeremiah 2. A Commentary on the Book of the Prophet Jeremia. Chapters 26–52*
(Hermeneia; Philadelphia: Fortress Press, 1989) 151, suggests רְכָכִים "softening", cf.
Isa. 1:6. Carroll, *Jeremiah – A Commentary*, p. 580, rearranges the verse: "There is no
one judging your case. (You don't have) remedies for your open wound; you don't
have new skin", cf. "Daughter of Egypt" in Jer. 46:11, whereas B. A. Bozak, *Life 'Anew':
A Literary-Theological Study of Jer. 30–31* (AnBib, 122; Rome: Editrice Pontificio Istituto Biblico, 1991) 49–50, interprets the wound as spiritual, explained as a mixed
metaphor.

[153] The causative condition is expressed by the subjunctive conjunction כִּי "for". עַל
רֹב עֲוֹנֵךְ עָצְמוּ חַטֹּאתָיִךְ is not transmitted in LXX. Some commentaries regard this as
dittography, cf. 30:14, while others regard it as left out in LXX due to haplography.

[154] זעק imperf. qal ms "cry", whereas the rest of vv. 12–15 is addressed to 2fs "you".
זעק "cry" in laments, see Pss. 142:2; 6, 107:13; 19.

the hope of healing or as an accusation of unfair treatment. The deity answers the question himself: her hurt is incurable and grievous (cf. v. 12) and she is punished by him because of her great and numerous sins (cf. v. 14). No reply is expected from her, for her situation is inevitable and hopeless. Interwoven in YHWH's lament for her terrible state are statements of its cause: she is stricken by pain, wounds and desolation (vv. 12–15) due to her sins and the deity's punishment (vv. 14–15).

Then YHWH changes the situation so that her enemies, who had been an instrument in his punishment of her, shall go into captivity because they have devoured, spoiled and preyed on her.[155] The punishment is reversed when compared to what had happened to Judah before (cf. v. 10). The judgment of her enemies implies her vindication. In addition, her state of illness is turned around as she is promised healing (v. 17).[156] What none did in v. 13, YHWH does in v. 17: he will make her broken body whole again. Whereas in vv. 12–15 her wounds are depicted as incurable due to her sins, and also as caused by YHWH, in v. 17 the deity promises unconditional healing. In v. 17 more reasons are given for her fate in the past, quoting the contemptuous speech of her neighbours. They have called her an outcast and said: "Zion, she for whom no one cares!"[157] (cf. YHWH's lament over her state in v. 14). The hopelessness and desolation contrast with the reversal by YHWH: the ill and forsaken outcast Zion shall be healed (vv. 16–17). YHWH's lament over the woman is addressed to "you" (2fs) from v. 12 onwards, and only in v. 17 is the woman first named Zion.

---

[155] Holladay, *Jeremiah 2*, p. 151, claims that the conjunction לָכֵן "therefore" lacks any logical connection to the preceding and reads לְכִי, an archaic form of לָךְ "for you". Carroll, *Jeremiah – A Commentary*, p. 581, maintains the conjunction לָכֵן "therefore", but sees no logical connection between v. 15 and v. 16, while Bozak, *Life 'Anew'*, p. 54, claims that לָכֵן might work as an adversative conjunction, not by its denotation, but by its connotation of "therefore" in v. 16. G. L. Keown, P. L. Scalise and T. G. Smothers, *Jeremiah 26–52* (WBC, 27; Dallas: Word Books, 1995) 97; 100, regard it as "surprisingly logical": לָכֵן "therefore" typically signals the beginning of a judgment following an indictment, but here the judgment is directed towards the enemies, which means the vindication of Zion.

[156] The conjunction כִּי works as a strong asseveration, cf. v. 14b. In vv. 13–14, עלה "restore" and רפא "heal" are related to the negation אֵין "no" and מַכָּה "wound" is incurable, whereas in v. 17 healing and restoration (רפא and עלה) of מַכּוֹת "wounds" are promised.

[157] In v. 17b, yet another conjunction כִּי follows, here with a causative force.

In Jer. 30:12–17, YHWH addresses "you" (2fs) as a personification
of Zion. YHWH laments her broken body and violated relationships
(vv. 12–14).[158] She who suffers from fatal injury is also abandoned by
her lovers and taunted by her enemies, and her deity is acting like a
cruel one. Fluctuating explanations are conveyed for her fate.[159] The
grievous and incurable wounds are explained as self-inflicted due to
her sin (vv. 14–15, cf. Isa. 53:4–6). YHWH is made her enemy who has
stricken her because of her sinfulness (vv. 14–15, cf. Isa. 53:4–6) and
yet external enemies are blamed for what has happened (vv. 16–17, cf.
Isa. 53:7–9). In all cases a reversal of her state is expressed, as YHWH
will strike her enemies and heal her incurable wounds (cf. Isa. 53:5).[160]
The single female figure of Zion personifies the people; her fate and
the people's go hand in hand, and illness/healing (vv. 12–15; 17) and
desolation/vindication (vv. 14; 16) are blurred beyond separation.

5.11.8. *Jer. 15:18*

15:18 לָמָּה הָיָה כְאֵבִי נֶצַח וּמַכָּתִי אֲנוּשָׁה מֵאֲנָה הֵרָפֵא
הָיוֹ תִהְיֶה לִי כְּמוֹ אַכְזָב מַיִם לֹא נֶאֱמָנוּ:

15:18:   Why is my pain unceasing and my wound incurable! It refuses
to be healed!
You are indeed for me like a deceitful brook – water you cannot
trust!

---

[158] Cf. Jer. 8:21–22 (5.11.4.) and 10:19–20 (5.11.5.).

[159] W. Brueggemann, "The 'Uncared for' Now Cared for (Jer. 30:12–17): A Methodological Consideration", *JBL* 104 (1985) 419–428, reads within Ricourian categories
of suspicion and retrieval. The suspicion in vv. 12–15 is the "plucking up and tearing
down" whereas the retrieval in vv. 16–17 is "the planting and building" – with the
same God and the same people, the same poet and the same poem. Holladay, *Jeremiah
2*, pp. 158–160, relates vv. 12–15 to the survivors of the Northern Kingdom during
615–609 BCE, and vv. 16–17 to the time just before the fall of Jerusalem. Carroll,
Jeremiah – A Commentary, p. 582, regards the two different kinds of explanation as
belonging to separate sections (vv. 12–15 and 16–17) and as only loosely connected.
Keown, Scalise and Smothers, *Jeremiah 26–52*, p. 97:
> The imagery [of vv. 12–17] suits the condition of Judah and Jerusalem resulting
> from conquest by the Babylonians, but the personal connotations of the motifs
> typical of the individual lament genre free this poem to address readers long after
> the sixth century BC. Words repeated in different parts of the poem form the
> links in its unified structure.

[160] For a brief overview of the history of research into Jer. 30–31, called "Book of
Consolation", see Bozak, *Life 'Anew'*, pp. 1–6, and W. McKane, "The Composition of
Jeremiah 30–31" in M. V. Fox, V. A. Hurowitz, A. Hurvitz, M. L. Klein, B. J. Schwartz
and N. Shupak (eds), *Texts, Temples, and Traditions: A Tribute to Menahem Haran*
(Winona Lake, IN: Eisenbrauns, 1996) 187–194.

In two לָמָה "why" questions in Jer. 15:18, a speaking "I" laments his unceasing and incurable wounds. The desperation of his questions is underlined by a further comment on the lack of any prospect of healing, followed by an accusation of YHWH.[161] Through a comparison to a deceitful brook, he accuses the unreliable deity.

The "I" lament begins in v. 15 with a protestation of innocence, followed by an admonition of YHWH to take revenge on "my" enemies. The "I" laments his suffering despite his fidelity. He depicts his past delight in being called by YHWH (v. 16), in contrast to his disappointment at his unreliable God (v. 18). He also tells of the way in which he has separated himself from those around him, avoiding the company of merrymakers (v. 17). YHWH responds to his troubled prophet by suggesting that he needs to repent (v. 19). YHWH offers a conditional promise: if he returns, YHWH will return to him. Carroll comments on the implication of a charge of infidelity in the summons to repent: Jeremiah, not YHWH, has failed![162] YHWH claims that Jeremiah has to "utter what is precious rather than what is worthless". The deity also explains how he is reliable, promising Jeremiah deliverance from his enemies: they will be the ones to come back to "you"; "you" shall not go back to them (v. 19). Here, YHWH addresses the speaker, but not his complaint.[163] YHWH will protect Jeremiah and save him from his enemies. Alternatively, the conditional promise of v. 19 might express how Jeremiah is stricken by the same as the people, because of their transgressions. He might both personify the people and become their victim.[164]

---

[161] The speaker's incurable pain (אָנוּשׁ, cf. 17:9; 16, 30:12) elsewhere refers to the community's devastation (אָנוּשׁ לְשִׁבְרֵךְ in 30:12, cf. 8:21). Moreover, "his" desperate lament over unceasing and incurable wounds corresponds to the people's lament in 14:17–19 (מַכָּה "wound" of the people, v. 17), in both instances formulated as questions.

[162] Carroll, *Jeremiah – A Commentary*, p. 334.

[163] Carroll, *Jeremiah – A Commentary*, p. 333.

[164] M. S. Smith, *The Laments of Jeremiah and Their Context: A Literary and Redactional Study of Jeremiah 11–20* (SBLMS, 42; Atlanta: Scholars Press, 1990) 53:

> The prophetic lament read in conjunction with the people's lament also emphasises judgement against the people. Indeed, reading the prophetic lament in this manner has the force of identifying the people as Jeremiah's enemies. Judgement against the people are reinforced by the relationship between 15:11–14 and 15:15–18.

L. Stulman, *Order Amid Chaos: Jeremiah as Symbolic Tapestry* (Biblical Seminar, 57; Sheffield: Sheffield Academic Press, 1998) 120–136, argues that the suffering in Jeremiah is not explained as due to foreigners ("enemies", "the north" or Babel), but "is most often associated with malevolent forces *within* the community structures"

Although many links might be seen to Isa. 53, Jer. 15 is even more complex. In Jer. 15, fluctuating explanations are offered for the prophet's suffering beyond any prospect of healing: it is both self-imposed and due to the unjust. Jeremiah both personifies the people and is their victim. He might suffer the same fate as the people, who have turned away from their deity, but he also suffers because of his prophetic task.[165] The troubled prophet is in conflict with both his people and

---

(p. 128, his italics), such as priests, (pseudo-) prophets, kings and leaders, as well as YHWH. H.-J. Hermisson, "Jeremias dritte Konfessionen (Jer. 15, 10–21)", *ZTK* 96 (1999) 1–21, focuses on the prophetic office, with the prophet regarded as bearer of the divine word. His task is to announce words which will bring disaster, and simultaneously he has to wait to see them fulfilled.

[165] Discussions concerning the so-called "laments of Jeremiah" in Jer. 11:18–12:6, 15:10–21, 17:12–18, 18:18–23, 20:7–18 (both delimitations and labels, e.g. laments, complaints, confessions, poems, are disputed) touch upon debates about the possibility of establishing connections between a historical Jeremiah and the character in the Book of Jeremiah. Different approaches to these texts might be roughly grouped into "historical auto-biographical approaches", approaches related to a corporate "I" and "editorial readings".

W. Baumgartner, *Die Klagegedichte des Jeremia* (BZAW, 32; Giessen: Alfred Töpelmann, 1917), regards the texts as personal laments modeled after the individual laments in the Psalms. According to him, the confessions reflect the inner struggle of Jeremiah, and thus are mainly auto-biographical. W. L. Holladay, *Jeremiah 1. A Commentary on the Book of the Prophet Jeremiah. Chapters 1–25* (Hermeneia; Philadelphia: Fortress Press, 1986) 358, also regards them as "a series of deeply personal laments" from Jeremiah to YHWH preserved because he spoke for the people in their common despair and because they were intended to affirm how YHWH made his prophetic office valid. McKane, *A Critical and Exegetical Commentary on Jeremiah*, sees them as "testimony to the exceptional nature of [Jeremiah's] individuality and the fineness of his spiritual texture: only an individual who had made the community's brokenness his own could have spoken like this" (p. xciii). Reventlow, *Liturgie und prophetisches Ich bei Jeremia*, emphasises the relationship between the confessions and the cultic lament (cf. Baumgartner). He sees the prophet as cultic mediator between nation and God, i.e. the individual speaking in the laments is liturgical and representative in character: the laments were communal laments reflecting the concerns of the community. Cf. 5.11.4. nn. 139–140. According to Carroll, *Jeremiah – A Commentary*, the laments are intended to justify the destruction of the community and the voices of protest represent Jerusalem or the community challenging the justice of such a catastrophe:

> The difficulty with the theological understanding of suffering suggested by the exposition of the laments in terms of Jeremiah's suffering is that the tradition resolutely presents suffering as the judgement of Yahweh against the wicked. If a new understanding of suffering is to be found in the "confessions", then it conflicts with the central theme of the book. This is but one conflict with the tradition which emerges as a result of making that tradition a unified representation of the sayings and deeds of one person (whether historical or created by the editors) (p. 334).

In R. P. Carroll, *Jeremiah* (OTG; Sheffield: JSOT Press, 1989), the Book of Jeremiah is regarded as a post-Exilic composition from Palestine which is edited by Deuteronomistic redactors. Carroll regards the Jeremiah figure as a conglomeration of a society's experiences in and after the Exile. Jeremiah is a product of different layers in the tradi-

his deity. Jeremiah laments his unceasing and incurable pain caused by his faithfulness to YHWH and YHWH responds with a call for repentance and offers a conditional promise (v. 19). The vindication of the prophet is not conveyed as healing, but as speech (v. 19) and the submission of his enemies (vv. 12–14; 20–21).[166]

5.11.9. *Lam. 1:12–13*

1:12 לוֹא אֲלֵיכֶם כָּל־עֹבְרֵי דֶרֶךְ הַבִּיטוּ וּרְאוּ
אִם־יֵשׁ מַכְאוֹב כְּמַכְאֹבִי אֲשֶׁר עוֹלַל לִי
אֲשֶׁר הוֹגָה יְהוָה בְּיוֹם חֲרוֹן אַפּוֹ:
[13] מִמָּרוֹם שָׁלַח־אֵשׁ בְּעַצְמֹתַי וַיִּרְדֶּנָּה
פָּרַשׂ רֶשֶׁת לְרַגְלַי הֱשִׁיבַנִי אָחוֹר
נְתָנַנִי שֹׁמֵמָה כָּל־הַיּוֹם דָּוָה:

tion about the time from Josiah to the fall of Jerusalem. This tradition about a certain time in the past ("the Exile") becomes a decisive pattern for the ideology in the present text. The presentation of the prophet is a depiction of the humiliations of the nation. The "laments of Jeremiah" have close thematic and literary links to the individual psalms of lament, the Book of Job as well as the servant in Isa. 40–55. Carroll nuances his view somewhat in his later article, "The Book of J: Intertextuality and Ideological Criticism" in A. R. P. Diamond, K. M. O'Connor and L. Stulmann (eds), *Troubling Jeremiah* (JSOTSup, 260; Sheffield: Sheffield Academic Press, 1999) 239, n. 45.

T. Polk, *The Prophetic Persona: Jeremiah and the Language of the Self* (JSOTSup, 32; Sheffield: JSOT Press, 1984), offers a synchronic reading of the prophetic figure. He emphasises the poetic language of the prophetic texts, which are emotional and ambiguous. Polk reads the prophetic figure in the Book of Jeremiah as a theological paradigm, where Jeremiah stands in a simultaneous relationship to YHWH and the nation: through a holistic approach to the tradition, Jeremiah appears as a created "prophetic persona", mediating the redactors' wish to convince the audience about "how things are" in society.

For brief overviews of the history of research into these texts, see K. M. O'Connor, *The Confessions of Jeremiah: Their Interpretation and Role in Chapters 1–25* (SBLDS, 94; Atlanta: Scholars Press, 1988) 1–4, and Smith, *The Laments of Jeremiah and Their Context*, pp. xiii–xxi.

[166] Traditionally, the Book of Jeremiah has been regarded as a writing from the time between the Assyrian downfall and the Babylonian growth (ca. 640–570). The texts consist of a blend of poetry and prose, comprehensive "biographical" material, told in 1cs and 3ms and a mix as concerns both chronology and genre. Readings of the book are characterised by biographical, historical, psychological and editorial interests. See overviews of the recent research into the Book of Jeremiah by R. P. Carroll, "Surplus of Meaning and the Conflict of Interpretations: A Dodecade of Jeremiah Studies (1984–1995)", *CRBS* 4 (1996) 115–159, and R. P. Carroll, "Century's End: Jeremiah Studies at the Beginning of the Third Millenium", *CRBS* 8 (2000) 18–58. Among studies referred to in these articles, Holladay, *Jeremiah 1* and *Jeremiah 2* might be counted among the "historical Jeremiah" interpreters, and Carroll, *Jeremiah – A Commentary*, as sceptical about establishing connections between a historical Jeremiah and the character in the book, whereas McKane, *A Critical and Exegetical Commentary on Jeremiah*, might be somewhere in between these points of view.

1:12: You there, all who pass by on the road – observe and see:
Is there any pain like my pain, which is being brought upon me,
with which YHWH deeply afflicted me on the day of his fierce
anger?

1:13: From on high he sent fire, he made it go deep into my bones.
He spread a net for my feet, he turned me back.
He left me desolate; faint all day long.

In Lam. 1:12, a speaking "I" calls upon passers-by to see her distress.[167]
She describes her pain by questioning its incomparability and explains
what has been done to her and by whom: her pain cannot be compared to anyone else's, and she has been stricken by YHWH "on the
day of his fierce anger" (v. 12).[168] She offers more details about what
the deity has done to her: the affliction he has brought upon her comes
both from above and below and has stricken her both inside and out;
her bones are burning[169] and her feet ensnared (v. 13).[170] Her crisis is
all-embracing and she has no chance to disappear; she is desolate and
totally broken.[171]

---

[167] Whereas vv. 1–11 are 3ms narrator's speech about the woman-city, vv. 12ff (and
vv. 9c; 11c) are 1cs, that is, the woman-city's speech. In the phrase אֲלֵיכֶם לוֹא, לוֹא
has been understood as the exclamation לוּ "O", or the negation לֹא "not", or the
phrase has been textually emended. For various suggestions, see J. Renkema, *Lamentations* (Historical Commentary on the Old Testament; Leuven: Peeters, 1998) 153–154.
I support Renkema: "Since לֹא [read לוּ] in an imperative context usually carries a
nuance of urgency (cf. Gen 23:13) and given that אֲלֵיכֶם clearly suggests address, both
words together serve to attract attention and to introduce the imperatives of the following colon" (p. 154).
[168] For מַכְאֹב "pain", "illness", "sorrow", cf. Lam. 1:18 and 5.11.1. n. 115.
[169] For עֶצֶם "bone" as the place of suffering, cf. Isa. 38:13 (see 5.11.14.), Pss. 22:15
(see 5.11.12.), 38:4 (see 5.11.11.). רדה (imperf. cons. qal 3ms) "to rule", with 3fs suff; in
MT אֵשׁ (f) is subject for the masc. predicate. With support in LXX, Peshitta and others, Hillers, *Lamentations*, p. 72, and Renkema, *Lamentations*, pp. 160–161, emend to
וַיִּרְדֶּנָּה (imperf. hi. 3ms *energicus* of ירד "go down", assuming an interchange between
ו and י, with וַיּוֹרְדֶנָּה as original form [cf. Lam. 1:16]) and YHWH as subject: "and sank
it into my bones" or "he made it go into my bones".
[170] Hillers, *Lamentations*, p. 89, explains spreading a net as "an exceptionally common image in the Old Testament", and refers to God's spreading a net for men also
in Jer. 50:24, Ezek. 12:13, 17:20, 32:2, Hos. 7:12, cf. Ps. 94:13. Berlin, *Lamentations*,
p. 57, claims that this imagery does not relate to hunting, but to a military implement,
cf. Ezek. 12:13, 17:20, 19:8, Hos. 7:12.
[171] שׁמם (pt. qal fs) "be desolate", cf. about "her gates" in Lam. 1:4, "her" children
in 1:16, the lamenting man in 3:11, Zion in Isa. 54:1. For שׁמם about land, see 5.8.1.
n. 54 and 5.11.5. n. 144.
B. B. Kaiser, "Poet as 'Female Impersonation': The Image of Daughter and Zion as
Speaker in Biblical Poems of Suffering", *JR* 67 (1987) 176, argues for the prominence
of Jerusalem personified as a menstruating woman in Lam. 1, emphasising vocabulary
such as נִידָה "abhorrent thing" (vv. 8; 17, cf. Lev. 12:2; 5, 15:19–26; 33, 18:19, 20:21,

After the appeal for pity in vv. 12–13, she acknowledges her sin in passing (v. 14). The burden of her sins is beyond her strength to bear and is forced upon her by YHWH.[172] The deity has also handed her over to enemies (vv. 14–15). She concludes her many accusations concerning what YHWH has done to her: she weeps and has no one to comfort or revive her; her sons are desolate and her enemy mighty (v. 16). In v. 17 Zion is not speaking, but mentioned. The narrator expresses her lack of a comforter (cf. v. 15), as well as YHWH's causing of military collapse. Jerusalem is overthrown and has become an abhorrence. This echoes v. 16, providing the narrator's comments on her preceding address.

The woman's "I" speech continues in vv. 18–22. Vv. 18–19 are addressed to כָּל־עַמִּים "all peoples", and conclude the accusations made against YHWH in vv. 12–15; 17. In a transition from pain to trust, YHWH is justified in his acts because she has sinned (v. 18). Then again an appeal for pity is raised to the passers-by to see her distress (cf. v. 12), which is expanded by recounting that her young women and men have been exiled, her lovers have deceived her and her priests

---

Ezra 9:11, Ezek. 7:19ff, 18:6, 22:10, 36:17), טָמְאָה "uncleanness" (v. 9, cf. 4:15) and דָּוָה "faint" (v. 13, related to menstruation in Lev. 12:2, 15:33, 20:18). For דְּוַי "faint" or "sick", cf. Isa. 1:5, Jer. 8:18, Lam. 1:22, 5:17, Job 6:7, Ps. 41:4. K. M. O'Connor, "Lamentations" in C. A. Newsom and S. H. Ringe, S. H. (eds), *The Women's Bible Commentary* (London: SPCK Press, 1992) 180, emphasises the sexual assault: "As daughter Zion gives voice to her sufferings, she describes herself in language that today calls to mind the circumstances of a battered woman. She is abused, beaten, and tortured by the one whom she trusted. She bitterly laments her sorrows and names their source." Cf. G. Baumann, "Prophetic Objections to YHWH as the Violent Husband of Israel: Reinterpretations of the Prophetic Marriage Metaphor in Second Isaiah (Isaiah 40–55)" in Brenner, *Prophets and Daniel*, pp. 97–98. Berlin, *Lamentations*, pp. 20–21; 53–54, claims that נִידָה (of נוד) "banished" of v. 8 and נִדָּה (of נדד) "a menstruating woman" of v. 17 are not from the same root. She argues that v. 9 does not refer to menstruation, and that exegetes have misunderstood the nature of menstrual impurity: menstruation is not a sin; it causes ritual, but not moral, impurity (cf. Lev. 15:19–24). However, Berlin also sees a play of נוד of v. 8 and נדד of v. 17 in v. 9: "It may be best to conclude that all three associations adhere to the word, and the dominant one shifts as we proceed from line to line – from the consequences of sin, to the scorn of others, to the idea of nakedness and impurity in her skirts" (p. 54). Hillers, *Lamentations*, p. 70, translates נִידָה (of נוד) "shake heads" in v. 8, cf. hi. in Jer. 18:16, Ps. 44:15.

[172] MT נִשְׂקַד in v. 14 is a *hapax legomenon*, 4QLamᵃ renders נשקד "to keep watch", supported by mss. Berlin, *Lamentations*, pp. 43; 46, translates v. 14a: "My yoke of transgression was fashioned" and explains: "I have chosen a neutral word to convey that a yoke is being made." Renkema, *Lamentations*, pp. 163–164, reads שׂקד ni. perf. as a *terminus technicus* for the fastening of a yoke, while Hillers, *Lamentations*, pp. 62; 73, emends to שׁקד and translates "Watch is kept over my steps".

and elders have perished (vv. 18–19). In a blending of the calamities of the woman and the city, the absence of help is expressed.

After the indirect accusation of YHWH in the summons to the passers-by (vv. 12–19), the "I" speaks directly to YHWH in a lament turning into an appeal (vv. 20–22). YHWH is admonished to see her distress both inside her body and outside in the house (v. 20, cf. vv. 9; 11). The catastrophe is all-embracing; both the woman and the city are stricken inwardly and outwardly. Her enemies take delight in her distress (v. 21, cf. v. 15). In addition to her admonition of YHWH, a turning point appears, as she appeals to the deity to take revenge on her enemies in the way he has punished her (vv. 21–22). Additionally, she depicts her state of illness – due to her sins (vv. 20; 22). She does not beg for Israel's restoration. Her only hope is that her enemies will suffer like her, rather than she will cease to suffer (v. 22).

In the "I" lament from v. 12 onwards, Zion repeatedly names YHWH as the one who has afflicted her. This affliction is all-embracing and her pain cannot be compared to anyone else's (vv. 12–13; 18). Her heart is turned over inside her, she is encircled by death both outside by the sword and inside her sick heart (vv. 20–22).[173] Moreover, the city is desolate, her priests groan and her young girls are grieving (v. 19, cf. vv. 4–6), her young men and women have disappeared (vv. 15; 18) and she is haunted and despised by enemies (vv. 14–17; 21, cf. 3; 5–11).

---

[173] C. Westermann, *Lamentations. Issues and Interpretation* (Minneapolis: Fortress Press, 1994) 140:

> Those who are speaking in this text are at the same time both the lamenters and the lamented. Zion, taking up her lament as a solitary and defenseless woman, also represents a multitude – the whole city and its inhabitants. Correspondingly, Zion herself can say "my sighs are countless" while someone else can speak of her suffering and note that "she groans and turns away". Zion both laments and is lamented. The change between singular and plural is a way of expressing the fact that the lamenters can be viewed as either a unit (Zion) or a conglomeration.

Miller, "Reading Voices", questions the commonly held notion that the 3ms narrator in Lam. 1 stands outside of the poem and thereby offers the reader an "objective" perspective. In this regard, he refers to Dobbs-Allsopp ("impartial"), Hillers ("external, objective"), Provan ("uninvolved"), Kaiser ("impersonal") and Lanahan ("objective"). Miller himself "draw[s] on Bakhtin's notion of the polyphonic text in an effort to explore the interpretive possibilities that open up when one chooses to privilege nei-ther voice, but instead takes seriously the existence of two 'independent and unmerged voices and consciousnesses'" (p. 394). Thus, Miller describes both speakers as literary constructions or personifications. Also, Heim, "The Personification of Jerusalem and the Drama of Her Bereavement in Lamentations", treats the more theoretical implica-tions of the trope personification.

The woman's appeal to the passers-by for compassion in 1:13ff follows a lament in which Zion is not speaking but mentioned. In vv. 1–11, her present downfall, pain and despair are contrasted with her past greatness, cf. v. 1: "How lonely the city sits that was once full of people! How like a widow she has become, she that was great among the peoples!" Her despair is related to her state as a widow, former princess and slave girl (v. 1), forsaken by lovers and deceived by friends (vv. 2; 8, cf. v. 19), exiled and pursued (vv. 3; 5; 6; 7), desolate (v. 4), despised (vv. 7; 8; 11), an abhorrence (v. 8, cf. v. 17), impure (v. 9) and robbed (v. 10), with her children and princes forced to depart (vv. 5–6), her sanctuary invaded (v. 10) and her people starving (v. 11) – all due to the multitude of her transgressions (v. 8, cf. vv. 5; 9; 14).[174] In the presentation of her fate in vv. 1–11, YHWH is mentioned only once, where it is said that the deity has caused her sufferings due to her sins (v. 5). Within the narrator's telling of vv. 1–11, in vv. 9c; 11c her voice appears. In reported speech, she admonishes the deity to see her affliction and shame.[175] In relation to vv. 1–11, the "I" speech from v. 12 onwards expands on the depiction of the catastrophe by also telling that she is like the dead (v. 20), a mourning and forsaken mother (vv. 16; 20), suffering from pain, illness and despair (vv. 12–13; 18; 22), a yoked ox (v. 14) and a vineyard (v. 15).

---

[174] T. Linafelt, "Zion's Cause: The Presentation of Pain in the Book of Lamentations" in T. Linafelt (ed), *Strange Fire: Reading the Bible After the Holocaust* (Biblical Seminar, 71; Sheffield: Sheffield Academic Press, 2000) 267–268, comments on how biblical scholars have focused on the interpretation of pain and suffering in Lamentations by explaining them as resulting from the guilt of the sufferer. According to him, the disturbing and accusatory passages of e.g. Lam. 1 and 2 have been read in passing "in favor of the few passages that seem to evidence hope through penitence and a reconciliation with God" (p. 267). Due to this, more attention has been given to the "Suffering Man" in Lam. 3 (cf. 5.11.4. n. 140) than to the presentation of the pain and suffering of the woman in Lam. 1 and 2. Linafelt presents three biases to explain the focus on the suffering man in Lam. 3 over the suffering woman of Lam. 1–2: 1) a male bias towards the male figure of ch. 3; 2) a Christian bias toward the suffering man based on the perceived similarity to the figure of Christ; and 3) a broader emphasis on the reconciliation with God rather than confrontation (p. 268). Linafelt wants to show that Lam. 1 and 2 are (re-read with contemporary survival literature) "more about the *expression* of suffering than the meaning behind it, more about the vicissitudes of *survival* than the abstractions of sin and guilt, more about *protest* as a religious posture than capitulation or confession", p. 279, his italics.

[175] This is expressed by a sg imp. to YHWH in 1:9 ("See") and double in v. 11 ("See and pay attention"). These are chiastically repeated in v. 12, directed to the passers-by.

Lam. 1 has two speakers: a narrator (3ms) in vv. 1–9b; 10–11b; 15c; 17 and a speaking "I" in vv. 9c; 11c–15b; 16; 18–22, further identified by name as Jerusalem (vv. 7; 8; 17), Zion (3fs, vv. 4; 6 [Daughter of];17), Judah (3fs, vv. 3; 15 [Daughter of]) and Jacob (v. 17). The account alternates between telling about a city and a woman, interwoven with accusations against YHWH. Common to all is that they have lost their dignity. Central to the depiction of the woman's misery is her suffering from illness, injury and pain (vv. 12–13; 18; 20; 22) – and that this has been brought upon her by the deity due to her sin (vv. 8; 14; 18; 20; 22). Heim describes the complexity of the personifications in Lam. 1:

> Personification helps to conceptualize and verbalize pain…In Lamentations 1 four types of personalities emerge: the individual sufferer, the suffering community, others, and God. The individual sufferer and the suffering community have been combined through the personification of Jerusalem, the "others" have turned from "lovers" into "enemies" and God has turned from somebody to complain about into someone to talk to, even though that discourse is still restricted to complaints and almost vindictive pleas for the enemies' punishment (vv. 21–22). This latter shift…is crucial: from talking to "others" and to one another *about* God as an enemy, suffering Jerusalem as a community turns again to her God in talking about her enemies.[176]

In the terrifying description of a woman's pain in Lam. 1, she works as a personification and the injury as a blurred metaphor of bodily, political and theological crises and diagnoses. Like "him"/"us" in Isa. 53, "her" suffering is both self-imposed through the people's turning away and brought upon "her" by YHWH: she suffers from guilt and is punished by the deity. And unlike Isa. 53, there is no prospect of healing.

5.11.10. *Lam. 2:13*

מָה־אֲעִידֵךְ מָה אֲדַמֶּה־לָּךְ הַבַּת יְרוּשָׁלַם 2:13
מָה אַשְׁוֶה־לָּךְ וַאֲנַחֲמֵךְ בְּתוּלַת בַּת־צִיּוֹן
כִּי־גָדוֹל כַּיָּם שִׁבְרֵךְ מִי יִרְפָּא־לָךְ:

2:13: What example shall I hold up to you, with what shall I compare you, daughter of Jerusalem?
       To what can I liken you to comfort you, young girl, daughter of Zion?
       For vast as the sea is your wound. Who shall heal you?

---

[176] Heim, "The Personification of Jerusalem and the Drama of Her Bereavement in Lamentations", p. 141, his italics.

In Lam. 2:13, a narrator (3ms) addresses "you" (2fs), more closely identified as הַבַּת יְרוּשָׁלַ͏ִם "the daughter of Jerusalem" and בְּתוּלַת בַּת־צִיּוֹן
"young girl, daughter of Zion". The narrator asks three questions as
to the comparability of her misery: what example to hold up, what to
compare her with and what to liken her to comfort her. The answer is
that there is nothing to which the narrator can compare her: her שֶׁבֶר
"wound" is as vast as the sea.[177] Her state is destructive, infinite, and
she is inconsolable.

The narrator's address to Zion continues in v. 14, where the unlikely
possibility of healing is rejected: the destruction is the result of false
prophecies that prevent repentance. Also, Jerusalem's guilt is alluded
to. Her shame is expressed in the passers-by's contempt of her (v.
15, cf. 1:12), and enemies' taunts and torture of Jerusalem (v. 16).
God does what he said he would (v. 17). The narrator expresses that
the deity caused the misery of Jerusalem because of her sins (vv. 14;
17), in which Zion is calling on the deity for help (vv. 18–19). The
question "Who shall heal you?" in v. 13 does not ask for any answer
but "none", as the following verses suggest: the prophets have failed,
the deity destroys and the passers-by and enemies increase both her
shame and her misery. Heim comments that in Lam. 2:13–19 the narrator speaks *to* Jerusalem, in which "hints at a connection between the
speaker and Jerusalem are conspicuously absent, suggesting a lesser
degree of identification".[178]

In Lam. 2:1–12, the personified Jerusalem is broken up into representative members of the community: rulers (v. 2), king, princes,
prophets and priests (vv. 6; 9), elders and maidens (v. 10), babies (v.
11), mothers and wounded men (v. 12). The description of the destruction in Lam. 2 has many references to architectural elements: footstool
(v. 1), dwellings (v. 2), strongholds (vv. 2; 5), palaces (v. 5), booth and
tabernacle (v. 6), walls and temple (v. 7), gates and their bars (v. 9)
and streets (v. 11).[179] Some of these have human characteristics: altar
and sanctuary are scorned and rejected (v. 7) and wall and rampart

---

[177] שֶׁבֶר "breaking", depicting *illness*, see Lam. 2:11; 13, 3:47–48, 4:10 and 5.11.4.
n. 137.

[178] Heim, "The Personification of Jerusalem and the Drama of Her Bereavement in
Lamentations", p. 147.

[179] Heim, "The Personification of Jerusalem and the Drama of Her Bereavement in
Lamentations", p. 142.

mourn (v. 8).[180] The members of the community, the architecture and institutions have all been destroyed.

In Lam. 2, two speakers appear: the narrator in vv. 1–19 (addressing the reader in vv. 1–12 about Jerusalem, and addressing Zion in vv. 13–19) and Jerusalem herself in vv. 20–22. The narrator is identified in "I" speech in vv. 11–12 in which he expresses his own feelings: "My eyes are spent…my stomach churns…because of the destruction of the daughter, my people." In v. 12a babies are quoted by the narrator. In vv. 20–22, the personified Jerusalem herself prays to the deity for help in a catastrophe which is total – young and old are lying dead in the streets and the deity invited the attackers to witness and participate in the destruction. She prays so the deity shall see the misery and destruction of the people, but no consolation is indicated. Heim emphasises the narrator's direct speech to Jerusalem in Lam. 2, with the narrator attempting to comfort both himself and the city. Heim describes a threefold address: through the emotional language, the individual can demonstrate empathy with his community, conceptualise Jerusalem's grief and enable Zion to enter into dialogue (with herself, the poet, the passers-by, enemies and God):

> By personifying his own city as another person, the narrator becomes able not only to *speak about* her torment, but also to represent her and *speak for her.* He becomes an interlocutor who is able to express the communal grief, exhort, encourage, and console (ch. 3)…by distinguishing himself from his community, the poet is enabled to enter into dialogue with Fair Zion. Not only can he speak *to* Fair Zion *from outside,* as someone who has a wider perspective on the suffering endured by everybody, but, more importantly, he is someone who can *listen* to Fair Zion. And, conversely, Fair Zion is enabled to express herself, and in doing so can listen to her own expression of pain and anguish![181]

The comparisons of Lam. 2:13 are reminiscent of Lam. 1:12: "Is there any pain like my pain?" Whereas Lam. 1:1–11 concerned the catastrophe that afflicted Zion, in Lam. 2 the cause of the disaster is dwelled upon, cf. 2:1: "How the Lord in his anger has treated daughter of

---

[180] Heim, "The Personification of Jerusalem and the Drama of Her Bereavement in Lamentations", p. 139, and Berlin, *Lamentations*, p. 75.

[181] Heim, "The Personification of Jerusalem and the Drama of Her Bereavement in Lamentations", pp. 142–143, his italics.

Zion…"[182] Her present state is the result of the Lord's punishment of her sin.[183]

Although many links might be seen to Isa. 53, Lam. 2 is even more complex. The personification in particular is much more developed, as the daughter of Zion is related to the city's inhabitants, architecture and institutions. As regards themes, both Lam. 2:13 and Isa. 53 concern suffering and sin, but while Isa. 53 also mediates coming healing, Lam. maintains the grief. One might conclude with Berlin:

> The poet [in Lam. 2:13] cannot console Jerusalem, and in fact, the verses that follow only prolong the description of sin and suffering. Lamentations is not a book of consolation; it is a book that refuses to console, keeping the moment of grief always in focus.[184]

To this huge theme, it might be added that "Jerusalem does not speak with one voice",[185] rather different focuses are conveyed within an atmosphere of grief.

5.11.11. *Psalm 38:4–9*

38:4 אֵין־מְתֹם בִּבְשָׂרִי מִפְּנֵי זַעְמֶךָ אֵין־שָׁלוֹם בַּעֲצָמַי מִפְּנֵי חַטָּאתִי:
5 כִּי עֲוֺנֹתַי עָבְרוּ רֹאשִׁי כְּמַשָּׂא כָבֵד יִכְבְּדוּ מִמֶּנִּי:
6 הִבְאִישׁוּ נָמַקּוּ חַבּוּרֹתָי מִפְּנֵי אִוַּלְתִּי:
7 נַעֲוֵיתִי שַׁחֹתִי עַד־מְאֹד כָּל־הַיּוֹם קֹדֵר הִלָּכְתִּי:
8 כִּי־כְסָלַי מָלְאוּ נִקְלֶה וְאֵין מְתֹם בִּבְשָׂרִי:
9 נְפוּגוֹתִי וְנִדְכֵּיתִי עַד־מְאֹד שָׁאַגְתִּי מִנַּהֲמַת לִבִּי:

38:4: There is no soundness in my flesh because of your indignation; there is no health in my bones because of my sin.

38:5. For my iniquities have gone into my head; they weight like a burden too heavy for me.

---

[182] יָעִיב is *hapax legomenon*, often taken as a denominative verb from עָב "cloud", i.e. "cover with clouds". Berlin, *Lamentations*, pp. 61; 66, takes it to be a verbal form of תּוֹעֵבָה "abomination", i.e. "make loathsome", Hillers, *Lamentations*, pp. 93; 96 suggests "with contempt", based on Arab. cognates. For this and other suggestions, see Hillers, pp. 96–97.

[183] The Book of Lamentations is a reflection of the destruction of Jerusalem in 586 BCE. It is a mixed composition of laments with a variety of speakers and widespread use of personifications. For an overview, see C. W. Miller, "The Book of Lamentations in Recent Research", *CBR* 1 (2002) 9–29.

[184] Berlin, *Lamentations*, p. 73.

[185] Heim, "The Personification of Jerusalem and the Drama of Her Bereavement in Lamentations", p. 149, concerning Lam. 1:9–11, but the statement might be broadened to concern the Book of Lamentations as a whole.

38:6: My wounds grow foul and fester because of my foolishness.

38:7: I am utterly bowed down and prostrate; all day long I go around mourning.

38:8: For my loins are filled with burning and there is no soundness in my flesh.

38:9: I am utterly spent and crushed; I groan because of the tumult of my heart.

An "I" laments his totally broken state, the whole body affected: the flesh (vv. 4; 8), bones (v. 4), head (v. 5), loins (v. 8), heart (vv. 9; 11) and eyes (v. 11). His wounds grow foul (v. 6), he is in pain (vv. 8; 9; 18, cf. v. 17), has no strength (v. 11) and is despairing (v. 9). He is utterly bowed down and prostrate (v. 7), spent, crushed (v. 9), constantly mourning (v. 7), deaf and dumb (vv. 14–15).[186]

The lament is introduced by a prayer to YHWH: the speaking "I" explains his sickness as due to YHWH's discipline (v. 2). A petition not to be made to suffer anymore is followed by a depiction of his striking by the deity's arrows of illness and hand (v. 3). The despairing man addresses YHWH, explaining his state as due to זַעְמֶךָ "your indignation" (v. 4, cf. קֶצְפְּךָ "your wrath" and חֲמָתֶךָ "your harm" in v. 1) and חַטָּאתִי "my sin" (vv. 4; 19), עֲוֹנֹתַי "my iniquities" (vv. 5; 19) and אִוַּלְתִּי "my foolishness" (v. 6).[187] In addition to confessing sin,

---

[186] For another reading of Ps. 38 with silence as its point of view, see 5.13.3.

[187] Craigie, *Psalms 1–50*, p. 303:

The link between sin and punishment is expressed most forcefully in the parallelism of v. 4, where divine indignation and human sin are linked as a primarily spiritual diagnosis of a physical complaint...[T]he poet's perception of the state of affairs [i.e. sickness = divine punishment] was not necessarily correct; he spoke and prayed from the dept of physical and mental despair, a situation within which it was easy for theological perspectives to go haywire. The facts were these: (a) he was terribly sick; (b) God, as omnipotent, must at the very least have permitted the sickness; (c) the psalmist had sinned as he freely confesses (v. 19). From the facts, he drew the "logical" conclusion that the sickness must be a consequence of sin.

F. Lindström, *Suffering and Sin: Interpretation of Illness in the Individual Complaint Psalms* (ConBOT, 37; Stockholm: Almqvist & Wiksell, 1994) regards everything said about sin in Ps. 38:4–6; 19 as due to a revision of the original psalm "with the purpose of making the poem applicable in a situation of penitence" (p. 241). He explains YHWH's wrath according to a pedagogical model where wrath is the means for discipline (p. 242). This is based on what he calls a literary-critically oriented and contextual analysis, where his arguments are mainly related to *metri causa* and terminology. I agree with M. L. Barré's review of Lindström, *Suffering and Sin* in *RBL* 06/26/2000:

The most salient weakness inheres in the methodology Lindström employs throughout the book. Passages that ill comport with his viewpoint are declared "redactional" with little or no reference to objective controls such as textual evidence. This flawed methodology appears perhaps most clearly in chapter 6, where

however, the "I" claims his innocence as regards those around him (vv. 20–21). His sickness (vv. 3–11; 18–19) is depicted within a more comprehensive description of a humiliating state, as forsaken by friends (v. 12), pursued or scorned by enemies (vv. 13; 17; 20–21) and abandoned by YHWH (vv. 22–23). The psalm opens and closes with prayer, in addition to a prayer in v. 16.

Ps. 38 does not convey the characteristic turning point of the lament psalms, but in v. 16 the "I" prays that YHWH must hasten to turn to the petitioner. There is no change in tone, and no thanksgiving in anticipation of healing.[188] Both in the introduction and at the end, the "I" turns to the deity in the only hope still left to him: that the one who has inflicted his wound will also heal (vv. 2; 16; 22–23). Most of the prayers are based on negations and accusations. The "I" is begging the deity not to rebuke, punish (v. 2) or forsake him (v. 22). Finally, he raises an urgent call: "Make haste to help me, YHWH, my salvation" (v. 23) – without any sign of divine response.[189] Two explanations are offered for his hard times: God caused his illnesses and they were due to his sins. The separation from YHWH and his despairing illness are closely related; accusation and self-accusation stand side by side. Even though in his wrath YHWH has caused his illness (v. 2) and has forsaken him (vv. 22–23), he continues to pray despite his despair. In this reading of Ps. 38, illness has been especially focused upon, as well as the explanation offered for the illness: it is due to the sin of the speaking "I" and the anger of the deity. In this psalm, illness is a part of a more comprehensive state of despair related to the absence of God and the threat of enemies. The illness is both self-imposed due to sin and brought about by YHWH: the "I" suffers from guilt and is punished by YHWH, but there is no healing and no personification; the "I" is an implicit figure of identification, functioning as a representation of the many.[190]

---

he must deal head-on with psalms that are generally thought to contain reference to sin as the cause of the psalmist's suffering. Lindström's treatment of Ps. 38 is an illustrative example of this.

[188] Craigie, *Psalms 1–50*, p. 302.

[189] Craigie, *Psalms 1–50*, p. 302.

[190] Gunkel, the early Mowinckel, Birkeland, Seybold etc. operate with a sub-category of the individual psalms of lament called "psalms of illness", e.g. Pss. 6, 13, 30, 31, 32, 35, 38, 39, 41, 51, 69, 73, 88, 91, 102, 103, Isa. 38:9–20. Of these, the psalmist admits his sin in Pss. 38:3ff, 39:8; 11 and also YHWH is thought of as responsible for the illness, e.g. Pss. 38:1–2, 39:10–11. Gunkel, *Die Psalmen übersetzt und erklärt* regarded the hostility of the enemies, e.g. 31, 35, 51, 71, as due to their interpretation

5.11.12. *Ps. 22:15–18*

22:15 כַּמַּיִם נִשְׁפַּכְתִּי וְהִתְפָּרְדוּ כָּל־עַצְמוֹתָי
הָיָה לִבִּי כַּדּוֹנָג נָמֵס בְּתוֹךְ מֵעָי:
16 יָבֵשׁ כַּחֶרֶשׂ כֹּחִי וּלְשׁוֹנִי מֻדְבָּק מַלְקוֹחָי
וְלַעֲפַר־מָוֶת תִּשְׁפְּתֵנִי:
17 כִּי סְבָבוּנִי כְּלָבִים עֲדַת מְרֵעִים הִקִּיפוּנִי
כָּאֲרִי יָדַי וְרַגְלָי:
18 אֲסַפֵּר כָּל־עַצְמוֹתָי הֵמָּה יַבִּיטוּ יִרְאוּ־בִי:

22:15: I have been poured out like water, and all my bones have been disjointed.

22:16: My mouth is dried up like a potsherd and my tongue sticks to my jaws;
you lay me in the dust of death.

22:17: For dogs have surrounded me; evil people have encompassed me, my hands and feet were exhausted.

22:18: I count all my bones; they stare and look at me!

An "I" depicts his feeling of being completely poured out and disjointed (vv. 15; 18), dried up, close to death[191] and exhausted (vv. 16–18). In addition to his bodily conditions and despair, he is threatened by enemies described as bulls (v. 13), lions (v. 14), dogs and evil people (v. 17). The complaint of vv. 13–19 is preceded by a presentation of his surroundings (vv. 7–9), in which he recounts his neighbours' gloom at his misery and their expressed hostility. His fellows scorn and taunt him because his deity has left him.

Ps. 22 alternates between lament (vv. 1–3; 7–10; 13–19), prayer (vv. 12; 20–22), praise and thanksgiving (vv. 4–6; 9–11; 23–32). In vv. 2–3 invocation and complaint are expressed in three appeals to God, followed by an accusation of forsakenness, and a description of his own struggle to establish contact with his God (v. 3). In vv. 4–6 an affirmation of trust is offered by alluding to the fathers' trust and YHWH's delivery in the past. After his complaint of his neighbours' treatment of him (vv. 7–9), he again expresses trust in his God (vv. 10–11, cf. v. 2) and prays for help from the deity (v. 12). After complaining

---

of the illness as a sign of the guilt and god-forsakenness of the sufferer, cf. Job 19:13–22. O. Keel, *Feinde und Gottesleugner: Studien zum Image der Widersacher in den Individualpsalmen* (SBM, 7; Stuttgart: Katholisches Bibelwerk GmbH, 1969) 18–19, has critizised the vagueness in Gunkel's account of how illness was logically related in prayer to the accusation of enemies or to an indictment of enemies for folly or for abandoning faith in God. For a brief overview of "psalms of illness", see Day, *Psalms*, pp. 25–27.

[191] On death, cf. vv. 21; 30 and 5.14. In 5.8.4, Ps. 22 is read in relation to neighbours' gestures.

about his bodily condition and his treatment by his neighbours (vv. 13–19), he again prays for a response from YHWH (v. 20), as well as for deliverance from enemies (vv. 21–22). The prayer ends with an expression of trust in v. 22. Finally, the "I" turns to thanksgiving, addressed to YHWH (v. 23) and to a collective (vv. 24–27).

In Ps. 22, no explanation is offered for the illness of the "I". The "I" does not confess any sin and does not pray for healing – unlike in Isa. 53, which concerns both sin and healing. The deity is absent and enemies are present: he is forsaken by YHWH (vv. 1–3; 12; 20) and despised by enemies (vv. 7–8; 12–14; 17–19). In this psalm, illness is a part of a more comprehensive state of despair related to the absence of God and the threat of enemies. The (metaphor of) sickness goes hand in hand with desperation and isolation beyond separation. The "I" is an implicit figure of identification for the many. Irrespective of the identity of the person, it might be a representative figure. The identification of him appears through interaction with others, as one who suffers, and who represents the people in his suffering. The relation between the "I" and the community is not a personification, neither is it a question of historical biography; rather, it is a figure of identification.

5.11.13. *Job 2:7*

2:7 וַיֵּצֵא הַשָּׂטָן מֵאֵת פְּנֵי יְהֹוָה וַיַּךְ אֶת־אִיּוֹב
בִּשְׁחִין רָע מִכַּף רַגְלוֹ עַד קָדְקֳדוֹ׃

> 2:7: The Satan went out from YHWH's presence and smote Job with grievous sores from the sole of his foot to the top of his head.

In Job 2:7, the Satan went away from YHWH and smote Job with the agreed שְׁחִין רָע "grievous sores", which can imply various diseases of the skin.[192] The Satan is named as the source of Job's affliction, which is all-embracing: his whole body is smitten. Job is already sitting among the ashes, the site of mourning, when the disease is inflicted upon him (v. 8). He scratches his sores with potsherds (v. 8). Job's wife advises him to "curse God and die" (v. 9, cf. the Satan's prediction in 1:11 and 2:5).[193] Job answers that YHWH gives and takes (v. 10, cf. 1:21).

---

[192] Cf. a list of the illnesses in the book of Job in J. E. Hartley, *The Book of Job* (NICOT; Grand Rapids: Eerdmans, 1988) 82.

[193] R. N. Whybray, *Job* (Readings; Sheffield: Sheffield Academic Press, 1998) 34, comments that since the advice of Job's wife echoes the Satan's predictions in 1:11, 2:5 she has been called "the mouthpiece of Satan". Also the Satan disappears after

He rebukes his wife for giving him such wicked advice. The narrator concludes: Job did not commit any sin with his lips in his reaction to the affliction (cf. 1:22).[194]

Job 2:7 belongs to the second dialogue between YHWH and the Satan (2:1–7a), followed by Job's afflictions (vv. 7b–10).[195] The deity asks the Satan where he comes from, and he answers that he has been wandering around on the earth (v. 2, cf. 1:7). YHWH asks whether the Satan has seen his blameless and upright servant, Job (v. 3, cf. 1:8). The Satan replies by challenging the deity to test Job with an attack on his body unto death (vv. 4–5), since the previous test failed (i.e. the sudden reversal of material fortune in 1:11). The Satan suggests that the deity stretch out his hand and touch Job's body. The Satan believed that if Job became life-threateningly afflicted, Job would curse God (vv. 4–5). In v. 3 the deity reminds the Satan that he urged him to destroy Job חִנָּם "without cause", but finally he allows Job to be tested (v. 6).

Vv. 11–13 introduce the arrival of Job's three friends, his partners in the dialogue that occupies the greater part of the book. They arrive לָנוּד־לוֹ וּלְנַחֲמוֹ "to grieve and comfort him" (v. 11). When they see him, his appearance is so changed that they do not recognize him, and when they do, they begin mourning for him as for one dead (vv. 12–13). The second test is an intensification of the first. The cause/effect law is broken when the blameless and upright Job becomes life-threateningly afflicted.[196] Job's illness is brought about by the Satan on behalf of YHWH. Like the psalmists in Pss. 22 and 38, the Job figure has been taken as representative of all who suffer.[197]

---

chapter 2. Elsewhere in the Hebrew Bible, the Satan is only mentioned in Zech. 3:1–2 and 1 Chron. 21:1.

[194] Clines, *Job 1–20*, p. 55, compares Job's silent reaction here to the psalmist in Ps. 39:2–4 (cf. 5.13.4.).

[195] The Prologue of Job 1–2 is composite of a depiction of Job's piety (1:1–5), first dialogue between YHWH and the Satan (vv. 6–12), first test (vv. 13–22: disaster announced to Job), second dialogue between YHWH and the Satan (2:1–6), second test (vv. 7b–11: afflictions of Job), arrival of Job's friends (vv. 11–13). The second dialogue between YHWH and the Satan (2:1–7) has many verbal repetitions of the first.

[196] Cf. 2.3.8.3. n. 178.

[197] Clines, *Job 1–20*, p. 18:

> If indeed Job is everyman – and the core of the book convinces us of that – is the cause of his suffering the cause of all innocent suffering, and was the day of the heavenly dialogue not some moment of archaic time but a timeless day in which the same scene [1:6–12: The Satan and God: first encounter] is perpetually reenacted?

5.11.14. *Isa. 38*

In Isa. 38:1–8, we are told that the Judean king, Hezekiah, has been stricken by illness and threatened with death, as well as the circumstances of his recovery. Vv. 9–22 consist of the king's thanksgiving song and its aftermath. He is life-threateningly ill, and Isaiah the prophet tells him he shall die (v. 1). The pious Hezekiah prays to YHWH, complaining that he sees this as unjust (vv. 2–3). The prophet tells the king that YHWH has heard his prayer. The deity promises the king he shall live fifteen more years (v. 5) and that he shall protect both the king and the city against the Assyrian king (v. 6). After the king's illness and recovery are recounted, Hezekiah is promised a sign to show that the deity will do what he has said (vv. 7–8). Hezekiah thanks YHWH with a song of thanksgiving, which is introduced as follows:

38:9 מִכְתָּב לְחִזְקִיָּהוּ מֶלֶךְ־יְהוּדָה בַּחֲלֹתוֹ וַיְחִי מֵחָלְיוֹ:

> 38:9: A writing[198] belonging to Hezekiah king of Judah when he was sick
> and became well.

Hezekiah laments his untimely death in a variety of metaphors: he must go into the gates of שְׁאוֹל (v. 10) and is unable to see YHWH in אֶרֶץ הַחַיִּים "the land of the living" or see human beings from the grave (v. 11). His distress is presented in terms of illness, pain and the proximity of death (vv. 10–13; 15–16, cf. vv. 1–2). He depicts his

---

Hartley, *The Book of Job*, pp. vii:
> The message of the Book of Job plays a vital role in the theology of the canon...I
> believe that Isaiah was so inspired by the account of Job that Job served as one of
> his models in his portrait of the Suffering Servant. Since Isaiah's Servant Songs
> play a vital role in the NT's interpretation of Jesus' mission, the tie between those
> Songs and the Book of Job binds this book even more tightly to the NT message
> of Christ's redemptive work.

Hartley is generally eager to find parallels between the Book of Isaiah and the Book of Job (e.g. pp. 13–15), and regards the righteous sufferer as "the most significant theme common to both books" (p. 14). On this relation, he concludes: "[I]t seems most likely that the author of Job wrote before Isaiah, for he only alludes to the vicarious merit of innocent suffering; Isaiah develops this theme fully" (p. 15). On vicarious suffering, see 2.2.4 and 2.3.8.3. Whybray, *Job*, p. 14, emphasises in the Book of Job YHWH's concern with all his human creatures, as exemplified by his relation to the non-Israelite Job, while Clines, p. 10, comments on the possible openness as regards Job's identity, as the book says nothing about this. Job might, for instance, be an Israelite in diaspora.

[198] BHSapp and several commentators emend MT to מִכְתָּם, a kind of "Davidic" psalm, cf. Pss. 16:1, 56:1, 57:1, 58:1, 59:1, 60:1. 1QIsaᵃ supports MT, while LXX has the ambiguous προσευχὴ Εζεκιου "A Prayer of Hezekiah".

helplessness, complaining that YHWH is responsible for his bad condition, but still cries to the deity for help (vv. 12–14). He begs for healing and is certain of being answered (vv. 14–17a). In v. 17 Hezekiah depicts that YHWH is behind both the past humiliation and the coming vindication. In a turning point to praise for salvation, his healing is related to the forgiveness of sin:

38:17 הִנֵּה לְשָׁלוֹם מַר־לִי מָר
וְאַתָּה חָשַׁקְתָּ נַפְשִׁי מִשַּׁחַת בְּלִי
כִּי הִשְׁלַכְתָּ אַחֲרֵי גֵוְךָ כָּל־חֲטָאָי:

> v. 17: Behold, bitterness that was bitter to me has become peace.[199]
> But you have held me back[200] from the pit of destruction.[201]
> For you have put all my sins behind your back.

After the turning point to healing, remission of sins is reckoned among his vindications: peace, life, and not the grave (v. 17). The whole is concluded: death and שְׁאוֹל are cut off from the deity and do not praise him (v. 18), but the living give thanks and confess his faithfulness (v. 19) as "all" shall praise YHWH in his house (v. 20). Isaiah then asks to press figs on the boil, as the sign the pious Hezekiah had asked to go to the temple (vv. 21–22).

In this thanksgiving, a change appears between the speaking "I" mentioning and addressing the Lord: in vv. 10–11; 17–19, the "I" is speaking to "you", in vv. 12–13 the "I" is speaking to "you" and about "him", in vv. 14; 16 the "I" invokes the Lord, in v. 15 the "I" is talking about "him" and in v. 20 the Lord is mentioned – and the address is suddenly in the plural.

In vv. 9–22, Hezekiah depicts what he has lived through: from humiliation (vv. 10–17a) to vindication (vv. 17b–20). In a combination of lament and thanksgiving, elements of sickness, near-death experiences

---

[199] Watts, *Isaiah 34–66*, p. 55, Blenkinsopp, *Isaiah 1–39*, pp. 480–481y, and many others suggest either deleting the second מָר or replacing it with מְאֹד, cf. 1QIsaᵃ מאודה.

[200] Oswalt, *The Book of Isaiah: Chapters 1–39*, p. 680, n. 12: "MT has [חָשַׁקְתָּ], 'you loved', which is possible, but very unlikely. LXX has [καὶ ἀπέρριψας ὀπίσω μου] 'delivered', which lends support to the original [חָשַׂק], 'hold back', 'spare'. Cf. Watts, *Isaiah 34–66*, p. 55. Blenkinsopp, *Isaiah 1–39*, p. 480, translates: "but now in love you have preserved my life".

[201] Blenkinsopp, *Isaiah 1–39*, pp. 480–481z: "For MT [מִשַּׁחַת בְּלִי] 1QIsaᵃ has [מִשַּׁחַת כְּלִי] 'from the pit of annihilation'."

and recovery are involved.[202] As in Isa. 53, the metaphor of sickness conveys a blurring of bodily, political and theological crises and diagnoses, but the connection between sickness and sin is less explicit, as it is mentioned only in passing (v. 17b). Hezekiah expresses his own sins, but not as a "confession". More emphatically articulated is his feeling of being unjustly punished by YHWH. A connection between king and people is underlined in words against the Assyrians in v. 6. As the king's sickness precedes the events recorded in Isa. 36–37, the promises of recovery for Hezekiah is joined by promises that the city will be saved. Hezekiah's life and reign had been threatened by illness and the Assyrian siege. Through the presentation of the Assyrian king as a common enemy, king Hezekiah becomes a representative and a symbol of the nation, i.e. the variation of personification called the Body Politic.[203] Here, the illness might be diagnosed as both self-

---

[202] Blenkinsopp, *Isaiah 1–39*, p. 484: "The psalm attributed to Hezekiah belongs to the familiar type of thanksgiving hymn for deliverance from danger and death (e.g. Ps 107) and contains nothing peculiar to Hezekiah's situation."

[203] It has been claimed that the sequences of events in Isa. 38 (related to their context) are due to theological rather than chronological reasons, where Hezekiah's rescue from death is related to the untimely death of Sennacherib (Isa. 37:38), as Hezekiah's sickness and recovery should precede the survival of Jerusalem (38:6, 39:1). Isa. 37 is a blend of words of doom to Assyria and words of salvation to Judah. The words of doom to Assyria talk of the death of the Assyrians (v. 36) and their king Sennacherib's (v. 38), as well as their futile gods (v. 38). The Assyrians' and their king's "incurable" humiliations are contrasted with King Hezekiah's illness and healing in Isa. 38. Sweeney, *Isaiah 1–39 with an Introduction to Prophetic Literature*, p. 501 argues that "the question of the historicity of Hezekiah's illness is irrelevant, the literary portrayal of his illness takes an overwhelming importance."

P. R. Ackroyd, "An Interpretation of the Babylonian Exile: 2 Kgs 20, Isaiah 38–39", *SJT* 27 (1974) 329–352, sees Hezekiah as representing the people, in which the king's situation is like the nation's near death in exile, but eventual restoration. Also Oswalt, *The Book of Isaiah: Chapters 1–39*, pp. 672; 681, takes the king as representing the people, but claims that the stress is not so much upon the restoration as upon the fallibility of the king and the people who, despite the present reprieve, must issue in coming destruction. J. H. Coetzee, "The 'Song of Hezekiah' (Isaiah 38:9–20): A Doxology of Judgement from the Exilic Period", *Old Testament Essays* 2/3 (1989) 15 sees "a striking relationship between the lengthened life of Hezekiah and the continued existence of the City of Jerusalem (cf. 38:5–6; 39)."

Seitz, *Zion's Final Destiny*, p. 208, regards Isa. 36–39 as part of a pre-Exilic corpus of First Isaiah, "the pivot on which the entire tradition process turns, explaining the puzzle of Isaiah's growth…and much of the shape and character of Second Isaiah…" He emphasises how the trust, restoration and praise of Hezekiah are a model of what will happen to the sick and sinful Zion, cf. Isa. 1:5–6 (pp. 176–182). Seitz sees an analogy between Isa. 52:13–53:12 and the illness of Hezekiah, based on his idea that Zion is the servant of YHWH (pp. 202–204). Contrary to what most scholars have claimed, Seitz argues that the Isaiah version of this story is earlier than the version in 2 Kgs 20:1–11 (pp. 162–176, supporting Smelik). For a critique of Seitz's study, see

imposed in Hezekiah's and the people's turning away and brought about by YHWH: the king and his people suffer guilt and are punished by YHWH, and they are promised recovery.

5.11.15. *Summing Up*

In Isa. 53, bodily conditions of pain appear in a variety of humiliations: he was ill, despised, isolated, even dead. This is not only a matter of illness as the wounds are also brought about by others. He was stricken with illness by God and this was due to "our" sins. Thus, the diagnosis and explanation consist of a blurring of bodily and theological concerns. Moreover, diagnoses of both human beings ("he" and "we") and a collective people ("we", that is, Israel) are made. By a personification, the actors are revealed through a pattern of elements surrounding the figure(s) of "he"/"we", where the personifier "he" and the personified "we" are blurred by different accentuations: the healing is gained for "us" by the punishment of "him" (v. 5b). Whereas an identification between "him" and "us" is revealed in the common illness, the question of "his" guilt, as well as "his" healing, is in some ways left open. Also, no explanation is given for the turning point towards healing.

While the relation between illness and sin is conveyed in confessional "we" speech in Isa. 53:4–6 and in YHWH speech in 53:8; 12, in 1:5–6 the diagnosis is made by YHWH. The desperate situation of the people is presented in a personification of the community as a wounded body, with a blurring of an address to a plurality, i.e. "you" (2mpl) and a depiction of a sick body. In Isa. 1:5–6, 53 and also in Hos. 5:13, illness is presented both as brought about by others and as self-imposed – related to delusion. "He" and "we" (Isa. 53), "you" (Isa. 1:5–6) and Ephraim and Judah (Hos. 5:13) all suffer illness as a result of guilt and are punished by YHWH. In Isa. 53 and Hos. 5, prospects

---

D. M. Carr, "What Can We Say about the Tradition History of Isaiah? A Response to Christopher Seitz's *Zion's Final Destiny*" (SBLSP, 31; Atlanta: Scholars Press, 1992) 583–597, and Sweeney, pp. 497–502. R. Kasher, "The Sitz im Buch of the Story of Hezekiah's Illness and Cure (II Reg 20,1–11; Isa 38,1–22)", *ZAW* 113 (2001) 41–55, argues that it is possible to reconstruct an original story older than both 2 Kgs 20 and Isa. 38, and that both versions have received some harmonised additions at a later stage. Williamson, *The Book Called Isaiah*, pp. 202–211, claims that the Isaiah passage has adapted Kings to its new focus. Whereas the Kings account focuses on the individual Hezekiah, the Isaiah version presents the king as typologically representing the restoration of the community. On the Body Politic, see 4.7.3.5.

of healing are also conveyed. In Hos 5:13, different kinds of personifications are at play: Ephraim and Judah personify land and people,
while Assyria is personified by its king.

Just as "he" interacts with "us" in Isa. 53, so in Jer. 8:21–22 a dialogue appears between "I" and בַּת־עַמִּי "the daughter of my people".
In Jer. 8, an "I" laments the city's fate. The speaker is sick and in deep
sorrow, hearing the cry of בַּת־עַמִּי "the daughter of my people" all over
the land (vv. 18–19). Attempts are made to blame the deity for being
absent, but the people's own fault is also admitted: they have followed
other deities. In a female personification, the misery of בַּת־עַמִּי "the
daughter of my people" is depicted as שֶׁבֶר (v. 21), with both the illness of the daughter and the destruction of the city indicated. The
speaking "I" of 8:21–22 has been identified as Jeremiah as spokesman
for the community: because of the suffering of the people, Jeremiah is
gripped by dismay. The identification of this "I" lies in his interaction
with others; he is one who suffers from his people's wounds. He is not
a personification, but represents and identifies with the people.

In Jer. 10, a variety of voices and actors appear in depictions of crises: in a lament over a woman in a besieged city (vv. 17–18), a person
broken with illness and bereaved of his children and with his tent scattered (vv. 19–20), shepherds and their scattered flock (vv. 21–22) and
Jacob's lament (vv. 23–24). Similar to Isa. 53, the illness seems to be
both self-imposed (cf. v. 19) and caused by others (v. 21) – in Isa. 53
the deity has punished and in Jer. 10. the leaders are blamed. In Jer. 10
and in the "I" and "we" lament in Jer. 14, the disaster and devastation
of land and people are mixed. The prophet describes the suffering of
the people of the city as the suffering of an incurably wounded woman.
She becomes a personification through a set of complex transformations in the relation between "I" (the prophet), Judah, Zion and "us".
Judah, Zion and "we" suffer from guilt and are punished by YHWH.
False prophets (vv. 13–16), the people (v. 20) and YHWH (v. 19) are
all depicted as responsible for the catastrophe. Unlike in Isa. 53, there
is no promise of healing in either Jer. 10 or Jer. 14.

In Jer. 30:12–17, YHWH addresses "you" (2fs) as a personification
of Zion. YHWH laments her fatal injury, her abandment by her lovers,
her enemies' taunting and her deity acting like a cruel one (vv. 12–14).
Fluctuating explanations are given for her fate. The incurable wounds
are explained as self-inflicted due to her sin (vv. 14–15, cf. Isa. 53:4–6),
YHWH has stricken her because of her sinfulness (vv. 14–15, cf. Isa.
53:4–6) and external enemies are also blamed for what has happened

(vv. 16–17, cf. Isa. 53:7–9). In all cases a reversal of her state is promised, as YHWH will act against her enemies and offer healing (cf. Isa. 53:5). The female figure of Zion personifies the people; her fate and the people's fate go hand in hand, with illness/healing (vv. 12–15; 17) and humiliation/vindication (vv. 14; 16) blurred beyond separation. Jer. 8, 10, 14 and 30 all convey female personifications of בַּת־עַמִּי "the daughter of my people".

In Jer. 15, fluctuating explanations are offered for the prophet's suffering beyond any prospect of healing: his suffering is both self-imposed and due to the unjust. Jeremiah both personifies the people and is their victim. He might suffer the same fate as the people, who have turned away from their deity, but he also suffers because of his prophetic task. The prophet laments the pain which his faithfulness to YHWH has caused and the deity responds by asking for repentance and offers a conditional promise (v. 19). The vindication of Jeremiah is not promised in terms of healing, but in terms of speech (v. 19) and the submission of his enemies (vv. 12–14; 20–21). The discussions about the "laments of Jeremiah" are challenged by similar questions to the debate about the servant in Second Isaiah, for instance, regarding the possibility of establishing connections between a historical Jeremiah and the character in the Book of Jeremiah, as well as between the humiliations of him and the people.

In the terrifying description of a woman's pain in Lam. 1, she works as a personification and the injury works as a metaphor blurring bodily, political and theological crises and diagnoses. Like "him"/"us" in Isa. 53, "her" suffering is both self-imposed through the people's turning away and brought upon "her" by YHWH: she suffers from guilt and is punished by the deity. Whereas Lam. 1:1–11 concerns what happened to Zion, in Lam. 2 the cause of the disaster is dwelt upon (cf. 2:1). When compared to Isa. 53, the personification of Lam. 2 is more complex, as the daughter of Zion is related to the city's inhabitants, architecture and institutions. As regards themes, both Lam. 1–2 and Isa. 53 concern suffering and sin, but while Isa. 53 also mediates coming healing, Lam. maintains the grief.

In Ps. 38, the psalmist offers two explanations for his bad times: God caused his illnesses and they were due to his sins. The separation from YHWH and his despairing illness are closely related; accusation and self-accusation stand side by side. In Ps. 22, no explanation is offered for the psalmist's illness. He neither confesses sin nor prays for healing, unlike in Isa. 53 in which both sin and healing are indicated. As in

Ps. 38, illness becomes part of a more comprehensive state of despair related to the absence of God and the threat of enemies. The (metaphor of) sickness goes hand in hand with desperation and isolation beyond separation. In both Pss. 38 and 22, the psalmist becomes an implicit figure of identification for the many. The identification of him appears in his interaction with others; he is one who suffers, and who represents the people in his suffering. In Job 2, illness is brought upon the pious servant Job by the Satan on behalf of YHWH. The cause/effect law is broken when the blameless man becomes life-threateningly afflicted. Also the Job figure has been taken as a representative of all who suffer.

In the pious king Hezekiah's lament and thanksgiving in Isa. 38, elements of sickness, near-death experiences and recovery are involved. As in Isa. 53, the metaphor of sickness conveys a blurring of bodily, political and theological crises, but the connection between sickness and sin is less explicit. Hezekiah mentions his sins only in passing. More emphatically articulated is his feeling of the unjust treatment by YHWH. Through the presentation of the Assyrian king as a common enemy, king Hezekiah becomes a representative and a symbol of the nation, i.e. the variation of personification called the Body Politic. Here, the illness might be diagnosed as both self-imposed and brought about by others: the king and his people suffer from guilt because they have turned away from and they are punished by YHWH. Also, they are promised recovery.

In Isa. 53, a man suffers illness, pain and contempt. In a personification, the intimate and devastating metaphor of illness depicts the people as ill – or injured. As in most of the other texts referred to in this chapter, a cause/effect relation appears between illness and sin, as a diagnosis is given: the people are ill due to sin. In this relation of illness and sin, a blurring of bodily, political and theological diagnoses and crises is at work. The illness is both self-imposed and brought about by YHWH. In Isa. 53, illness becomes part of a more comprehensive depiction of a situation of uttermost distress related to punishment for sin, i.e. a multi-layered description of the crisis: sickness, contempt, isolation, injustice, death and unworthy burial.[204] Taking the historical dimension

---

[204] As regards metaphors of illness in general in the Hebrew Bible, Lindström, *Suffering and Sin*, p. 26, comments on the tense combinations of metaphors and how the

into consideration, the Exile becomes a theological interpretation of
"something which has happened" in most of the texts referred to.[205]

In this chapter, different kinds of personifications and represen-
tations of the people have been presented: the community of Israel,
Ephraim and Judah ("he"/"we") as a wounded body (Isa. 53, 1:5–6,
Hos 5:13), Zion as a woman (Jer. 8, 10, 14, 30, Lam 1, 2), Assyria and
Israel as their kings (Hos. 5, Isa. 38), the prophet on behalf of society
(Jer. 8, 15) and the psalmists and Job representing those who suffer
(Pss. 22, 38, Job 2). The interrelationships existing between characters
of different texts are a highly important dimension of intertextuality.[206]
The task is not to search for an *Urtext* or original meaning. In viewing
every text as a sign, the writer's individual, authorial voice disappears
in favour of the effects of difference and the process of differentiation
itself only to emerge in the guise of the new text, sign and writing.

5.12. "...AND THUS YHWH STRUCK HIM BY THE INIQUITY OF ALL OF US"

5.12.1. *Isa. 53:5–6*

53:5 וְהוּא מְחֹלָל מִפְּשָׁעֵנוּ מְדֻכָּא מֵעֲוֹנֹתֵינוּ
מוּסַר שְׁלוֹמֵנוּ עָלָיו וּבַחֲבֻרָתוֹ נִרְפָּא־לָנוּ:
6 כֻּלָּנוּ כַּצֹּאן תָּעִינוּ אִישׁ לְדַרְכּוֹ פָּנִינוּ
וַיהוָה הִפְגִּיעַ בּוֹ אֵת עֲוֹן כֻּלָּנוּ:

53:5:   But he was wounded because of our transgressions and injured
        because of our iniquities;
        chastisement was upon him for our healing and by his wound is
        recovery for us.
53:6:   All of us like sheep went astray; everyone turned his own way
        and thus YHWH struck him by the iniquity of all of us.

In Isa. 53:5 "we" explain his and "our" fate: the humiliation which has
stricken him is a punishment from YHWH because of "our" sin. In
v. 3, his illness is connected to the shame related to others' reactions,
including the reactions of the speaking, witnessing "we". In v. 4a, an

---

depictions of affliction are conveyed through diverse metaphors in a circular way, i.e.
the different aspects and dimensions of suffering/humiliation intertwine. He asks: "Is
it wise to break apart such circles in order to forge them into causal chains?"
    [205] Cf. 2.3.3. n. 142.
    [206] Müller, "Interfigurality", p. 101.

identification of fate between him and "us" is disclosed in a common
illness. In a personification, the actors are revealed through a repetition of elements surrounding the figure(s) of "he"/"we", with a blurring of the personifier "he" and the personified "we" (cf. 4.8.2.2.). In
v. 4b, "our" past explanation of his fate as caused by YHWH is offered,
whereas in v. 5a "we" acknowledge that the illnesses he and "we"
carried are a result of פְּשָׁעֵנוּ "our transgressions" and עֲוֹנֹתֵינוּ "our
iniquities". In v. 6 כֻּלָּנוּ "all of us" compare themselves to sheep gone
astray, modifying the comparison with an explanation: everybody was
breaking away by going their own way.[207] In a final and concluding
statement, "our" confession of transgression and the explanation for
his fate appear (v. 6b, cf. v. 5): he was ill due to "our" sin and the
punishment is brought upon him by YHWH. The illness is explained
as punishment of sins, framed by a distancing, where he is depicted
as wounded and "we" as sinners. In this reflection on "our" own guilt,
the awareness of having been chastised by God and the admission
of having been struck are prompted by "our" own delusion and self-
accusation on account of the previous failure to recognise him. After
his and "our" illnesses and sins are described and explained (vv. 3–5a),
his wounds are described as chastisement for "our" rehabilitation
(v. 5b). In the relation between his punishment and wounds and "our"
healing, both restitution of illness and reconciliation as opposed to sin
might be indicated: both "we" and he shall be healed.

Then, in v. 8 a depiction of his humiliations as one who has been
unjustly treated is interrupted by a question about his fate and its relation to דּוֹרוֹ "his time" and עַמִּי "my people". It appears that his wounds
are due to פֶּשַׁע עַמִּי "the transgression of my people" (cf. vv. 5–6).[208]
The speaking "I" is identified as YHWH and the sinners as the deity's
people.[209] In v. 9 his humiliations are deepened, with a depiction of his
death and unworthy tomb.[210] He is buried with רְשָׁעִים "wicked ones",

---

[207] On people in delusion as צֹאן "sheep", see Isa. 13:14, Jer. 23:1–3, 25:34–36, 50:6;
17, Ezek. 34:6; 8; 10; 12; 17; 22; 31, Zech. 13:7. On people as sheep, cf. 5.13.2. n. 244,
on YHWH as shepherd, see 5.8.3. n. 65, and on kings or leaders as shepherds, see
5.11.5. n. 143.
[208] On scholarly discussions of מֵעֹצֶר וּמִמִּשְׁפָּט לֻקָּח, see 3.10.11 n. 115 and Appendix 5 and on מִפֶּשַׁע עַמִּי נֶגַע לָמוֹ, see 3.10.11. nn. 122–123.
[209] See 3.10.17.3. עַמִּי "my people" appears in YHWH speech in Isa. 40:1 (cf. 5.12.5.),
43:20, 47:6, 49:13, 51:4; 16; 22, 52:4–6.
[210] For רְשָׁעִים "wicked ones", see 48:22, 55:7 (sg, cf. אָוֶן אִישׁ "evil man"); vb. hi.
"condemn as guilty" in 50:9, 54:1. For humiliating death and unworthy tomb, see
5.14.1.

echoing the consequences of sin: being struck due to the transgression of עַמִּי "my people", he is reckoned among the wicked ones. This striking of him is despite his having committed neither violence nor treachery. A *waw* in v. 10 connects to v. 9 by way of contrast and is followed by a depiction of his illness and its explanation: it was due to YHWH's pleasure and to sin.[211] The depiction of sin continues in v. 11: עֲוֹנֹתָם הוּא יִסְבֹּל "he carried their iniquities", echoing מַכְאֹבֵינוּ סְבָלָם "he carried our sicknesses" in v. 4. As a man who carries illness is a sick man (v. 4), a man who carries sin is a sinner (v. 11, cf. vv. 5; 6; 8; 10). Also in v. 12, his past is explained within a similar semantic field: תַּחַת אֲשֶׁר הֶעֱרָה לַמָּוֶת נַפְשׁוֹ "because he was slain to death"; הוּא חֵטְא־פֹּשְׁעִים נִמְנָה "he was reckoned with transgressors"; רַבִּים נָשָׂא "he bore the sin of many" (cf. vv. 4; 11) and לַפֹּשְׁעִים יַפְגִּיעַ "he was struck because transgressors"; the two last phrases echo the relation between illness and sin in v. 5.[212]

The past situation of illness, sin and punishment is interrupted by and contrasted with a completely opposite situation in the future in vv. 10b; 11; 12a, where he shall be blessed with descendants and live long (v. 10), see, be satisfied by his knowledge, called עַבְדִּי "my servant", make רַבִּים "many" righteous (v. 11) and succeed over רַבִּים "many" and עֲצוּמִים "numerous" (v. 12). Both the past and the future are explained as חֵפֶץ יְהוָה "YHWH's pleasure" (v. 10).

In Isa. 53, a whole range of expressions for transgression appears: פְּשָׁעֵנוּ "our transgressions" and עֲוֹנֹתֵינוּ "our iniquities" (v. 5); כֻּלָּנוּ כַּצֹּאן תָּעִינוּ "all of us like sheep went astray"; אִישׁ לְדַרְכּוֹ פָּנִינוּ "everyone turned his own way"; עֲוֹן כֻּלָּנוּ "the iniquity of all of us" (v. 6); פֶּשַׁע עַמִּי "the transgression of my people" (v. 8); רְשָׁעִים "wicked ones" (v. 9); עֲוֹנֹתָם הוּא יִסְבֹּל "he carried their iniquities" (v. 11); פֹּשְׁעִים נִמְנָה "he was reckoned with transgressors"; הוּא חֵטְא־רַבִּים נָשָׂא "he bore the sin of many" and לַפֹּשְׁעִים יַפְגִּיעַ "he was struck by transgressors" (v. 12). Although inseparable, sin, guilt and punishment are explained through different accentuations. In 53:1ff, an identification between him and "us" appears within a relation to sin and punishment, where the punishment is related to him, and the sin to "us". Moreover, "our" sin is related both to his and "our" illnesses. "We" both confess guilt and have brought upon "ourselves" "our" own punishment. The

---

[211] אִם־תָּשִׂים אָשָׁם נַפְשׁוֹ is disputed, see Appendix 6.
[212] Cf. 3.10.15. nn. 154–155.

sufferings have a twofold effect: they are both the penalty for sins and the means of reconciliation and restoration. The personified humiliated and restored Israel in the past, present and future is addressed and mentioned in sg ("he", עַבְדִּי "my servant") and pl ("we", רַבִּים "many", עֲצוּמִים "numerous", עַמִּי "my people"). These are variations on a blurring of signifiers and signifieds.

5.12.2. *Isa. 42:24–25*

42:24 מִי־נָתַן לִמְשׁוֹסֶה יַעֲקֹב וְיִשְׂרָאֵל לְבֹזְזִים
הֲלוֹא יְהוָה זוּ חָטָאנוּ לוֹ
וְלֹא־אָבוּ בִדְרָכָיו הָלוֹךְ וְלֹא שָׁמְעוּ בְּתוֹרָתוֹ:
²⁵ וַיִּשְׁפֹּךְ עָלָיו חֵמָה אַפּוֹ וֶעֱזוּז מִלְחָמָה
וַתְּלַהֲטֵהוּ מִסָּבִיב וְלֹא יָדָע וַתִּבְעַר־בּוֹ וְלֹא־יָשִׂים עַל־לֵב:

42:24: Who surrendered Jacob to the plunder and Israel to the robbers?
Was it not YHWH, against whom we sinned,
in whose ways they were not willing to walk and whose law they would not obey?

42:25: He poured upon him the heat, his anger and the fury of war;
it consumed him round about, but he did not understand,
it burned him, but he did not take it to heart.

In two questions about the past in Isa. 42:24, the one who surrendered Jacob and Israel is asked for. The questions of who gave Israel and Jacob up to utter subjection and powerlessness in v. 24a are responded to by yet another question in v. 24b. After an interrogative, negating הֲלוֹא "Was it not...", the requested agent of v. 24a is identified as YHWH, with the appositional חָטָאנוּ לוֹ "against whom we sinned", establishing a relation between him and a speaking "we" through sin. After Jacob and Israel were mentioned in v. 24a, "we" appear as the interrogative voice in v. 24b. The abrupt transition to "we" makes the expression into "our" confession of sinning towards the deity. Apart from Isa. 53:1–6, the only place in Isa. 40–55 in which "we" speak is in 42:24.[213] This is followed by two more appositions to the question of

---

[213] In Isa. 47:4, 52:10 and 55:17, the expression "our God" appears as a more formulaic statement in the prophet's speech, cf. this formulation in the anonymous voice in 40:3; 8. In a trial speech in 41:22–23; 26, YHWH is speaking in the plural, i.e. including the people. See Conrad, *Reading Isaiah*, pp. 83–116, esp. pp. 94ff.

Westermann, *Isaiah 40–66*, p. 113, suggests that the prophet seems to confess his own sin along with the people's in 42:24a. Since there is nothing similar elsewhere in what he defines as the *Grundschicht* in Isa. 40–55, he regards this as a later addition. Further, he argues that 42:24c must be a later addition because it is prose and it lacks

v. 24b, which is also an answer. In the appositions, both predicates are
negated: וְלֹא־אָבוּ בִדְרָכָיו הָלוֹךְ "they were not willing to walk his ways"
and לֹא שָׁמְעוּ בְּתוֹרָתוֹ "they did not obey his law" (cf. 53:5–6).[214] The
subject "we" in v. 24b abruptly changes to "they" in v. 24c. With the
appositions, "we" rebuke "ourselves" for not having trusted YHWH,
not walking in his ways and disobeying his law. The calamities were
permitted by YHWH in response to their disobedience: due to sin,
delusion and disobedience, the deity gave up his people to "plunder
and robbers".

After the questions in v. 24a are answered, YHWH's treatment
of "him" is deepened (v. 25): the deity brought his wrath and fury
upon "him", who neither understood this nor took it to heart. As in
v. 24, faithlessness and sin are expressed. By "his" obstinacy and the
wrath of YHWH, both "he" and the deity have brought about the
misery. Whereas most of v. 24 concerns what "we"/"they" did not do
to YHWH, v. 25 concerns the deity's reaction to "him": "we" sinned,
"they" neither walked in his ways nor listened his law (v. 24), "he" neither understood YHWH's wrath nor took it to heart (v. 25). Even the
deity's war did not make Israel understand. YHWH is the defendant
and "we" are confessing; they have sinned and the deity has punished.
Hearing is key as regards both past and future: when the people did
not listen to the words of YHWH, misery was caused, but if they listen, a better future might come, cf. the rhetorical question in v. 23.[215]
Characteristic of the many changes in the addressing and mentioning
of "you" (v. 23), Jacob (v. 24), Israel (v. 24), "we" (v. 24), "they" (v. 24)
and "he" (v. 25) is that all are presented through a relation to sin and
punishment: YHWH surrendered Jacob and Israel to plundering and
brought upon "him" his wrath, whereas "we" sinned and "they" neither walked in YHWH's ways nor listened to his law. This is reminiscent of the relation between the wounds and chastisement of "him"
and "our" sins in Isa. 53:3ff. "We", "they" and "he" did not recognise

---

any connection with what precedes it because it reverts to 3ms. He connects v. 24c
to v. 21, which he also regards as a later addition, supported by Schoors, *I am God
your Saviour*, pp. 206–207, and H. C. Spykerboer, *The Structure and Composition of
Deutero-Isaiah with Special Reference to the Polemics against Idolatry* (Meppel: Krips
Repro, 1976) 98.

[214] תּוֹרָה "instruction", "law" in Isa. 42:24 is connected to delusion; in 42:4, 51:4 it is
related to YHWH's מִשְׁפָּט "justice" and in 42:21 (cf. 51:7) to צִדְקוֹ "his righteousness".

[215] Also immediately before, in 42:18–20; 22, Israel is diagnosed as blind and deaf,
cf. 5.9.2.

the implications of what they had experienced, the fatal connection between suffering and guilt. YHWH's wrath is a reaction to Israel's guilt, because they did not understand. A blurring of personifier and personified "you" emerges, – or is created –, when some sort of identification between Jacob, Israel, "we", "they" and "he" is disclosed: Jacob and Israel were punished by YHWH (v. 24), "we" sinned, "they" neither walked in his ways nor listened to his law (v. 24) and "he" neither understood YHWH's wrath nor took it to heart (v. 25). While in Isa. 53 there are many pronounced expressions demonstrating a turn-around to future vindication, in Isa. 42 this is not as explicit, although it is alluded to in the rhetorical questions related to listening in the future in v. 23.

5.12.3. *Isa. 43:22–28*

43:22 וְלֹא־אֹתִי קָרָאתָ יַעֲקֹב כִּי־יָגַעְתָּ בִּי יִשְׂרָאֵל:
²³ לֹא־הֵבִיאתָ לִּי שֵׂה עֹלֹתֶיךָ וּזְבָחֶיךָ לֹא כִבַּדְתָּנִי
לֹא הֶעֱבַדְתִּיךָ בְּמִנְחָה וְלֹא הוֹגַעְתִּיךָ בִּלְבוֹנָה:
²⁴ לֹא־קָנִיתָ לִּי בַכֶּסֶף קָנֶה וְחֵלֶב זְבָחֶיךָ לֹא הִרְוִיתָנִי
אַךְ הֶעֱבַדְתַּנִי בְּחַטֹּאותֶיךָ הוֹגַעְתַּנִי בַּעֲוֹנֹתֶיךָ:
²⁵ אָנֹכִי אָנֹכִי הוּא מֹחֶה פְשָׁעֶיךָ לְמַעֲנִי וְחַטֹּאתֶיךָ לֹא אֶזְכֹּר:
²⁶ הַזְכִּירֵנִי נִשָּׁפְטָה יָחַד סַפֵּר אַתָּה לְמַעַן תִּצְדָּק:
²⁷ אָבִיךָ הָרִאשׁוֹן חָטָא וּמְלִיצֶיךָ פָּשְׁעוּ בִי:
²⁸ וַאֲחַלֵּל שָׂרֵי קֹדֶשׁ וְאֶתְּנָה לַחֵרֶם יַעֲקֹב וְיִשְׂרָאֵל לְגִדּוּפִים:

43:22: But me have you not called upon, Jacob, that you have wearied
yourself with me, Israel.

43:23: You have not brought me sheep for your burnt offerings
and with your sacrifices have you not honoured me.
I have not burdened you with meal offerings or wearied you with
frankincense.

43:24: You have not bought me sweet cane with money,
and with the fat of your sacrifice have you not satisfied me.
But you have burdened me with your sins and you have wearied
me with your iniquities.

43:25: I, I am He who blots out your transgression for my own sake
and your sins I will not remember.

43:26: Put me in remembrance, let us argue together;
set forth your case that you may be proved right.

43:27: Your first father sinned and your spokesmen rebelled against me.

43:28: That is why I profaned the princes of the sanctuary,
why I delivered Jacob to utter destruction and Israel to insult.

In Isa. 43:22–28, indictments are addressed in "I" speech to "you" (2ms), who is further identified as Jacob and Israel (v. 22). YHWH is calling upon them, accusing them of not calling upon him, but being weary (v. 22) and not bringing him offerings, honouring him (v. 23) or satisfying him with sacrifices (v. 24). In addition to the statements about what Jacob and Israel have not done, the deity expresses what he himself has not required: he has neither burdened him with offerings nor wearied him with frankincense. Then YHWH expresses what "you" have done: "you have burdened me with your sins" and "wearied me with your iniquities" (v. 24b).[216] The verbs עבד (hi.) "burden" and יגע (hi.) "weary" in v. 24b are repetitions, with variations, of v. 23b: I, YHWH, have not burdened "you" with offerings, but you have burdened me with your sin. It was not service (worship) you gave to me, rather you served me with your sins instead of sacrifice. Additionally: I have not wearied you with frankincense (v. 23), but you have wearied me with your iniquities.[217] You have not called upon me, but wearied yourself with me (v. 22).[218] YHWH has neither claimed offerings nor sacrifices of honour; they have brought him their sins and burdened the deity with the weight of their transgressions.[219] In

---

[216] The prep. בְּ in בְּחַטֹּאותֶיךָ "your sins" and בַּעֲוֺנֹתֶיךָ "your iniquities" is causal, explaining the cause of the burdening of YHWH. Cf. 5.12.4. n. 223.

[217] יגע (qal in v. 22, hi. in v. 23). In v. 23 and v. 24 the same verb forms in the same order appear (עבד hi. "burden", יגע hi. "weary"), but the subjects and objects are reversed; while v. 23 has negations, v. 24 has affirmations. Westermann, *Isaiah 40–66*, p. 131, explains how this word play implies that YHWH is made into a servant. Blenkinsopp, *Isaiah 40–55*, p. 231, also comments on the word play of עבד in vv. 23–24, which he relates to Israel's inauthentic sacrifice to YHWH:

> "I did not burden you (also: make you serve liturgically) with the cereal offering"; "you burdened me (also: offered service to me – suffix as indirect object) with your sins"; in other words: you served me up your sins instead of sacrifice; your sins got through to me, but your sacrifice did not.

Israel's cultic service towards YHWH is expressed with עבד qal "serve" in Exod. 3:12, 4:23, 7:16, 8:16, 9:1; 13, 10:3; 7; 8; 11; 24; 26, 12:31. Israel's false service towards YHWH and its apostasy and worshipping of other Gods are frequently expressed by עבד. On the root עבד, see also 5.17. n. 324.

[218] It has been asked whether 43:22–24 are a reproach of Israel on account of its sacrifices. The cult is central to the text, but both the divine ordering of the cult and its factuality are denied: all cultic acts are preceded by לֹא, see T. Booij, "Negotiation in Isaiah 43:22–24", *ZAW* 94 (1982) 390. Cultic language does not play a prominent role in Isa. 40–55. Apart from 43:23–24, Lebanon's cult is critizised in 40:16, idol production is an issue in 44:15 and perhaps the fire in 50:11. 43:22–28 might also be related to a prophetic critique of the sacrificial system, cf. Isa. 1:10–17, 66:3, Jer. 6:20, 7:5–10; 21–26, Amos 5:21–24, Hos. 6:6, Mic. 6:3–8, Mal. 1:13, 2:17.

[219] Koole, *Isaiah III. Vol. 2*, p. 337, comments that no guilt or sin offerings are mentioned in the enumerations of offerings. He describes briefly the different offerings mentioned: עֹלָה "burnt offerings" is expressive of atonement, זֶבַח "sacrifice" may encompass the whole system, but particularly bloody offerings of sin, מִנְחָה "gift"

the explanation offered in v. 25, a fatal connection between suffering and guilt appears. Then YHWH offers forgiveness through his self-presentation. The deity affirms what he will do and not do for the future: he blots out their transgressions and will not remember their sins (v. 25). According to YHWH, this is not due to Israel's serving of sacrifices, confessions of sin or return to obedience, but takes place לְמַעֲנִי "for my sake".

Vv. 22–25 present contrasts between what Israel and YHWH did and did not do in the past, and what YHWH will do in the future. After the deity has been arguing with his people in vv. 22–25, in v. 26 YHWH takes them to court. His forgetting of the people's past (v. 25) is contrasted with his appeal to them to remind him of their past (v. 26). After having confronted his people with their mistaken worship (vv. 23–24), the possibility manifests itself that YHWH could have forgotten, i.e. Israel is given a chance to justify herself.

In vv. 27–28 the indictment includes the whole past of Israel as the sins of אָבִיךָ הָרִאשׁוֹן "your first father" and מְלִיצֶיךָ "your spokesmen" are also considered. The indictments against the ancestors and leaders are not primarily about their cultic praxis, but their חָטָא "sin" and פֶּשַׁע "transgression" in general, echoing פְּשָׁעֶיךָ "your transgressions" and חַטֹּאתֶיךָ "your sins" in v. 25. The people's whole mistaken history is alluded to. Due to these sins, שָׂרֵי קֹדֶשׁ "the princes of the sanctuary" were profaned,[220] and Jacob and Israel destroyed and insulted. The punishment which YHWH brought upon the people and the sanctuary is explained. YHWH defends himself against an implied charge that he has abandoned Israel during its bad times by blaming Israel's sins. Just as YHWH was justified in the destruction of Israel's sinful ancestors (vv. 26–28), so too is this present chastisement of the people deserved.

---

represents an offering of oil, wine and grain expressing worship and praise, and לְבוֹנָה "incense" and קָנֶה "sweet cane" represent various expensive elements that contribute to the air of sacredness in worship.

[220] The translation of שָׂרֵי קֹדֶשׁ in Isa. 43:28 is disputed. Oswalt, *The Book of Isaiah: Chapters 40–66*, pp. 157; 162 and Blenkinsopp, *Isaiah 40–55*, p. 229, translate "the princes (or rulers) of the sanctuary". Koole, *Isaiah III. Vol. 1*, pp. 351–352, translates "Therefore I profaned the holy priests", while Goldingay and Payne, *A Critical and Exegetical Commentary on Isaiah 40–55. Vol. 1*, p. 316, translate "And I profane sacred leaders". שָׂרִים "princes" are paralleled with מְלָכִים "kings" in Isa. 49:7 and related to heads of the priestly houses in 1 Chron. 24:5. For חלל (pi.) "profane" with YHWH as subject, cf. Isa. 47:6. Westermann, *Isaiah 40–66*, p. 130, deletes שָׂרֵי קֹדֶשׁ וְאֶתְּנָה, translating thus "So I delivered Jacob to utter destruction and Israel to reviling".

In this YHWH speech, the people personified are addressed as
Jacob and Israel (v. 22) and "you" (2ms, vv. 22–28). The relationship between YHWH and Israel is depicted in terms of a contrast
between weariness and serving, where the people's mistaken service is
alluded to, but Israel's sins are not discounted (vv. 22–24). A relation
appears between sacrifice and "your" (2ms) חֲטָא "sin" (vv. 24–25),
עָוֹן "iniquity" (v. 24) and פֶּשַׁע "transgression" (v. 25). The perspective is broadened to include also the past, as חֲטָא "sin" of your first
fathers and פֶּשַׁע "transgression" of your spokesmen (vbs., v. 27) are
considered. In-between, the forgiveness of YHWH now transcends
her earlier transgressions (v. 25). Through his punishment and forgiveness of Israel, YHWH reveals who he and Israel are. Israel is an
instrument for YHWH (in his forgiveness, cf. v. 25): it is not YHWH
who is an instrument for Israel (cf. v. 24b). Like Isa. 53 and 42:24–25,
43:22–28 is characterised by the many changes in the addressing of
"you", "Jacob" and "Israel" (v. 22), and the mentioning of the sins of
"you" (vv. 24–25), "your first father", "spokesmen" (v. 27), "princes of
sanctuary", Jacob and Israel (v. 28), with interwoven relations of identification concerning personification and sin. Like in these other texts,
a turning point to reconciliation and a promising future is expressed.
In Isa. 53 it occurs because of YHWH's pleasure; in chap. 43 it occurs
for the deity's לְמַעַן "sake". But whereas Isa. 53 dwells upon the sins,
the punishment and the restoration, chap. 43 focuses more upon the
sin, the mistaken service, as well as the forgiveness.

5.12.4. *Isa. 50:1*

50:1 כֹּה אָמַר יְהוָה
אֵי זֶה סֵפֶר כְּרִיתוּת אִמְּכֶם אֲשֶׁר שִׁלַּחְתִּיהָ
אוֹ מִי מִנּוֹשַׁי אֲשֶׁר־מָכַרְתִּי אֶתְכֶם לוֹ
הֵן בַּעֲוֺנֹתֵיכֶם נִמְכַּרְתֶּם וּבְפִשְׁעֵיכֶם שֻׁלְּחָה אִמְּכֶם׃

50:1: Thus says YHWH:
       Where is then the letter of divorce of your mother with which I
       sent her away?
       Or which of my creditors is it to whom I have sold you?
       See, for your iniquities you were sold and for your transgressions
       your mother was sent away.

In Isa. 50, the deity is quoted as asking two questions touching upon
the relationship between him and the addressee "you" (2mpl). The first
question concerns a letter of divorce with which YHWH is supposed
to have sent אִמְּכֶם "your mother" away, thus ending his relationship

with her.[221] The second question concerns the creditors whom YHWH is supposed to have sent "you", as if the deity is not willing to take responsibility for the children.

The two questions are chiastically responded to, as the first answer concerns the selling of the children and the second the sending away of the mother. However, the questions are not really answered: it is not stated where the letter of divorce is or who the creditors are.[222] Rather, the responses regard the reason for the selling and the divorce: "you" were sold and "your mother" was sent away because of "your" iniquities.[223] Neither the selling nor the divorce is denied in the replies, but it does not matter where the letter of divorce is or who the creditors are: "your mother" has been sent away and "you" were sold, whether the creditors or the letter of divorce exist or not. Both responses are conveyed in the passive: it is not stated that it was YHWH who sent the mother away or sold the children. The responsibility is placed on the children, and the consequences both upon the mother, who becomes a divorcee, and the children, who are sold. The mother is not held responsible for either her own or the children's fate. She is punished by an annulment of her marital relationship and by having her children sold, but this is not explained as due to her transgressions. The description of the faithless Israel in 50:1 is contrasted with a presentation of the faithful servant in 50:5; 7. Interestingly, no scholar has with fear or trembling identified the woman of 50:1 as one

---

[221] סֵפֶר כְּרִיתוּת "letter of divorce" is related to the verb שׁלח (pi.) in Deut. 24:1–3 and Jer. 3:8, cf. Gen. 21:14, Deut. 22:19, 2 Sam. 13:16, and Abma, *Bonds of Love*, p. 71. The description of the people as a rejected wife is also depicted in Isa. 54, and a divorce in Hos. 2. In Isa. 54, no sin is mentioned, only the husband YHWH's wrath (v. 8).

[222] Muilenburg, "The Book of Isaiah: Chapters 40–66", p. 580, claims that YHWH has not exercised any issuing of a bill of divorce and also that the deity has no creditors. Also, Blenkinsopp, *Isaiah 40–55*, p. 315, argues that the accusation that YHWH has divorced the mother is false so there is no bill of divorce. He claims that when it comes to the creditors, the real reason for the disaster is the moral failure of Israel, cf. 40:2 (5.12.5.), 42:22; 24–25 (5.12.2.), 43:27–28 (5.12.3.), 46:8. Abma, *Bonds of Love*, pp. 66–74, rejects form-critical readings of Isa. 50:1–3 as a trial speech, where the point at issue is whether the actions of the accused were justified. YHWH answers his own questions: he has never issued a bill of divorce and he is under no obligation of debt to anyone to sell his children. This is due to Israel's iniquities alone.

[223] The prep. בְּ in בַּעֲוֺנֹתֵיכֶם "your iniquities" and בְּפִשְׁעֵיכֶם "your transgressions" has a causal meaning, explaining the cause of the selling and sending away of "you" and "your mother". Cf. this construction in Isa. 43:24 (cf. 5.12.3. n. 216) and 53:5 (בַּחֲבֻרָתוֹ "by his wound"), cf. 3.10.8. n. 104.

or another historical individual suffering vicariously.[224] Some scholars have, however, commented on a distinction between the fate of the woman and that of her children. Abma, for instance, depicts the distinction between the portrayal of Zion and her children as pervasive in Isa. 49–55: while Zion is depicted as a lamentable figure (49:14–21, 51:17–20, 54:1–4), her children are described as disobedient (50:1–2, 10–11, 53:4–7).[225] Baumann adds a critical gender dimension to her presentation of the relation between Zion and her children:

> The female figure is the one who bore the consequences of her children's misbehaviour…In Isa. 50.1, there is a denial of YHWH's divorce from Jerusalem. She is not a sinner; her children are to blame. The imagery of Jerusalem remains, however, within the framework of the patriarchal marriage. Nonetheless, only YHWH plays an active role, whereas the wife is completely passive and is being acted upon.[226]

The questions in 50:1 might be a response to an accusation raised against YHWH by the addressee, "you". YHWH is the defendant, husband and father who answers charges from his children about his rejection of them and their mother.[227] The response in v. 1 does not answer the questions raised, and might indicate that the questions are regarded as based on misunderstandings about the state of the mother and the children. What is indicated, however, is that the misery is due to "your" transgressions. The mother and the children are a composite personification of the people, where the transition between "her" suffering and "your" transgressions is reminiscent of the relation between "him" and "us" in Isa. 53:4–5: just as "she" was sent away because of "your" sins (50:1), so too "he" bore "our" illnesses (53:4a) due to "our"

---

[224] Steck identifies a vicarious suffering of Zion at a redactional level in the *EJL*, see 2.2.5.

[225] Abma, *Bonds of Love*, pp. 73–74, n. 80.

[226] Baumann, "Prophetic Objections to YHWH as the Violent Husband of Israel", p. 106, cf. Willey, *Remember the Former Things*, p. 203. Baumann further compares the fate of the wife Zion to the fate of the servant in Isa. 53 (pp. 115–116), cf. 5.12.6. n. 235. A. Brenner, "Identifying the Speaker-in-the-Text and the Reader's Location in the Prophetic Texts: The Case of Isaiah 50" in A. Brenner and C. Fontaine (eds), *A Feminist Companion to Reading the Bible: Approaches, Methods and Strategies* (Sheffield: Sheffield Academic Press, 1997) 147, reads Isa. 50 as a dialogue "between Yhwh, the implied speaker-in-the-text of vv. 1–3, and that section's implied audience, which becomes a [metaphorical] *female* speaking voice in the passage's latter part", her italics. When reading vv. 4–9 (11), Brenner's feminist critique starts with the echo of the repressed mother-wife-slave.

[227] Cf. Isa. 54:7–9, where YHWH is depicted as a returning husband, see 5.15.5.

sins (53:5). When compared to Isa. 53, the personification of Isa. 50 is similar but not identical: in Isa. 50 "she" and "her" children are related within family categories, whereas in Isa. 53 the relation between "him" and "us" is more abstract. Unlike Isa. 53, there are no expressions for a turning point to future healing or vindication in 50:1, and there are no expressions for forgiveness, as in chap. 43.

5.12.5. Isa. 40:1–2

40:1 נַחֲמוּ נַחֲמוּ עַמִּי יֹאמַר אֱלֹהֵיכֶם:
² דַּבְּרוּ עַל־לֵב יְרוּשָׁלַם וְקִרְאוּ אֵלֶיהָ
כִּי מָלְאָה צְבָאָהּ כִּי נִרְצָה עֲוֹנָהּ
כִּי לָקְחָה מִיַּד יְהוָה כִּפְלַיִם בְּכָל־חַטֹּאתֶיהָ:

40:1: Comfort, comfort my people, says your God.
40:2: Speak to the heart of Jerusalem and cry to her
        that her time of service has ended, that her iniquity is paid for;
        that from YHWH's hand she has received double for all her sins.

Through the double imperative of "comfort!" and its echoes "speak!" and "cry!" in Isa. 40:1,[228] YHWH instructs his messengers, who are addressed in the plural. What shall be cried? נַחֲמוּ נַחֲמוּ עַמִּי "Comfort, comfort my people" and tell Jerusalem that YHWH forgives her. The relationship between עַמִּי "my people" and אֱלֹהֵיכֶם "your God" is at issue. The collective עַמִּי "my people" is paralleled by Jerusalem and "she". The change in the people's status from past to future is described in three כִּי clauses in v. 2: מָלְאָה צְבָאָהּ "her service has ended",[229] נִרְצָה עֲוֹנָהּ "her iniquity is paid"[230] and לָקְחָה מִיַּד יְהוָה כִּפְלַיִם בְּכָל־חַטֹּאתֶיהָ "from YHWH's hand she has received double for all her sins".[231] In

---

[228] The consolation of Israel is a passing tone in Isa. 40–55, see 40:1, 49:13, 51:3; 12; 19, 52:9. All these references to נחם appear in descriptions of Zion/Jerusalem. Except for 40:1, YHWH is the subject.

[229] S. A. Geller, "A Poetic Analysis of Isaiah 40:1–2", HTR 77 (1984) 413–420, reads כִּי as "because"…"echo[ing] a lover's ardent pleadings". For צְבָא ([most often masc., but fem. also in Dan. 8:12] with 3fs suff.) as military service, see e.g. 2 Sam. 3:23, as battle see 1 Sam. 28:1, as hired labour see Job 7:1.

[230] For רצה (ni.), a hypothetical רצה II "expiated" has been assumed in connection with עָוֹן, with a suggested cultic setting, cf. Lev. 26:41; 43, where the verb is used in qal in a description of how the people shall pay for עֲוֹנָם "their transgressions" (cf. Lev. 26:34, and in 1:4 with כֻּפָּר). H. J. Stoebe, "Überlegung zu Jesaja 40,1–11", TZ 40 (1984) 104–113, offers an alternative translatiom: רצה "gefallen haben", cf. his cultic interpretation of צְבָא.

[231] G. von Rad, "כִּפְלַיִם in Jes. 40:2=Äquivalent?", ZAW 79 (1967) 80–82, follows M. Tsevat, "Alalkhiana", HUCA 29 (1958) 125–126, arguing that כִּפְלַיִם can be understood here as a legal term meaning "equivalent", "double", and refers to a (synonymous)

these two verses we are presented with Israel's past and future, and an event regarded as already come is proclaimed; a great change from judgment to salvation is accomplished. What makes the cry one of good news is the earlier fate of Jerusalem: she has sinned and suffered; the people have been abandoned by YHWH. Her fate is not explained as a misfortune, but as a penalty, given by YHWH, for sin (cf. Isa. 53). The salient point is that it belongs to their past. A turning point for Israel is proclaimed, as they are forgiven. Her hard times, which were the result of sins, have become the source of comfort. The time of punishment is ended. It might be illuminating to compare vv. 1–2 and vv. 9–10. Both passages contain a double instruction to a messenger: v. 2 concentrates on the end of the time of punishment, and v. 9 on YHWH's return to his people: הִנֵּה אֱלֹהֵיכֶם "See, your God!" The focus is turned from paying for guilt and release in vv. 1–2 to joy and salvation in vv. 9–10.[232]

In Isa. 40:1–2, the people are mentioned in a female personification, whereas the city of Jerusalem is called "her". Like "he"/"we"/"my people"/"many" in Isa. 53, Jerusalem has sinned and suffered. And like them, she experiences a turning point to vindication. Whereas in 53 the focus is on how "he" and "we" suffered illness due to their sin and

---

מִשְׁנֶה as a "terminus technicus des Schuldrechtes" in Deut. 15:18 and Jer. 16:16. Thus, in Isa. 40:2 it is announced that Jerusalem has now paid "the equivalent", that is "the appropriate penalty". A. Phillips, "Double for all her Sins", ZAW 94 (1982) 130–132, reads כִּפְלַיִם in Isa. 40:2 as expressing the doubling of Jerusalem's punishment, "thereby involving a second innocent generation in no way responsible for the events leading to the exile". This is further connected to his view of Isa. 53: "It is through their ['the second innocent generation's] vicarious suffering that the glorious future envisaged by the prophet is to be realised." With regard to Jerusalem's צָבָא and עָוֹן in 40:2, which comprise the whole people, I do not find such a splitting up of the people reasonable. Phillips also refers to a proposal by W. Tom, "Welke is de Zin van het 'dubbel ontvangen' uit Jesaja 40.2?", GThT 59 (1959) 122–123, who argues that כפל in Exod. 26:9, 28:16, 39:9 and Job 41:5 indicates something placed exactly on top of its counterpart, which in Isa. 40:2 could indicate that Jerusalem's sins were wholly covered: the people sinned and paid, and now both her forgiveness and consolation are absolute. On beth pretii, see 3.10.8. n. 104.

[232] There have been many suggestions as to which genre to assign to Isa. 40:1–8(11), for instance: prologue, prophetic call narrative, divine directives to a circle of prophets, divine directives to angelic heralds, Heroldinstruktion, Der Liturgie des Neujahrsfestes. For an overview, see Seitz, "The Divine Council", pp. 229–247. Readings of Isa. 40:1ff are clearly connected to scholars' view of the composition of Isa. 1–66, see 2.3.2. and 5.11.2. n. 128. Darr, Isaiah's Vision and the Family of God, pp. 35–45, employs the figurative language with respect to children and women as a new entrance into themes and concerns in the Book of Isaiah. She redefines the concerns of the fate of Jerusalem in Isa. 40:1–11 as "care and commitment" rather than as exile and restoration.

how they shall be healed, in chap. 40 we are told that she has suffered hard times due to her sin.

5.12.6. *Excursus: Servant and Zion*

Readings of the "servant texts" in Isa. 40–55 have often been disturbed by the apprehension of an assumed inconsistency in the description of the servant. A comparison with the female personifications within Isa. 40–55 can illuminate a previously neglected, but nevertheless conspicuous rhetorical dimension in the texts. There is little doubt among scholars that the female personifications in Isa. 40–55 represent the people, i.e. the city of Jerusalem/Zion. Like in the "servant texts", the female personifications also draw an ambiguous image of the "person". The female personifications of Isa. 40–55(66) do not have any "genealogy", but her "biography" and "future prospects" are parallel to the servant's story of humiliation and vindication. Central to the Zion texts are the return of YHWH and that of the people to Zion. Prominent in the female personification is her role as mother, where the humiliation is described as the loss of children and childlessness, and her vindication as the return of her sons and daughters. The woman is described as called, redeemed, delivered, not rejected, or forgotten, having her children gathered in and begetting descendants.[233] Also, the female personification of the people depicts that the woman is or shall be comforted by YHWH. In Isa. 40–55, a female personification is also presented as Daughter of Babylon. This personification shares some features with the depiction of the female personification of the people of Jerusalem in Isa. 40–55, e.g. being barren and a widow (47:9).[234]

A numerical change similar to the one between "he" and "we" in Isa. 53 appears in the female personifications, in the relation between Zion and her children (49:17–26, 51:18; 20, 54:1–4). It should further be emphasised that the "servant texts" and the female personifications are ambiguous in relation to sin and suffering. The woman has paid double for all her sins (40:2) and suffered for the sins of her

---

[233] She is קרא "called" (54:6), גאל "redeemed" (49:26, 54:5; 8), ישע "delivered" (43:12, 49:25, i.e. "your children"), לא מאס "not rejected" (54:6), לא שכח "not forgotten" (49:15), on ingathering, see 5.15.5. nn. 297 and 302, on descendants, see 5.15. 4.–6.

[234] Within Isa. 1–66, the fate of a land, city or people is depicted woman (e.g. as daughter, mother or whore) in 1:21–26, 7:14, 10:30, 13:8, 21:3, 23:4–12; 15–18, 26:17, 40:2; 9–11, 47, 49:14–26, 50:1–3, 51:3; 11–23, 52:1–2, 54:1–10, 57:6–13, 66:1–10.

children (50:1), just as the servant has sinned (44:22) and will bear
the transgressions of the many (53:11). In Isa. 40:1–2, the people are
mentioned in a female personification, with Jerusalem called "her".
Like "he"/"we"/"my people"/"many" in Isa. 53, Jerusalem has sinned
and suffered. And like them, she experiences a turning point towards
vindication. Whereas in Isa. 53 the focus was placed on the way in
which "he" and "we" suffered illness due to their sin and how they
shall become healed, in Isa. 40 her hard times are due to her sin.

Between Isa. 53 and 50 an oscillation appears between male and
female personifications, e.g. servant and Zion. In 53:2–6, a relation
between the wounds and chastisement of "him" and the sins of "us"
is prominent, as well as a moment of identification between them, i.e.
the crossing point between the story of "him" and the story of "us".
One peculiarity in the personification is that the figure of personification (mother, servant) is related to "the people" (53:8: "my people", cf.
vv. 5–6: "we", v. 11: "many", v. 12: "many") or "her children" (50:1).
Both the male and female personifications are texts which contain frequent changes, ambiguities and paradoxes. At the same time as the
texts about the servant and about the woman clearly show distinctive
features, we also find significant communication links between these
personification texts and the rest of Isa. 40–55, regarding both literary
motifs and themes.[235]

---

[235] On the relation between servant and Zion, see L. E. Wilshire, "The Servant-City:
A New Interpretation of the 'Servant of the Lord' in the Servant Songs of Deutero-
Isaiah", *JBL* 94 (1975), 356–367, J. F. A. Sawyer, "Daughter of Zion and Servant of
the Lord in Isaiah: A Comparison", *JSOT* 44 (1989) 89–107, P. T. Willey, "The Ser-
vant of YHWH and Daughter Zion: Alternating Visions of YHWH's Community"
(SBLSP, 34; Atlanta: Scholars Press, 1995) 267–303, Willey, *Remember the Former
Things*, B. J. Stratton, "Engaging Metaphors: Suffering with Zion and the Servant in
Isaiah 52–53" in S. E. Fowl (ed), *The Theological Interpretation of Scripture: Classic and
Contemporary Readings* (Blackwell Readings in Modern Theology; Oxford: Blackwell,
1997) 219–237, B. G. Webb, "Zion in Transformation: A Literary Approach to Isaiah"
in Clines, Fowl and Porter, *The Bible in Three Dimensions*, pp. 65–84, K. Jeppesen,
"Mother Zion, Father Servant: A Reading of Isaiah 49–55" in McKay and Clines, *Of
Prophets' Visions and the Wisdom of Sages*, pp. 109–125, K. P. Darr, "Two Unifying
Female Images in the Book of Isaiah" in L. M. Hopfe (ed), *Uncovering Ancient Stones:
Essays in Memory of H. Neil Richardson* (Winona Lake, IN: Eisenbrauns, 1994) 17–30,
Korpel, "The female servant of the Lord in Isaiah 54", pp. 153–167, Berges, "Per-
sonifications and Prophetic Voices of Zion in Isaiah and Beyond", pp. 54–82, A. van
der Woude, "Can Zion Do without the Servant in Isaiah 40–55?", *Calvin Theological
Journal* 39 (2004) 109–116.

On the Zion tradition in the Book of Isaiah in general, see Biddle, "The Figure of
Lady Jerusalem", O. H. Steck, "Zion als Gelände und Gestalt" in Steck, *Gottesknecht
und Zion*, pp. 126–145, O'Connor, "'Speak Tenderly to Jerusalem'", pp. 281–294, and

5.12.7. *Summing Up*

Isa. 40–55 presents declarations of sin and judgment, hope and salvation. These sixteen chapters, often labelled "prophet" or "book of consolation", are interwoven with promises, discussions, disputations, persuasions, admonitions, calls, invitations, interrogations, accusations, invectives, negotiations and laments. Just as salvation was hidden in the prophets' words of doom, so too the judgment of YHWH is hidden in the good news. Israel is still desolate, despised, dispersed, oppressed, deaf, blind, shamed, guilty and rebellious. The presentations of the people's transgressions are only of a general character in Isa. 40–55. Closely related to sin are different ways of expressing the punishment, for instance, illness and death (53), YHWH's wrath and war (42:25), destruction and insult (43:28), divorce and the selling of children (50:2) and צָבָא "time of service" (40:2).

At issue are the ways of YHWH with Israel and vice versa, with the relation between the deity and his people depicted by themes such as sin, return and forgiveness: YHWH has punished his people because of their sin and now the punishment is over. The duties of YHWH's servant are to see, listen, understand, take YHWH's word to heart and walk in his ways, and YHWH's duty is the forgiveness of people's sins, cf. 40:1–2, 43:25, 44:22 and 53:5; 11; 12 (and in a variation in Isa. 48:9).

In 42:23–24, YHWH rebukes his people because they have not trusted him, but they have sinned, walked their own ways and not listened to his law. This is the reason why YHWH had to punish them. The deity is the defendant, and the people are addressed in many different ways as Jacob and Israel (v. 24), "they" (v. 22; 24), "you" (2mpl, v. 23), "we" (v. 24) and "he" (v. 25). Like Isa. 53 and 42:24–25, 43:22–28 is also characterised by the many changes in the addressing of "you", Jacob and Israel (v. 22), and the mentioning of the sins of "you" (vv. 24–25), "your first father", "spokesmen" (v. 27), "princes of sanctuary", Jacob, and Israel (v. 28), where relations of identification in terms of personification and sin appear.

Common to the texts referred to in this chapter is a confusion between personifier and personified (cf. similar oscillation in Isa. 48:1–2). In all these instances, the relation between the personified

---

A. Labahn, "Metaphor and Intertextuality: 'Daughter of Zion' as a Test Case", *SJOT* 17 (2003) 49–67.

people ("he", "she", Jacob, Israel, Jerusalem) and the people as a group ("we", "they") is presented through the theme of sin.[236] Apart from in Isa. 50, a turning point towards reconciliation and a promising future is expressed. In 53 it occurs because of YHWH's pleasure, in 42:23 it is related to the people's possible hearing, and in 43 it takes place לְמַעַן "for the sake of" the deity. Isa. 53 is endlessly augmented by the transposition of other texts into it: 42:24–25, 43:22–28, 50:1, 40:1–2. Whereas Isa. 53 dwells upon sin, punishment and restoration, Isa. 42 focuses upon sin and the punishment and alludes to a turning point in the future, and Isa. 43 dwells upon the mistaken service and the forgiveness. Isa. 40 concerns how the hard times due to sin are over and YHWH has returned, while Isa. 50 explains the misery as due to "your" transgressions. Unlike Isa. 53, there are no expressions for a turning point towards future healing or vindication in Isa. 50:1, and there are no expressions for forgiveness, as in Isa. 43.

5.13. "...LIKE A SHEEP LED TO SLAUGHTERING...HE DID NOT OPEN HIS MOUTH"

5.13.1. *Isa. 53:7*

53:7 נִגַּשׂ וְהוּא נַעֲנֶה וְלֹא יִפְתַּח־פִּיו
כַּשֶׂה לַטֶּבַח יוּבָל וּכְרָחֵל לִפְנֵי גֹזְזֶיהָ נֶאֱלָמָה
וְלֹא יִפְתַּח פִּיו:

53:7: He was oppressed, and he was humble(d), but he did not open his mouth,
like a sheep led to slaughtering and like a ewe which is dumb before her shearers,
and he did not open his mouth.

---

[236] R. Youngblood, "A New Look at Three Old Testament Roots for 'Sin'" in G. A. Tuttle (ed), *Biblical And Near Eastern Studies: Essays in Honour of William Sanford LaSor* (Grand Rapids: Eerdmans, 1978) 201–205, lists many examples where חָטָא, עָוֹן and פֶּשַׁע are associated with הלך "walk", דֶּרֶךְ "way", סוּר "turn aside", שׁוּב "turn to/ from", אֹרַח "path" and expressions for the people's "walking astray" elsewhere in Isa. 40–55, cf. מרה "rebellious" in Isa. 50:5 (i.e. the servant as *not* rebellious), Israel as בגד "dealing treacherously" in 48:8, as well as "walking astray", "blind", "deaf", "not listening". Cf. K. P. Darr, "Isaiah's Vision and the Rhetoric of Rebellion" (SBLSP, 33; Atlanta: Scholars Press, 1994) 847–882, on sin in Isa. 1–66. It is a misunderstanding that words, e.g. the vocabulary of sin, are concepts with the same meaning every time they appear in the Hebrew Bible (cf. similar critique regarding concepts of election in 5.8.2. n. 60).

In Isa 53:7, a man is depicted as being oppressed and humble(d), to which he reacts with silence. The situation is described by the paired similes of שֶׂה "a sheep" led to slaughtering and רָחֵל "a ewe" which is dumb before her shearers. In the comparisons no statements about actions or afflictions are made, only about the passivity of שֶׂה "a sheep" and the silence of רָחֵל "a ewe".[237] The silence is his reaction to a situation in which he was humbled or humble, showing his lack of opposition and protest when he fell into the hands of others. The slaughtering and shearing become parts of a more comprehensive depiction of silence as/and humbleness, as his silence is how he reacts (or does not react) to his neighbours' treatment of him. No reason is given for why he is treated so badly.[238]

In 53:7, a personification becomes identified through interaction with vv. 6; 8. His silence compared to that of שֶׂה "a sheep" and רָחֵל "a ewe" evokes the comparison in v. 6 in which the speaking "we" liken themselves to lost צֹאן "sheep": everybody is breaking away and going their own way. In a concluding statement, a confession of "our" own transgressions includes an explanation of his fate: he was stricken by YHWH due to "our" transgressions.[239] In v. 8, a question regards the relation of דּוֹרוֹ "his time" to "his" fate, in which "his" time is ignorant or indifferent. In a second question, נֶגַע לָמוֹ "his wound" is explained as due to פֶּשַׁע עַמִּי "the transgression of my people", and an asymmetrical relation appears between the punishment of "him" and the transgression of עַמִּי "my people". In a personification, the actors are revealed through a repetition of elements surrounding

---

[237] Rignell, "Isa. LII 13–LIII 12", p. 89, n. 2, relates Isa. 53:7 to the sacrifice terminology he finds elsewhere in 52:13–53:12: "[הַשֶּׂה] in liii 7 has the definite article, possibly with specific reference to the paschal lamb". Rignell identifies the servant as the exile generation which had to endure vicarious suffering. Oswalt, *The Book of Isaiah: Chapters 40–66*, p. 392, also briefly alludes to sacrifice. He identifies the servant as "an individual, almost certainly the Messiah, who will be the ideal Israel. Through his obedient service to God, Israel will be enabled to perform the service of blessing the nations that had been prophesied in Gen. 12:3 and elsewhere" (p. 108). Blenkinsopp, *Isaiah 40–55*, p. 351, sees a hint of the vocabulary of sacrifice in the image of a sheep being led to the slaughter. He regards אָשָׁם of 53:10 as the most explicit statement of this, see Appendix 6. However, most scholars refute any sacrificial terminology in Isa. 53, cf. Duhm in 2.1.4., Hermisson in 2.2.3. n. 82, Janowski in 2.2.4. n. 93 and Koole, *Isaiah III. Vol. 2*, p. 302.

[238] In Isa. 42:2, "he" shall "neither cry nor lift up his voice, nor make it heard in the street", in relation to the execution of מִשְׁפָּט "justice". See Linafelt, "Speech and Silence in the Servant Passages", pp. 199–209, and on senses in 5.9.2. and 5.9.3.

[239] פגע, cf. 3.10.15. n. 155 and Appendix 8.

"him" and עַמִּי "my people", where the personifier "he" and the personified עַמִּי "my people" are blurred and the sin and punishment are
introduced. What might seem to be an innocent submission is not so
in a broader context.

In v. 9 a relation is made to speaking: it is claimed that "there was no
deceit in his mouth" and no violence. "His" lack of deceit and violence
is related to a situation in which "he" is handed over to others, related
to death and an unworthy tomb (cf. 5.14.1.). The silence motifs in
vv. 7; 9 might also be related to the speaking voices in the personification of 53:1ff, where the "we" are speaking about "him" and "themselves", while "he" is not making himself heard.[240]

5.13.2. *Jer. 11:18–19*

11:18 וַיהוָה הוֹדִיעַנִי וָאֵדָעָה אָז הִרְאִיתַנִי מַעַלְלֵיהֶם: [19] וַאֲנִי כְּכֶבֶשׂ
אַלּוּף יוּבַל לִטְבוֹחַ וְלֹא־יָדַעְתִּי כִּי־עָלַי חָשְׁבוּ מַחֲשָׁבוֹת נַשְׁחִיתָה
עֵץ בְּלַחְמוֹ וְנִכְרְתֶנּוּ מֵאֶרֶץ חַיִּים וּשְׁמוֹ לֹא־יִזָּכֵר עוֹד:

11:18:   And YHWH made it known to me and I knew; then you showed
         me their (bad) deeds.
11:19:   But I was like a tame lamb led to the slaughter. I did not know it
         was against me they devised schemes, saying, "Let us destroy the
         tree with its fruit, let us cut him off from the land of the living,
         that his name be remembered no more".

In Jer. 11:18, an "I" tells that YHWH introduced him to knowledge
in the past, and that the deity, addressed as "you", warned the speaking "I" against the activities of some unknown enemies. Then the "I"
provides a flashback to his past, in which he likens himself to כֶּבֶשׂ
אַלּוּף, "a tame lamb", modified by an explanation: like this lamb being
led to the slaughter, he was unaware of the threat to his life (v. 19).[241]
The speaker's ignorance is expressed, as it was before YHWH made
known to him the bad plan his enemies had made for him. After his
explanation of the situation, he quotes his enemies. In this quotation,
a tree and its destruction becomes an image of their scheming against
him: they shall wipe out his name and cut him off from the land of the

---

[240] In Isa. 52:15, kings' reactions to "his" vindication are expressed as silence, cf.
5.8.1.
[241] יוּבַל (perf. ho.), i.e. no agents named, cf. imperf. ho. in Isa. 53:7. חָשְׁבוּ מַחֲשָׁבוֹת
"schemed schemes", "devise evil against", cf. Jer. 18:18, 49:30.

living.[242] Nothing is said about why he shall be so treated. The imagery might, however, be related to vv. 16–17. In the image of a green tree, YHWH's calling of Judah in the past is depicted, but also how he shall set fire to the tree and its branches shall be consumed. This judgment of Judah is due to their apostasy (v. 17). What YHWH is planning to do to the community (v. 16), Jeremiah's enemies are planning to do to him. Since Jeremiah is unaware of the plans of his enemies, he reacts neither with opposition nor protest.[243]

In an appeal to YHWH for vindication over his enemies, the prophet turns to the future (v. 20). He trusts YHWH and appeals to the deity's justice and revenge. The "I" speech of the prophet in vv. 18–20 is followed by answers from YHWH in vv. 21–23. Here, the enemies of the addressee "you" are identified as "the men of Anathoth, who seek your life". Again, the enemies are quoted as threatening him with death if he continues prophecying in the name of YHWH (cf. v. 19). This threat is followed by YHWH's judgment of the enemies of Jeremiah: their warriors will die by the sword, and their sons and daughters by famine with no remnant left (vv. 22–23).

In a dialogue between the prophet and YHWH in Jer. 11:18–12:3, the prophet depicts the humiliations he has experienced from his enemies as a tool of YHWH. Whereas Jeremiah compares himself to a tame lamb, his enemies present him as a "tree with strength". The

---

[242] שחת (imperf. hi. 1cpl) "let us destroy" and כרת (imperf. qal 1cpl) "let us cut off", cf. נִגְזַר מֵאֶרֶץ חַיִּים "cut off from the land of the living" in Isa. 53:8, see 3.10.11. n. 121.

[243] Carroll, *Jeremiah – A Commentary*, p. 279, comments that as the tree can be both individual and collective (cf. v. 21 below), the image of the tame lamb in v. 19 could also refer to the ignorance of speaker and the community about to be slaughtered. Oswalt, *The Book of Isaiah: Chapters 40–66*, p. 392, explains the difference between Isa. 53:7 and Jer. 11:19:

> Interestingly, Jeremiah uses the metaphor of the lamb led to the slaughter to describe himself in 11:19, but there the context shows that the point is one of trusting naïveté in which the animal has no idea of what is about to happen to it. Here [Isa 53:7] the issue being emphasized is not unknowingness, but willing submission to what lies ahead.

Blenkinsopp, *Isaiah 40–55*, p. 353:

> [A]t this point (beginning with Isa. 53:7) the language points unmistakably to physical violence resulting in death. That Jeremiah survived in spite of claiming in one of his "confessions" to have been led like a lamb to be slaughtered (Jer. 11:19) provides no support for the view that the prophetic servant survived his ordeal [cf. Whybray]. In fact it indicates the contrary, since it is clear that Jeremiah's enemies intended his death…(11:19b). Unlike Jeremiah, however, the servant *was* cut off from the land of the living (53:8b), his italics.

sheep image used to describe the prophet in 11:18–19 appears in a
variation about his enemies in 12:3, where the prophet asks the deity
to drive them out like sheep to slaughter. Whereas Jeremiah laments
his ignorance, the humiliation of the enemies is presented as due to
their own transgression.[244]

Jer. 11:18–19 does not concern a personification, but a person in
crisis.[245] As in Jer. 15:18 (cf. 5.11.8.), Jeremiah laments the suffering
his faithfulness to YHWH has caused and YHWH responds with a
call for repentance and a reaffirmation of his calling. In Jer. 11:18–19,
the prophet depicts himself as a tame lamb being led to slaughter –
unaware of the threat to his life. The prophet regards himself as faithful and righteous and YHWH as unfair, whereas the deity explains his
suffering as deserved. In Isa. 53, what might seem to be innocent submission is not so in a broader context. At the end, there is a contrast
between the silence of Isa. 53:7 and Jer. 11:18–19, where the prophet
is speaking.

5.13.3. *Ps. 38:14–15*

38:14 וַאֲנִי כְחֵרֵשׁ לֹא אֶשְׁמָע וּכְאִלֵּם לֹא יִפְתַּח־פִּיו:
15 וָאֱהִי כְּאִישׁ אֲשֶׁר לֹא־שֹׁמֵעַ וְאֵין בְּפִיו תּוֹכָחוֹת:

> 38:14: But I am like the deaf, I do not hear, and like the mute, who can-
> not open his mouth.
> 38:15: Truly, I am like one who does not hear and in whose mouth is
> no retort.

In Ps. 38:14–15 a suffering "I" expresses his deafness and muteness.
This is surrounded by depictions of his treatment by his enemies and
his deity. The lament is introduced by the appeal of the speaking "I" to
YHWH to cease dealing with him in anger (vv. 2–3), with an additional
depiction of the afflictions he has brought upon him, the whole body
seemingly stricken (vv. 4–9; 11; 18). Interwoven with this complaint
is also a confession of sin (vv. 5; 19), as he considers his afflictions as
deserved due to his transgressions. Added to his affliction is his aban-

---

[244] For people as צֹאן "sheep" in relation to slaughtering, cf. Jer. 25:34–36, 50:45,
Ps. 44:23 (cf. v. 12), Zech. 10:2, 11:4; 7, Prov. 7:22, whereas Jer. 11:19 concerns כְּבֶשׂ
"lamb". See on people as sheep in 5.12.1. n. 207, kings or leaders as shepherds in
5.11.5. n. 143 and YHWH as shepherd in 5.8.3. n. 65.
[245] Jer. 11:18–12:3 is one "lament of Jeremiah", see 5.11.8. n. 165. The figure Jeremiah and his relation to the people have been widely discussed, cf. 5.11.8. nn. 164–
165, and 5.11.4. n. 139.

donment by friends and desertion by kinsmen (v. 12) and the scorn
and persecution by enemies (vv. 13; 17) who are many and hate him
without cause (v. 20). As a reaction to their assaults, he becomes deaf
and mute (vv. 14–15). Without offering any opposition, he submits to
their afflictions by trusting in God (v. 16). In v. 17 his silence might
be explained as a way of not giving the enemies an opportunity to
boast about his afflictions. By keeping silent, he shows them his trust
in YHWH. He trusts that the deity shall break his silence by answering
him (v. 16) and that YHWH knows that he has been striving for that
which is good (v. 21). Totally abandoned by YHWH, in his despair
he continues to pray – even though no answer has appeared so far.
YHWH is his only hope of deliverance (vv. 22–23, cf. vv. 2; 10; 16).
The lamenting one does not boast of his own perfection, but pleads
righteousness in the face of certain accusations, while confessing his
own guilt.[246] A contrast between the silence of Isa. 53:7 and Ps. 38 is
that while "he" is silent in Isa. 53:7, in Ps. 38 the "I" does speak. Ps. 38
does not present a personification, rather the speaking "I" is a figure
of identification.[247]

5.13.4. *Ps. 39:3*

39:3 נֶאֱלַמְתִּי דוּמִיָּה הֶחֱשֵׁיתִי מִטּוֹב וּכְאֵבִי נֶעְכָּר:

39:3: I was dumb, silent, speechless; my distress grew worse.

In Ps. 39:3, the speaking "I" recounts how he kept quiet and muz-
zled himself. When keeping silent, he refrained from sinning and so
avoided giving the wicked an opportunity to hear him complain to
his God (v. 2, cf. vv. 9; 11). The silence added distress to his suffering;
the longer he kept silent, the more it became like a fire within him –
and he began to speak (v. 4). Since life is transitory and YHWH his
only hope for deliverance (vv. 5–8), he confesses his sins, which stand
between him and his hope, and begs not to be made the scorn of the
fool (v. 9, cf. v. 11). He becomes silent again, knowing how YHWH
acts (v. 10). YHWH's acts are related to his fate as an ill, sinful and

---

[246] For a lamenting one expressing innocence as regards his enemies, see e.g. Pss.
5:13, 7:4–6; 10, 26:4–6, 27:12, 31:19, 35:7; 19, 69:5, 73:13; 15, 109:2, 119:69; 78; 86, Job
9:17, Lam 3:52. Also in these texts, the lamenting one pleads righteousness in the face
of certain accusations, while confessing his own guilt.

[247] In 5.11.11., another reading of Ps. 38 is offered, with illness as its point of
view.

transitory human being. The silence hinders sinful complaining and expresses trust in YHWH, in the face of evildoers and suffering. He knows that like death, sin and punishment are inescapable for everyone (v. 12), and in this he reminds YHWH that he, like his ancestors, is a passing guest in life (v. 13). Then he again admonishes YHWH to remain hidden (v. 14)! Although much of Ps. 39 concerns silence in suffering, it ends with a cry of pain (cf. Ps. 88 in 5.14.6.). Like in Ps. 38, so too in Ps. 39 the "I" does not present a personification, but the speaking "I" is a figure of identification.

5.13.5. *Summing Up*

In Isa. 53:7, slaughtering and shearing become parts of a more comprehensive depiction of silence as/and humbleness, as "his" silence is related to how he reacts (or does not react) to his neighbours' treatment of him: without offering any protest or opposition, he has fallen into the hands of others. No reason is given for why he is treated so badly. In a personification, the actors are revealed through a repetition of elements surrounding "him" and עַמִּי "my people", where the personifier "he" and the personified עַמִּי "my people" become blurred. Here, sin and punishment are also introduced, and "he" loses his innocence. What might seem to be innocent submission is not so in a broader context.

Jer. 11:18–19 does not concern a personification, but a person in crisis. Jeremiah laments the suffering his faithfulness to YHWH has caused and the deity responds with a call for repentance and a reaffirmation of his calling. In Jer. 11:18–19, the prophet depicts himself as a tame lamb being led to slaughter – unaware of the threat to his life. He regards himself as righteous and YHWH as unfair, while the deity explains this suffering as deserved. At the end, a contrast between the silence of Isa. 53:7 and Jer. 11:18–19 is that the prophet *is* speaking.

In Pss. 38:14–15 and 39:3, silence might become a way for protecting YHWH towards the enemies, while still trusting the deity, despite suffering. In both psalms the silent one may be a sinner. The lamenting one does not boast of his own perfection, but pleads righteousness in the face of certain accusations, while he may confess his own guilt. A contrast between the silence of Isa. 53:7 and Pss. 38–39 is that while "he" is silent in Isa. 53:7, the psalmists in Pss. 38–39 do speak. Pss. 38–39 do not present a personification, but the speaking "I" is a figure of identification.

5.14. "He was given his grave with wicked ones..."

5.14.1. *Isa. 53:9*

53:9 וַיִּתֵּן אֶת־רְשָׁעִים קִבְרוֹ וְאֶת־עָשִׁיר בְּמֹתָיו
עַל לֹא־חָמָס עָשָׂה וְלֹא מִרְמָה בְּפִיו:

53:9: He was given his grave with wicked ones and with a rich (?) in his death
although he had not done any violence and there was no deceit in his mouth.

In Isa. 53:9, a humiliation is related to an unworthy tomb, with the dead one classified with רְשָׁעִים "wicked ones" and עָשִׁיר "a rich" (?).[248] No explanation is given for why he is offered a disgraceful grave. Rather, the lack of any reason is noted: this took place even though he had behaved neither violently nor deceitfully.[249]

After he has been struck by illness, scorn and contempt, he reaches the ultimate defeat: death. The catastrophe, which until now has seemed endless, is now all-consuming and irrevocable: after death there is no hope. Elsewhere he is cut off from the land of the living (53:8) and slain to death (53:12). In v. 8 "his" death is explained as due to פֶּשַׁע עַמִּי "the transgression of my people"; in v. 12 "he" is classified with פֹּשְׁעִים "transgressors". In a personification the actors are revealed through a repetition of elements surrounding "him", where the personifier "he" and the personified עַמִּי "my people" become blurred (cf. 4.8.3.3.). Here, death works as a metaphor, a figure of deviation, departing from its lexically codified usage.[250] The semantic order is displaced, transformed and changed. In this, not only is his nearness

---

[248] רֶשַׁע "wicked" in 48:22, in 55:7, alluding to unfaithful Israelites, and רשע (vb.) in 50:9 (cf. 5.16.2.). For discussions of the rendering of בְּמֹתָיו, see 3.10.12. n. 127 and for the translation of עָשִׁיר "rich" and other readings, see 3.10.12. n. 126. Gottwald, *The Hebrew Bible*, p. 539, claims that in the psalms "'rich' and 'wicked' are often spoken in the same breath", and argues that a context of socioeconomic oppression has been retained in the texts, as it is in the prophetic and wisdom literature.

[249] For חָמָס "violence" and מִרְמָה "deceit", cf. Zeph. 1:9, Ps. 55:10; 12, and Mic. 6:12, which also includes richness (cf. Jer. 5:27, Hos. 12:8–9). For מִרְמָה "deceit" and רֶשַׁע "wicked", cf. e.g. Prov. 12:5, Mic. 6:11, Ps. 109:2. In Ps. 38:13, enemies mediate treachery (cf. 5.11.11. and 5.13.3.), and in Zeph. 3:13, "no tongue of deceit shall be found in their [the rest of Israel's] mouth...".

[250] In Isa. 51:12 YHWH admonishes the perishable man not to fear death, cf. v. 14. Death is not punishment and is contrasted with a coming vindication. In v. 6 the peoples shall die like mosquitoes while Israel shall be restored.

to death indicated, but the very death itself is depicted: yes, the servant did really die![251]

5.14.2. *Amos 5:2*

5:2 נָפְלָה לֹא־תוֹסִיף קוּם בְּתוּלַת יִשְׂרָאֵל
נִטְּשָׁה עַל־אַדְמָתָהּ אֵין מְקִימָהּ:

5:2: She is fallen, no more to rise, young girl Israel;
    forsaken on her land, with no one to raise her up.

In Am. 5:2, an elegy of Israel is recited: בְּתוּלַת יִשְׂרָאֵל "young girl Israel" has fallen, is forsaken and is prematurely stripped of her vitality.

---

[251] In the Servant Song research, there has been a comprehensive debate whether the servant died or not. Most scholars conclude that the servant did really die. North, *The Suffering Servant in Deutero-Isaiah*, pp. 148–149, comments on the servant's death:

> No one would dream of taking the descriptions of death in liii.7ff. otherwise than literally, unless he were first determined to identify the Servant with some historical individual of whom he could not claim that he died a violent death. Of course, on the collective theory the death is allegory. There is no inconsistency in this, since the whole is allegory. But as soon as we begin to pick and choose, taking part literally and part figuratively, we are out of touch with reality. The song describes an actual death and burial of the Servant.

Hermisson, "Das vierte Gottesknechtslied im deuterojesajanischen Kontext", p. 16 (the quotation is taken from ET, p. 37, his italics), claims,

> [I]t is difficult to say to what extent individual traits should be interpreted biographically. But to me it seems certain…that the Servant really died an ignominious death and was shamefully buried. This does *not* then simply involve the common metaphor of the Psalms that severely ill and suffering people already find themselves "in the grip of death". The text explicitly states that this was the death of an innocent person (v. 9b).

Concerning v. 10, in which the servant, after his death and burial, is promised descendants and a long life, Hermisson warns against introducing the thought of a resurrection from the dead. He further claims,

> [I]f one respects the largely metaphorical language of the text, then this much can be said: YHWH will acknowledge his Servant even beyond death and the grave; death imposes no limit upon his fellowship with God; God holds his Servant fast; and the turn of salvation that he helped to effect will also reach him: indeed, God will exalt him to the highest place (p. 17, ET p. 39).

To me, Hermisson's bringing in of the metaphorical qualities of the language in v. 10, but not when it comes to the servant's death in v. 9, seems like an *ad hoc* argument. Also arguing, based on a relation between literal and metaphorical, Whybray, *Thanksgiving for a Liberated Prophet*, reaches an opposite conclusion: "The mass of statements in the poem about the Servant [=the prophet Second Isaiah], taken together, makes it quite clear that he was subjected to violence and humiliation, but that these stopped short of his death" (p. 106). Whybray depicts Isa. 53 as an individual thanksgiving. Both in this genre and in the individual laments, "there are frequent references to the speaker's *nearness to death*", p. 120, his italics. Cf. 3.10.11. n. 121. For an overview of the debate about "the servant's death", see Whybray, pp. 79–106.

Her untimely downfall makes the situation even more tragic.[252] In v. 1 a call to listen to the prophet is raised. קִינָה "a dirge" follows, a lament for the dead, in this case over Israel, conveyed in "I" speech and addressed to "you" (fs).[253] The funerary lament is intoned in the perfect tense as if the death and destruction have already occured: בְּתוּלַת יִשְׂרָאֵל "young girl Israel" has fallen and is "no more to rise" (v. 2). This is followed by the formulaic "For thus said the Lord YHWH", before the deity is quoted and a reason for the dirge is offered: Israel will suffer an overwhelming military defeat (v. 3). Within this destruction only ten percent will remain for the future of the people (v. 3, cf. v. 15).[254] In this personified lamentation, the prophet utters a funerary dirge for the whole people, conveying both his own and the deity's sorrow at the devastation of Israel.

Vv. 4–6 contrast with the dirge: they also begin with a formulaic introduction with an identification of the addressee "House of Israel" before the deity is quoted: seek YHWH and you shall live (vv. 4; 6, cf. vv. 14–15): life and death are thus at stake. The admonition to seek the Lord, including a conditional hope, is addressed to "you" (2mpl). Then more admonitions follow, this time formulated negatively: seek not Bethel, Gilgal or Beer-Sheba (v. 5). If they do not seek the Lord, the anger of the deity shall rise against the House of Joseph (v. 6). The exhortations to seek YHWH and live present repentance as a way of restoring the relationship with the deity (cf. 4:6–11). Amos 5:1–15 concerns Israel's behaviour. In vv. 16–17, a coming judgment of the oppressors is portrayed in an image of the land being filled with funerals. There shall be מִסְפֵּד "lamentation" (mentioned three times) and cries of הוֹ־הוֹ "woe, woe" in squares and streets, farms and vineyards. Also, in v. 18 a הוֹ "woe" cry, normally pronounced over the dead, is

---

[252] S. M. Paul, *Amos* (Hermeneia; Minneapolis: Fortress Press, 1991) 160.

[253] H. M. Barstad, *The Religious Polemics of Amos: Studies in the Preaching of Am 2, 7B-8; 4,1–13; 5, 1–27; 6, 4–7; 8,14* (VTSup, 34; Leiden: E. J. Brill, 1984) 77, n. 4 offers a whole range of examples of the use of the *qynh* metre in prophets' preaching of doom.

[254] Paul, *Amos*, p. 161. Barstad, *The Religious Polemics of Amos*, p. 77, rejects the idea of the references to the hundred and the ten that are left as an expression of an idea of a "remnant". He argues:

As is the case with the description of the shepherd who rescues a pair of legs or a bit of an ear from the lion's mouth (3,12) and of the man that carries the bones out of the ruined house (6,10), the purpose of the description of the prophet in 5,3 is to describe the total annihilation of the Israelites.

pronounced over a living audience.[255] In Amos 5, death appears within
a rhetorical discourse: it is not the actual death of a human being that
is bewailed, rather a warning of the people's imminent destruction is
given.[256] In Isa. 53 death is unworthy and a punishment for sin (but also
a turning point towards promises of a prolonged life and descendents
is indicated, cf. 53:10 and 5.15.1.); in Amos 5, the funerary lament is
intoned as if the death and destruction have already happened, but
there is a conditional hope that death might not occur.

5.14.3. *Jer. 22:18–19*

22:18 לָכֵן כֹּה־אָמַר יְהוָה אֶל־יְהוֹיָקִים בֶּן־יֹאשִׁיָּהוּ מֶלֶךְ יְהוּדָה
לֹא־יִסְפְּדוּ לוֹ הוֹי אָחִי וְהוֹי אָחוֹת לֹא־יִסְפְּדוּ לוֹ הוֹי אָדוֹן וְהוֹי הֹדֹה:
[19] קְבוּרַת חֲמוֹר יִקָּבֵר סָחוֹב וְהַשְׁלֵךְ מֵהָלְאָה לְשַׁעֲרֵי יְרוּשָׁלָ͏ִם:

22:18:   Therefore, thus said YHWH concerning Jehoiakim son of Joshiah,
         king of Judah:
         They shall not mourn for him, "Woe, brother! Woe, sister!"
         They shall not mourn for him, "Woe, lord! Woe, his majesty!'"
22:19:   He shall have the burial of an ass, dragged out and left lying
         outside the gates of Jerusalem.

In Jer. 22:18, a formulaic לָכֵן כֹּה־אָמַר יְהוָה "Therefore, thus said
YHWH" is followed by an identification of Jehoiakim, son of Josiah.
Then a judgment of Jehoiakim is stated: none shall mourn at his death
and his burial will be like an animal's (vv. 18b–19). None shall express
הוֹי "woe!" of mourning at the loss of a brother, a sister or a king. The
king's body will be thrown outside the gates without a worthy burial.
No explanation is given for the king's fate.

לָכֵן "therefore" in v. 18 relates the judgment to the previous verses:
in v. 13, a הוֹי "woe!" cry introduces an accusation adressed to an individual (vv. 13–17). The building of large houses using unpaid labour
and built לֹא־צֶדֶק "without righteousness" and לֹא מִשְׁפָּט "without

---

[255] K. J. Dell, "The Misuse of Forms in Amos", *VT* 45 (1995) 56–57: "The fall of
Israel, usually announced as coming in the future, is treated as a judgment that has
already taken place and the calamity is celebrated as though it had already occurred by
the singing of a funeral song for the nation", with reference also to Fohrer.

[256] The Book of Amos consists mainly of words of doom on Israel, but also dox-
ologies, words against the nations and some "biographical" material. While earlier
scholarship on Amos was characterised by form- and redactional-critical analyses of
shorter units, recently focus has been brought to larger rhetorical units and synchronic
(not a-historical!) analyses. For an overview of the most recent discussions, see R. F.
Melugin, "Amos in Recent Research", *CRBS* 6 (1998) 65–101.

justice" is condemned (vv. 13–15). Also, a contrast is made between
a just father taking care of the needy and an unjust son who does
not (vv. 15b–17). In 22:13–19 there is movement in the speech: in vv.
13–14, 3ms forms dominate, and in vv. 15–17, which is addressed in
2ms, the addressee is identified as a king. In vv. 18–19, judgment is
announced upon the more closely identified king Jehoiakim.[257]

In Jer. 22, accusations are directed towards the kings and people of
Judah. A fluid relation appears between the royal house and city. Jer.
22 offers examples of death and disgraceful burial as humiliations of
kings: Shallum (vv. 10–12), Jehoiakim (vv. 18–19) and Coniah (vv.
24–30). Jerusalem and her shepherds and lovers shall become scattered by the wind and birth pangs will come over her (vv. 21–23).
While the city is threatened with punishment because of its wickedness and apostasy in the breaking of the covenant and idolatry (vv.
9; 21), no charge is raised to explain the kings' fate. Due to the close
connection between the fates of kings and people, it seems appropriate
to read them as variations of a personification, where the fates of the
kings (that is, the lack of funerary laments on their death) are expressions for the catastrophe of the people.[258] As in Isa. 53, the humiliations take place because of unjust behaviour. In the (lack of) funerary
lament in Jer. 22:18, death is a metaphor in relation to punishment:
the הוֹי "woe!" of mourning becomes הוֹי "woe!" of accusation, representing the cry of the accuser, YHWH. Furthermore: it is the very
absence of הוֹי "woe!" which is the point in Jer. 22:18.[259]

5.14.4. Isa. 14:9–11; 15; 18–20

14:9 שְׁאוֹל מִתַּחַת רָגְזָה לְךָ לִקְרַאת בּוֹאֶךָ
עוֹרֵר לְךָ רְפָאִים כָּל־עַתּוּדֵי אָרֶץ
הֵקִים מִכִּסְאוֹתָם כֹּל מַלְכֵי גוֹיִם׃
10 כֻּלָּם יַעֲנוּ וְיֹאמְרוּ אֵלֶיךָ
גַּם־אַתָּה חֻלֵּיתָ כָמוֹנוּ אֵלֵינוּ נִמְשָׁלְתָּ׃
11 הוּרַד שְׁאוֹל גְּאוֹנֶךָ הֶמְיַת נְבָלֶיךָ

---

[257] In Jer. 22:10, an admonition to lament for the one who will go into exile and be
buried abroad is raised (cf. v. 19). The king is addressed by name: King Shallum, son
of Josiah (v. 11, Jehoahaz). In vv. 24–27 the humiliation of Coniah (Jehoiakin), son
of Jehoiakim and his descendants is described as death in exile. He is compared to a
broken pot (v. 28), stripped and childless (vv. 28–30). As in the depiction of Jehoiakim's fate in vv. 18–19, no explanation is offered for Coniah's fate.

[258] Cf. the Body Politic in 4.7.3.5.

[259] Carroll, *Jeremiah – A Commentary*, pp. 430–431.

תַּחְתֶּיךָ יֻצַּע רִמָּה וּמְכַסֶּיךָ תּוֹלֵעָה׃....
אַךְ אֶל־שְׁאוֹל תּוּרָד אֶל־יַרְכְּתֵי־בוֹר׃.... ¹⁵
כָּל־מַלְכֵי גוֹיִם כֻּלָּם שָׁכְבוּ בְכָבוֹד אִישׁ בְּבֵיתוֹ׃ ¹⁸
וְאַתָּה הָשְׁלַכְתָּ מִקִּבְרְךָ כְּנֵצֶר נִתְעָב ¹⁹
לְבוּשׁ הֲרֻגִים מְטֹעֲנֵי חָרֶב יוֹרְדֵי אֶל־אַבְנֵי־בוֹר כְּפֶגֶר מוּבָס׃
לֹא־תֵחַד אִתָּם בִּקְבוּרָה כִּי־אַרְצְךָ שִׁחַתָּ עַמְּךָ הָרָגְתָּ ²⁰
לֹא־יִקָּרֵא לְעוֹלָם זֶרַע מְרֵעִים׃

14:9:   שְׁאוֹל beneath is stirred up to meet you when you come,
        it rouses the shades to greet you, all who were leaders of the
        earth;
        it raises from their thrones all who were kings of the nations.
14:10: All of them will speak and say to you:
        "You too have become as weak as we! You have become like
        us!"
14:11: Brought down to שְׁאוֹל is your pomp, the sound of your harps;
        maggots are the bed beneath you, and worms are your cover-
        ing....
14:15: But to שְׁאוֹל are you brought down, to the depths of the pit.....
14:18: All the kings of the nations, all of them, lie in honour in their
        own tombs.
14:19: But you are cast out, away from your grave, like a loathed
        untimely birth,[260]
        clothed with the slain, those pierced by the sword,
        who go down to the stones of the pit, like a dead body trodden
        under foot.
14:20: You will not be joined with them in burial,
        because you have destroyed your land, you have slain your
        people.
        May the descendants of the evildoers nevermore be named.

In Isa. 14:9–10, the Babylonian king is addressed with expectations of
how, when he goes down to שְׁאוֹל, all the leaders and kings of the earth
raise up as in homage, but address him in a taunt: when descending
into שְׁאוֹל he is like them. His disgrace is strengthened by a contrast
with his former greatness: he goes down with his pomp and harps to
maggots and worms (v. 11). Then follows a mocking comparison of
the kings's downfall from heaven to הֵילֵל בֶּן־שָׁחַר "the shining one,
son of Dawn" (v. 12). The kings's thoughts are quoted: he would climb
to the heavens to sit on his throne and become like the Most High

---

[260] כְּנֵצֶר נִתְעָב "like a loathed untimely birth", lit. "abominable branch". LXX has
ὡς νεκρὸς ἐβδελυγμένος "as a loathsome corpse", which might be due to a reading of
נֵצֶל instead of נֵצֶר.

(vv. 13–14). He attempts to be like God but is fallen to שְׁאוֹל (v. 15). He wishes to ascend בְּיַרְכְּתֵי צָפוֹן "to the furthest reaches of the north" (v. 13) but goes down אֶל־יַרְכְּתֵי־בוֹר "to the depths of the pit" (v. 15, cf. vv. 9; 11).

Yet another comparison is made, where those who see him going down to שְׁאוֹל question his present state compared to his past, when the earth shook and kings trembled at him, he laid waste to the world and its cities and did not let his prisoners go free (vv. 16–17). His final disgrace is depicted: the peoples' kings are laid in honour in their tombs (v. 18) whereas he is denied a decent burial (vv. 19–20). He shall be cast down from his tomb which he seems never to have entered. He shall not be united with the peoples' kings in the grave and he will forever be denied a name because he shall never beget descendants (vv. 19–20). This is a judgment for his destruction of his own people and land (cf. vv. 6; 16–17).[261] In vv. 21–23, a sacrifice for his sons is prepared due to the transgressions of their father. After this taunt it is expressed that it is YHWH who rises up against Babylon and causes their downfall, in which name and offspring shall be cut off (vv. 22–23, cf. vv. 19–20).[262]

Isa. 14:3–4 is addressed to "you" (2ms), that is, Israel, who is instructed to utter הַמָּשָׁל הַזֶּה "this taunt song" against the king of Babylon. This shall occur יוֹם הָנִיחַ יְהוָה "the day that YHWH gives rest". The song addresses the Babylonian king as "you" (2ms, vv. 8–13; 15–16; 19–20) and the king is also quoted in "I" speech (vv. 13–14). It begins with a אֵיךְ "how" (cf. v. 12) concerning the downfall of the oppressor, and YHWH's breaking of the staff of the wicked and the rod of the tyrant, which had earlier stricken the peoples (vv. 4–6). Whereas the whole earth, cypresses and cedars rejoice at the king's downfall (vv. 7–8), שְׁאוֹל stirs up when he goes down and all the leaders of the earth and kings of the peoples greet him. The instruction

---

[261] G. A. Yee, "The Anatomy of Biblical Parody: The Dirge Form in 2 Samuel 1 and Isaiah 14", *CBQ* 50 (1988) 565–586, reads Isa. 14 as a parody of a dirge form more closely identified as 2 Sam. 1: "As such, it does not appear after the death of a hero but during the life of a tyrant. The dirge parody functions as prophecy, announcing the certain death of an oppressive ruler as if it had already taken place" (p. 581). Yee refers to many other parodies of dirge forms in the prophetic literature (n. 41). Oswalt, *The Book of Isaiah: Chapters 1–39*, p. 316, explains Isa. 14 as a mockery of the lament form, and as such the song for the dead is a song of joy, not grief, cf. Dell, "The Misuse of Forms in Amos", p. 50.

[262] On offspring, see 5.15.

to taunt the king of Babylon in vv. 3–4 is part of the restoration of Israel and the overthrow of Babylon as an act of YHWH (vv. 22–23). The mocking character is reinforced in vv. 21–23 by an admonition to slaughter the king's sons rather than mourn for his loss. The king is addressed as "you" until v. 21, where an imp. pl appears, whereas vv. 22–23 returns to 2ms, where statements by YHWH are made. These are, however, connected to the preceding by references to the sons of the king of Babylon. The close connection with the words of doom for Babylon makes this a variation of a personification, where the fate of the king is related to the fate of the people.

In v. 1, in 3ms statements about YHWH's actions with Israel are contrasted to those of Babylon. The deity will forgive Jacob and again choose Israel. Peoples shall bring the people of Israel home and serve them in their own land (v. 2), and YHWH shall give his people rest from עֶצֶב "sorrow", רֹגֶז "trouble" and הָעֲבֹדָה הַקָּשָׁה "the hard service" (v. 3). Israel shall be restored and shall rule over its former oppressors. The taunt song (vv. 4–23) is followed by words of doom for Assyrians (vv. 24–27) and Philistines (vv. 28–32) and words of salvation for Israel (v. 32).[263]

In Isa. 14, death appears within a personification of Babylonian pride and arrogance.[264] In a combination of lament over the dead and the song of derision, the Babylonian king is scorned and humiliated by a pitiful death and unworthy tomb. His final disgrace is contrasted with his former powerful position. The humiliation takes place due to his hubris. The dirge does not present the greatness of the king, but his disgrace, followed by the death of his sons and the end of his dynasty as a consequence of his oppressive politics. Like their king, the Babylonian people shall also perish. In an oscillation between words of salvation for Israel (vv. 1–4a) and words of doom for the peoples, the doom of the peoples strengthens the vindication of Israel (14:1–3 ["you"]; 22; 32)[265] This taunt of the Babylonian king becomes

---

[263] In vv. 26–27 universalistic perspectives are expressed, as YHWH's hand stretches out over all the peoples.

[264] Oswalt, *The Book of Isaiah: Chapters 1–39*, p. 311.

[265] Many suggestions have been made concerning the identity of the king in Isa. 14, e.g. kings of Babylon (Nebuchadrezzar II, Nabonidus), Assyrian kings (Sargon I/II, Sennacherib, Tiglath-pileser III, Shalmanezer V) and Alexander the Great. For an overview, see Sweeney, *Isaiah 1–39 with an Introduction to Prophetic Literature*, pp. 232–238, who identifies the king as Sargon II, and Blenkinsopp, *Isaiah 1–39*, pp.

yet another variation of a disgraceful death like the one depicted in Isa. 53.[266]

5.14.5. Ezek. 32:18–21

32:18 בֶּן־אָדָם נְהֵה עַל־הֲמוֹן מִצְרַיִם וְהוֹרִדֵהוּ
אוֹתָהּ וּבְנוֹת גּוֹיִם אַדִּרִם אֶל־אֶרֶץ תַּחְתִּיּוֹת אֶת־יוֹרְדֵי בוֹר:
19 מִמִּי נָעַמְתָּ רְדָה וְהָשְׁכְּבָה אֶת־עֲרֵלִים:
20 בְּתוֹךְ חַלְלֵי־חֶרֶב יִפֹּלוּ חֶרֶב נִתָּנָה מָשְׁכוּ אוֹתָהּ וְכָל־הֲמוֹנֶיהָ:
21 יְדַבְּרוּ־לוֹ אֵלֵי גִבּוֹרִים מִתּוֹךְ שְׁאוֹל אֶת־עֹזְרָיו
יָרְדוּ שָׁכְבוּ הָעֲרֵלִים חַלְלֵי־חָרֶב:

32:18: Son of man, wail over the Egyptian army and send it[267] down – her and the daughters of the majestic nations, to the land of the netherplace, to those who have gone down to the pit.

32:19: Whom do you surpass in loveliness? Go down and lie to rest with the uncircumcised.

32:20: Among those slain by the sword they shall fall. The sword has been appointed; draw her and all her armies.

32:21: To him will speak the strong leaders[268] from the midst of שְׁאוֹל and with his helpers. They descended, lay down, the uncircumcised, slain by sword.

286–287, who concludes that, due to the stereotypical language of the depiction, it is difficult to identify any historical Babylonian king, cf. Oswalt, *The Book of Isaiah: Chapters 1–39*, p. 314: "[T]he attempt to identify a precise historical figure is probably futile."

[266] Williamson, *The Book Called Isaiah*, pp. 165–168, regards Deutero-Isaiah as the redactor responsible for joining Isa. 13:2–22 and 14:4b-21 (23) together by adding 13:1 and 14:1–4a. Blenkinsopp, *Isaiah 1–39*, p. 272:

It is…likely that the Babylonian poems 13:1–14:23 were at some stage of the editorial process placed where they are to make the point that the prophetic history about Judah and Assyria recorded in chs. 1–12 provides the essential clues to interpreting the course of events during the time, much closer to the reader, of Neo-Babylonian ascendancy.

Cf. C. T. Begg, "Babylon in the Book of Isaiah" in Vermeylen, *The Book of Isaiah*, pp. 121–125.

Isa. 13–23 contains oracles against various foreign nations and against the rulers in Jerusalem (22:1–25) and are regarded as a mix of eighth-century proclamations and oracles dated to post-Exilic Israel. On discussions of the Book of Isaiah, cf. 2.3.2., 5.8.2. n. 55 and 5.11.2. n. 128.

[267] אוֹתָהּ "it" (fem) is often emended to אַתְּ (personal pronoun 2msg) "you"; see, for instance, D. I. Block, *The Book of Ezekiel. Chapters 25–48* (NICOT; Grand Rapids: Eerdmans, 1998) 215 n. 12. For further text-critical discussions of v. 18, cf. L. C. Allen, *Ezekiel 20–48* (WBC, 28; Dallas: Word Books, 1994) 134 n. 18a.

[268] אֵלֵי גִבּוֹרִים lit. "the rams of the mighty (men)".

בֶּן־אָדָם "Son of man" is addressed and directed to wail, i.e. Ezekiel is given the task of ironically grieving over the coming fate of Egypt's army (vv. 18–20, cf. vv. 4–5).[269] The admonition to נְהֵה "wail" belongs to the language of the mourning of the dead,[270] here applied to "her and the daughters of the majestic nations", who shall go down אֶל־ אֶרֶץ תַּחְתִּיּוֹת "to the land of the netherplace" among those who went down to the בּוֹר "pit".

A rhetorical question challenges Egypt's self-esteem as the loveliest nation in the world, and is followed by contrasting mocking expressions about how she shall go to the uncircumcised to lie among those slain by the sword (vv. 19–20). The uncircumcised and the victims of the sword represent the dead that are not buried with their families, and so in שְׁאוֹל are regarded as occupying a separate place of dishonour (v. 21, cf. v. 27). The lowest place in the world is called אֶרֶץ תַּחְתִּיּוֹת "land of the netherplace" (v. 18, cf. v. 24 and Isa. 14:15), בּוֹר "pit" (v. 18, cf. Isa. 14:15; 19) and שְׁאוֹל (v. 21, cf. Isa. 14:9; 11; 15), where the Egyptians come to their ignomious end.

Ezek. 32:17–32 is an oracle of judgment against Egypt or Pharaoh, though without any clear accusation.[271] From v. 22 onwards, Egypt's companions in שְׁאוֹל are presented. The majestic nations of v. 18 are further identified as Assyria (vv. 22–23), Elam (vv. 24–25), Meshech-Tubal (vv. 26–27), Edom (v. 29) and Sidon (v. 30) – all related to dishonorable death. The direct address is dropped from v. 20 until v. 28.[272] The Assyrian king and his men have fallen by the sword and

---

[269] MT Ezek. 32:17–32 are beset with textual corruptions, difficulties and inconsistencies and LXX has a different rendering in many places, cf. Block, *The Book of Ezekiel. Chapters 25–48*, pp. 212–213.

[270] The verb occurs elsewhere in Mic. 2:4 and 1 Sam. 7:2 only, but the noun is more common, cf. Jer. 9:17–19, 31:15, Amos 5:16 and the *hapax* forms in Ezek. 2:10 and 27:32.

[271] The Book of Ezekiel is composite of message of judgment (1–24), oracles against foreign nations (25–32) and oracles of salvation (33–48). The oracles against the nations (25–32) are arranged in seven groups. Ezek. 32:18–21 is the last of the seven sayings. In the book, the fall of Jerusalem in 587 BCE works as a dividing point between judgment and consolation. The book draws on prophetic, priestly and other biblical traditions. For an overview of traditional approaches, see K. P. Darr, "Ezekiel Among the Critics", *CRBS* 2 (1994) 9–24. In addition to traditional historical-critical analyses, gender, psychoanalytical, rhetorical and anthropological studies, among others, have recently been conducted on the Book of Ezekiel, see R. L. Kohn, "Ezekiel at the Turn of the Century", *CBR* 2 (2003) 9–31.

[272] Block, *The Book of Ezekiel. Chapters 25–48*, pp. 222–223, presents linguistic similarities between the nations mentioned in Ezek. 32:22–30. He also comments on how

are in tombs in the remotest reaches of the pit. In contrast to a glorious past, they are now dishonoured with a violent death (vv. 21–23). Also Elam and her army have fallen by the sword and have gone down uncircumcised to the netherworld. Their glorious past is also contrasted with their dishonourable death (vv. 24–25). Meshech-Tubal is classified with the uncircumcised and those slain by the sword – and like the other peoples, this happens "although they had spread their terror in the land of living" (vv. 26–28). Edom with all her rulers, the princes of the north and Sidonians (vv. 29–30) share the very same fate in both past and present as Egypt, Assyria, Elam and Meshech-Tubal. The oracle ends with a reminder of what shall happen to Pharaoh: he and his army shall also be laid in the midst of those uncircumcised and slain by the sword (vv. 31–32).

The Egyptians are assigned the same dishonourable fate as the other peoples. Again, a word of doom for a foreign nation has elements of a personification, where the fate of Pharaoh is identical to the fate of the people of Egypt.[273] In Ezek. 32, death appears within mocking expressions.

5.14.6. *Ps. 88:4–8*

88:4 כִּי־שָׂבְעָה בְרָעוֹת נַפְשִׁי וְחַיַּי לִשְׁאוֹל הִגִּיעוּ׃
5 נֶחְשַׁבְתִּי עִם־יוֹרְדֵי בוֹר הָיִיתִי כְּגֶבֶר אֵין־אֱיָל׃
6 בַּמֵּתִים חָפְשִׁי כְּמוֹ חֲלָלִים שֹׁכְבֵי קֶבֶר
אֲשֶׁר לֹא זְכַרְתָּם עוֹד וְהֵמָּה מִיָּדְךָ נִגְזָרוּ׃
7 שַׁתַּנִי בְּבוֹר תַּחְתִּיּוֹת בְּמַחֲשַׁכִּים בִּמְצֹלוֹת׃
8 עָלַי סָמְכָה חֲמָתֶךָ וְכָל־מִשְׁבָּרֶיךָ עִנִּיתָ סֶּלָה׃

88:4: For I am sated with trouble; I am brought near to שְׁאוֹל.
88:5: I am counted among those who go down to the pit,
     I am like a man who has no strength,[274]

---

each entry except Egypt and Sidon is portrayed in the feminine. Egypt is portrayed as both fem. (vv. 17; 20b) and masc. (vv. 19–21) (p. 224).

[273] Dell, "The Misuse of Forms in Amos", p. 50, regards Ezek. 32 among her examples of a mocking, prophetic dirge directed against a foreign nation. With its combination of a taunt song and a lament over the dead, "the paradoxical form of the ironical dirge makes the threat more severe".

[274] אֱיָל is a *hapax legomenon*, often taken as the Aram. loan word "help", supported by LXX, Pesh, BDB, but also "strength", see M. E. Tate, *Psalms 51–100* (WBC, 20; Dallas, Texas: Word Books, 1990) 396 n. 5e.

88:6: like those חָפְשִׁי[275] among the dead, like the slain that lie in the grave,
like those whom you remember no more, for they are cut off from your hand.

88:7: You have put me in the depths of the pit in the regions dark and deep.[276]

88:8: Your wrath lies heavy upon me and you overwhelm (me) with all your waves.

In Ps. 88:4, the psalmist is sated with troubles with a life on the brink of death and שְׁאוֹל.[277] He feels that he is reckoned with those going down to the בּוֹר "pit" and that he is like a strong man who has lost his strength (v. 5), like those forsaken among the dead and like those slain that lie in the grave (v. 6) – not remembered but cut off from the deity (v. 6).[278] He complains that the deity has put him in the darkness at the bottom of the pit (v. 7), and that YHWH's wrath rests upon him and his waves afflict him (v. 8, cf. vv. 17–18).

Ps. 88 is an individual lament – or prayer – addressed to יְהוָה אֱלֹהֵי יְשׁוּעָתִי "YHWH, the God of my salvation!"[279] An introductory petition is raised in a cry for help which goes unheard (vv. 2–3). The speaker has prayed day and night but feels forsaken. The address conveys a continuing faith in YHWH, although the deity has not responded. After he has depicted his life as being like those who are dead and forgotten by the deity (vv. 4–8), he continues by telling how YHWH has caused his friends to distance themselves from him and how he has become תּוֹעֵבוֹת "abominable" (vv. 9; 19) and his eyes have "grown weak from

---

[275] חָפְשִׁי usually means "free", supported by LXX and Pesh., but it has been difficult to acquire a meaningful understanding of this in Ps. 88:6. Tate, *Psalms 51–100*, p. 396, n. 6a, regards בַּמֵּתִים חָפְשִׁי "set free among the dead" in an ironic sense as a key expression of the whole psalm (pp. 402–403). F.-L. Hossfeld and E. Zenger, *Psalms 2 – A Commentary* (Hermeneia; Minneapolis: Fortress Press, 2005) 390 n. e, translate "one expelled", intending to "bring the negative connotations of this 'release' to awareness".

[276] בְּמַחֲשַׁכִּים בִּמְצֹלוֹת lit. "in the dark (places) in the depths", cf. v. 19 חֹשֶׁךְ "darkness".

[277] K.-J. Illman, "Psalm 88 – A Lamentation without Answer", *SJOT* 1 (1991) 116, comments on the expression "I am at the brink of שְׁאוֹל": "This motif is common in lamentation texts [cf. Pss. 30:4, 107:18b; Isa. 38:10; Job 33:22a] but it is uncommonly broadly depicted here [4b.5–8.17–19, cf. 11–13]."

[278] Ni. גזר, cf. Isa. 53:8, see 3.10.11. n. 121.

[279] On the genre of Ps. 88, see a discussion in W. S. Prinsloo, "Psalm 88: The Gloomiest Psalm?", *Old Testament Essays* 5 (1992) 332–345. Ps. 88 has, among others, been regarded as belonging to the "psalms of illness", see a brief overview in Prinsloo, pp. 337–338, and Tate, *Psalms 51–100*, p. 399.

suffering" (v. 10). The last part of v. 10 relates back to vv. 2–3 and reiterates the praying of the psalmist.

In vv. 11–13 rhetorical questions expecting negative answers are conveyed. The questions regard the netherworld as a place without the wonderful deeds of YHWH and without praise for him.[280] שְׁאוֹל is the place of מֵתִים "the dead ones", of רְפָאִים "shades", of קֶבֶר "grave", בָּאֲבַדּוֹן "in Abaddon", חֹשֶׁךְ "darkness" and בְּאֶרֶץ נְשִׁיָּה "in the land of forgetfulness". The questions intensify the complaint of the speaker, in an urgent need for divine intervention for one who is already near to שְׁאוֹל and reckoned among those on their way to the pit of death.

The complaint continues in vv. 14–19. The psalmist returns to complaining about an unanswered morning prayer (v. 14). In two לָמָה "why" questions, a feeling of being spurned by God and that God is hiding his face is expressed (v. 15). No hints are given that the questions might be answered. Further depictions of the dark situation are added: long-term affliction[281] until death, overwhelming divine wrath and annihilation by God's terrors, which surround him like water (vv. 16–18). In addition, the deity has caused him to be forsaken by lovers and friends (vv. 15; 19), ending with מַחְשָׁךְ "darkness". As in vv. 7–9, in vv. 17–19 it is made clear that the deity is responsible for the trouble. In Ps. 88 there are no exclamations of praise.

Ps. 88 has been called the gloomiest of all the individual psalms.[282] The psalmist's dark situation is, among other things, depicted as a disgraceful death (vv. 3; 5; 15) and an unworthy tomb (vv. 4–6; 11), with the added dimension that this is caused by YHWH (vv. 7–9; 15–19). He depicts his feeling rejected by God, interwoven with a conviction that YHWH cannot let this happen. The psalm ends with a cry of pain. There is no turning point towards trust in YHWH or exclamations of praise, no confession of sin, only YHWH's anger[283] and expressions of the feeling of being treated unjustly by God.

---

[280] Cf. Isa. 38:18–19 in 5.11.14.

[281] Tate, *Psalms 51–100*, p. 400:
> The metaphorical language of sickness is sufficiently varied enough to encompass the statements in Ps 88…Sickness involves an increased danger of death and heightens the awareness of the nearness of dying. Death language is "stereotypically associated with the image of sickness" [quoting Seybold and Mueller]…On the other hand, there appears to be no language in Ps 88 which *necessitates* a direct reference to illness, his italics.

[282] Prinsloo, "Psalm 88", pp. 333–334, M. E. Tate, "Psalm 88", *RevExp* 87 (1990) 91.

[283] R. C. Culley, "Psalm 88 Among the Complaints" in L. Eslinger and G. Taylor (eds), *Ascribe to the Lord* (JSOTSup, 67; Sheffield: JSOT Press, 1988) 301:

5.14.7. *Summing Up*

In this chapter we have examined depictions of the way one is buried –
or not buried at all. In Isa. 53:9, humiliation is related to an unworthy tomb where the dead one is classified with רְשָׁעִים "wicked ones"
and עָשִׁיר "a rich" (?). This occured although he had behaved neither
violently nor deceptively. He is also cut off from the land of the living
(v. 8) and slain to death (v. 12). In v. 8 "his" death is explained as due
to פֶּשַׁע עַמִּי "the transgression of my people"; in v. 12 "he" is classified
with פֹּשְׁעִים "transgressors".

In Amos 5, death appears within a rhetorical discourse: it is not the
actual death of a human being that is bewailed: rather, a warning of
the people's imminent destruction is raised. In Isa. 53 death is unworthy and a punishment for sin, while in Amos 5 the funeral lament is
intoned as if the death has already taken place, but there is a conditional hope that it might not occur.

In Jer. 22, a judgment on Jehoiakim is stated: none shall mourn
at his death and his burial will be like an animal's (vv. 18b–19). The
kings's body will be thrown outside the gates without a proper burial.
While in vv. 9; 21 the city is threatened with punishment because of
the people's wickedness, no charge is raised to explain the kings' fate.
Due to the close connection between the fates of king and people,
this becomes a variation of a personification, where the fate of the

---

By focusing on the anger of YHWH as the sole source of the suffering of the victim and not mentioning punishment as the reason for the action of the deity, one
may be led to another explanation [that is, different from the traditional "rescue
pattern in the psalms and elsewhere in OT"]. This may be what is happening in
the song of the Suffering Servant in Isa. 52:14 [!]–53:12. Here Yahweh afflicts an
innocent person but the suffering has some purpose. It will benefit others. Rescue
remains a central issue since the victim, although he is not aware of it, will be
the instrument of rescue. However, the framework of suffering as punishment for
wrongdoing is still retained because the suffering of the innocent party is taken to
be the punishment which should have been laid on others, and there is no hint
of this kind of understanding in Psalm 88.

Culley offers another possible way of understanding Ps. 88:

By focusing on the action of the deity as the sole source of the difficult situation
with no role left for outside forces, the enemies which evoke the problem of evil,
Psalm 88 poses a painful and difficult dilemma: how to account for the rage and
destruction demonstrated by the deity, especially since the anger of Yahweh is
not explained by the sin of the victim. These are some of the issues the Book of
Job explored (p. 302).

In the Book of Job, different aspects of death are depicted, see, for instance, death
before the proper time (10:19, 20:11, 22:16) and the blessing of dying in full rigour
(5:26, 21:32).

king is an expression of the catastrophe of the people. In the (lack of)
funerary lament in Jer. 22:18, death becomes a metaphor in relation
to punishment.

In a combination of lament over the dead and the song of derision,
in Isa. 14 the Babylonian king is scorned and humiliated by a pitiful
death and unworthy tomb. The humiliation occurs due to his hubris
and is contrasted with his former powerful position. Like their king,
the Babylonian people shall also perish. The taunt of the Egyptian Pharaoh in Ezek. 32 becomes yet another variation of a disgraceful death.
Both in Isa. 14 and in Ezek. 32 a word of doom upon a foreign nation
has elements of a personification, where the fate of the king/Pharaoh
is identical with the fate of Babylon/Egypt. In both instances, death
appears within mocking expressions.

Dell argues that in the prophetic literature traditional forms of
speech are "misused" by being appropriated for purposes other than
those for which they were normally employed, for instance, the use of
funeral lament for purposes other than the actual rites for the dead.[284]
She comments:

> [T]he style of the dirge has affected the form of the oracle concerning
> the Servant of YHWH in Isa. lii 13–liii 12. In this case…the content is
> completely reversed; as Fohrer writes, "the description of need and the
> death of the Servant provide the basis for the salvation that has been
> achieved through him".[285]

In Ps. 88, the psalmist depicts his dark situation as, among other
things, a disgraceful death (vv. 3; 5; 15) and an unworthy tomb (vv.
4–6; 11) caused by YHWH (vv. 7–9; 15–19). He feels rejected by God,
but is also convinced that YHWH cannot let this happen. However,
there are no exclamations of praise, no confession of sin, only expressions of the feeling of being treated unjustly. Certainly, "intertextual
links" should not be drawn too far as regards the individual psalms
of lament and Isa. 53, but Ps. 88 is a telling example of how death
works as a metaphor, departing from its lexically codified usage. Death
appears within a stereotypical language of lament related to individuals (kings like Jehoiakim in Jer. 22, the Babylonian king in Isa. 14 and
the Pharaoh of Egypt in Ezek. 32 and psalmist in Ps. 88) and personifications (Israel in Isa. 53 and Amos 5) in extreme situations. Texts

---

[284] Dell, "The Misuse of Forms in Amos", pp. 59–60.
[285] Dell, "The Misuse of Forms in Amos", p. 50.

on disgraceful burials in this chapter also convey personifications and
close connections between king and land (Jer. 22, Isa. 14, Ezek. 32).

5.15. "…HE SHALL SEE OFFSPRING…"

5.15.1. *Isa. 53:10b*

53:10 יִרְאֶה זֶרַע יַאֲרִיךְ יָמִים

53:10:…he shall see offspring and live long.

In Isa. 53:10, dimensions of hope and expectation are expressed: "he"
shall see descendants and live a long life. In spite of all the humiliations he has lived through, he shall "rise from death" and emerge with
dignity. With reproduction and offspring, the future is promising.[286]
No direct reason is given for "his" turning point from humiliation to
vindication, apart from the statement that both are due to חֵפֶץ יְהוָה
"YHWH's pleasure" (v. 10).

A personification here is composite of "he" and "his" offspring,
which together are the collective people of Israel, and is similar (but
not identical) to "he" and "we" in 53:1–6. In 53:1–6, "he" and "we" are
related through illness, sin and rehabilitation; in v. 10 the depiction of
"him" and "his" offspring indicates family relations.

5.15.2. *Isa. 44:3–4*

44:3 כִּי אֶצָּק־מַיִם עַל־צָמֵא וְנֹזְלִים עַל־יַבָּשָׁה
אֶצֹּק רוּחִי עַל־זַרְעֶךָ וּבִרְכָתִי עַל־צֶאֱצָאֶיךָ:
⁴וְצָמְחוּ בְּבֵין חָצִיר כַּעֲרָבִים עַל־יִבְלֵי־מָיִם:

44:3: For I will pour water on the thirsty and streams on the dry
ground.
I will pour my spirit upon your offspring and my blessing on your
descendants.
44:4: They shall spring up in green grass, like willows by flowing
streams.

---

[286] Mowinckel, *He That Cometh*, p. 205, interprets Isa. 53:10b as an expression for
resurrection, arguing that a dead man could certainly not have children or live long, cf.
Elliger, "Jes. 53:10", pp. 228–233, Bentzen, *King and Messiah*, pp. 54; 59; 62, E. Haag,
"Das Opfer des Gottesknechts (Jes. 53:10)", *TTZ* 86 (1977) 81–98, Gerlemann, *Studien
zur alttestamenlichen Theologie*, pp. 38–60. For an overview, see Whybray, *Thanksgiving for a Liberated Prophet*, pp. 79–92, esp. 80–81, and Haag, *Der Gottesknecht
bei Deuterojesaja*, pp. 191–195. Cf. Hermisson in 5.14.1. n. 251.

In Isa. 44:3, a speaking "I" introduces an addressee "you" (2ms) and promises the tranformation of צָמֵא "thirsty" and יַבָּשָׁה "dry ground", upon which "I" will pour מַיִם "water" and נֹזְלִים "streams". V. 3b links closely with v. 3a, as אֶצֹּק "I will pour" is repeated, but where the elements in transformation are זַרְעֶךָ "your offspring" and צֶאֱצָאֶיךָ "your descendants", upon which the speaking "I" will pour רוּחִי "my spirit" and בִּרְכָתִי "my blessing".[287] In the outpouring, מַיִם "water", נֹזְלִים "streams", רוּחִי "my spirit" and בִּרְכָתִי "my blessing" are life-giving. A doubleness of both זֶרַע "offspring" and צֶאֱצָאִים "descendants" in v. 3b appears when related to v. 3a: water and streams make זֶרַע "seed" come up after the drought and give growth to צֶאֱצָאִים "what springs from the earth".[288] זֶרַע "seed" and צֶאֱצָאִים "what springs from the earth" refer to the sowing both of seed and of the offspring of the addressee. In v. 4, both the metaphors of nature (v. 3a) and of descendants (v. 3b) are echoed. In the outpouring of water, spirit and blessings, growth and fertility are related to the future. The descendants shall survive, blossom and multiply.

V. 3 motivates the encouragement of v. 2b not to fear, which is addressed to Jacob, "my servant", Israel, "my chosen"[289] and Jeshurun. It is addressed by YHWH as Israel's "former", "maker" and "helper". Thus, both re-election and re-creation are expressions of YHWH returning to his people with care. Here, an assurance of descendants is expressed in the metaphor of the fertility of the soil, and water is

---

[287] On YHWH's בְּרָכָה "blessing" of Israel and its offspring, see Isa. 19:24–25, 51:2, 61:9, 65:23, and YHWH's proclamation of צֶדֶק "righteousness" to the offspring of Jacob and Israel in Isa. 45:19; 25.

[288] Cf. זֶרַע "seed" in 55:10 and צֶאֱצָאִים "offspring" in 42:5, related to a vegetable sphere. For water and blossoming in dry ground, see e.g. Isa. 32:2; 15–16, 35:1–2; 6–7, 41:17–20, 43:19–20, 48:21, 49:10, 51:3, 55:1, 66:12. A "wilderness motif" in Isa. 40–55 is treated in Barstad, *A Way in the Wilderness*. He opposes the traditional identification of an "Exodus motif" in Isa. 40–55, as in e.g. B. W. Anderson, "Exodus Typology in Second Isaiah" in B. W. Anderson and W. Harrelson (eds), *Israel's Prophetic Heritage: Essays in Honour of James Muilenburg* (New York: Harper & Brother, 1962) 177–195, K. Kiesow, *Exodustexte im Jesajabuch: Literarkritische und motivgeschichtliche Analysen* (OBO, 24; Fribourg: Éditions Universitaires, 1979), R. E. Watts, "Consolation or Confrontation? Isa. 40–55 and the Delay of the New Exodus", *TynBul* 41 (1990) 31–59, Ceresko, "The Rhetorical Strategy of the Fourth Servant Song", pp. 42–55, Steck, *Gottesknecht und Zion*, R. Abma, "Travelling from Babylon to Zion: Location and its Function in Isaiah 49–55", *JSOT* 74 (1997) 3–28, A. Johnston, "A Prophetic Vision of an Alternative Community: A Reading of Isa. 40–55" in Hopfe, *Uncovering Ancient Stones*, pp. 31–40.

[289] On servant, see 5.8.2. n. 58 and 5.17. n. 324, on election, see 5.8.2. n. 60.

aligned with the spirit as the source of life.[290] As in 53:10, the personification is composite of family terms with a relation between "you"
and "your" offspring.

The depiction of the future as descendants and offspring that shall
survive, blossom and multiply might be contrasted with the depiction
of the man's misery in Isa. 53:2, likening his past to יוֹנֵק "a shoot" and
שֹׁרֶשׁ "a root" in dry ground. Through associations of progeny, blossoming and prosperity, attention is drawn to the potential of growth
and hope. Further signs of drought and desert bring associations of
feeble and perishable plants prematurely stripped of their vitality and
splendor. The comparison is modified by a portrayal of his miserable
bodily appearance. In the interaction between the similes and adjacent
explanations, we can see that the insignificant little plant has hardly
any future.

5.15.3. *Isa. 48:18–19*

48:18 לוּא הִקְשַׁבְתָּ לְמִצְוֺתָי
וַיְהִי כַנָּהָר שְׁלוֹמֶךָ וְצִדְקָתְךָ כְּגַלֵּי הַיָּם:
[19] וַיְהִי כַחוֹל זַרְעֶךָ וְצֶאֱצָאֵי מֵעֶיךָ כִּמְעֹתָיו
לֹא־יִכָּרֵת וְלֹא־יִשָּׁמֵד שְׁמוֹ מִלְּפָנָי:

48:18: If only you had heeded my commandments!
Then your peace would have flowed like a river and your righteousness like the waves of the sea.

48:19: Your offspring would have been like the sand and the descendants of your loins like its grains;
its name would never be cut off or destroyed from before me.

In "I" speech, YHWH addresses "you" (2ms) and reminds "you" of
what might have been if "you" had paid attention to his מִצְוֺת "com-
mands": "שְׁלוֹמֶךָ 'your peace' would be like a river and צִדְקָתְךָ 'your
righteousness' like the waves of the sea" (v. 18).[291] The promises of an
unfulfilled wish are expanded by an abundance of descendants and
a great name (v. 19). The blessings on "you" are compared to נָהָר
"a river" and יָם "a sea" (v. 18), and likened to חוֹל "sand" and מְעֹת

---

[290] Cf. the pairing of זֶרַע "offspring" and צֶאֱצָאִים "descendants" in Isa. 43:5, 44:3,
61:9, 65:23 and Job 5:25 (cf. 5.15.7.).

[291] צְדָקָה and שָׁלוֹם are paired also in 56:1, 59:9; 16; 17, 61:10–11, 63:3.

"grains"[292] (v. 19) – all being immeasurable and uncountable. The promises of blessings are related to שְׁלוֹמֶךָ "your peace", צִדְקָתֶךָ "your righteousness", זַרְעֶךָ "your offspring" and צֶאֱצָאֵי מֵעֶיךָ "the descendants of your loins". To the promises of well-being and great expansion are added an allusion to a present threat: whereas vv. 18b–19a are positively formulated and say what would have happened, v. 19b is negative and states what would not happen: "its name would never be cut off or destroyed from before me".[293] Receiving offspring and descendants, the name shall also live in the future. Not only the well-being and numerical strength of Israel are at stake but also its very survival.

However, the reproachful tone of YHWH to "you" in v. 18 implies critique. Conveyed as an unfulfilled wish, it appears as a lament by YHWH about the obstinacy of his people: "If you had followed my words…but you did not…" The punishment of Israel could not have been avoided.

The "I" speech to "you" (2ms) about "your" offspring is placed in the middle of an argument beginning in v. 17. YHWH's complaint in vv. 18–19 is embedded within the words of the formulaic כֹּה־אָמַר יְהוָה גֹּאַלְךָ קְדוֹשׁ יִשְׂרָאֵל "Thus says the Lord, your redeemer, Israel's Holy one",[294] followed by a self-presentation: "I am YHWH your God", with appellatives depicting the deity as teacher and guide. In these appellatives, the addressee is prepared to pay attention and is admonished to accept his instructions and follow his way. The addressee is reminded of what might be if they listen to YHWH and of what will be for those who do not (vv. 17–19). In a personification, the blessings on "you" are compared to נָהָר "a river" and יָם "a sea" (v. 18), and likened to חוֹל "sand" and מְעֹת "grains" (v. 19), all being immeasurable and uncountable. As in Isa. 53:10 and 44:3, the personification is composite of family terms with a relation between "you" and "your" offspring.

---

[292] 1QIsaᵃ renders וצאצאי כמעיו "the descendants like its grain", which might be due to haplography of the MT מֵעֶיךָ "your loins" (confused with כְּמֵעָיו "like its grain"), which is a *hapax legomenon*, see Koole, *Isaiah III. Vol. 1*, p. 596.

Cf. the promise of זֶרַע "offspring" to the patriarchs in the book of Genesis. The promise of descendants is closely connected to the people, see Gen 12:2, 26:4, 48:4 and Hos. 2:1, cf. the address "offspring of Abraham" in Isa. 41:8, 2 Chron. 20:7, Ps. 105:6, and the recollection of the blessing of children to Abraham and Sarah in Isa. 51:2.

[293] שֵׁם "name" and זֶרַע "offspring" appear together in Isa. 66:22 (see 5.15.6.), 1 Sam. 24:22, in Isa. 14:22 (cf. 5.14.4.) parallel with children and grandchildren.

[294] גֹּאַלְךָ "your redeemer" and קְדוֹשׁ יִשְׂרָאֵל "Israel's Holy one", see 5.8.2. n. 55.

5.15.4. *Isa. 49:16–21*

49:16 הֵן עַל־כַּפַּיִם חַקֹּתִיךְ חוֹמֹתַיִךְ נֶגְדִּי תָּמִיד:
¹⁷ מִהֲרוּ בָּנָיִךְ מְהָרְסַיִךְ וּמַחֲרִבַיִךְ מִמֵּךְ יֵצֵאוּ:
¹⁸ שְׂאִי־סָבִיב עֵינַיִךְ וּרְאִי כֻּלָּם נִקְבְּצוּ בָאוּ־לָךְ
חַי־אָנִי נְאֻם־יְהוָה כִּי כֻלָּם כָּעֲדִי תִלְבָּשִׁי וּתְקַשְּׁרִים כַּכַּלָּה:
¹⁹ כִּי חָרְבֹתַיִךְ וְשֹׁמְמֹתַיִךְ וְאֶרֶץ הֲרִסֻתֵיךְ
כִּי עַתָּה תֵּצְרִי מִיּוֹשֵׁב וְרָחֲקוּ מְבַלְּעָיִךְ:
²⁰ עוֹד יֹאמְרוּ בְאָזְנַיִךְ בְּנֵי שִׁכֻּלָיִךְ
צַר־לִי הַמָּקוֹם גְּשָׁה־לִּי וְאֵשֵׁבָה:
²¹ וְאָמַרְתְּ בִּלְבָבֵךְ מִי יָלַד־לִי אֶת־אֵלֶּה
וַאֲנִי שְׁכוּלָה וְגַלְמוּדָה גֹּלָה וְסוּרָה וְאֵלֶּה מִי גִדֵּל
הֵן אֲנִי נִשְׁאַרְתִּי לְבַדִּי אֵלֶּה אֵיפֹה הֵם:

49:16: See, I have graven you on my palms, your walls are always before me.
49:17: Your sons hasten to come, your destroyers and your wasters, they go forth from you.
49:18: Lift up your eyes and see around you, they all gather and come to you.
As I live, says YHWH, surely, you will put all of them on as an ornament
and you will bind them on like a bride.
49:19: Surely, your wasted and ruined places and your destroyed land –
Surely, now you will be too narrow for the inhabitant and your devourers will be far off.
49:20: They will say in your ears, your sons of which you were bereft:
The place is too narrow for me, make room for me, so that I shall dwell!
49:21: And you will say in your heart: Who has begotten these for me?
And I was bereaved and barren, exiled and deserted – and these, who has raised them?
See, I was left alone, where then have all these come from?

In Isa. 49:16 YHWH explains his relationship to a woman who is on his hand and whose walls are before him. Her sons hasten to come (vv. 17–18),[295] whereas her destroyers and destruction disappear (vv. 17; 19). Her children will be like a bride's ornament (v. 18). Her ruined places and destroyed land shall beget so many children that Zion becomes too crowed and too narrow (vv. 19–20) and her time as barren, rejected and desolate (vv. 20–21) is past. The peoples and nations shall bring her sons and daughters, kings and queens shall foster them and grovel in the dust to her (vv. 22–23). She will recognise that YHWH is the

---

[295] 1QIsaᵃ renders בֹּנָיִךְ "your builders" in v. 17.

Lord (v. 23) and she will be rescued from the tyrant (vv. 24–26).[296] The depiction of the fate of the woman and the city is interwoven beyond separation, as the promises of the future concern the rehabilitation of the woman, the rebuilding of the city and its population (vv. 17–21) and the return of the exiled (vv. 22–26).

Isa. 49:16–21 is preceded by a memory from Zion's time of humiliation, where she is quoted, lamenting her feeling of having been abandoned and forgotten by YHWH (v. 14). She is answered by a question and an assurance which together tell her that a woman would sooner forget her child than YHWH Zion (v. 15). Vv. 16–21 are composite of a mixture of ingathering, promises of descendants and the future of the nation: prosperity and expansion. The background is former barrenness and desolation, exile and ruin (vv. 19–21). As in Isa. 53:10, 44:3 and 48:19, the rehabilitation of the people (and land) is depicted in a personification composed of parent and descendants, but unlike the previous masculine personifications, this one is about a woman, formerly barren, desolate and driven away, now with plenty of children and a rebuilt land.[297]

5.15.5. Isa. 54:1–3

54:1 רָנִּי עֲקָרָה לֹא יָלָדָה פִּצְחִי רִנָּה וְצַהֲלִי לֹא־חָלָה
כִּי־רַבִּים בְּנֵי־שׁוֹמֵמָה מִבְּנֵי בְעוּלָה אָמַר יְהוָה:
²הַרְחִיבִי מְקוֹם אָהֳלֵךְ וִירִיעוֹת מִשְׁכְּנוֹתַיִךְ יַטּוּ אַל־תַּחְשֹׂכִי
הַאֲרִיכִי מֵיתָרַיִךְ וִיתֵדֹתַיִךְ חַזֵּקִי: ³כִּי־יָמִין וּשְׂמֹאול תִּפְרֹצִי
וְזַרְעֵךְ גּוֹיִם יִירָשׁ וְעָרִים נְשַׁמּוֹת יוֹשִׁיבוּ:

54:1: Sing, you barren one, who never bore,
  break forth into singing, cry aloud, you who were not in labour;
  for the children of the desolate will be more than the children of her that is married,
  says YHWH.
54:2: Broaden the place of your tent and let the tent-cloths of your dwellings be stretched out;[298]
  do not hold back, lengthen your cords and strengthen your pegs.

---

[296] Cf. words against the nations, see 5.8.5.
[297] Descriptions of YHWH's ingathering of his people occur in a masc. personification in Isa. 41:9, 43:5, 49:5, in fem. personifications in 49:18, 54:7 and in a shepherd/flock motif in 40:11.
[298] נטה (jussive 3mpl) "spread out", "stretch out", "extend". LXX has imp. fs in accordance with the rest of the verbs in the sentence, which are 3fpl imperf. Since a similar change of subject occurs in v. 3 and because pl can be understood as a collective "they", MT might be preserved.

> 54:3: For to the right and to the left you will break out;
> your offspring will inherit from the nations and inhabit the destroyed cities.

In Isa. 54:1 a woman addressed as barren, childless and desolate is admonished to sing, break forth into singing and cry aloud because she shall beget a large family. This threefold appeal to rejoice anticipates the reversal of her fortune. Her barrenness, childlessness[299] and desolation[300] belong to the past; now, she will have more children than the married one. Then the imagery turns to "your" tent and dwelling (v. 2). In a detailed description of how to put up a tent, she is admonished to stretch out her tents in width and length.[301] She shall expand to right and left and her offspring shall take possession of the place of the peoples and populate desolate cities (v. 3). Not only shall her children be gathered, but she will also expand.[302] Vv. 1–3 are hymnic, expressing a turning point from humiliation to vindication as a previously childless woman begetting children who will inhabit the desolate cities, as utterances for the repopulation and restoration of the city.

The appeal to rejoice over her future prospects is followed by an admonition not to fear, as the disappointment and shame of her youth and widowhood shall belong to the past (vv. 4; 6).[303] The expression

---

[299] For lack of descendants as humiliation, see fem. personifications in Isa. 49:16–26, 51:17–23, 66:1–10, and in Lam. 1:5; 16; 20–22, 2:22, 5:3, as well as Sidon in 23:4 and the daughter of Babylon in Isa. 47:8–9. On barren women begetting children: Sarah (Gen. 11:30), Rebecca (Gen. 25:21, cf. 27:45), Rachel (Gen. 29:31, cf. Jer. 31:15), the wife of Manoah (Judg. 13:2), Hannah (1 Sam. 1:6–11), cf. Ps. 113:9. On men bereaved of children, see e.g. Jacob (Gen. 43:14), Chonia (Jer. 4:31, 22:30), threat against David (33:21), King Jehoiachim (36:30), king of Babel (Ps. 21:11, Isa. 14:22–23, cf. 5.14.4.), Job 18:19.

[300] שָׁמֵם, cf. about cities in v. 3, and 5.8.1. n. 50 and 5.11.5. n. 144.

[301] Cf. Isa. 33:20 and Jer. 10:20 (5.11.5.).

[302] For ingathering from north, south, etc. cf. 43:6, 49:12, 60:4. Beuken, "Isaiah 54", pp. 37–42, argues that the tent imagery and the motif of the barren woman in Isa. 54:1–3 are modeled on the matriarch Sarah. He also finds a periodisation: patriarchal time (vv. 1–3), pre-Exilic time in the land with YHWH as husband and Zion as wife (vv. 4–10) and Exilic time with Zion as city (vv. 11–17). I find this periodisation somewhat forced.

[303] The paradoxical expressions עֲלוּמִים "girlhood" and אַלְמְנוּת "widowhood" are often interpreted as references to the slavery in Egypt or all the pre-Exilic sufferings as the period of youth, and the Babylonian Exile as the period of widowhood, cf. Muilenburg, "The Book of Isaiah: Chapters 40–66", p. 635, Koole, Isaiah III. Vol. 2, p. 360. Steck, "Zion als Gelände und Gestalt", explains the widowhood of Zion as meaning that her husband YHWH is temporarily dead and arises from the dead when remarrying her. Abma, Bonds of Love, p. 98, opposes such interpretations:

בֹּשֶׁת עֲלוּמַיִךְ "shame of your youth" in v. 4 might be the only utterance alluding to a possible explanation for her misery in the past in this pericope. The husband, who is YHWH and who was angry (v. 8), returns to her as her creator and redeemer, called Lord of the hosts, Israel's Holy one and the God of all the earth (vv. 5; 6; 7). He who hid בְּשֶׁצֶף קֶצֶף "in a flood of wrath" (v. 8) will return to her with רַחֲמִים גְּדֹלִים "great compassion" (v. 7), חֶסֶד עוֹלָם "everlasting kindness" (v. 8), חַסְדִּי "my kindness", בְּרִית שְׁלוֹמִי "my covenant of peace" and as מְרַחֲמֵךְ "your compassionate one" (v. 10). He swears that he will refrain from being angry with her or rebuking her (v. 9). He begs her to forget the past (v. 4) and live in peace (v. 10).[304] Zion and Israel merge and the distinction between people and city disappears.[305] In, for example, the ingathering of v. 7, the husband is concerned about his wife and the deity about his people.[306]

The text focuses on the *present* misery of Zion and the *present* reversal of this situation. In this light the images of "girlhood" and "widowhood" may constitute a parallel pair and provide two descriptions of *one* central point, the miserable situation of Zion. In this light the chronological interpretation is not particularly convincing and it seems that the text can be explained in a more obvious way by treating the images of "girlhood" and "widowhood" as two amplifying poetic images rather than as sequential descriptions of Zion's situation (her italics).

[304] Blenkinsopp, *Isaiah 40–55*, p. 365:
The well-established thematic link between covenant and marriage makes vv 9–10 an appropriate nexus between Zion as woman and Zion as city. The covenant with Noah is introduced in order to affirm the oath... [A] closer examination shows that the language in 54:9–10 is quite different from Gen 9:8–17. The key term is not [בְּרִית עוֹלָם] but [בְּרִית שָׁלוֹם] which, in the context of making of treaties and agreements, implied establishing good relations or reconciliation by restoring relations of amity that had been severed – hence the translation "covenant of friendship".

שָׁלוֹם "peace" has a wide range of uses in Isa. 40–55: 41:3 (safely, related to Cyrus' way), 45:7 (vs רָע "evil"), 48:18 (paralleled with צְדָקָה "righteousness"); 22 (no peace for the wicked), 52:7 (related to טוֹב מְבַשֵּׂר "good tidings"), 53:5 ("healing"), 54:13 ("peace", "well-being"), 55:12 (parallel with שִׂמְחָה "joy"). On שָׁלוֹם, cf. 5.11.1. n. 119 and 5.15.3. n. 291.

[305] Abma, *Bonds of Love*, p. 101.

[306] Baumann, "Prophetic Objections to YHWH as the Violent Husband of Israel", pp. 88–120, describes the differences between the marriage metaphor in Hosea, Jeremiah and Ezekiel on the one hand, and in Second Isaiah on the other: 1. In Second Isaiah, the metaphor appears in oracles of salvation (sometimes mixed with other forms) and not in proclamation of punishment (with Isa. 47 as exception). 2. YHWH's wife Zion is no longer the recipient of the punishment of the deity. On the other hand, YHWH regrets what he has done
The theological model used to explain the exile is being transformed by Second Isaiah, and this prophetic school creates a new model by changing the social roles

Then her state is presented as afflicted and not comforted (v. 11), before returning to the future of the city: YHWH will make foundations, shields, gates and walls of precious stones (vv. 11–12). Moreover, her children shall be taught and be prosperous,[307] and she will be established in צְדָקָה "righteousness" and שָׁלוֹם "peace" (v. 14). Both the desolate woman and the destroyed land shall be restored; the children have a role in both her life and the life of the city.[308] No explanation for the turning point is given and the reason for her misery is only alluded to by the expression בֹּשֶׁת עֲלוּמַיִךְ "shame of your youth" in v. 4.

5.15.6. *Isa. 66:7–11*

66:7 בְּטֶרֶם תָּחִיל יָלָדָה
בְּטֶרֶם יָבוֹא חֵבֶל לָהּ וְהִמְלִיטָה זָכָר:
⁸מִי־שָׁמַע כָּזֹאת מִי רָאָה כָּאֵלֶּה
הֲיוּחַל אֶרֶץ בְּיוֹם אֶחָד אִם־יִוָּלֵד גּוֹי פַּעַם אֶחָת
כִּי־חָלָה גַּם־יָלְדָה צִיּוֹן אֶת־בָּנֶיהָ:
⁹הַאֲנִי אַשְׁבִּיר וְלֹא אוֹלִיד יֹאמַר יְהוָה
אִם־אֲנִי הַמּוֹלִיד וְעָצַרְתִּי אָמַר אֱלֹהָיִךְ:
¹⁰שִׂמְחוּ אֶת־יְרוּשָׁלַ͏ִם וְגִילוּ בָהּ כָּל־אֹהֲבֶיהָ
שִׂישׂוּ אִתָּהּ מָשׂוֹשׂ כָּל־הַמִּתְאַבְּלִים עָלֶיהָ:
¹¹לְמַעַן תִּינְקוּ וּשְׂבַעְתֶּם מִשֹּׁד תַּנְחֻמֶיהָ
לְמַעַן תָּמֹצּוּ וְהִתְעַנַּגְתֶּם מִזִּיז כְּבוֹדָהּ:

66:7:   Before she was in labour she gave birth;
        before her pains came upon her she was delivered of a son.
66:8:   Who has heard such a thing? Who has seen such things?
        Shall a land be born in one day? Shall a nation be brought forth in one moment?
        For as soon as Zion was in labour she brought forth her sons.
66:9:   Shall I bring to the birth and not cause to bring forth? says the Lord.

---

of husband and wife. YHWH remains the husband, but he no longer violates his wife. Zion remains the wife, but she is no longer the guilty part (p. 116).

[307] 1QIsaᵃ renders בוניכי "your builders".

[308] Abma, *Bonds of Love*, p. 91, comments on how interpretations traditionally identify

the heart of the text…outside of the verses with explicit female imagery (vv. 1–6) and that central motifs in the text are circumscribed with such general terms as "love" or "renewal of the covenant". The specific female imagery and the metaphorical language in the passage tend to be played down.

She mentions Beuken (1974), Sawyer (1989) and Darr (1994) as exceptions. On relations between Isa. 53 and 54, see Muilenburg, "The Book of Isaiah: Chapters 40–66", p. 632, Wilshire, "The Servant-City", Sawyer, "Daughter of Zion and Servant of the Lord in Isaiah", Korpel, "The Female Servant of the Lord in Isaiah 54", pp. 153–167, Koole, *Isaiah III. Vol. 2*, pp. 374–375.

Shall I, who cause to bring forth, shut the womb? says your
God.
66:10: Rejoice with Jerusalem and be glad for her, all you who love her;
rejoice with her in joy, all you who mourn over her;
66:11: that you may suck and be satisfied with her consoling breasts;
that you may drink deeply with delight from the abundance of
her glory.

Isa. 66:7 switches abruptly from the judgment in vv. 1–6 to speak of
the wonderful birth before the onset of labour and its pain. The unbelievable and unprecedented nature of this is expressed in six questions
pertaining to the miracle of the land's and people's sudden appearance, and YHWH's ability to let a mother conceive a child, concluding
that Zion has delivered her children in a moment (vv. 8–9). In the
questions, the fate of the land, the people, the woman and her children
are mixed beyond separation. The restoration is expressed in an overwhelming image of a woman's painless labour by the will of YHWH,
who appears as the midwife.

Then a group, more closely identified as "you (2mpl) who love
Jerusalem", is addressed and admonished to be glad over her, as their
mourning over her is at an end (v. 10). The description of the future is
developed in all its sensuality as they shall all be nurtured and sated by
her breast, sucking and rejoicing at her great glory and be carried and
cared for by her (vv. 11–12). YHWH will bring peace over her (v. 12)[309]
and comfort them like a mother (v. 13), but bring his wrath upon their
enemies (vv. 14–18). He shall further gather "all peoples and tongues"
to see his glory on his holy mountain in Jerusalem (vv. 18–20). Coming generations shall stand before YHWH's eyes for ever (v. 22). After
the deity's manifestation (vv. 1–2), a contrasting of pious and wicked,
and a polemic against idols (vv. 3–5), a blossoming image follows of
descendants as an expression of the coming prosperity of the land.

Isa. 66:7–11 is a female personification of the people with vindication expressed as descendants, but unlike all the previous texts about
descendants, v. 7 concerns the past. The only allusion to former misery
is the mention of mourning in v. 10. As in Isa. 54, attention is drawn
as much to the mother as to her children. Related to survival, birth
might be opposed to death, as in Isa. 53. As in the previous personifications, a relation between parent and offspring is described, where

---

[309] On the wide range of uses of שָׁלוֹם in Isa. 40–55, see 5.11.1. n. 119, 5.15.3.
n. 291 and 5.15.5. n. 304.

the wonderous new creation is depicted as both one child (v. 7), more than one child (v. 8) and a people being born (v. 8). Again, the blurring between children and city is beyond separation. The promise of descendants within Isa. 40–55 (66) is widespread in depictions of the coming greatness of Israel. This is a most effective image for the coming restoration of the nation.

5.15.7. *Job 5:25 and 42:12–17*

5:25 וְיָדַעְתָּ כִּי־רַב זַרְעֶךָ וְצֶאֱצָאֶיךָ כְּעֵשֶׂב הָאָרֶץ׃

> 5:25: You will know that your offspring will be many; your descendants like the grass of the earth.

In Job 5:25 a great family is a sign of YHWH's blessings on the pious. His offspring will flourish like the grass of the earth. A doubleness of both זֶרַע "offspring" and צֶאֱצָאִים "descendants" appears, as this concerns both children and seed.[310] This appears in a list of earthly blessings, promising Job secure dwelling (v. 24) and death at a ripe old age (v. 26).[311] These utterances appear within Eliphaz' first speech (4:1–5:27), in which he seeks to encourage Job to hope that the pious man may find a way out of his sufferings and form a better relationship with God. Eliphaz explains Job's suffering and loss of everything as due to the limitation and sinfulness of all creatures. In God, Job will find the peace and quiet he desires and God will bless his whole life. At the end of this speech Eliphaz confirmed the truth of his words by referring to the tradition of the wise.[312] And at the end of the Book of

---

[310] זֶרַע "offspring" and צֶאֱצָאִים "descendants" are also coupled in Job 21:8 and Isa. 44:3, 48:19, see 5.15.2. n. 288.

[311] Vs unworthy death in 5.14., esp. 5.14.6. n. 283.

[312] Whybray, *Job*, p. 49, comments on how Eliphaz has to:

> admit that between the two opposites of righteous and wicked there is a third category to which Job belongs: that of the person who is neither wholly innocent nor irredeemably wicked, but whose faults are redeemable. But there is an underlying irony in all this. Eliphaz was quite unaware that he had shifted his position: he ended his speech in utter confidence that he had faithfully represented the voice of traditional wisdom. There is also a more profound irony in that the mysterious voice that declared that no human being is absolutely pure missed the whole issue that is the principal concern of the book: that it is not human innocence that is being questioned, but divine justice.

Clines, *Job 1–20*, p. 154, describes the speech as operating on two levels:

> Occasionally, the two levels merge, as when Eliphaz's conventional piety and rhetoric lead him into remarks that are totally inappropriate or even positively

Job, Job is granted exactly what Eliphaz says he will get if he accepts the deity. As a great contrast to the prologue, in the epilogue (42:7–17) the outcome of Job's bereavement is numerous progeny, with God's blessing and restoration of him:

42:12 וַיהוָה בֵּרַךְ אֶת־אַחֲרִית אִיּוֹב
מֵרֵאשִׁתוֹ וַיְהִי־לוֹ אַרְבָּעָה עָשָׂר אֶלֶף צֹאן וְשֵׁשֶׁת אֲלָפִים גְּמַלִּים
וְאֶלֶף־צֶמֶד בָּקָר וְאֶלֶף אֲתוֹנוֹת:
13וַיְהִי־לוֹ שִׁבְעָנָה בָנִים וְשָׁלוֹשׁ בָּנוֹת:
14וַיִּקְרָא שֵׁם־הָאַחַת יְמִימָה וְשֵׁם הַשֵּׁנִית קְצִיעָה וְשֵׁם הַשְּׁלִישִׁית
קֶרֶן הַפּוּךְ:15וְלֹא נִמְצָא נָשִׁים יָפוֹת כִּבְנוֹת אִיּוֹב בְּכָל־הָאָרֶץ וַיִּתֵּן
לָהֶם אֲבִיהֶם נַחֲלָה בְּתוֹךְ אֲחֵיהֶם:16וַיְחִי אִיּוֹב אַחֲרֵי־זֹאת
מֵאָה וְאַרְבָּעִים שָׁנָה וַיִּרְא אֶת־בָּנָיו וְאֶת־בְּנֵי בָנָיו אַרְבָּעָה
דֹרוֹת:17וַיָּמָת אִיּוֹב זָקֵן וּשְׂבַע יָמִים:

42:12: YHWH blessed Job's later life more than his earlier life. He had fourteen thousand sheep, six thousand camels, a thousand yoke of oxen and a thousand donkeys.

42:13: And he had seven sons and three daughters.

42:14: He named his daughters: the first Jemimah, the second Keziah and the third Keren-Happuch.

42:15: No women in all the earth were more beautiful than Job's daughters and their father gave them an inheritance with their brothers.

42:16: After this Job lived one hundred and forty years; he saw his children and their children, four generations –

42:17: Job died, old and full of years.

In Job 42:12–17 Job's rehabilitation is described. Job's property in the prologue (1:3) is doubled (cf. 42:10; 12). He begets seven sons and three daughters (cf. 1:3). After all the sufferings and humiliations Job has lived through, he, the most humiliated one, is promised the most beautiful daughters in the land! The daughters are named and receive an inheritance. Job lives for 140 years, sees his children's children up to four generations (v. 16) and dies ripe in age (v. 17). He was not punished for sins; it was his innocence that was put on trial and he is restored because he has passed the test.

---

painful to Job (cf. on 4:7, 5:4; 19; 25; 26). On the upper level, then, these chapters present a speech of encouragement to Job, on the deeper level, they are an indictment of the cruelty of narrow dogma.

5.15.8. *Summing Up*

In Isa. 53:10, dimensions of hope and expectation are expressed: "he" shall see descendants and live a long life. With reproduction and off-spring, the future is promising. In Isa. 44:3–4 a doubleness of זֶרַע "off-spring" and צֶאֱצָאִים "descendants" appears, referring to the sowing both of seed and of the offspring of the addressee. In the outpouring of water, spirit and blessings, growth and fertility are related to the future. The descendants shall survive, blossom and multiply. A varia-tion appears in Isa. 48, with the blessings of "your" offspring compared to נָהָר "a river" and יָם "a sea" (v. 18), and likened to חוֹל "sand" and מֵעֹת "grains" (v. 19), all being immeasurable and uncountable. As in Isa. 53:10 and 44:3, the personification is composite of family terms with a relation between "you" and "your" offspring, and growth and fertility are related to a promising future.

Yet another variation appears in Isa. 49:14–26, which is composite of a mixture of ingathering and the promise of descendants and the prosperous future of the nation. The background is former barrenness and exile (vv. 19–21). As in Isa. 53:10, 44:3 and 48:19, the rehabilita-tion of the people is depicted in a personification composed of par-ent and descendants, but unlike the previous ones, the personification here is a woman, formerly barren, desolate and driven away, now with plenty of children and a rebuilt land. Isa. 54:1–3 also convey a turn-ing point from humiliation to vindication expressed as a previously childless woman obtaining children who will inhabit the desolate cit-ies. Both the desolate woman and the destroyed land shall be restored; the children have a role in both her life and the life of the city. No explanation for the turning point is given and the reason for her mis-ery is only alluded to by the expression בֹּשֶׁת עֲלוּמַיִךְ "shame of your youth" in v. 4.

Isa. 66:7–11 is a female personification of the people where vindica-tion is expressed as descendants, but unlike all the previous texts about descendents, v. 7 concerns the past. The only allusion to former misery is the mention of mourning in v. 10. As in Isa. 54, attention is paid as much to the mother as to her children. As in Isa. 53, birth might be related to survival as opposed to death. As in the previous personifi-cations, a relation between parent and offspring is expressed, where the wonderous new creation is depicted as one child (v. 7), more than one child (v. 8) and a people being born (v. 8). Again, the blurring of children and city is beyond separation.

In Eliphaz speech in Job 5:25, he claims that a great family is a sign of YHWH's blessings on the pious. In a list of blessings, Job is promised that his offspring will flourish like the grass of the earth, he will live safely (v. 24) and shall die at a ripe old age (v. 26). Eliphaz explains Job's suffering as due to the limitation and sinfulness of all creatures. By God Job will find the peace and quiet he desires and God will bless his whole life. This is exactly what Job receives at the end: the most beautiful daughters in the land. Job was not punished for sins; it was his innocence that was put on trial, and he is restored because he has passed the test (42:7–17).

The promises of descendants and a long life might be seen as a turning point after the death of the servant in Isa. 53:9. In spite of all the humiliations he has lived through, he shall "rise from death" and emerge in dignity. With reproduction and offspring, the future is promising. No direct reason is given for "his" turning point from humiliation to vindication, apart from the statement that both are due to חֵפֶץ יְהוָה "YHWH's pleasure" (v. 10).

5.16. "The righteous one, my servant, will cause the many to be righteous..."

5.16.1. *Isa. 53:11*

53:11...יַצְדִּיק צַדִּיק עַבְדִּי לָרַבִּים...

53:11b: The righteous one, my servant, will cause the many to be righteous...

In "I" speech in Isa. 53:11, צַדִּיק עַבְדִּי "the righteous one, my servant" is held up as the tool of vindication for the present and the future, which shall benefit both "himself" and הָרַבִּים "the many". "He" and הָרַבִּים "the many" are related within a common fate of righteousness, but with different focuses, as "he" is righteous and "my" servant and will cause הָרַבִּים "the many" to be righteous.[313]

Other expressions for "his" future are that "he" shall succeed (52:13, 53:10), be healed (53:5), beget descendants and live long (v. 10), see and

---

[313] Koole, *Isaiah III. Vol. 2*, pp. 332–333, refers to ethical or salvific interpretations, but claims himself that צדק (hi.) is a forensic term everywhere in OT except in Dan. 12:3. C. Begg, "Zedekiah and the Servant", *ETL* 62 (1986) 393–398, sees an allusion to, but no identification with, Zedekiah in relation to the servant in Isa. 53:11.

be satisfied by his knowledge (v. 11) and allot numerous to spoiling (v. 12). Also, the future of הָרַבִּים "the many", עֲצוּמִים "numerous", גּוֹיִם רַבִּים "many peoples", מְלָכִים "kings" and "we" is expressed: in 52:15 he יַזֶּה ('will startle'?) גּוֹיִם רַבִּים "many peoples" before him, מְלָכִים "kings" shall shut their mouth and "they" shall see and understand what is neither told nor heard. In 53:12 the speaking YHWH will allot הָרַבִּים "the many" to "him" and "he" shall allot עֲצוּמִים "numerous" to spoiling, and in 53:5b ("he") and "we" shall be healed and recover. The righteous servant previously humiliated by shame and punished because of sins is now declared righteous, is rehabilitated and has "his" honour restored.

This might be seen in contrast to Isa. 53:8, depicting how "he" is treated badly by others: מֵעֹצֶר וּמִמִּשְׁפָּט לֻקָּח "By restraint (?) and by execution (?) he was taken". Later in the verse, "his" bad experiences of the past are explained as due to sin: נִגְזַר מֵאֶרֶץ חַיִּים "he was cut off from the land of the living" and מִפֶּשַׁע עַמִּי נֶגַע לָמוֹ "because of the transgression of my people was his stroke".

5.16.2. *Isa. 50:8–9*

50:8 קָרוֹב מַצְדִּיקִי מִי־יָרִיב אִתִּי נַעַמְדָה יָּחַד
מִי־בַעַל מִשְׁפָּטִי יִגַּשׁ אֵלָי׃
⁹ הֵן אֲדֹנָי יְהוִה יַעֲזָר־לִי מִי־הוּא יַרְשִׁיעֵנִי
הֵן כֻּלָּם כַּבֶּגֶד יִבְלוּ עָשׁ יֹאכְלֵם׃

50:8: He who vindicates me is near. Who will contend with me? Let us
stand up together.
Who is my adversary? Let him come near to me.

50:9: See, the Lord YHWH helps me; who will declare me guilty?
See, all of them will wear out like a garment, the moth will eat
them up.

In Isa. 50:8, "I" speech is framed by the language of legal proceedings. In a forensic context, one who is accused is trusting in the deity. He is waiting for YHWH, who is near and will vindicate him. After this declaration of trust, the "I" challenges his adversaries to a legal battle with two questions and two admonitions. The questions concern who will contend and who is his adversary;[314] the admonitions are to "stand up

---

[314] רִיב (noun) "legal proceedings brought against another party" and corresponding verb, cf. 41:11; 21, 49:25, בַּעַל מִשְׁפָּטִי "my adversary", cf. 41:1. Cf. אַנְשֵׁי רִיבֶךָ "those who contend with you" in 41:11. מִשְׁפָּט has a wide range of meanings; "judicial

together" and "come near".[315] These legal proceedings brought against adversaries are followed by yet another assurance of trust in YHWH, contrasted with yet another question: מִי־הוּא יַרְשִׁיעֵנִי "who will declare me guilty" (v. 9).[316] Then the adversaries are condemned by a comparison to the wearing out of a piece of clothing and being eaten by moths. Within this cluster of legal language, a contrast between צדק (hi) and רשע (hi) is framed. The speaking "I" declares his righteousness and dares anyone to condemn him.

In vv. 4–7 the "I" recounts that he has been instructed by YHWH in his commision in spite of opposition. אֲדֹנָי יְהוִה "The Lord YHWH" has given him a disciple's voice יָעֵף...יָעִיר "to refresh the dispirited" (v. 4). The deity makes him listen and he has been neither obstinate nor drawn back (vv. 4–5). He was struck by enemies and helped by the deity (vv. 6–7).

In v. 10, four מִי "who" questions are asked, with the מִי "who" identified in contrasting pairs: מִי בָכֶם יְרֵא יְהוָה "who among you fear YHWH", שֹׁמֵעַ בְּקוֹל עַבְדּוֹ "listens to the voice of his servant" (cf. vv. 4–5), הָלַךְ חֲשֵׁכִים "walks in darkness" and וְאֵין נֹגַהּ לוֹ "has no light". This addressee shall trust in and rely on YHWH his God.[317] In contrast to the promise made to those who fear YHWH in v. 10, v. 11 is addressed to קֹדְחֵי אֵשׁ "those who kindle fire",[318] i.e. those who live by their own lights. They have judgment proclaimed to them: לְמַעֲצֵבָה תִּשְׁכָּבוּן "You shall lie down in torment."

In a personification, the vindication of YHWH's disciple is expressed. When carrying out his task, he was humiliated by his enemies, but

---

sentence" (Isa. 42:1, 51:4), "lawsuit" (40:14, 41:1, 50:8, 53:8 (?), 54:17) and "right" (40:27, 49:4).

[315] עמד (imperf. qal 1cpl) "stand"; forensically "take part in legal proceedings", see 44:11, 47:13, נגשׁ (imperf. qal) "initiate the proceedings", cf. 41:1; 21–22 (hi.), 45:20–21 (htp., hi.).

[316] רשע (imperf. hi 3ms and 1sg suffix), cf. 54:17. רשע, cf. 48:22, 53:9, 55:7.

[317] In v. 10, the servant title appears. Duhm delimits 50:4–9 as the third servant song, cf. 2.1.3. This is treated by Steck in 2.2.2. In Isa. 42:6, i.e. Duhm's second servant song, YHWH says about the servant: אֲנִי יְהוָה קְרָאתִיךָ בְצֶדֶק "I, YHWH, have called you in righteousness…" On קרא "call" used for Israel, see 5.8.2. n. 60.

[318] The parallel מְאַזְּרֵי זִיקוֹת is disputed. מְאַזְּרֵי (pi. pt. pl. cstr. of אזר) "girding" is supported by Tg., Vulg, Watts, Isaiah 34–66, pp. 194a; 196, Oswalt, The Book of Isaiah: Chapters 40–66, p. 328 n. 44, while Westermann, Isaiah 40–66, p. 232, Whybray, Isaiah 40–66, p. 154, Blenkinsopp, Isaiah 40–55, p. 318, Koole, Isaiah III. Vol. 2, p. 130, Baltzer, Deutero-Isaiah, p. 338, among others, emend to מְאִירֵי (אור "light") "alight", supported by Syr. LXX renders κατισχύετε. זִיקוֹת is a hapax legomenon. While v. 10 addresses in sg., v. 11 has pl.

YHWH interferes as the judge and advocate of his elected against them. The speaking "I" emphasises his non-obstinacy (v. 5, cf. 53:7; 9). In vv. 6–7 his adversaries smite him and spit on him; in vv. 8–9 they are presented within a legal battle, where "he" is right (cf. "he" and הָרַבִּים "the many" in 53:11) – and not them (cf. רַבִּים "many" and עֲצוּמִים "numerous" in 53:12).[319]

5.16.3. Isa. 41:2

41:2 מִי הֵעִיר מִמִּזְרָח צֶדֶק יִקְרָאֵהוּ לְרַגְלוֹ
יִתֵּן לְפָנָיו גּוֹיִם וּמְלָכִים יַרְדְּ יִתֵּן כֶּעָפָר חַרְבּוֹ כְּקַשׁ נִדָּף קַשְׁתּוֹ:

41:2: Who roused one from the east that claims righteousness at every step;
delivers up nations to him and beats down kings beneath him?
He makes their swords like dust, their bows like windblown chaff.

In a מִי "who" question in Isa. 41:2, it is asked who roused a man of righteousness,[320] identified as מִמִּזְרָח "from the east". Two more questions about his success are raised: "Who delivers up nations to him and beats down kings beneath him?" The Persian king Cyrus possesses righteousness and the nations are defeated by him.[321] He pursues them, he goes in peace and does not touch the way with his feet (v. 3). The foreign king Cyrus becomes some sort of a Body Politic who acts on behalf of YHWH to the profit of Israel and against the nations.

In a trial speech in Isa. 41, YHWH addresses אִיִּים "coastlands" and לְאֻמִּים "peoples", telling them to gather for הַמִּשְׁפָּט "the judgment"; be silent and then speak (v. 1). The power of YHWH is proclaimed: he is the creator and the only one unlike the peoples, who are defeated by

---

[319] A variation of a legal dispute appears in Isa. 50:1–3 (see 5.12.4.). The legal proceedings are conveyed in a fem. personification, with the relation between Israel and YHWH depicted as a marriage and a divorce. Here, juridical language is used about the past and humiliation of Israel.

[320] קרא in 41:1 has been taken as either קרא I "call", cf. Watts, Isaiah 34–66, p. 97, Oswalt, The Book of Isaiah: Chapters 40–66, p. 76, Koole, Isaiah III. Vol. 2, pp. 136–137, or קרא II "meet", cf. Westermann, Isaiah 40–66, p. 62, Baltzer, Deutero-Isaiah, p. 87, Whybray, Isaiah 40–66, p. 61, and Blenkinsopp, Isaiah 40–55, p. 195b.

[321] Kissane, The Book of Isaiah, pp. 29–30, and Torrey, The Second Isaiah, pp. 310–316, take "one from the east" to be Abraham, G. H. Jones, "Abraham and Cyrus: Type and Anti-Type", VT 22 (1972) 304–319, argues that although the reference is to Cyrus, it is based on the Abraham tradition, while J. D. Smart, History and Theology in Second Isaiah: A Commentary on Isaiah 35, 40–66 (Philadelphia: Westminster Press, 1965) 68–69, interprets the person as an eschatological figure.

him (vv. 4–5). YHWH's uniqueness is further conveyed by a polemic against the futile gods of the nations (vv. 6–7). Vv. 8ff is addressed to Israel, "my servant", Jacob, "whom I have chosen, offspring of Abraham, my friend" etc. and an admonition: "Fear not!" as well as promises that YHWH is the God of Israel. The similarities with Isa. 53 are striking: the Servant/Cyrus as YHWH's elected possesses the deity's righteousness. Also, this is contrasted with the nations, for whom this righteousness is absent.[322]

5.16.4. *Summing Up*

In Isa. 53:11b, the righteous servant previously humiliated by shame and punished because of sins is declared righteous and has his honour restored. In YHWH speech, he is held up as the tool of vindication for the present and the future, which shall benefit both himself and הָרַבִּים "the many": he is righteous and a servant and will cause הָרַבִּים "the many" to be righteous.

In a personification of Isa. 50:8–9, the vindication of YHWH's disciple is expressed. When carrying out his task, he was humiliated by his enemies, but YHWH interferes as the judge and advocate of his elected against them. The speaking "I" emphasises his non-obstinacy (v. 5, cf. 53:7; 9). In vv. 6–7 his adversaries smite him and spit on him; in vv. 8–9 they are presented within a legal battle, in which he is right (cf. "he" and הָרַבִּים "the many" in 53:11) and not them (cf. רַבִּים "many" and עֲצוּמִים "numerous" in 53:12). Also the similarities between Isa. 53 and 41:2 are striking: the Servant/Cyrus as YHWH's elected possesses the deity's righteousness. Also, this is contrasted with the nations, for whom this righteousness is absent. The Persian king Cyrus becomes some sort of a Body Politic acting on behalf of YHWH to the profit of Israel and against the nations. Righteousness in Isa. 40–55 appears

---

[322] In a trial scene in Isa 43:9, גּוֹיִם "nations" and לְאֻמִּים "peoples" are summoned as witnesses to what the deity has said and done. Through this testimony the gods will have to be justified. The nations and their futile gods are contrasted with YHWH and Israel as his witnesses and servant (v. 10). In an overwhelming manifestation of YHWH in vv. 10–12, it is expressed who YHWH is; the only God and Saviour, who has power in history, expressed in a word of doom towards Babylon (v. 14) and in the creation (v. 15), cf. v. 26. Polemics about idols have been regarded as "later additions" to *Isa. 40–55 (cf. 2.3.3.).

in personifications, depicted as possessed by YHWH's elected, e.g. the servant Israel, and also by an individual like the Persian king Cyrus.[323]

5.17. "SEE, MY SERVANT SHALL PROSPER..."

52:13 הִנֵּה יַשְׂכִּיל עַבְדִּי יָרוּם וְנִשָּׂא וְגָבַהּ מְאֹד:

> 52:13: See, my servant shall prosper and be exalted, he shall be lifted and be very high!

The interjection הִנֵּה "See!" appears in an address to an implied "you", whose attention is drawn to the adjacent utterance. The utterance concerns the prosperity of עַבְדִּי "my servant". הִנֵּה "See!" indicates that any response to this utterance involves a more active capacity than that of immediate listening, as there is also a prospective future to be perceived: עַבְדִּי "my servant"'s exaltation shall become visible!

The dynamic factor in the history of Israel comes from the tension between YHWH's demands and Israel's response. The relation between YHWH and Israel is depicted in different manners: YHWH is the deity and Israel his people; YHWH is the master and Israel his servant; YHWH is the husband and Israel his wife; YHWH is shepherd and Israel his flock. The deity punishes his people (Zion, Jerusalem, Israel) and also arrogant rulers, cities and nations (Babylon, idols, etc.). And YHWH also vindicates his people; their fate lies with its God, not with an undiscerning instrument of divine aggression. In this "dichotomy", the Persian king and saviour Cyrus appears "in-between".

The servant in Isa. 40–55 has a wide range of shades of meanings. Israel's relationship of servanthood to YHWH will at last be brought into being as YHWH will.[324] Because the people have not served their

---

[323] J. J. Scullion, "Righteousness (OT)", *ABD* 5 (1992) 724, reminds us: "The OT text must not be read through the eyes of the Reformation controversies about "righteousness" and "justification", or even through Paul's letters to the Romans and Galatians." Cf. Westermann, *Isaiah 40–66*, p. 231, on Isa. 50:8–9:

> The certainty that God is on his side (corresponding to the "certainty of being answered" in the Psalms) is now expressed in a different, and very forceful, way, by means of terms taken from a legal process. The same form was used by Paul in a similar situation to express the same conviction (Rom. 8.31ff.)

and Goldingay, *The Message of Isaiah 40–55*, p. 411.

[324] In Isa. 40–55, עֶבֶד "servant" is mentioned as עַבְדִּי "my servant" in 41:8; 9, 42:1; 19, 43:10, 44:1–2; 21, 45:4, 49:3; 6, 52:13, 53:11, as עַבְדּוֹ "his servant" in 44:26, 48:20, 49:5, 50:10, as עֶבֶד מֹשְׁלִים "servant of rulers" in 49:7 (see 5.8.2.) and as עֲבְדֵי יְהוָה

lord obediently, the disobedient servant remains hard pressed by his sentence of punishment and still suffers under it. When YHWH crushed him, he had no excuse, escape, or rescue. The people's debased situation is related to their delusion, transgression, forgetting, blindness, deafness. The survival and vindication of Israel among the peoples is anticipated after the experience of destruction. YHWH's condemnation of Israel has reached its end, and is followed by a restoration of the people. The time of bliss awaiting Israel beyond sentence and punishment is depicted, as her glorious future is presented. YHWH has called his servant and "he" shall call him, YHWH "serves" his servant and "he" shall serve him; YHWH glorifies his servant and "he" shall glorify him.[325] The positive side of Israel's relation towards YHWH is further depicted by prominent words of honour, such as chosen, created, ingathered,[326] redeemed,[327] neither rejected nor forgotten,[328] but helped, strengthened, upheld, guarded and delivered.[329] As YHWH's

---

"servants of YHWH" in 54:17. Elsewhere in the Book of Isaiah, a whole range of servants are related to YHWH: 20:3 (Isaiah), 22:20 (Eliakim son of Hilkiah), 24:2, 36:9; 11, 37:24; 35 (David), 56:6 ("foreigners who attach themselves to YHWH"), 63:17, 65:8; 9; 13–14; 15, cf. 14:2 (Israel shall make עַמִּים "other peoples" serve them, cf. 49:7).

About the servant motif within the Book of Isaiah, see Orlinsky, *The So-Called "Servant of the Lord" and "Suffering Servant" in Second Isaiah*, Mettinger, *Farewell to the Servant Songs*, p. 44, nn. 77–79, H. Leene, *De stem van de knecht als metafoor: Beschouwingen over de compositie van Jesaja 50* (Kampen: Kok, 1980), K. Jeppesen, "From 'You, my Servant' to 'The Hand of the Lord is with my Servants': A Discussion of Is 40–66", *SJOT* 1 (1990) 113–129, and J. Werlitz, "Vom Knecht der Lieder zum Knecht des Buches: Ein Versuch über die Ergänzungen zu den Gottesknechtstexten des Deutero-jesajabuches", *ZAW* 109 (1997) 30–43. The root עבד is also a common term in the Hebrew Bible both to express political subjugation, see 5.8.2. n. 58, and in relation to worship, see 5.12.3. n. 217.

[325] The servant is depicted as כבד "glorified" in masc. personifications in 43:4, 49:5, פאר "glorify" also appears in masc. personifications in 44:23, 49:3, 55:5 (i.e. in whom I will reveal my glory, cf. 43:7).

[326] On "elected" and "called", see 5.8.2. n. 60, on "serve", see 5.17. n. 324, and on ingathering, see 5.15.5. nn. 297 and 302.

[327] The servant is depicted as גאל "redeemed" by YHWH in 41:14, 43:1, 44:6; 22–24, 48:17; 20, 49:7, whereas the people (pl) are depicted as redeemed by YHWH in 41:14, 43:14, 44:6, 47:4, 51:10, 52:3; 10, and in fem. in 49:26, 54:5; 8.

[328] The servant is depicted as לא מאס "not rejected" in 41:9 and in a variation in a fem. personification in 54:6. He is also described as נשה "not forgotten" in 44:21 and in a fem. personification as שכח "forget" in 49:15.

[329] The servant is presented as עזר "helped" by his God in 41:10; 13; 14 cf. 44:2, 49:8, 50:7; 9, and as אמץ "strengthened" in 41:10, חזק "made strong" in 41:13, cf. 42:6, as well as as "upheld" תמך in 41:10, 42:1. In 51:18, the fem. personification is presented as lacking strength. The servant is נצר "guarded" by YHWH in 42:6, 49:8 and ישע "delivered" in 43:12 and in pl 45:17; 22 and in a fem. personification in 49:25 (that is, "your children").

servant, the people shall no longer walk their own ways but YHWH's, and perform his will by being obedient. In choosing to end, instead of beginning with, this intertextual reading of Isa. 52:13–53:12 with the servant motif, this is not because I have read a triumphalist agenda into the text; rather, the opposite: I have chosen this order because I do not want the text to be overshadowed by the servant discourse. Due to the scholarly consensus since Duhm that this and three other texts are so-called "servant songs", distinct from the rest of Isa. 40–55, readers have become participants in a narrow discursive space restricting signifying practices. The servant motif is part of the personification, but I do not want it to dominate my reading.

CHAPTER SIX

SUMMING UP

6.1. Identifications of Isa. 52:13–53:12

In an extraordinary way, Duhmian readings of Isa. 52:13–53:12 seem to be a matter of re-covering the meaning of the text through some kind of homage to his "Servant Song" thesis. Due to the scholarly consensus since Duhm, readers have become participants in a narrow discursive space restricting signifying practices. However, the Duhmian readings of Isa. 52:13–53:12 are not as homogenous as one would have expected. Within this discursive space different interpretations of the identities of actors and events in Isa. 52:13–53:12 are offered. This might illuminate both the complexity in the text and in the readings of it.

Isa. 52:13–53:12 is encircled by proclamations and exhortations to Zion/Jerusalem to prepare for a return and restoration of people and land (51:17–52:12 and 54). הִנֵּה "See!" in 52:13 follows a prediction of messengers announcing peace, YHWH's revelation and admonition to depart in joy.[1] Also, the war language of 53:12 might be interesting in relation to the war motif of 52:1–2; 11–12, which is addressed to Zion/Jerusalem (52:1–2; 8–9). However, the limit of the text cannot be determined by an outside that coincides with a naive empirical or objective delimitation, unit or reality. In our instance, the deictic הִנֵּה "See!" works as a chosen sign of departure.[2]

It has been my aim in this study to focus our understanding of the conventions and operations of modes of discourse. Isa. 52:13–53:12 is a particularly apt case for this pursuit. In this text, many discourses are at play, and the interplay of scholarly and textual discourses is remarkably clear. I will give some illustrations of this from the three different

---

[1] Spykerboer, *The Structure and Composition of Deutero-Isaiah*, p. 177, explains הִנֵּה as a "connecting particle". הִנֵּה also appears in YHWH's presentation of Israel's vindication in 41:15 ("you" [2ms] address), and in YHWH's introduction of "the new things" in 42:9 (cf. הֵן in 43:19). Janowski describes a connection between הֵן in 42:1 and הִנֵּה in 52:13 as a הֵן formula, cf. 2.2.3. n. 84.

[2] On delimitation, cf. 3.9. and. 4.8.5. n. 94.

readings I have presented in this study; at a linguistic, narrative and an intertextual level:

6.2. Isa. 52:13–53:12 on a Linguistic Level

On a linguistic level, Isa. 52:13–53:12 is beset with textual uncertainties. However, what may be discerned are relationships of YHWH, "I", "he", "you", "we", עַמִּי "my people", רַבִּים "many", עֲצוּמִים "numerous", פֹּשְׁעִים "transgressors", גּוֹיִם רַבִּים "many peoples" and מְלָכִים "kings". In first- and third-person speech, "I", "we" and anonymous voices tell about and question broken and restored relationships between YHWH, "he", "we", "you" and "they".

In the YHWH proclamations in 52:13–15 and 53:11–12, YHWH, "I", "he", צַדִּיק עַבְדִּי "the righteous one, my servant", "you", רַבִּים "many", עֲצוּמִים "numerous", גּוֹיִם רַבִּים "many peoples" and מְלָכִים "kings" are identified in relation to each other. רַבִּים "many", for instance, are identified as the nations, in relation to the servant as the collective Israel, a messenger of God or an individual, for instance, the Messiah. רַבִּים "many" are also identified as the Israelites, in relation to the servant as the "Jews of the diaspora", or as the Gola community of Zion. רַבִּים "many" are further taken to embrace both Israel and the nations, in relation to the servant as the generation of the exile through which the nations had suffered vicariously, or as "the righteous remnant of the people". רַבִּים "many" are further interpreted as the Israelites in 52:14; 53:11–12 and the nations in 52:15, in relation to the servant interpreted as the prophet. Finally, רַבִּים "many" are identified as the disciples of the servant, that is, the prophet.

The relationship between "him" and "us" in 53:1–6 is most often explained as a contrast between "his" suffering in innocence and "our" sin. "We" are most often identified as a collective, that is, the whole Israel, the nations or the whole world. However, also individual interpretations are offered, such as the "we" as the prophet or one or more disciples of the prophet. Also the abundance of suggestions concerning the identity of the servant can be outlined in two groups: individual and collective. Some tendencies might be seen in the identifications of the relation between "him" and "us": Those scholars who take the servant to be the collective Israel might identify the "we" as the nations. Those who regard the servant to be either the faithful part of Israel or an individual, take the "we" to be the nations or Israel in general.

Other scholars characterise the text as enigmatic and its actors as not identifiable.

Certain tendencies might be seen in the readings of Isa. 52:13–53:12, for instance, the identification of רַבִּים "many" might be related to the discussions of universalism or particularism, while the dualistic interpretation of the relation between "him" and "us" is related to a concept of vicarious suffering. While most scholars take the concept of vicarious suffering as being central to Isa. 53, a few deny that vicarious suffering is indicated. For some, אָשָׁם in 53:10 constitutes the very core of the text, while others delete it because they regard the half-line as too corrupt to make sense in this instance.

6.3. Isa. 52:13–53:12 on a Narrative Level

A narrative reading activates forces in the text on a level other than the linguistic one, and shows what a story *does*, its performative dimension. A central element in this is the way in which the reader is a self-involved participant in the text. On a narrative level, "I", "we" and "anonymous" voices have spoken in repetitions, reinforcements, culminations and assurances. The heuristic distinction between a sequence of events labelled *story* and the presentation of the events labelled *narration* has appeared to be fruitful. By this distinction, the rhetorics of the narrative show how shifting and unstable discourses interact with other discourses without any stable terms. In both *story* and *narration*, as well as in the relation between them, rhetorics of temporality, agency and causality are key. In this narrative reading it becomes clear that the trope of personification is complex enough to justify a careful reading.

In a narrative reading of Isa. 52:13–53:12, we are challenged to attempt to make "I", "him", "us", עַמִּי "my people", (הָ)רַבִּים "(the) many", גּוֹיִם רַבִּים "many peoples", מְלָכִים "kings", עֲצוּמִים "numerous" and פֹּשְׁעִים "transgressors" all givens of a single situation and yet we are doomed to fail by the dissolution of binary oppositions. As readers we make certain assumptions about the participants in the text, but then our expectations are thwarted as we see that in the relation between narrator and actor a situation arises in which the levels of *story* and *narration* produce an unavoidable collision. Between the prediction of vindication in 52:13; 15, 53:5b; 10b; 11; 12a and the description of the very background for this in 52:14, 53:2–5a; 6–10a; 11ad; 12bc, a dramatic tension emerged which can never disappear completely: the humiliation and vindication of sinners and the righteous in past and future are explained as both undeserved and highly deserved. Also, the future is not so bright for everyone. In 52:15 he יַזֶּה (will startle?) many peoples before him, kings shall shut their mouth, etc.; in 53:12 "he" shall allot numerous to spoiling.

In "our" story about "him", the contrasting relationship between the ill, lonely and solitary one and "our" testimony to "him" at a distance is salient (53:2–3). However, in telling about the common fate of "him" and "us" (v. 4a), "we" appear as both narrator and actor. In a fluid relation between "him" and "us", "we", in "our" self-questioning and self-consciousness, are continually self-displacing. The turning point in "our" sense of reality is expressed through echoes from v. 3 in v. 4, related to the common diagnosis. In a personification, the actors are disclosed through a repetition of elements surrounding the figure(s) "he"/"we", where the personifier "he" and the personified "we" become blurred. The story plays ironically against "our" earlier assumptions about "him" and "his" illnesses. After the testimony "we" gave about the ill man's fate, where "we" took offence at "his" illness and devastating appearance (vv. 2–3), the diagnosis is repeated with variation, where suddenly "we" are also deeply involved (v. 4a). This turn-around is in "us" seeing "him" as "us" instead of a devastating other. Suddenly we are in a double story or in crossing stories, that is, the story about "him" and that which appears to be about "us", where not only contrast, but also a common fate is created – or revealed. Thus, חֳלָיֵנוּ הוּא נָשָׂא "he bore our illnesses…" expresses how both "he" and "we" are ill (v. 4). And when הוּא מְחֹלָל מִפְּשָׁעֵנוּ "he was wounded because of our transgressions…" (v. 5), the punishment is explained in terms of an identification between "him" and "us", with various accentuations, with sin, guilt and punishment inseparable. V. 5b explains the punishment of "him": מוּסַר שְׁלוֹמֵנוּ עָלָיו וּבַחֲבֻרָתוֹ נִרְפָּא־לָנוּ׃ "chastisement was upon him for our healing…" It is not only "he" who is ill, and it is not only "we" who have sinned: both parties are ill, have sinned and shall be healed. As such, the dominant reading of Isa. 53 as a text about "vicarious suffering" is rejected.

6.4. ISA. 52:13–53:12 ON AN INTERTEXTUAL LEVEL

In Isa. 52:13–53:12, talk of servant, exaltation, disfigurement, vision, questioning, contempt, desolation, illness, striking, sin, punishment, healing, delusion, oppression, silence, death, burial, descendants, wealth and vindication moves readers to understandings of relationships of YHWH, "I", "he", "you", "we", "many", "numerous", "transgressors", "people", "many peoples" and "kings". In an intertextual reading of Isa. 53, the trope of personification has been in focus, where nation, people and city speak and are spoken to in patterns which alternate between presentations of individuals and collectives. In Isa. 40–55, "I", "we", "you", "he", "she" and "they" are speaking and are spoken to. The people are also named as Jacob, Israel, Jeshurun and Zion, as well as designated as friend, messenger, servant, woman and mother. I have not pursued Isa. 52:13–53:12's relation to particular prior texts, a historical background or an author's intention, but the text's participation in a discursive space. I have concentrated on the humiliations and vindications of fates and fortunes in the past, present and future in Isa. 40–55 and elsewhere in the prophetic literature, Psalms and Lamentations. In addition to other biblical texts, secondary literature has also participated. The scholarly concept of *Gottesknechtlied*, for instance, is one of many intertexts, *Stellvertretung* another, exile a third. In this intertextual reading, a variety of conventions derived from Isa. 53 and other texts have appeared as constituents of themes, tropes and displacements. Some discourses might be dominant in Isa. 40–55, others in the Book of Isaiah, others in the Hebrew Bible. I will illustrate this with the depiction of the servant's death in Isa. 53. In the Servant Song research, there has been a comprehensive debate whether the servant died or not. Most scholars conclude that the servant did really die. In 53:9, a humiliation is related to an unworthy tomb where the dead one is classified with רְשָׁעִים "wicked ones" and עָשִׁיר "a rich" (?). This happened although he had behaved neither violently nor deceptively. He is also cut off from the land of the living (v. 8) and slain to death (v. 12). His death is explained as due to פֶּשַׁע עַמִּי "the transgression of my people" (v. 8) and he is classified with פֹּשְׁעִים "transgressors" (v. 12). Read with Am. 5, Jer. 22, Isa. 14 and Ps. 88, we have seen how death works as a metaphor, a figure of deviation. Death appears within a stereotypical language of lament related to individuals (kings such as Jehoiakim in Jer. 22, the Babylonian king in Isa. 14 and the Pharaoh of

Egypt in Ezek. 32 and psalmist in Ps. 88) and personifications (Israel in Isa. 53 and Amos 5) in extreme situations. Traditional forms of speech might be appropriated in other ways than as funeral lament in rites for the dead.[3]

6.5. Personification Once More

In this study, we have indeed glimpsed the complexity inherent in formalising so usual, and at first so seemingly transparent, a trope as personification. It appears to be a powerful and widespread literary trope in the Hebrew Bible, both in its poetical as well as in its more prosaic parts. Perhaps a personification is not as tedious, obvious and simple as it has been reckoned to be in biblical exegesis. Something has probably been lost in the earlier superficial treatment of this trope. A theoretical rehabilitation of personification is needed. Heim depicts how a careful reading of the trope of personification may also give us an impression of the cultural, political and theological constructions which the texts represent:

> Th[e] representative function explains why the personified Jerusalem can be depicted in surprisingly different roles, which at times appear to be mutually exclusive. She is wife, prostitute, divorcee, widow, mother, daughter, and so on, thus impersonating the various individuals suffering distress…[The personification] transforms the Jerusalem community into an interlocutor who can perform different roles in the complex dialogue which dramatizes the bereavement of the survivors in Jerusalem – both on an individual and on a corporate level.[4]

---

[3] Dell, "The Misuse of Forms in Amos", pp. 59–60.

[4] Heim, "The Personification of Jerusalem and the Drama of Her Bereavement in Lamentations", pp. 138; 144. E. S. Said, "The Clash of Ignorance", *The Nation* (October 22, 2001 Issue), points also to a danger of personification, exemplified by B. Lewis, "The Roots of Muslim Rage", *The Atlantic Monthly* (September 1990 Issue) and S. Huntington, "The Clash of Civilizations?", *Foreign Affairs* 72 (1993) 22–49. Said claims:

> In both articles, the personification of enormous entities called "the West" and "Islam" is recklessly affirmed, as if hugely complicated matters like identity and culture existed in a cartoonlike world where Popeye and Bluto bash each other mercilessly, with one always more virtuous puligist getting the upper hand over his adversary. Certainly neither Huntington nor Lewis has much time to spare for the internal dynamics and plurality of every civilization, or for the fact that the major contest in most modern cultures concerns the definition or interpretation of each culture, or for the unattractive possibility that a great deal of demagogy and downright ignorance is involved in presuming to speak for a whole religion or civilization. No, the West is the West, and Islam Islam.

It might be useful to illustrate the trope of personification by complementary readings of the "servant" and Zion texts. Both the male and the female personifications draw an ambiguous image of the "person". A numerical change similar to the one between "he" and "we" in Isa. 53 appears in the female personifications, in the relation between Zion and her children (49:17–26, 51:18; 20, 54:1–4). Moreover, both the male and the female personifications are ambiguous in relation to sin and suffering. The woman has both paid doubly for all her sins (40:2) and suffered for the sins of her children (50:1), just as the servant has sinned (44:22) and will bear the transgressions of the many (53:11). Like "he"/"we"/"my people"/"many" in Isa. 53, in a female personification in Isa. 40:1–2 Jerusalem has sinned and suffered. And like them, she experiences a turning point towards vindication. Whereas in Isa. 53 the focus was placed on how "he" and "we" suffered illness due to their sin and how they shall become healed, in Isa. 40 her hard times, which are due to her sin, are over. A peculiarity in both Isa. 53 and the female personification of chap. 50 is that the personification figure (mother, servant) is related to "the people" (53:8 "my people", cf. vv. 5–6: "we", v. 11: "many", v. 12: "many", "numerous") or "her children" (50:1). Both the male and female personifications are texts which contain frequent changes, ambiguities and paradoxes.

6.6. Concluding Remarks

Biblical scholarship is influenced by the traditional historical-critical method and post-modern perspectives. Postmodern perspectives have lead to an expansion of scholars' horizon, contributing to an increased attention on reading and construction of knowledge. While some practitioners of these approaches regard them as mutually exclusive, others consider them possible to combine.[5] Both camps have a common task in being both critical and self-critical, which becomes challenged by each other when it comes to issues of, for instance, historiography and context of reading. Scholars from different parties might have a

---

[5] On recent contributions on the discussion of the relationship between traditional historical-critical method and post-modern perspectives, see J. J. Collins, *The Bible after Babel: Historical Criticism in a Postmodern Age* (Grand Rapids: Eerdmans, 2005), S. Weitzman, "Rebuilding the Tower of Babel", *JQR* 98 (2008) 103–112 and Aichele, Miscall and Walsh, "An Elephant in the Room".

conversation about such joint topics, in which each might learn something from each other.

This study has focused on our understanding of the conventions and operations of modes of discourse. Isa. 52:13–53:12 has appeared to be an apt case for this pursuit. In this text, many discourses are at play, and the interplay of scholarly and textual discourses is remarkably clear. As well as a textual, a narrative and an intertextual reading of Isa. 53, interpretations of interpretations, metanarratives and interpretive institutions are also presented. Due to the comprehensive history of interpretation of the text, studying Isa. 53 is intriguing in many ways. The text has been multifariously interpreted within biblical studies and theology in Judaism and Christianity, in which readers and reading communities have contemplated experiences or visions of humiliation, suffering, sin, atonement, forgiveness, vindication and resurrection. In biblical research, the classical Duhmian questions about Isa. 53 have dominated the readings of the text, read through lenses of *Gottesknecht*, *Ebed-Jahwe-Lied*, *Stellvertretung* and "Servant Song Research". The servant ideologeme involves a hegemonic domination of some interpretations over others. However, we have also seen that there is no undisputed consensus or unified methodology, but a complex heterogeneity of ideas within readings of Isa. 53. Although the Duhmian paradigm is strong, it has not led to a coherent reading. The text does not possess a meaning unique to itself and different forces are at work. Different strategies of reading produce different pursuits and identifications of the servant of Isa. 53. Every reading is contextual and situated. This concerns the German common-sense reading(s), constructed on a legacy of more than one hundred years of German-speaking theological (Protestant) readings, as much as feminist, liberation theological and narratological readings, to mention but some. The question of "who is the servant" in Isa. 53 is challenged and any supposed self-integrity to the text is contested. Also, a traditional concept of originality is exploded. To paraphrase Barthes, one could claim, "Isa. 53 is neither a unit nor a work that can be held in the hand!"

APPENDIX 1
יַשְׂכִּיל IN 52:13

The translation of יַשְׂכִּיל (imperf. 3ms hi of שׂכל) in Isa. 52:13 has been widely discussed. It has been related to insight, wisdom, prosperity and success. The word has also been emended and even omitted.[1] Most scholars, but not all, connect שׂכל (hi) to the servant's exaltation.

A common rendering of יַשְׂכִּיל in 52:13 is "to have success" or "prosper".[2] In this sense, Koole sees a connection to leaders of Israel such as Joshua (Josh. 1:7–8), David (1 Sam. 18:5, 14–15), Solomon (1 Kgs 2:3) and Hezekiah (2 Kgs 18:7), with שׂכל (hi) and צלח paralleled in expressions regarding the manner in which the deity was with them, cf. Isa. 53:10. Also, in a portrayal of the Messiah in Jer. 23:5–6, שׂכל (hi) is parallel with עָשָׂה מִשְׁפָּט וּצְדָקָה "to execute justice and righteousness" in the world; cf. מִשְׁפָּט in Isa. 42:4, 49:4, 50:8 and צדק in 53:11.[3]

יַשְׂכִּיל in Isa. 52:13 has also been ascribed the meaning "act with insight".[4] Rignell comments:

> [יַשְׂכִּיל] is usually translated by "success", but it would be preferable to find in the word some indication that the Servant has aquired a deeper experience, or that he shows evidence of an increased knowledge (as a result of his existence). A similar expression is התבוננו at the end of lii 15.[5]

---

[1] Duhm, *Das Buch Jesaia*, p. 355.

[2] See, for instance, Kutsch, *Sein Leiden und Tod – unser Heil*, pp. 15–16, Westermann, *Isaiah 40–66*, p. 253, Orlinsky, *The So-Called "Servant of the Lord" and "Suffering Servant" in Second Isaiah*, p. 18, n. 1, Blenkinsopp, *Isaiah 40–55*, pp. 344; 346b, Hermisson, "Das vierte Gottesknechtlied im deuterojesajanischen Kontext", p. 6 (ET p. 23).

[3] Koole, *Isaiah III. Volume 2*, p. 264. Haag, "Das Opfer des Gottesknechts", p. 87, comprehends a war context for Josh. 1:7–8, 1 Sam. 18:5; 14; 15; 2 Kgs 18:7, Jer. 10:21, 23:5, 50:9, as well as Isa. 52:13. This is connected to his interpretation of the servant as a charismatic leader of the people (p. 83).

[4] LXX renders συνήσει "have insight" and Vulg. *intelliget* "understand". Ekblad, *Isaiah's Servant Poems according to the Septuagint*, p. 179, concerning LXX: "The Lord's forming of the servant with understanding is parallel with his showing the servant light (53:11)."

[5] Rignell, "Isa. LII 13–LIII 12", pp. 87–88.

Torrey interprets יַשְׂכִּיל nominally as "the wise One".[6] Clines suggests that the meanings "have success" and "be wise" are combined in יַשְׂכִּיל in 52:13, translating the verb as "his wisdom prospers".[7] Oswalt also reads both meanings into this verb:

> [I]t is saying that he will both know and do the right things in order to accomplish the purpose for which he was called (Isa. 42:1, 49:2–3, 50:7–9). Whatever the intervening intimations of failure might be (49:4), the Servant and the world should know that he will not fail.[8]

However, not all exegetes connect יַשְׂכִּיל to the servant's exaltation. Blau explains double meanings of the root שׂכל as "understand" and "put crossways", and connects the second meaning to an Arab. cognate translated as "rope", thus rendering יַשְׂכִּיל "to be bound".[9] Driver also finds the usual interpretation of יַשְׂכִּיל "he will prosper" problematic, because the vindication is first described at the end of the text, and because שׂכל (hi) represents an inadequate description of the servant's circumstances, as its meaning is related to "worldly success", and not the more relevant צלח (hi) "prosper" in 53:10.[10] Therefore, he revocalizes to יִשָּׂכֵל (ni) "he will be bound", which he supports by an Akk. cognate translated as "bandage", "scarf", a Hebr. cognate שִׂכֵּל "crossed" (e.g. the hands) and an Arab. cognate translated as "bound", "tied". Driver claims that the following verbs refer to the lifting up of the servant after being bound as a form of punishment, such as

---

[6] Torrey, *The Second Isaiah*, p. 415: "This is one of the prophet's own poetical designations of Israel, the Servant, similar to *Meshullam*, the Perfected One, 42:19 …and *Yeshurun*, 44:2." He also draws attention to דֵּעְתוֹ in 53:11 in this connection. Torrey is supported by H. L. Ginsberg, "The Oldest Interpretation of the Suffering Servant", *VT* 3 (1953) 403, and J. Day, "[דַּעַת] Humiliation in Isaiah LIII 11 in the Light of Isaiah LIII 3 and Daniel XII 4, and the Oldest Known Interpretation of the Suffering Servant", *VT* 30 (1980) 100.

[7] Clines, *I, He, We and They*, p. 14, cf. Muilenburg, "The Book of Isaiah: Chapters 40–66", p. 616, Westermann, *Isaiah 40–66*, p. 258, Whybray, *Isaiah 40–66*, p. 169, and the more eccentric reading by K. Baltzer, "Jes. 52,13: Die 'Erhöhung' des 'Gottes-Knechtes'" in L. Bormann, K. D. Tredici and A. Standhartiger (eds), *Religious Propaganda and Missionary Competition in the New Testament World* (NTSupp, 74; Leiden: E. J. Brill, 1994) 45–56.

[8] Oswalt, *The Book of Isaiah: Chapters 40–66*, p. 378. Whybray, *Isaiah 40–66*, p. 169, claims that the two meanings "to understand" and "to be successful" may be combined here, but that "to prosper", "be successful" predominates.

[9] J. Blau, "Über Homonyme und angeblich Homonyme Wurzeln II", *VT* 7 (1957) 101.

[10] Driver, "Isaiah 52:13–53:12", pp. 90–91.

hanging,[11] and translates 52:13: "Lo! my servant shall be bound and lifted up, he shall be raised aloft, very high".[12] Williamson rejects Driver's interpretation by arguing that שׂכל (hi) is not limited to "worldly success", referring to Josh 1:7; 8 and 1 Sam. 18:14, and by claiming that it is not uncommon in the Hebrew Bible to state the result of an action first and then trace the path by which this result is attained.[13]

---

[11] Driver, "Isaiah 52:13–53:12", p. 105:
The *double entendre* thus implied in the following clause, namely "he shall be exalted and lifted up and shall be very high" is similar to that which Jesus uses when he says "I, if I be lifted up from earth, will draw all men unto myself" [Gen. 12:32], which may indeed be based on a recollection of this very passage.
Driver identifies the servant as "some unknown Jew, whether teacher or preacher or prophet, whose message inflamed and alarmed his fellow-country men or perhaps the Babylonian authorities against him".

[12] Driver, "Isaiah 52:13–53:12", p. 103. J. Morgenstern, "The Suffering Servant-A New Solution", *VT* 11 (1961) 313, emends to יֻשְׂכַּל "he is suspended; he is hanging", expressing the ill treatment of him.

[13] Williamson, *The Book Called Isaiah*, pp. 265–266.

APPENDIX 2
עָלָיו...יַזֶּה IN 52:15

The translation of the verb יַזֶּה עַל in Isa. 52:15 is highly disputed, and the rendering has been regarded as both cryptic and corrupt. Also, the role of יַזֶּה within the parallelism is disputed. The proposals can be grouped into two camps: those who read יַזֶּה as a 3ms vb with the servant as its subject and גּוֹיִם רַבִּים as object; and those who emend it to a 3mpl verb with גּוֹיִם רַבִּים as its subject. The two most usual suggestions are to read the verb as either נזה I "sprinkle" or נזה II "cause to leap", i.e. "startle".

i.   נזה I "SPRINKLE"

A few scholars read נזה I (3ms hi) as "sprinkle", with "he" as the subject acting towards the object גּוֹיִם רַבִּים "many peoples" in 52:14.[14] Others emend the verb to the plural, making גּוֹיִם רַבִּים "many peoples" the subject.[15] The root נזה has also been emended to יזה "besprinkle".[16]

---

[14] E. J. Young, "The Intepretation of [יַזֶּה] in Isaiah 52:15", *WTJ* 3 (1941) 125–132, Muilenburg, "The Book of Isaiah: Chapters 40–66", pp. 617–618. נזה I (hi) signifies "sprinkle" in most cases in BH. נזה is a marked ritual term in the Pentateuch. Isa. 52:15 is the only case where the verb appears with a personal object. In the other occurences of נזה "sprinkle" in BH, the object of the verb is the liquid that is being sprinkled, and the thing being sprinkled on is preceded by a prep such as עַל.

[15] Nyberg, "Smärtornas man", pp. 47–48, translates as "Many peoples offer sacrifices of purifying (for his sake)...", i.e. they attempt to protect themselves from the infection spread by the servant, thought of as a leprous man. This is supported by North, *The Second Isaiah*, p. 235. On Nyberg's suggestion, Lindblom, *The Servant Songs in Deutero-Isaiah*, p. 40, comments: "[I]s it really probable that we have here the extremely rare construction where a verb in singular is followed by a *personal* subject in the plural? The translation 'will be amazed' or the like is pure guesswork based on the presumed meaning of the context" (his italics).

[16] Lindblom, *The Servant Songs in Deutero-Isaiah*, pp. 40–42, labels יזה as a ritual *terminus technius* in MT. He further claims that MT gave the word another sense than the one it usually has, translating Isa. 52:15a:

He will besprinkle many peoples, i.e. purify them from their sin." He continues: "It is a well-known fact that the Massoretes frequently employ peculiar constructions objectionable to us both from a lexical and from a syntactical point of view. It

ii. נזה II "cause to leap", i.e. "startle"

In נזה II "cause to leap", i.e. "startle", "he" may be the subject and גּוֹיִם רַבִּים "many peoples" the object. The sg proposals related to נזה II include "scatter"[17] and "startle".[18] The verb is also emended to pl. The suggestions in the pl include נזה II "startle"[19] and "leap up",[20] or

---

is moreover to be observed that ritual terms in particular vary greatly in their constructions, e.g. the roots כפר, רצה and so on

(pp. 40–41). יזה is not preserved in the Hebrew Bible, but forms part of two proper names: יְזַוְאֵל "he who is besprinkled by God", i.e. "he who is purified by God from sin" (1 Chron. 12:3) and יִזִּיָּה (pi) "he whom YHWH has purified from sin" (Ezra 10:25). Lindblom argues that the stem consequently has a transitive sense with personal objects. He adds that the correspondence between the two members of comparison is not absolutely logical, and translates: "as many (before) were appalled at you, so he (in the future) will purify many nations [i.e. 'from their sin']" (p. 41). In Isa. 52:13–15, he interprets the servant as the personified Israel, regarding which he emphasises that Israel's task is to mediate welfare to the nations (p. 52). Kaiser, *Der königliche Knecht*, pp. 86; 91, supports Lindblom. Kaiser is supported by Hertzberg, "Die 'Abtrünningen' und die 'Vielen'", p. 103.

[17] T. C. Vriezen, "The Term Hizza: Lustration and Consecration", *OTS* 7 (1950) 204: "The Ebed is said to make many (or large) nations retreat in great fear to all sides by his marvelous victory." He bases his interpretation of יַזֶּה as "scatter" on the figure of the scattering of enemies in Ps. 68:1–2, and the description of the nations as "a drop from a bucket" in Isa. 40:15. Further, whereas the term is mainly used of liquid, either in a metaphorical or in a literal sense, flood is also used of the bursting in of an army and for a horse rushing into battle (Jer. 8:6). A similar interpretation is held by Gerlemann, *Studien zur alttestamentlichen Theologie*, p. 40, who relates נזה to a war context, and so reads יזה in Isa. 52:15 as *zerstreut*, i.e. the servant overpowers the nations so they have to run away in all directions. Gerlemann reads Isa. 52:13–53:12 as a biography of David as the servant (p. 44).

[18] Whybray, *Isaiah 40-66*, p. 170, Koole, *Isaiah III. Vol. 2*, p. 271 ("so he will cause many nations to leap up"), Blenkinsopp, *Isaiah 40–55*, pp. 345–346f ("so will he astonish many nations").

[19] Driver, "Isaiah 52:13–53:12", p. 92, emends to יַזֶּה, which he supports with an Arab. cognate "leap" and LXX. He translates v. 15a: "So now mighty nations shall be startled." Cf. Clifford, *Fair Spoken and Persuading*, p. 173.

[20] Snaith, *Isaiah 40-66*, p. 161. He argues for a parallel between יזה "to leap up" and קפץ פה "shut mouth" in 52:15 and the pair in Job 29:8–9, that is, "to clasp one's hand over one's mouth in silence" and "to leap to one's feet" (pp. 161–162). Watts, "The Meaning of [עָלָיו יִקְפְּצוּ מְלָכִים פִּיהֶם] in Isaiah LII 15", pp. 327–335, claims that Snaith does not make any attempt to derive his observation concerning the Gentiles' amazement from the text itself. Watts argues that the focus is not the "astonishment" in itself but the event which caused it (p. 328), cf. 5.8.1. n. 54.

emendations to רגז "be excited",[21] זוח "agitate",[22] ירג "astonish"[23] and בזה "despise".[24]

I find the text obscure, and would emphasise the uncertain meaning of יַזֶּה in Isa. 52:15. However, the suggestion of נזה II "startle" might be a tenable assumption as a parallel to the following "kings shall shut their mouth" (as well as to the other astonishment motifs in the context).[25]

---

[21] G. F. Moore, "On יזה in Isaiah LII.15", *JBL* 9 (1890) 216–222, claims that the antithesis between v. 14 and v. 15 and the structure of v. 15 require a plural verb with רַבִּים as subject. Influenced by Vss, he "restores" יזה to יִרְגְּזוּ "were excited" (cf. Deut. 2:25, Isa. 64:1 and Jer. 33:9 or alternatively יַחְפְּזוּ, cf. Deut. 20:3 or יֵחָפֵזוּ, 1 Sam. 23:23 and Ps. 48:6). He also mentions possible similar corruptions in 1 Sam. 14:14 and Ps. 48:6. Moore' proposal has been supported by Duhm, *Das Buch Jesaia*, p. 356. Hermisson, "Das vierte Gottesknechtslied im deuterojesaianischen Kontext", p. 6, n. 13 (ET p. 23, n. 13), also recommends the conjectural emendation to יִרְגְּזוּ "become agitated". He comments further, p. 9 (ET p. 29, incl. n. 42):

> The parallelism shows that in place of the MT's term יַזֶּה there must have stood another term, denoting astonishment, wonder, or even excitement, as in most English versions, where the servant will "startle" (NRSV, NJPS) the nations, or the nations will be "astonished" (NJB) or will "marvel" at him (NIV margin; cf. LXX θαυμάσονται). The popular interpretation of the MT's reading יַזֶּה as suggesting an atonement ritual (KJV, NASB, NIV: the Servant will "sprinkle" many nations) is opposed not only by the linguistic usage and parallelism, but by the flow of the text… Against the above translations, the hiphil of נזה followed by an accusative object does not mean "to sprinkle (an implied fluid) on an object", such as the nations (גּוֹיִם), but simply "to sprinkle (the fluid)", where the fluid either stands as the direct object in the accusative (Lev. 16:15, Num 8:7, 19:219) or, more frequently, follows the partitive מִן ("sprinkel *some of* the blood/oil", etc.). The object upon which or toward which the fluid is sprinkled is then always preceded by one of the prepositions עַל, אֶל, אֶל נכח, or לִפְנֵי, it never appears as the verb's direct object (his italics).

Hermisson (n. 43) also refers to Janowski, who has rejected the notion that the text has any cultic context.

[22] Kutsch, *Sein Leiden und Tod – unser Heil*, p. 17, proposes the emendation יְזוּחוּ, which he supports with Sir. 8:11, translating *sich ereifern*, and relates to wrath in Isa. 28:21, Ps. 4:5, and Prov. 29:9.

[23] Westermann, *Isaiah 40–66*, pp. 253; 259, with reference to LXX θαυμάσονται ἔθνη πολλὰ ἐπ' αὐτῷ "many people will marvel (cause to wonder) at him". LXX renders נזה as intrans. instead of the trans. in MT. LXX reading is based on a verb in pl, making ἔθνη πολλὰ the subject (and not the object, as in MT). No other ancient versions have such a rendering. Clines, *I, He, We and They*, pp. 11; 14–15, translates "astonished" without arguing either for which root he reads (neither נזה I nor II has been translated as "astonished" by any other scholars) or for his emendation of the verb to pl.

[24] J. Leveen, "יזה in ISAIAH LII. 15", *JJS* 7 (1956) 93–94, emends יַזֶּה to יִבְזֻהוּ "(many nations) shall despise him", which he argues fits the parallelism better, and is also more appropriate in the context, cf. נִבְזֶה in 53:3.

[25] Kaiser, *Der königliche Knecht*, pp. 91–92, illuminates this motif through the occurences in lament psalms and hymns, where it is expressed how the enemies of as well as "everyone who passes by", the praying one, mock and makes mouth at him.

APPENDIX 3
כְּמַסְתֵּר פָּנִים מִמֶּנּוּ IN 53:3

The nominal clause of Isa. 53:3a is introduced by a conjunctive *waw* and a particle of comparison which heads a noun (ms) מַסְתֵּר "hiding". The noun is derived from סתר (hi pt) "hide", "conceal". The object of the clause is פָּנִים "faces" which by its pl form implies a pl also for the impersonal (sg) phrase כְּמַסְתֵּר "like hiding one(s)". This is followed by a prep. phrase with the disjunctive prep. מִן "from", "away from" and 3ms suffix. The whole phrase might be translated "…and like a hiding of faces from him", "as one from whom the faces (are) hidden", "like hiding one(s)" or "there is hiding of faces". 1QIsaᵃ reads מסתר, (pt. hi.), while most vrss render MT sg. מַסְתֵּר in the pl. As we shall see, the servant, YHWH or those around him have been taken to be the subject of the clause.

i. Servant as Subject

LXX renders ὅτι ἀπέστραπται τὸ πρόσωπον αὐτοῦ, making the servant the subject. The form here was assumed to be from סור "turn away".[26] Dahood argues that the verb formation with infixed /-t-/ remained alive through the biblical period, citing the LXX translation of הִסְתֵּר פָּנָיו. He claims that MT is *scriptio defectiva* which ought to be repointed מַסְתֵּר (pt. hi.) with the servant as subject: he turned away because of his ugliness, cf. Isa. 50:6.[27] Thomas also borrows support from LXX and the versions, rendering כְּמַסְתֵּר פָּנִים מִמֶּנּוּ "as a man who hid his face from us", which he reads as a parallel to חֲדַל אִישִׁים in the first line.[28]

---

[26] Barr, *Comparative Philology and the Text of the Old Testament*, p. 253, explains this as a stylistic preference in Greek, which has nothing to do with the original Hebrew form. According to him, the "hiding" of the face is a Hebrew religious idiom.

[27] Dahood, "Phoenician Elements in Isaiah 52:13–53:12", p. 67. Cf. Clines, *I, He, We and They*, p. 16, n. 23.

[28] Thomas, "A Consideration of Isaiah LIII", p. 123.

ii. YHWH as Subject

Elliger, Heller and Friedman argue that YHWH is the subject in the expression כְּמַסְתֵּר פָּנִים מִמֶּנּוּ.[29] Friedman shows that this is the case in nearly all other occurrences of the expression. Further, he reads the phrase not in parallel with the preceding v. 3a, but with its counterpart in the following v. 4a, in which the servant is described as being regarded as "stricken, smitten by God and afflicted" (cf. Targum). He comments that in the two exceptions in which humans are the subjects of the expression, i.e. Ex. 3:6 and Isa. 50:6, both identify פָּנִים with pronominal suffixes.[30]

iii. Those Who Are Around "Him" as Subject

Driver reads the sg מַסְתֵּר as pl: "…an object from which men turn their gaze."[31] Nyberg explains מַסְתֵּר פָּנִים מִמֶּנּוּ as an archaism, where the prefix מַה is identical to the interrogative and relative pronoun מַה, originating from an earlier time when this מַה was indifferent to genus.[32] כְּמַסְתֵּר פָּנִים מִמֶּנּוּ "like a hiding of face from him" corresponds to נִבְזֶה וַחֲדַל אִישִׁים in v. 3a, i.e. the isolation of him from those around him further emphasises men's contempt for him. אִישִׁים in the previous clause might be the subject of the expression כְּמַסְתֵּר פָּנִים מִמֶּנּוּ.[33]

---

[29] Elliger, *Deuterojesaja in seinem Verhältnis zu Tritojesaja*, pp. 9–10, J. Heller, "Hiding of the Face: A Study of Isa. 53:3", *Communio Viatorum* 1 (1958) 263–266, and E. R. Friedman, "The Biblical Expression [מַסְתֵּר פָּנִים]", *HAR* 1 (1977) 139–148.

[30] Friedman, "The Biblical Expression [מַסְתֵּר פָּנִים]", pp. 146–147.

[31] Driver, "Isaiah 52:13–53:12", p. 103. See also Whybray, *Isaiah 40–66*, pp. 174–175.

[32] Nyberg, "Smärtornas man", p. 51.

[33] This implies that we are dealing with a pl. subject with a sg pt. This reading might be further supported by the fact that the pl אִישִׁים is a rare form in the Hebrew Bible, as the sg אִישׁ followed by a sg verb is the most common, see among others GKC § 96.

יָדַע IN 53:3 AND 53:11

The assumption that the verb יָדַע does not always mean "to know" in the Hebrew Bible goes back a long way.[34] In modern biblical scholarship, Thomas maintained that the meaning "to know" does not fit the context in many verses in the Hebrew Bible, and spoke for a root יָדַע II with the sense of "to rest", "to be still", "quiet", "at ease", and in an extended sense as "to be submissive", "humiliated" (qal) for some of these occurences (and "to make quiet", "submissive", "to be humiliated", "to punish" [hi]).[35] The philological basis provided by Thomas is the supposed homonymous Arab. cognate root "to become still", "quiet", "at rest". He also drew attention to renderings in the versions as well as to some Jewish commentaries regarding a supposed יָדַע II. As we shall see below, a יָדַע II has been suggested for either וִירוּעַ חֹלִי in Isa. 53:3 or בְּדַעְתּוֹ in v. 11, or both places. In both instances, it is primarily the extended sense "humiliate" which has been suggested.

i. 53:3: וִידוּעַ חֹלִי

Thomas' thesis is supported by Driver, who thus renders וִידוּעַ חֹלִי (pt. pass. qal) "humbled", "disciplined by sickness" in Isa. 53:3.[36] Driver argues that if the verb "to know" is used, a comparison with the same form in Deut. 1:13; 15 should imply the translation "known", "famous for sickness", which he finds absurd.[37] Thomas' thesis has also been applied to 53:3 by North, Emerton, Day and Clines, and more

---

[34] J. A. Emerton, "A Consideration of Some Alleged Meanings of [ידע] in Hebrew", *JSS* 15 (1970) 145–180, refers to examples from Jewish and Samaritan commentators and lexicographers, ancient versions, rabbinic medieval renderings and biblical scholars from seventeenth century and onwards.

[35] D. W. Thomas, "The root ידע in Hebrew", *JTS* 35 (1934) 298–306 and many further articles, see an overview in W. Johnstone, "YDʻ II, 'Be Humbled, Humiliated'?", *VT* 41 (1991) Appendix 1.

[36] Driver, "Linguistic and Textual Problems", pp. 48–49.

[37] Driver, "Isaiah 52:13–53:12", pp. 93; 101–102; 104. This was also followed up by Thomas himself in later articles, see an overview in Johnstone, "YDʻ II, 'Be Humbled, Humiliated'?", n. 7 and Appendix 1.

hesitantly by Muilenburg and Whybray.[38] Ackroyd speaks of a possible ambiguity concerning the meaning: "In 53:3, its use could suggest both humiliation and intimacy, the divergent forms could preserve the two alternatives."[39] Apart from by Westermann, Thomas' thesis seems not to have been accepted by German scholarship.[40]

Johnstone has most recently scrutinized the Arabic evidence proposed by Thomas' thesis.[41] He claims that the Arab. root to which Thomas refers offers no support for a possible Hebrew ידע II to which Thomas explains:

> [T]here is…at least a *prima facie* case on grounds of morphology and meaning against this appeal to Arabic. The Arab. verb in Form I is used both intransitively and transitively but neither usages seems to provide obvious support for the theory: the stative *wadu'a*, "be at rest etc.", accords ill with the passive participle in Isa. liii 3; common use of the active (from which a passive participle would be expected) do not appear to yield the requested sense…As far as Isa. liii 3 is concerned, the most that one might claim on this basis might be "left", perhaps even, "abandoned" [to sickness].[42]

Johnstone's main objection to Thomas' studies is that he fails to examine the Arab. root in its context, and thus ends up with interpretations based on the Hebrew root unsupported by the Arab. root. Johnstone does not have objections to Thomas' thesis that there is an equivalent with Arabic *wadu'a* "be still", "at rest". What he objects, is the postulated extended sense in hi. leading to "humiliate".

---

[38] North, *The Second Isaiah*, pp. 237–238, Emerton, "A Consideration of Some Alleged Meanings of [ידע] in Hebrew", p. 176, Day, "[דֵּעָה] 'Humiliation' in Isaiah LIII 11", pp. 97–98, Clines, *I, He, We and They*, p. 21, Muilenburg, "The Book of Isaiah: Chapters 40–66", p. 620, Whybray, *Thanksgiving for a Liberated Prophet*, p. 58, n. 115. Concerning Isa. 53:3, this reading has even been adopted by the NEB, which renders וִידוּעַ חֹלִי "humbled by sufferings".

[39] P. R. Ackroyd, "Meaning and Exegesis" in P. R. Ackroyd and B. Lindars (eds), *Words and Meanings: Essays Presented to David Winton Thomas* (Cambridge: Cambridge University Press, 1968) 13–14.

[40] Westermann, *Isaiah 40–66*, p. 254.

[41] Johnstone, "YD' II, 'Be Humbled, Humiliated'?", pp. 49–62. Earlier, Barr, *Comparative Philology and the Text of the Old Testament*, pp. 19–25; 325; 328, also problematised the philological basis of this.

[42] Johnstone, "YD' II, 'Be Humbled, Humiliated'?", pp. 49–50.

Emerton accepts Johnstone's rejection of the part of Thomas' theory which is based on the meaning of a supposed Hebrew cognate derived from a misunderstanding of the Arabic.[43] After having deleted the Arabic evidences for Thomas' thesis, Emerton reconsiders the other arguments for the thesis, namely the ancient versions as well as some rabbinic medieval renderings. Unlike in his earlier reading of Isa. 53:3, he now comments:

> Isa. 53:3 comes from an important passage, but [וְיִדוּעַ חֹלִי] is not a serious problem, since the first word can be understood as a pa'ul form meaning "knowing" (GK §50 *f*), or 1QIsa^a's reading as an active participle [יודע] can be accepted.[44]

Interestingly, the main argument in Thomas' and his successors' interpretations, that the meaning "to know" did not fit the context, has vanished.

Reider proposes that six passages, in which the current meaning ידע "to know" does not fit well, have been corrupted during transmission by a change of ר to רעע.[45] Whereas this in most cases leads to the root רעע "to break", in Isa. 53:3 the change from ר to ע leads to a different root, ירע "to be weak". Thus, he emends it to וְירוּעַ חֹלִי "weak from sickness". By applying an Arab. cognate, Goldmann translates it as "to put", "to lay down", and in Isa. 53:3 as "laid down by illness".[46]

ii. 53:11: דַּעַת

As seen as regards 53:3 above, Thomas' thesis about a supposed ידע II in the Hebrew Bible has supporters, defenders and critics. Although the same methodological principles are valid for the phrase בְּדַעְתּוֹ (prep. בְּ, noun fs cstr. of דַּעַת "knowledge", "insight", 3ms suff.) "by his

---

[43] J. A. Emerton, "A Further Consideration of D. W. Thomas' Theories About [ידע]", *VT* 41 (1991) 145–163.

[44] Emerton, "A Further Consideration of D. W. Thomas' Theories About [ידע]", pp. 160–161. D. F. Payne, "Old Testament Exegesis and the Problem of Ambiguity", *ASTI* 5 (1967) 60–63; 67, shows how the Qumran reading יודע (active pt qal) in 53:3 corresponds to the LXX rendering.

[45] J. Reider, "Etymological Studies: ידע, ירע, and רעע", *JBL* 66 (1947) 315–317.

[46] M. D. Goldmann, "The Root ידע and the Verb 'to know' in Hebrew", *Australian Biblical Review* 3 (1953) 46–47.

knowledge" in 53:11 as well, the problems are more complex here due to the possible textual corruption of the verse. Driver applied Thomas' thesis also to 53:11:

> Thus, [דַעַת] "humiliation" catches up [יִדוֹע חֱלִי] "humbled by suffering" in v. 3; for "knowledge" here is off the point, whatever sense may be read into it, as something parallel to "the travails of his soul" is required.[47]

Further, Thomas and Driver have been supported by Allen, and more modestly by Emerton and Day,[48] whereas their view has been modified by Gelston[49] and Williamson.[50] In his reconsideration of Thomas' thesis, Emerton, after having accepted the tradional rendering of ידע I in 53:3, comments:

> In verse 11, [בְּדַעְתּוֹ] is more of a problem, because it is not clear what the servant is supposed to have known (not even אוֹר is added after [יִרְאֶה] with IQIsa). Perhaps [בְּרָעָתוֹ], "in his misery" should be read; but this is a difficult chapter, and [בְּדַעְתּוֹ] is but one of a number of problems.[51]

---

[47] Driver, "Isaiah 52:13–53:12", pp. 101–102. This was followed up by Thomas himself in many later articles, see an overview in Johnstone, "YDʻ II, 'Be Humbled, Humiliated'?", Appendix 1.

[48] L. C. Allen, "Isaiah LII 11 and its Echoes", *Vox Evangelica* 1 (1962) 24–28, Emerton, "A Consideration of Some Alleged Meanings of [ידע] in Hebrew", p. 174: "…Thomas offers an intelligible rendering of the whole verse, and of the passage as a whole. Nevertheless, the verse is undoubtedly difficult, and caution is needed in using it as evidence for Thomas' theory." Day, "[דַעַת] 'Humiliation' in Isaiah LIII 11", pp. 97–103.

[49] A. Gelston, "Some Notes on Second Isaiah", *VT* 21 (1971) 525, reconstructs the line:

> [T]he construction [בדעתו] with יצדיק at the beginning of the second line, as well as having precedents of the Targum and the Vulgate, picks up both the use of ידע in v. 3 and the argument in vv. 4–6 that the servant's suffering are vicarious: "By his humiliation/chastisment shall my servant justify the many and he shall bear their iniquities/guilt/penalties."

[50] H. G. M. Williamson, "[דַעַת] in Isaiah LIII 11", *VT* 28 (1978) 118–122, agrees with Thomas in relating דַעַת in 53:11 to a supposed ידע II. However, whereas Thomas and also Driver here gave דַעַת the extended sense "humiliation", Williamson proposes "rest", thus supporting P. A. D. Boer (1956).

[51] Emerton, "A Further Consideration of D. W. Thomas's Theories About [ידע]", pp. 160–161.

Westermann, who supported Thomas and Driver concerning 53:3, leaves 53:11 untranslated – as too obscure.[52] The same is true of Whybray, who expresses some doubt as to 53:11.[53] Reicke translates it as "his obedience…",[54] Müller "good",[55] while Dahood refers to יָדַע III, translating דַּעְתּוֹ "his sweat".[56]

---

[52] Westermann, *Isaiah 40–66*, p. 255.

[53] Whybray, *Thanksgiving for a Liberated Prophet*, p. 71, n. 168.

[54] B. Reicke, "The Knowledge of the Suffering Servant" in F. Maass (ed), *Das Ferne und Nahe Wort: Festschrift Leonhard Rost zur Vollendung seines 70. Lebensjahres am 30. November 1966 gewidmet* (BZAW, 105; Berlin: Töpelmann, 1967) 186ff., i.e. the servant's knowledge implies his obedience.

[55] H.-P. Müller, "Ein Vorschlag zu Jes. 53:10f", *ZAW* 81 (1969) 378–379 (*sein Gut*).

[56] Dahood, "Phoenician Elements in Isaiah 52:13–53:12", p. 72. He explains דַּעַת as יָדַע III which is a Canaanite form translated "sweat". He also reorganises the verse and translates it as "he was soaked by his sweat".

מֵעֹצֶר וּמִמִּשְׁפָּט IN 53:8

The translation of the expression מֵעֹצֶר וּמִמִּשְׁפָּט has been widely discussed. The proposed translations include:

i. "without protection (of kin) and without due legal procedure" by Driver, who states that the root עצר "hardly connotes oppression".[57] He supports his suggestion with Arab. cognates for "asylum", "refuge", "dependent on the family" and "kinsmen". Koole offers an alternative: "from protection (?) and justice", which he explains thus: "[T]he Servant, though he fulfils this justice, v. 9b, for the sake of others, for whom he suffers vicariously, vv. 4ff., perishes without justice."[58]

ii. "without restraint and without moderation" by Dahood, with the following explanation: "The apparent synonymy with [מֵעֹצֶר] suggests this nuance of [מִמִּשְׁפָּט], which is witnessed in…Prov. 13:16, 28:5, Eccl. 8:5–6, cf. Eccl. 16:23."[59]

iii. "from prison and law court" by Thomas, who refers to Peshitta and עצר (vb.) "shutting up" in prison, cf. 2 Kgs 17:4; Jer. 33:1, 39:15, and מִשְׁפָּט meaning "seat of judgement" in Deut 25:1, 1 Kgs 7:7, Isa. 38:6.[60]

iv. "from (royal) power and administration" by Ackroyd,[61] cf. his interpretation of דּוֹר as "assembly", "community" in Isa. 53:9, i.e. the grouping to which the servant belongs. Ackroyd refers to Judg. 18:7 for עצר as "inherited (royal) authority", and מִשְׁפָּט as the "royal prerogative" or "that justice which kings administer" in 1 Sam. 8:9; 11.

---

[57] Driver, "Isaiah 52:13–53:12", p. 94.

[58] Koole, *Isaiah III. Vol. 2*, pp. 303–304, the quotation is taken from p. 304.

[59] Dahood, "Phoenician Elements in Isaiah 52:13–53:12", p. 69.

[60] D. W. Thomas, "A Consideration of Isaiah LIII in the Light of Recent Textual and Philological Study" in H. Cazelles et al. (eds), *De Mari à Qumrân. L' Ancien Testament. Son mileu. Ses Écrits. Ses relectures juives. Hommage à Mgr. J. Coppens* (BETL, 24; Gembloux: J. Duculot, 1969) 124.

[61] Ackroyd, "The Meaning of Hebrew דּוֹר Considered", p. 7.

v.   "from oppression and from judgment" by Hermisson and Oswalt.[62]

vi. "out of exclusion and condemnation" by Baltzer.[63]

vii. "from (after) imprisonment (arrest) and trial" by Whybray and in a variation by Westermann.[64]

Others take it as hendiadys:

viii. "from his just position of power" by Ahlström.[65]

ix. "isolation due to the regulation of the law" by Nyberg, who sees a connection between נָגוּעַ in Isa. 53:4, which according to him means that the servant is smitten by leprosy, and so עֹצֶר is a description of ritual isolation from social intercourse, cf. Lev. 13–14.[66]

x.   "By oppressive acts of judgment" by Blenkinsopp.[67]

The different renderings of the prepositions depend on the interpretations of the nouns of the prep. phrases. The alternatives can be sorted into the following groups:

i.   causal: "as a result of", "by", "because of".[68]

ii. separative: "from".[69]

iii. privative: "without".[70]

---

[62] Hermisson, "Das vierte Gottesknechtlied im deuterojesajanischen Kontext", p. 7 (ET p. 26), Oswalt, *The Book of Isaiah: Chapters 40–66*, p. 390.

[63] Baltzer, *Deutero-Isaiah*, p. 393.

[64] Whybray, *Thanksgiving for a Liberated Prophet*, pp. 99–100, cf. Westermann, *Isaiah 40–66*, 254: "from prison and judgment".

[65] G. W. Ahlström, "Notes on Isaiah 53:8f", *BZ NF* 13 (1969) 97.

[66] Nyberg, "Smärtornas man", p. 53.

[67] Blenkinsopp, *Isaiah 40–55*, p. 345.

[68] e.g. Blenkinsopp, *Isaiah 40–55*, pp. 345; 348.

[69] He was taken away, deprived of his right, referring to the unfair treatment of him (cf. מִן "from" with לָקַח in Isa. 40:2, 44:15, 49:24, 51:22), e.g. Oswalt, *The Book of Isaiah: Chapters 40–66*, p. 390, Koole, *Isaiah III. Vol. 2*, pp. 303–305, Hermisson, "Das vierte Gottesknechtlied im deuterojesajanischen Kontext", p. 7 (ET p. 26).

[70] e.g. Driver, "Isaiah 52:13–53:12", p. 94, Dahood, "Phoenician Elements in Isaiah 52:13–53:12", pp. 64; 69.

APPENDIX 6
אִם־תָּשִׂים אָשָׁם נַפְשׁוֹ IN 53:10

The half-line אִם־תָּשִׂים אָשָׁם נַפְשׁוֹ is corrupt, disputed and untranslatable; it has been both emended and neglected. The syntax (e.g. the
particle אִם as temporal or conditional) and the interpretation of the
term אָשָׁם are also problematic. Also, the 3ms suffix in נַפְשׁוֹ is inconsistent with the 2ms vb תָּשִׂים. For some scholars, אָשָׁם constitutes the
very core of the text, while others delete it. MT is supported by 1QIsaᵃ.
The centrality of the half-line is related to scholars' interpretations of
the vicarious suffering in Isa. 53.

i. Scholars Who Emend the Text

Interestingly, in his pursuit of the historical biography of the servant,
a concept of vicarious suffering was not of great importance to Duhm.
Also his treatment of the textual problems of 53:10 is interesting. He
emends תָּשִׂים to יָשִׂים and אָשָׁם to מָשָׁם "Lust", and interprets the
expression *Lust der Seele* as a parallel to children.[71] He translates 53:10
as: "Doch Jahwe gefiels, ihn zu reinigen, Neu sprossen zu lassen sein
Alter; Die Lust seiner Seele wird er sehen, Samen lang von Leben."[72]

Elliger emends דְּכָאוֹ to דֻּכְּאוֹ "humiliated" and אִם־תָּשִׂים to וְהוּא
שָׂם, thus וְהוּא שָׂם אָשָׁם נַפְשׁוֹ וַיהוָה חָפֵץ דַּכְּאוֹ.[73] Begrich supports
Elliger's emendation to דֻּכְּאוֹ "humiliated". He also changes the two
letters ת and ם: דֻּכְּאוֹ הֶחֱלִים אֵת שָׂם אָשָׁם נַפְשׁוֹ "he healed the one
who made himself a sacrifice for sin".[74] Begrich is supported by, e.g.,
Driver and Westermann.[75]

---

[71] Duhm, *Das Buch Jesaia*, p. 365,
[72] On Duhm, see also 2.1.4. n. 57.
[73] Elliger, "Jes. 53:10", pp. 228–233. On his emendation to דֻּכְּאוֹ "humiliated", see
3.10.13. n. 131.
[74] Begrich, *Studien zu Deuterojesaja*, pp. 58; 64.
[75] Driver, "Isaiah 52:13–53:12", pp. 98–101, and Westermann, *Isaiah 40–66*,
p. 254f.

Dahood emends אִם־תָּשִׂים to שִׂימָה אֱמֶת "certainly was (his life) made", with references to the emphatic אֱמֶת in Isa. 42:3 and 43:9,[76] cf. Battenfield and Hermisson.[77]

Müller follows Greßmann's conjecture in 53:10a.[78] Müller regards v.10a and v. 11bβ as duplicates, and also maintains that v. 10ab can be reconstructed by means of v. 10bβ and v. 11aα. Thus, he restores 53:10: וַיהוָה חָפֵץ דַּכְּאוֹ מֵחֲלִי וְחַצִּיל מֵעֲמָל נַפְשׁוֹ.

ii. Scholars Who See Parallels Between Lev. 16 and Isa. 53

Ruppert,[79] Mettinger[80] and Blenkinsopp[81] claim that like the scapegoat, the servant bears the guilt of Israel, which is surmounted through his vicarious "guilt death". Blenkinsopp translates: "If his life is laid down as a guilt offering...", and argues:

> It seems that it was the vocabulary of sacrifice that provided the prophetic author with the means for expressing this discovery about the significance of the Servant's suffering. The most explicit statement is that he served a function analogous to a reparation-or trespass-offering ([אָשָׁם] 53:10a). According to ritual prescription, the [אָשָׁם] was an animal, either a ram without blemish, a lamb, or a goat offered for sacrifice as a means of expiating for certain kinds of voluntary or involuntary sin (Lev 5:1–26 [5:1–6:7]; 7:2; 14:24). The Isaian poet does not state the analogy in formal terms or explore it at length, but it is hinted at elsewhere in the poem in the image of sheep being led to the slaughter (53:7b) and the pouring out of the life-blood (cf. Ps 141:8, the same verb, also with נֶפֶשׁ). The statement that the Servant bore the community's sin also echoes the scapegoat ritual (Lev 16), in which one of the two animals is sacrificed as an atoning sin-offering [חַטָּאת], and the other carries all the community's iniquities into a solitary, literally, "cut-off land"

[76] Dahood, "Phoenician Elements in Isaiah 52:13–53:12", p. 71.

[77] J. R. Battenfield, "Isaiah LII 10: Taking an 'If' out of the Sacrifice of the Servant", *VT* 32 (1982) 485 and Hermisson, "Das vierte Gottesknechtlied im deuterojesajanischen Kontext", p. 8 (ET p. 28): "yet he truly made (אֱמֶת שָׂם) his life the means of wiping out guilt".

[78] Müller, "Ein Vorschlag zu Jes. 53:10f", pp. 377–380.

[79] L. Ruppert, "Schuld und Schuld-lösen nach Jesaja 53" in G. Kaufmann (ed), *Schulderfahrung und Schuldbewältigung: Christen im Umgang mit der Schuld* (SPK, 21; Paderborn, 1982) 21–22; 27–28.

[80] Mettinger, *Farewell to the Servant Songs*, p. 41. Mettinger adds Ezek. 4 as a variation on this idea: the prophet lying a certain number of days on each side thus bearing the sins of the people (vv. 4–6).

[81] Blenkinsopp, *Isaiah 40–55*, p. 351.

אֶרֶץ גְּזֵרָה), recalling the Servant's being cut off from the land of the living (נִגְזַר מֵאֶרֶץ חַיִּים 53:8b).[82]

iii. Scholars Who Regard אָשָׁם as the Core of Isa. 53

Kutsch distinguishes between אָשָׁם as an atonement sacrifice and as a non-sacrificial action removing sin (*Sühneleistung*), cf. 1 Sam. 6:4; 8; 17.[83] According to him, the giving of the life of the Servant effects the atonement.

Fohrer suggests the death of the Servant is equal to a sacrificial offering; the Servant is like a sacrificial animal:

> Seiner Bestimmung nach handelt es sich um das Opfer eines Einzelmenschen, der es durch den Priester darbringen ließ, wenn er sich unwissentlich gegen eines der göttlichen Gebote vergangen hatte. Dabei war der Blutritus, nach dem das Blut des Opfertiers ringsherum an den Altar gesprengt wurde, wohl der wichtigste Akt der Opferhandlung. Auch das Blut des "Knechtes Jhwhs" war bei seiner Hinrichtung vergossen worden, und diese Hinrichtung wird in Jes 53,10 mit der Opfer-handlung gleichgesetzt. Der Knecht war das Opfertier, das Gott als der amtierende Priester "schlug", d. h. schlachtete, da ihm dies "gefiel", d. h. da er den Knecht als opferwürdig annahm.[84]

Janowski regards אָשָׁם "wiping out guilt" (*Schuldtilgung*) as a key term in Isa. 53:10a.[85] He claims that as a part of God's plan, the servant surrenders his life as an אָשָׁם, which is a "wiping out" provided when the guilty realise their guilt and take responsibility for it. Since this is precisely what the exilic community does not do, the servant does it for them.[86] He ascribes the origin of אָשָׁם not to a cultic context, but to "contexts in which…guilt-incurring encroachments and their reparation are the theme [cf. Gen. 26:10, 1 Sam. 6:3–4, 8:17]".[87] In contrast to offering חַטָּאת "sin", the term אָשָׁם relates to conscious transgression

---

[82] Blenkinsopp, *Isaiah 40–55*, p. 351.
[83] Kutsch, *Sein Leiden und Tod – unser Heil*, pp. 32–33. He translates the half-line: "…'er aber setzte' sein Leben als Sühneleistung ein."
[84] G. Fohrer, "Stellvertretung und Schuldopfer in Jes 52,13–53,12" in G. Fohrer, *Studien zu alttestamentlichen Texten und Themen (1966–1972)* (BZAW, 155; Berlin: W. de Gruyter, 1981) 41.
[85] Janowski, "Er trug unsere Sünden", p. 43 (ET p. 69).
[86] Janowski, "Er trug unsere Sünden", p. 43 (ET p. 69).
[87] Janowski, "Er trug unsere Sünden", p. 43. The quotation is taken from ET pp. 68–69.

or error, according to Janowski. In v. 10, אָשָׁם explains the servant's surrendering of his life as a wiping out of guilt:

> Israel, which is in no position to take over the obligation arising from its guilt [*Schuldverpflichtung*], must be released from this obligation to have a future. This liberation comes from an innocent one who surrenders his life according to YHWH's "plan" (v. 10a, b) and as a consequence of his own ministry (vv. 7–9). "Surrender of *one's own life* as a means of wiping out guilt" [*Schuldtilgung*] is therefore identical with "taking over the consequences of *others actions*".[88]

Also Hägglund regards the interpretation of אִם־תָּשִׂים אָשָׁם נַפְשׁוֹ as "of great significance for the whole understanding of the servant's work",[89] and offers the following translation: "if his life is made to guilt." He argues that "[t]he term אָשָׁם should neither be understood against its priestly background in Lev 5, nor should it be seen as a compensatory payment".[90]

iv. Scholars Who Regard the Half-line as Untranslatable

The untranslatability of אִם־תָּשִׂים אָשָׁם נַפְשׁוֹ in Isa. 53:10 is most clearly expressed by Orlinsky:

> The expression…in the first part of the verse is both of uncertain meaning and corrupt – and this is any interpretation of the verse as a whole, so that the translators and commentators render this passage on the basis of emendation, whether implicit or explicit. None of these translations may be used for any theory.[91]

Whybray comments that the participle אִם has either a temporal or a conditional sense ("when" or "if"); there are no cases in which אִם with the imperfect refers to a past event.[92] He concludes:

---

[88] Janowski, "Er trug unsere Sünden", p. 43. The quotation is taken from ET p. 69, his italics. Cf. 2.2.4. n. 94.

[89] Hägglund, *Isaiah 53 in the Light of Homecoming after Exile*, p. 67.

[90] Hägglund, *Isaiah 53 in the Light of Homecoming after Exile*, p. 73.

[91] Orlinsky, *The So-Called "Servant of the Lord" and "Suffering Servant" in Second Isaiah*, p. 61, n. 1.

[92] Whybray, *Thanksgiving for a Liberated Prophet*, p. 65. He claims further:
But to put the supposed "guilt-offering" of the Servant in the future or present…is to make nonsense of the thought of the passage. Whatever it is that the Servant, according to this chapter, does for those who call themselves "we", it has already been done and belongs to the past.

> The whole line (...) presents many difficulties...It is sufficient to con-
> clude, especially in view of the remarkable possibilities of metathesis,
> haplography and dittography which this sequence of letters must have
> presented to a succession of scribes, that the text is so uncertain that
> 53:10 cannot properly be used to support any theory of the vicarious
> suffering of the servant.[93]

I regard the half-line as so corrupt that it is impossible to render a
proper translation.

---

[93] Whybray, *Thanksgiving for a Liberated Prophet*, p. 66.

APPENDIX 7
צַדִּיק IN 53:11

צַדִּיק has been explained as:

i. An adverb: according to Reicke, the servant justifies or vindicates "righteously".[94]

ii. An adjective describing the servant: "my righteous servant". Usually in Hebrew, the adjective follows the noun, but it might also be read as a noun, as "the righteous one, (who is) my servant" or "my servant, (who is) righteous".[95]

iii. Several scholars suggest that צַדִּיק should be deleted as a dittography, e.g. Gelston[96] and Hermisson[97] (cf. Whybray and Blenkinsopp below). The repetition of the root צדק in 53:11b is rendered in all the versions and might be explained as a word play. Reicke explains יַצְדִּיק צַדִּיק as *figura etymologica*, where "a denominative verb is supplemented by the noun from which it is derived, to secure a marked accuracy".[98]

The root צדק has been given both an ethical and a forensic meaning. Additionally, the verb has been interpreted as transitive, intransitive and external hi:

For rhythmical and grammatical reasons, Driver restores the text by placing צַדִּיק "righteous" before יַצְדִּיק as צֶדֶק "righteousness", which implies that the verb gains an object parallel to the "restored" אוֹר in the parallel clause.[99] After his restorations, he translates v. 11: "After his pains he shall be flooded with light, through his humiliation he shall win full justification; so shall my servant justify many, himself bearing the penalty for their guilt".

---

[94] Reicke, "The Knowledge of the Suffering Servant", pp. 189–190.

[95] Waltke and O'Connor, *An Introduction to Biblical Hebrew Syntax*, § 11.4.3b. GKC §132b, explains this relation as appositional, with the attribute preceding the noun.

[96] Gelston, "Some Notes on Second Isaiah", pp. 517–527.

[97] Hermisson, "Das vierte Gottesknechtlied im deuterojesajanischen Kontext", p. 8, n. 39 (ET p. 28, n. 39).

[98] Reicke, "The Knowledge of the Suffering Servant", p. 190.

[99] Driver, "Isaiah 52:13–53:12", p. 101.

Muilenburg interprets יַצְדִּיק as having forensic connotations of "to be accounted righteous": "The primary meaning is of acquittal; the many are declared innocent even though they were in reality guilty".[100] Blenkinsopp translates "By his knowledge my servant will vindicate the many", with the following explanation: "Omitting [צַדִּיק], which overburdens the verse and was either inserted by error on account of the similar [יַצְדִּיק] or by a scribe who wished to identify the [עֶבֶד] with the [צַדִּיק] in Isa. 57:1."[101] Oswalt translates "The Righteous One, my Servant, will justify many...", and interprets "righteousness" as a synonym for deliverance from Isa. 40 onwards.[102] Regarding 53:11b, he claims: "This man is the Deliverer who fulfills all the promises of deliverance for the people."[103]

North translates "[he] shall bring righteousness to many", adding: "[T]here is no need... to invoke the Pauline and Lutheran Protestant doctrine of justification by faith."[104] Whybray also reads צַדִּיק as an internal hi. and comments that "no attempt to elucidate them can be regarded as more than tentative".[105] In another study, he also claims:

> If יצדיק ל means "act righteously", ל indicates the indirect object and לרבים means "for the many" or "in relation to the many", which makes adequate sense. If יצדיק means "brought to a state of salvation", ל here indicates the direct object. This usage in biblical Hebrew is almost entirely post-exilic, though its occurrence in the sixth century BC cannot be ruled out as impossible. לרבים therefore perhaps makes the former interpretation of יצדיק slightly more probable than the latter, but cannot be said to be decisive.[106]

Also Westermann reads יַצְדִּיק as an internal hi., and translates 53:11b as: "As a righteous one my servant shall justify many",[107] as well as Reicke: "[T]he servant proves to be truly righteous to the advantage of the multitude".[108] Janowski translates "By his knowledge (of God) the

---

[100] Muilenburg, "The Book of Isaiah: Chapters 40–66", p. 630.
[101] Blenkinsopp, *Isaiah 40–55*, pp. 346; 348.
[102] Oswalt, *The Book of Isaiah: Chapters 40–66*, pp. 399; 404.
[103] Oswalt, *The Book of Isaiah: Chapters 40–66*, p. 404. Cf. Koole, *Isaiah III. Vol. 2*, p. 327, and Ruppert, "'Mein Knecht, der Gerechte, macht die Vielen gerecht, und ihre Verschuldungen-er trägt sie'".
[104] North, *The Second Isaiah*, p. 244.
[105] Whybray, *Isaiah 40–66*, pp. 180–181.
[106] Whybray, *Thanksgiving for a Liberated Prophet*, p. 71, n. 176.
[107] Westermann, *Isaiah 40–66*, pp. 255; 267–268.
[108] Reicke, "The Knowledge of the Suffering Servant", pp. 188–190.

righteous one, my Servant, will justify the many",[109] while Steck does not offer a translation of Isa. 53:11, while his interpretation is similar to Janowski's.[110]

Dahood: "MT [יַצְדִּיק צַדִּיק עַבְדִּי] yields sense when [צַדִּיק] is interpreted as a divine appellative, and [עַבְדִּי] parsed as the direct object with the third person suffix-y, precisely as in 52:13 [הִנֵּה יַשְׂכִּיל עַבְדִּי]."[111] Thus, he renders the half-line: "But the Just One will vindicate his servant".[112]

For an overview of the discussion, also in relation to the LXX, see Sapp.[113]

[109] Janowski, "Er Trug unsere Sünden", p. 33, n. 20 (ET p. 56, n. 20).

[110] Steck, "Aspekte des Gottesknechts in Jes. 52,13–53,12", p. 38. Hermisson, "Das vierte Gottesknechtlied im deuterojesajanischen Kontext", p. 8 (ET p. 28) translates "my servant shall make righteous the many" without further comment. In his own words, Hermisson just "passe[es] over the somewhat complicated exegesis of the last two verses…" and claims that "the result is very simple" (p. 19, ET p. 41).

[111] Dahood, "Phoenician Elements in Isaiah 52:13–53:12", p. 72.

[112] Dahood, "Phoenician Elements in Isaiah 52:13–53:12", p. 72.

[113] Sapp, "The LXX, 1QIsa, and MT Versions of Isaiah 53 and the Christian Doctrine of Atonement", pp. 173–176.

APPENDIX 8

יַפְגִּיעַ לֹ IN 53:12

i. "Intercede"

Thelle has categorised all occurrences of פגע in BH, in which the larg-
est category consist of verses bearing the meaning "fall upon someone,
to kill or inflict violence".[114] She places Isa. 53:12 in the same category
as do most exegetes: "plead", "beg", "make entreaty", together with
the other hi. occurrences: Isa. 59:16, Jer. 15:11, 36:25. However, she
comments that there are many problems with the interpretation of
Isa. 53:12.[115] יַפְגִּיעַ לֹ in Isa. 53:12 has almost unanimously been translated as "intercede" and interpreted as an expression for vicarious
suffering, although many comment on the difficulties of this interpretation, cf. Westermann, who translates: "[he] made intercession for
the transgressors", explaining that hi. of פגע with the prep. בְּ "to cause
to light upon" in Isa. 53:6 becomes "to make entreaty", cf. Jer. 36:25.[116]
Westermann continues:

> Used absolutely it means "to intervene", as in Isa. 59:16. This does not
> mean, as some editors imagine, that he made prayers of intercession for
> them, but that with his life, his suffering and his death, he took their
> place and underwent their punishment in their stead

cf. Muilenburg,[117] Kutsch,[118] Hermisson,[119] Clifford,[120] Blenkinsopp[121]
and Koole.[122]

Dahood regards the Qumran rendering a defective hi. and renders
v. 12b as "[he] made entreaty for the rebellious".[123]

Payne comments that neither Torrey nor Driver, in their comments
on the word play in Deutero-Isaiah, attend to the repeated root פגע

---

[114] Thelle, *Ask God*, p. 242.
[115] Thelle, *Ask God*, p. 242. The sixth and last hi occurrence of פגע, Job 36:32, is
unclear.
[116] Westermann, *Isaiah 40–66*, p. 255.
[117] Muilenburg, "The Book of Isaiah: Chapters 40–66", p. 631.
[118] Kutsch, *Sein Leiden und Tod – unser Heil*, p. 14.
[119] Hermisson, "Das vierte Gottesknechtlied im deuterojesajanischen Kontext",
p. 9 (ET p. 29).
[120] Clifford, *Fair Spoken and Persuading*, p. 175.
[121] Blenkinsopp, *Isaiah 40–55*, p. 346.
[122] Koole, *Isaiah III. Vol. 2/Isaiah 49–55*, p. 336.
[123] Dahood, "Phoenician Elements in Isaiah 52:13–53:12", pp. 64; 72–73.

in 53:6; 12.[124] Payne comments: "It is my view that having used the word recently (in verse 6), the writer found it came readily to mind at verse 12, though now in a different sense". Whybray also argues for an intended word play between 53:6 and v. 12:

> Yahweh imposed (הפגיע) upon the Servant a punishment which he did not deserve (verse 6), whereas the Servant יפגיע (interceded) for the sinners (verse 12). The word-play is intended to bring out the contrast between the behaviour of the Servant and his fellows.[125]

ii. "Intervene"

Hägglund argues against the common translation "intercede", and suggest rather "intervene", which he regards as more open and with less theological implications. According to him, this understanding fits better with the context: in Isa. 53, the servant is silent and does not perform any active action.[126]

iii. "Fall upon"

Snaith translates v. 12b as "And-with-reference-to-the-rebels it-was-caused-to light (on him)".[127] He explains:

> We find here no thought of "interceding for" the rebels, and no vicarious suffering in the sense that the Servant suffered in order to save the rebels. The writer is stating the plain fact that the Servant did not deserve the suffering and disaster, and because he did not deserve it, it must necessarily be the case that he will prosper and triumph... It is unfortunate that the English Versions... have "made intercession for" in 53:12, because this phrase involves conscious and deliberate self-sacrifice for others and a pleading with God on their behalf. No one would dream that the same verb (and also the *hiph'il* form) is used in v. 6 and there

---

[124] Payne, "Characteristic Word-Play in 'Second Isaiah'", p. 215, n. 1. Also Ceresko, "The Rhetorical Strategy of the Fourth Servant Song", who mentions most repetitions in Isa. 52:13–53:12, does not comment on this one.

[125] Whybray, *Thanksgiving for a Liberated Prophet*, p. 60. Cf. Raabe, "The Effect of Repetition in the Suffering Servant Song", pp. 78; 80, Bergey, "The Rhetorical Role of Reiteration in the Suffering Servant Poem", pp. 181; 186.

[126] Hägglund, *Isaiah 53 in the Light of Homecoming after Exile*, pp. 80–81, cf. Clines, *I, He, We and They*, p. 14, and Oswalt, *The Book of Isaiah: Chapters 40–66*, pp. 399; 406–407.

[127] Snaith, *Isaiah 40–55*, p. 148.

translated "laid on him". We hold that the verb should be translated in the same way in both cases.[128]

Barré claims that the verb might be ho., which he supports with LXX, and thus he translates v. 12b as: "their transgression was made to fall upon him", cf. his translation of v. 6: "Yet Yahweh caused the iniquity of all of us to fall upon him."[129] I would also emphasise the repetition of words, which is so widespread in our text, and support the same meaning, i.e. that "he" was stricken in both v. 6 and v. 12.

Steck claims that an alleged intercession here would contradict the consistent picture in this text of the servant as silent and passive.[130] He further refers to Elliger, who reads a pass. ni (cf. 1QIsaᵃ), thus rendering: "und für ihre Frevel getroffen war".[131]

---

[128] Snaith, *Isaiah 40–55*, p. 149.
[129] Barré, "Textual and Rhetorical-Critical Observations on the Last Servant Song", pp. 6;27.
[130] Steck, "Aspekte des Gottesknechts in Jes. 52,13–53,12", p. 31, n. 38.
[131] Elliger, "Nochmals textkritisches zu Jes. 53", pp. 143–144.

BIBLIOGRAPHY

Abma, R., *Bonds of Love: Methodic Studies of Prophetic Texts with Marriage Imagery (Isaiah 50:1-3 and 54:1-10, Hosea 1-3, Jeremiah 2-3)* (Studia Semitica Neerlandica; Assen: Van Gorcum, 1999).
——, "Travelling from Babylon to Zion: Location and its Function in Isaiah 49-55", *JSOT* 74 (1997) 3-28.
Ackroyd, P. R., *Exile and Restoration: A Study of Hebrew Thought of the Sixth Century BC* (OTL; London: SCM Press, 1968).
——, "The Meaning of Hebrew דוֹר Considered", *JSS* 13 (1968) 3-10.
——, "Meaning and Exegesis" in P. R. Ackroyd and B. Lindars (eds), *Words and Meanings: Essays Presented to David Winton Thomas* (Cambridge: Cambridge University Press, 1968) 1-14.
——, "An Interpretation of the Babylonian Exile: 2 Kgs 20, Isaiah 38-39", *SJT* 27 (1974) 329-352.
——, "Isaiah i-xii: Presentation of a Prophet" in W. Zimmerli (ed), *International Organization for the Study of the Old Testament: Congress Volume Göttingen 1977* (VTSup, 29; Leiden: E.J. Brill, 1978) 16-48.
Adam, A. K. A. (ed), *Handbook of Postmodern Biblical Interpretation* (St. Louis, Missouri: Chalice Press, 2000).
Adams, J. W., *The Performative Nature and Function of Isaiah 40-55* (London: T. & T. Clark: 2006).
Ahlström, G. W., "Notes on Isaiah 53:8f", *BZ NF* 13 (1969) 95-98.
Aichele, G., et al. (eds), *The Postmodern Bible: The Bible and Culture Collective* (New Haven: Yale University Press, 1995).
Aichele, G., and Phillips, G. A., "Introduction: Exegesis, Eisegesis, Intergesis", *Semeia* 69/70 (1996) 7-18.
Aichele, G., Miscall, P. D., and Walsh, R., "An Elephant in the Room: Historical-Critical and Postmodern Interpretations of the Bible", *JBL* 128 (2009) 383-404.
Albright, W. F., "The High Place in Ancient Palestine", *International Organization for the Study of the Old Testament: Congress Volume Strasbourg 1956* (VTSup, 4; Leiden: E. J. Brill, 1957) 242-258.
Allen, G., *Intertextuality* (The New Critical Idiom; London: Routledge, 2000).
Allen, L. C., *Ezekiel 20-48* (WBC, 28; Dallas: Word Books, 1994).
——, "Isaiah LII 11 and its Echoes", *Vox Evangelica* 1 (1962) 24-28.
——, "Isaiah LIII 2 Again", *VT* 21 (1971) 490.
Alonso Schökel, L., *A Manual of Hebrew Poetics* (Subsidia Biblica, 11; Rome: Editrice Pontificio Istituto Biblico, 1988).
——, "Isaiah" in R. Alter and F. Kermode (eds), *The Literary Guide to the Bible* (London: Fontana Press, 1989) 165-183.
Alter, R., *The Art of Biblical Poetry* (New York: Basic Books, 1985).
Althusser, L., "Ideology and Ideological State Apparatuses (Notes towards an Investigation)" in L. Althusser, *Lenin and Philosophy and Other Essays* (Transl. from the French by B. Brewster. London: New Left Books, 1971) 121-173. First published in *La Pensee*, 1970.
Amador, J. D. H., "Where Could Rhetorical Criticism (Still) Take Us", *CRBS* 7 (1999) 195-222.
Anderson, B. W., "Exodus Typology in Second Isaiah" in B. W. Anderson and W. Harrelson (eds), *Israel's Prophetic Heritage: Essays in Honour of James Muilenburg* (New York: Harper & Brother, 1962) 177-195.

Anderson, F. I., and Freedman, D. N., *Hosea: A New Translation with Introduction and* Commentary (AB, 24; New York: Doubleday, 1980).
——, *Micah: A New Translation with Introduction and* Commentary (AB, 24E; New York: Doubleday, 2000).
Attridge, D., "Language as History/History as Language: Saussure and the Romance of Etymology" in D. Attridge, G. Bennington and R. Young (eds), *Post-Structuralism and the Question of History* (Cambridge: Cambridge University Press, 1987) 183–211.
Bailey, D. P., "Concepts of Stellvertretung in the Interpretation of Isaiah 53" in Bellinger and Farmer, *Jesus and the Suffering Servant*, pp. 223–250.
——, "The Suffering Servant: Recent Tübingen Scholarship on Isaiah 53" in Bellinger and Farmer, *Jesus and the Suffering Servant*, pp. 251–259.
Bakhtin, M. M., *Problems of Dostoevsky's Poetics* (Edited and translated by C. Emerson; introduction by W.C. Booth. Theory and History of Literature, 8; Manchester: Manchester University Press, 1984).
——, "Discourse in the Novel" in M. M. Bakhtin, *The Dialogic Imagination: Four Essays* (Edited by M. Holquist; translated by C. Emerson and M. Holquist. University of Texas Press Slavic Series, 1; Austin: University of Texas Press, 1981) 259–422.
Bal, M., *Narratology: Introduction to the Theory of Narrative* (Toronto: University of Toronto Press, 1997. 2. edition, complete revision of the first edition from 1985).
Baltzer, K., *Deutero-Isaiah* (Hermeneia; Minneapolis: Fortress Press, 2001).
——, "Jes. 52,13: Die 'Erhöhung' des 'Gottes-Knechtes'" in L. Bormann, K. D. Tredici and A. Standhartiger (eds), *Religious Propaganda and Missionary Competition in the New Testament World* (NTSupp, 74; Leiden: E. J. Brill, 1994) 45–56.
Barker, M., *The Risen Lord: The Jesus of History as the Christ of Faith* (Current Issues in Theology; Edinburgh: T. & T. Clark, 1996).
Barr, J., *Old and New in Interpretation: A Study of the Two Testaments* (London: SCM Press, 1966).
——, *Comparative Philology and the Text of the Old Testament* (London: SCM Press, 1983. Reprint, first published: Oxford: Oxford University Press, 1968).
——, *The Semantics of Biblical Language* (London: SCM Press, 1991. Reprint, first published: Oxford: Oxford University Press, 1961).
——, "The Synchronic, the Diachronic and the Historical: A Triangular Relationship?" in J. de Moor (ed), *Synchronic or Diachronic? A Debate on Method in Old Testament Exegesis* (OTS, 34; Leiden: E. J. Brill, 1995) 1–14.
Barré, M. L., "[אֶרֶץ חַיִּים] – 'The Land of the Living'?", *JSOT* 41 (1988) 37–59.
——, "Textual and Rhetorical-Critical Observations on the Last Servant Song (Isa. 52:13–53:12)", *CBQ* 62 (2000) 1–27.
——, "Review: F. Lindström, *Suffering and Sin: Interpretation of Illness in the Individual Complaint Psalms* (ConBOT, 37; Stockholm: Almqvist & Wiksell, 1994)", *RBL* 06/26/2000.
Barrick, W. B., "The Funerary Character of the 'High-Places' in Ancient Palestine: A Reassessment", *VT* 25 (1975) 565–595.
Barstad, H. M., *The Religious Polemics of Amos: Studies in the Preaching of Am 2, 7B-8; 4,1–13; 5, 1–27; 6, 4–7; 8,14* (VTSup, 34; Leiden: E. J. Brill, 1984).
——, *A Way in the Wilderness: The "Second Exodus" in the Message of Second* Isaiah (Journal of Semitic Studies. Monograph Series, 12; Manchester: Manchester University Press, 1989).
——, *The Myth of the Empty Land: A Study in the History and Archaeology of Judah During the "Exilic" Period* (Symbolae Osloenses. Fasc. Suppl., 28; Oslo: Scandinavian University Press, 1996).
——, *The Babylonian Captivity of the Book of Isaiah: "Exilic" Judah and the Provenance of Isaiah 40–55* (The Institute for Comparative Research in Human Culture. Serie B: Skrifter CII; Oslo: Novus Forlag, 1997).

——, "The Future of the 'Servant Songs': Some Reflections on the Relationship of Biblical Scholarship to its own Tradition" in S. E. Balentine and J. Barton (eds), *Language, Theology, and The Bible: Essays in Honour of James Barr* (Oxford: Clarendon Press, 1994) 261–270. Slightly revised and translated version of "Tjenersangene hos Deuterojesaja: Et eksegetisk villspor", *Norsk teologisk tidsskrift* 83 (1982) 235–244.

——, "No Prophets? Recent Developments in Biblical Prophetic Research and Ancient Near Eastern Prophecy" in Davies, *The Prophets*, pp. 106–126.

——, "History and The Hebrew Bible" in L. L. Grabbe (ed), *Can a "History of Israel" Be Written?* (JSOTSup, 245=European Seminar in Historical Methodology, 1; Sheffield: Sheffield Academic Press, 1997) 37–64.

Barthes, R., *Mythologies* (Selected and translated from the French by A. Lavers. London: Vintage, 1972. Original title: *Mythologies*, Paris: Editions du Seuil, 1957).

——, *Image-Music-Text* (Essays selected and translated by S. Heath. London: Fontana Press, 1977).

——, *S/Z* (Translated by R. Miller. Preface by R. Howard. Oxford: Blackwell, 1998. Original title: *S/Z* published in French in 1973 by Éditions du Seuil, Paris).

——, *The Pleasure of the Text* (Oxford: Blackwell, 1990. Translated from the French by R. Miller; with a note on the text by R. Howard. Original title: *Le plaisir du texte*, Paris: Editions du Seuil, 1973).

——, "Introduction to the Structural Analysis of Narratives" in Barthes, *Image-Music-Text*, pp. 79–124.

——, "The Struggle with the Angel: Textual Analysis of Genesis 32:22–32" in Barthes, *Image-Music-Text*, pp. 125–141.

——, "The Death of the Author" in Barthes, *Image-Music-Text*, pp. 142–148.

——, "From Work to Text" in Barthes, *Image-Music-Text*, pp. 155–164.

——, "Theory of the Text" in Young, *Untying the Text*, pp. 32–47.

Barton, J., *Reading the Old Testament: Method in Biblical Study* (London: Darton, Longman and Todd, 1996. 2. rev. ed. First published: London: Darton, Longman and Todd Ltd., 1984).

——, "Natural Law and Poetic Justice in the Old Testament", *JTS* 30 (1979) 1–14.

——, "Classifying Biblical Criticism", *JSOT* 29 (1984) 19–35.

Battenfield, J. R., "Isaiah LII 10: Taking an 'If' out of the Sacrifice of the Servant", *VT* 32 (1982) 485.

Bauman, R., *A World of Others' Words: Cross-Cultural Perspectives in Intertextuality* (London: Blackwell, 2004).

Baumann, G., "Prophetic Objections to YHWH as the Violent Husband of Israel: Reinterpretations of the Prophetic Marriage Metaphor in Second Isaiah (Isaiah 40–55)" in Brenner, *Prophets and Daniel*, pp. 88–120.

Baumgartner, W., *Die Klagegedichte des Jeremia* (BZAW, 32; Giessen: Alfred Töpelmann, 1917).

Beal, T. K., "Ideology and Intertextuality: Surplus of Meanings and Controlling the Means of Production" in Fewell, *Reading Between Texts*, pp. 27–39

Becking, B., and Korpel, M. C. A. (eds), *The Crisis of Israelite Religion: Transformation of Religious Tradition in Exilic and Post-Exilic Times* (OTS, 42; Leiden: E. J. Brill, 1999).

Begg, C. T., "Zedekiah and the Servant", *ETL* 62 (1986) 393–398.

——, "Babylon in the Book of Isaiah" in Vermeylen, *The Book of Isaiah*, pp. 121–125.

Begrich, J., *Studien zu Deuterojesaja* (TBü, 20; München, Chr. Kaiser Verlag, 1969).

——, "Das priesterliche Heilsorakel", *ZAW* 11 (1934) 81–92.

Bellinger Jr., W. H., and Farmer, W. R. (eds), *Jesus and the Suffering Servant: Isaiah and Christian Origins* (Harrisburg: Trinity Press, 1998).

Ben-Zvi, E., "The Prophetic Book: A Key Form of Prophetic Literature" in M. A. Sweeney and E. Ben-Zvi (eds), *The Changing Face of Form Criticism for the Twenty-First Century* (Grand Rapids: Eerdmans, 2003) 276–297.

Bentzen, A., *King and Messiah* (Oxford: Blackwell, 1970).

Benveniste, E., *Problems in General Linguistics* (Miami Linguistic Series, 8; Coral Gables: University of Miami Press, 1971. Translated by M. E. Meek. Original title: *Problèmes de linguistique générale*, Paris, 1966).

Berges, U., *Das Buch Jesaja: Komposition und Endgestalt* (Herders Biblische Studien, 16; Freiburg: Herder, 1998).

——, "Personifications and Prophetic Voices of Zion in Isaiah and Beyond" in de Moor, *The Elusive Prophet*, pp. 54–82.

Bergey, R. L., "The Rhetorical Role of Reiteration in the Suffering Servant Poem (Isa. 52:13–53:12)", *JETS* 40 (1997) 177–188.

Berkhofer Jr., R. F., *Beyond the Great Story: History as Text and Discourse* (Cambridge, MA: Belknap Press of Harvard University Press, 1995).

Berlin, A., *The Dynamics of Biblical Parallelism* (Bloomington: Indiana University Press, 1985).

——, *Lamentations: A Commentary* (OTL; Louisville, KY: Westminster/John Knox Press, 2002).

Beuken, W. A. M., "Isaiah 54: The Multiple Identity of the Person Addressed" in J. Barr (ed), *Language and Meaning: Studies in Hebrew Language and Biblical Exegesis* (OTS, 19; Leiden: E. J. Brill, 1974) 29–70.

Biddle, M. E., "The Figure of Lady Jerusalem: Identification, Deification and Personification of Cities in the Ancient Near East" in K. Lawson Younger Jr., W. W. Hallo and B. F. Batto (eds), *The Biblical Canon in Comparative Perspective* (Scripture in Context, IV; Lewiston, NY: Edwin Mellem Press, 1991) 173–187.

——, "Lady Zions Alter Egos: Isaiah 47:1–15 and 57:6–13 as Structural Counterparts" in Melugin and Sweeney, *New Visions of Isaiah*, pp. 124–139.

Blau, J., "Über Homonyme und angeblich Homonyme Wurzeln II", *VT* 7 (1957) 98–102.

Blenkinsopp, J., *A History of Prophecy in Israel: From the Settlement in the Land to the Hellenistic Period* (Philadelphia: Westminster Press, 1983).

——, *Isaiah 1–39: A New Translation with Introduction and Commentary* (AB, 19; New York: Doubleday, 2000).

——, *Isaiah 40–55: A New Translation with Introduction and Commentary* (AB, 19A; New York: Doubleday, 2002).

——, *Opening the Sealed Book: Interpretations of the Book of Isaiah in Late Antiquity* (Grand Rapids: Eerdmans, 2006).

——, "Second Isaiah-Prophet of Universalism", *JSOT* 41 (1988) 83–103.

Block, D. I., *The Book of Ezekiel. Chapters 25–48* (NICOT; Grand Rapids: Eerdmans, 1998).

Boadt, L., "Intentional Alliteration in Second Isaiah", *CBQ* 45 (1983) 353–363.

Booij, T., "Negotiation in Isaiah 43:22–24", *ZAW* 94 (1982) 390–400.

Bond, S. L., "What, Me Suffer? Women's Suspicions and the Servant Songs: Lectionary Readings for Epiphany, Year A.", *Quarterly Review* 18 (1998) 299–317.

Bozak, B. A., *Life 'Anew': A Literary-Theological Study of Jer. 30–31* (AnBib, 122; Rome: Editrice Pontificio Istituto Biblico, 1991).

Brenner, A., (ed), *A Feminist Companion to the Latter Prophets* (A Feminist Companion to the Bible, 8; Sheffield: JSOT Press, 1995).

—— (ed), *Prophets and Daniel* (A Feminist Companion to the Bible, Second Series, 8; Sheffield: Sheffield Academic Press, 2001).

——, "Identifying the Speaker-in-the-Text and the Reader's Location in the Prophetic Texts: The Case of Isaiah 50" in A. Brenner and C. Fontaine (eds), *A Feminist Companion to Reading the Bible: Approaches, Methods and Strategies* (Sheffield: Sheffield Academic Press, 1997) 136–150.

Breslauer, S. D., "Power, Compassion, and the Servant of the Lord in Second Isaiah", *Encounter* 48 (1987) 163–178.

Brett, M. G. (ed), *Ethnicity and the Bible* (Biblical Interpretation Series, 19; Leiden: E. J. Brill, 1996).

——, "Nationalism and the Hebrew Bible" in J. W. Rogerson, M. Davies and M. D. Carroll (eds), *The Bible in Ethics: The Second Sheffield Colloquium* (JSOTSup, 207; Sheffield: Sheffield Academic Press, 1995) 136–163.

——, "Interpreting Ethnicity: Method, Hermeneutics, Ethics" in Brett, *Ethnicity and the Bible*, pp. 3–22.

Brooks, P., *Reading for the Plot: Design and Intention in Narrative* (Cambridge, MA: Harvard University Press, 1998).

Broyles, C. C., and Evans, C. A. (eds), *Writing and Reading the Scroll of Isaiah: Studies of an Interpretive Tradition. Volumes 1–2* (VTSup 70, 2; Leiden: E. J. Brill, 1997).

Brueggemann, W., *Isaiah 40–66* (Westminster Bible Companion; Louisville, KY: Westminster/John Knox, 1998).

——, "The 'Uncared for' Now Cared for (Jer. 30:12–17): A Methodological Consideration", *JBL* 104 (1985) 419–428.

Burnett, F. W., "Historiography" in Adam, *Handbook of Postmodern Biblical Interpretation*, pp. 106–112.

Calderone, P. J., "HDL-II in Poetic Texts", *CBQ* 23 (1961) 451–460.

——, "Supplementary Note on HDL-II", *CBQ* 24 (1962) 412–419.

Carr, D. M., "Reaching for Unity in Isaiah", *JSOT* 57 (1993) 61–80.

——, "Reading Isaiah from Beginning (Isaiah 1) to End (Isaiah 65–66): Multiple Modern Possibilities" in Melugin and Sweeney, *New Visions of Isaiah*, pp. 188–218.

——, "What Can We Say about the Tradition History of Isaiah? A Response to Christopher Seitz's *Zion's Final Destiny*" (SBLSP, 31; Atlanta: Scholars Press, 1992) 583–597.

Carroll, R. P., *Jeremiah – A Commentary* (OTL; London: SCM Press, 1986).

——, *Jeremiah* (OTG; Sheffield: JSOT Press, 1989).

——, "Prophecy and Society" in R. E. Clements (ed), *The World of Ancient Israel* (Cambridge: Cambridge University Press, 1991) 203–225.

——, "The Myth of the Empty Land", *Semeia* 59 (1992) 79–93.

——, "Surplus of Meaning and the Conflict of Interpretations: A Dodecade of Jeremiah Studies (1984–1995)", *CRBS* 4 (1996) 115–159.

——, "Poets No Prophets: A Response to 'Prophets through the Looking Glass'" in Davies, *The Prophets*, pp. 43–49.

——, "Deportation and Diasporic Discourses in the Prophetic Literature" in J. M. Scott (ed), *Exile: Old Testament, Jewish, and Christian Conceptions* (Supplements to the Journal for the Study of Judaism, 56; Leiden: E. J. Brill, 1997) 63–85.

——, "Blindsight and the Vision Thing: Blindness and Insight in the Book of Isaiah" in Broyles and Evans, *Writing and Reading the Scroll of Isaiah. Vol. 1*, pp. 79–93.

——, "The Book of J: Intertextuality and Ideological Criticism" in A. R. P. Diamond, K. M. O'Connor and L. Stulmann (eds), *Troubling Jeremiah* (JSOTSup, 260; Sheffield: Sheffield Academic Press, 1999) 220–243.

——, "Century's End: Jeremiah Studies at the Beginning of the Third Millenium", *CRBS* 8 (2000) 18–58.

Ceresko, A. R., "The Rhetorical Strategy of the Fourth Servant Song (Isaiah 52:13–53:12): Poetry and the Exodus-New Exodus", CBQ 56 (1994) 42–55.

Chatman, S., *Story and Discourse: Narrative Structure in Fiction and Film* (Ithaca, NY: Cornell University Press, 1989. First published: Ithaca: Cornell University Press, 1978).

Childs, B. S., *Isaiah: A Commentary* (OTL; Louisville, KY: Westminster/John Knox Press, 2001).

——, *The Struggle to Understand Isaiah as Christian Scripture* (Grand Rapids: Eerdmans, 2004).

Christensen, D. L., "Nations", *ABD* 4 (1992) 1037–1049.

Clayton, J., and Rothstein, E., "Figures in the Corpus: Theories of Influence and Inter-textuality" in J. Clayton and E. Rothstein (eds), *Influence and Intertextuality in Literary History* (Wisconsin: University of Wisconsin Press, 1991) 3–36.

Clements, R. E., *A Century of Old Testament Study* (Guildford: Lutterworth Press, 1983).

Clifford, R. J., *Fair Spoken and Persuading: An Interpretation of Second Isaiah* (Theological Inquieries; New York: Paulist Press, 1984).

Clines, D. J. A., *I, He, We, and They: A Literary Approach to Isaiah 53* (JSOTSup, 1; Sheffield: JSOT Press, 1983).

——, *Job 1–20* (WBC, 17; Dallas: Word Books, 1989).

——, *The Sheffield Manual for Authors and Editors in Biblical Studies* (Sheffield: Sheffield Academic Press, 1997).

——, Fowl, S. E. and Porter, S. E., (eds), *The Bible in Three Dimensions: Essays in Celebration of Forty Years of Biblical Studies in the University of Sheffield* (JSOTSup, 87; Sheffield: JSOT Press, 1990).

Coetzee, J. H., "The 'Song of Hezekiah' (Isaiah 38:9–20): A Doxology of Judgement from the Exilic Period", *Old Testament Essays* 2/3 (1989) 13–26.

Cohan, S., and Shires, L. M., *Telling Stories: A Theoretical Analysis of Narrative Fiction* (New Accents; London: Routledge, 1997).

Collins, A. Y., "The Suffering Servant: Isaiah Chapter 53 as a Christian Text" in R. Brooks and J. J. Collins. (eds), *Hebrew Bible or Old Testament? Studying the Bible in Judaism and Christianity* (Christianity and Judaism in Antiquity, 5; Notre Dame: University of Notre Dame Press, 1990) 201–206.

Collins, J. J., *The Bible after Babel: Historical Criticism in a Postmodern Age* (Grand Rapids: Eerdmans, 2005).

——, "The Suffering Servant: Scapegoat or Example?", *Proceedings of the Irish Biblical Association* 4 (1980) 59–67.

Conrad, E. W., *Reading Isaiah* (Overtures to Biblical Theology, 27; Minneapolis: Fortress Press, 1991).

——, "The 'Fear not' Oracles in Second Isaiah", *VT* 34 (1984) 129–152.

——, "Prophet, Redactor and Audience: Reforming the Notion of Isaiah's Formation" in Melugin and Sweeney, *New Visions of Isaiah*, pp. 142–160.

Conroy, C., "The 'Four Servant Poems' in Second Isaiah in Light of Recent Redaction-Historical Studies" in C. McCarthy and J. F. Healey (eds), *Biblical and Near Eastern Essays: Essays in Honour of Kevin J. Cathcart* (JSOTSup, 375; Sheffield: Continuum, 2004) 80–94.

Cover, R. C., "Sin, Sinners (OT)", *ABD* 6 (1992) 31–40.

Craigie, P. C., Kelley, P. H., and Drinkard Jr., J. F., *Jeremiah 1–25* (WBC, 26; Dallas: Word Books, 1991).

——, *Psalms 1–50* (WBC, 19; Waco, TX: World Books, 1983).

Croatto, J. S., "Exegesis of Second Isaiah from the Perspective of the Oppressed; Paths to Reflection" in F. F. Segovia and M. A. Tolbert (eds), *Reading From This Place 2: Social Location and Biblical Interpretation in Global Perspective* (Minneapolis: Fortress Press, 1995) 219–236.

Croft, S. J. L., *The Identity of the Individual in the Psalms* (JSOTSup, 44; Sheffield: JSOT Press, 1987).

Cross, F. M., "The Council of Yahweh in Second Isaiah", *JNES* 12 (1953) 274–277.

Culler, C., *Structuralist Poetics: Structuralism, Linguistics and the Study of Literature* (London: Routledge, 1975).

——, *Ferdinand de Saussure* (Ithaca, NY: Cornell University Press, 1986. Rev. ed. First published: London: Fontana, 1976).

——, *The Pursuit of Signs: Semiotics, Literature, Deconstruction* (London: Routledge, 1992. First published: London: Routledge and Kenan Paul, 1981).

——, "Preface" in F. de Saussure, *Course in General Linguistics*, pp. xi–xxv.

Culley, R. C., and Overholt, T. W. (eds), *Anthropological Perspectives on Old Testament Prophecy* (Semeia, 21; Chico: Scholars Press, 1982).

Culley, R. C., "Psalm 88 Among the Complaints" in L. Eslinger and G. Taylor (eds), *Ascribe to the Lord* (JSOTSup, 67; Sheffield: JSOT Press, 1988) 289–302.

Currie, M., *Postmodern Narrative Theory* (Transitions; Hampshire: Macmillan, 1998).

Dahood, M. J., "Phoenician Elements in Isaiah 52:13–53:12" in H. Goedicke (ed), *Near Eastern Studies in Honor of William Foxwell Albright* (Baltimore: Johns Hopkins, 1971) 63–73.

——, "Isaiah 53,8–12 and Massoretic Misconstructions", *Bib* 63 (1982) 566–570.

Darr, K. P., *Isaiah's Vision and the Family of God* (Literary Currents in Biblical Interpretation; Louisville, KY: Westminster/John Knox Press, 1994).

——, "Isaiah's Vision and the Rhetoric of Rebellion" (SBLSP, 33; Atlanta: Scholars Press, 1994) 847–882.

——, "Ezekiel Among the Critics", *CRBS* 2 (1994) 9–24.

——, "Two Unifying Female Images in the Book of Isaiah" in Hopfe, *Uncovering Ancient Stones*, pp. 17–30.

Davies, G. I., "Etymology of [הִשְׁתַּחֲוָה]", *VT* 29 (1979) 493–495.

——, "The Destiny of the Nations in the Book of Isaiah" in Vermeylen, *The Book of Isaiah*, pp. 93–120.

Davies, P. R., and Clines, D. J. A. (eds), *Among the Prophets: Language, Image and Structure in the Prophetic Writing* (JSOTSup, 144; Sheffield: JSOT Press, 1993).

Davies, P. R. (ed), *The Prophets* (Biblical Seminar, 42; Sheffield: Sheffield Academic Press, 1996).

——, *In Search of "Ancient Israel"* (JSOTSup, 148; Sheffield: JSOT Press, 1992).

——, "Do Old Testament Studies Need A Dictionary?" in Clines, Fowl and Porter, *The Bible in Three Dimensions*, pp. 321–335.

——, "'Pen of Iron, Point of Diamond' (Jer. 17:1): Prophecy as Writing" in E. Ben-Zvi and M. H. Floyd (eds), *Writings and Speech in Israelite and Ancient Near Eastern Prophecy* (SBLSS, 10; Atlanta: SBL, 2000) 65–81.

Day, J., *Psalms* (OTG; Sheffield: JSOT Press, 1990).

——, "[דַּעַת] Humiliation in Isaiah LIII 11 in the Light of Isaiah LIII 3 and Daniel XII 4, and the Oldest Known Interpretation of the Suffering Servant", *VT* 30 (1980) 97–103.

de Man, P., *The Resistance to Theory* (Foreword by W. Godzich. Theory and History of Literature, 33; Minneapolis: University of Minnesota Press, 1993. First published: Minneapolis: University of Minnesota 1986).

de Moor, J. C. (ed), *The Elusive Prophet: The Prophet as a Historical Person, Literary Character and Anonymous Artist. Papers Read at the Eleventh Joint Meeting of The Society of the Old Testament Study and Het Oudtestamentisch Werkgezelschap in Nederland en België held at Soesterberg 2000* (OTS, 45; Leiden: E. J. Brill, 2001).

de Regt, L. J., "Person Shift in Prophetic Texts. Its Function and its Reading in Ancient and Modern Translations" in de Moor, *The Elusive Prophet*, p. 214–231.

de Saussure, F., *Course in General Linguistics* (Introduction by J. Culler, edited by C. Bally and A. Sechehaye in collaboration with A. Reidlinger, translated from the French by W. Baskin. Glasgow: Collins, 1974. First published: *Cours de linguistique générale*, 1915).

Deist, F. E., "The Prophets: Are We Heading for a Paradigm Switch?" in V. Fritz (ed), *Prophet und Prophetenbuch: Festschrift für Otto Kaiser zum 65. Geburtstag* (BZAW, 185; Berlin: W. de Gruyter, 1989) 1–18.

——, "On 'Synchronic' and 'Diachronic': Wie es eigentlich gewesen", *JNSL* 21 (1995) 37–48.

——, "Contingency, Continuity and Integrity in Historical Understanding: An Old Testament perspective" in V. P. Long (ed), *Israel's Past in Present Research: Essays on Ancient Israelite Historiography* (Sources for Biblical and Theological Study, 7; Winona Lake, IN: Eisenbrauns, 1999) 373–390.

Dell, K. J., "The Misuse of Forms in Amos", *VT* 45 (1995) 45–61.

Delorme, J., "Intertextualities about Mark" in S. Draisma (ed), *Intertextuality in Biblical Writings: Essays in Honor of Bas van Iersel* (Kampen: Kok, 1989) 35–42.

Dempsey, C. J., *The Prophets: A Liberation-Critical Reading* (A Liberation-Critical Reading of the Old Testament; Minneapolis: Fortress Press, 2000).

Derrida, J., *Of Grammatology* (Translated by G. C. Spivak. Baltimore: Johns Hopkins University Press, 1976. Original title: *De la grammatologie*, Paris: Les Editions de minuit, 1967).

——, *Speech and Phenomena and Other Essays on Husserl's Theory of Sign* (Translated, with an introduction, by D. B. Allison; preface by N. Garver. Evanston: Northwestern University Press, 1973. Original title: *La voix et le phénomène*, Paris: Presses Universitaires de France, 1967).

——, "Structure, Sign and Play in the Discourse of the Human Science" in J. Derrida, *Writing and Difference* (Translated, with an Introduction and Additional Notes by A. Bass. London: Routledge, 1995. First published: London: Routlege and Kegan Paul Ltd, 1978) 278–293.

Dobbs-Allsopp, F. W., "Rethinking Historical Criticism", *BibInt* 7 (1999) 235–271.

Driver, S. R., and Neubauer, A., *The Fifty-Third Chapter of Isaiah according to the Jewish Interpreters I–II* (LBS; New York: Ktav, 1969).

Driver, G. R., "Linguistic and Textual Problems: Isaiah I–XXXIX", *JTS* 38 (1937) 36–50.

——, "Once Again Abbreviations", *Textus* 4 (1964) 76–94.

——, "Isaiah 52:13–53:12: 'The Servant of the Lord'" in M. Black and G. Fohrer (eds), *In Memoriam Paul Kahle* (BZAW, 103; Berlin: Alfred Töpelmann, 1968) 90–105.

Duhm, B., *Die Theologie der Propheten als Grundlage für die innere Entwicklungsgeschichte der israelitischen Religion* (Bonn: Marcus, 1875).

——, *Das Buch Jeremia* (KHAT, 11; Freiburg: Mohr, 1901).

——, *Das Buch Jesaia übersetzt und erklärt* (HKAT; Göttingen: Vandenhoeck & Ruprect, 1902, 2. ed. First ed. published in 1892).

——, *Israels Propheten* (Lebensfrage, 26; Tübingen: J. C. B. Mohr {Paul Siebeck} 1916).

Eagleton, T., *Literary Theory. An Introduction: A Study in Marxist Literary Theory* (Cambridge, MA: Blackwell, 1996. 2. edition, first published 1983).

Eaton, J. H., *Kingship and the Psalms* (Biblical Seminar, 3; Sheffield: JSOT Press, 1986).

——, *The Psalms: A Historical and Spiritual Commentary with an Introduction and New Translation* (London: T. & T. Clark, 2005).

Eidevall, G., *Grapes in the Desert: Metaphors, Models, and Themes in Hosea 4–14* (ConBOT, 43; Stockholm: Almqvist & Wiksell, 1996).

Eißfeldt, O., *Der Gottesknecht bei Deuterojesaja (Jes. 40–55) im Lichte der israelitischen Anschauung von Gemeinschaft und Individuum* (Beiträge zur Religionsgeschichte der Altertums, 2; Halle: Niemeyer, 1933).

——, "The Ebed-Jahweh in Isaiah xl–lv", *ExpTim* 44 (1933) 261–268.

Ekblad, E. R., *Isaiah's Servant Poems according to the Septuagint: An Exegetical and Theological Study* (Contributions to Biblical Exegesis and Theology, 23; Leuven: Peeters, 1999).

Elliger, K., *Deuterojesaja in seinem Verhältnis zu Tritojesaja* (BZWANT, 11; Stuttgart: W. Kohlhammer, 1933).

——, *Deuterojesaja. 1. Teilband Jesaja 40,1–45,7* (BK XI/1; Neukirchen-Vluyn: Neukirchener Verlag, 1978).

——, "Jes. 53:10: 'alte crux – neuer Vorschlag'", *MIO* 15 (1969) 228–233.

——, "Nochmals textkritisches zu Jes. 53" in Schreiner, *Wort, Lied und Gottesspruch*, pp. 137–144.

Emerton, J. A., "A Consideration of Some Alleged Meanings of [ידע] in Hebrew", *JSS* 15 (1970) 145–180.

——, "A Further Consideration of D. W. Thomas' Theories About [ידע]", *VT* 41 (1991) 145–163.

Engnell, I., "Till frågan om Ebed Jahve-sångarna och den lidande Messias hos 'Deutero-jesaja'", *SEÅ* 10 (1945) 31–64. Revised translation: "The 'Ebed Yahweh Songs' and the 'Suffering Messiah' in Deutero-Isaiah'", *BJRL* 31 (1948) 54–93.

Fewell, D. N. (ed), *Reading Between Texts: Intertextuality and the Hebrew Bible* (Literary Currents in Biblical Interpretation; Louisville, KY: Westminster/John Knox Press, 1992).

Fish, S., *Is There a Text in This Class? The Authority of Interpretive Communities* (Cambridge, MA: Harvard University Press, 1980).

Fishbane, M. A., *Biblical Interpretation in Ancient Israel* (Oxford: Oxford University Press, 1985).

Flint, P. W., "The Isaiah Scrolls from the Judean Desert" in Broyles and Evans, *Writing and Reading the Scroll of Isaiah. Vol. 2*, pp. 481–498.

Floyd, M. H., and Haak, R. D. (eds), *Prophets, Prophecy, and Prophetic Texts in Second Temple Judaism* (Library of Hebrew Bible/Old Testament Studies, 427; New York: T. & T. Clark, 2006).

Fohrer, G., *Das Buch Jesaja: Kap. 40–66* (ZBK; Zürich: Zwingli Verlag, 1964).

——, "Stellvertretung und Schuldopfer in Jes 52,13–53,12" in G. Fohrer, *Studien zu alttestamentlichen Texten und Themen (1966–1972)* (BZAW, 155; Berlin: W. de Gruyter, 1981) 24–43.

Foucault, M., *The Archaeology of Knowledge and The Discourse on Language* (Translated by A. M. S. Smith. New York: Pantheon Books, 1972. Original title: *L'archéologie du savoir*, first published: Paris: Éditions Gallimard, 1969).

——, *The Order of Things: An Archaeology of the Human* Sciences (Routledge Classics; London: Routledge, 2002. Original title: *Les mots et les choses*, first published: Paris: Éditions Gallimard, 1966).

——, *The History of Sexuality. Vol. 1: An Introduction* (New York: Vintage, 1980. Original title: *Histoire de la sexualité*, first published: Paris: Éditions Gallimard, 1976).

——, "The Order of Discourse" in Young, *Untying the Text*, pp. 52–64.

Franke, C. A., "Is DI 'PC': Does Israel have Most Favored Nation Status? Another Look at 'The Nations' in Deutero-Isaiah" (SBLSP, 38; Atlanta: Scholars Press, 1999) 272–291.

Friedman, E. R., "The Biblical Expression [מַסְתֵּר פָּנִים]", *HAR* 1 (1977) 139–148.

Funkelstein, A., "Basic Types of Christian Anti-Jewish Polemics in the Later Middle Ages", *Viator* 2 (1971) 373–383.

Galambush, J., *Jerusalem in the Book of Ezekiel: The City as YHWH's Wife* (SBLDS, 130; Atlanta: Scholars Press, 1992).

Gelston, A., "Some Notes on Second Isaiah", *VT* 21 (1971) 517–527.

——, "Universalism in Second Isaiah", *JThS* 43 (1992) 377–398.

——, "Review: O. H. Steck, *Gottesknecht und Zion: Gesammelte Aufsätze zu Deuterojesaja* (Forschungen zum Alten Testament, 4; Tübingen: J. C. B. Mohr {Paul Siebeck}, 1992)", *JSS* 40 (1995) 117–118.

Geller, S. A., "A Poetic Analysis of Isaiah 40:1–2", *HTR* 77 (1984) 413–420.

——, "Cleft Sentences with Pleonastic Pronoun: A Syntactic Construction of Biblical Hebrew and Some of its Literary Uses", *JANES* 20 (1991) 15–33.

Genette, G., *Narrative Discourse: An Essay in Method* (Ithaca, NY: Cornell University Press, 1980).

Gerlemann, G., *Studien zur alttestamentlichen Theologie* (Franz Delitzsch-Vorlesungen 1978, Neue Folge; Heidelberg: Lambert Schneider, 1980).

Gesenius, W., Kautzsch, E. and Cowley, A. E., *Gesenius' Hebrew grammar* (2nd English ed. rev. in acc. with the twenty-eight German ed. 1909. Oxford: Clarendon Press, 1963).

Gignillat, N., "Who is Isaiah's Servant? Narrative Identity and Theological Potentiality", *SJT* 61 (2008) 125–136.

Ginsberg, H. L., "The Oldest Interpretation of the Suffering Servant", *VT* 3 (1953) 400–404.

Gitay, Y., *Prophecy and Persuasion: A Study of Isaiah 40–48* (Forum Theologiae Linguisticae, 14; Bonn: Lingustica Biblica, 1981).

——, "Deutero-Isaiah: Oral or Written?", *JBL* 99 (1980) 185–197.

Glover, G. L., *Getting a Word in Edgewise: A New Historicist Interpretation of Deutero-Isaiah's Idol Rhetoric* (Princeton: Princeton Theological Seminary, 1999).

Goldingay, J., and Payne, D., *A Critical and Exegetical Commentary on Isaiah 40–55. Volume I–II* (ICC; London: T. & T. Clark, 2006).

——, *The Message of Isaiah 40–55: A Literary-Theological Commentary* (London: T. & T. Clark, 2005).

——, *Isaiah* (NIBCOT; Massachusetts: Hendrickson, 2001).

——, *God's Prophet, God's Servant: A Study in Jeremiah and Isaiah 40–55* (Exeter: Pater Noster, 1984).

——, "Isaiah 42.18–25", *JSOT* 67 (1995) 43–65.

Goldmann, M. D., "The Root ידע and the Verb 'to know' in Hebrew", *Australian Biblical Review* 3 (1953) 46–47.

Gordon, R. P. (ed), *"The Place is Too Small for Us": The Israelite Prophets in Recent Scholarship* (Sources for Biblical and Theological Study, 5; Winona Lake, IN: Eisenbrauns, 1995).

——, "Isa. LII 2", *VT* 20 (1970) 491–492.

——, "From Mari to Moses: Prophecy at Mari and in Ancient Israel" in McKay and Clines, *Of Prophets' Visions and the Wisdom of Sages*, pp. 63–79.

Gottwald, N. K., *The Hebrew Bible – A Socio-Literary Introduction* (Philadelphia: Fortress Press, 1985).

——, "Social Class and Ideology in Isaiah 40–55: An Eagletonian Reading", *Semeia* 59 (1992) 43–57.

——, "Ideology and Ideologies in Israelite Prophecy" in Reid, *Prophets and Paradigms*, pp. 136–149.

Grabbe, L. L. (ed), *Leading Captivity Captive: "The Exile" as History and Ideology* (JSOTSup, 278= European Seminar in Historical Methodology, 2; Sheffield: Sheffield Academic Press, 1998).

Greimas, A. J., "Elements of a Narrative Grammar", *Diacritics* 7 (1977) 23–40.

Guillaume, A., "Some Readings in the Dead Sea Scroll of Isaiah", *JBL* 76 (1957) 41–42.

Gumperz, J. J., and Levinson, S. C., "Rethinking Linguistic Relativity", *Current Anthropology* 32 (1991) 613–623.

Gunkel, H., *Die Psalmen übersetzt und erklärt* (Göttingen: Vandenhoeck & Ruprecht, 1929).

——, "Knecht Jahwes", *RGG* III (1912) 1540–1543.

Gunn, D. M., and Fewell, D. N., *Narrative in the Hebrew Bible* (The Oxford Bible Series; Oxford: Oxford University Press, 1993).

Haag, E., "Das Opfer des Gottesknechts (Jes. 53:10)", *TTZ* 86 (1977) 81–98.

Haag, H., *Der Gottesknecht bei Deuterojesaja* (Erträge der Forschung, 233; Darmstadt: Wissenschaftliche Buchgesellschaft, 1985).

Hägglund, F., *Isaiah 53 in the Light of Homecoming after Exile* (Forschungen zum Alten Testament, 2. Reihe; 31, Tübingen: J. C. B. Mohr {Paul Siebeck}, 2008).

Hall, S., "Introduction, Who Needs 'Identity'?" in P. de Gay, J. Evans and P. Redman (eds), *Identity: A Reader* (London: SAGE Publications, 2002) 15–30.

Hartley, J. E., *The Book of Job* (NICOT; Grand Rapids: Eerdmans, 1988).

Hegermann, H., *Jesaja 53 in Hexapla, Targum und Peschitta* (BFCT, 2. Reihe, 56. Band; Gütersloh: C. Bertelsmann, 1954).

Heim, K., "The Personification of Jerusalem and the Drama of Her Bereavement in Lamentations" in R. S. Hess and G. J. Wenham (eds), *Zion, City of Our God* (Grand Rapids: Eerdmans, 1999) 129–169.

Heller, J., "Hiding of the Face: A Study of Isa. 53:3", *Communio Viatorum* 1 (1958) 263–266.

Hermisson, H.-J., *Studien zu Prophetie und Weisheit: Gesammelte Aufsätze* (Forschungen zum Alten Testament, 23; Tübingen: J. C. B Mohr {Paul Siebeck}, 1998).

——, "Einheit und Komplexität Deuterojesajas: Probleme der Redaktionsgeschichte von Jes. 40–55" in Hermisson, *Studien zu Prophetie und Weisheit*, pp. 132–157. First published in Vermeylen, *The Book of Isaiah*, pp. 287–312.

——, "Israel und der Gottesknecht bei Deuterojesaja" in Hermisson, *Studien zu Prophetie und Weisheit*, pp. 197–219. First published in *ZTK* 79 (1982) 1–24.

——, "Jeremias dritte Konfessionen (Jer. 15, 10–21)", *ZTK* 96 (1999) 1–21.

——, "Das vierte Gottesknechtslied im deuterojesajanischen Kontext" in Janowski and Stuhlmacher, *Der leidende Gottesknecht*, pp. 1–25, ET H.-J. Hermisson, "The Fourth Servant Song in the Context of Second Isaiah" in Janowski and Stulmacher, *The Suffering Servant*, pp. 16–47.

Hertzberg, H. W., "Die 'Abtrünningen' und die 'Vielen': Ein Beitrag zu Jesaja 53" in A. Kutschke (ed), *Verbannung und Heimkehr. Beiträge zur Geschichte und Theologie Israels im 6. und 5. Jahrhundert v. Chr.: Festschrift für W. Rudolph* (Tübingen: J. C. B. Mohr {Paul Siebeck}, 1961) 97–108.

Hillers, D. R., *Micah* (Hermeneia; Philadelphia: Fortress Press, 1984).

——, *Lamentations* (AB, 7A; New York: Doubleday, 1992).

Hillis Miller, J., "The Two Allegories" in M. W. Bloomfield (ed), *Allegory, Myth, and Symbol* (Harvard English Studies, 9; Cambridge, MA: Harvard University Press, 1982) 355–370.

——, "Narrative" in F. Lentricchia and T. McLaughin (eds), *Critical Terms for Literary Study* (Chicago: University of Chicago Press, 1995) 66–70.

Holladay, C. R., and Hayes, J. H., *Biblical Exegesis: A Beginner's Handbook* (London: SCM Press, 1988).

Holladay, W. L., *Jeremiah 1. A Commentary on the Book of the Prophet Jeremiah. Chapters 1–25* (Hermeneia; Philadelphia: Fortress Press, 1986).

——, *Jeremiah 2. A Commentary on the Book of the Prophet Jeremiah. Chapters 26–52* (Hermeneia; Philadelphia: Fortress Press, 1989).

Hollenberg, D. E., "Nationalism and 'The Nations' in Isaiah 40–55", *VT* 19 (1969) 35–36.

Holter, K., *Second Isaiah's Idol-Fabrication Passages* (Beiträge zur biblischen Exegese und Theologie, 28; Frankfurt am Main: Peter Lang, 1995).

Hooker, M. D., *Jesus and the Servant: The Influence of the Servant Concept of Deutero-Isaiah in the New Testament* (London: SPCK Press, 1959).

Hopfe, L. M. (ed), *Uncovering Ancient Stones: Essays in Memory of H. Neil Richardson* (Winona Lake, IN: Eisenbrauns, 1994).

Hossfeld, F.-L., and Zenger, E., *Psalms 2 – A Commentary* (Hermeneia; Minneapolis: Fortress Press, 2005).

Houtman, C., Prinsloo, W. S., Watson, W. G. E., and Wolters, A., "Editorial preface (I)" in Koole, *Isaiah Part III. Volume 1/Isaiah 40-48*, pp. ix–xi.

Huntington, S., "The Clash of Civilizations?", *Foreign Affairs* 72 (1993) 22–49.

Illman, K.-J., "Psalm 88 – A Lamentation without Answer", *SJOT* 1 (1991) 112–120.

Jacobs, M. R., "Bridging the Times: Trends in Micah Studies since 1985", *CBR* 4 (2006) 293–329.

Jahnow, H., *Das hebräische Leichenlied im Rahmen der Völkerdichtung* (BZAW, 36; Giessen: Alfred Töpelmann, 1923).

Jakobson, R., *Selected Writings III: Poetry of Grammar and Grammar of Poetry* (The Hague: Mouton, 1981).

——, *Language in Literature* (Cambridge, MA: Belknap Press, 1987).

——, "Two Aspects of Language and Two Types of Aphasic Disturbances" in R. Jakobson and M. Halle, *Fundamentals of Language* (Janua Linguarum. Series Minor, 1; The Hague: Mouton, 1971. 2. rev. ed. First edition 1956) 69–96.

Janowski, B., and Stuhlmacher, P. (eds), *Der leidende Gottesknecht: Jesaja 53 und seine Wirkungsgeschichte mit einer Bibliographie zu Jes 53* (Forschungen zum Alten Testament, 14; Tübingen: J. C. B. Mohr {Paul Siebeck}, 1996). ET: B. Janowski and P. Stulmacher (eds), *The Suffering Servant: Isaiah 53 in Jewish and Christian Sources* (Grand Rapids: Eerdmans, 2004).

——, "Vorwort" in Janowski and Stuhlmacher, *Der leidende Gottesknecht*, pp. III–IV. ET: B. Janowski and P. Stuhlmacher, "Preface" in Janowski and Stulmacher, *The Suffering Servant*, pp. vii–viii.

Janowski, B., *Stellvertretung: Alttestamentliche Studien zu einem theologischen Grundbegriff* (Stuttgarter Bibel-Studien, 165; Stuttgart: Katholisches Bibelwerk, 1997).

——, "Er trug unsere Sünden: Jes. 53 und die Dramatik der Stellvertretung" in Janowski and Stuhlmacher, *Der leidende Gottesknecht*, pp. 27–48. ET B. Janowski, "He Bore Our Sins: Isaiah 53 and the Drama of Taking Another's Place" in Janowski and Stulmacher, *The Suffering Servant*, pp. 48–74. First published in German in *ZTK* 90 (1993) 1–24.

Jaworski, A., and Coupland, N., "Editors' Introduction to Part Five" in A. Jaworski and N. Coupland (eds), *The Discourse Reader* (London: Routledge, 1999) 407–414.

Jefferson, A., "Structuralism and Post-Structuralism" in Jefferson and D. Robey (eds), *Modern Literary Theory: A Comparative Introduction* (London: BT Batsford, 1996) 92–121.

Jeppesen, K., "From 'You, my Servant' to 'The Hand of the Lord is with my Servants': A Discussion of Is 40–66", *SJOT* 1 (1990) 113–129.

——, "Mother Zion, Father Servant: A Reading of Isaiah 49–55" in McKay and Clines, *Of Prophets' Visions and the Wisdom of Sages*, pp. 109–125.

Joachimsen, K., "Steck's Five Stories of the Servant in Isaiah lii 13– liii 12, and Beyond", *VT* 57 (2007) 210–224.

Johnston, A., "A Prophetic Vision of an Alternative Community: A Reading of Isa. 40–55" in Hopfe, *Uncovering Ancient Stones*, pp. 31–40.

Johnstone, W., "YD' II, 'Be Humbled, Humiliated'?", *VT* 41 (1991) 49–62.

Jones, G. H., "Abraham and Cyrus: Type and Anti-Type", *VT* 22 (1972) 304–319.

Joüon, P., and Muraoka, T., *A Grammar of Biblical Hebrew* (Subsidia Biblica, 14/II; Rome: Editrice Pontificio Istituto Biblico, 1996).

Kabasele, F. L., and Grey, N., "Isaiah 52:13–53:12: An African Perspective" in Levinson and Levinson, *Return to Babel*, pp. 101–106.

Kaiser, B. B., "Poet as 'Female Impersonation': The Image of Daughter and Zion as Speaker in Biblical Poems of Suffering", *JR* 67 (1987) 164–183.

Kaiser, O., *Der königliche Knecht: Eine traditions-geschichtlich-exegetische Studie über die Ebed-Jahwe-Lieder bei Deuterojesaja* (FRLANT, 70; Göttingen: Vandenhoeck & Ruprecht, 1962).

Kaminsky, J. S., *Corporate Responsibility in the Hebrew Bible* (JSOTSup, 196; Sheffield: Sheffield Academic Press, 1995).

——, *Yet I Loved Jacob: Reclaiming the Biblical Concept of Election* (Nashville: Abingdon Press, 2007).

——, "The Concept of Election and Second Isaiah: Recent Literature", *BTB* 31 (2001) 134–144.

Kasher, R., "The Sitz im Buch of the Story of Hezekiah's Illness and Cure (II Reg 20,1–11; Isa 38,1–22)", *ZAW* 113 (2001) 41–55.

Keel, O., *Feinde und Gottesleugner: Studien zum Image der Widersacher in den Individualpsalmen* (SBM, 7; Stuttgart: Katholisches Bibelwerk GmbH, 1969).

Keown, G. L., Scalise, P. L., and Smothers, T. G., *Jeremiah 26–52* (WBC, 27; Dallas: Word Books, 1995).

Kiesow, K., *Exodustexte im Jesajabuch: Literarkritische und motivgeschichtliche Analysen* (OBO, 24; Fribourg: Éditions Universitaires, 1979).

Kissane, E. J., *The Book of Isaiah: Translated from a Critically Revised Hebrew Text with Commentary* (Dublin: Browne and Nolan, 1941–43).

Knohl, I., *The Messiah Before Jesus: The Suffering Servant of the Dead Sea Scrolls* (California: University of California Press, 2000).

Koch, K., "Gibt es eine Vergeltungs-Dogma", *ZTK* 52 (1955) 1–42.

——, "Der Spruch 'Sein Blut bleibe auf seinem Haupt' und die israelitische Auffassung vom vergossenen Blut", *VT* 12 (1962) 396–416.

Kohn, R. L., "Ezekiel at the Turn of the Century", *CBR* 2 (2003) 9–31.

Komlosh, J., "The Countenance of the Servant of the Lord, Was it Marred?", *JQR* 65 (1974/75) 217–220.

Koole, J. L., *Isaiah. III. Volume 1/Isaiah 40–48* (HCOT; Leuven: Peeters, 1997).

——, *Isaiah III. Volume 2/Isaiah 49–55* (HCOT; Leuven: Peeters, 1998).

Korpel, M. C. A., and Moor, J. C., *The Structure of Classical Hebrew Poetry: Isa. 40–55* (OTS, 41; Leiden: E. J. Brill, 1998).

——, "The Female Servant of the Lord in Isa. 54" in B. Becking and M. Dijkstra (eds), *On Reading Prophetic Texts: Gender-Specific and Related Studies in Memory of Fokkelin van Dijk-Hemmes* (Biblical Interpretation Series, 18; Leiden: E. J. Brill, 1996) 153–167.

Kratz, R. G., *Kyros im Deuterojesaja-Buch: Redaktions-geschichtliche Untersuchungen zu Entstehung und Theologie von Jes 40–55* (Forschungen zum Alten Testament, 1; Tübingen: J. C. B. Mohr {Paul Siebeck}, 1991).

——, "Israel in the Book of Isaiah", *JSOT* 31 (2006) 103–128.

Kraus, H.-J., *Geschichte der historisch-kritischen Erforschung des Alten Testaments* (Neukirchen-Vluyn: Neukirchener Verlag, 1982).

Krause, D., "A Blessing Cursed: The Prophet's Prayer for Barren Womb and Dry Breasts" in Fewell, *Reading Between Texts*, pp. 191–202.

Kreizer, L., "Suffering, Sacrifice and Redemption: Biblical Imagery in Star Trek" in J. E. Porter and D. L. McLaren (eds), *Star Trek and Sacred Ground: Explorations of Star Trek, Religion, and American Culture* (Albany: State University of New York, 1999) 139–163.

Kreuzer, S., "Zur Bedeutung und Etymologie von [השתחוה/השתחוי]ישתחוי", *VT* 35 (1985) 39–60.

Kristeva, J., *Revolution in Poetic Language* (Translated by M. Waller with an Introduction by L. S. Roudiez. New York: Columbia University Press, 1984. Original title: *La revolution du language poètique*, first published: Paris: Éditions du Seuill, 1974).

——, *Desire in Language: A Semiotic Approach to Literature and Art* (Edited by L. S. Roudiez; translated by T. Gora, A. Jardine and L. S. Roudiez. Oxford: Blackwell, 1980).

Kugel, J. L., *The Idea of Biblical Poetry: Parallelism and Its History* (New Haven: Yale University Press, 1981).

Kuhn, T. S., *The Structure of Scientific Revolutions* (Chicago: University of Chicago Press, 1970. 2nd ed, enlarged. 1st ed., Chiacago: University of Chicago, 1962).

Kuntz, J. K., "Engaging the Psalms: Gains and Trends in Recent Research", *CRBS* 2 (1994) 77–106.

——, "Biblical Hebrew Poetry in Recent Research. Part I", *CRBS* 6 (1998) 31–64.

——, "Biblical Hebrew Poetry in Recent Research. Part 2", *CRBS* 7 (1999) 35–79.

——, "The Form, Location, and Function of Rhetorical Questions in Deutero-Isaiah" in Broyles and Evans, *Writing and Reading the Scroll of Isaiah. Vol. 1*, pp. 121–141.

Kustár, Z., *"Durch seine Wunden sind wir geheilt": Eine Untersuchung zur Metaphorik von Israels Krankheit und Heilung im Jesajabuch* (BWANT, 159; Stuttgart: W. Kohlhammer Verlag, 2002).

Kutsch, E., *Sein Leiden und Tod – unser Heil: Eine Exegese von Jesaja 52,13–53,12* (BS, 52; Neukirchen-Vluyn: Neukirchener Verlag, 1967).

Kutscher, E. Y., *The Language and Linguistic Background of the Isaiah Scroll (IQIsa)* (StDJ, 6; Leiden: E. J. Brill, 1974).

Labahn, A., "Metaphor and Intertextuality: 'Daughter of Zion' as a Test Case", *SJOT* 17 (2003) 49–67.

Landy, F., *Hosea* (Readings; Sheffield: Sheffield Academic Press, 1995).

——, "The Construction of the Subject and the Symbolic Order: A Reading of the Last Three Suffering Servant Songs" in Davies and Clines, *Among the Prophets*, pp. 60–71.

Lechte, J., *Julia Kristeva* (London: Routledge, 1990).

Leene, H., *De stem van de knecht als metafoor: Beschouwingen over de compositie van Jesaja 50* (Kampen: Kok, 1980).

Leveen, J., "יזה in ISAIAH LII. 15", *JJS* 7 (1956) 93–94.

Lentricchia, F., *After the New Criticism* (Chicago: University of Chicago Press, 1980).

Levenson, J. D., "The Universal Horizon of Biblical Particularism" in Brett, *Ethnicity and the Bible*, pp. 143–169.

Levinson, P. P., and Levinson, J. R. (eds), *Return to Babel: Global Perspectives on the Bible* (Louisville, KY: Westminster/John Knox Press, 1999).

Lewis, B., "The Roots of Muslim Rage", *The Atlantic Monthly* (September 1990 Issue).

Likins-Fowler, D. G., "Sociological Functions of the Servant in Isaiah 52:13–53:12", *Proceedings-Eastern Great Lakes and Midwest Biblical Societies* 21 (2001) 47–59.

Linafelt, T., "Zion's Cause: The Presentation of Pain in the Book of Lamentations" in T. Linafelt (ed), *Strange Fire: Reading the Bible After the Holocaust* (Biblical Seminar, 71; Sheffield: Sheffield Academic Press, 2000) 267–268.

Lindblom, J., *The Servant Songs in Deutero-Isaiah: A New Attempt to Solve an Old Problem* (Lunds Universitets Årsskrift, N. F. Avd. 1, 47: 5; Lund: C. W. K. Gleerup, 1951).

Lindström, F., *Suffering and Sin: Interpretation of Illness in the Individual Complaint Psalms* (ConBOT, 37; Stockholm: Almqvist & Wiksell, 1994).

Liverani, M., "Nationality and Political Identity", *ABD* 4 (1992) 1031–1037.

Loewe, R., "Prolegomenon" in Driver and Neubauer, *The Fifty-third Chapter of Isaiah according to the Jewish Interpreters I–II*, pp. 1–8.

Lohfink, N., *Option for the Poor: The Basic Principle of Liberation Theology in the Light of the Bible* (Berkeley: BIBAL Press, 1987).

——, "'Israel' in Jes. 49,3" in Schreiner, *Wort, Lied und Gottesspruch*, pp. 217–229.

Lowth, R., *Lectures on the Sacred Poetry of the Hebrews. Vol. I* (The Major Works/ Robert Lowth; London: Routledge/Thoemmes Press, 1995. Translated from the Latin by R. Lowth. Original title: *De sacra poesi Hebraeorum*, London: Printed for J. Johnson, 1787).

Lozada, Jr., F., "Identity" in Adam, *Handbook of Postmodern Biblical Interpretation*, pp. 113–119.

Macintosh, A. A., *Hosea* (ICC; Edinburgh: T. & T. Clark, 1997).

Malamat, A., "The Secret Council and Prophetic Involvement" in R. Liwak and S. Wagner (eds), *Prophetie und geschichtliche Wirklichkeit im alten Israel: Festschrift für Siegfried Hermann zum 65. Geburtstag* (Stuttgart: W. Kohlhammer, 1991) 231–236.

Matheus, F., *Singt dem Herrn ein neues Lied: Die Hymnen Deuterojesajas* (Stuttgarter Bibel-Studien, 141; Stuttgart: Katholisches Bibelwerk, 1990).

Mays, J. L., "Past, Present, and Prospect in Psalm Study" in J. L. Mays, D. L. Petersen and K. H. Richards (eds), *Old Testament Interpretation. Past, Present and Future: Essays in Honour of Gene M. Tucker* (Old Testament Studies; Edinburgh: T. & T. Clark, 1995) 147–156.

McGinnis, C. M., and Tull, P. K. (eds), *"As Those who are Taught": The Interpretation of Isaiah from the LXX to the SBL* (SBLSS, 27; Atlanta: SBL, 2006).

——, "Remembering the Former Things: The History of Interpretation and Critical Scholarship" i McGinnis and Tull, *"As Those who are Taught"*, pp. 1–27.

McKane, W., *A Critical and Exegetical Commentary on Jeremiah* (ICC; Edinburgh: T. & T. Clark, 1986).

——, "The Composition of Jeremiah 30–31" in M. V. Fox, V. A. Hurowitz, A. Hurvitz, M. L. Klein, B. J. Schwartz and N. Shupak (eds), *Texts, Temples, and Traditions: A Tribute to Menaham Haran* (Winona Lake, IN: Eisenbrauns, 1996) 187–194.

McKay, H. A., and Clines, D. J. A. (eds), *Of Prophets' Visions and the Wisdom of Sages: Essays in Honour of R. Norman Whybray* (JSOTSup, 162; Sheffield: JSOT Press, 1993).

McKenzie, J. L., *Second Isaiah: Introduction, Translation, and Notes* (AB, 20; Garden City, NY: Doubleday, 1968).

McLaughlin, J. L., "Review: O. H. Steck, *Gottesknecht und Zion: Gesammelte Aufsätze zu Deuterojesaja* (Forschungen zum Alten Testament, 4; Tübingen: J. C. B. Mohr {Paul Siebeck}, 1992", *JBL* 113 (1994) 712–714.

Melugin, R. F., and Sweeney, M. A. (eds), *New Visions of Isaiah* (JSOTSup, 214; Sheffield: Sheffield Academic Press, 1996).

Melugin, R. F., *The Formation of Isaiah 40–55* (BZAW, 141; Berlin: W. de Gruyter, 1976).

——, "Reading the Book of Isaiah as Christian Scripture" (SBLSP, 35; Atlanta: Scholars Press, 1996) 188–203.

——, "Prophetic Books and the Problem of Historical Reconstruction" in Reid, *Prophets and Paradigms*, pp. 63–78.

——, "Figurative Speech and the Reading of Isaiah 1 as Scripture" in Melugin and Sweeney, *New Visions of Isaiah*, pp. 282–305.

——, "Israel and the Nations in Isa. 40–55" in H. T. C. Sun (ed), *Problems in Biblical Theology: Essays in Honor of Rolf Knierim* (Grand Rapids: Eerdmans: 1997) 249–264.

——, "The Book of Isaiah and the Construction of Meaning" in Broyles and Evans, *Writing and Reading the Scroll of Isaiah. Vol. 1*, pp. 39–55.

——, "Amos in Recent Research", *CRBS* 6 (1998) 65–101.

——, "Isaiah in the Worshipping Community" in M. P. Graham, R. R. Marrs and S. L. McKenzie (eds), *Worship and the Hebrew Bible: Essays in Honour of John T. Willis* (JSOTSup, 284, Sheffield: Sheffield Academic Press, 1999) 244–264.

Mendels, D., *The Rise and Fall of Jewish Nationalism: Jewish and Christian Ethnicity in Ancient Palestine* (AB Reference Library; New York: Doubleday, 1992).

Menn, E. M., "No Ordinary Lament: Relecture and the Identity of the Distressed in Psalm 22", *HTR* 93 (2000) 301–341.

Mesters, C., *The Mission of the People Who Suffer: The Songs of the Servant of God* (Cape Town: Theology Exchange Programme, 1990).

——, "The Servant of Yahweh: The Patient Endurance of the Poor, Mirror of God's Justice" in T. Okure, J. Sobrino and F. Wilfred (eds), *Rethinking Martyrdom* (Concilium, 2003/1; London: SCM Press, 2003) 67–74.

Mettinger, T. N. D., *Farewell to the Servant Songs: A Critical Examination of an Exegetical Axiom* (Scripta Minora. Regiae Societatis Humaniorum Literarum Lundensis, 3; Lund: C. W. K. Gleerup, 1982–1983).

Miller, C. W., "Reading Voices: Personification, Dialogism, and the Reader of Lamentations 1", *BibInt* 9 (2001) 393–408.

——, "The Book of Lamentations in Recent Research", *CBR* 1 (2002) 9–29.

Miller II, R. D., "Yahweh and His Clio: Critical Theory and the Historical Criticism of the Hebrew Bible", *CBR* 4 (2006) 149–168.

Mills, S., *Discourse* (The New Critical Idiom; London: Routledge, 2004).

Mintz, A., "The Rhetoric of Lamentations and the Representation of Catastrophe", *Prooftext* 2 (1982) 1–17.

Miscall, P. D., *Isaiah* (Readings; Sheffield: JSOT Press, 1993).
——, "Isaiah: The Labyrinth of Images", *Semeia* 54 (1992) 103–121.
——, "Isaiah: New Heavens, New Earth, New Book" in Fewell, *Reading Between Texts*, pp. 41–56.
Mitchell, W .J. T. (ed), *On Narrative* (Chicago: Chicago University Press, 1981).
Moon, C. H. S., "Isaiah 52:13–53:12: An Asian Perspective" in Levinson and Levinson, *Return to Babel*, pp. 107–113.
Moore, G. F., "On יזה in Isaiah LII.15", *JBL* 9 (1890) 216–222.
Morgenstern, J., "The Suffering Servant-A New Solution", *VT* 11 (1961) 292–320.
Morris, P. M., "Introduction" in P. M. Morris, *The Bakhtin Reader: Selected Writings of Bakhtin, Medvedev, Volosinov* (Edited by P. Morris, with a glossary compiled by G. Roberts. London: Arnold, 1996) 1–24.
Motyer, J. A., *The Prophecy of Isaiah: An Introduction and Commentary* (Illinois: Intervarsity Press, 1993).
Moyise, S., "Intertextuality and the Study of the Old Testament in the New Testament" in S. Moyise (ed), *The Old Testament in the New Testament: Essays in Honor of J. L. North* (JNTSSup, 198; Sheffield: 2000) 14–41.
Mowinckel, S., *He That Cometh* (Oxford: Blackwell, 1959).
——, "Der Knecht Jahwäs", *NTT* 3 (1921) 1–69.
Muilenburg, J., "The Book of Isaiah: Chapters 40–66", *IB* 5 (Nashville: Abingdon Press, 1956).
Müller, H.-P., "Ein Vorschlag zu Jes. 53:10f", *ZAW* 81 (1969) 378–379.
Müller, W. G., "Interfigurality: A Study on the Interdependence of Literary Figures" in Plett, *Intertextuality*, p. 101–121.
Mulzer, M., "Döderlein und Deuterojesaja", *BN* 66 (1993) 15–22.
Muraoka, T., *Emphatic Words and Structures in the Hebrew Bible* (Jerusalem: Magnes Press, 1985).
Murphy, R. E., "The Personification of Wisdom" in H. G. M. Williamson, J. Day and R. P. Gordon (eds), *Wisdom in Ancient Israel: Essays in Honour of J. A. Emerton* (Cambridge: Cambridge University Press, 1995) 222–233.
Niccacci, A., "Analysing Biblical Hebrew Poetry", *JSOT* 74 (1997) 77–93.
——, *The Syntax of the Verb in Classical Hebrew Prose* (JSOTSup, 86; Sheffield: JSOT Press, 1990).
Newsom, C. A., "Considering Job", *CRBS* 1 (1993) 87–118.
Nicholls, B. J., "The Servant Songs of Isaiah in Dialogue with Muslims", *Evangelical Review of Theology* 20 (1996) 168–177.
Niditch, S., "The Composition of Isaiah 1", *Bib* 61 (1980) 509–529.
Nielsen, K., *There is Hope for a Tree: The Tree as Metaphor in Isaiah* (JSOTSup, 65; Sheffield: JSOT Press, 1989).
——, *Bilderna och Ordet: Om Herrens tjänare och andra bilder i Gamla Testamente* (Örebro: Libris, 1998).
Nissinen, M., (ed), *Prophecy in its Ancient Near Eastern Context: Mesopotamian, Biblical, and Arabian Perspectives* (SBLSS, 13; Atlanta: SBL, 2000).
——, "Prophets and the Divine Council" in U. Hübner and E.-A. Knauf (eds), *Kein Land für sich allein: Studien zum Kulturkontakt in Kanaan, Israel/Palestina und Ebirnari für Manfred Weippert zum 65. Geburtstag* (Göttingen: Universitetsverlag Freiburg, 2002) 4–19.
——, "Introduction" in M. Nissinen (ed), *Prophets and Prophecy in the Ancient Near East* (Writings from the Ancient World, 12; Atlanta: SBL, 2003) 1–11.
North, C. R., *The Suffering Servant in Deutero-Isaiah: An Historical and Critical Study* (London: Oxford University Press, 1948).
——, *The Second Isaiah: Introduction, Translation and Commentary to Chapter XL–LV* (Oxford: Clarendon, 1964).
Nyberg, H. S., "Smärtornas man: En studie till Jes. 52,13–53,12", *SEÅ* 7 (1942) 5–82.

O'Connor, K. M., *The Confessions of Jeremiah: Their Interpretation and Role in Chapters 1–25* (SBLDS, 94; Atlanta: Scholars Press, 1988).

——, "Lamentations" in C. A. Newsom and S. H. Ringe (eds), *The Women's Bible Commentary* (London: SPCK Press, 1992) 178–182.

——, "'Speak Tenderly to Jerusalem': Second Isaiah Reception and Use of Daughter Zion", *Princeton Seminary Bulletin* 20 (1999) 281–294.

O'Kane, M., "Picturing 'The Man of Sorrows': The Passion-filled Afterlives of a Biblical Icon", *Religion and the Arts* 9 (2005) 62–100.

O'Kennedy, D. F., "Healing as/or Forgiveness? The Use of the Term [רפא] in the Book of Hosea", *Old Testament Essays* 14 (2001) 458–474.

Olley, J. W., "'The Many': How is Isa 53,12a to be Understood?", *Bib* 68 (1987) 330–356.

Orlinsky, H. M., *The So-Called "Servant of the Lord" and "Suffering Servant" in Second Isaiah* (VTSup, 14; Leiden: E. J. Brill, 1967).

——, *Essays in Biblical Culture and Bible Translation* (New York: Ktav, 1974).

——, "The So-Called 'Suffering Servant' in Isaiah 53" in H. M. Orlinsky, *Interpreting The Prophetic Tradition: The Goldenson Lectures 1955–1966* (New York: Ktav, 1969) 227–273.

——, "Nationalism – Universalism and Internationalism in Ancient Israel" in Orlinsky, *Essays in Biblical Culture and Bible Translation*, pp. 78–116.

——, "A Covenant of People, A Light of Nations' – a Problem in Biblical Theology" in Orlinsky, *Essays in Biblical Culture and Bible Translation*, pp. 166–186.

Oswalt, J. N., *The Book of Isaiah: Chapters 1–39* (NICOT; Grand Rapids: Eerdmans, 1986).

——, *The Book of Isaiah: Chapters 40–66* (NICOT; Grand Rapids: Eerdmans, 1998).

Overholt, T., *Channels of Prophecy: The Social Dynamics of Prophetic Activity* (Minneapolis: Fortress Press, 1989).

Parry, D. W., and Qimron, E., *The Great Isaiah Scroll (1QIsa): A New Edition* (STDJ, 32; Leiden: E. J. Brill, 1999).

Paul, S. M., *Amos* (Hermeneia; Minneapolis: Fortress Press, 1991).

Paxson, J. J., *The Poetics of Personification* (Literature, Culture, Theory, 6; Cambridge: Cambridge University Press, 1994).

Payne, D. F., "Characteristic Word-Play in 'Second Isaiah': A Reappraisal", *JSS* 12 (1967) 207–229.

——, "Old Testament Exegesis and the Problem of Ambiguity", *ASTI* 5 (1967) 48–68.

Phillips, A., "Double for all her Sins", *ZAW* 94 (1982) 130–132.

Phillips, G. A., "Sign/Text/Différance" in Plett, *Intertextuality*, pp. 78–97.

Pixley, J. V., "Isaiah 52:13–53:12: A Latin American Perspective" in Levinson and Levinson, *Return to Babel*, pp. 95–100.

Plett, H. F. (ed), *Intertextuality* (Research in Text Theory 15; Berlin: W. de Gruyter, 1991).

Polk, T., *The Prophetic Persona: Jeremiah and the Language of the Self* (JSOTSup, 32; Sheffield: JSOT Press, 1984).

Porter, S. E. and Pearson, B. W. R., "Isaiah through Greek Eyes: The Septuagint of Isaiah" in Broyles and Evans, *Writing and Reading the Scroll of Isaiah. Vol. 2*, pp. 531–546.

Porter, S. E., "Two Myths: Corporate Personality and Language/Mentality Determinism", *SJT* 43 (1990) 289–307.

Preuß, H. D., *Deuterojesaja: Eine Einführung in seine Botschaft* (Neukirchen-Vluyn: Neukirchener Verlag, 1976).

Prince, G., *A Grammar of Stories: An Introduction* (De proprietatibus litterarum: Series Minor, 13; The Hague: Mouton, 1973).

——, "Introduction to the Study of the Narratee" in J. P. Tompkins (ed), *Reader-Response Criticism: From Formalism to Post-Structuralism* (Baltimore: Johns Hopkins University Press, 1980) 7–25.

——, "On Narrative Studies and Narrative Genres", *Poetics Today* 11 (1990) 271–282.

Prinsloo, W. S., "Psalm 88: The Gloomiest Psalm?", *Old Testament Essays* 5 (1992) 332–345.

Pulikottil, P., *Transmission of Biblical Texts in Qumran: The Case of the Large Isaiah Scroll (1QISa)*, (JSPSup, 34; Sheffield: Sheffield Academic Press, 2001).

Quinn-Miscall, P. D., *Reading Isaiah: Poetry and Vision* (Louisville, KY: Westminster/ John Knox Press, 2001).

Rae, M., "Scripture and the Divine Economy", *Journal for Theological Interpretation* 1 (2007) 1–21.

Räisänen, H., "The Effective 'History' of the Bible: A Challenge to Biblical Scholarship?", *SJT* 45 (1992) 303–324.

Reicke, B., "The Knowledge of the Suffering Servant" in F. Maass (ed), *Das Ferne und Nahe Wort: Festschrift Leonhard Rost zur Vollendung seines 70. Lebensjahres am 30. November 1966 gewidmet* (BZAW, 105; Berlin: Töpelmann, 1967) 186–192.

Reid, S. B., (ed), *Prophets and Paradigms: Essays in Honor of Gene M. Tucker* (JSOT-Sup, 229; Sheffield: Sheffield Academic Press, 1996).

Reider, J., "Etymological Studies: ירע, ידע, and רעע", *JBL* 66 (1947) 315–317.

Rembaum, J. E., "The Development of a Jewish Exegetical Tradition Regarding Isaiah 53", *HTR* 75 (1982) 289–311.

Renkema, J., *Lamentations* (HCOT; Leuven: Peeters, 1998).

Reventlow, H. G., *Liturgie und prophetisches Ich bei Jeremia* (Gütersloh: Gerd Mohn, 1963).

——, "Die Prophetie im Urteil Bernhard Duhms", *ZTK* 85 (1988) 259–274.

Ricoeur, P., "Narrative Time" in Mitchell, *On Narrative*, pp. 165–186.

Rignell, L. G., "A Study of Isaiah Ch. 40–55" (Lunds universitets Årsskrift. N. F. Avd. 1. 52:5; Lund: C. W. K. Gleerup, 1956).

——, "Isa. LII 13–LIII 12", *VT* 3 (1953) 87–92.

Rimmon-Kenan, S., *Narrative Fiction: Contemporary Poetics* (New Accents; London: Routledge, 1989. First published: London: Methuen & Co. Ltd, 1983).

Robinson, H. W., *The Cross in the Old Testament* (London: SCM, 1955).

Roudiez, L. S., "Introduction" in Kristeva, *Desire in Language*, pp. 1–20.

Rogerson, J. W., "The Hebrew Conception of Corporate Personality: A Re-examination" in B. Lang (ed), *Anthropological Approaches to the Old Testament* (Issues in Religion and Theology, 8; Philadelphia: Fortress Press, 1985) 43–57.

Rosenbaum, M., *Word-Order Variation in Isaiah 40–55: A Functional Perspective* (Studia Semitica Neerlandica; Assen: Van Gorcum, 1997).

Rowley, H. H., *The Servant of the Lord and Other Essays on the Old Testament* (London: Lutterworth, 1952).

Rubinstein, A., "Isaiah LII 14 מִשְׁחַת and the DSIa Variant", *Bib* 35 (1954) 146–149.

Runions, E., *Changing Subjects: Gender, Nation and Future in Micah* (Playing the Texts, 7; Sheffield: Sheffield Academic Press, 2001).

Ruppert, L., "Schuld und Schuld-lösen nach Jesaja 53" in G. Kaufmann (ed), *Schulderfahrung und Schuldbewältigung: Christen im Umgang mit der Schuld* (SPK, 21; Paderborn, 1982) 17–34.

——, "'Mein Knecht, der Gerechte, macht die Vielen gerecht, und ihre Verschuldung-er trägt sie (Jes 53,11)': Universales Heil durch das stellvertretende Strafleiden des Gottesknechtes?", *BZ* 40 (1996) 1–17.

Ruprecht, E., *Die Auslegungsgeschichte zu den sogenannten Gottesknechtliedern im Buch Deuterojesaja unter metodischen Gesichtspunkten bis zu Bernard Duhm* (Unpubl. Diss., Heidelberg, 1972).

Said, E. S., "The Clash of Ignorance", *The Nation* (October 22, 2001 Issue).

Sapp, D. A., "The LXX, 1QIsa, and MT Versions of Isaiah 53 and the Christian Doctrine of Atonement" in Bellinger and Farmer, *Jesus and the Suffering Servant*, pp. 170–192.

Sawyer, J. F. A., *The Fifth Gospel: Isaiah in the History of Christianity* (Cambridge: Cambridge University Press, 1996).

——, "Daughter of Zion and Servant of the Lord in Isaiah: A Comparison", *JSOT* 44 (1989) 89–107.

——, "Isaiah" in J. Hayes (ed), *Dictionary of Biblical Interpretation. Vol. 1* (Nashville: Abingdon, 1999) 549–555.

Saydon, P. P., "The Use of Tenses in Deutero-Isaiah", *Bib* 40 (1959) 2960–301.

Schoors, A., *I am God your Saviour: A Form-Critical Study of the Main Genres in Is. xl–lv* (VTSup, 24; Leiden: E. J. Brill, 1973).

Schreiner, J. (ed), *Wort, Lied und Gottesspruch. Festschrift für Joseph Ziegler. Vol. II: Beiträge zu Psalmen und Propheten* (FzB, 1–2; Würzburg: Echter Verlag, 1972).

Schwartz, G., "…wie ein Reis vor ihm", *ZAW* 83 (1971) 256–257.

Scullion, J. J., "Righteousness (OT)", *ABD* 5 (1992) 724–736.

Seitz, C. R., *Zion's Final Destiny. The Development of the Book of Isaiah: A Reassessment of Isaiah 36–39* (Minneapolis: Fortress Press, 1991).

——, *Prophecy and Hermeneutics. Toward a New Introduction to the Prophets: Studies in Theological Interpretation* (Grand Rapids: Baker Academic Press, 2007).

——, "The Divine Council: Temporal Transition and New Prophecy in the Book of Isaiah", *JBL* 109 (1990) 229–247.

——, "Isaiah, Book of (First Isaiah)", *ABD* 3 (1992) 472–488.

Seow, C. L., "Hosea, Book of", *ABD* 3 (1992) 291–297.

Sheppard, G. T., "'Enemies' and the Politics of Prayer in the Book of Psalms" in D. Jobling, P. L. Day and G. T. Sheppard (eds), *The Bible and the Politics of Exegesis* (Cleveland: Pilgrim Press, 1991) 61–82.

——, "The Book of Isaiah: Competing Structures according to a Late Modern Description of Its Shape and Scope" (SBLSP, 31; Atlanta: Scholars Press, 1992) 549–582.

Ska, J. L., *'Our Fathers Have Told Us': Introduction to the Analysis of Hebrew Narratives* (Subsidia Biblica, 13; Rome: Editrice Pontificio Istituto Biblico, 1990).

Smart, J. D., *History and Theology in Second Isaiah: A Commentary on Isaiah 35, 40–66* (Philadelphia: Westminster Press, 1965).

Smend, R., *Deutsche Alttestamentler in drei Jahrhunderten* (Göttingen: Vandenhoeck & Ruprecht, 1989).

Smith, B. H., "Narrative Versions, Narrative Theories" in Mitchell, *On Narrative*, pp. 209–232.

Smith, M. S., *The Laments of Jeremiah and Their Context: A Literary and Redactional Study of Jeremiah 11–20* (SBLMS, 42; Atlanta: Scholars Press, 1990).

Snaith, N. H., *Isa. 40–55: A Study of the Teaching of the Second Isaiah and Its Consequences* (VT, 14; Leiden. E. J. Brill, 1967).

Soggin, J. A., "Tod und Auferstehung des leidenden Gottesknechtes – Jes. 53:8–10", *ZAW* 87 (1975) 346–355.

Sommer, B. D., *A Prophet Reads Scripture: Allusion in Isaiah 40–66* (Contraversions; Stanford: Stanford University Press, 1998).

——, "The Scroll of Isaiah as Jewish Scripture, or, Why Jews Don't Read Books" (SBLSP, 35; Atlanta: Scholars Press, 1996) 225–242.

Spieckermann, H., "Konzeption und Vorgeschichte des Stellvertretungsgedankens im Alten Testament" in J. A. Emerton (ed), *International Organization for the Study of the Old Testament: Congress Volume Cambridge 1995* (VTSup, 66; Leiden: E. J. Brill, 1997) 281–295, ET: H. Spieckermann, "The Conception and Prehistory of the Idea of Vicarious Suffering in the Old Testament" in Janowski and Stulmacher, *The Suffering Servant*, pp. 1–15.

Spykerboer, H. C., *The Structure and Composition of Deutero-Isaiah with Special Reference to the Polemics against Idolatry* (Meppel: Krips Repro, 1976).

Steck, O. H., *Wahrnehmungen Gottes im Alten Testament: Gesammelte Studien* (TBü, 70; Munich: Chr. Kaiser Verlag, 1982).

——, *Bereitete Heimkehr: Jesaja 35 als redaktionelle Brücke zwischen dem Ersten und dem Zweitem Jesaja* (Stuttgarter Bibel-Studien, 121; Stuttgart: Katholisches Bibelwerk, 1985).

——, *Gottesknecht und Zion: Gesammelte Aufsätze zu Deuterojesaja* (Forschungen zum Alten Testament, 4; Tübingen: J. C. B. Mohr {Paul Siebeck}, 1992).

——, *The Prophetic Books and their Theological Witness* (St. Louis, Missouri: Chalice Press, 2000).

——, "Bewahrheitungen des Prophetenworts. Überlieferungs-geschichtliche Skizze zu 1. Könige 22, 1–38" in H.-G. Geyer and J. M. Schmidt (eds), *"Wenn nicht jetzt, wann dann?". Aufsätze für Hans-Joachim Kraus zum 65. Geburtstag* (Neukirchen-Vluyn: Neukirchener Verlag, 1983) 87–96.

——, "Aspekte des Gottesknechts in Deuterojesajas 'Ebed-Jahwe-Liedern'" in Steck, *Gottesknecht und Zion*, pp. 3–21. First published in *ZAW* 96 (1984) 372–390.

Steck, O. H., "Aspekte des Gottesknechts in Jesaja 52,13–53,12" in Steck, *Gottesknecht und Zion*, pp. 22–43. First published in *ZAW* 97 (1985) 36–58.

——, "Zion als Gelände und Gestalt" in Steck, *Gottesknecht und Zion*, pp. 126–145. First published in *ZTK* 86 (1989) 261–281.

——, "Beobachtungen zu den Zion-Texten in Jesaja 51–54: Ein redaktionsgeschichtlicher Versuch" in Steck, *Gottesknecht und Zion*, pp. 96–125. First published in *BN* 46 (1989) 58–90.

——, "Die Gottesknechts-Texte und ihre redaktionelle Rezeption im Zweiten Jesaja" in Steck, *Gottesknecht und Zion*, pp. 149–172.

——, "Israel und Zion: Zum Probleme konzeptioneller Einheit und literarischer Schichtung in Deuterojesaja" in Steck, *Gottesknecht und Zion*, pp. 173–207.

——, "Der Gottesknecht als 'Bund' und 'Licht': Beobachtungen im Zweiten Jesaja", *ZTK* 90 (1993) 117–134.

——, "Prophetische Prophetenauslegung" in H. F. Geißer, H. J. Luibl, W. Mostert and H. Weder (eds), *Wahrheit der Schrift-Wahrheit der Auslegung: Eine Zürcher Vorlesungsreihe zu Gerhard Ebelings 80. Geburtstag am 6. Juli 1992* (Zürich: Theologischer Verlag Zürich, 1993) 198–244.

Stern, P., "The 'Blind Servant' Imagery of Deutero-Isaiah and Its Implications", *Bib* 75 (1994) 224–232.

Stienstra, N., *YHWH is the Husband of His People: Analysis of a Biblical Metaphor with Special Reference to Translation* (Kampen: Kok Pharos, 1993).

Stratton, B. J., "Engaging Metaphors: Suffering with Zion and the Servant in Isaiah 52–53" in S. E. Fowl (ed), *The Theological Interpretation of Scripture: Classic and Contemporary Readings* (Blackwell Readings in Modern Theology; Oxford: Blackwell, 1997) 219–237.

Stuart, D., *Hosea-Jonah* (WBC, 31; Waco, TX: Word Books, 1987).

Stulman, L., *Order Amid Chaos: Jeremiah as Symbolic Tapestry* (Biblical Seminar, 57; Sheffield: Sheffield Academic Press, 1998).

Sweeney, M. A., and Ben-Zvi, E. (eds), *The Changing Face of Form Criticism for the Twenty-First Century* (Grand Rapids: Eerdmans, 2003).

——, *Isaiah 1-4 and the Post-Exilic Understanding of the Isaianic Tradition* (BZAW, 171; Berlin: W. de Gruyter, 1988).

——, *Isaiah 1-39 with an Introduction to Prophetic Literature* (FOTL, 16; Grand Rapids: Eerdmans, 1996).

——, "The Book of Isaiah in Recent Research", *Currents in Research* 1 (1993) 141–162.

——, "On Multiple Settings in the Book of Isaiah" (SBLSP, 32; Atlanta: Scholars Press, 1993) 267–273.

——, "On the Road to Duhm: Isaiah in Nineteenth-Century Critical Scholarship" in McGinnis and Tull, *"As Those who are Taught"*, pp. 243–261.

——, "Reevaluating Isaiah 1-39 in Recent Critical Reseach", *Currents in Research* 4 (1996) 79–113.

——, "Review: B. Janowski and P. Stuhlmacher (eds), *Der leidende Gottesknecht: Jesaja 53 und seine Wirkungsgeschichte mit einer Bibliographie zu Jes 53* (Forschungen zum Alten Testament, 14; Tübingen: J. C. B. Mohr {Paul Siebeck}, 1996)", *CBQ* 68 (2006) 166–168.

Tate, M. E., *Psalms 51–100* (WBC, 20; Dallas, Texas: Word Books, 1990).

——, "Psalm 88", *RevExp* 87 (1990) 91–95.

Thelle, R. I., *Ask God: Divine Consultation in the Literature of the Hebrew Bible* (Beiträge zur biblischen Exegese und Theologie, 30; Frankfurt am Main: Peter Lang, 2002).

Thomas, D. W., "The root ידע in Hebrew", *JTS* 35 (1934) 298–306.

——, "Some Observations on the Hebrew Root [חדל]" (VTSup, 6; Leiden: E. J. Brill, 1957) 8–16.

——, "A Consideration of Isaiah LIII in the Light of Recent Textual and Philological Study" in H. Cazelles et al. (eds), *De Mari à Qumrân: L' Ancien Testament. Son mileu. Ses Écrits. Ses relectures juives. Hommage à Mgr. J. Coppens* (BETL, 24; Gembloux: J. Duculot, 1969) 119–126.

Thompson, M. P., "Reception Theory and the Interpretation of Historical Meaning", *History and Theory* 32 (1993) 248–272.

Todorov, T., *The Poetics of Prose* (Translated from the French by R. Howard; with a new foreword by J. Culler. Ithaca, New York: Cornell University Press, 1977. Original title: *La poetique de la prose*, published: Paris: Editions du Seuil, 1971).

Tom, W., "Welke is de Zin van het 'dubbel ontvangen' uit Jesaja 40.2?", *GThT* 59 (1959) 122–123.

Tomasino, A. J., "Isaiah 1.1–2.4 and 63–66, and the Composition of the Isaianic Corpus", *JSOT* 57 (1993) 81–98.

Tomes, R., "The Reason for the Syro-Ephraimite War", *JSOT* 59 (1993) 55–71.

Torrey, C. C., *The Second Isaiah: A New Interpretation* (Edinburgh: T. & T. Clark, 1928).

Tov, E., "The Text of Isaiah at Qumran" in Broyles and Evans, *Writing and Reading the Scroll of Isaiah. Vol. 2*, pp. 491–511.

Treves, M., "Isaiah 53", *VT* 24 (1974) 98–108.

Trible, P., *Texts of Terror: Literary-Feminist Readings of Biblical Narratives* (London: SCM Press, 2002. First published by Fortress Press, 1984).

Tsevat, M., "Alalkhiana", *HUCA* 29 (1958) 125–126.

Tucker, G. M., "The Futile Quest for the Historical Prophet" in E.E. Carpenter (ed), *A Biblical Itinerary. In Search of Method, Form, and Content: Essays in Honor of George W. Coats* (JSOTSup, 240; Sheffield: Sheffield Academic Press, 1997) 144–152.

Tull, P. K., "Intertextuality and the Hebrew Scriptures", *CRBS* 8 (2000) 59–90.

——, "One Book, Many Voices: Conceiving of Isaiah's Polyfonic Message" in McGinnis and Tull, *"As Those Who are Taught"*, pp. 279–314.

Ulrich, E., "Pluriformity in the Biblical Text, Text Groups, and Questions of Canon" in J. T. Barrera and L. V. Montaner, *The Madrid Qumran Congress. Proceedings on the International Congress on the Dead Sea Scrolls Madrid 18–21 March 1991* (STDJ, 11, 1; Leiden: E. J. Brill, 1992) 223–41.

——, "An Index to the Contents of the Isaiah Manuscripts from the Judean Desert" in Broyles and Evans, *Writing and Reading the Scroll of Isaiah. Vol. 2*, pp. 477–480.

Van der Kooij, A., "Isaiah in the Septuagint" in Broyles and Evans, *Writing and Reading the Scroll of Isaiah. Vol. 2*, pp. 513–529.

Van der Woude, A., "Can Zion Do without the Servant in Isaiah 40–55?", *Calvin Theological Journal* 39 (2004) 109–116.

Van Oorschot, J., *Von Babel zum Zion: Eine literarkritische und redaktionsgeschichtliche Untersuchung* (BZAW, 206; Berlin: W. de Gruyer, 1993).

Van Winkle, D. W., "The Relationship of the Nations to Yahweh and to Israel in Isaiah 40–55", *VT* 35 (1985) 446–458.

Vaughan, P., *The Meaning of "Bama" in the Old Testament: A Study of Etymological, Textual and Archaeological Evidence* (SNTSMS, 3; London: Cambridge University Press, 1974).

Vermeylen, J. (ed), *The Book of Isaiah* (BETL, 81; Leuven: Leuven University Press, 1989).

Vincent, J. M., *Studien zur literarischen Eigenart und zur geistigen Heimat von Jesaja, Kap. 40–48* (Beiträge zur biblischen Exegese und Theologie, 5; Frankfurt am Main: Peter Lang, 1977).

Volosinov, V. N. (and Bakhtin, M. M.), *Marxism and the Philosophy of Language* (Translated by L. Matejka and I. R. Titunik. Studies in Language, 1; New York: Seminar Press, 1973).

von Rad, G., "כְּפלִים in Jes. 40:2=Äquivalent?", *ZAW* 79 (1967) 80–82.

von Waldow, H. E., "The Message of Deutero-Isaiah", *Int* 22 (1968) 259–287.

Vriezen, T. C., "The Term Hizza: Lustration and Consecration", *OTS* 7 (1950) 201–235.

Waltke, B. K., and O'Connor, M., *An Introduction to Biblical Hebrew Syntax* (Winona Lake, IN: Eisenbrauns, 1990).

Watermann, L., "The Martyred Servant Motif of Is. 53", *JBL* 56 (1937) 27–34.

Watson, W. G. E., *Classical Hebrew Poetry: A Guide to its Techniques* (JSOTSup, 26; Sheffield: JSOT Press, 1984).

Watts, J. D. W., *Isaiah 1–33* (WBC, 24; Waco, Texas: World Books: 1985).

——, *Isaiah 34–66* (WBC, 25; Waco, Texas: World Books: 1987).

Watts, R. E., "The Meaning of [עָלָיו יִקְפְּצוּ מְלָכִים פִּיהֶם] in Isaiah LII 15", *VT* 40 (1990) 327–335.

——, "Consolation or Confrontation? Isa. 40–55 and the Delay of the New Exodus", *TynBul* 41 (1990) 31–59.

Webb, B. G., "Zion in Transformation: A Literary Approach to Isaiah" in Clines, Fowl and Porter, *The Bible in Three Dimensions*, pp. 65–84.

Weitzman, S., "Rebuilding the Tower of Babel", *JQR* 98 (2008) 103–112.

Werlitz, J., *Redaktion und Komposition: Zur Rückfrage hinter die Endgestalt von Jesaja 40–55* (BBB, 122; Berlin: Philo, 1999).

——, "Vom Knecht der Lieder zum Knecht des Buches: Ein Versuch über die Ergänzungen zu den Gottesknechtstexten des Deutero-jesajabuches", *ZAW* 109 (1997) 30–43.

Westermann, C., *Isaiah 40–66–A Commentary* (OTL; London: SCM Press, 1969. Translated by D. M. G. Stalker from the German *Das Buch Jesaja* [Das alte Testament Deutsch 19], first published by Vandenhoeck & Ruprecht, Göttingen, 1966).

——, *Sprache und Struktur der Prophetie Deuterojesajas* (Calwer theologische Monographien, A. 11; Stuttgart: Calwer Verlag, 1981).

——, *Lamentations: Issues and Interpretation* (Minneapolis: Fortress Press, 1994. Translated by C. Muenchow. Original title: *Die Klagelieder: Forschungsgeschichte und Auslegung*, Neukirchener-Vluyn: Neukirchener Verlag, 1990).

——, "Das Heilswort bei Deuterojesaja", *ET* 24 (1964) 355–373.

White, Hayden, "Historical Pluralism", *Critical Inquiry* 12 (1986) 480–493.

Whybray, R. N., *The Heavenly Counsellor in Isaiah xl 13–14: A Study of the Sources of the Theology of Deutero-Isaiah* (SOTSMS, 1; Cambridge: University Press, 1971).

——, *Isaiah 40–66* (NCB; London: Oliphants, 1975).

——, *Thanksgiving for a Liberated Prophet: An Interpretation of Isaiah Chapter 53* (JSOTSup, 4; Sheffield: JSOT, 1978).

——, *Job* (Readings; Sheffield: Sheffield Academic Press, 1998).

——, "Review: O. H. Steck, *Gottesknecht und Zion: Gesammelte Aufsätze zu Deuterojesaja* (Forschungen zum Alten Testament, 4; Tübingen: J. C. B. Mohr {Paul Siebeck}, 1992", *JTS* 45 (1994) 180–183.

Wilcox, P. and Paton-Williams, D., "The Servant Songs in Deutero-Isaiah", *JSOT* 42 (1988) 79–102.

Willey, P. T., *Remember the Former Things: The Recollection of Previous Texts in Second Isaiah* (SBLDS, 161; Atlanta: Scholars Press, 1997).

——, "The Servant of YHWH and Daughter Zion: Alternating Visions of YHWH's Community" (SBLSP, 34; Atlanta: Scholars Press, 1995) 267–303.

Williams, R. J., "The Passive Qal Theme in Hebrew" in J. W. Wevers and D. B. Redford (eds), *Essays on the Ancient Semitic World* (Toronto Semitic Texts and Studies; Toronto: University of Toronto Press, 1970) 43–50.

Williamson, H. G. M., *The Book Called Isaiah: Deutero-Isaiah's Role in Composition and Redaction* (Oxford: Clarendon Press, 1994).

——, "[דעת] in Isaiah LIII 11", *VT* 28 (1978) 118–122.

——, "Isaiah and the Holy One of Israel" in A. Rapoport-Albert and G. Greenberg (eds), *Biblical Hebrew, Biblical Texts: Essays in Memory of M. P. Weitzman* (JSOTSup, 333; Sheffield: Sheffield Academic Press, 2001) 22–38.

——, "Reclocating Isaiah 1:2–9" in Broyles and Evans, *Writing and Reading the Scroll of Isaiah. Vol. 1*, pp. 263–277.

Wilshire, L. E., "The Servant-City: A New Interpretation of the 'Servant of the Lord' in the Servant Songs of Deutero-Isaiah", *JBL* 94 (1975) 356–367.

Wolff, H. W., *Hosea: A Commentary on the Book of the Prophet Hosea* (Hermeneia; Philadelphia: Fortress Press, 1974).

——, *Jesaja 53 im Urchristentum* (Giessen: Brunnen Verlag, 1984).

Wuellner, W., "Where Is Rhetorical Criticism Taking Us?", *CBQ* 49 (1987) 448–463.

Yee, G. A., "The Anatomy of Biblical Parody: The Dirge Form in 2 Samuel 1 and Isaiah 14", *CBQ* 50 (1988) 565–586.

Young, E. J., "The Intepretation of [יזה] in Isaiah 52:15", *WTJ* 3 (1941) 125–132.

Young, R. (ed), *Untying the Text: A Post-Structuralist Reader* (Boston: Routledge & Kegan Paul, 1981).

Youngblood, R., "A New Look at Three Old Testament Roots for 'Sin'" in G. A. Tuttle (ed), *Biblical And Near Eastern studies: Essays in Honour of William Sanford LaSor* (Grand Rapids: Eerdmans, 1978) 201–205.

Zimmerli, W., "Zur Vorgeschichte von Jes. LIII" in W. Zimmerli (ed), *International Organization for the Study of the Old Testament: Congress Volume Rome 1986* (VTSup, 17; Leiden: E. J. Brill, 1969) 236–244.

Ziolkowski, J., (ed), *On Philology* (University Park, Pennsylvania: Pennsylvania State University Press, 1990).

INDEX OF BIBLE REFERENCES

INDEX OF AUTHORS

INDEX OF SUBJECTS

SUPPLEMENTS TO VETUS TESTAMENTUM

94. PAUL, S.M., R.A. KRAFT, L.H. SCHIFFMAN and W.W. FIELDS (eds.). *Emanuel.* Studies in Hebrew Bible, Septuagint, and Dead Sea Scrolls in Honor of Emanuel Tov. 2003. ISBN 90 04 13007 1

95. VOS, J.C. DE. *Das Los Judas.* Über Entstehung und Ziele der Landbeschreibung in Josua 15. ISBN 90 04 12953 7

96. LEHNART, B. *Prophet und König im Nordreich Israel.* Studien zur sogenannten vor klassischen Prophetie im Nordreich Israel anhand der Samuel-, Elija- und Elischa-Überlieferungen. 2003. ISBN 90 04 13237 6

97. LO, A. *Job 28 as Rhetoric.* An Analysis of Job 28 in the Context of Job 22-31. 2003. ISBN 90 04 13320 8

98. TRUDINGER, P.L. *The Psalms of the Tamid Service.* A Liturgical Text from the Second Temple. 2004. ISBN 90 04 12968 5

99. FLINT, P.W. and P.D. MILLER, JR. (eds.) with the assistance of A. Brunell. *The Book of Psalms.* Composition and Reception. 2004. ISBN 90 04 13842 8

100. WEINFELD, M. *The Place of the Law in the Religion of Ancient Israel.* 2004. ISBN 90 04 13749 1

101. FLINT, P.W., J.C. VANDERKAM and E. TOV. (eds.) *Studies in the Hebrew Bible, Qumran, and the Septuagint.* Essays Presented to Eugene Ulrich on the Occasion of his Sixty-Fifth Birthday. 2004. ISBN 90 04 13738 6

102. MEER, M.N. VAN DER. *Formation and Reformulation.* The Redaction of the Book of Joshua in the Light of the Oldest Textual Witnesses. 2004. ISBN 90 04 13125 6

103. BERMAN, J.A. *Narrative Analogy in the Hebrew Bible.* Battle Stories and Their Equivalent Non-battle Narratives. 2004. ISBN 90 04 13119 1

104. KEULEN, P.S.F. VAN. *Two Versions of the Solomon Narrative.* An Inquiry into the Relationship between MT 1 Kgs. 2-11 and LXX 3 Reg. 2-11. 2004. ISBN 90 04 13895 1

105. MARX, A. *Les systèmes sacrificiels de l'Ancien Testament.* Forms et fonctions du culte sacrificiel à Yhwh. 2005. ISBN 90 04 14286 X

106. ASSIS, E. *Self-Interest or Communal Interest.* An Ideology of Leadership in the Gideon, Abimelech and Jephthah Narritives (Judg 6-12). 2005. ISBN 90 04 14354 8

107. WEISS, A.L. *Figurative Language in Biblical Prose Narrative.* Metaphor in the Book of Samuel. 2006. ISBN 90 04 14837 X

108. WAGNER, T. *Gottes Herrschaft.* Eine Analyse der Denkschrift (Jes 6, 1-9,6). 2006. ISBN 90 04 14912 0

109. LEMAIRE, A. (ed.). *Congress Volume Leiden 2004.* 2006. ISBN 90 04 14913 9

110. GOLDMAN, Y.A.P., A. van der Kooij and R.D. Weis (eds.). *Sôfer Mahîr.* Essays in Honour of Adrian Schenker Offered by Editors of *Biblia Hebraica Quinta.* 2006. ISBN 90 04 15016 1

111. WONG, G.T.K. *Compositional Strategy of the Book of Judges.* An Inductive, Rhetorical Study. 2006. ISBN 90 04 15086 2

112. HØYLAND LAVIK, M. *A People Tall and Smooth-Skinned.* The Rhetoric of Isaiah 18. 2006. ISBN 90 04 15434 5

113. REZETKO, R., T.H. LIM and W.B. AUCKER (eds.). *Reflection and Refraction.* Studies in Biblical Historiography in Honour of A. Graeme Auld. 2006. ISBN 90 04 14512 5

114. SMITH, M.S. and W.T. PITARD. *The Ugaritic Baal Cycle.* Volume II. Introduction with Text, Translation and Commentary of KTU/CAT 1.3–1.4. 2009. ISBN 978 90 04 15348 6

115. BERGSMA, J.S. *The Jubilee from Leviticus to Qumran.* A History of Interpretation. 2006. ISBN-13 978 90 04 15299 1. ISBN-10 90 04 15299 7

116. Goff, M.J. *Discerning Wisdom*. The Sapiential Literature of the Dead Sea Scrolls. 2006. ISBN-13 978 90 04 14749 2. ISBN-10 90 04 14749 7

117. De Jong, M.J. *Isaiah among the Ancient Near Eastern Prophets*. A Comparative Study of the Earliest Stages of the Isaiah Tradition and the Neo-Assyrian Prophecies. 2007. ISBN 978 90 04 16161 0

118. Forti, T.L. *Animal Imagery in the Book of Proverbs*. 2007. ISBN 978 90 04 16287 7

119. Pinçon, B. *L'énigme du bonheur*. Étude sur le sujet du bien dans le livre de Qohélet. 2008. ISBN 978 90 04 16717 9

120. Ziegler, Y. *Promises to Keep*. The Oath in Biblical Narrative. 2008. ISBN 978 90 04 16843 5

121. Villanueva, F.G. *The 'Uncertainty of a Hearing'*. A Study of the Sudden Change of Mood in the Psalms of Lament. 2008. ISBN 978 90 04 16847 3

122. Crane, A.S. *Israel's Restoration*. A Textual-Comparative Exploration of Ezekiel 36–39. 2008. ISBN 978 90 04 16962 3

123. Mirguet, F. *La représentation du divin dans les récits du Pentateuque*. Médiations syntaxiques et narratives. 2009. ISBN 978 90 04 17051 3

124. Ruiten, J. van and J.C. Vos de (eds.). *The Land of Israel in Bible, History, and Theology*. Studies in Honour of Ed Noort. 2009. ISBN 978 90 04 17515 0

125. Evans, P.S. *The Invasion of Sennacherib in the Book of Kings*. A Source-Critical and Rhetorical Study of 2 Kings 18-19. 2009. ISBN 978 90 04 17596 9

126. Glenny, W.E. *Finding Meaning in the Text*. Translation Technique and Theology in the Septuagint of Amos. 2009. ISBN 978 90 04 17638 6

127. Cook, J. (ed.). *Septuagint and Reception*. Essays prepared for the Association for the Study of the Septuagint in South Africa. 2009. ISBN 978 90 04 17725 3

128. Kartveit, M. *The Origin of the Samaritans*. 2009. ISBN 978 90 04 17819 9

129. Lemaire, A., B. Halpern and M.J. Adams (eds.). *The Books of Kings*. Sources, Composition, Historiography and Reception. 2010. ISBN 978 90 04 17729 1

130. Galil, G., M. Geller and A. Millard (eds.). *Homeland and Exile*. Biblical and Ancient Near Eastern Studies in Honour of Bustenay Oded. 2009. ISBN 978 90 04 17889 2

131. Anthonioz, S. *L'eau, enjeux politiques et théologiques, de Sumer à la Bible*. 2009. ISBN 978 90 04 17898 4

132. Hugo, P. and A. Schenker (eds.). *Archaeology of the Books of Samuel*. The Entangling of theTextual and Literary History. 2010. ISBN 978 90 04 17957 8

133. Lemaire, A. (ed.). *Congress Volume Ljubljana*. 2007. 2010. ISBN 978 90 04 17977 6

134. Ulrich, E. (ed.). *The Biblical Qumran Scrolls*. Transcriptions and Textual Variants. 2010. ISBN 978 90 04 18038 3

135. Dell, K.J., G. Davies and Y. Von Koh (eds.). *Genesis, Isaiah and Psalms*. A Festschrift to honour Professor John Emerton for his eightieth birthday. 2010. ISBN 978 90 04 18231 8

136. Good, R. *The Septuagint's Translation of the Hebrew Verbal System in Chronicles*. 2010. ISBN 978 90 04 15158 1

137. Reynolds, K.A. *Torah as Teacher*. The Exemplary Torah Student in Psalm 119. 2010. ISBN 978 90 04 18268 4

138. van der Meer, M., P. van Keulen, W. Th. van Peursen and B. ter Haar Romeny (eds.). *Isaiah in Context*. Studies in Honour of Arie van der Kooij on the Occasion of his Sixty-Fifth Birthday. 2010. ISBN 978 90 04 18657 6

139. Tiemeyer, L.-S. *For the Comfort of Zion*. The Geographical and Theological Location of Isaiah 40-55. 2011. ISBN 978 90 04 18930 0

140/1. Lange, A., E. Tov and M. Weigold (eds.). *The Dead Sea Scrolls In Context*. Integrating the Dead Sea Scrolls in the Study of Ancient Texts, Languages, and Cultures. 2011. ISBN 978 90 04 18903 4

141. Halvorson-Taylor, M.A. *Enduring Exile*. The Metaphorization of Exile in the Hebrew Bible. 2011. ISBN 978 90 04 16097 2

142. Joachimsen, K. *Identities in Transition*. The Pursuit of Isa. 52:13–53:12. 2011. ISBN 978 90 04 20106 4